LIGHTER
THAN MY
SHADOW

LIGHTER
THAN MY
SHADOW

KATIE GREEN

Published by Jonathan Cape 2013

2 4 6 8 10 9 7 5 3 1

Copyright © Katie Green 2013

First published in Great Britain in 2013 by Jonathan Cape

Random House, 20 Vauxhall Bridge Road,
London, SW1V 2SA

www.capegraphicnovels.co.uk

Addresses for companies within The Random House Group Limited can be found at:
www.randomhouse.co.uk/offices.htm

The Random House Group Limited Reg. No. 954009

A CIP catalogue record for this book is available from the British Library.

ISBN 9780224090988

Printed and bound in China by C&C Offset Printing Co. Ltd.

Supported using public funding by
ARTS COUNCIL
ENGLAND
LOTTERY FUNDED

Work on this book was also supported
by The Authors' Foundation, administered by
The Society of Authors

This is a work of non-fiction. Except where permission has been given, all names have been changed.

For Mum
and Dad

and
Jemma

and
George

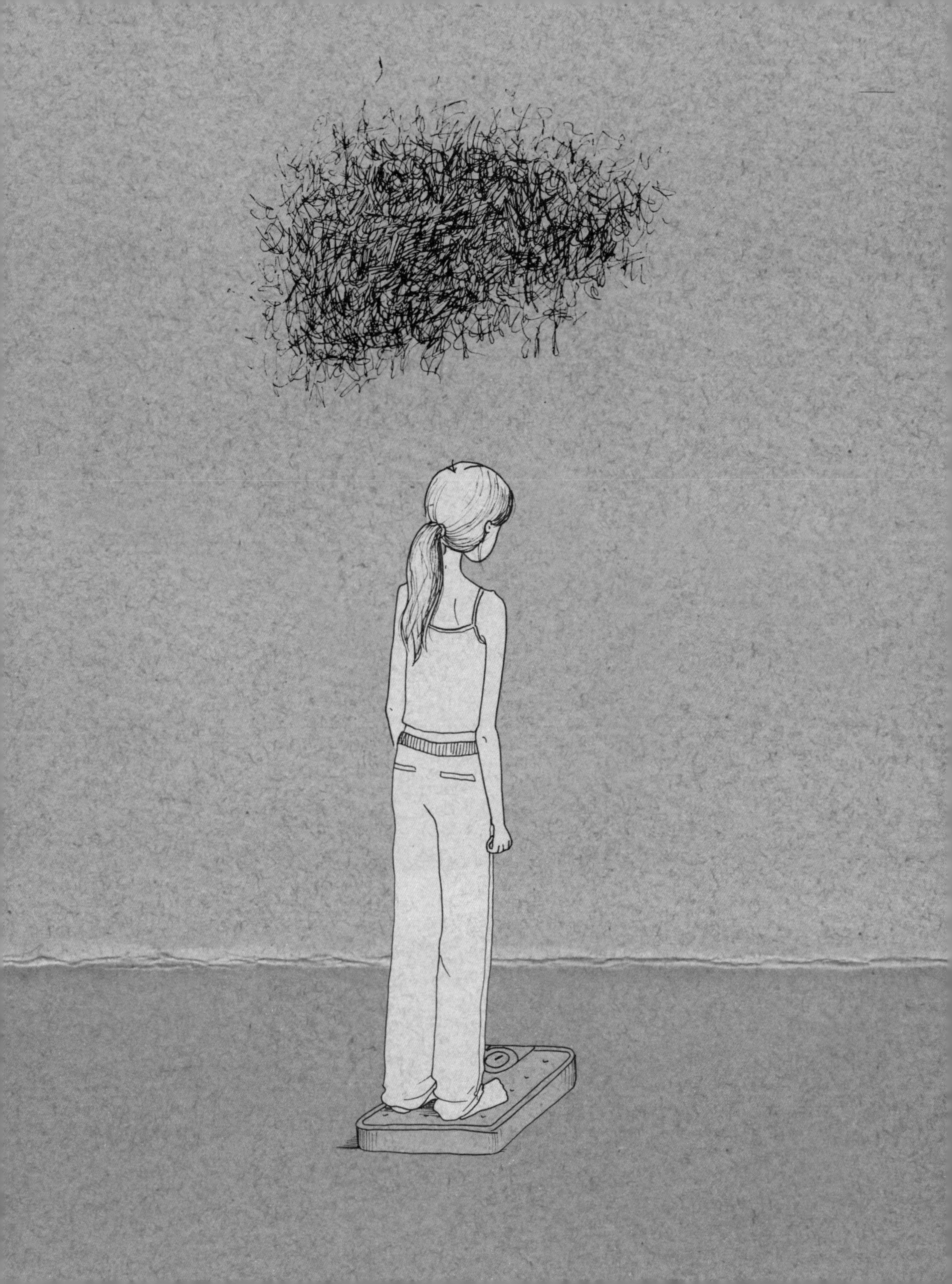

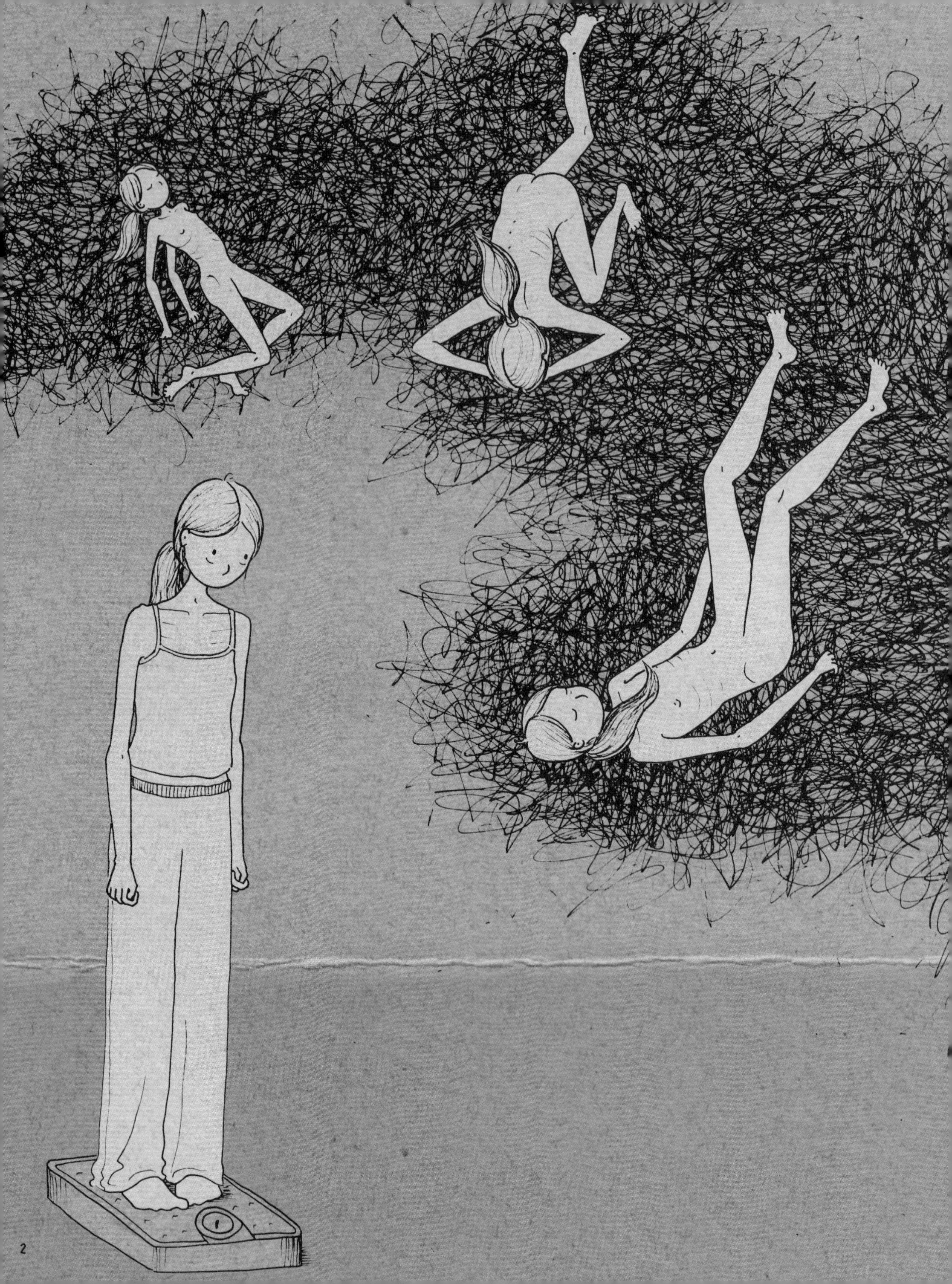

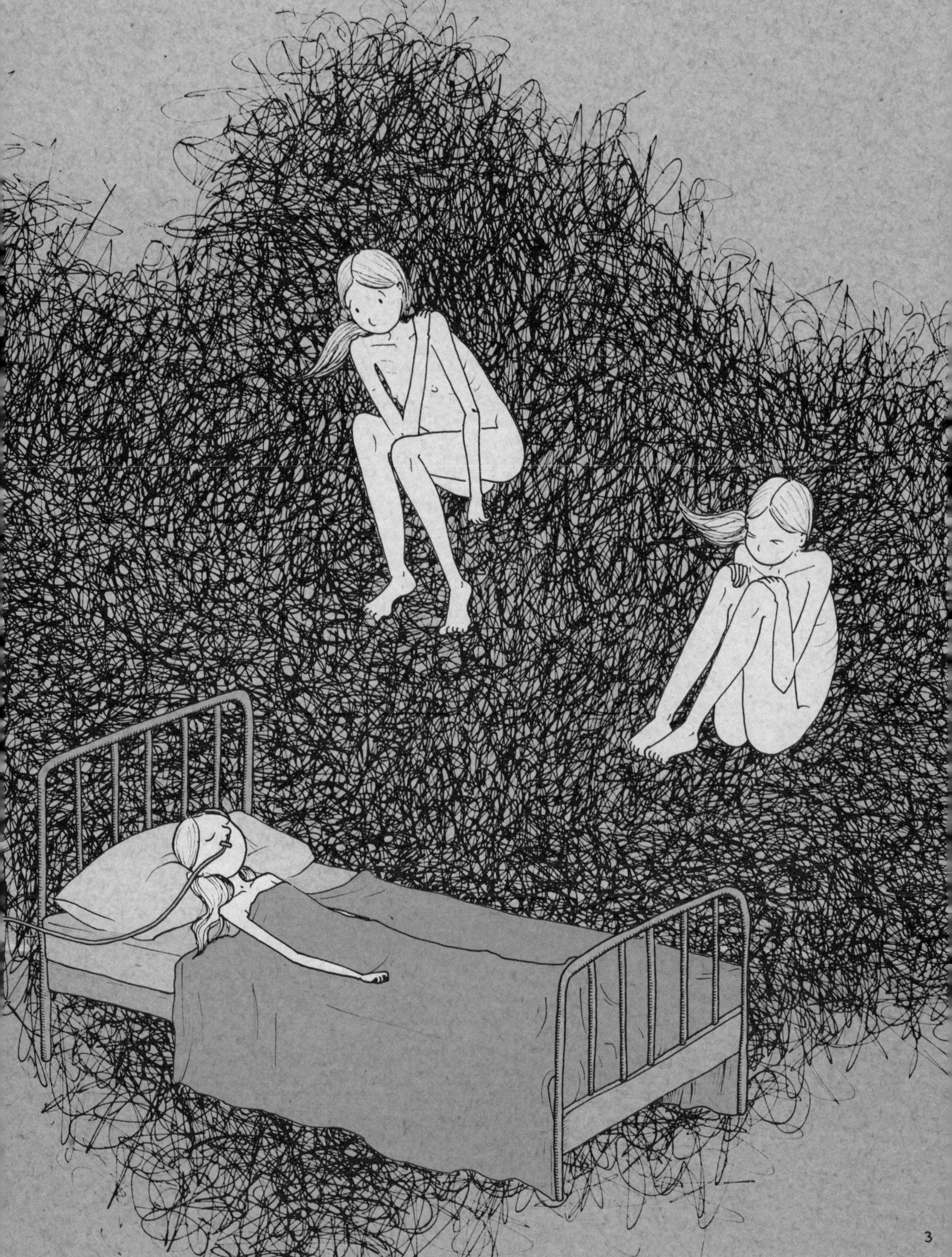

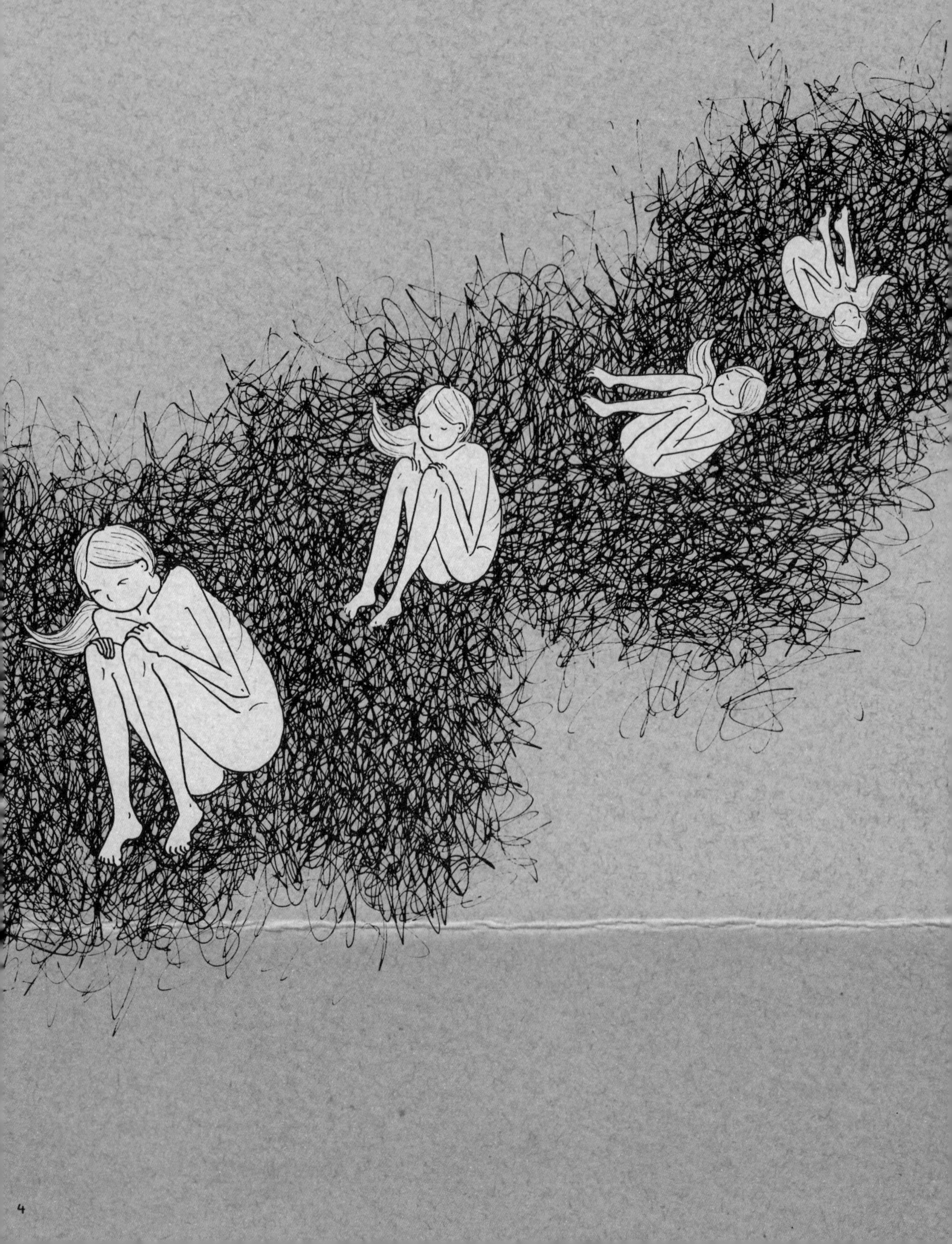

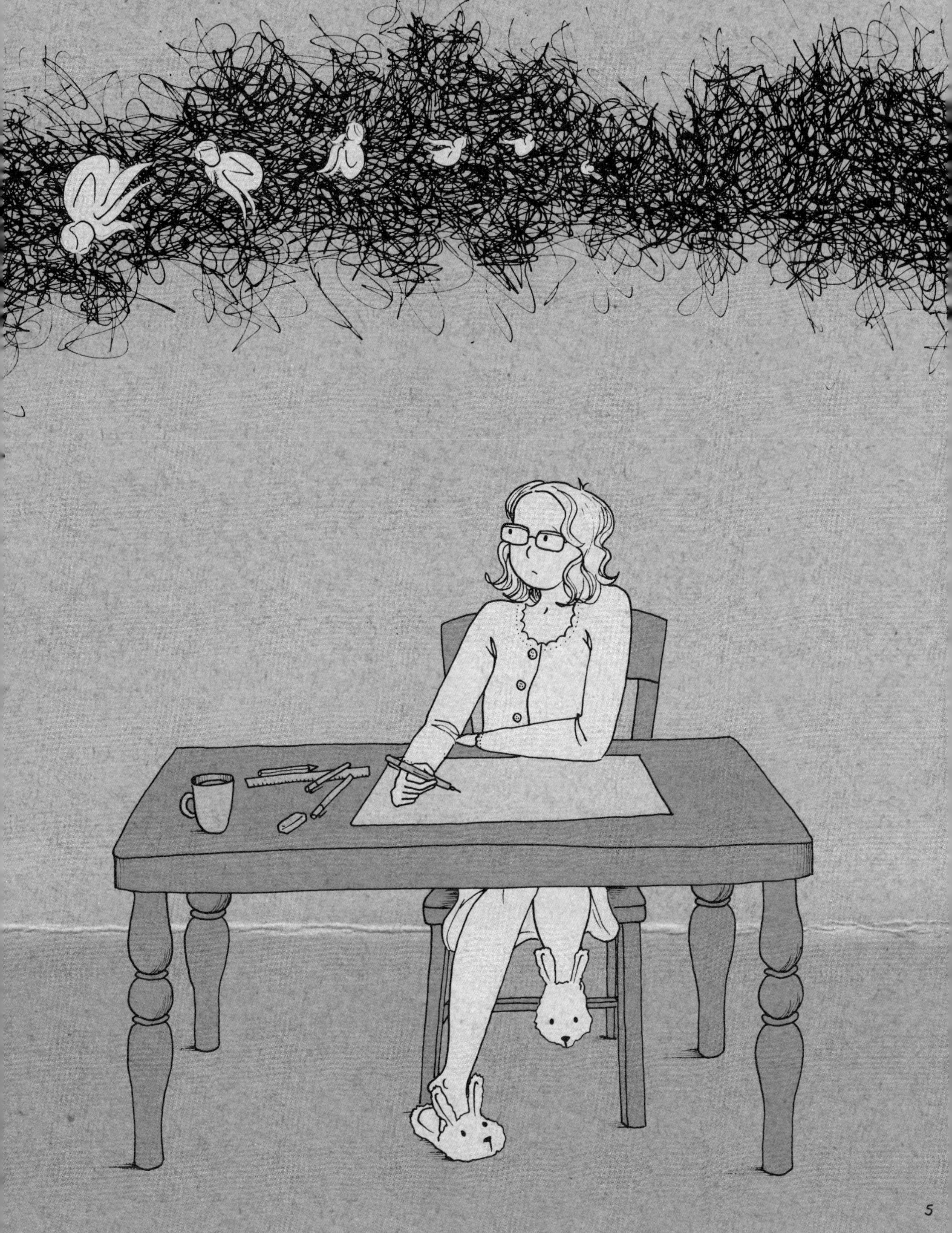

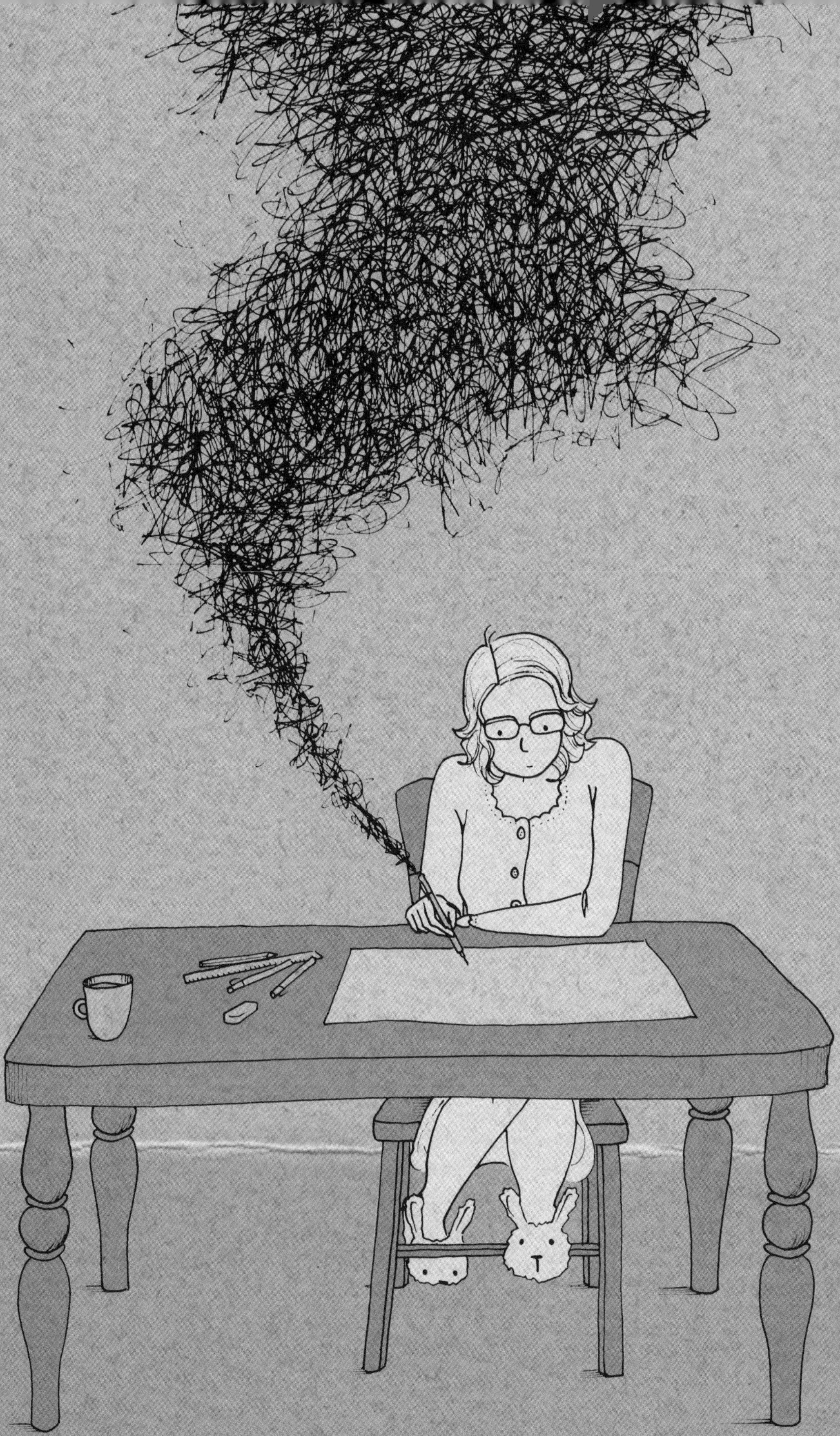

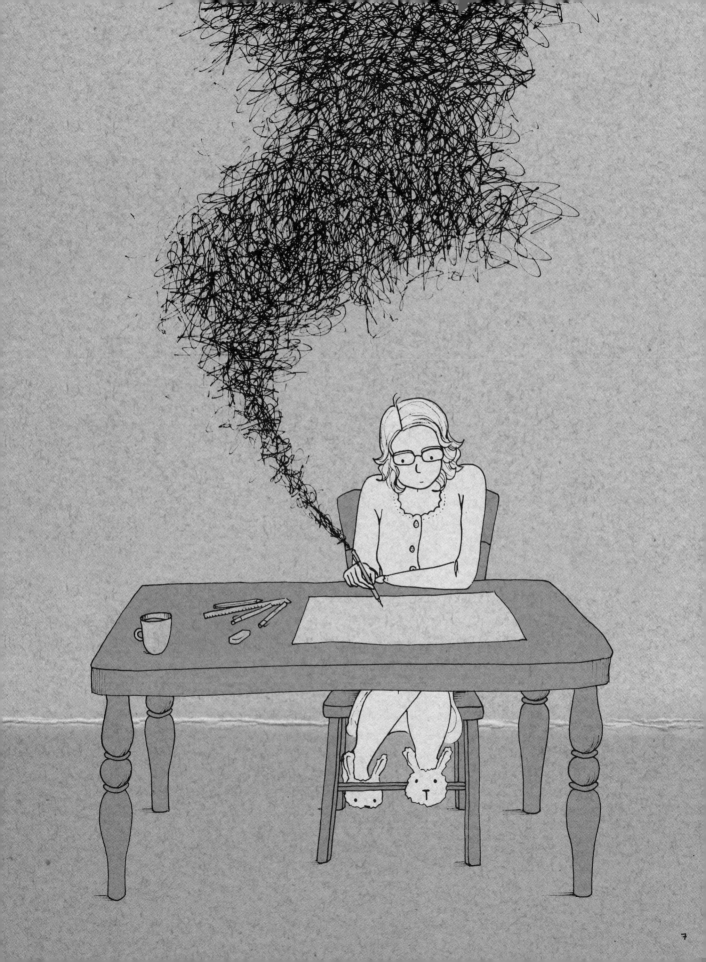

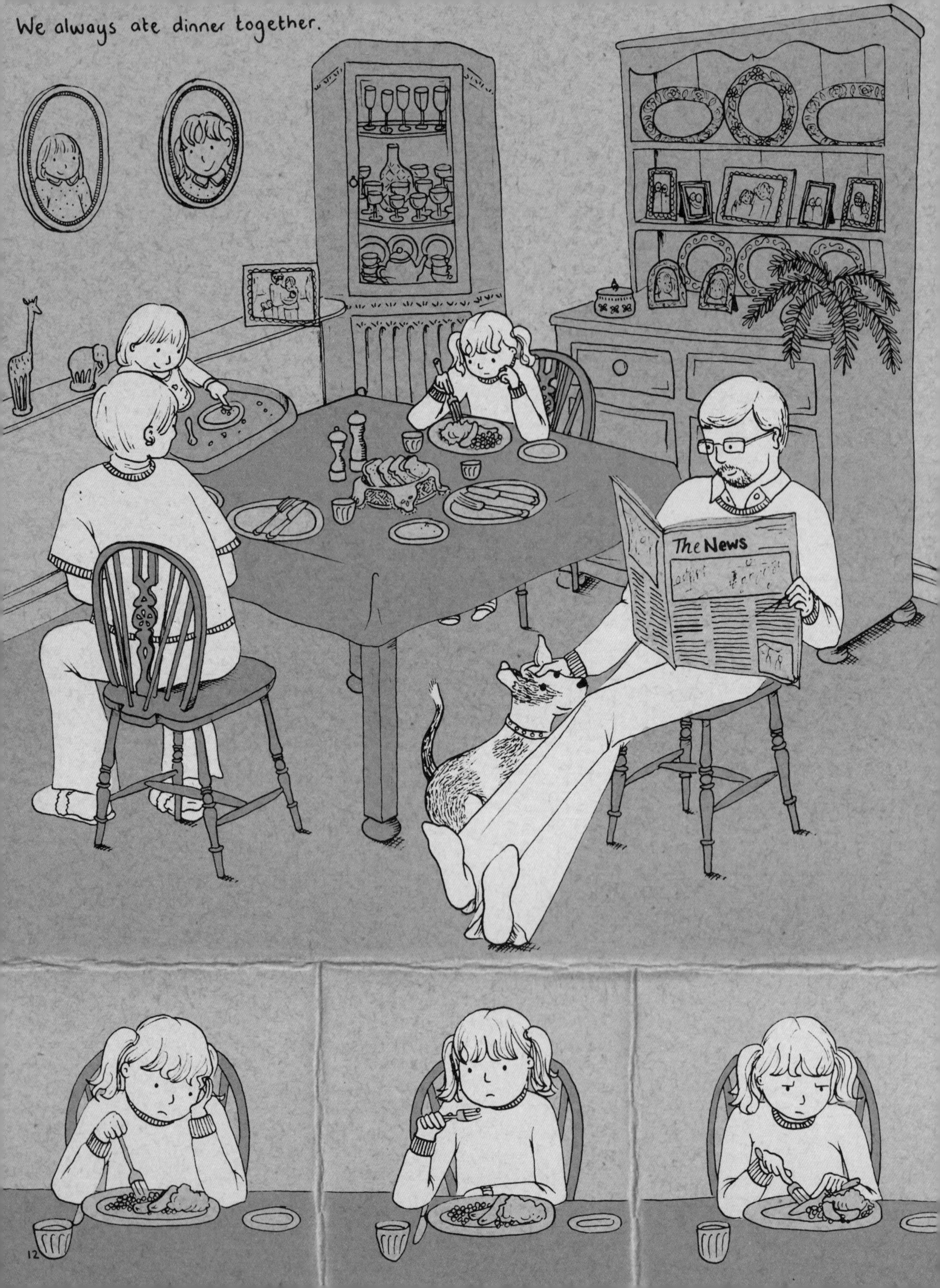
We always ate dinner together.
The News

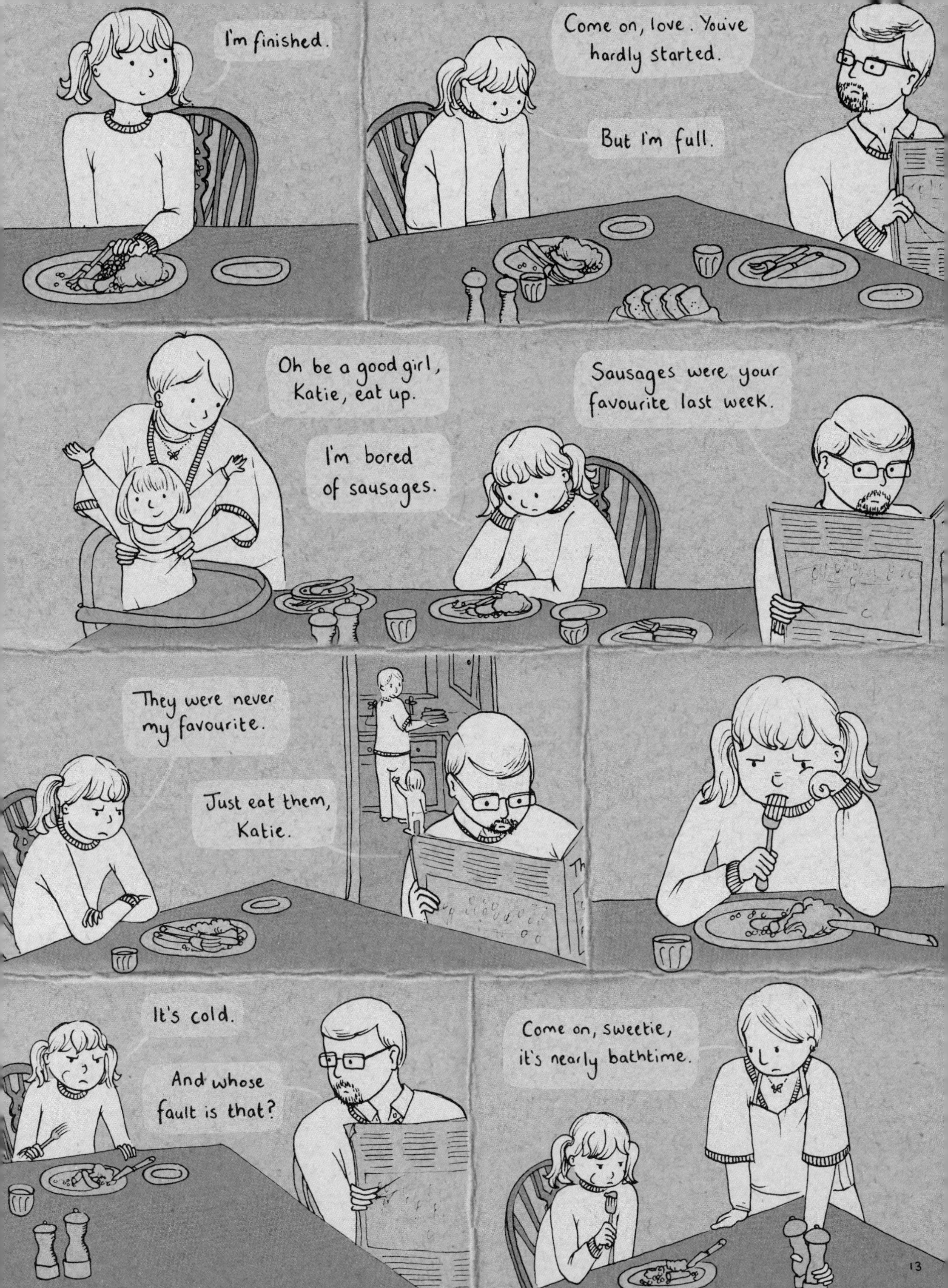
I'm finished.
Come on, love. You've hardly started.
But I'm full.
Oh be a good girl, Katie, eat up.
I'm bored of sausages.
Sausages were your favourite last week.
They were never my favourite.
Just eat them, Katie.
It's cold.
And whose fault is that?
Come on, sweetie, it's nearly bathtime.

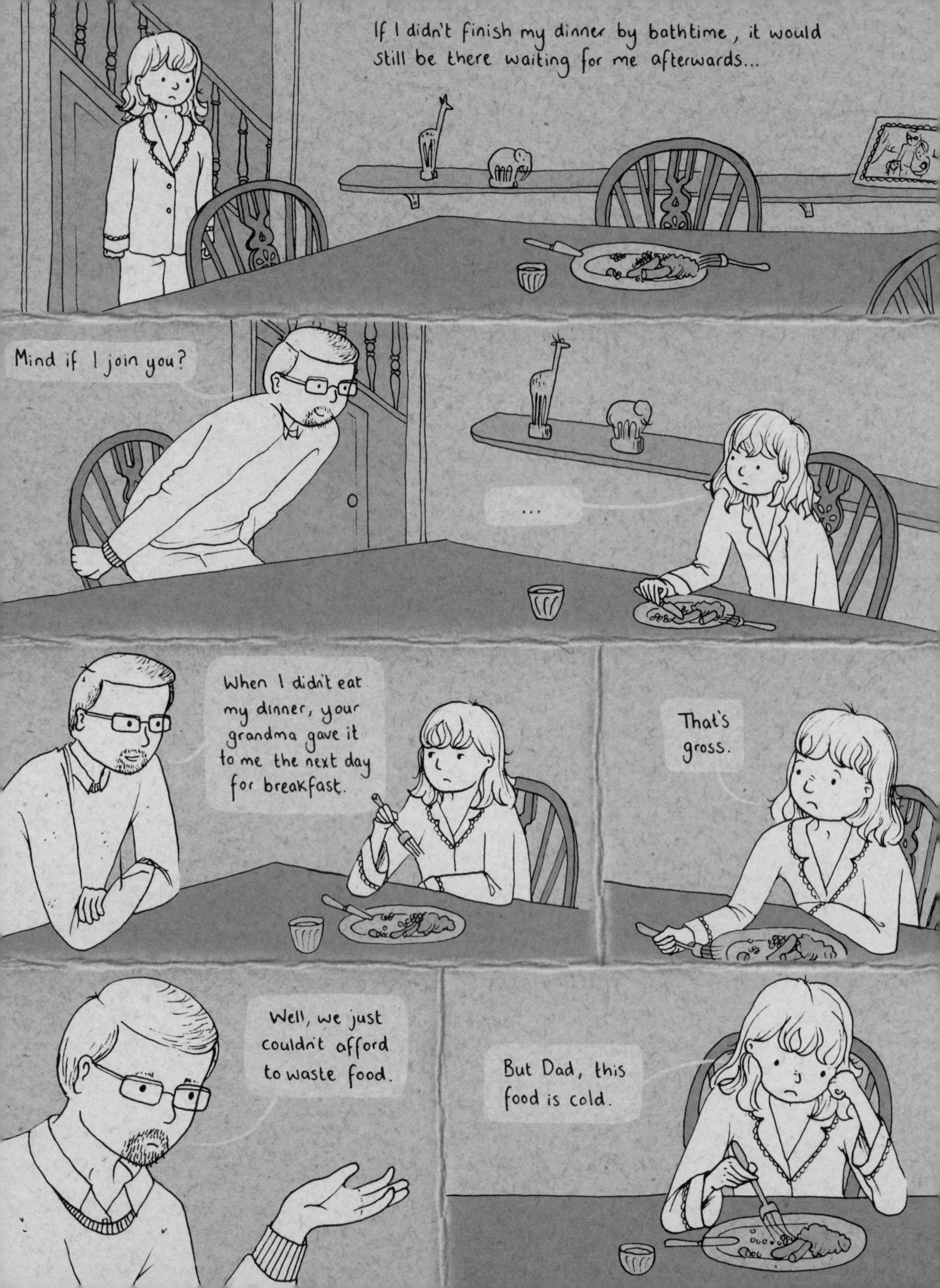
If I didn't finish my dinner by bathtime, it would still be there waiting for me afterwards...
Mind if I join you?
...
When I didn't eat my dinner, your grandma gave it to me the next day for breakfast.
That's gross.
Well, we just couldn't afford to waste food.
But Dad, this food is cold.

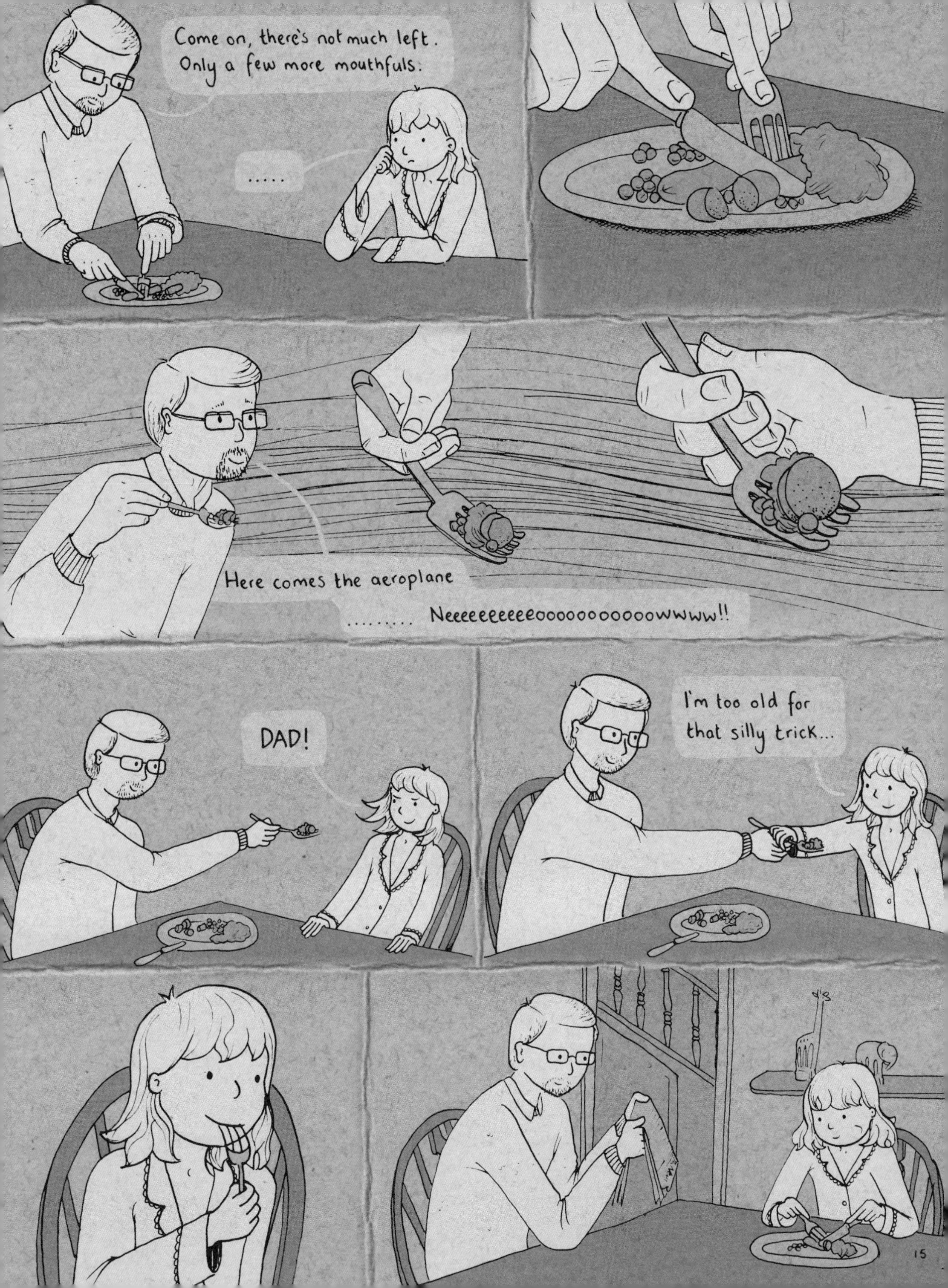
Come on, there's not much left. Only a few more mouthfuls.
.....
Here comes the aeroplane
.... Neeeeeeeeeeooooooooooowwww!!
DAD!
I'm too old for that silly trick...

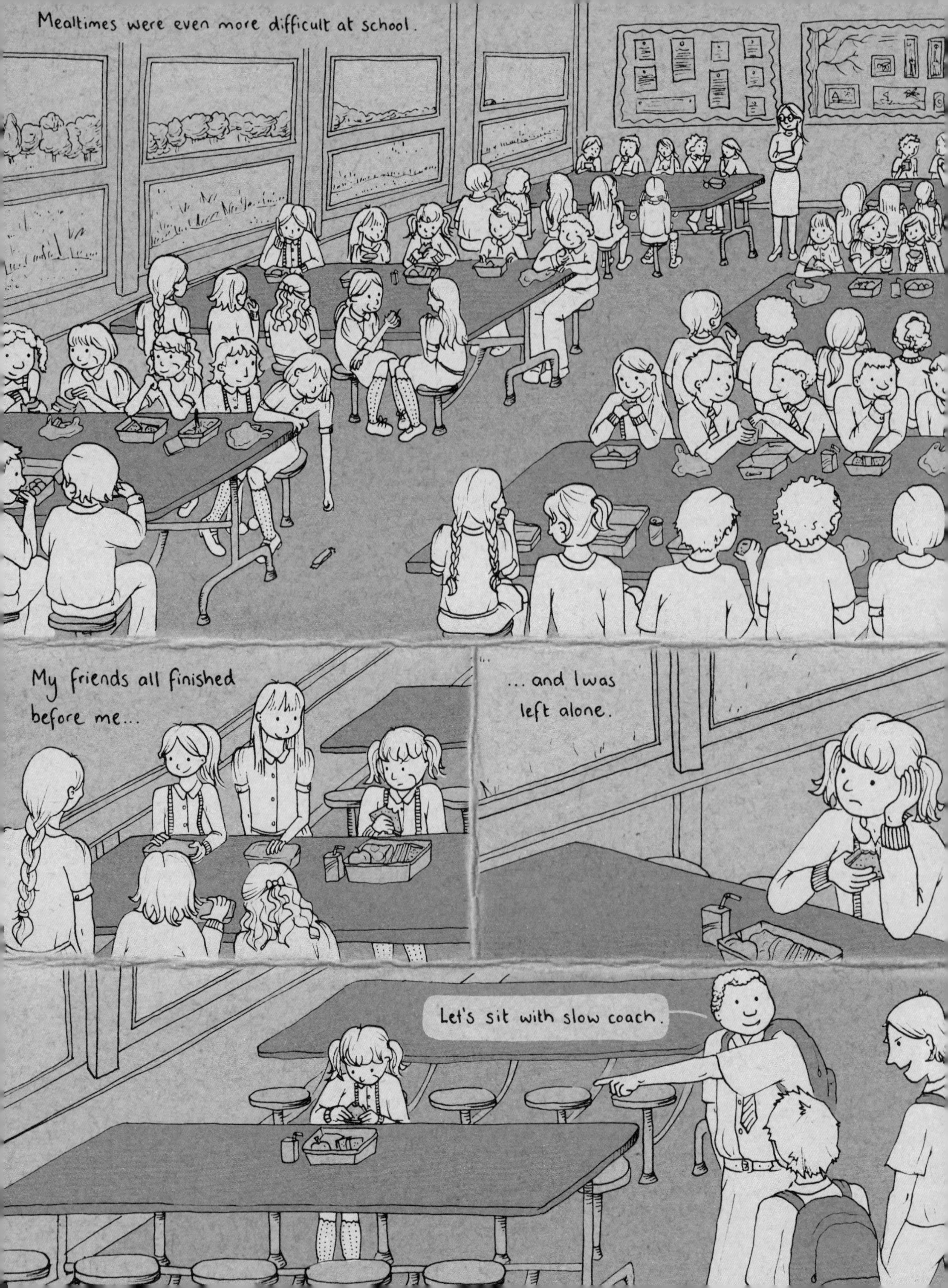
Mealtimes were even more difficult at school.
My friends all finished before me...
... and I was left alone.
Let's sit with slow coach.

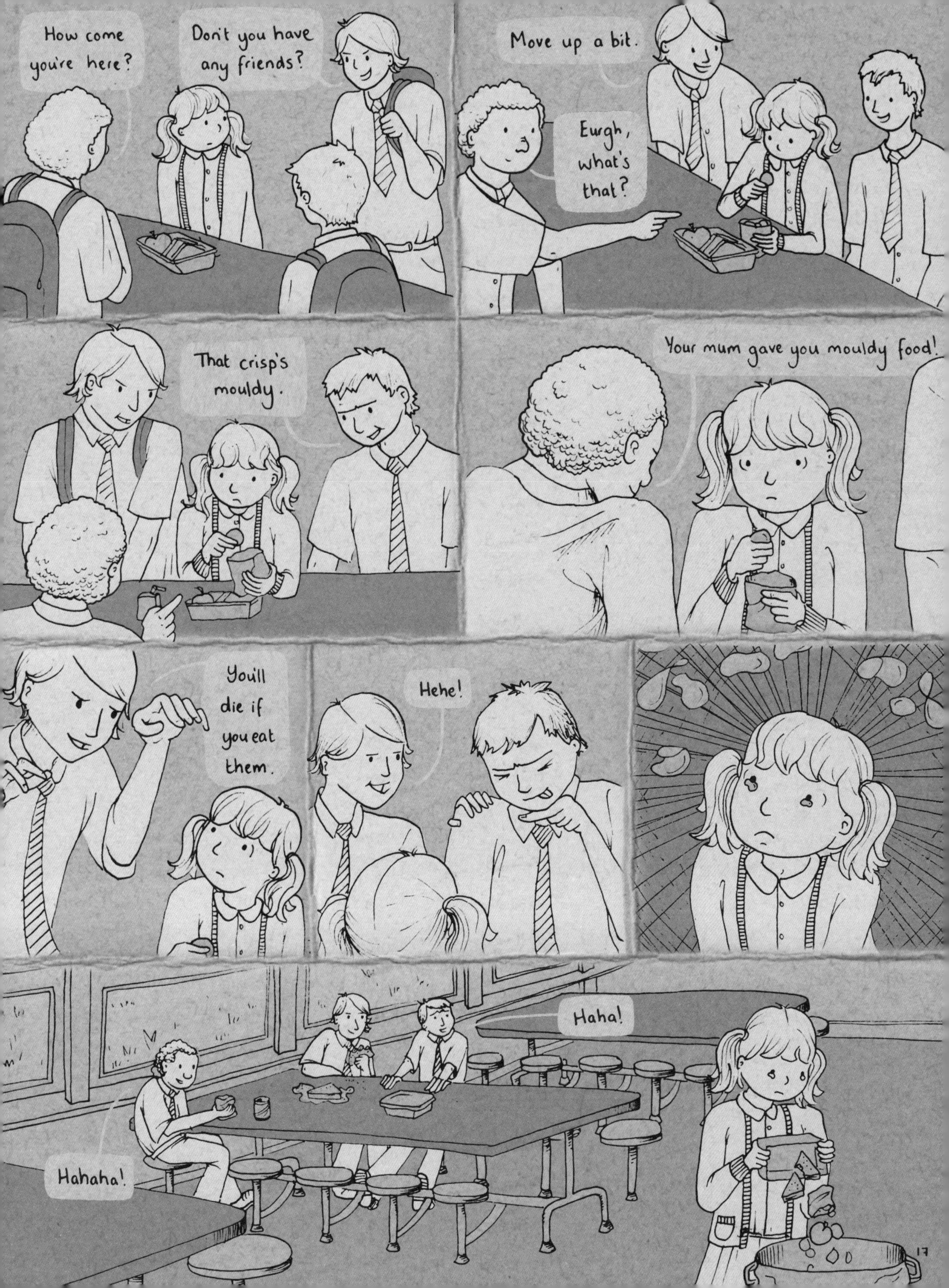
How come you're here?
Don't you have any friends?
Move up a bit.
Eurgh, what's that?
That crisp's mouldy.
Your mum gave you mouldy food!
You'll die if you eat them.
Hehe!
Haha!
Hahaha!

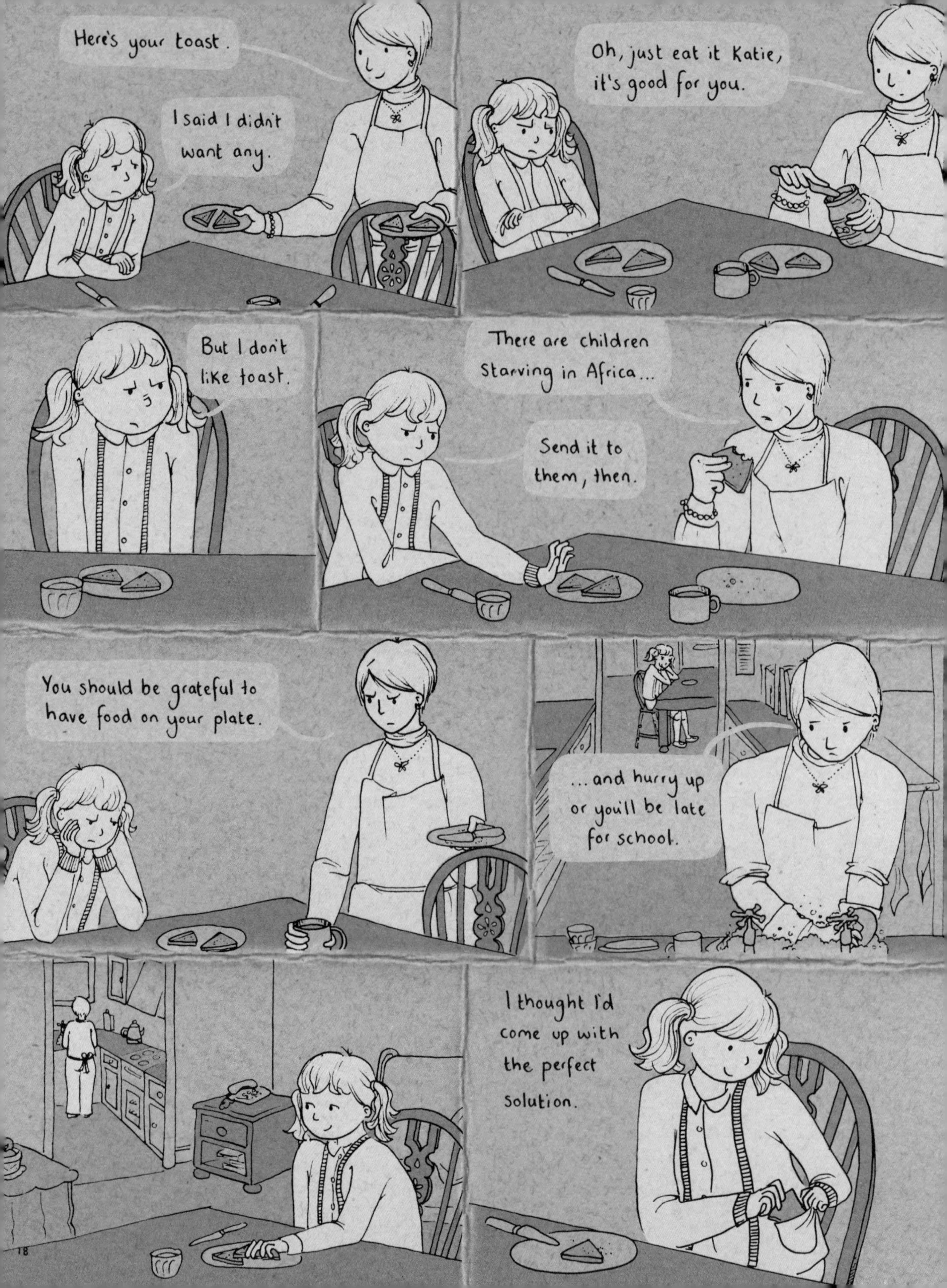

Here's your toast.
I said I didn't want any.
Oh, just eat it Katie, it's good for you.
But I don't like toast.
There are children starving in Africa...
Send it to them, then.
You should be grateful to have food on your plate.
...and hurry up or you'll be late for school.
I thought I'd come up with the perfect solution.

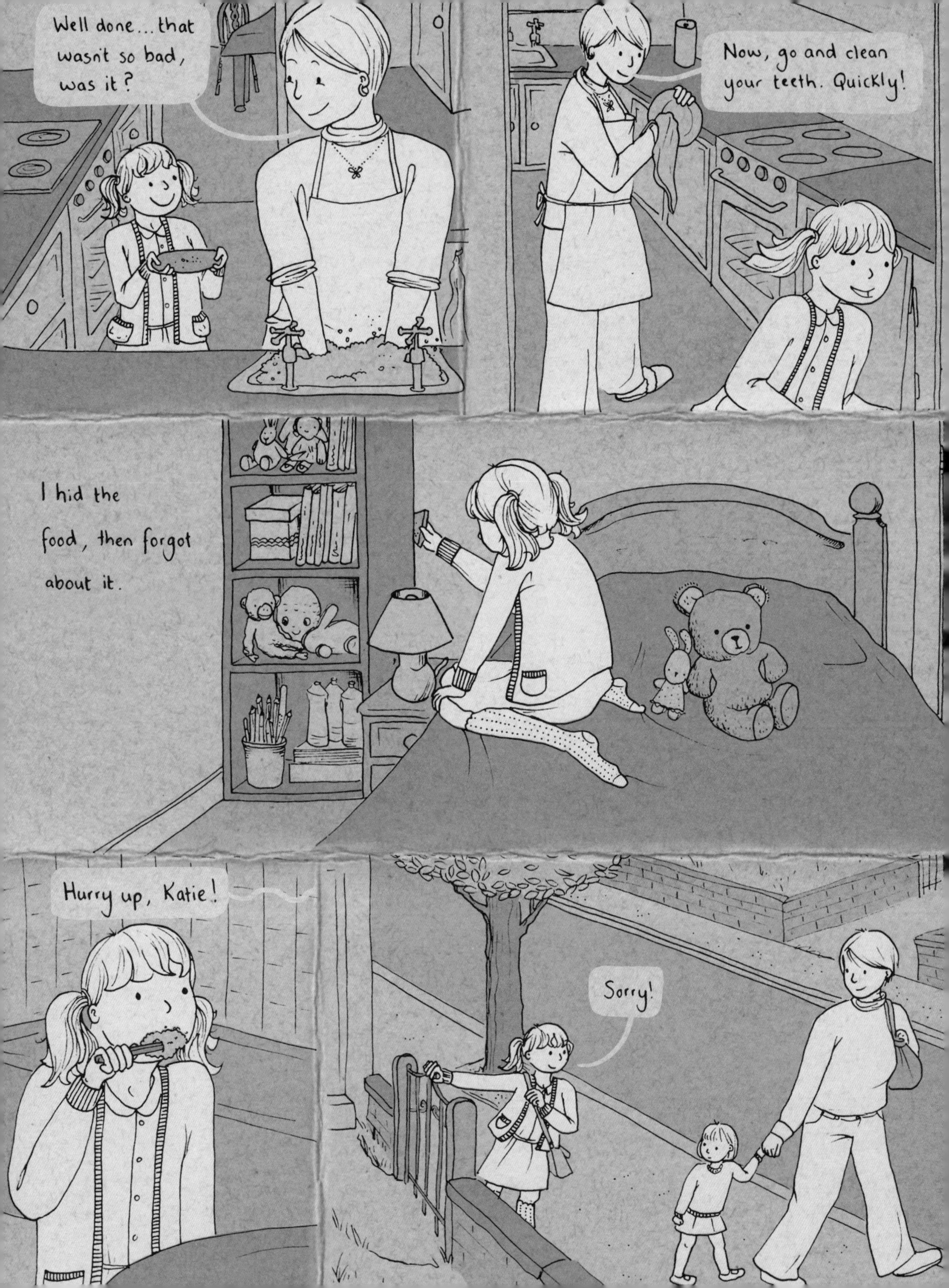
Well done... that wasn't so bad, was it?
Now, go and clean your teeth. Quickly!
I hid the food, then forgot about it.
Hurry up, Katie!
Sorry!

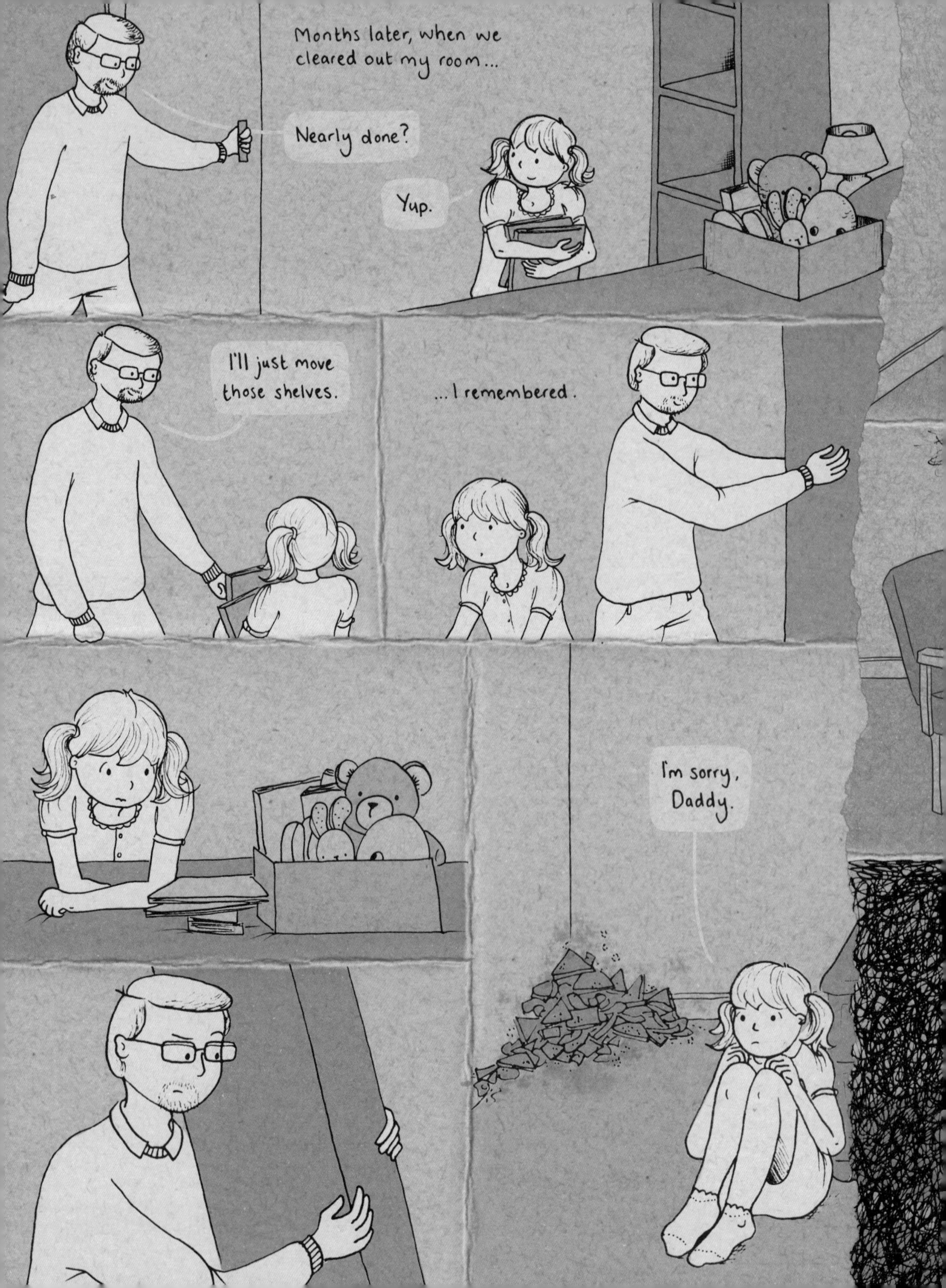

Months later, when we cleared out my room...
Nearly done?
Yup.
I'll just move those shelves.
...I remembered.
I'm sorry, Daddy.

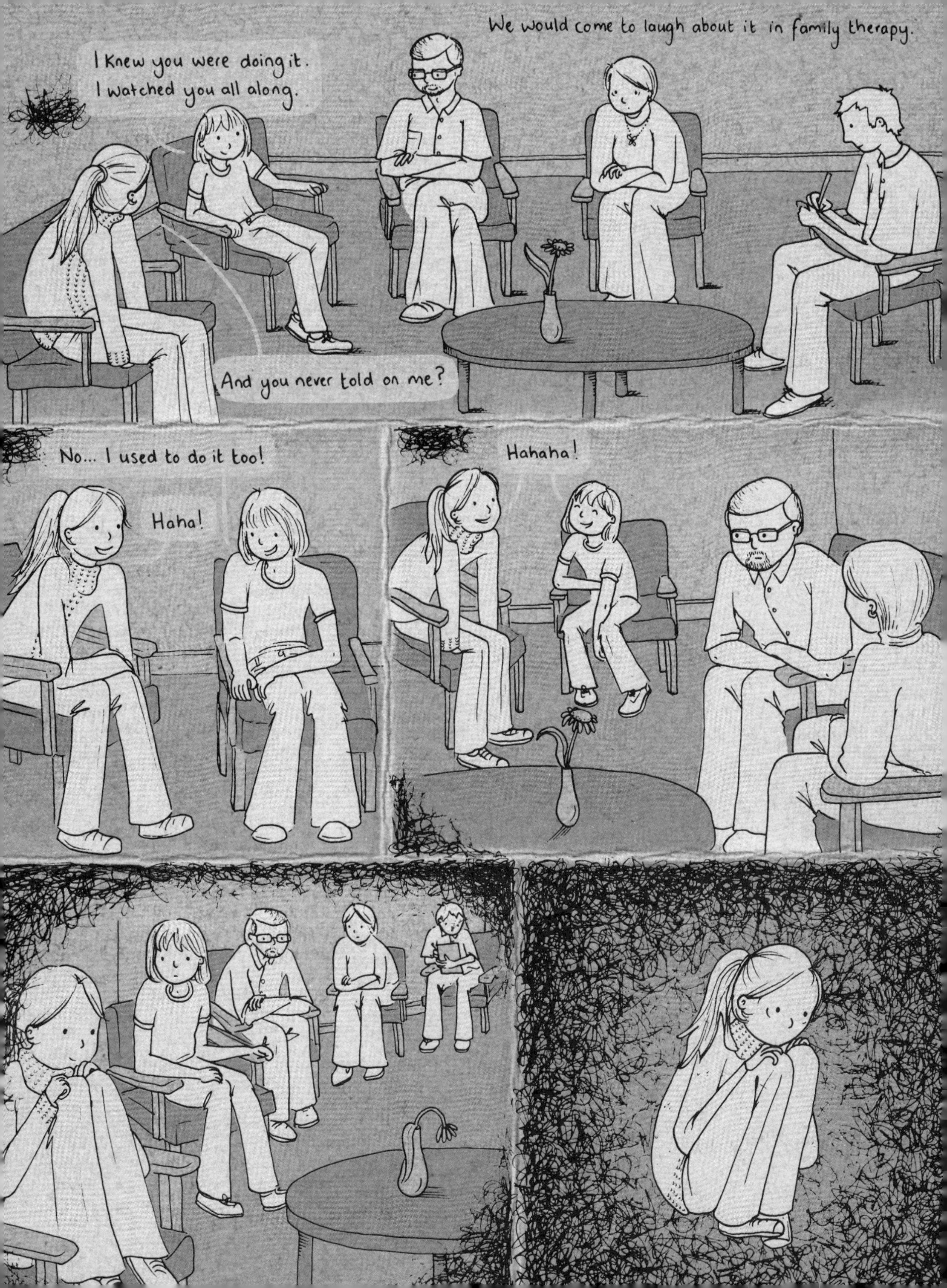
We would come to laugh about it in family therapy.
I knew you were doing it. I watched you all along.
And you never told on me?
No... I used to do it too!
Haha!
Hahaha!

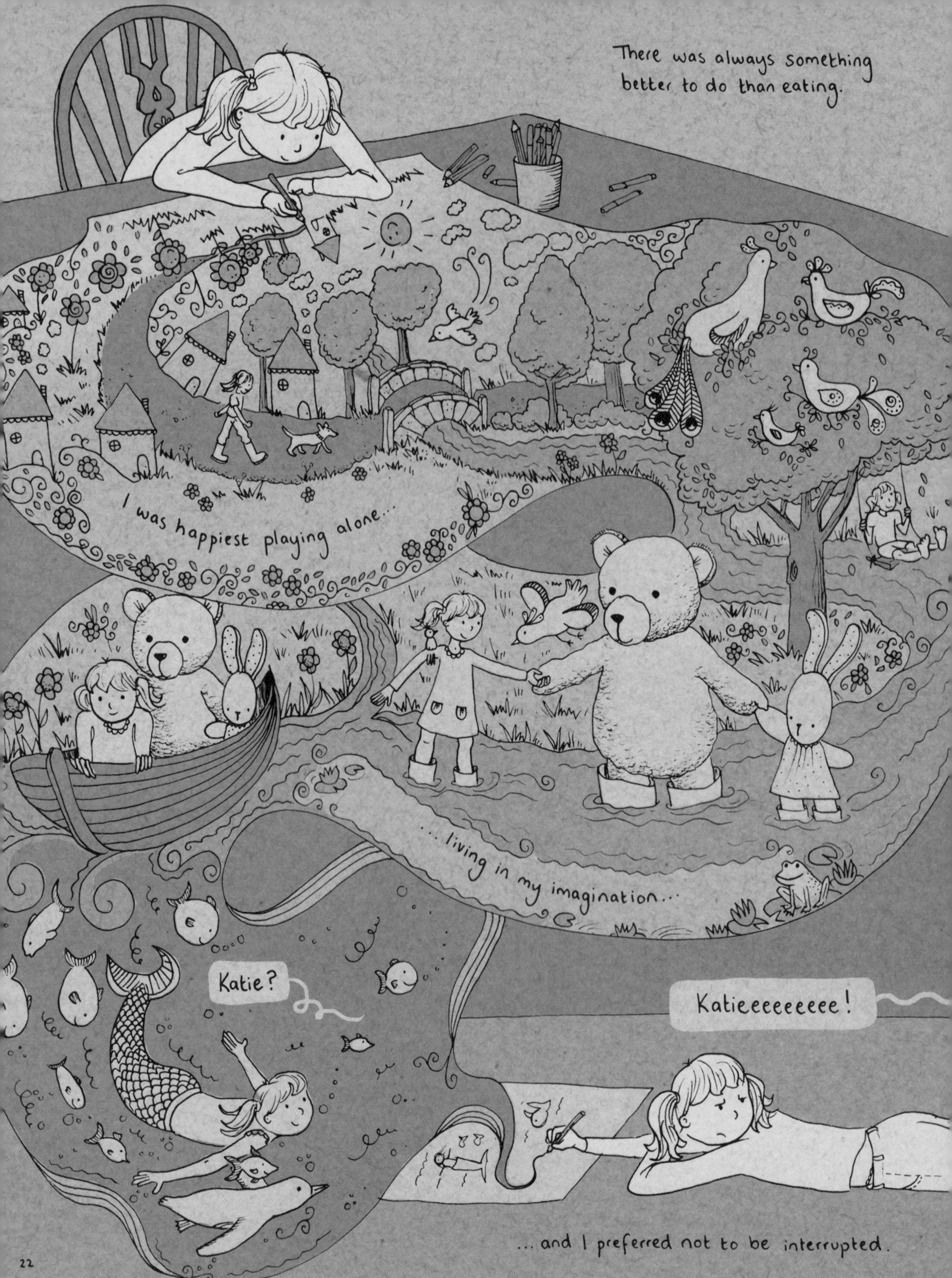

There was always something better to do than eating.
I was happiest playing alone...
... living in my imagination...
Katie?
Katieeeeeeee!
... and I preferred not to be interrupted.

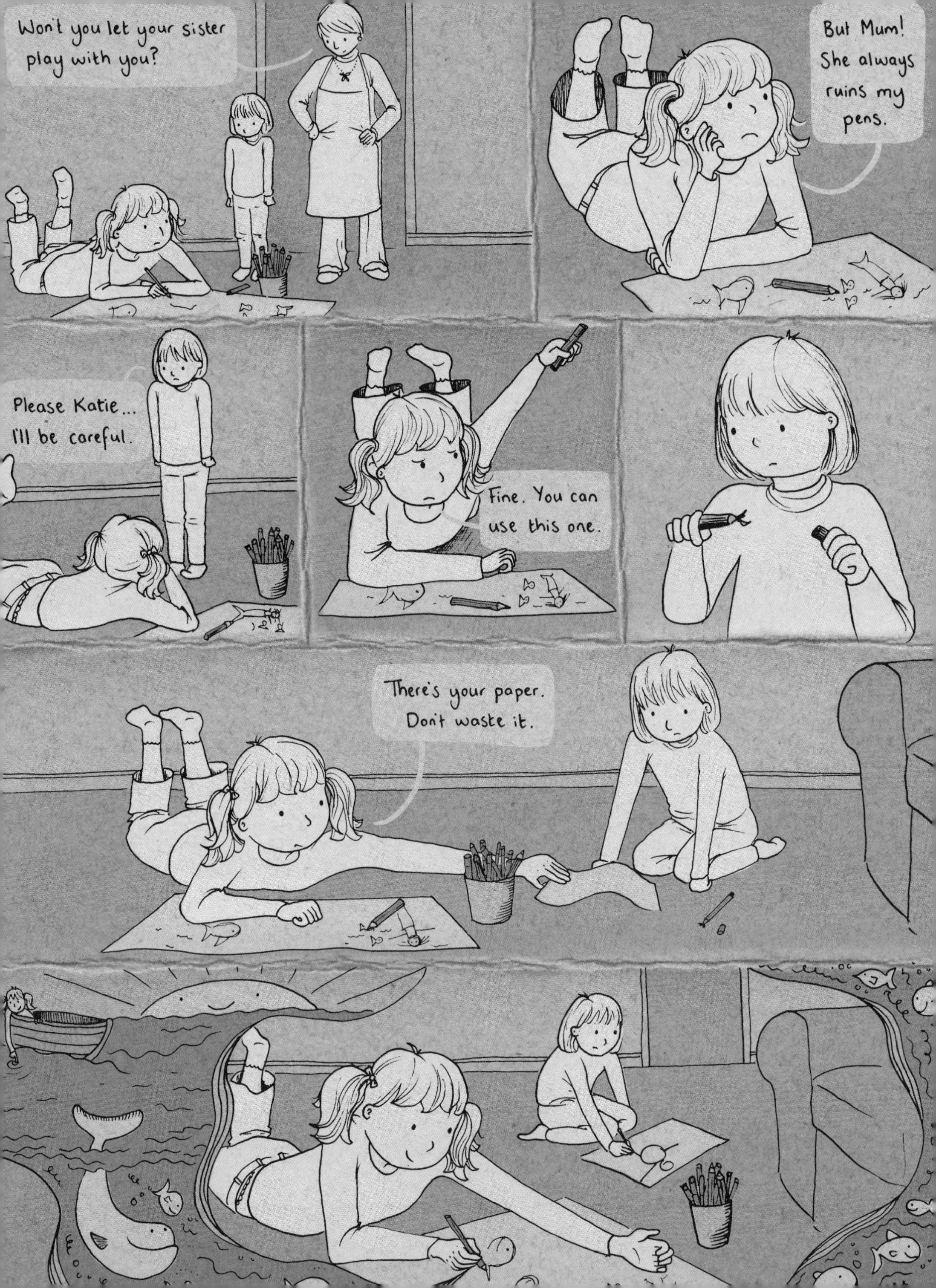
Won't you let your sister play with you?
But Mum! She always ruins my pens.
Please Katie... I'll be careful.
Fine. You can use this one.
There's your paper. Don't waste it.

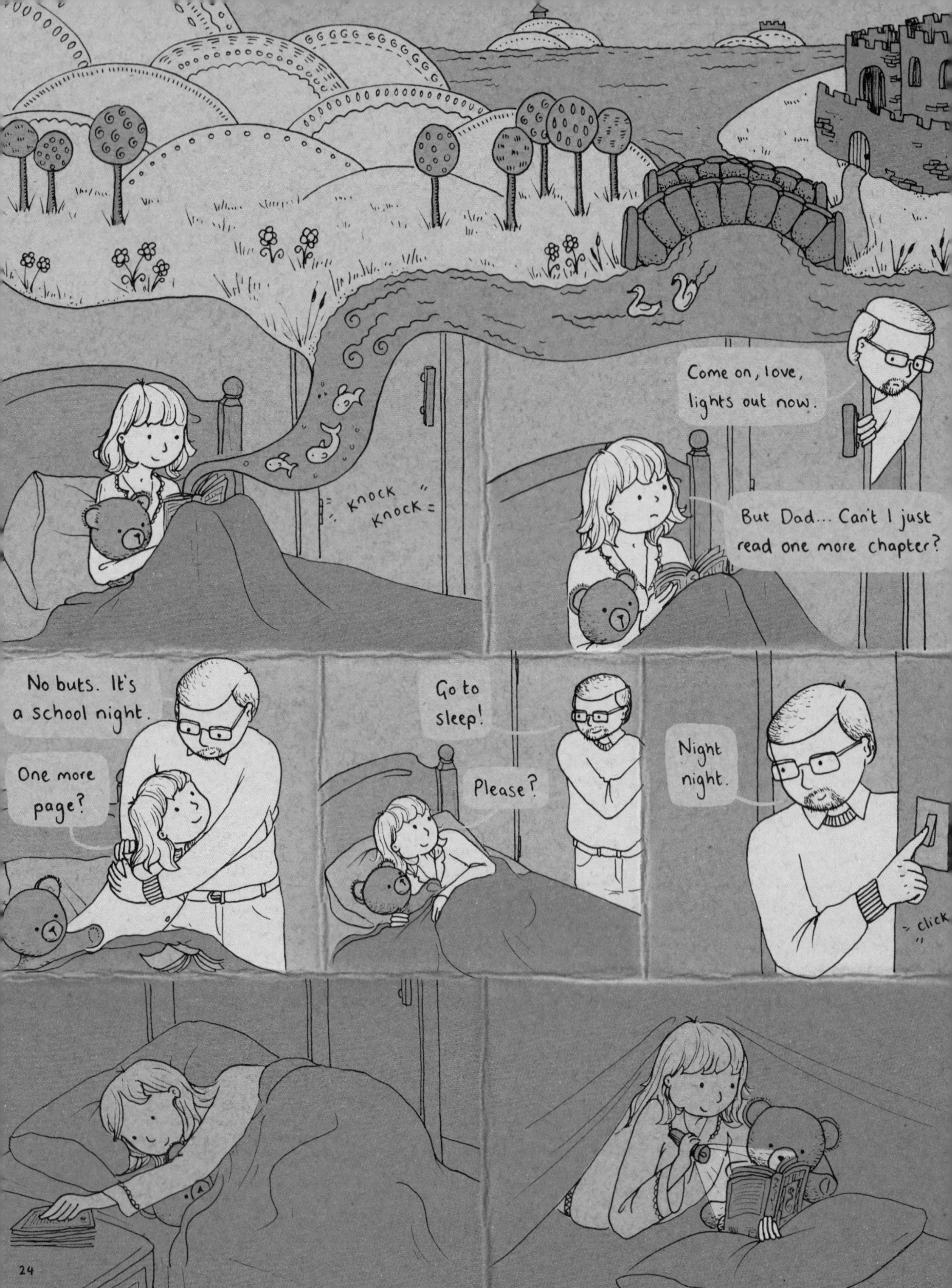
KNOCK KNOCK
Come on, love, lights out now.
But Dad... Can't I just read one more chapter?
No buts. It's a school night.
One more page?
Go to sleep!
Please?
Night night.
click

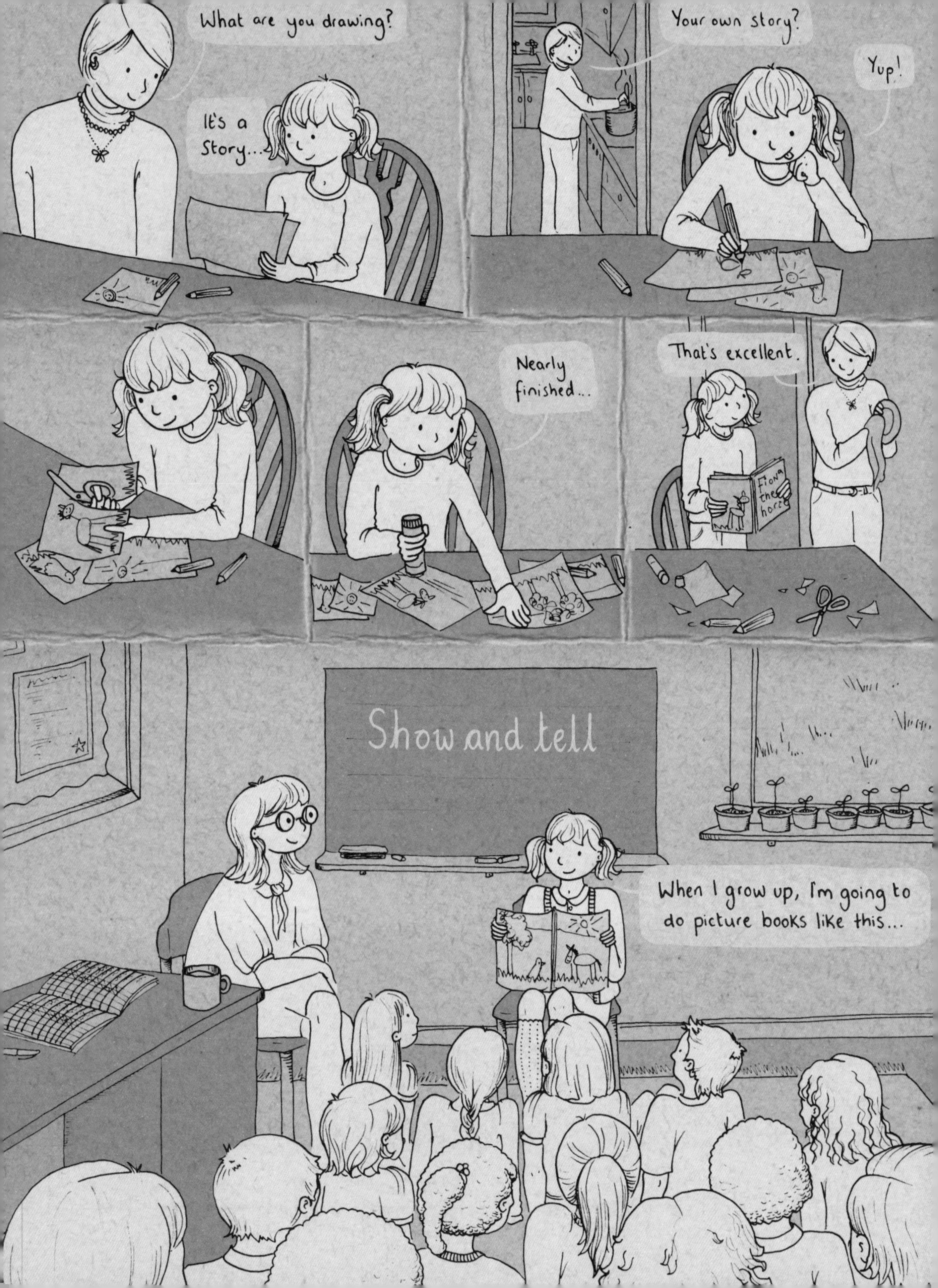
What are you drawing?
It's a Story...
Your own story?
Yup!
Nearly finished...
That's excellent.
Fiona the horse
Show and tell
When I grow up, I'm going to do picture books like this...

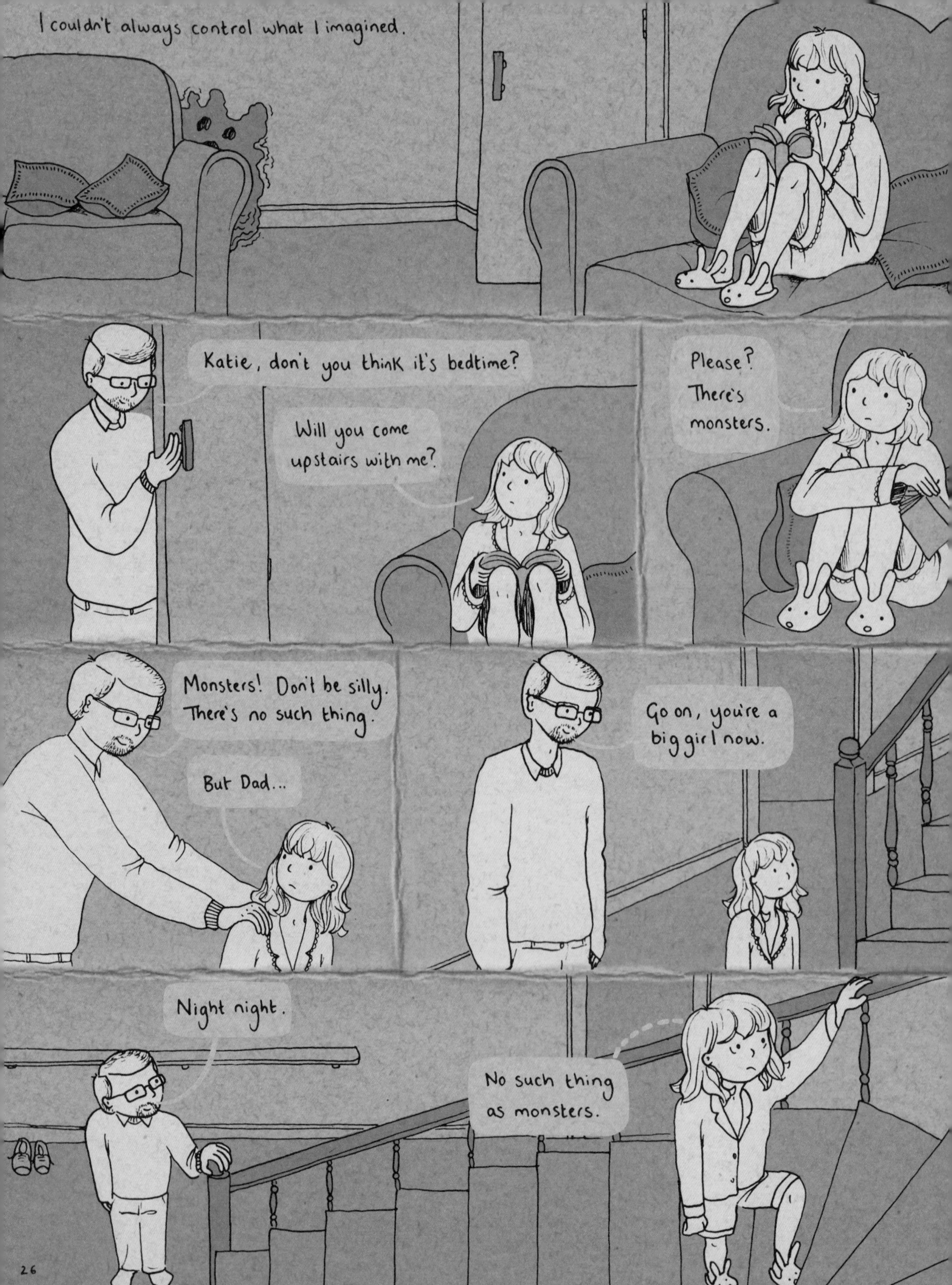
I couldn't always control what I imagined.
Katie, don't you think it's bedtime?
Will you come upstairs with me?
Please? There's monsters.
Monsters! Don't be silly. There's no such thing.
But Dad...
Go on, you're a big girl now.
Night night.
No such thing as monsters.

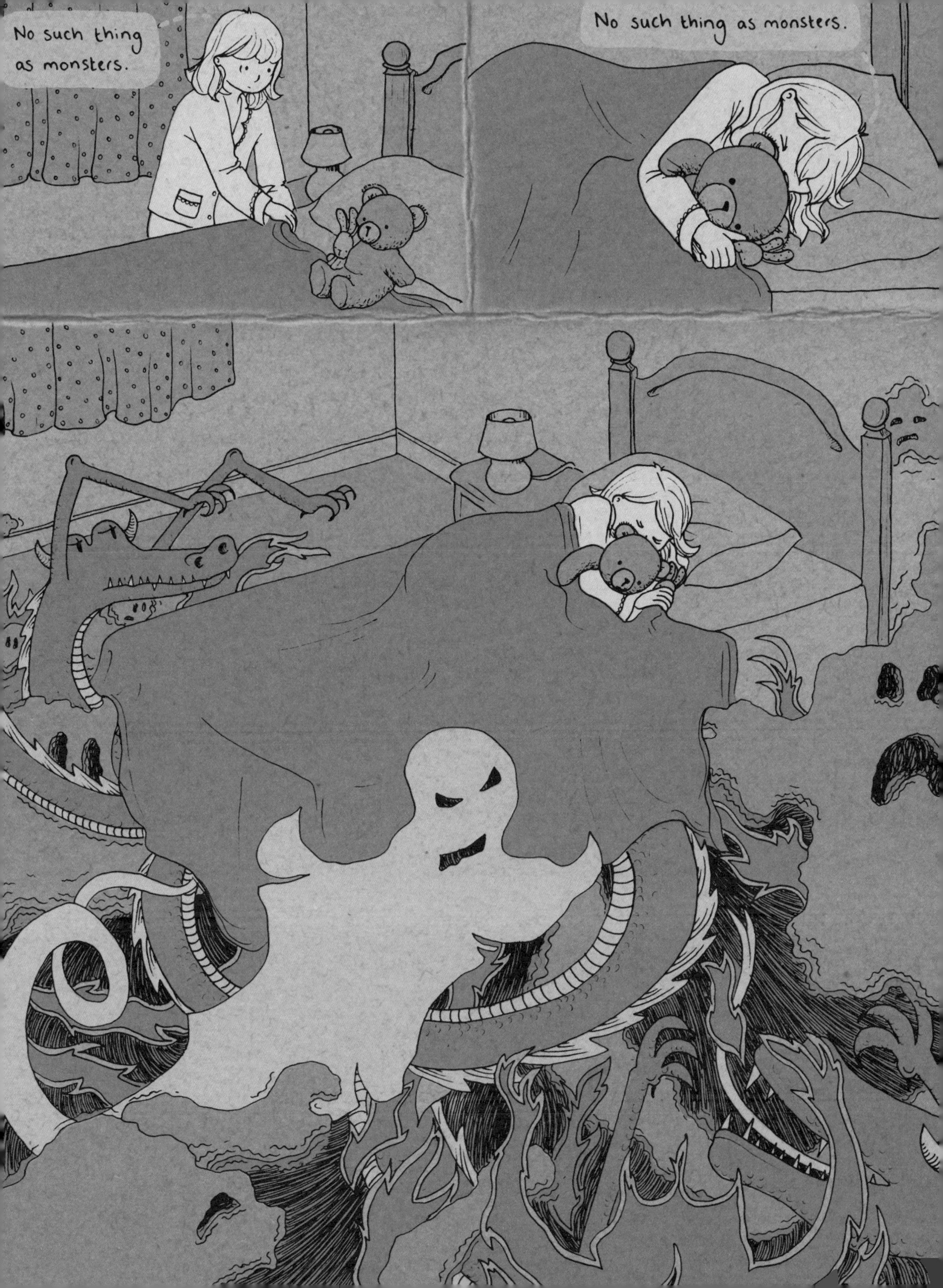
No such thing as monsters.
No such thing as monsters.

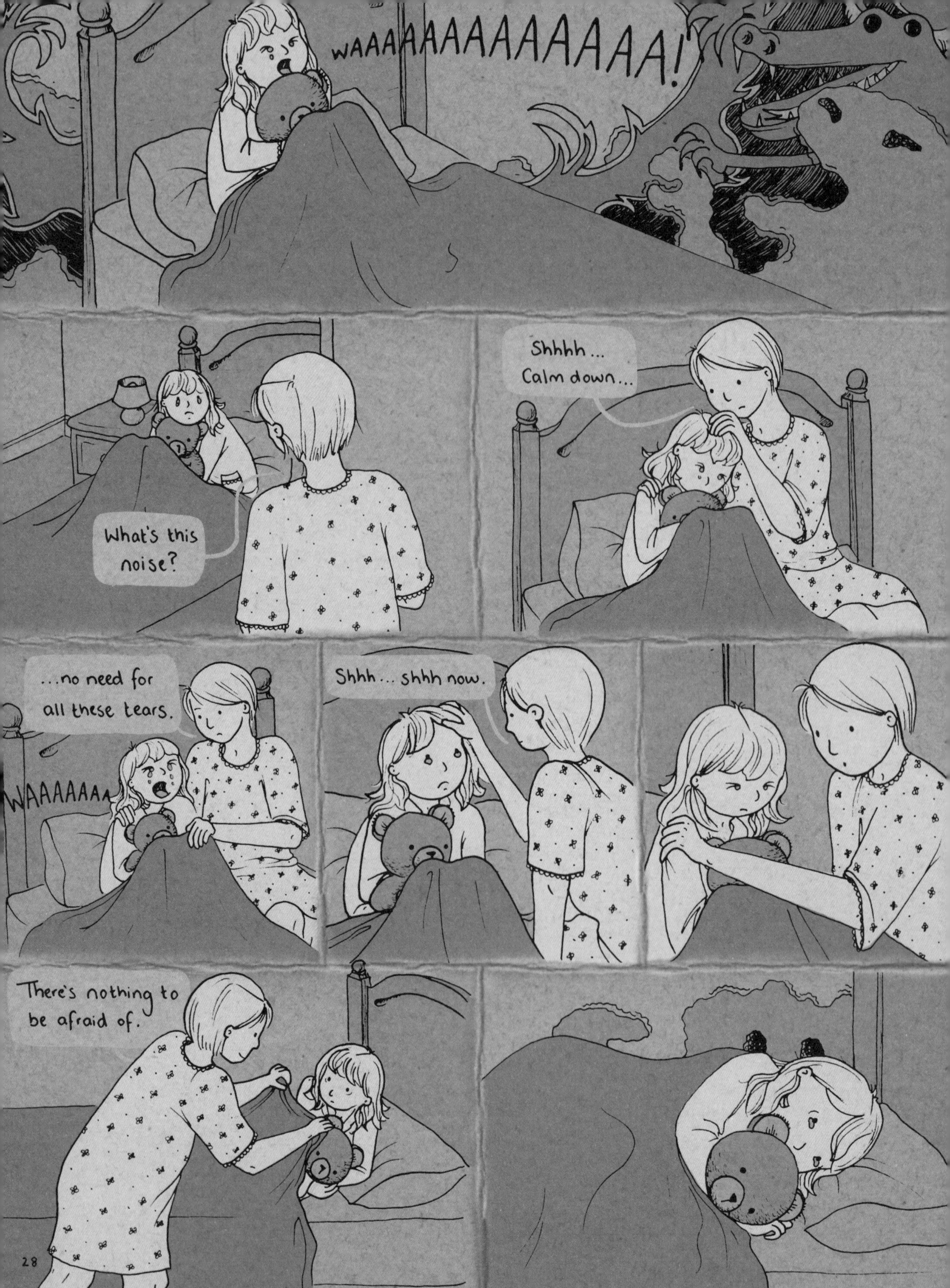
WAAAAAAAAAAAAA!
What's this noise?
Shhhh... Calm down...
...no need for all these tears.
WAAAAAAA
Shhh... shhh now.
There's nothing to be afraid of.

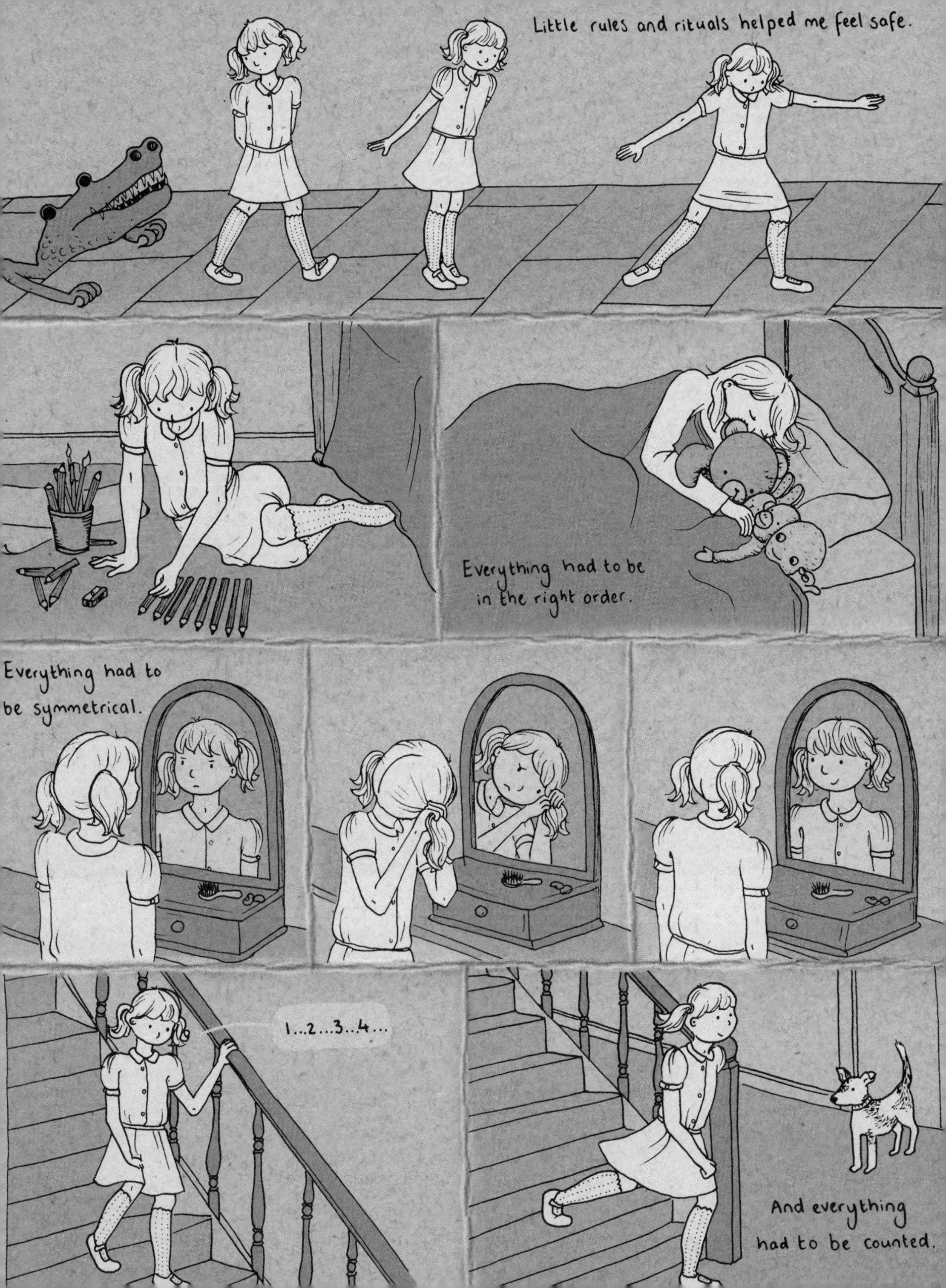
Little rules and rituals helped me feel safe.
Everything had to be in the right order.
Everything had to be symmetrical.
1...2...3...4...
And everything had to be counted.

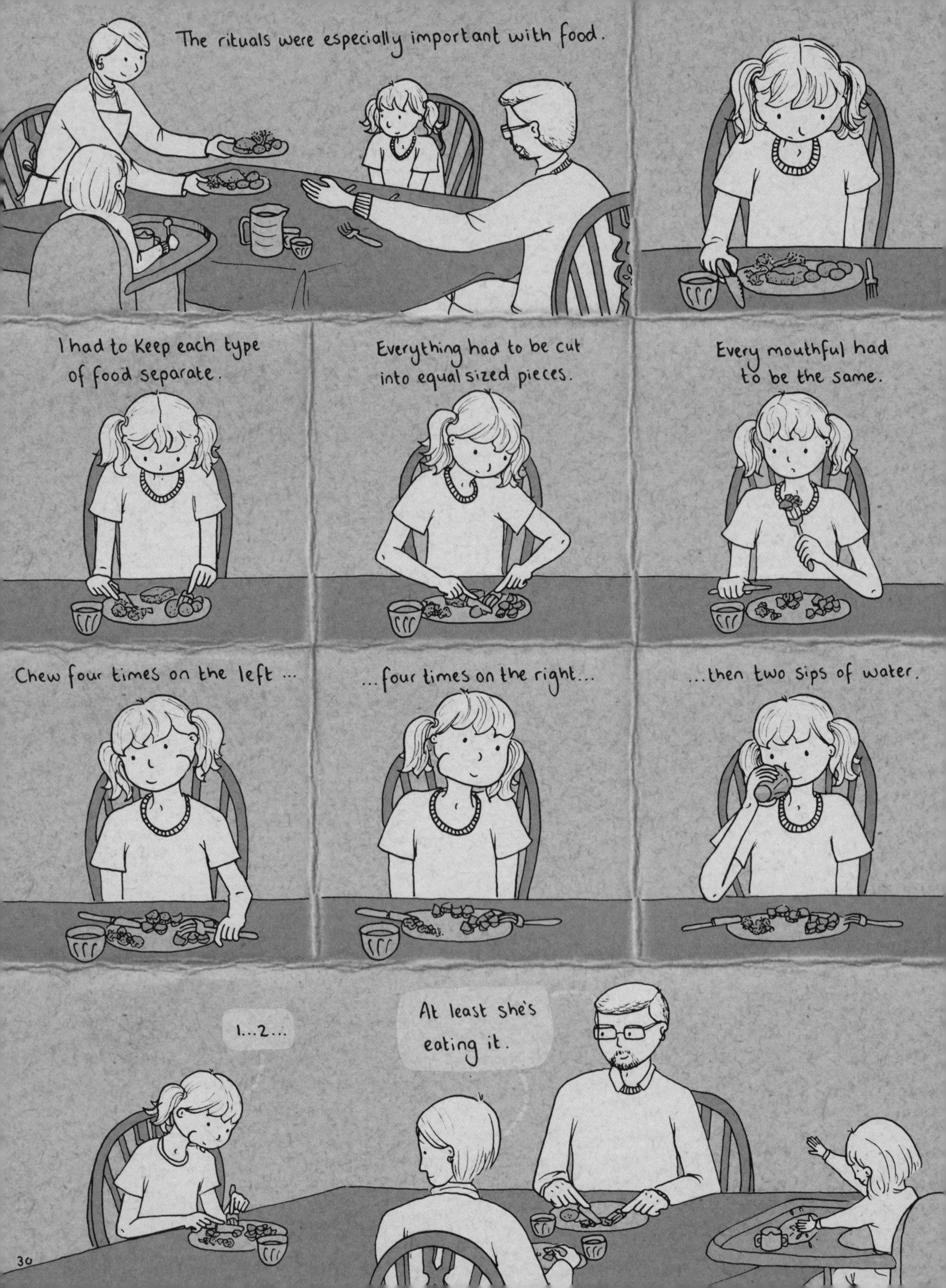
The rituals were especially important with food.
I had to keep each type of food separate.
Everything had to be cut into equal sized pieces.
Every mouthful had to be the same.
Chew four times on the left ...
... four times on the right...
... then two sips of water.
1...2...
At least she's eating it.

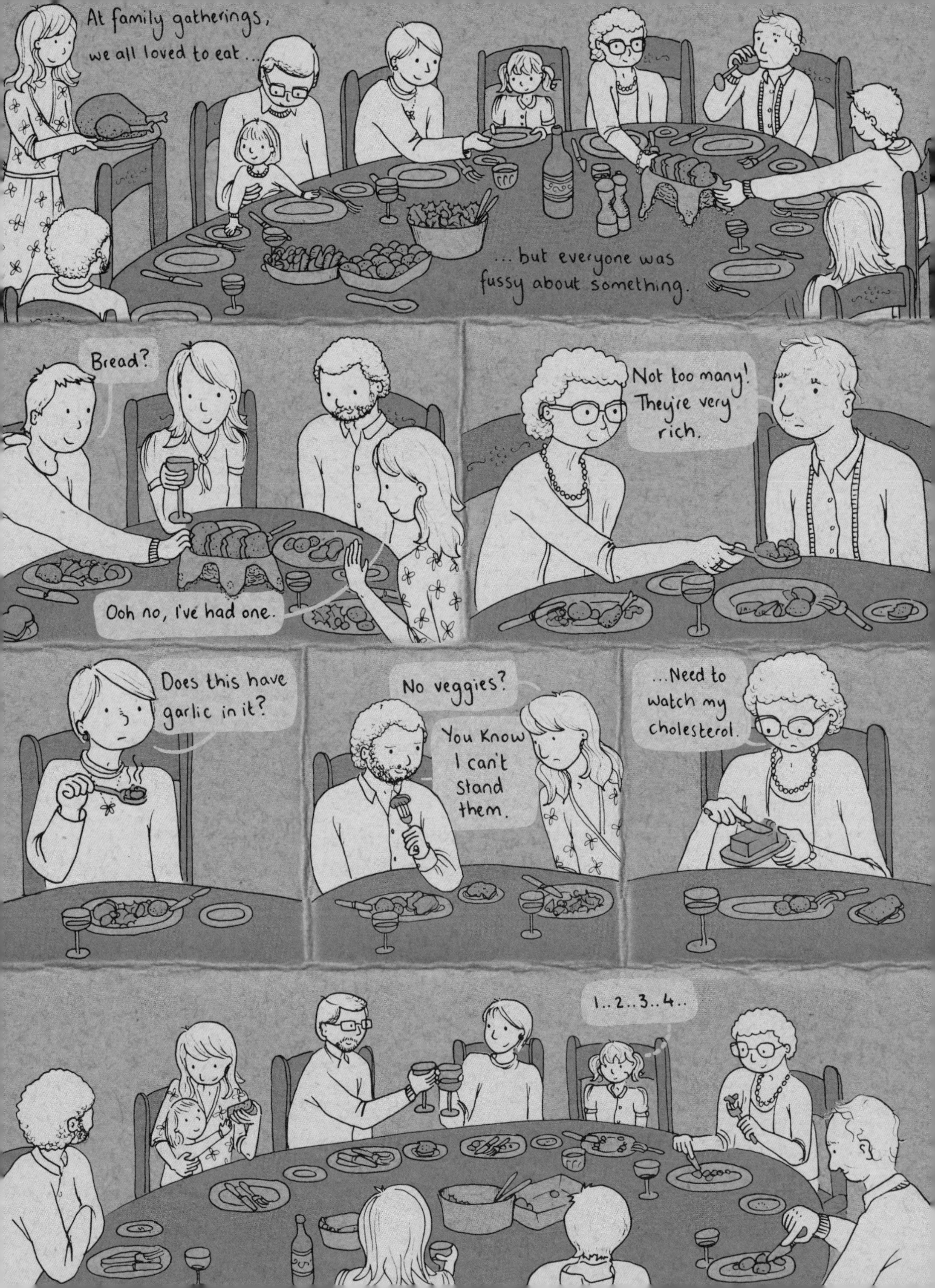
At family gatherings,
we all loved to eat...
... but everyone was fussy about something.
Bread?
Ooh no, I've had one.
Not too many! They're very rich.
Does this have garlic in it?
No veggies?
You know I can't stand them.
...Need to watch my cholesterol.
1..2..3..4..

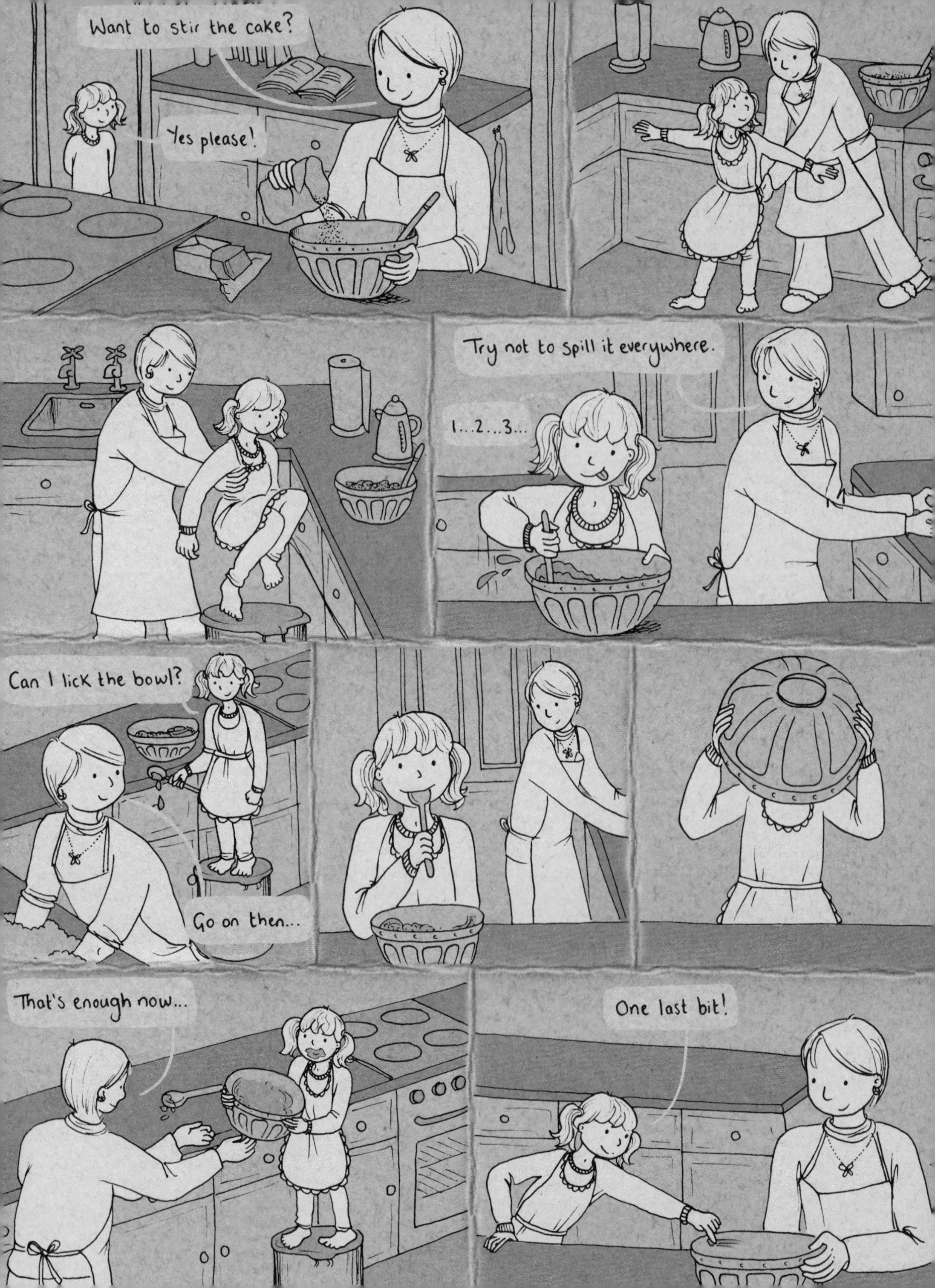
Want to stir the cake?
Yes please!
Try not to spill it everywhere.
1...2...3...
Can I lick the bowl?
Go on then...
That's enough now...
One last bit!

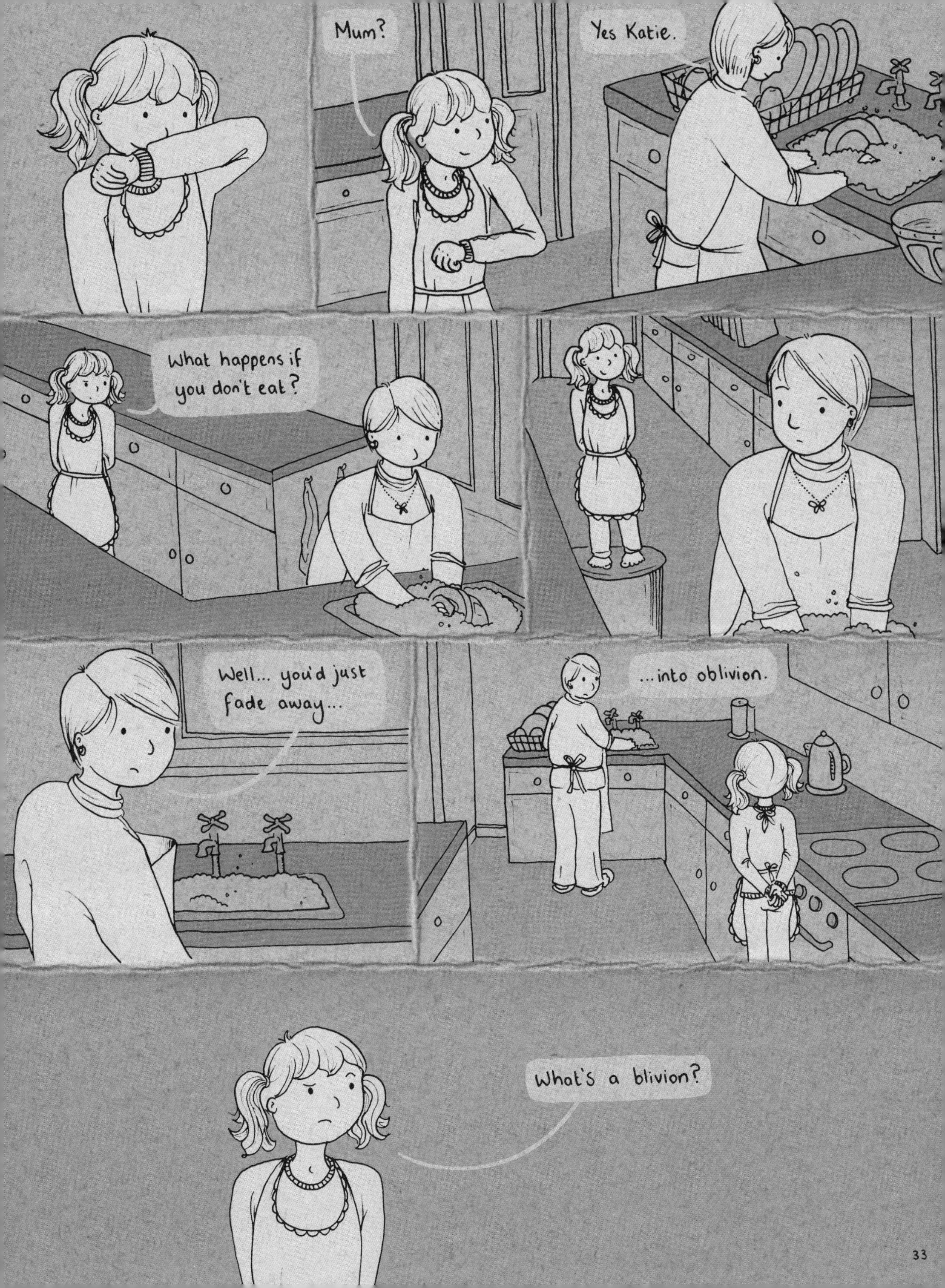

Mum?
Yes Katie.
What happens if you don't eat?
Well... you'd just fade away...
...into oblivion.
What's a blivion?

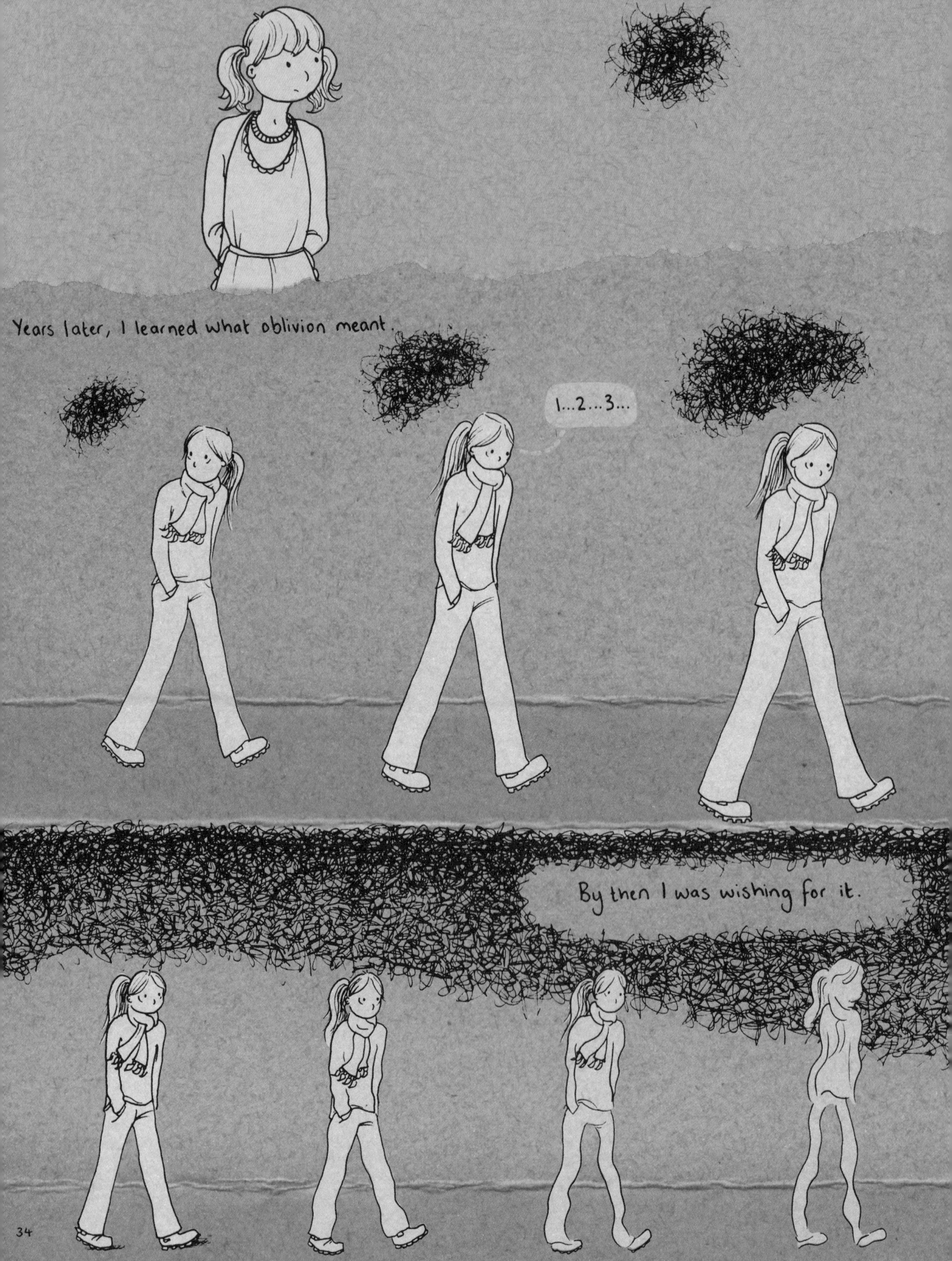
Years later, I learned what oblivion meant.
1...2...3...
By then I was wishing for it.

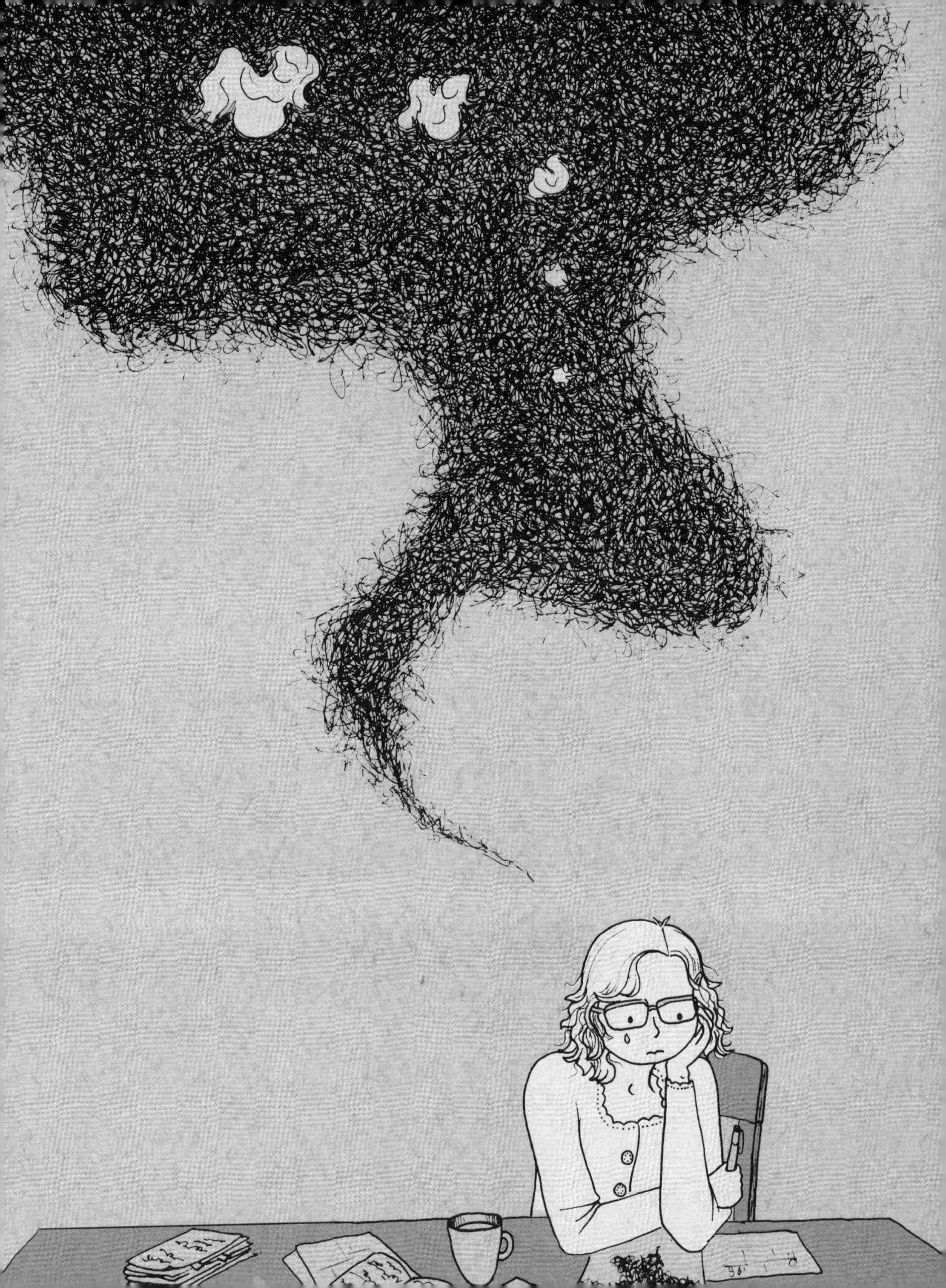

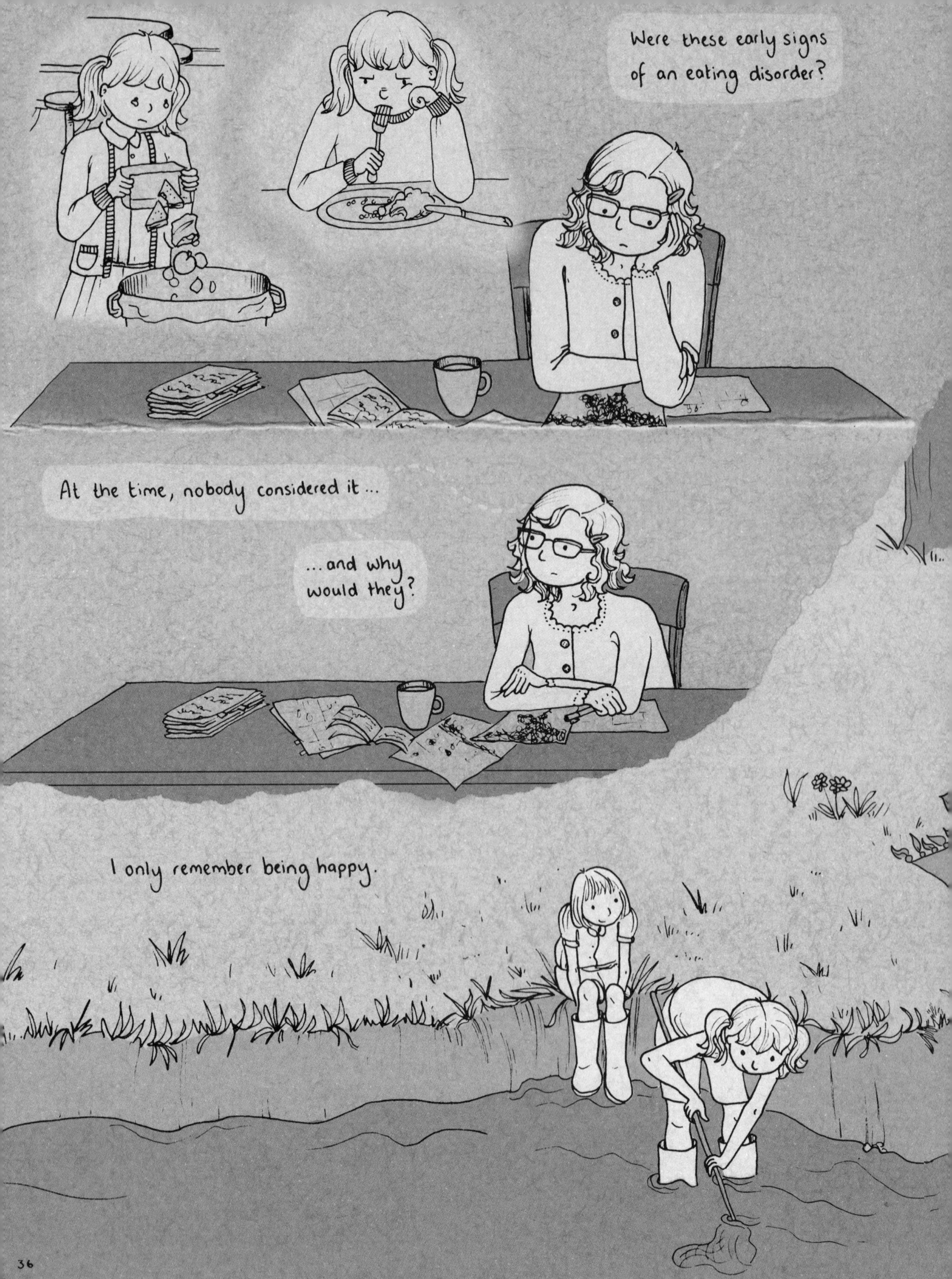
Were these early signs of an eating disorder?
At the time, nobody considered it ...
... and why would they?
I only remember being happy.

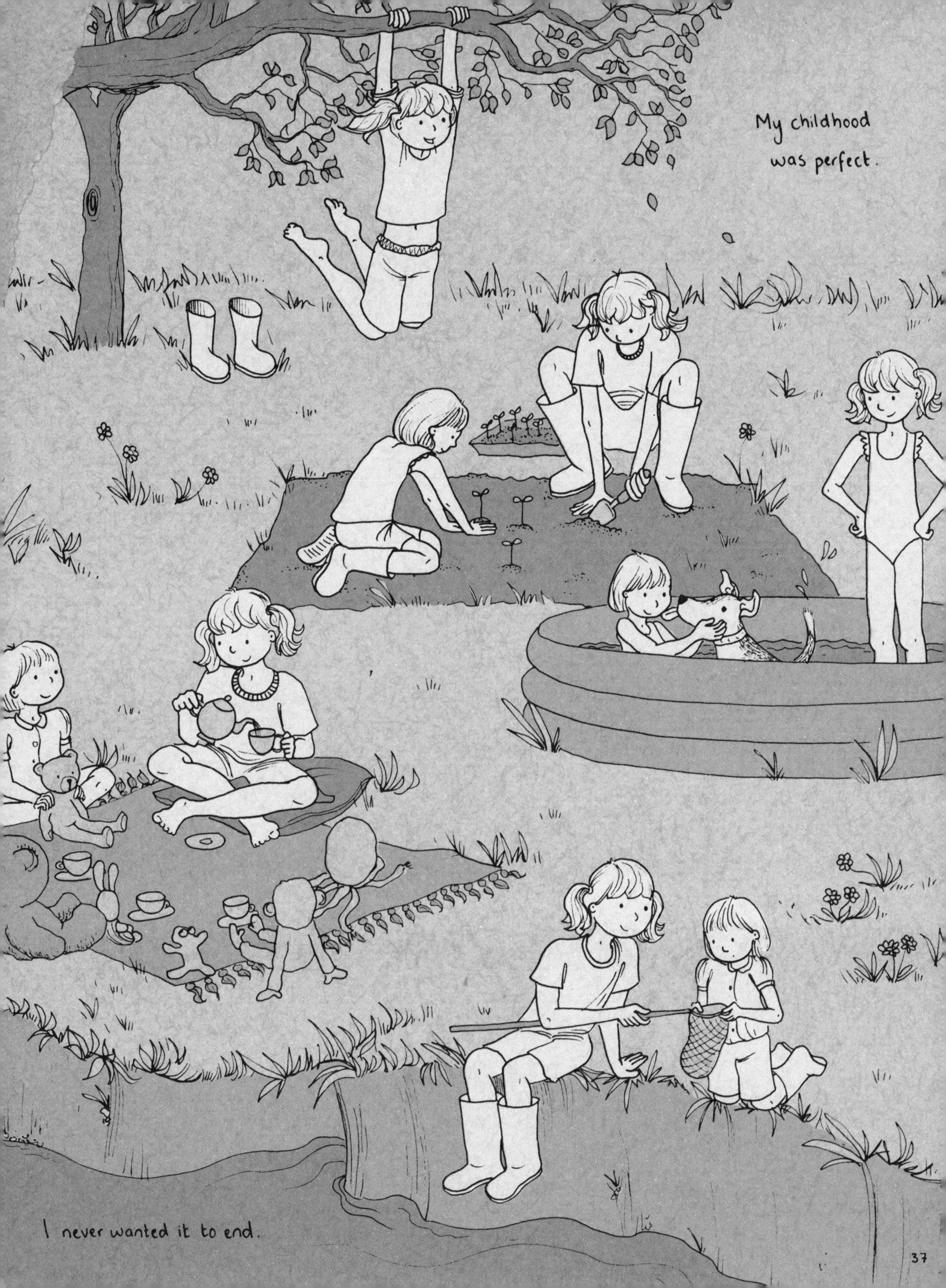
My childhood
was perfect.
I never wanted it to end.

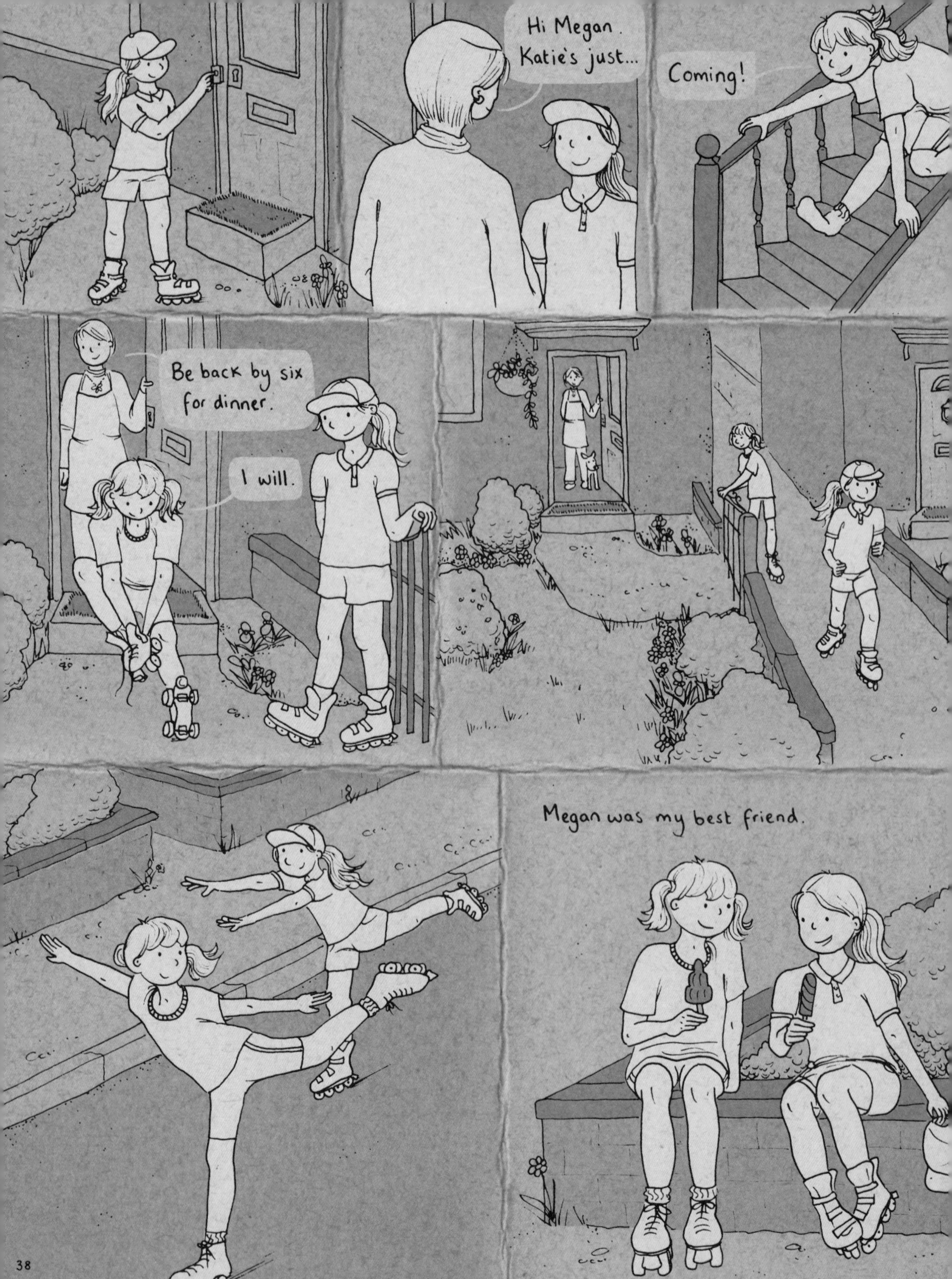
Hi Megan. Katie's just...
Coming!
Be back by six for dinner.
I will.
Megan was my best friend.

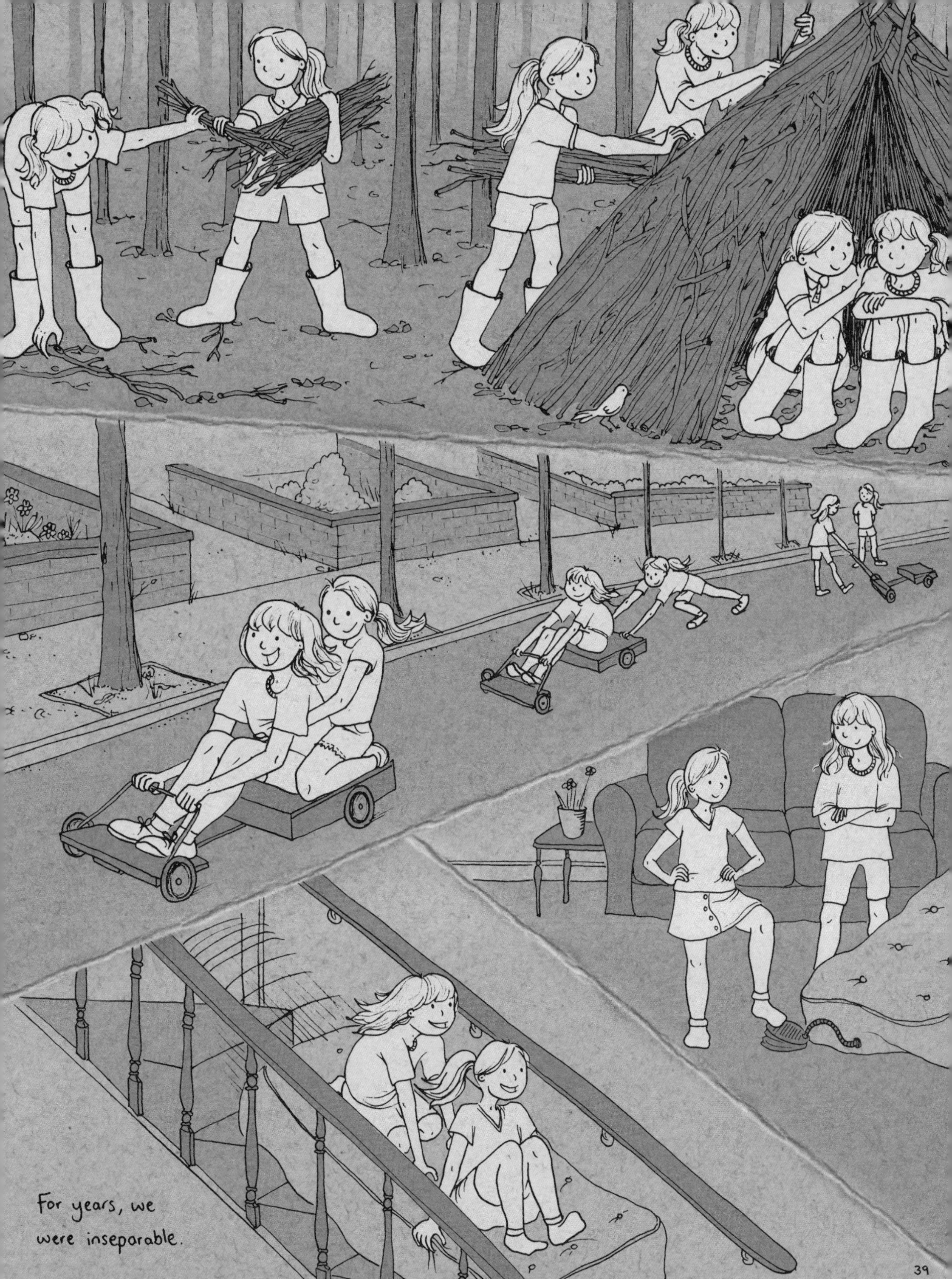
For years, we
were inseparable.

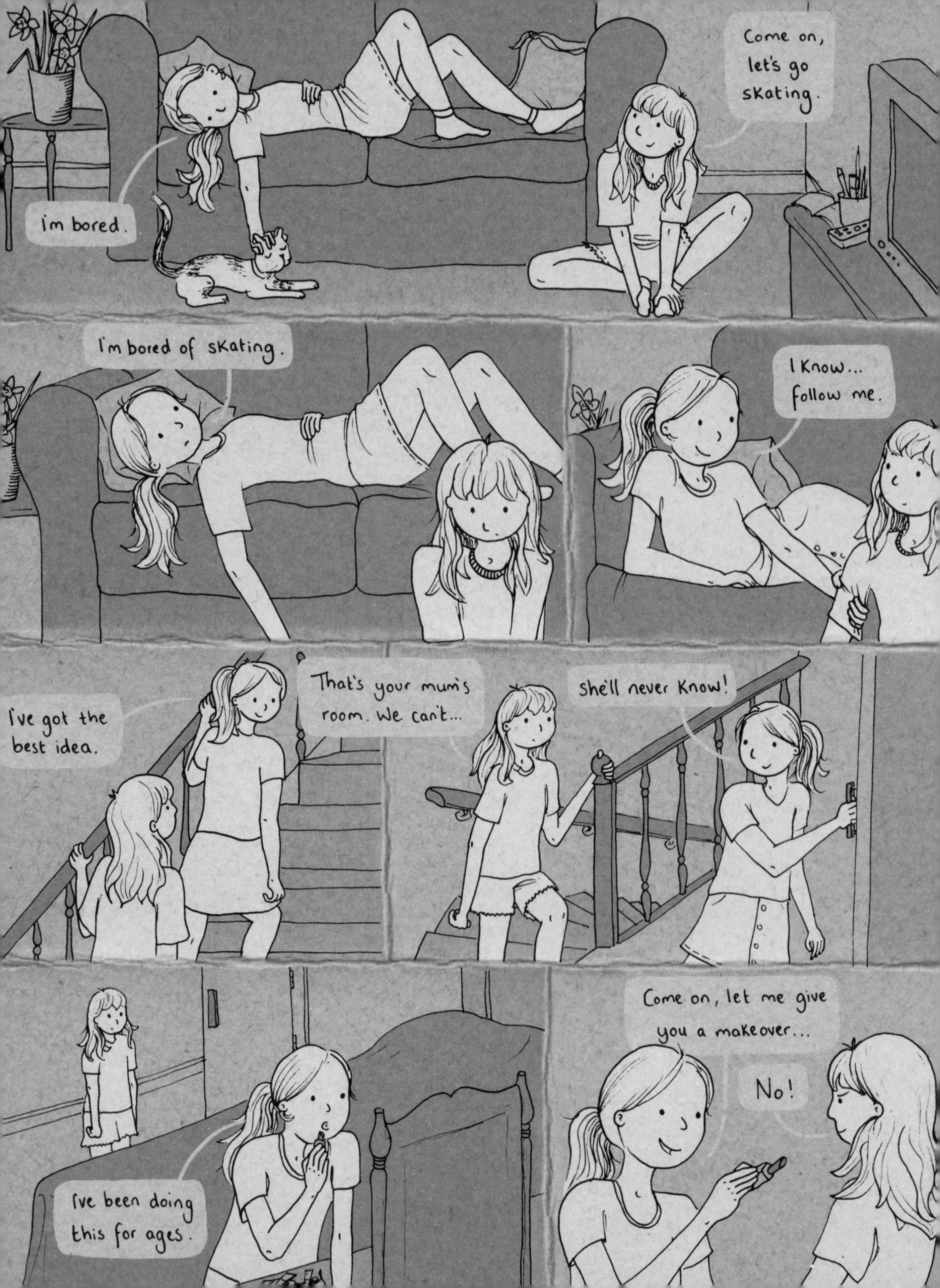

I'm bored.
Come on, let's go skating.
I'm bored of skating.
I know... follow me.
I've got the best idea.
That's your mum's room. We can't...
She'll never know!
I've been doing this for ages.
Come on, let me give you a makeover...
No!

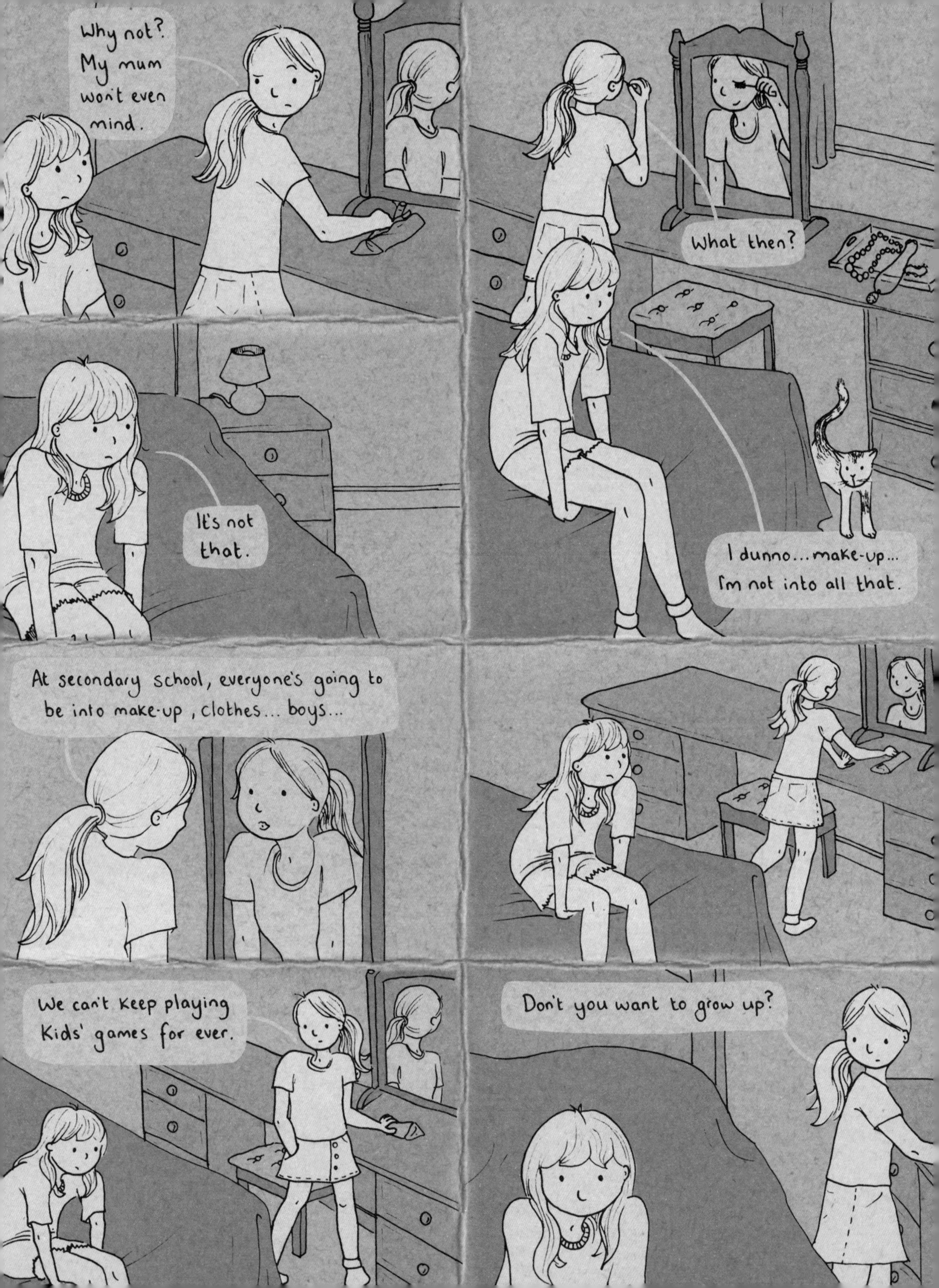

Why not? My mum won't even mind.
What then?
It's not that.
I dunno... make-up... I'm not into all that.
At secondary school, everyone's going to be into make-up, clothes... boys...
We can't keep playing kids' games for ever.
Don't you want to grow up?

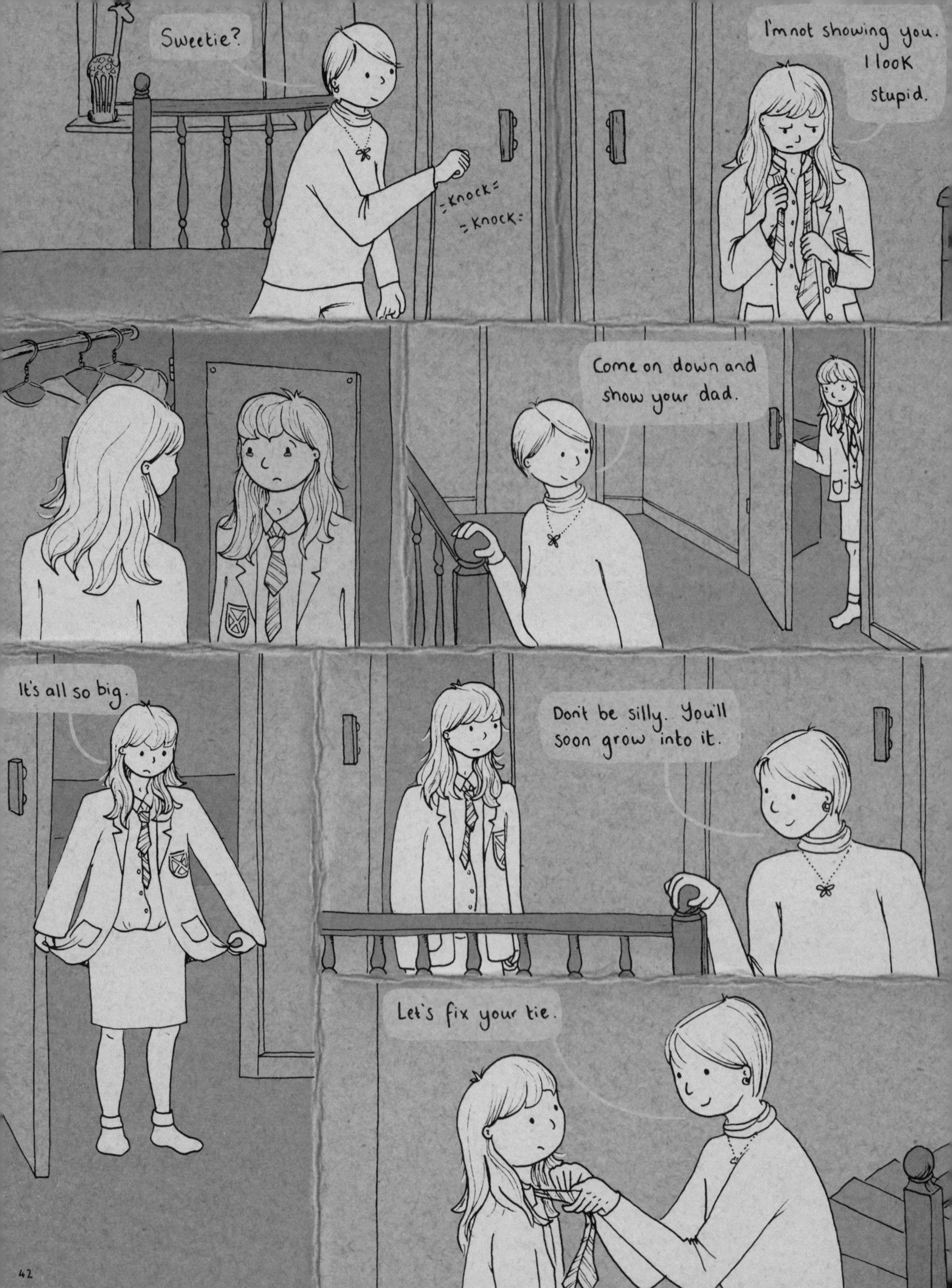
Sweetie?
=Knock=
=Knock=
I'm not showing you. I look stupid.
Come on down and show your dad.
It's all so big.
Don't be silly. You'll soon grow into it.
Let's fix your tie.

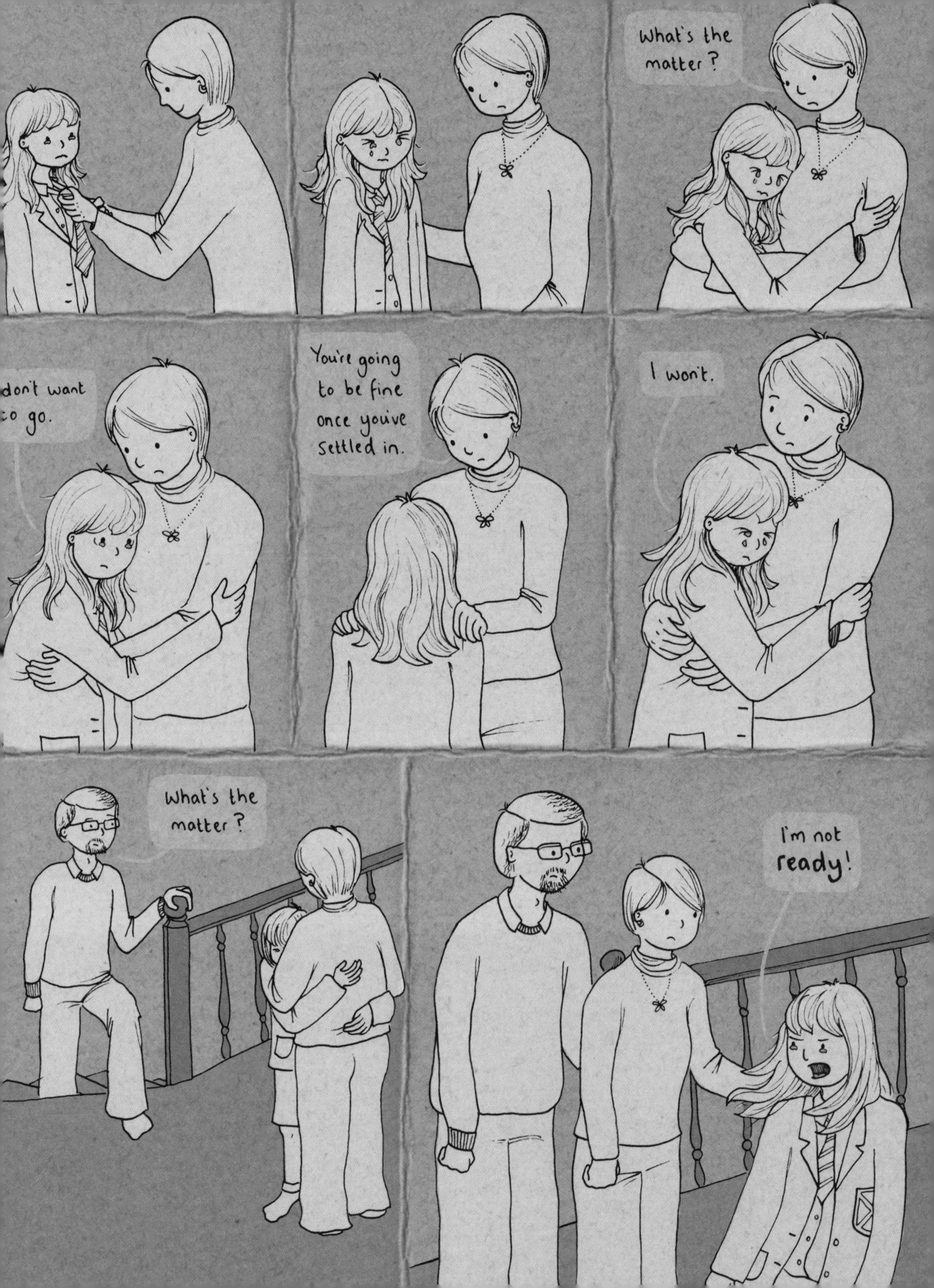
What's the matter?
don't want
to go.
You're going to be fine once you've settled in.
I won't.
What's the matter?
I'm not ready!

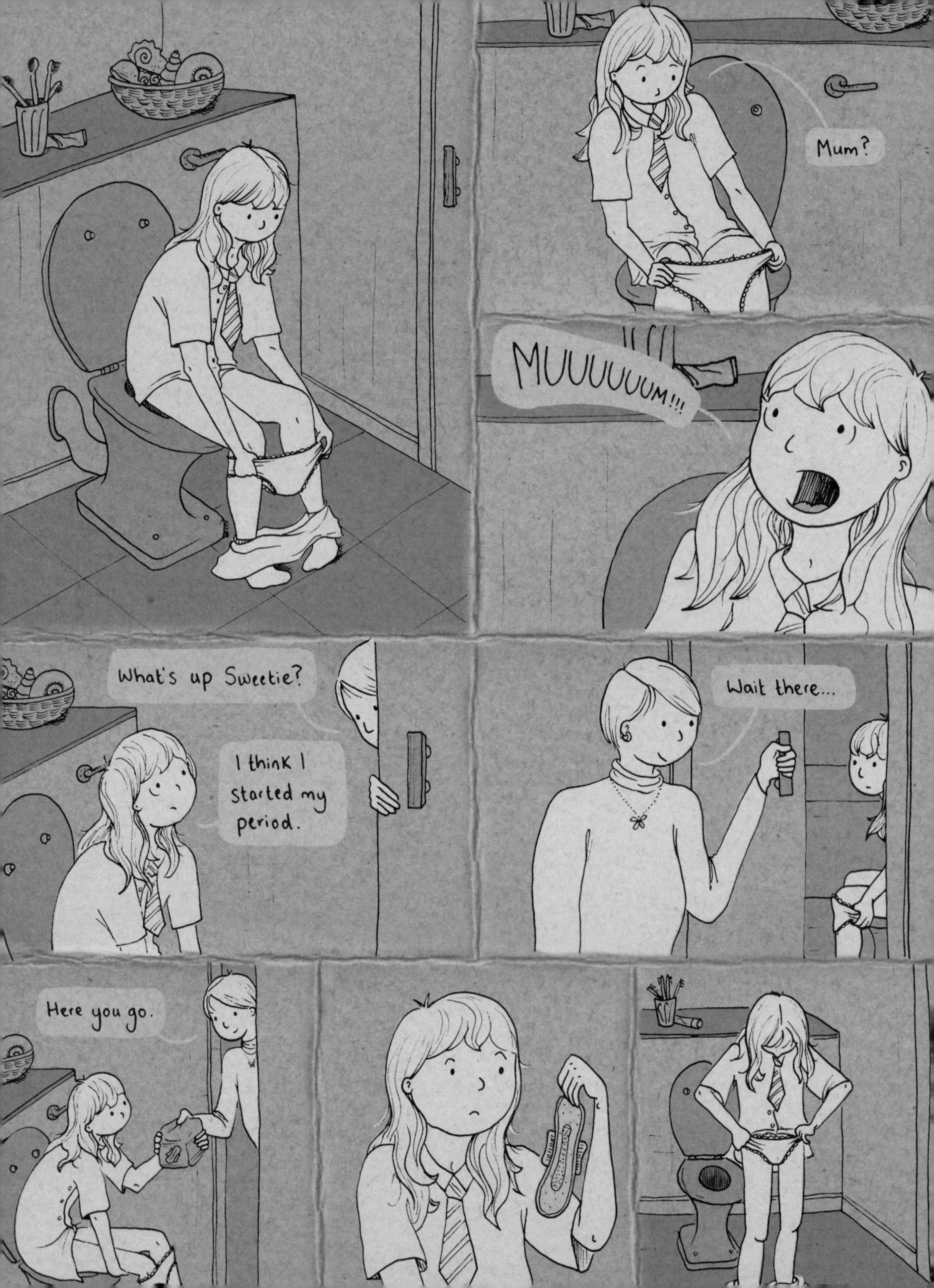
Mum?
MUUUUUUM!!!
What's up Sweetie?
I think I started my period.
Wait there...
Here you go.

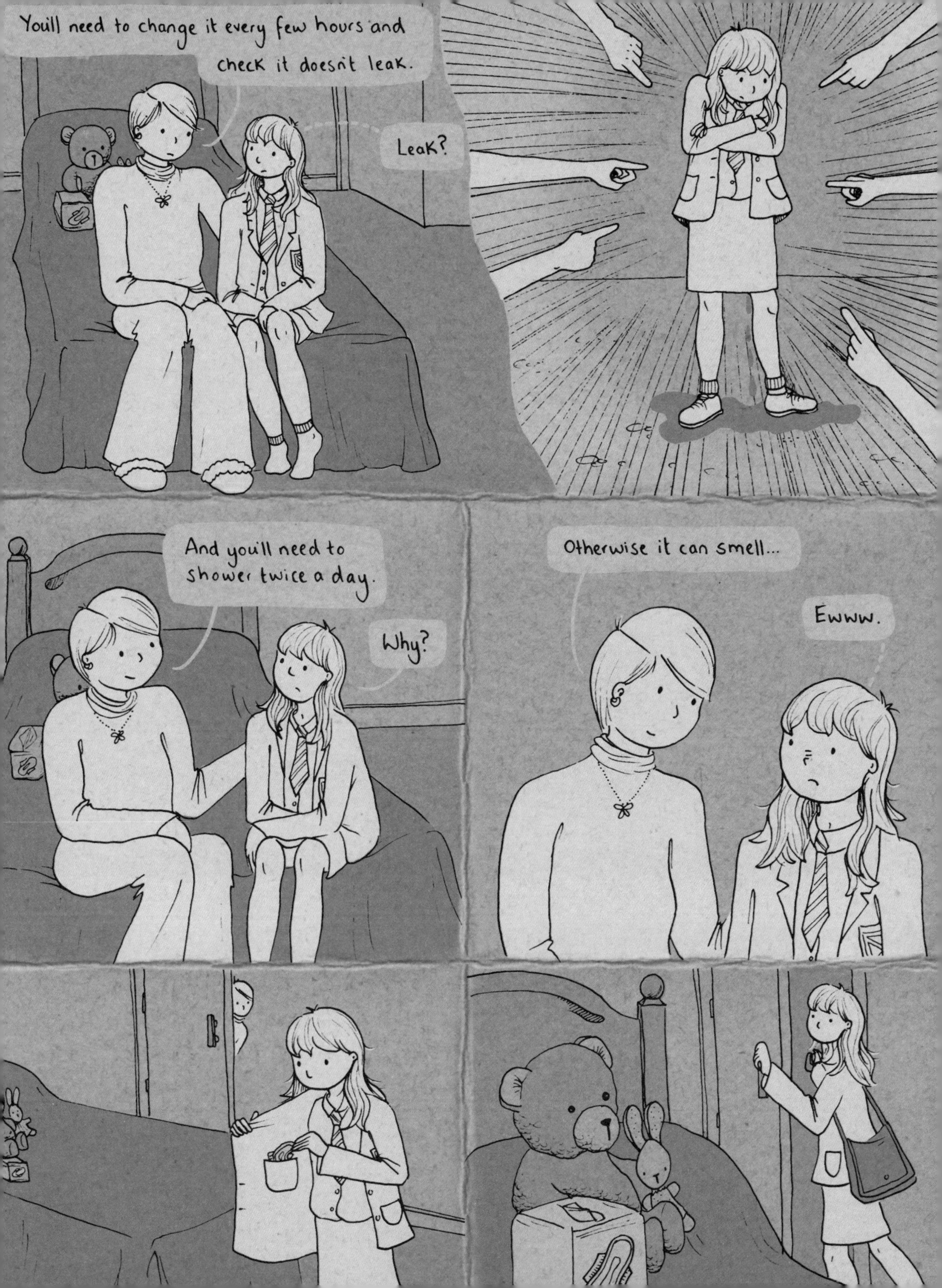
Youll need to change it every few hours and
check it doesn't leak.
Leak?
And you'll need to shower twice a day.
Why?
Otherwise it can smell...
Ewww.

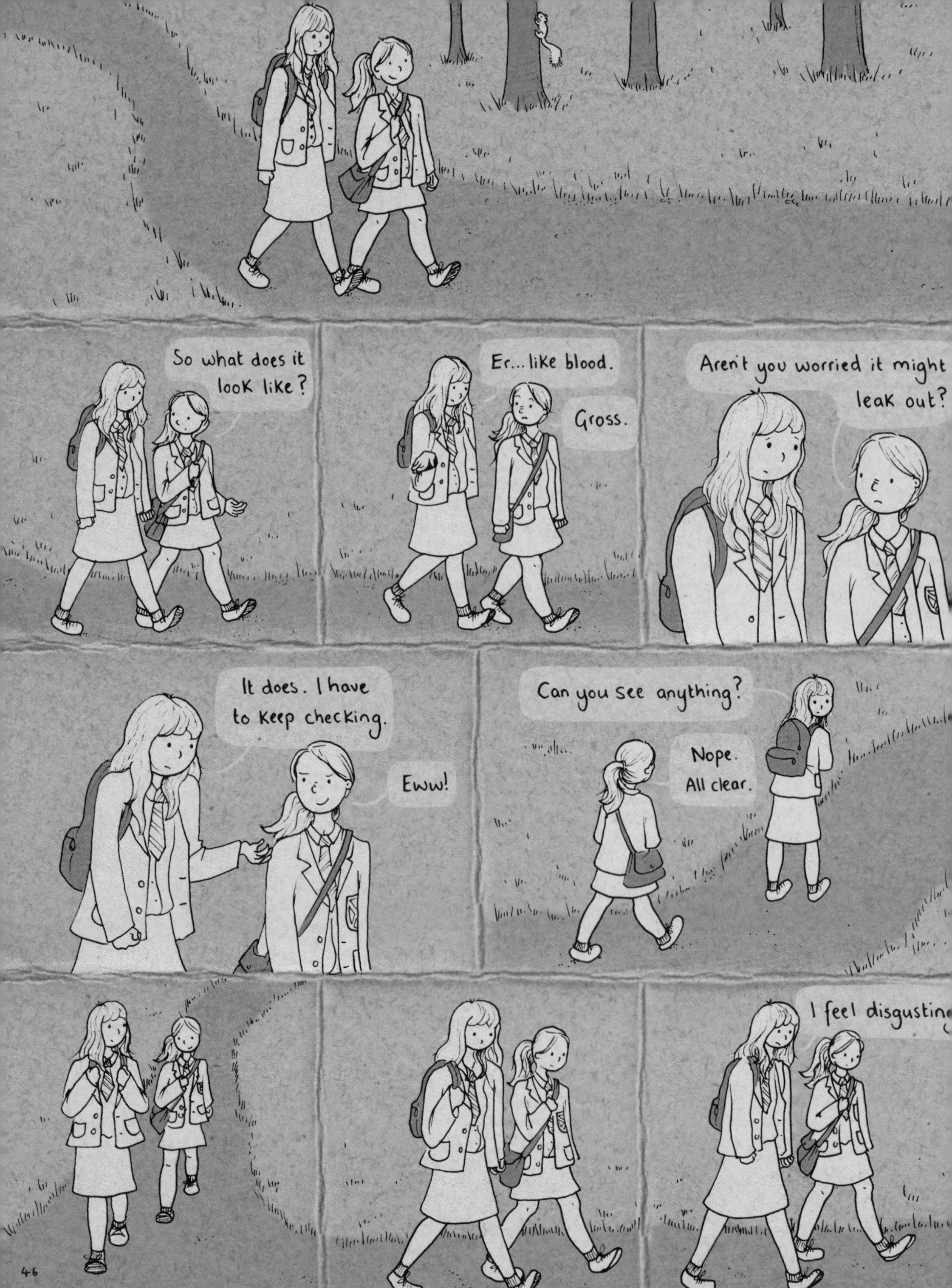
So what does it look like?
Er... like blood.
Gross.
Aren't you worried it might leak out?
It does. I have to keep checking.
Eww!
Can you see anything?
Nope. All clear.
I feel disgusting

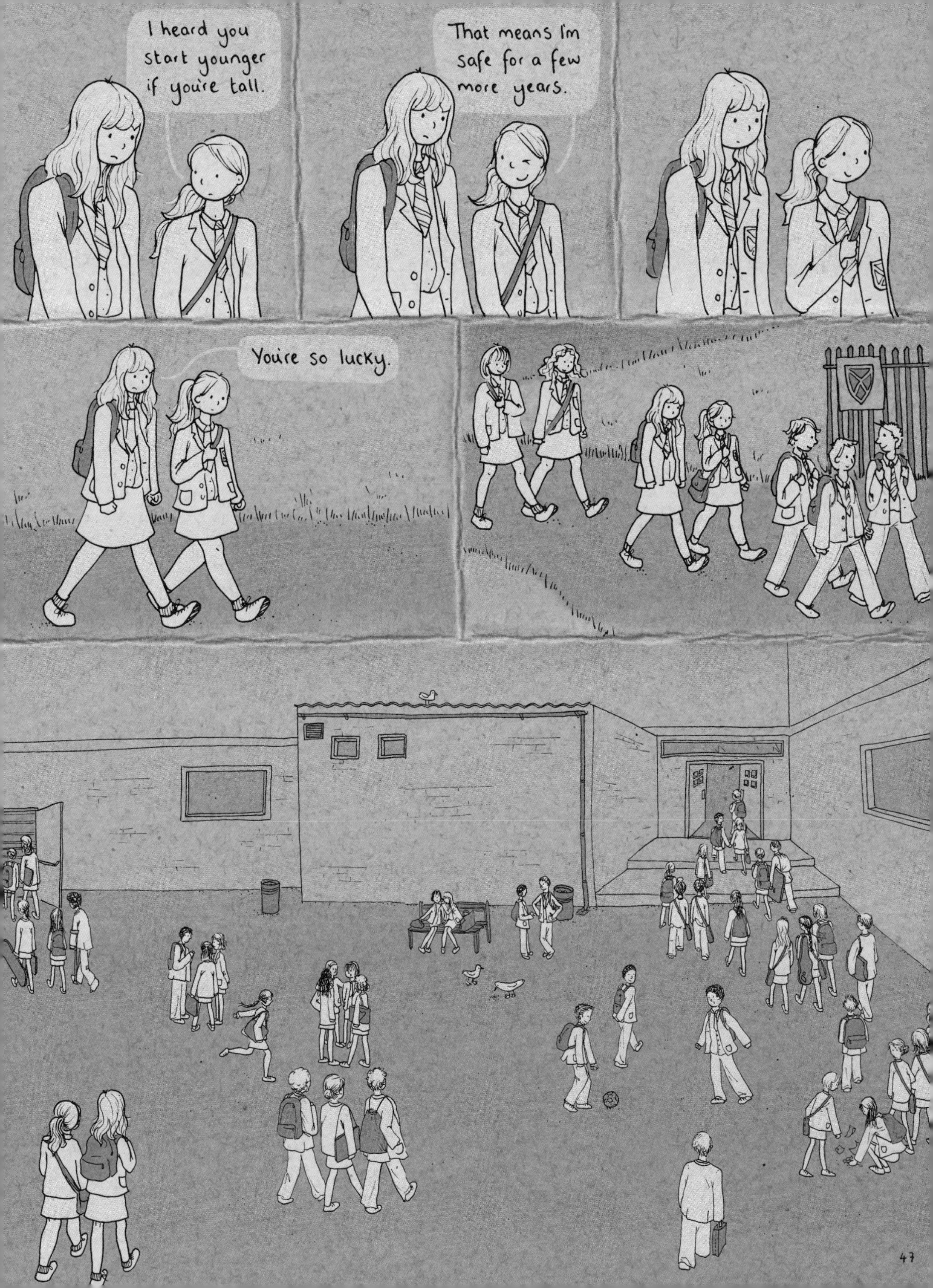
I heard you start younger if you're tall.
That means I'm safe for a few more years.
You're so lucky.

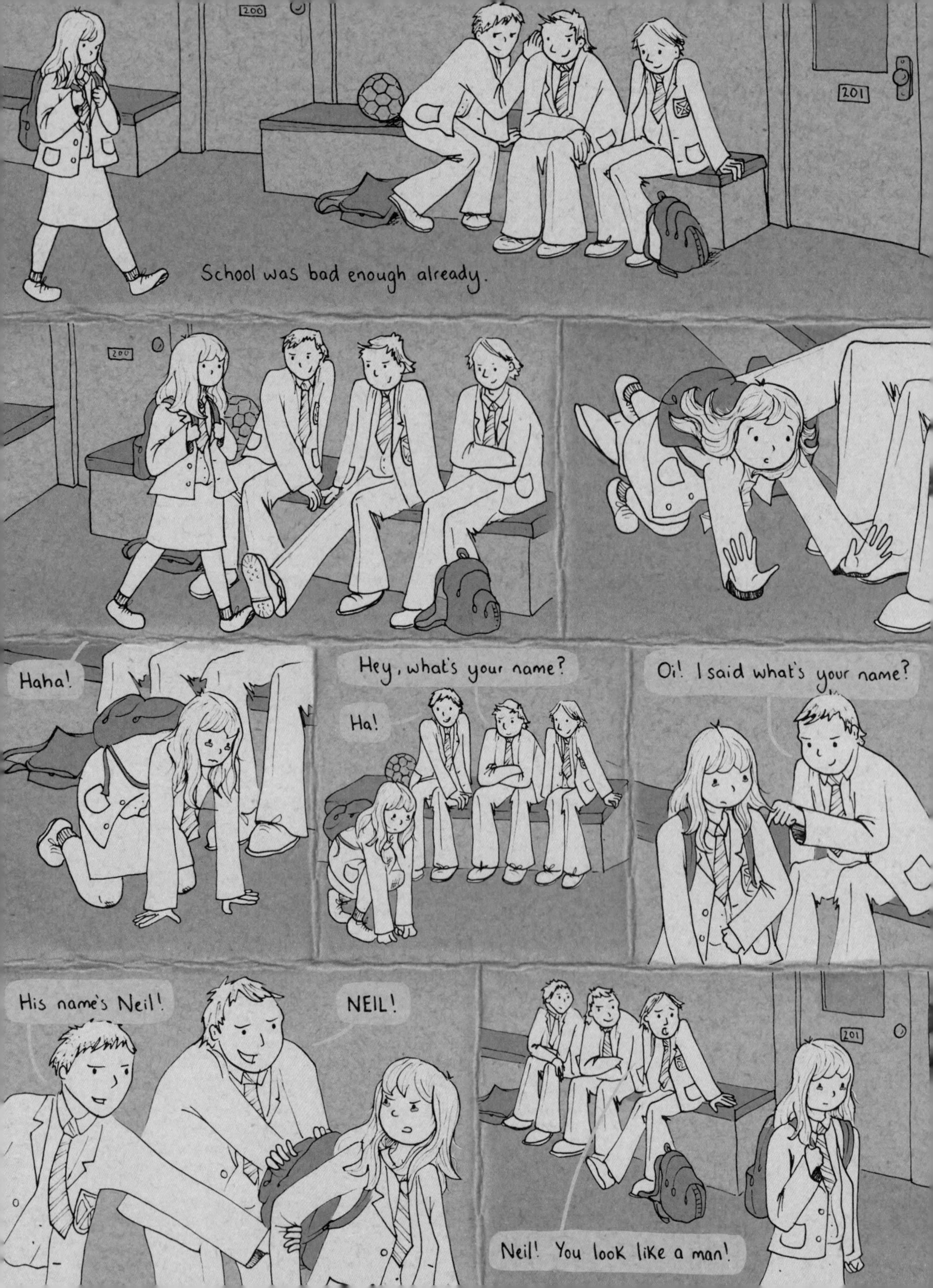
School was bad enough already.
Haha!
Hey, what's your name?
Ha!
Oi! I said what's your name?
His name's Neil!
NEIL!
Neil! You look like a man!

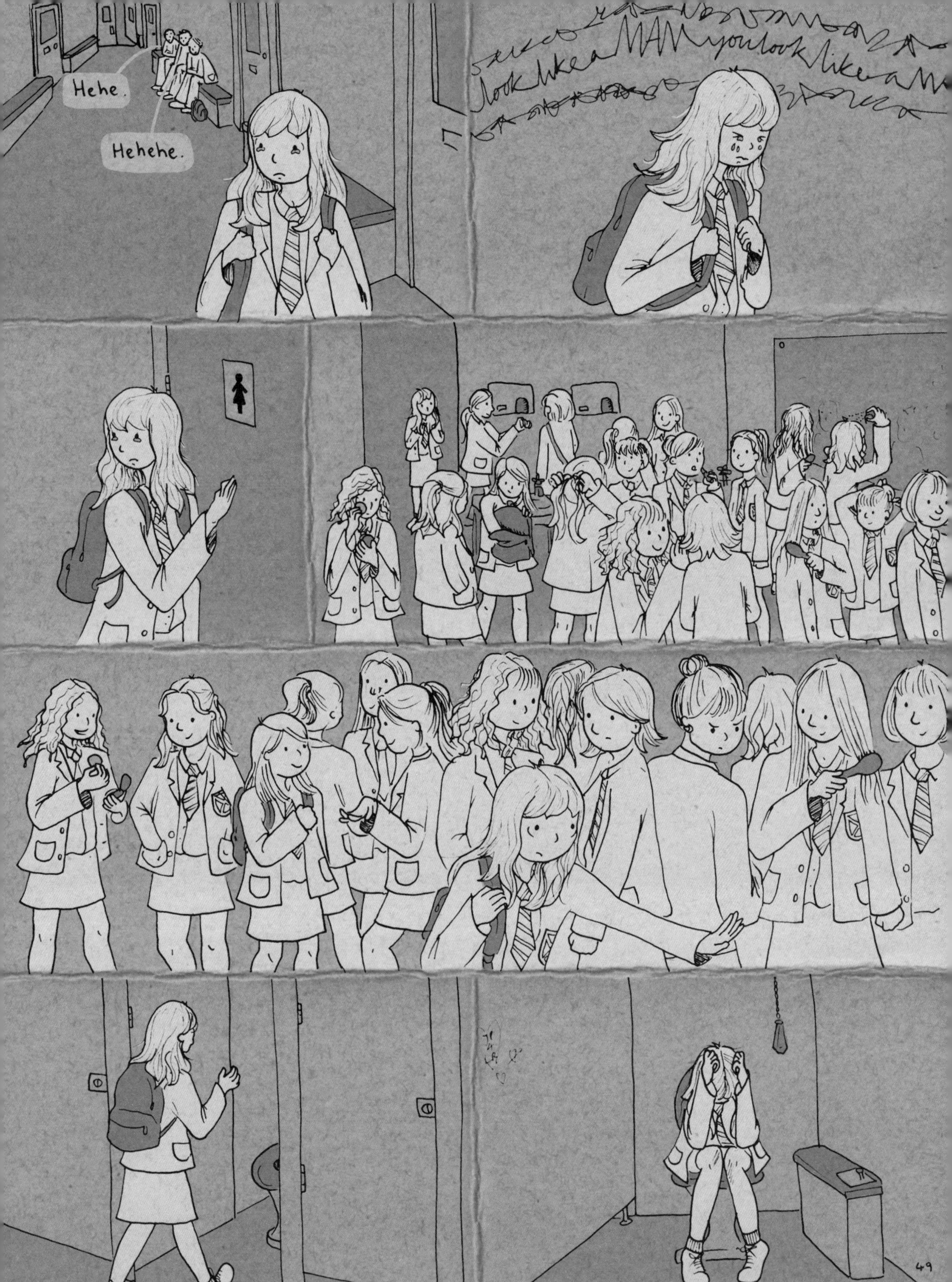
Hehe.
Hehehe.
look like a MAN you look like a

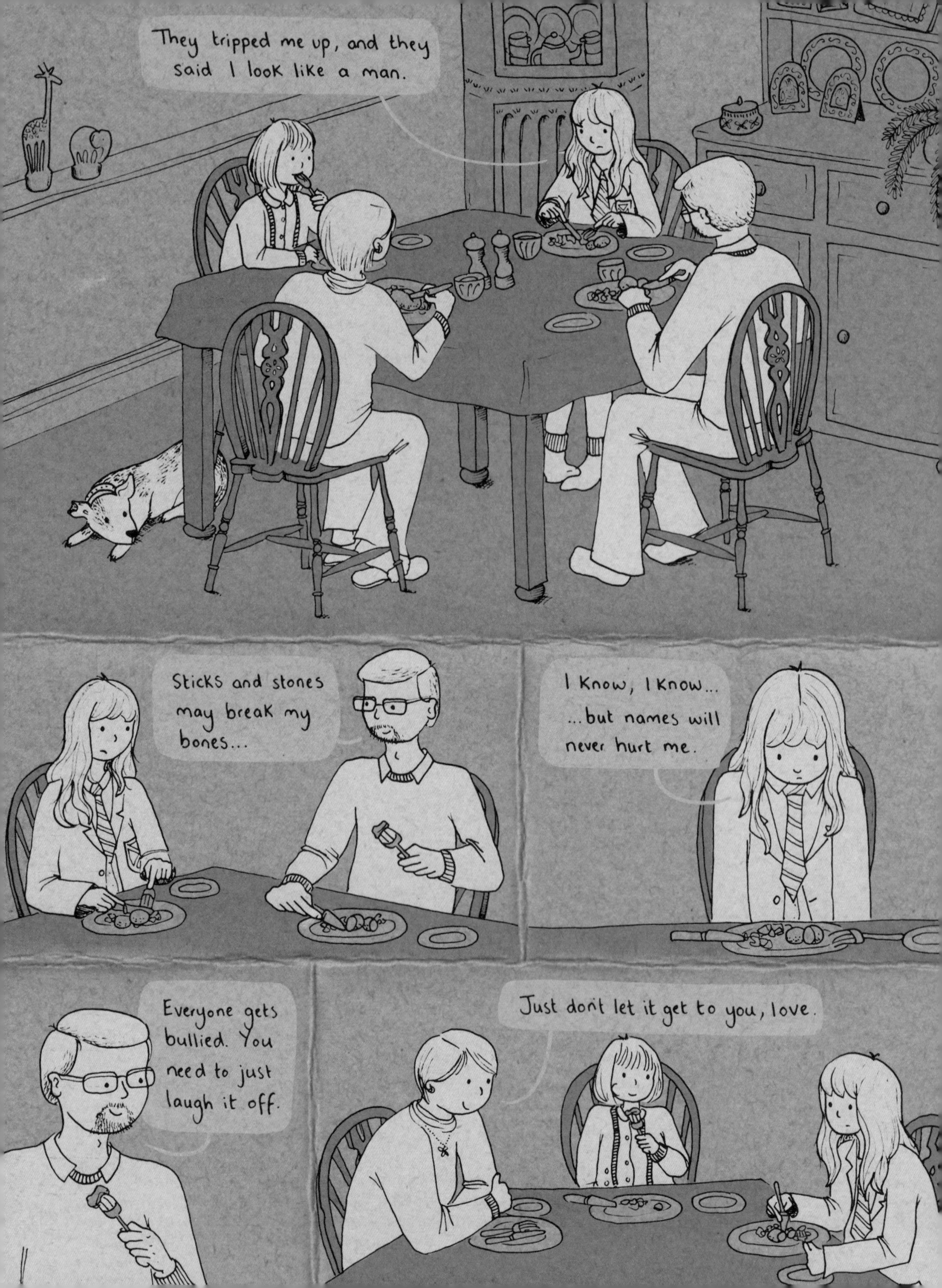
They tripped me up, and they said I look like a man.
Sticks and stones may break my bones...
I know, I know... ...but names will never hurt me.
Everyone gets bullied. You need to just laugh it off.
Just don't let it get to you, love.

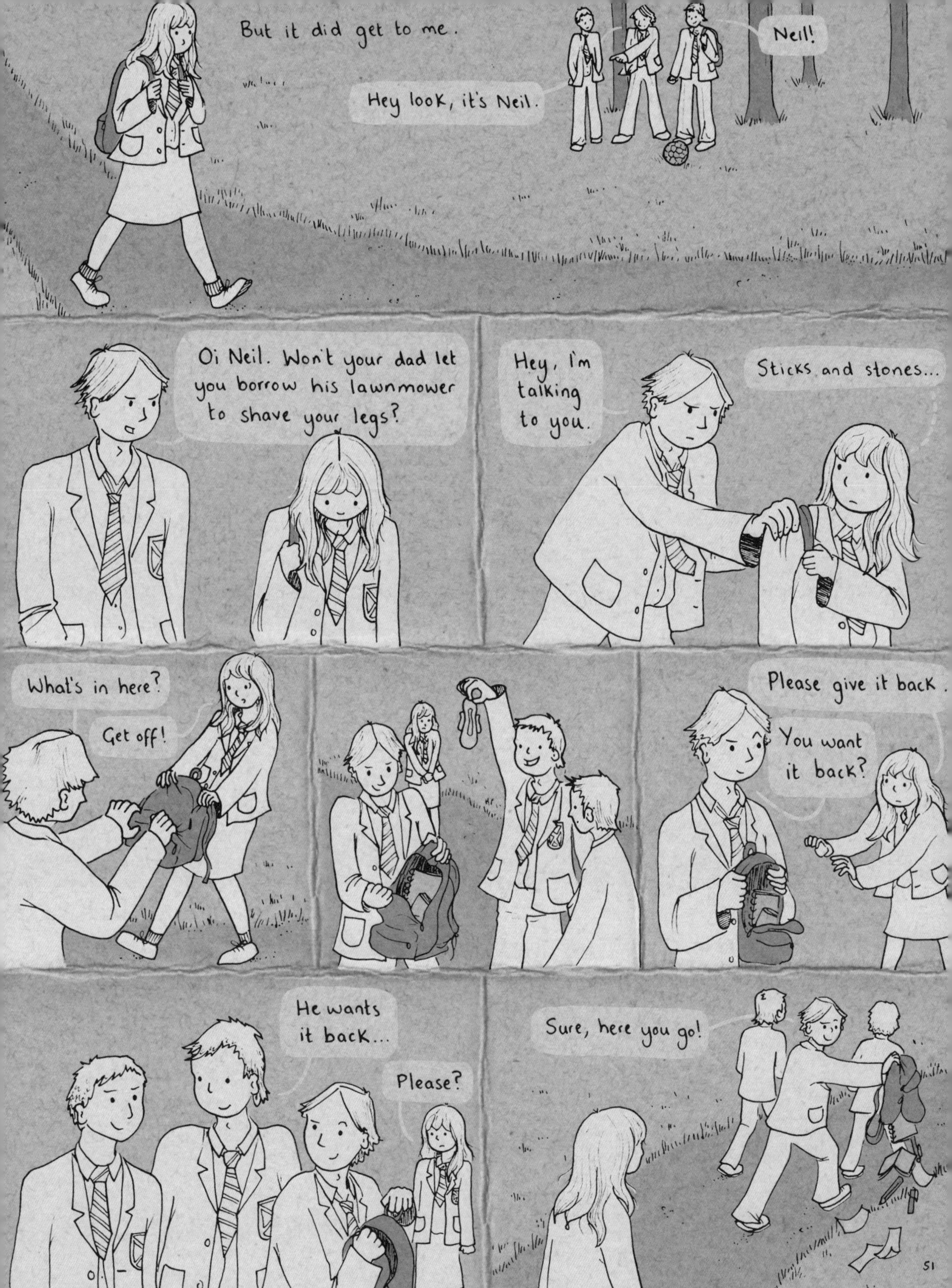
But it did get to me.
Neil!
Hey look, it's Neil.
Oi Neil. Won't your dad let you borrow his lawnmower to shave your legs?
Hey, I'm talking to you.
Sticks and stones...
What's in here?
Get off!
Please give it back.
You want it back?
He wants it back...
Please?
Sure, here you go!

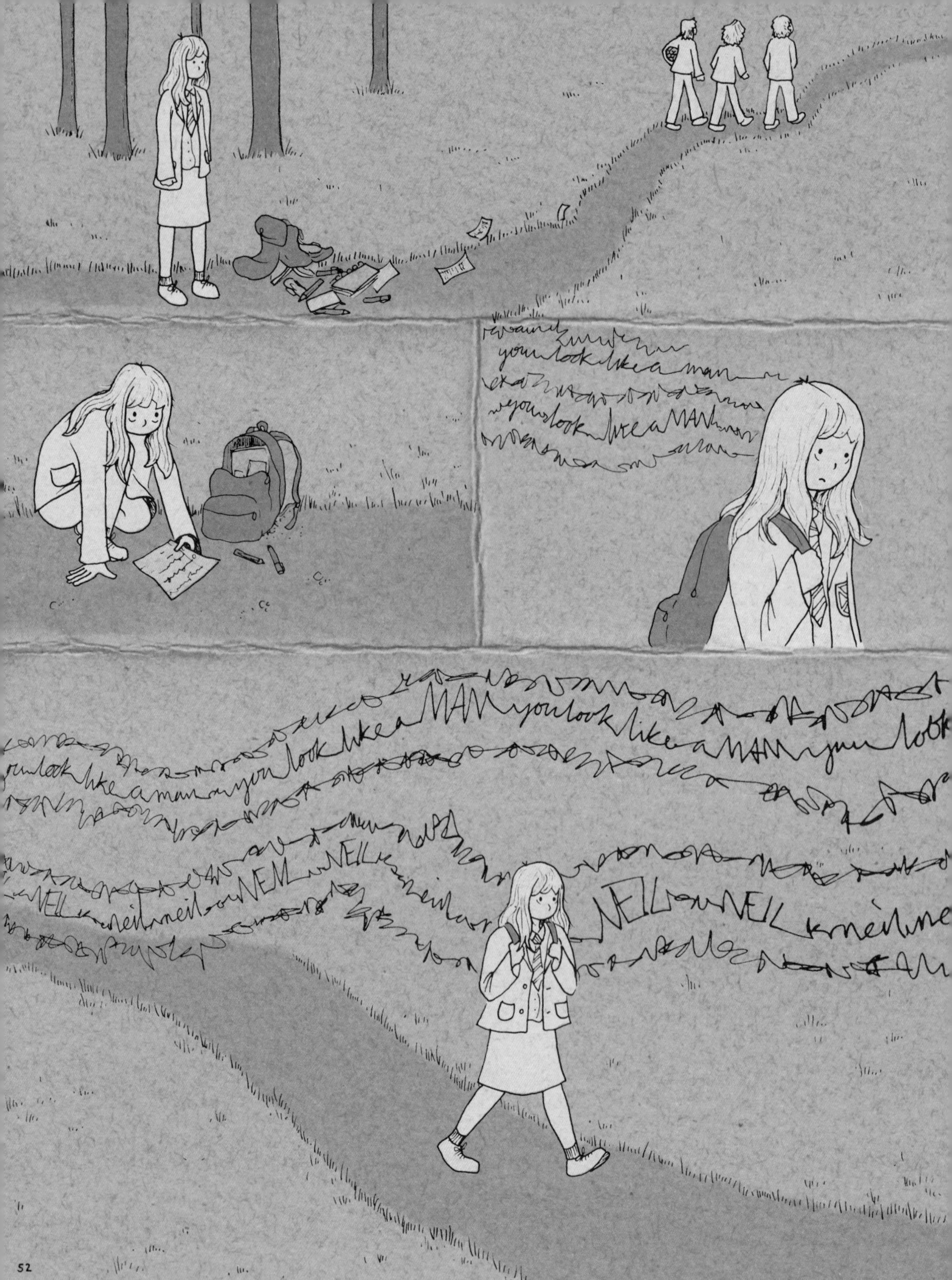
you look like a man
you look like a MAN
you look like a MAN you look like a MAN you look
you look like a man you look
NEIL NEIL
neil neil
NEIL NEIL neil

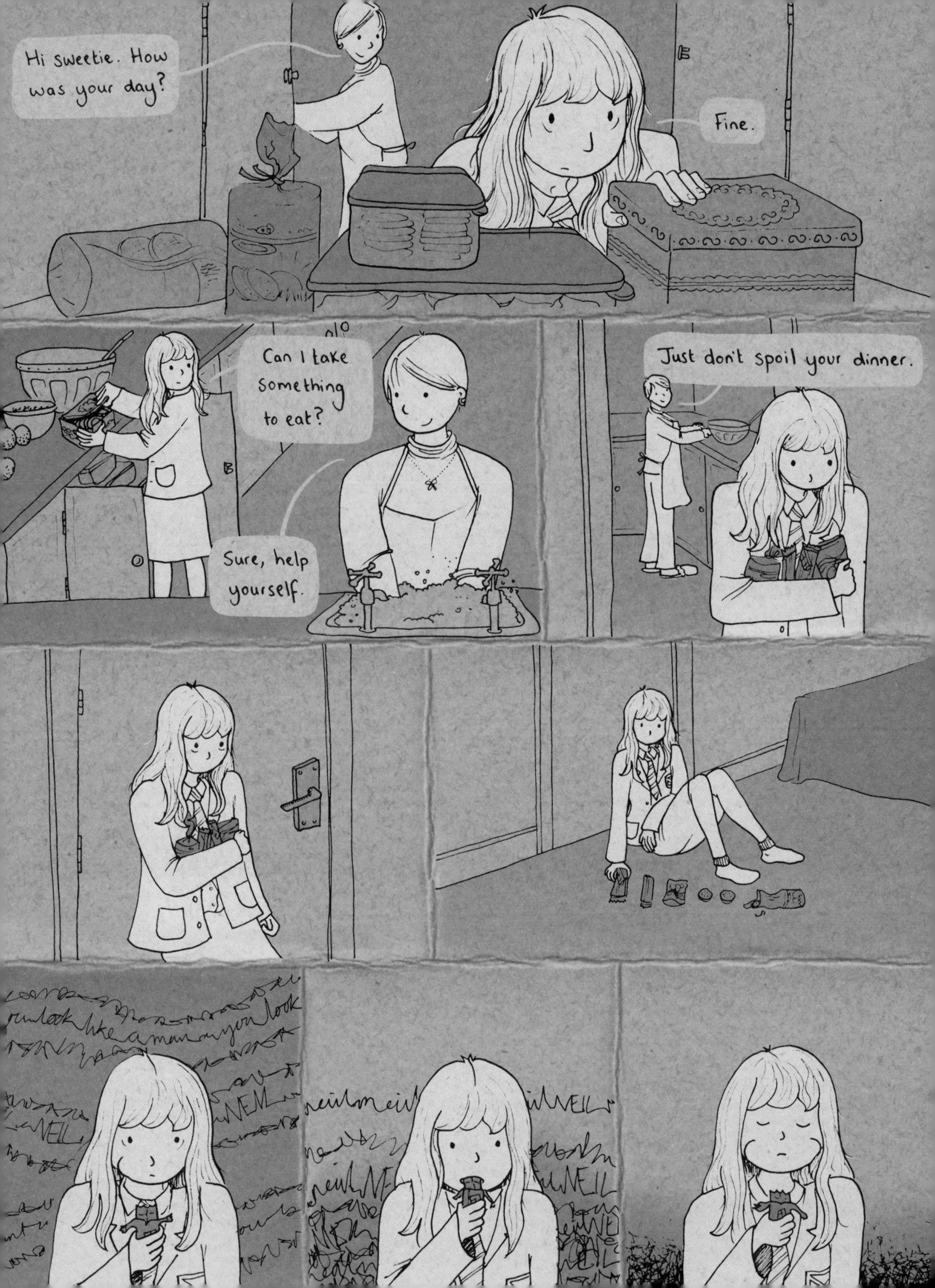
Hi sweetie. How was your day?
Fine.
Can I take something to eat?
Sure, help yourself.
Just don't spoil your dinner.

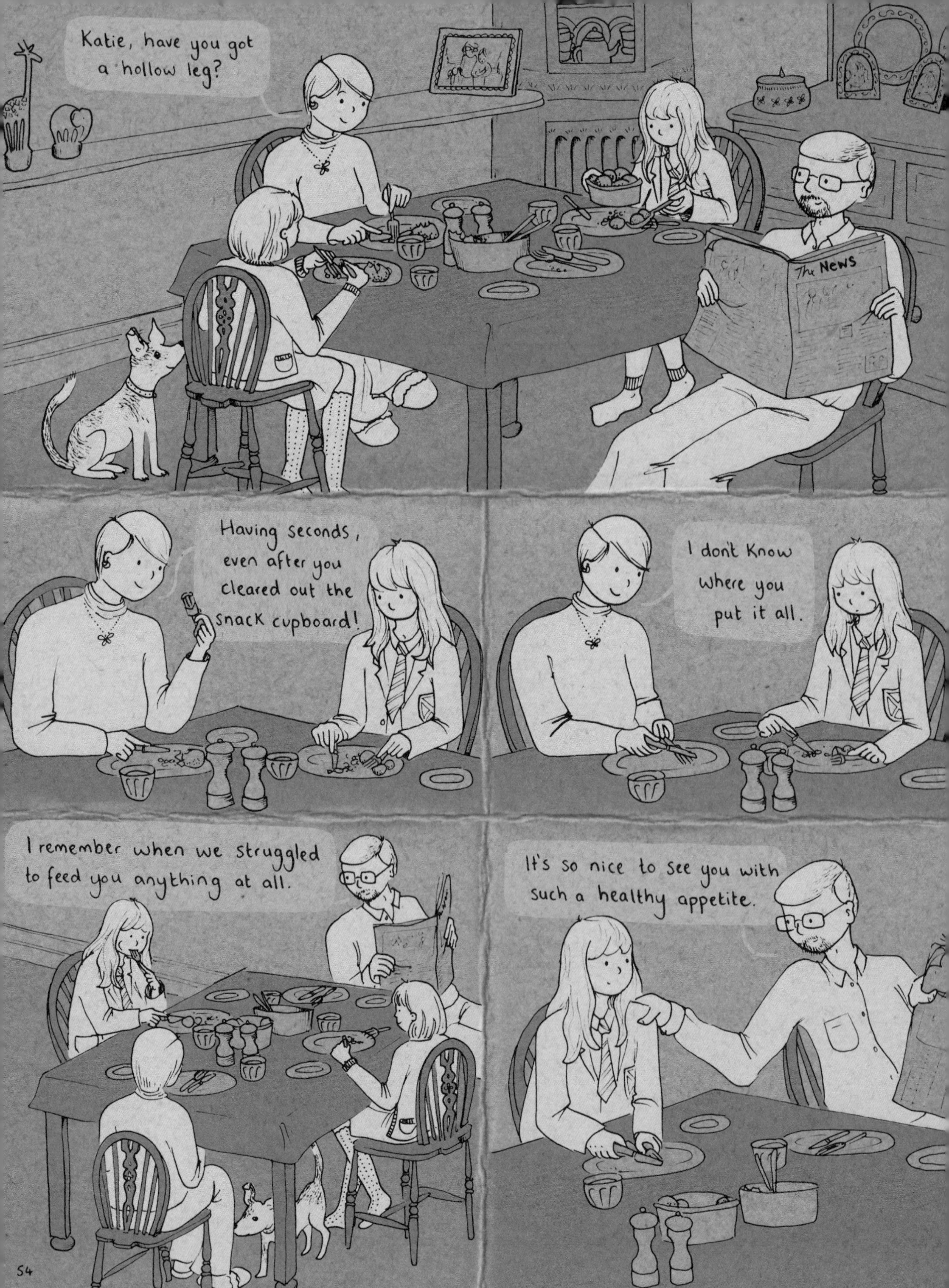
Katie, have you got a hollow leg?
Having seconds, even after you cleared out the snack cupboard!
I don't know where you put it all.
I remember when we struggled to feed you anything at all.
It's so nice to see you with such a healthy appetite.
The News

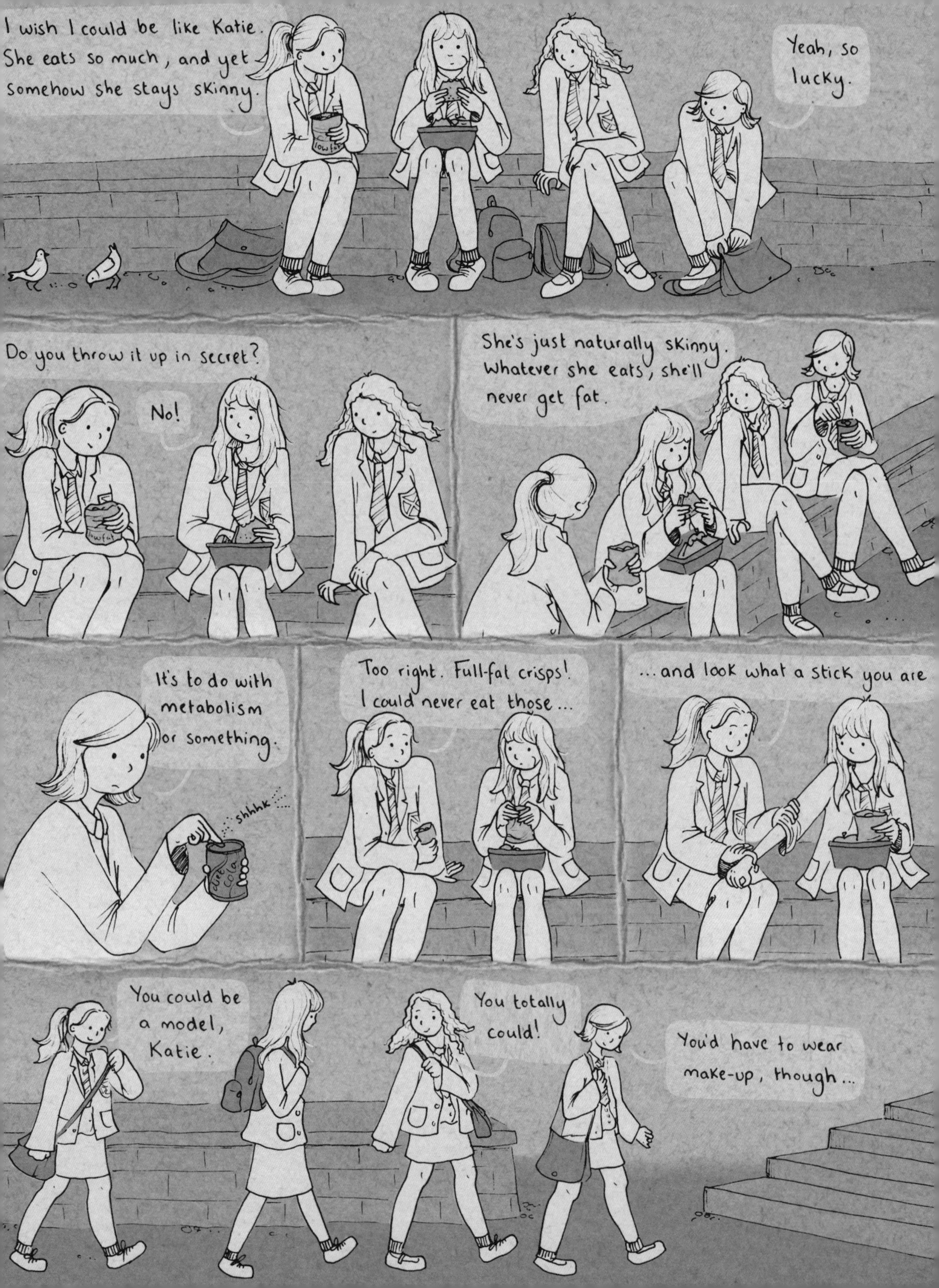
I wish I could be like Katie. She eats so much, and yet somehow she stays skinny.
Yeah, so lucky.
Do you throw it up in secret?
No!
She's just naturally skinny. Whatever she eats, she'll never get fat.
It's to do with metabolism or something.
shhhk
Too right. Full-fat crisps! I could never eat those...
...and look what a stick you are
You could be a model, Katie.
You totally could!
You'd have to wear make-up, though...
lowfat
diet cola

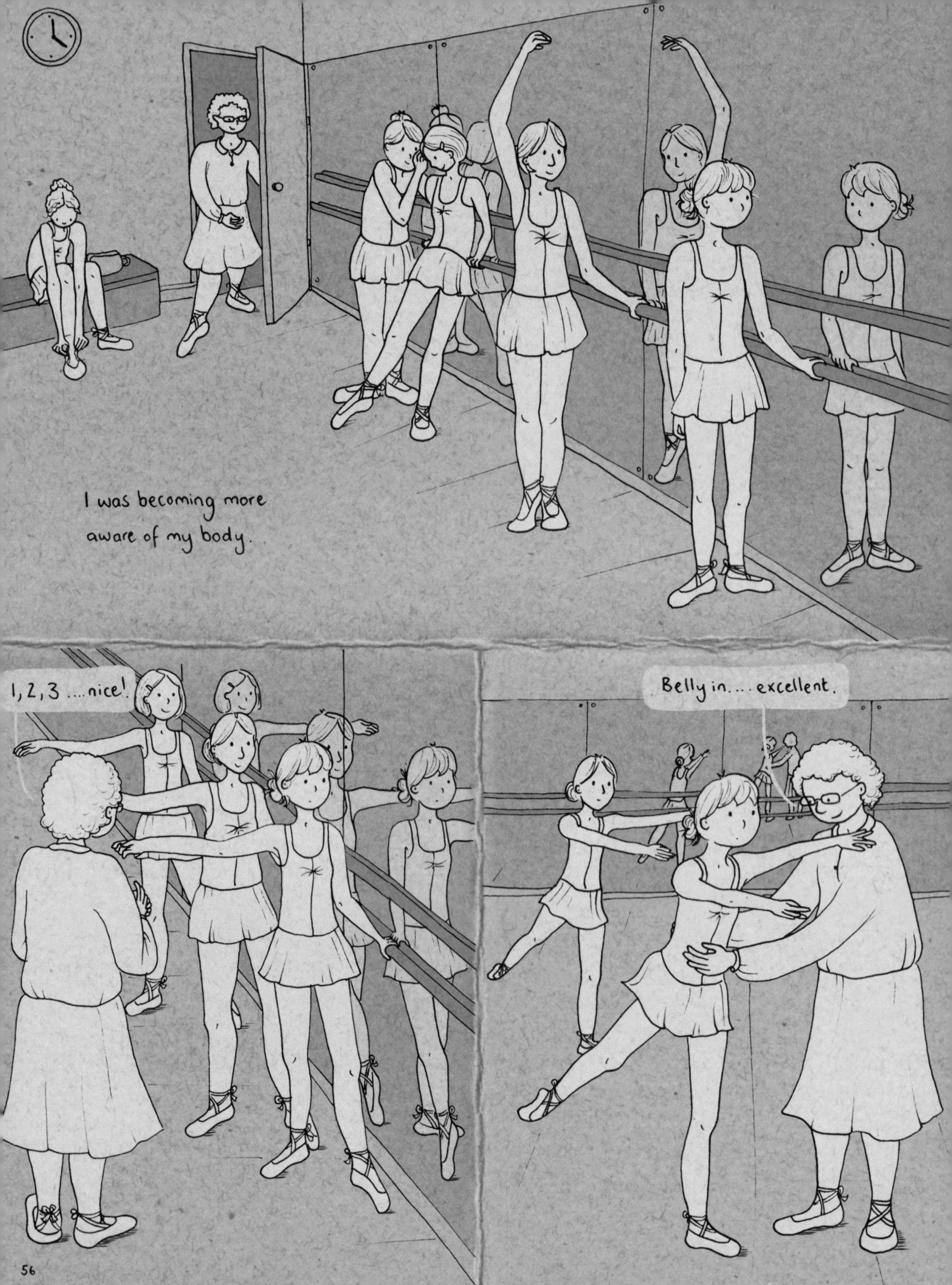
I was becoming more aware of my body.
1, 2, 3 .... nice!
Belly in.... excellent.

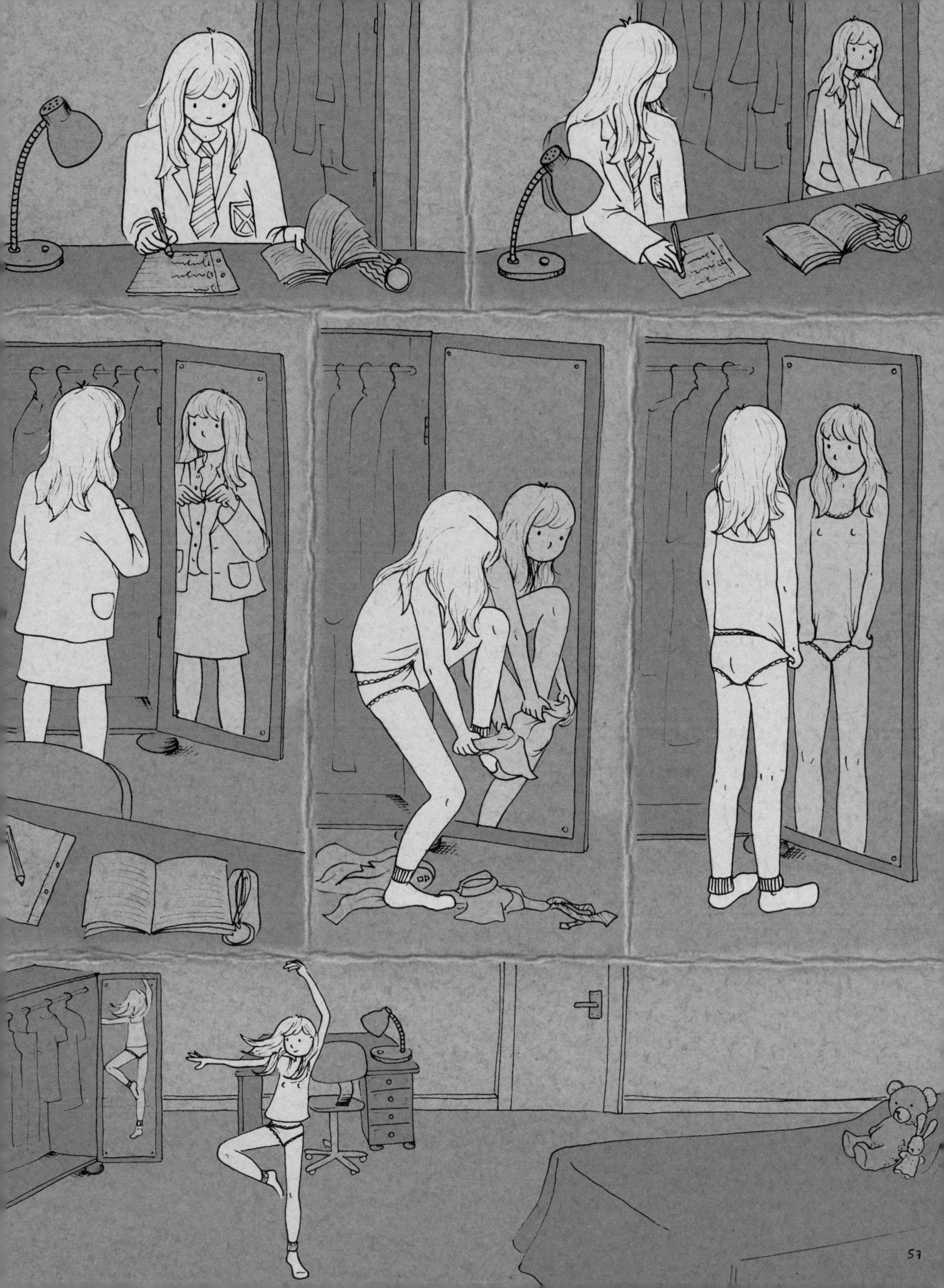

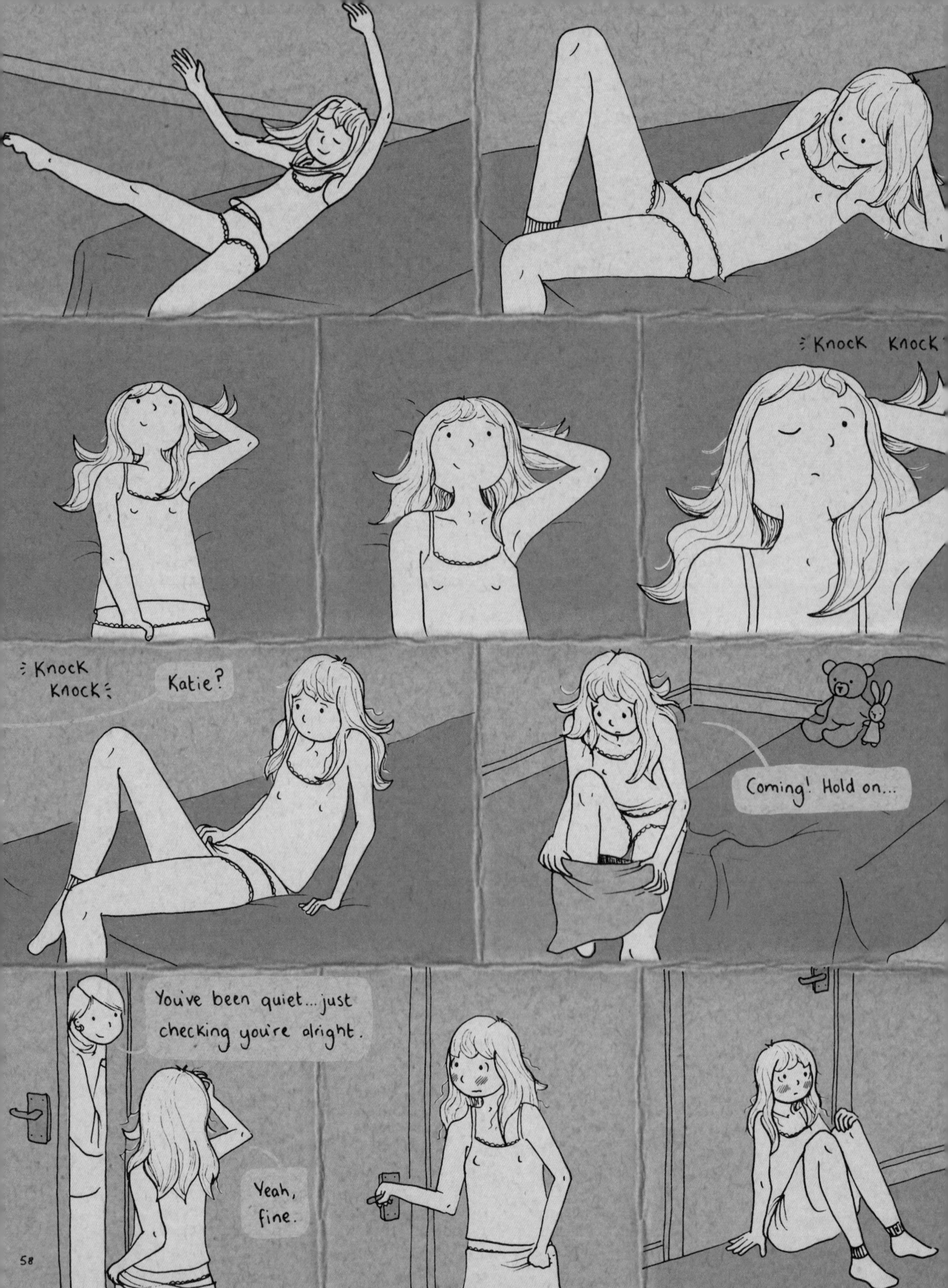
Knock Knock
Knock Knock
Katie?
Coming! Hold on...
You've been quiet... just checking you're alright.
Yeah, fine.

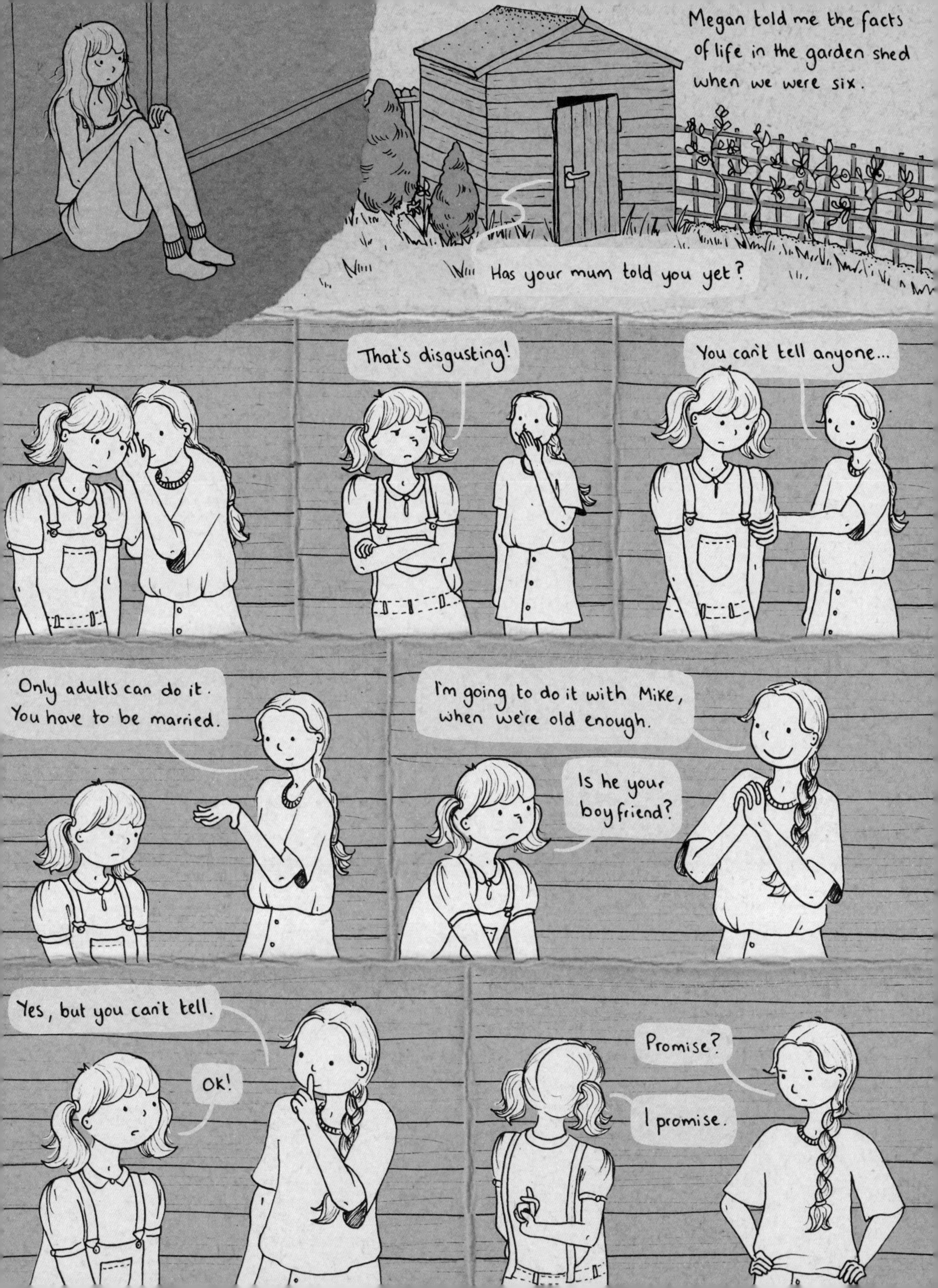
Megan told me the facts of life in the garden shed when we were six.
Has your mum told you yet?
That's disgusting!
You can't tell anyone...
Only adults can do it. You have to be married.
I'm going to do it with Mike, when we're old enough.
Is he your boyfriend?
Yes, but you can't tell.
OK!
Promise?
I promise.

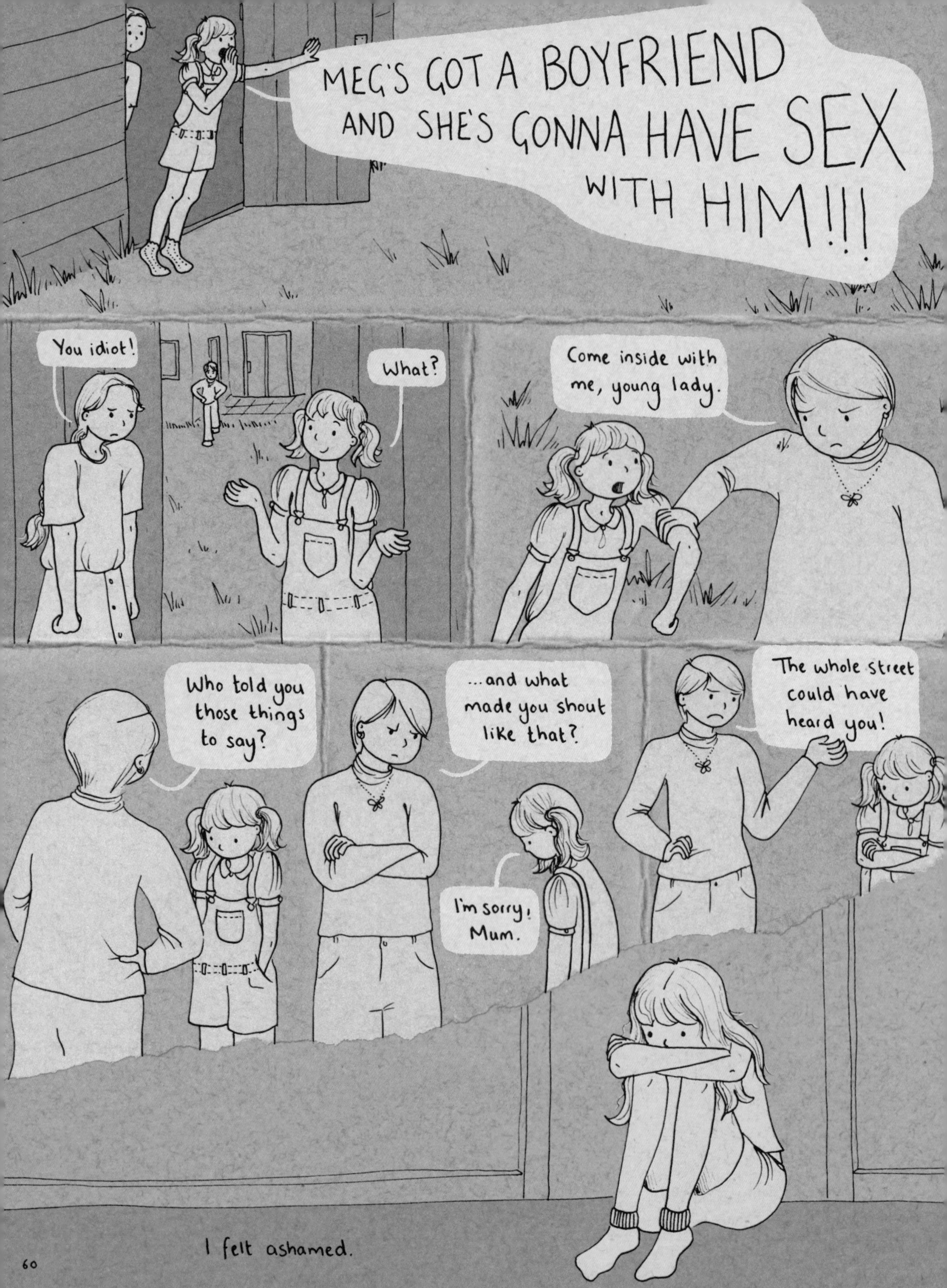

MEG'S GOT A BOYFRIEND AND SHE'S GONNA HAVE SEX WITH HIM!!!
You idiot!
What?
Come inside with me, young lady.
Who told you those things to say?
...and what made you shout like that?
The whole street could have heard you!
I'm sorry, Mum.
I felt ashamed.

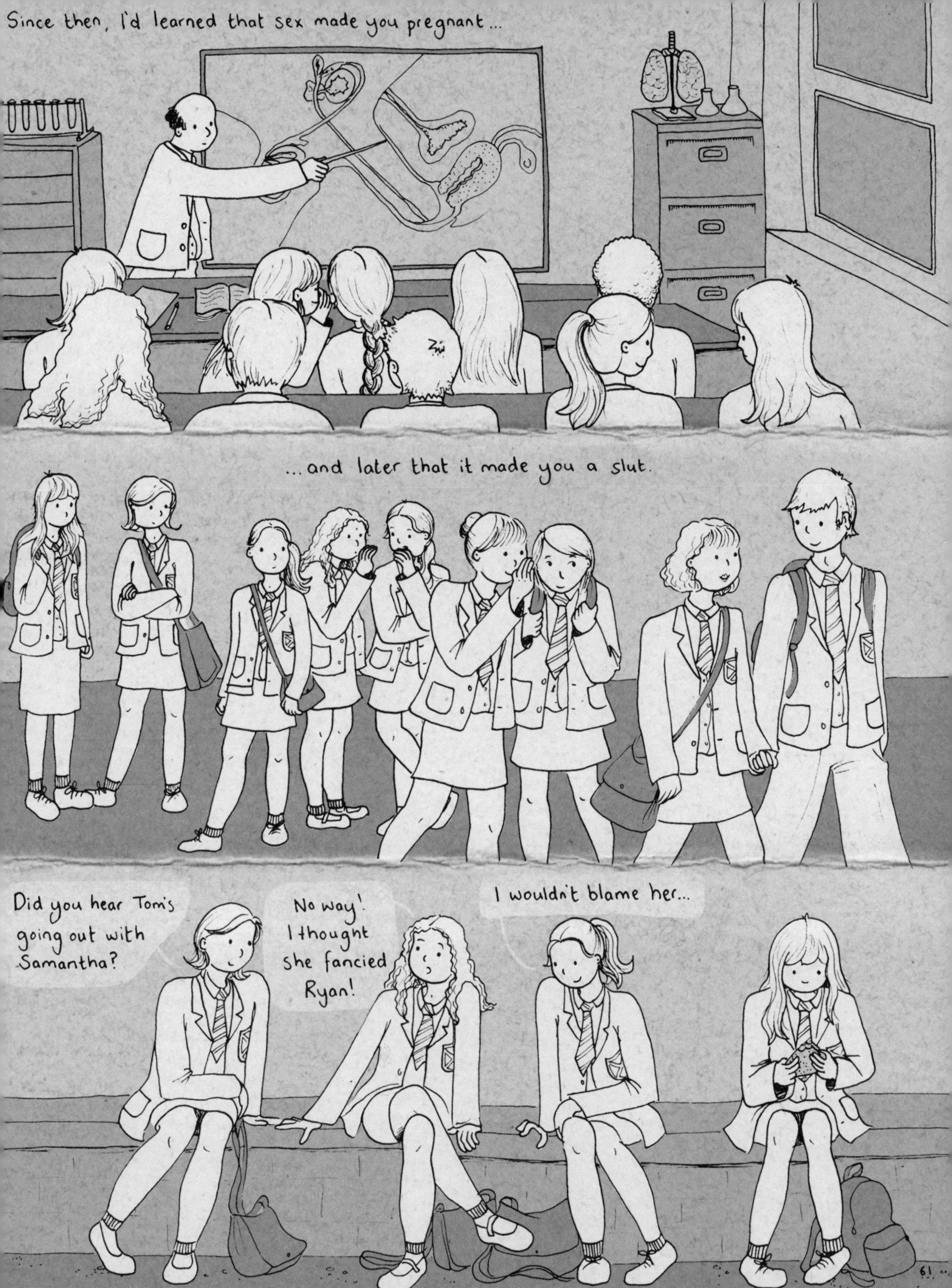
Since then, I'd learned that sex made you pregnant...
...and later that it made you a slut.
Zw
Did you hear Tom's going out with Samantha?
No way! I thought she fancied Ryan!
I wouldn't blame her...

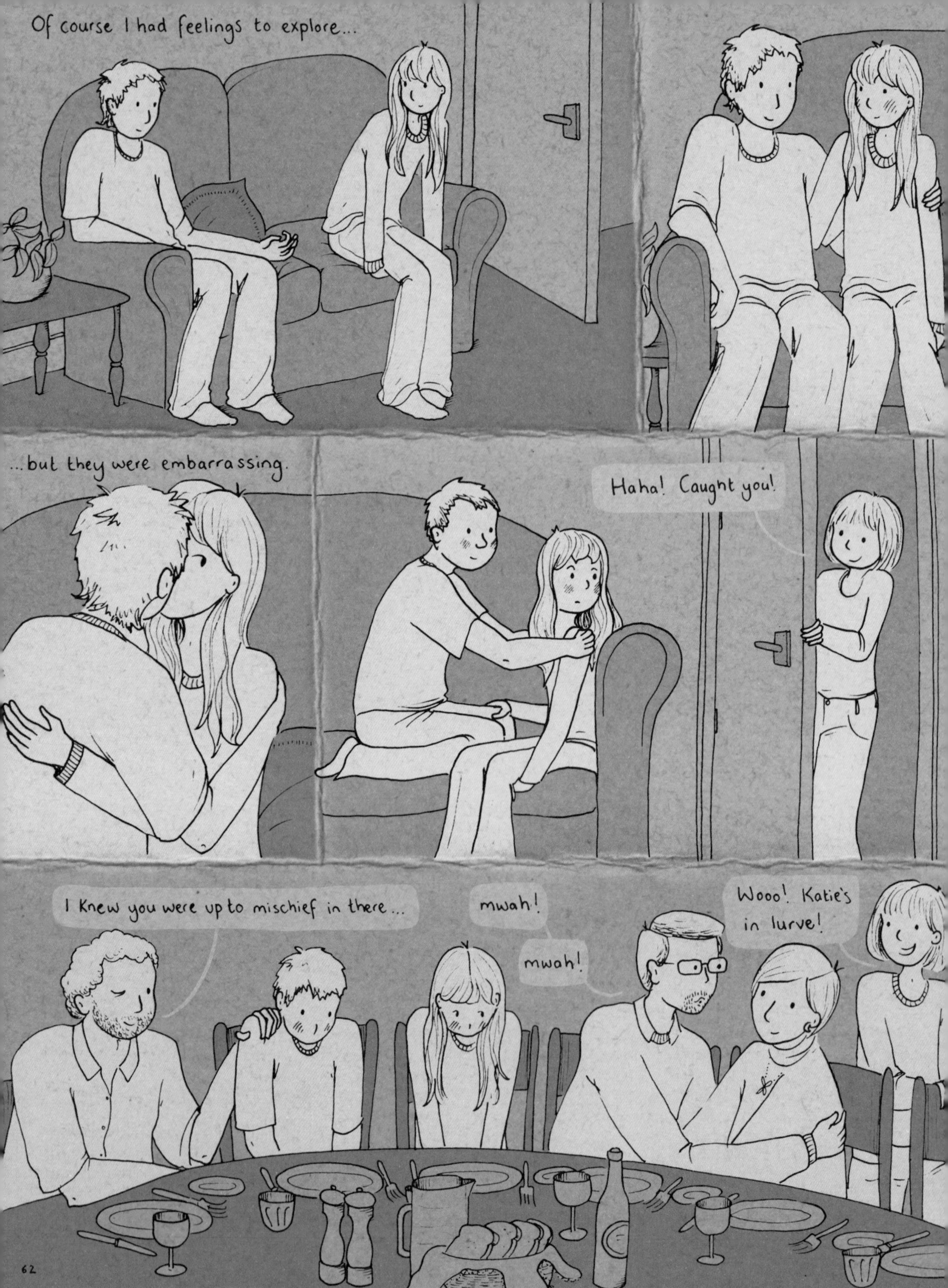
Of course I had feelings to explore...
...but they were embarrassing.
Haha! Caught you!
I knew you were up to mischief in there...
mwah!
mwah!
Wooo! Katie's in lurve!

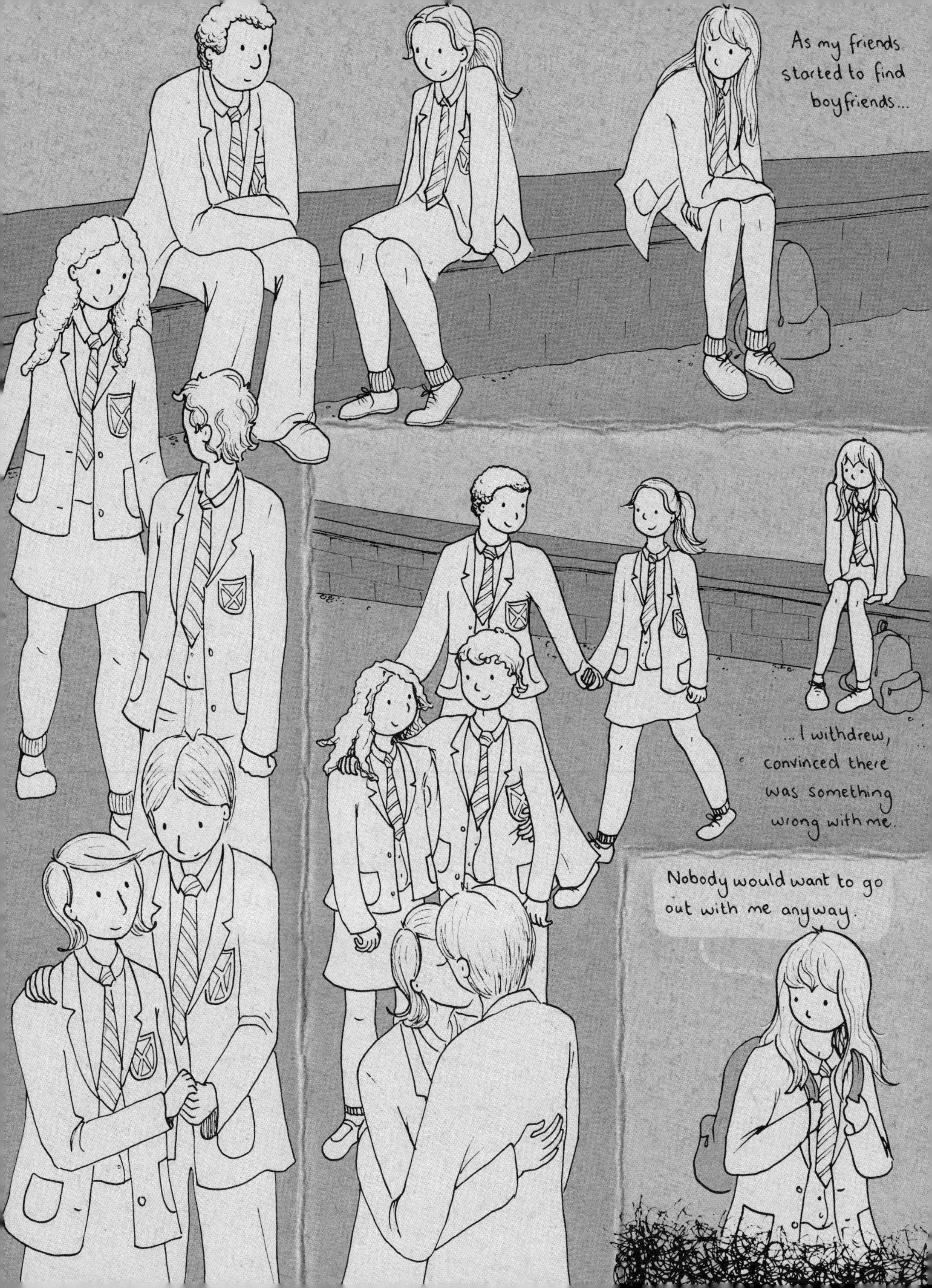
As my friends started to find boyfriends...
...I withdrew, convinced there was something wrong with me.
Nobody would want to go out with me anyway.

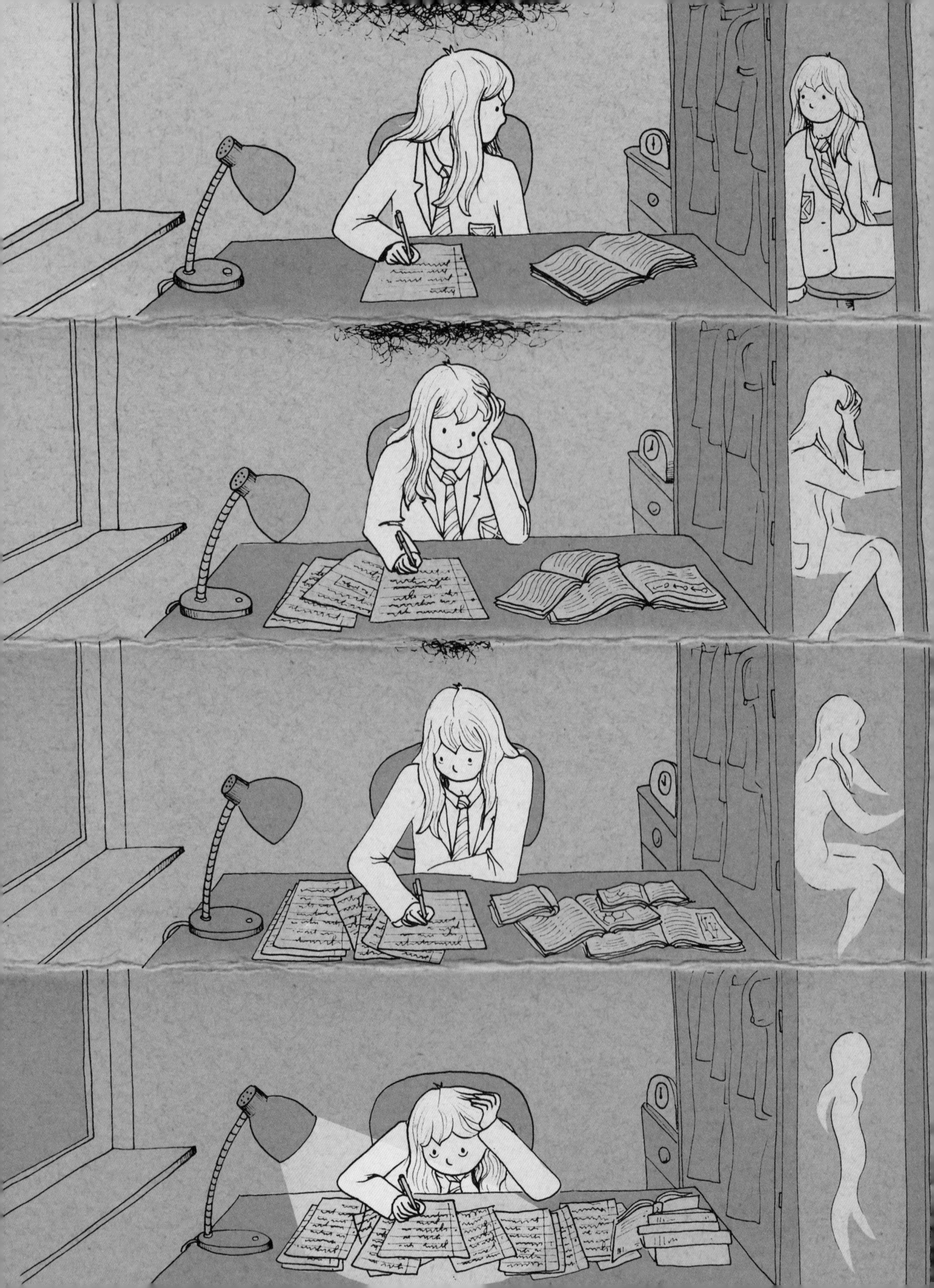

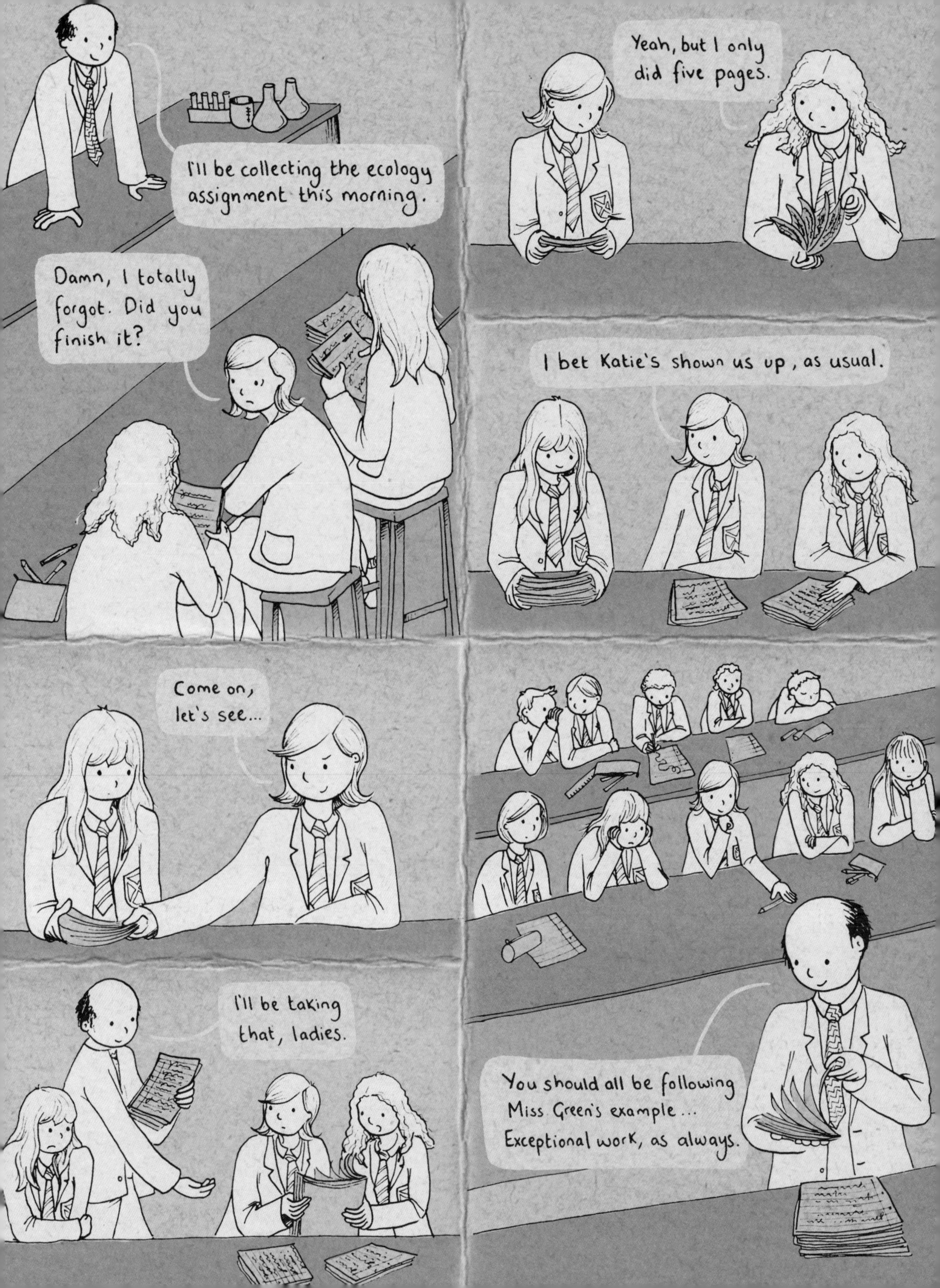
I'll be collecting the ecology assignment this morning.
Damn, I totally forgot. Did you finish it?
Come on, let's see...
I'll be taking that, ladies.
Yeah, but I only did five pages.
I bet Katie's shown us up, as usual.
You should all be following Miss Green's example... Exceptional work, as always.

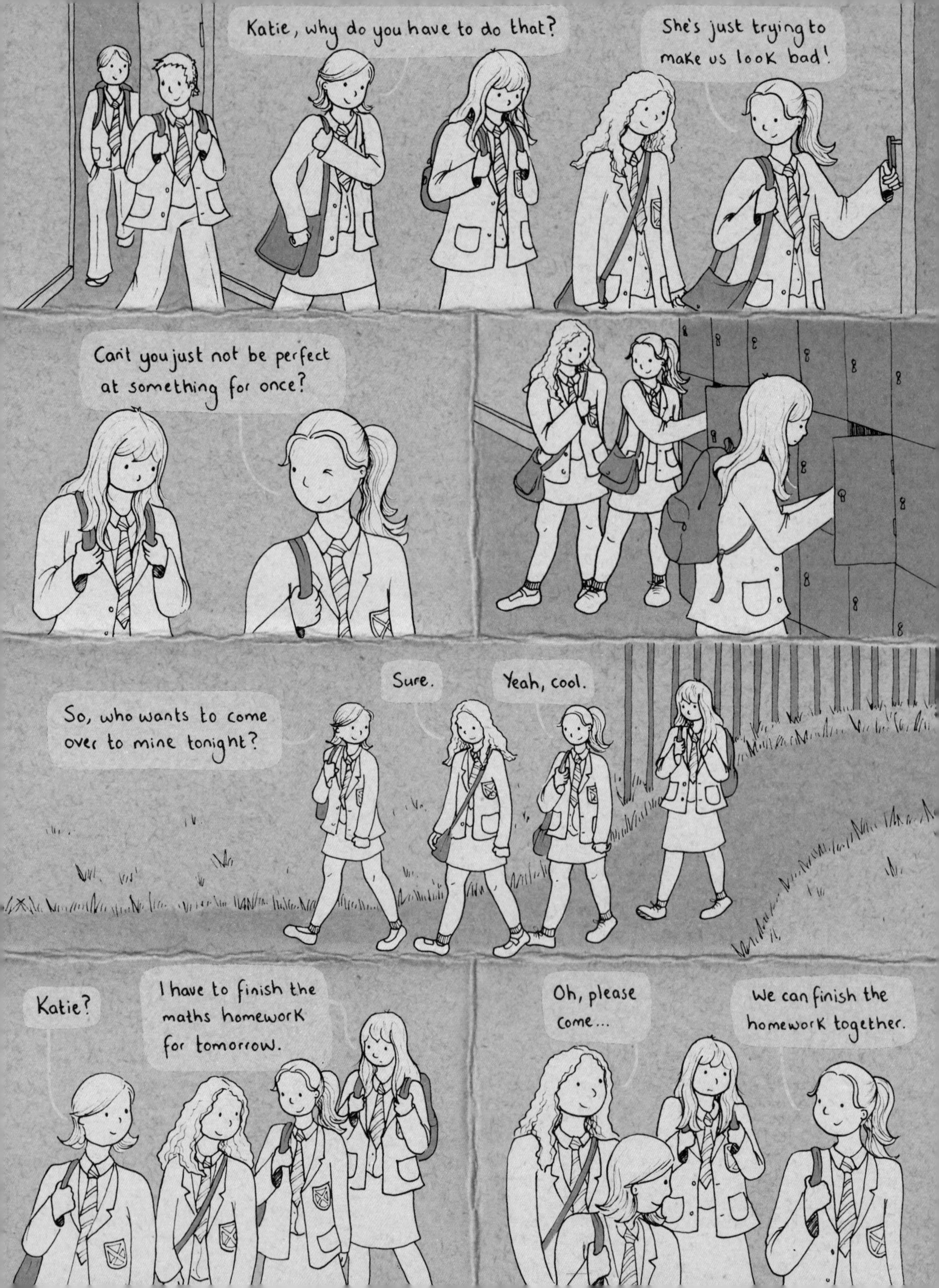
Katie, why do you have to do that?
She's just trying to make us look bad!
Can't you just not be perfect at something for once?
So, who wants to come over to mine tonight?
Sure.
Yeah, cool.
Katie?
I have to finish the maths homework for tomorrow.
Oh, please come...
We can finish the homework together.

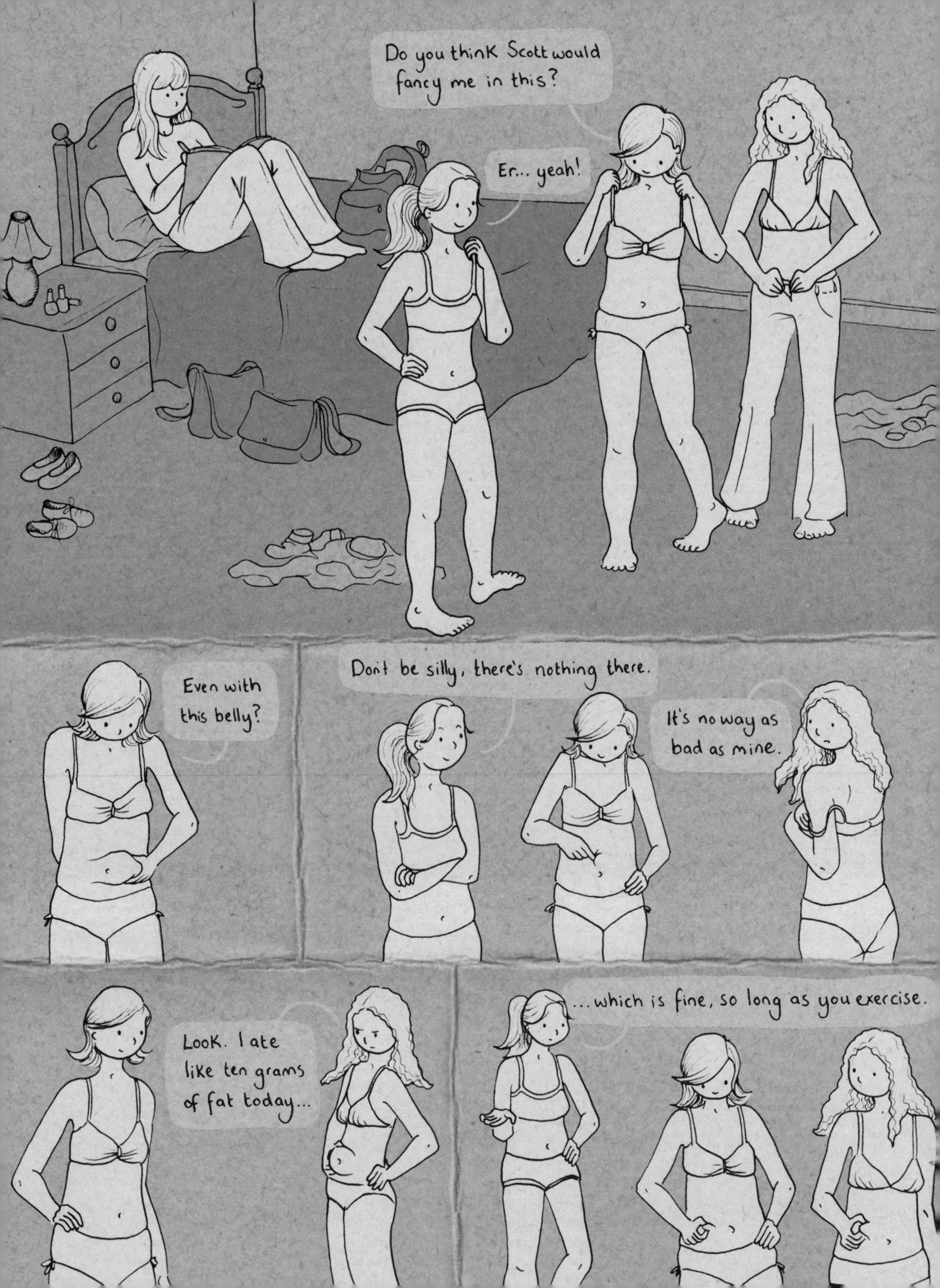
Do you think Scott would fancy me in this?
Er... yeah!
Even with this belly?
Don't be silly, there's nothing there.
It's no way as bad as mine.
Look. I ate like ten grams of fat today...
...which is fine, so long as you exercise.

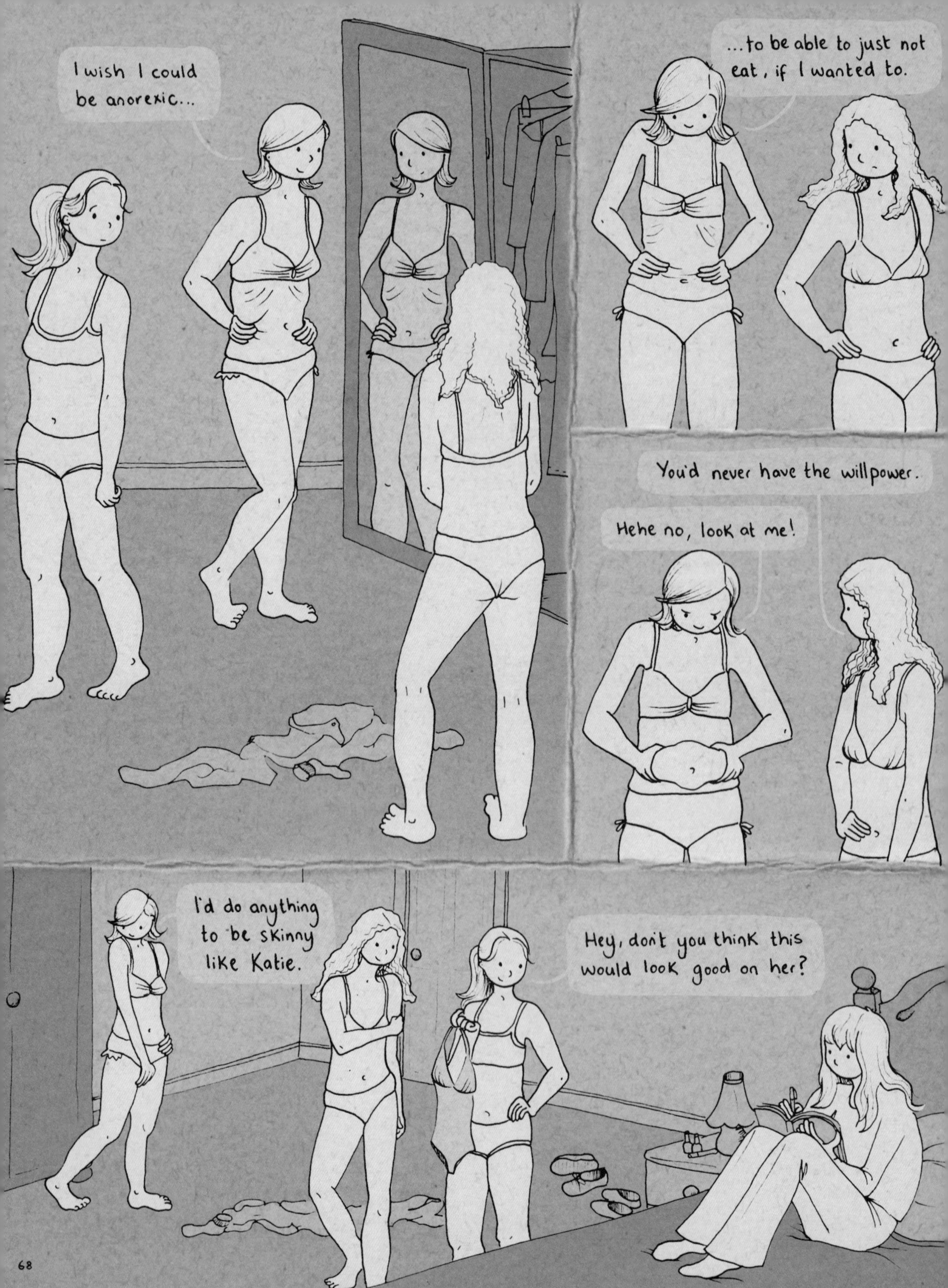
I wish I could be anorexic...
...to be able to just not eat, if I wanted to.
You'd never have the willpower.
Hehe no, look at me!
I'd do anything to be skinny like Katie.
Hey, don't you think this would look good on her?

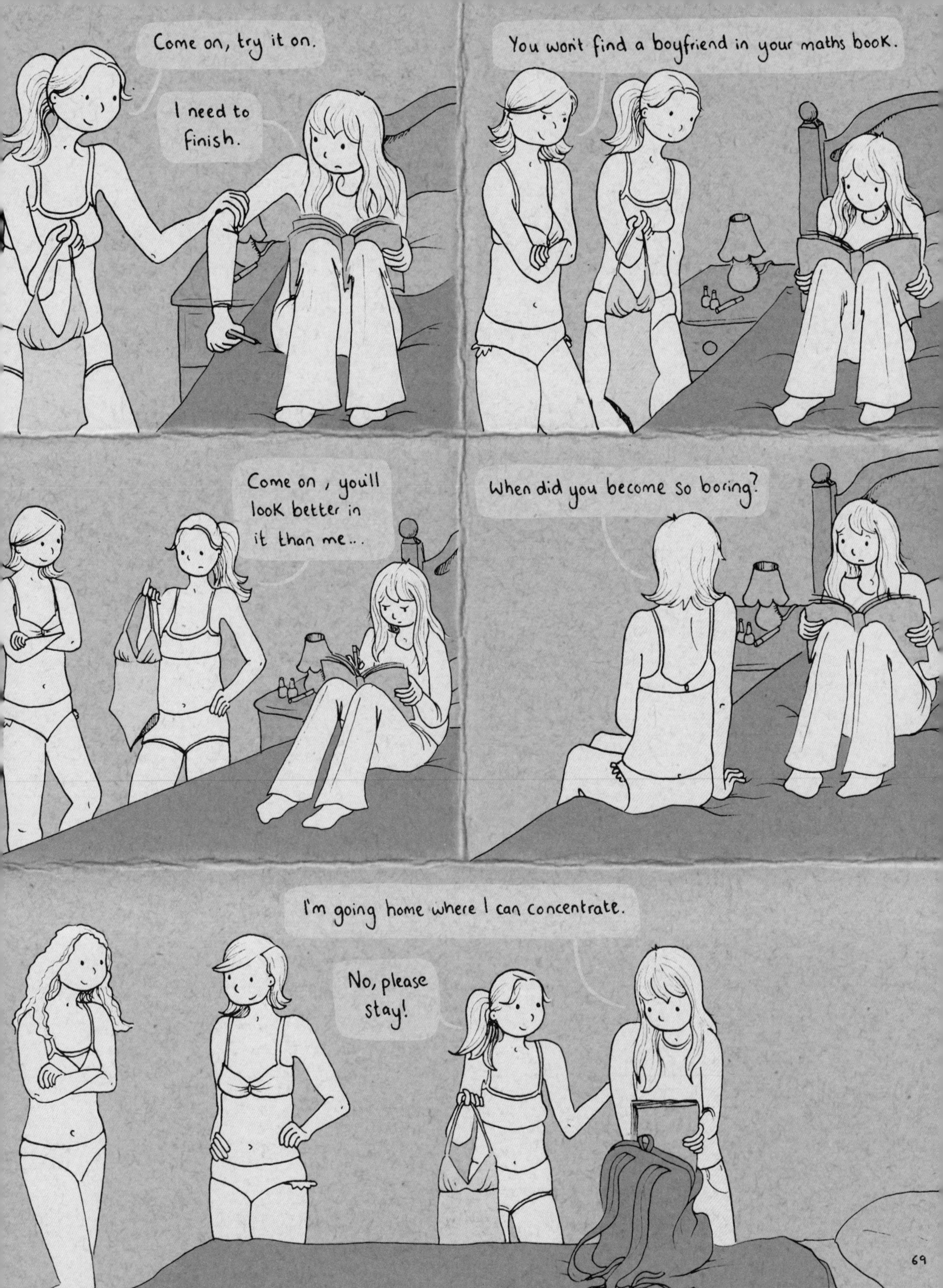
Come on, try it on.
I need to finish.
You won't find a boyfriend in your maths book.
Come on, you'll look better in it than me...
When did you become so boring?
I'm going home where I can concentrate.
No, please stay!

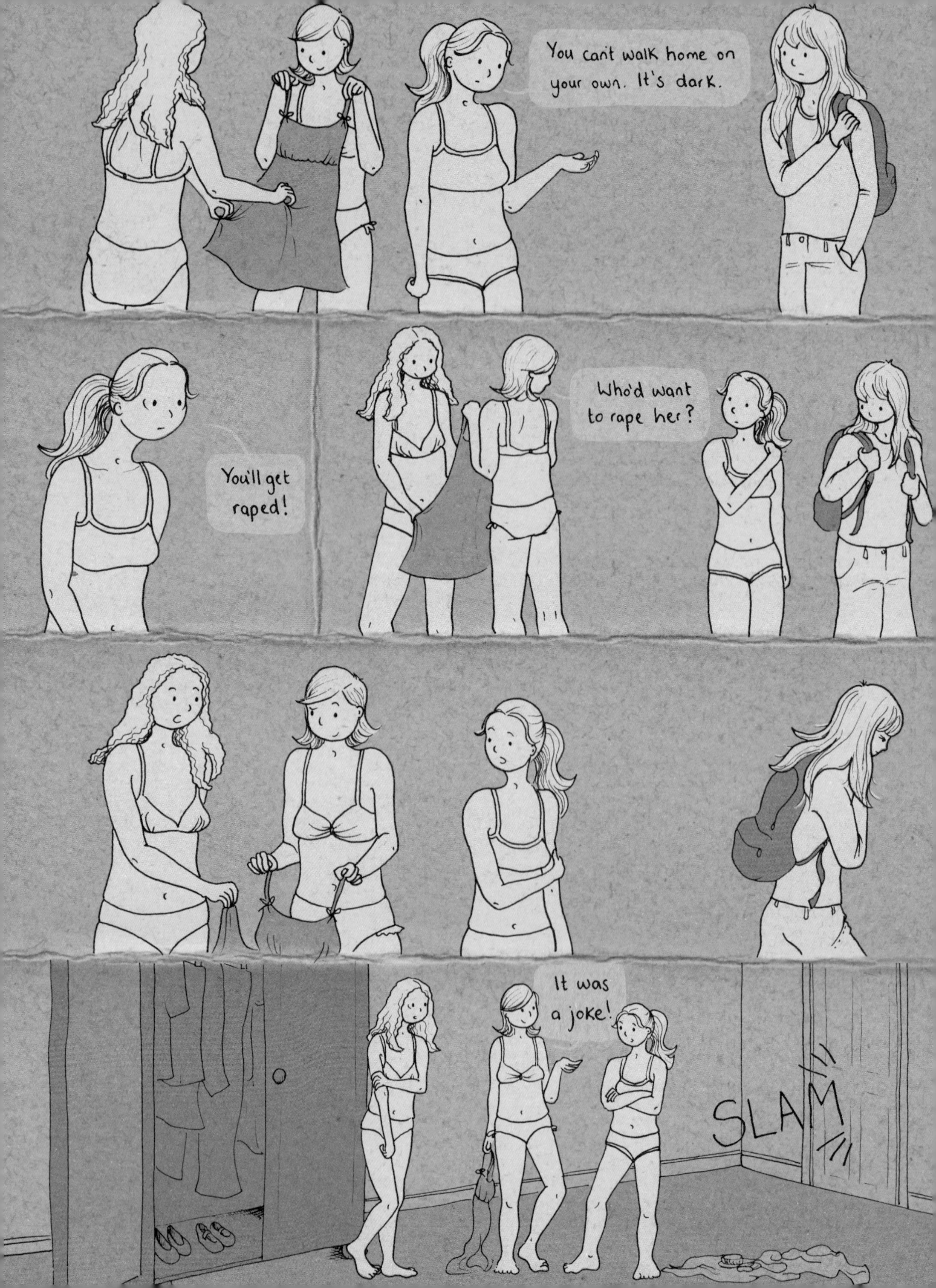
You can't walk home on your own. It's dark.
You'll get raped!
Who'd want to rape her?
It was a joke!
SLAM

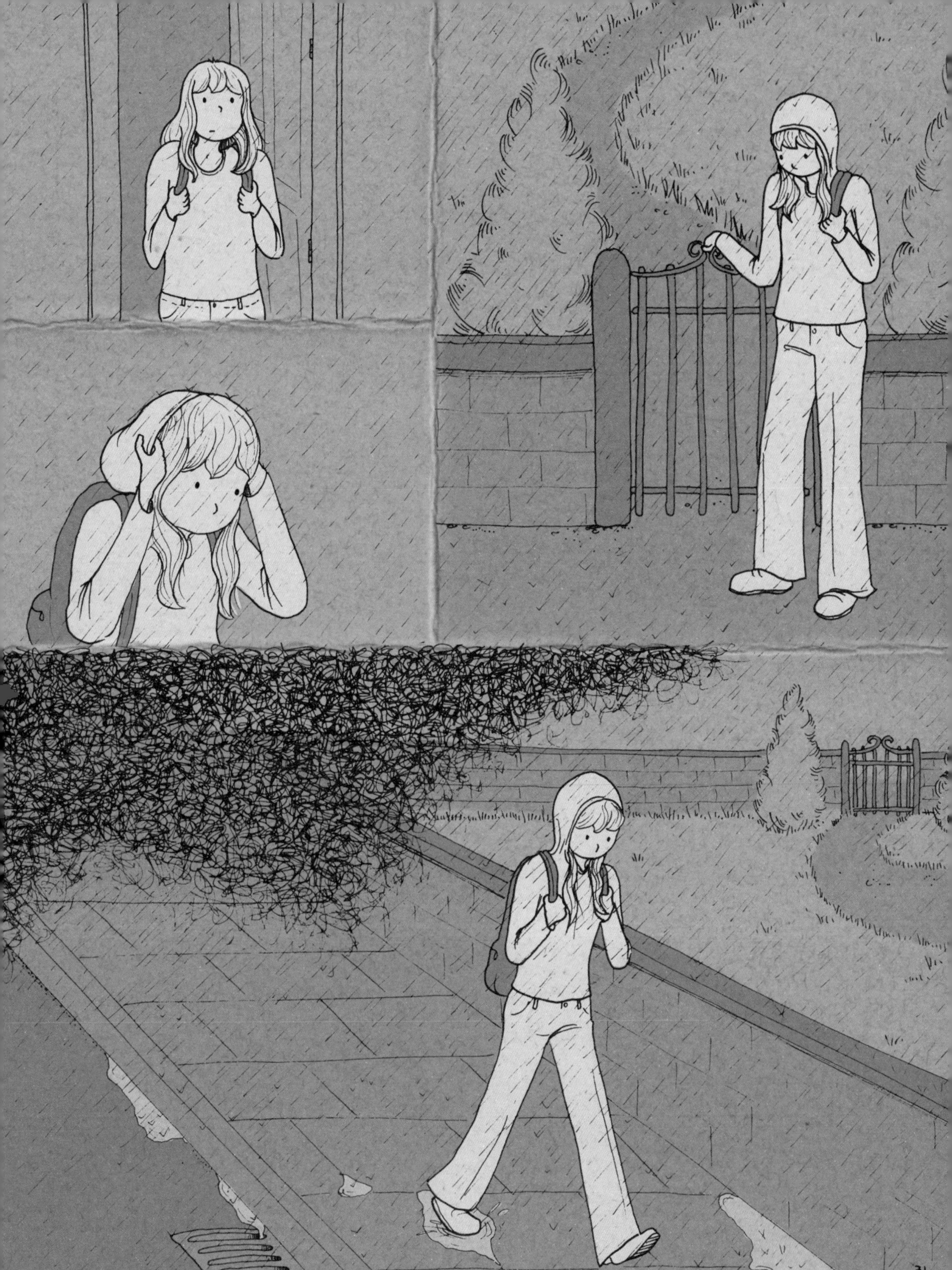

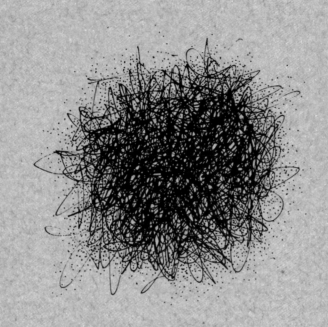

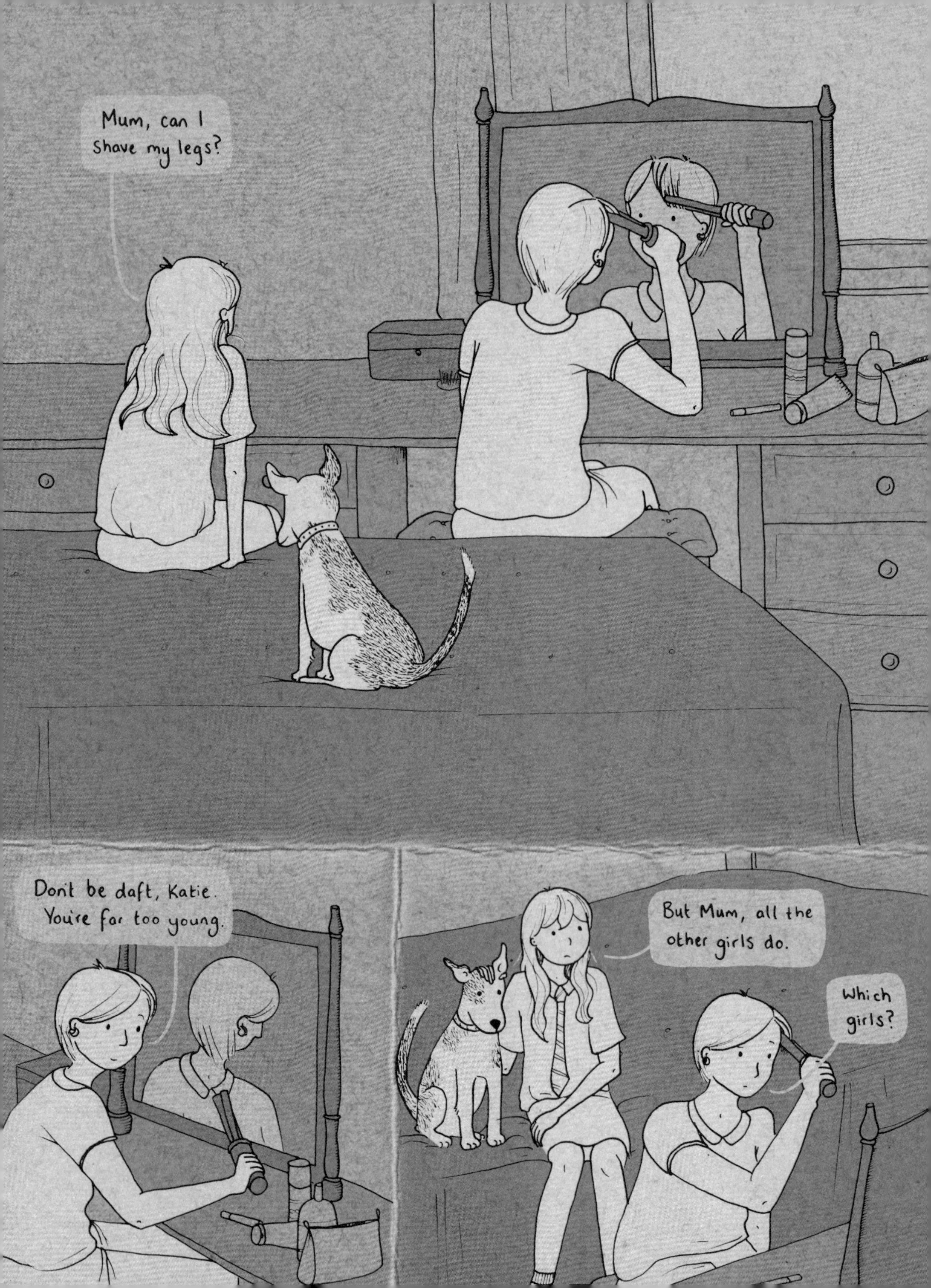
Mum, can I shave my legs?
Don't be daft, Katie. You're far too young.
But Mum, all the other girls do.
Which girls?

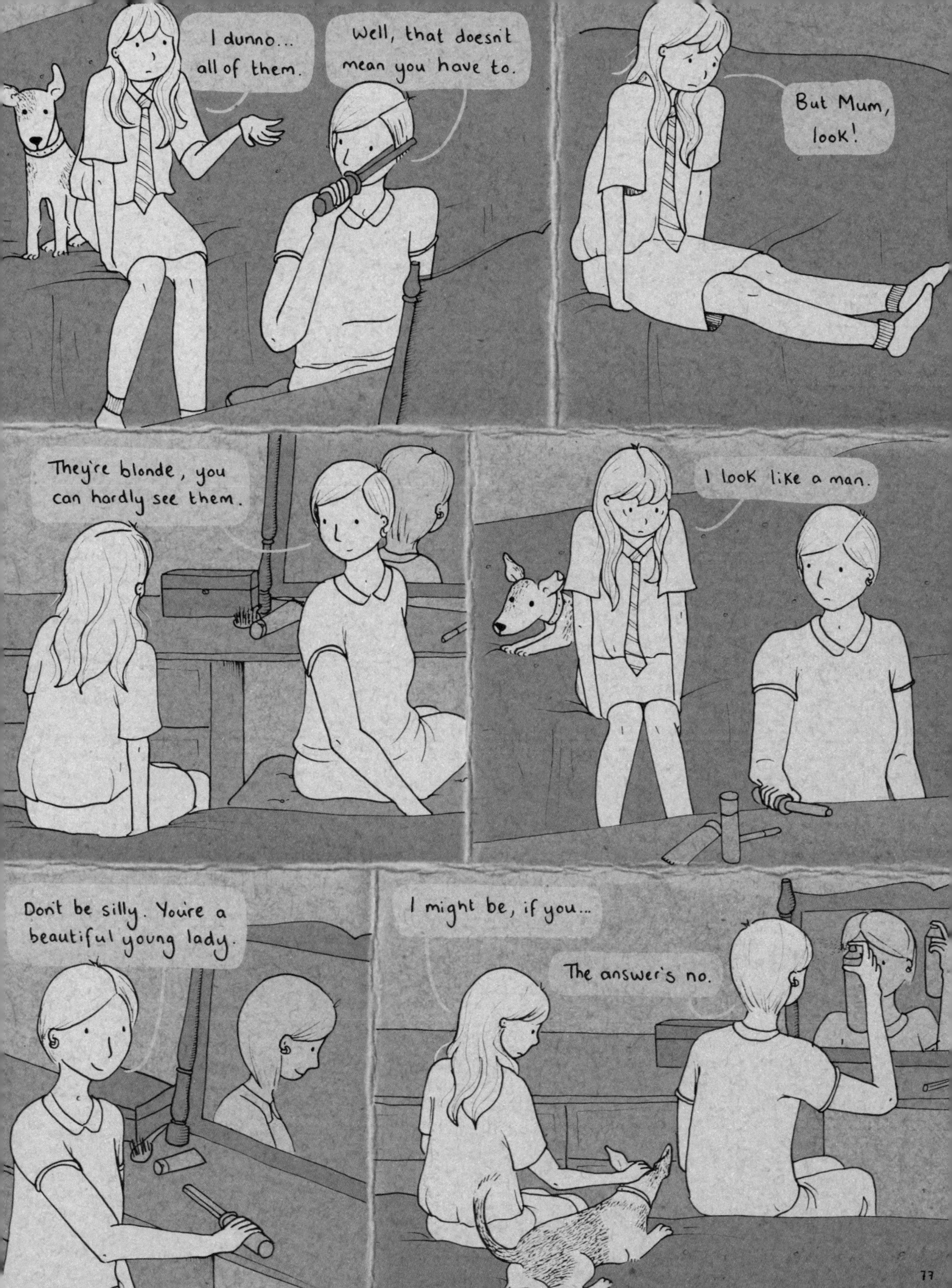
I dunno... all of them.
Well, that doesn't mean you have to.
But Mum, look!
They're blonde, you can hardly see them.
I look like a man.
Don't be silly. You're a beautiful young lady.
I might be, if you...
The answer's no.

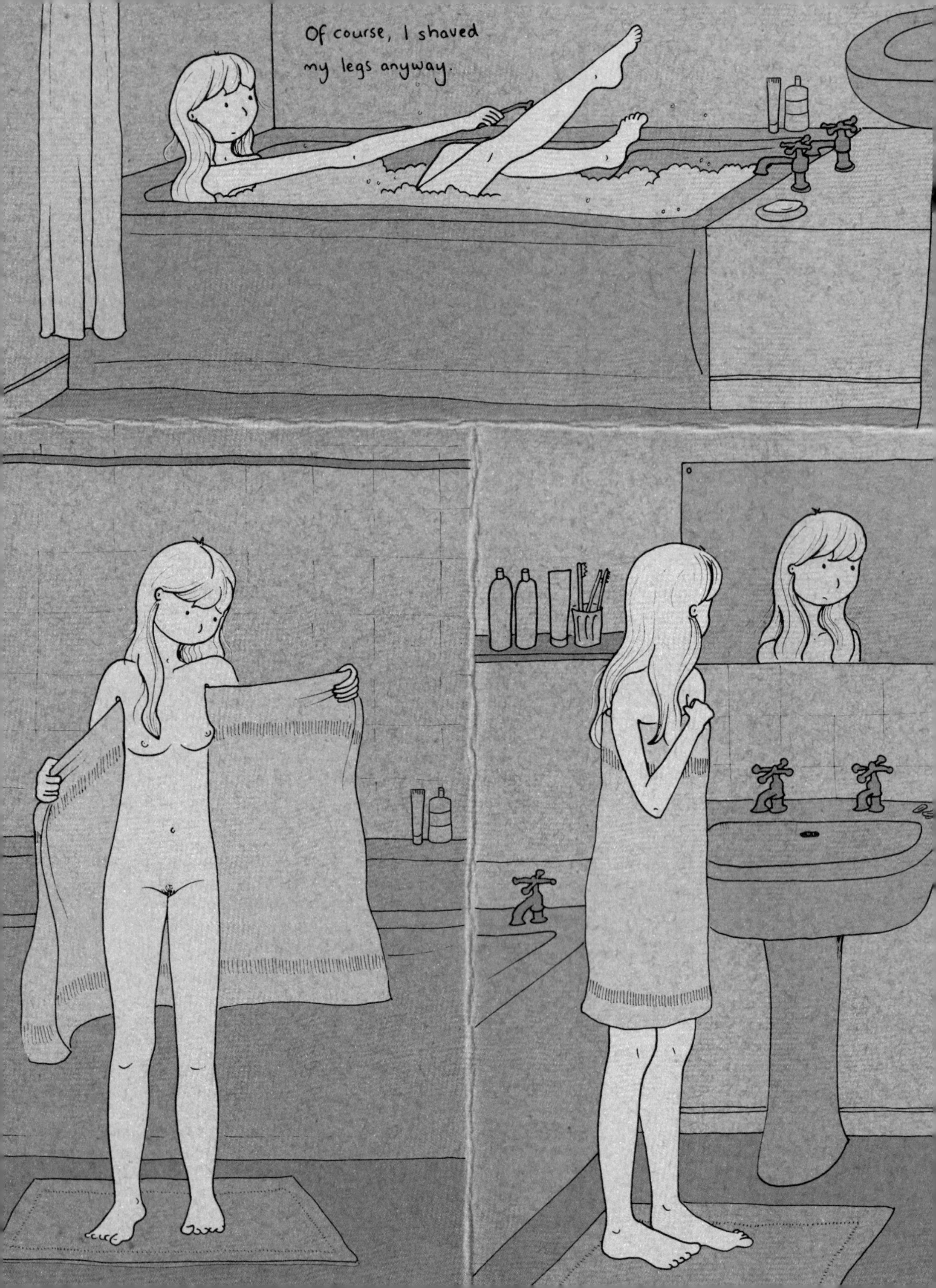
Of course, I shaved my legs anyway.

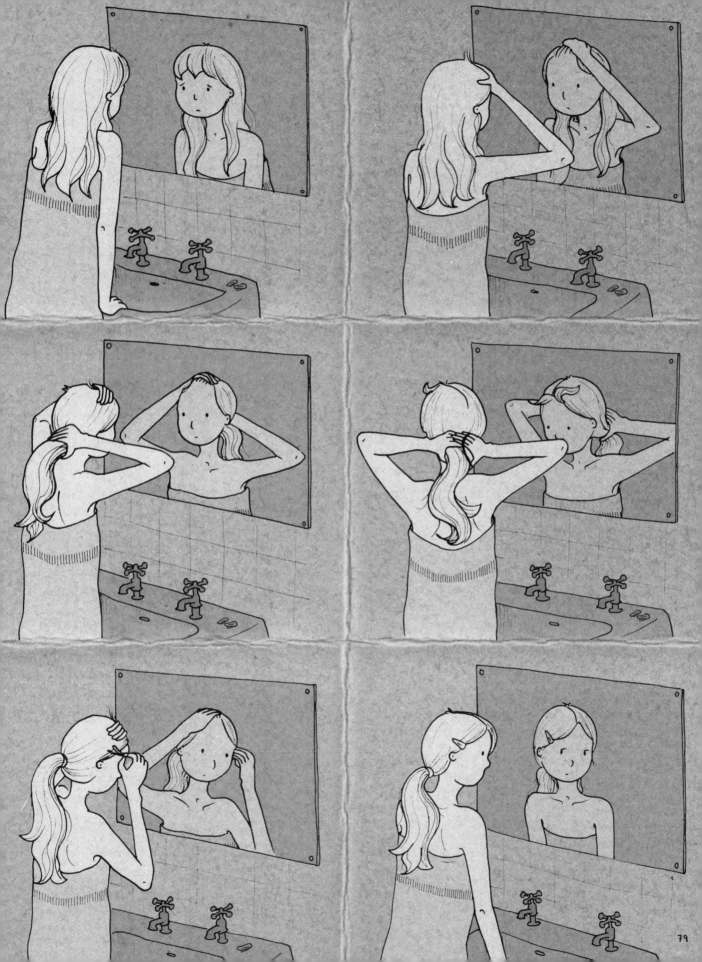

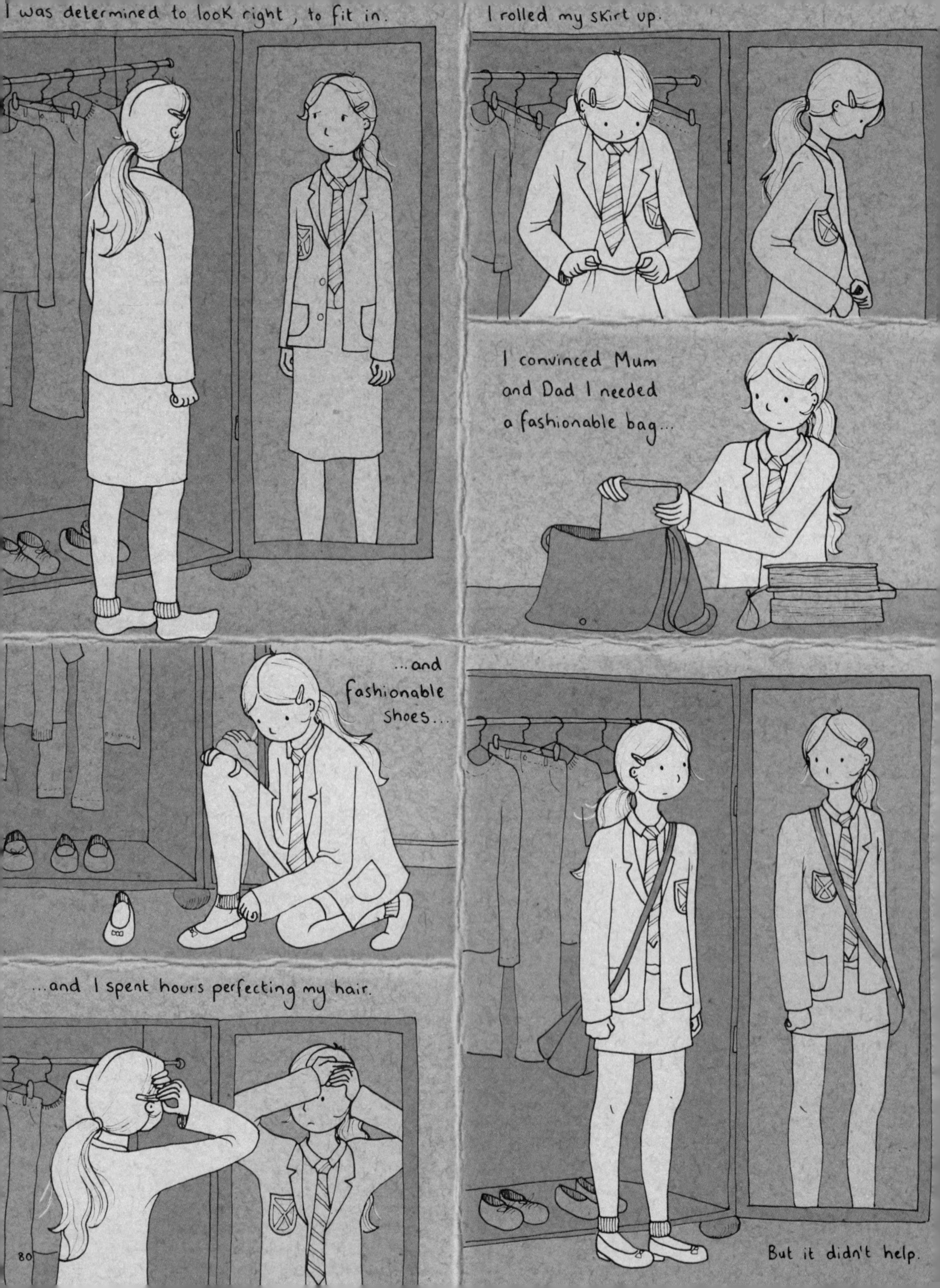
I was determined to look right, to fit in.
I rolled my skirt up.
I convinced Mum and Dad I needed a fashionable bag...
...and fashionable shoes...
...and I spent hours perfecting my hair.
But it didn't help.

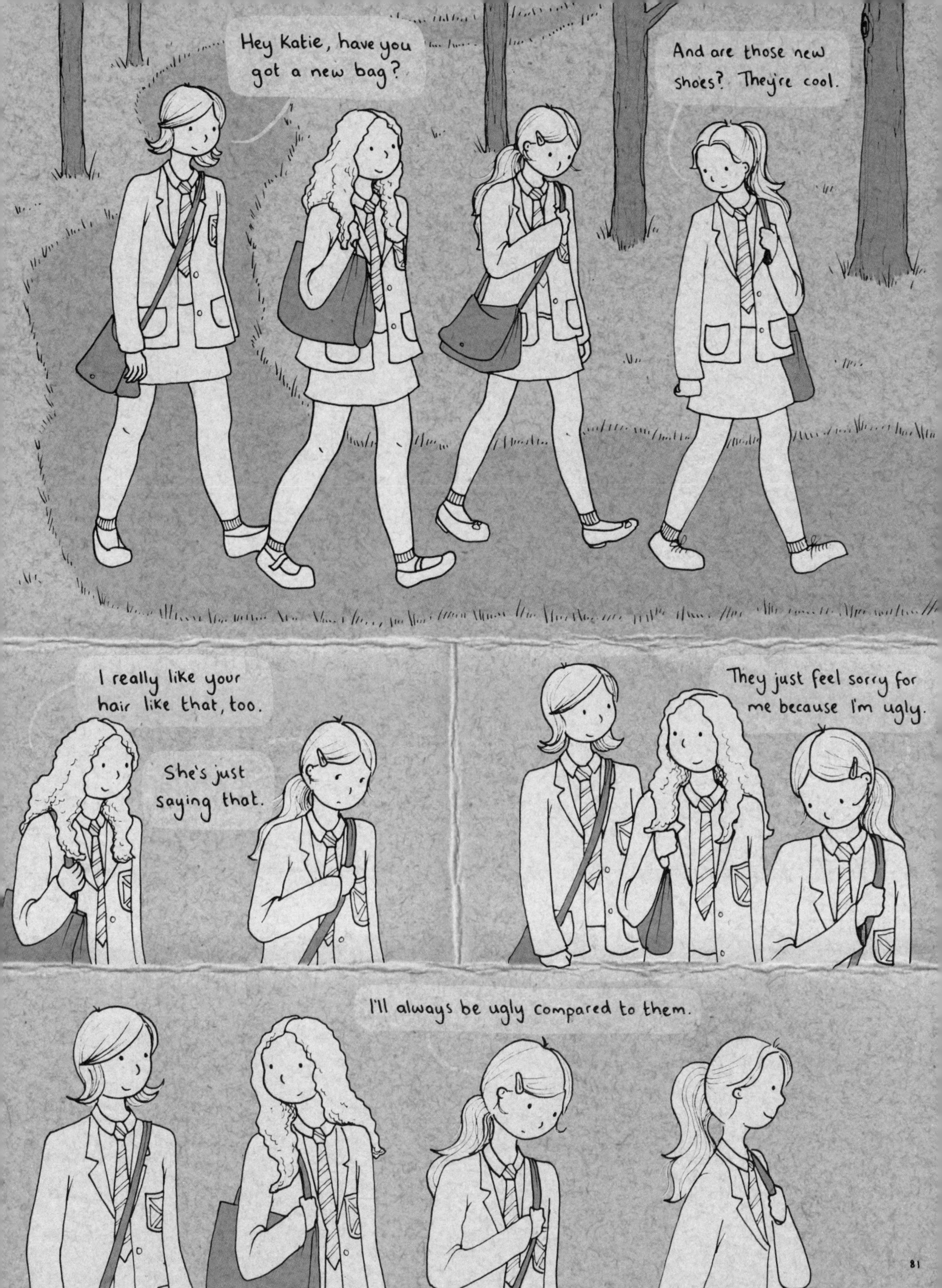
Hey Katie, have you got a new bag?
And are those new shoes? They're cool.
I really like your hair like that, too.
She's just saying that.
They just feel sorry for me because I'm ugly.
I'll always be ugly compared to them.

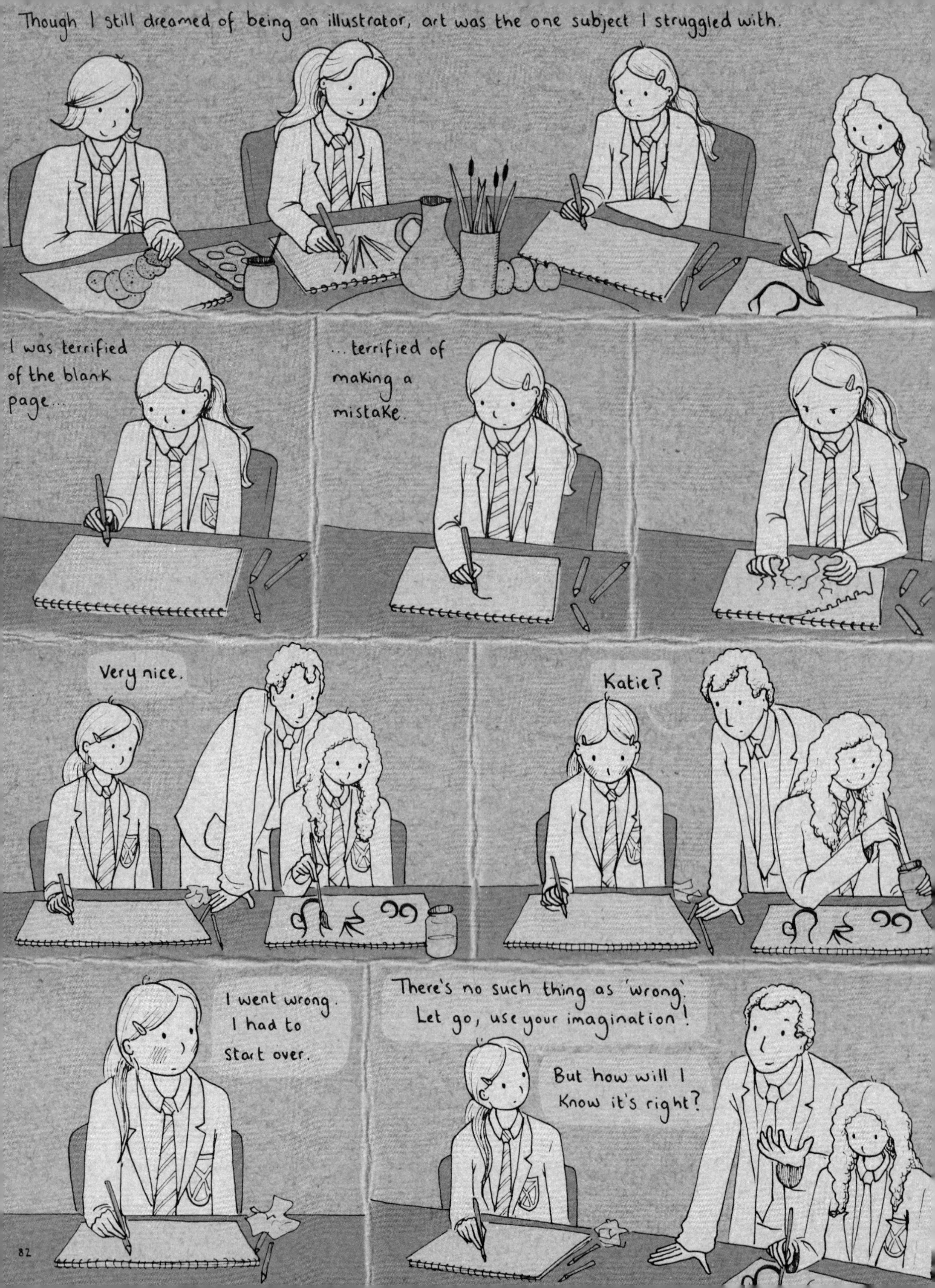
Though I still dreamed of being an illustrator, art was the one subject I struggled with.
I was terrified of the blank page...
...terrified of making a mistake.
Very nice.
Katie?
I went wrong. I had to start over.
There's no such thing as 'wrong'. Let go, use your imagination!
But how will I know it's right?

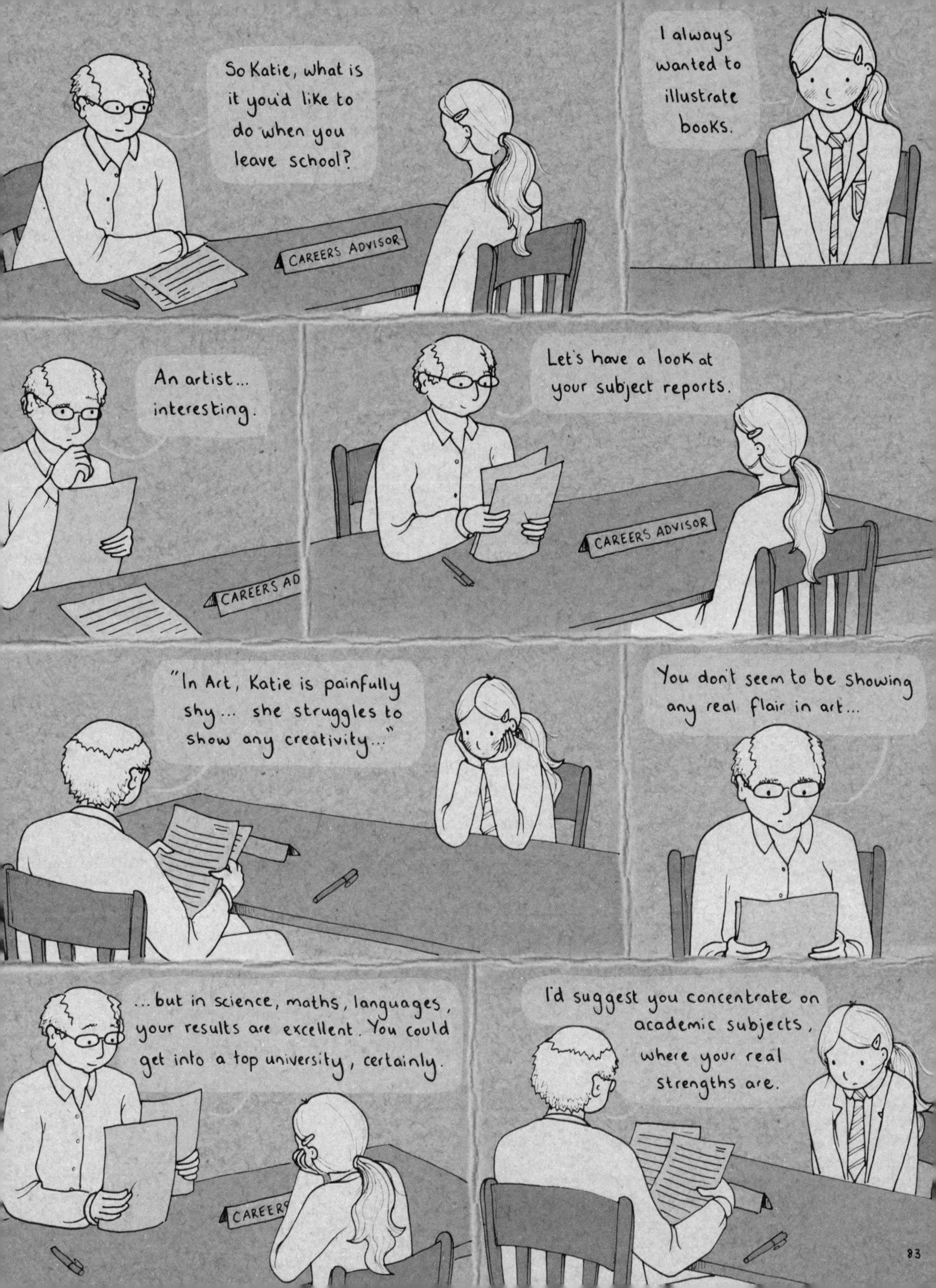
So Katie, what is it you'd like to do when you leave school?
CAREERS ADVISOR
I always wanted to illustrate books.
An artist... interesting.
CAREERS AD
Let's have a look at your subject reports.
CAREERS ADVISOR
"In Art, Katie is painfully shy... she struggles to show any creativity..."
You don't seem to be showing any real flair in art...
...but in science, maths, languages, your results are excellent. You could get into a top university, certainly.
CAREERS
I'd suggest you concentrate on academic subjects, where your real strengths are.

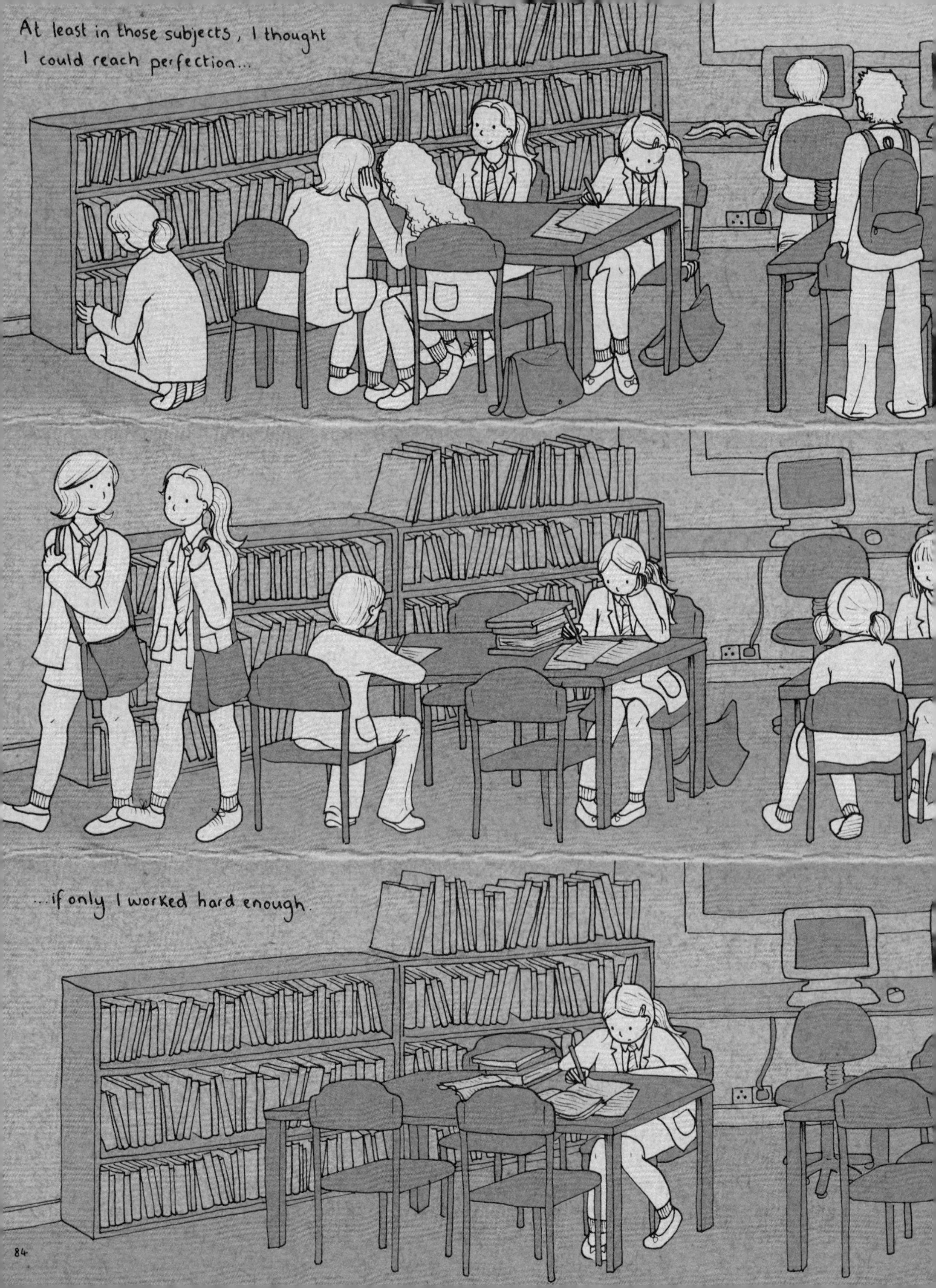
At least in those subjects, I thought I could reach perfection...
...if only I worked hard enough.

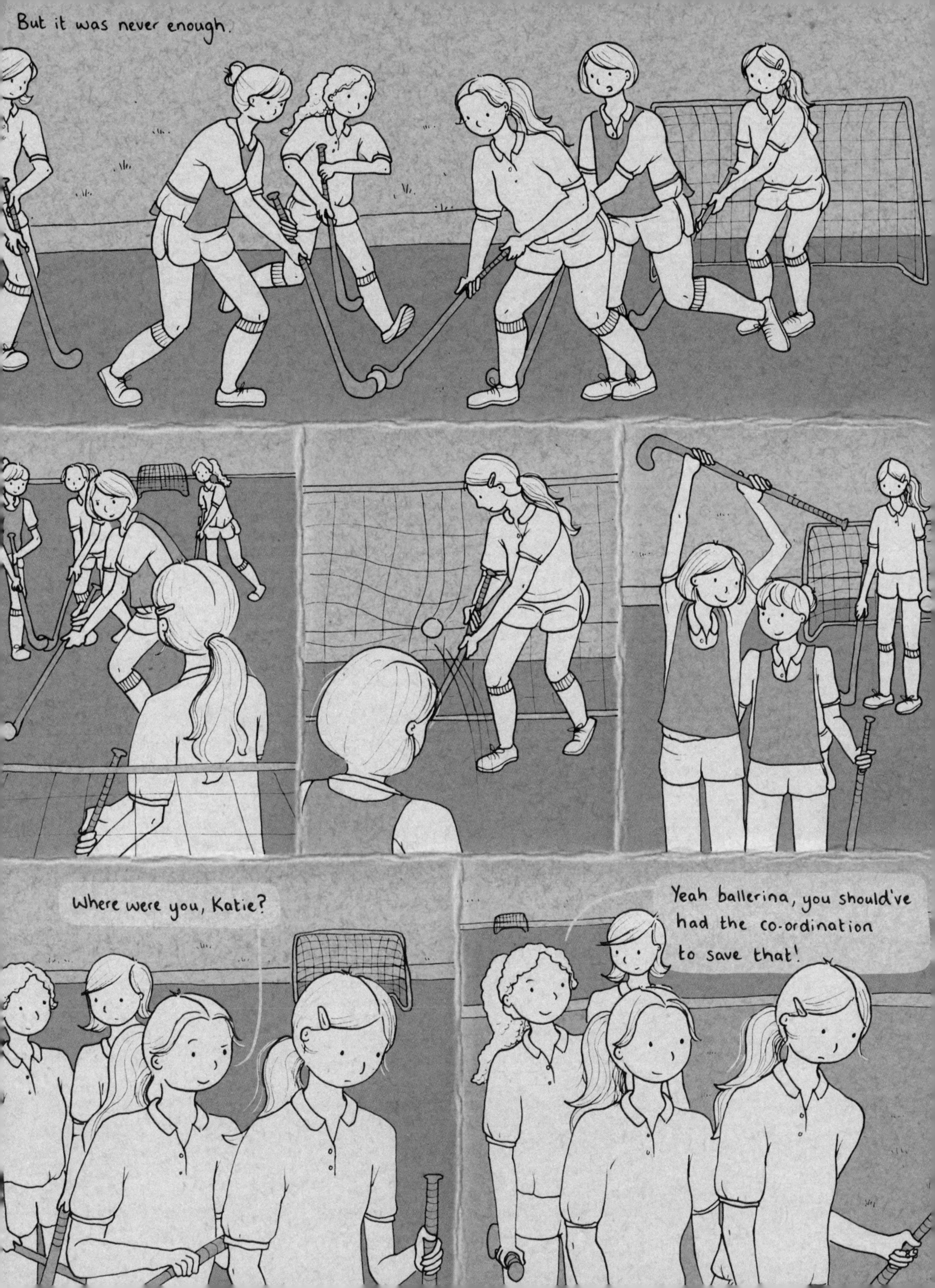
But it was never enough.
Where were you, Katie?
...
Yeah ballerina, you should've had the co-ordination to save that!

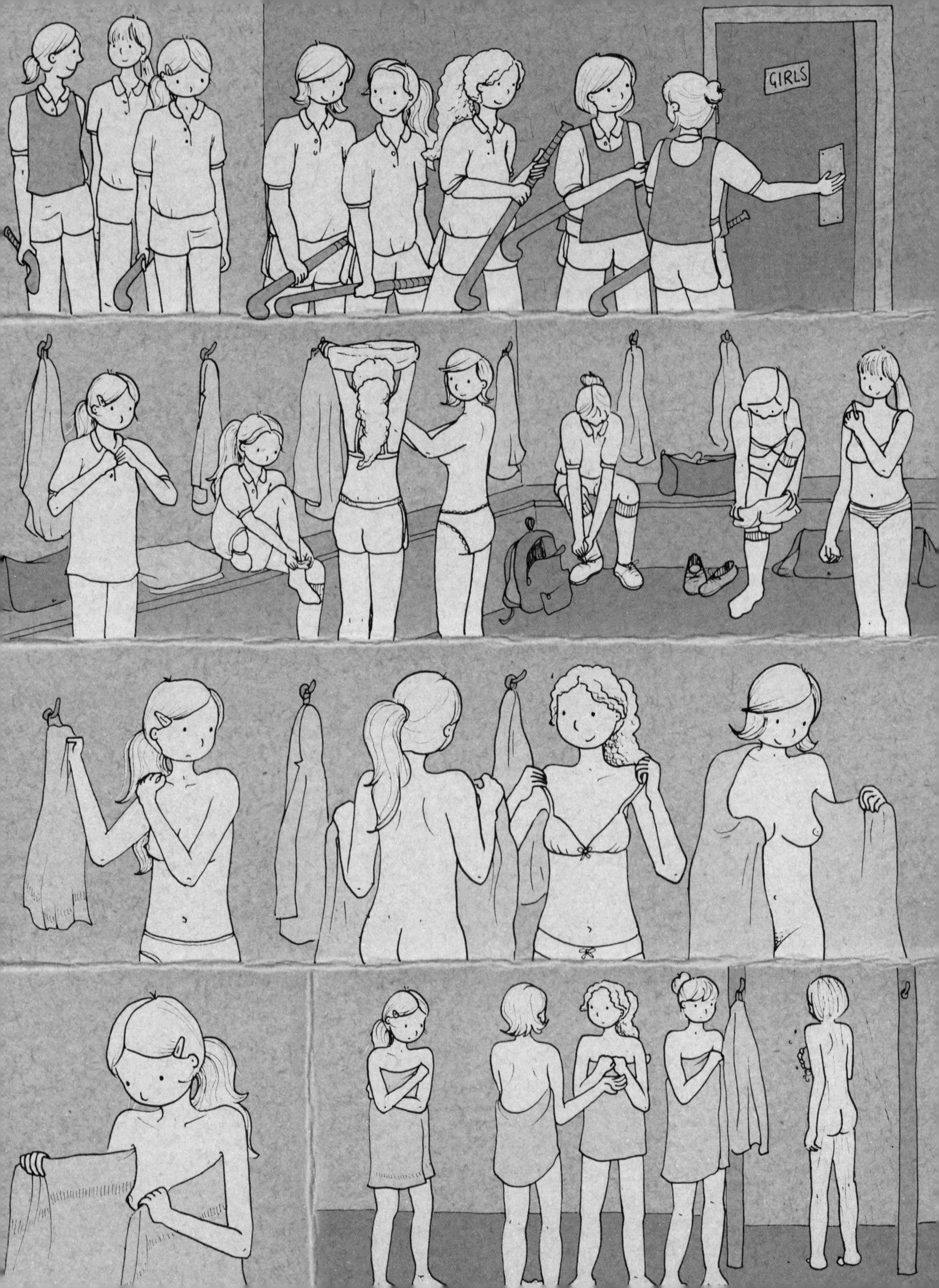
GIRLS

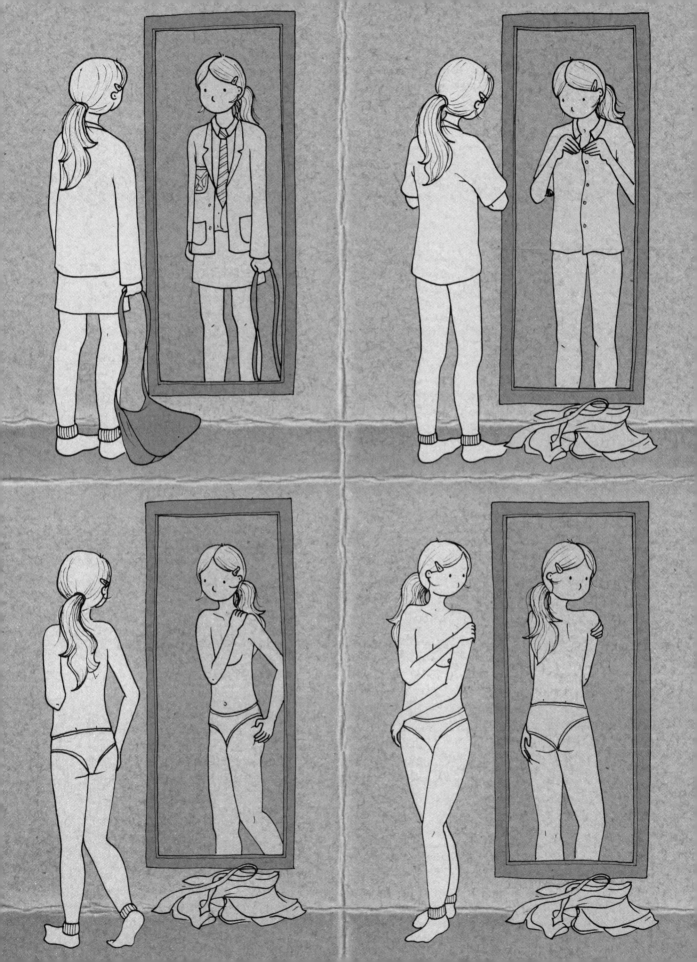

Suddenly, it seemed everyone had something to say about my body.

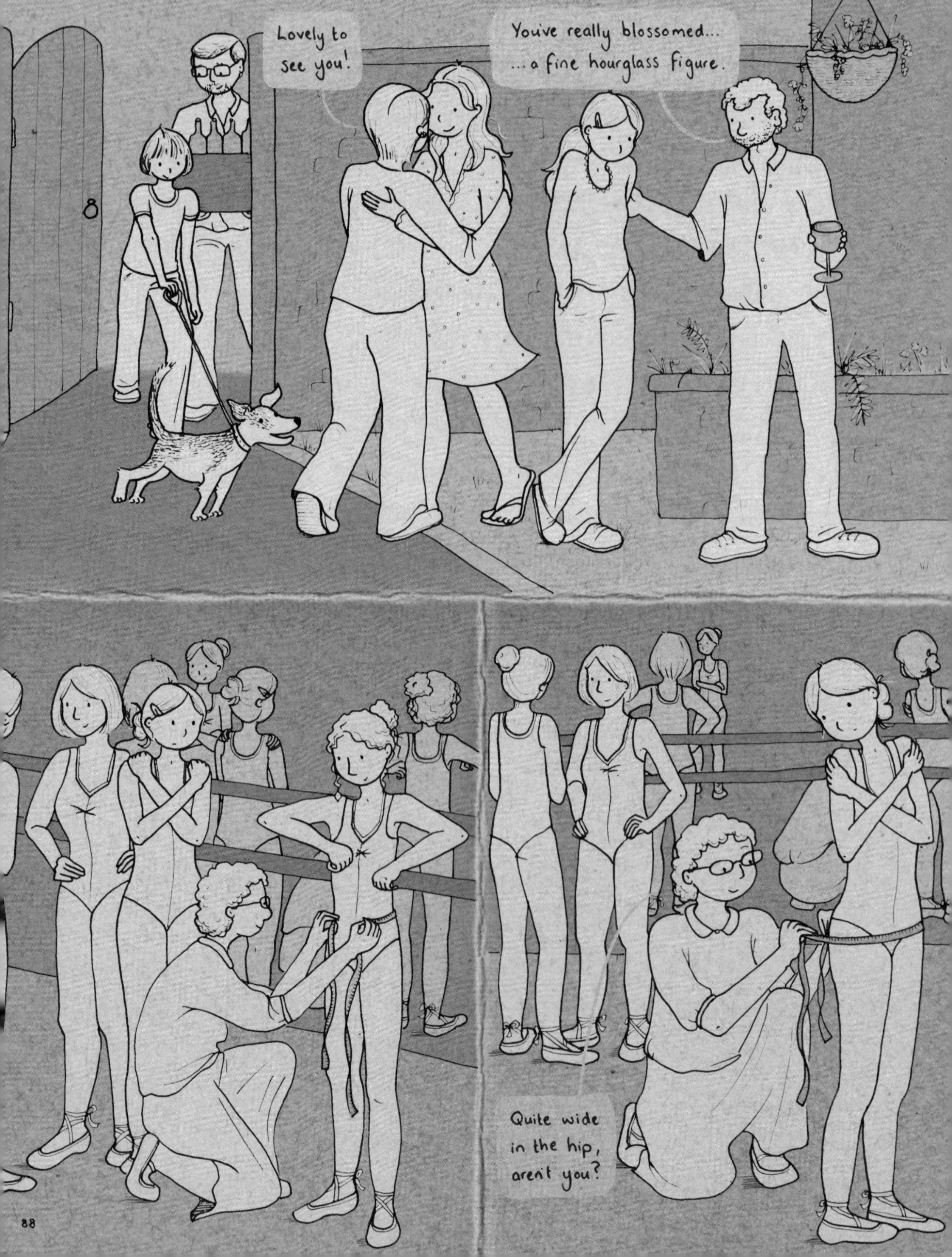

Lovely to see you!
You've really blossomed... ...a fine hourglass figure.
Quite wide in the hip, aren't you?

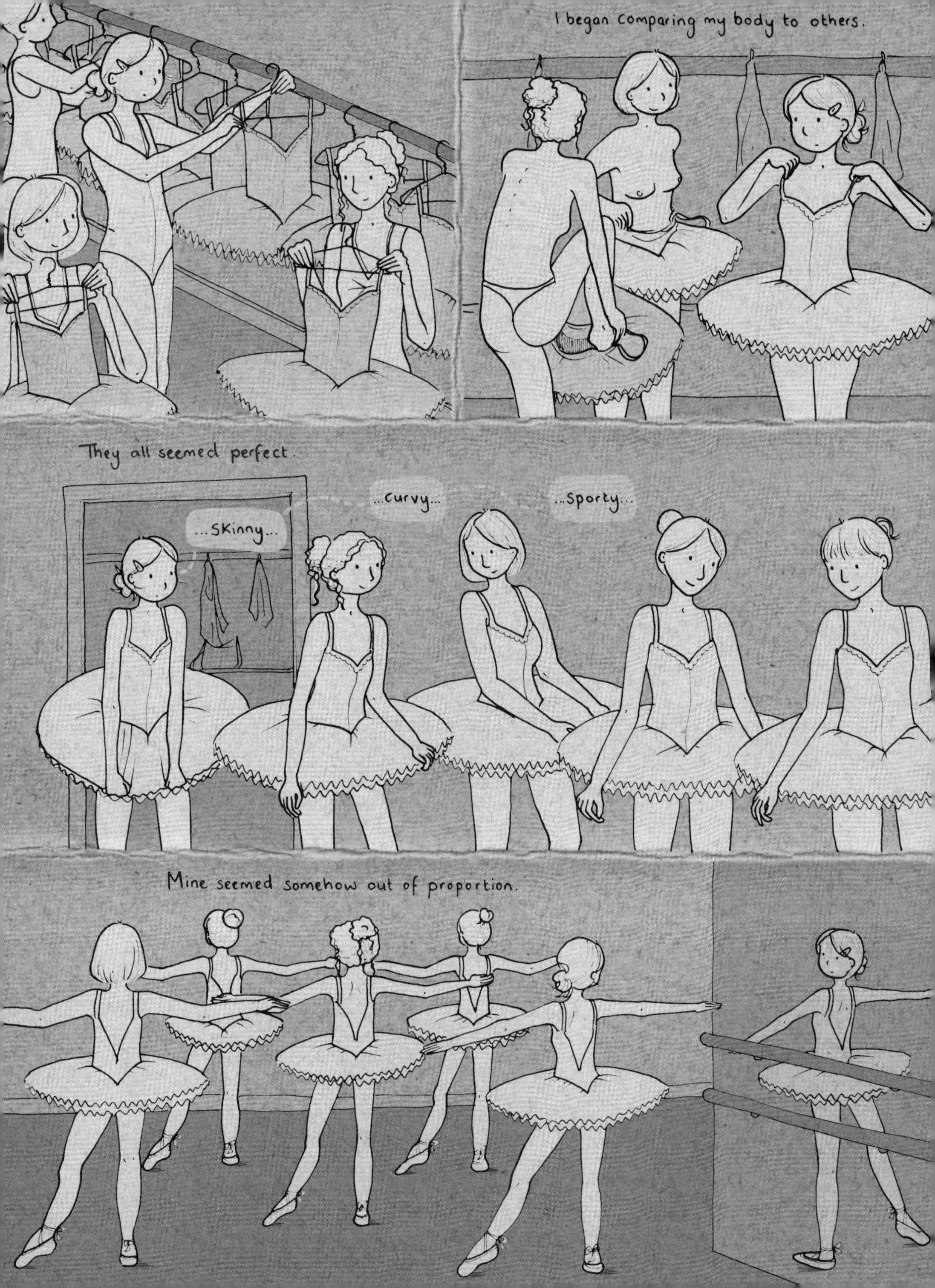

I began comparing my body to others.
They all seemed perfect.
...Skinny...
...curvy...
...sporty...
Mine seemed somehow out of proportion.

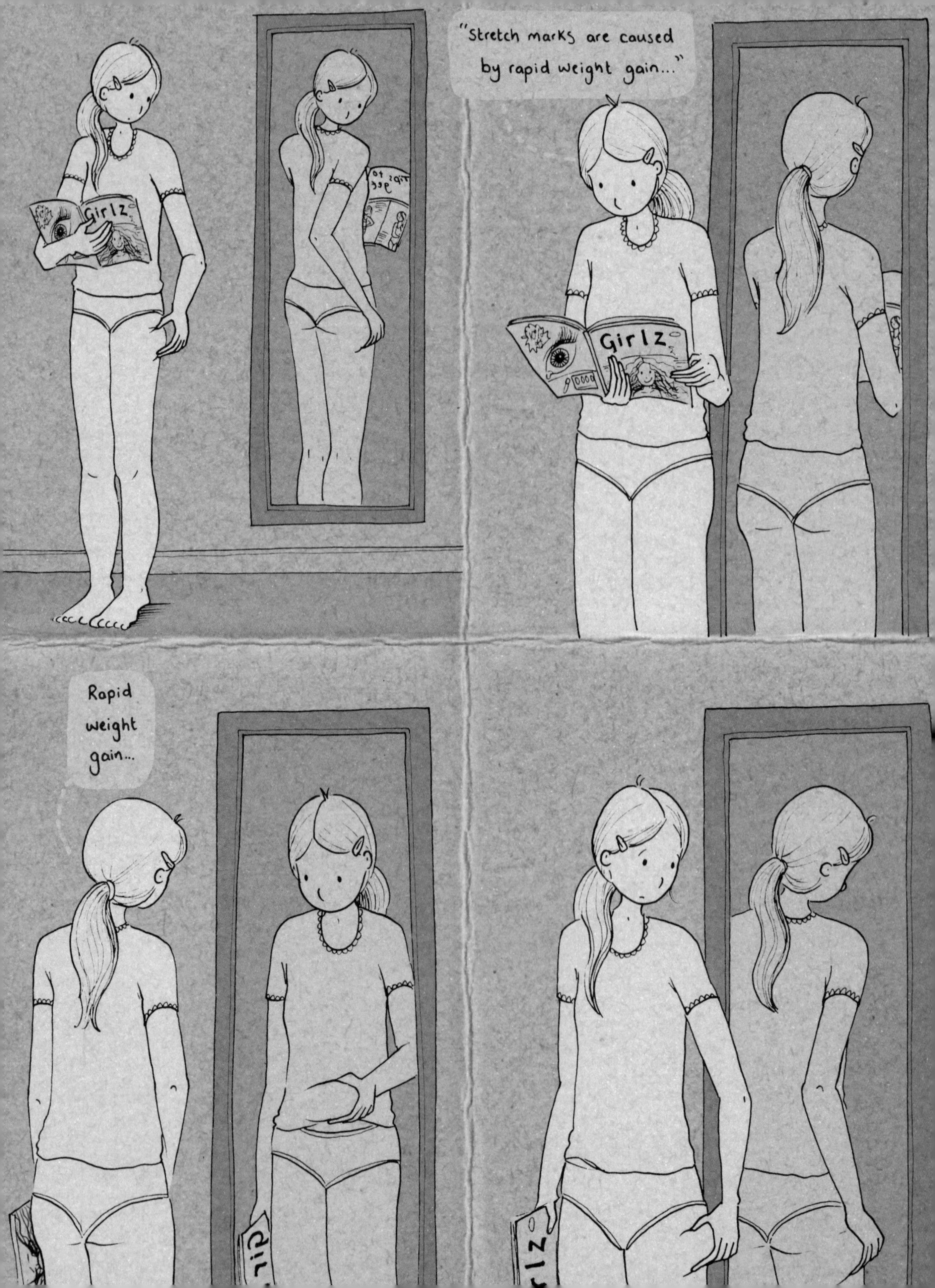
Girlz
"Stretch marks are caused by rapid weight gain..."
Girlz
Rapid weight gain...

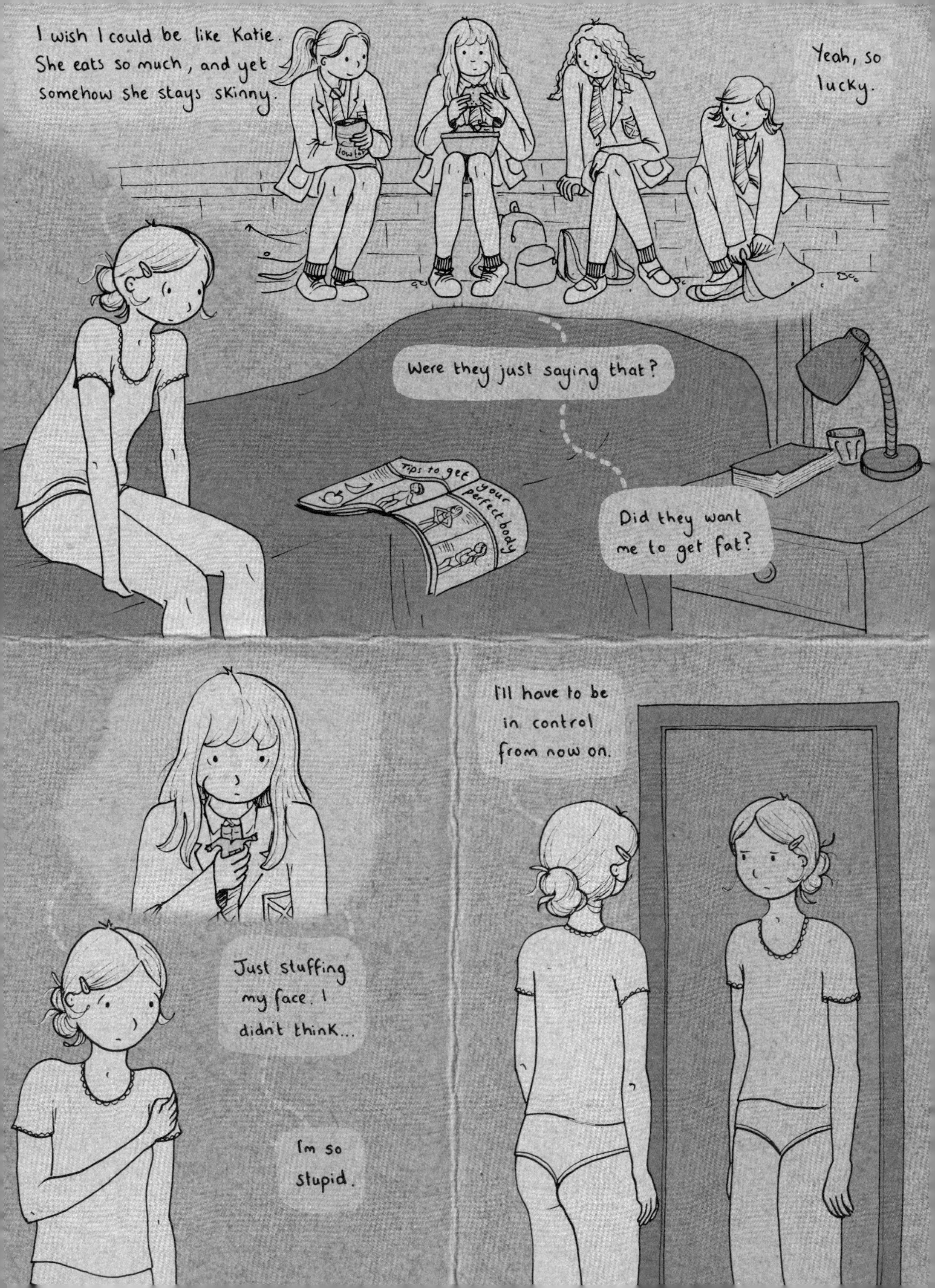
I wish I could be like Katie. She eats so much, and yet somehow she stays skinny.
low fat
Yeah, so lucky.
Were they just saying that?
Tips to get your perfect body
Did they want me to get fat?
Just stuffing my face. I didn't think...
I'm so stupid.
I'll have to be in control from now on.

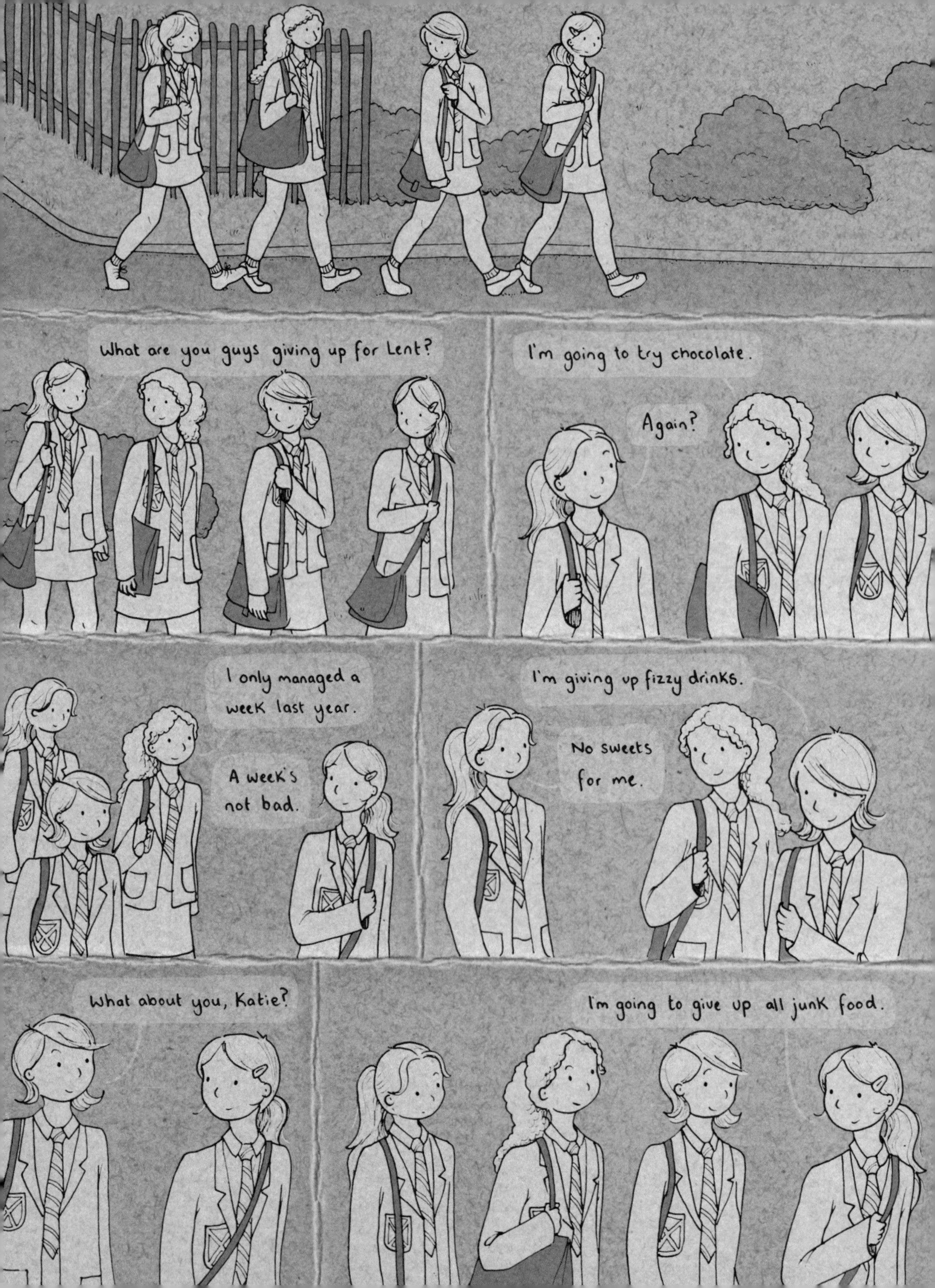
What are you guys giving up for Lent?
I'm going to try chocolate.
Again?
I only managed a week last year.
A week's not bad.
I'm giving up fizzy drinks.
No sweets for me.
What about you, Katie?
I'm going to give up all junk food.

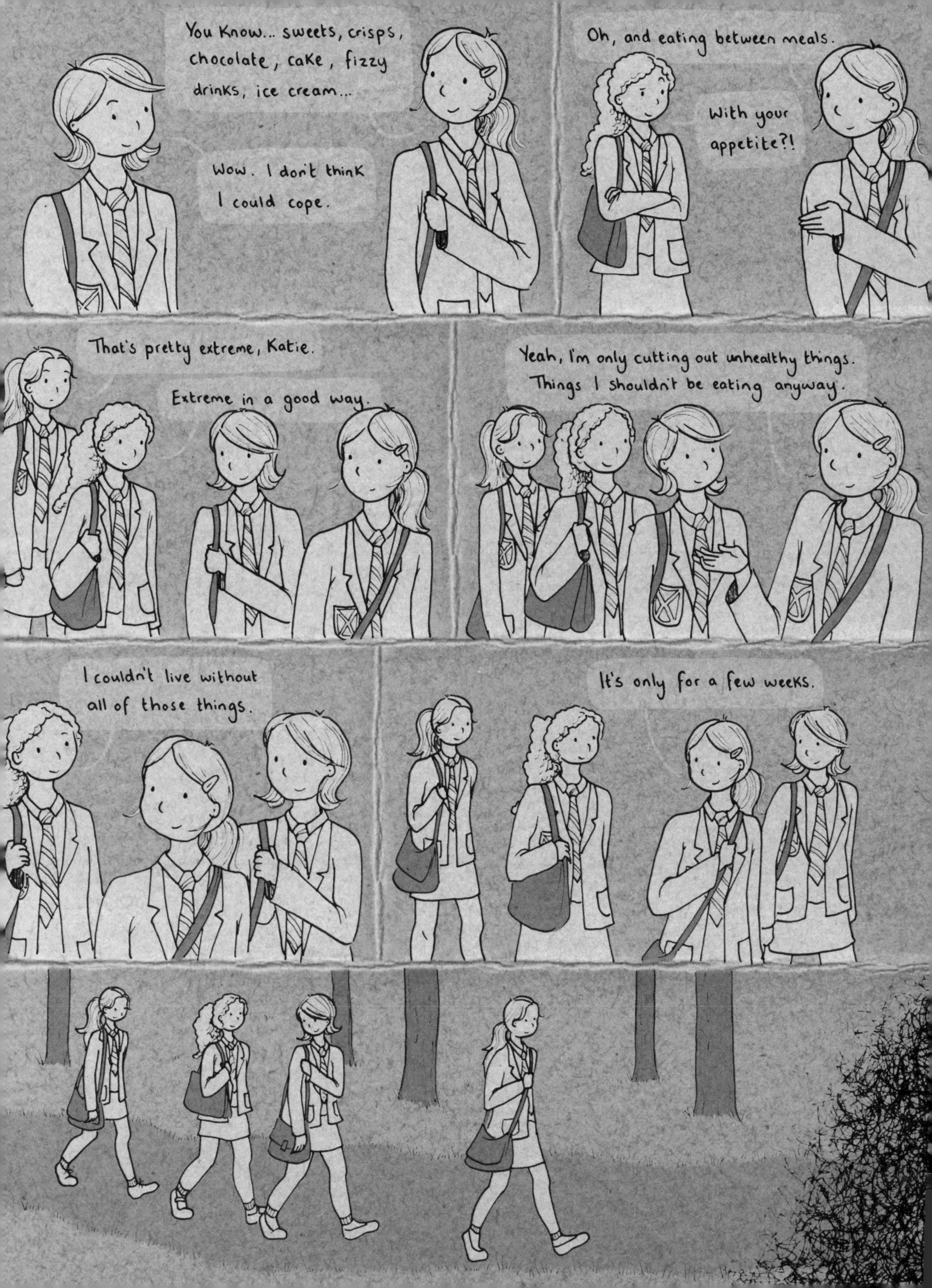
You Know... sweets, crisps, chocolate, cake, fizzy drinks, ice cream...
Wow. I don't think I could cope.
Oh, and eating between meals.
With your appetite?!
That's pretty extreme, Katie.
Extreme in a good way.
Yeah, I'm only cutting out unhealthy things. Things I shouldn't be eating anyway.
I couldn't live without all of those things.
It's only for a few weeks.

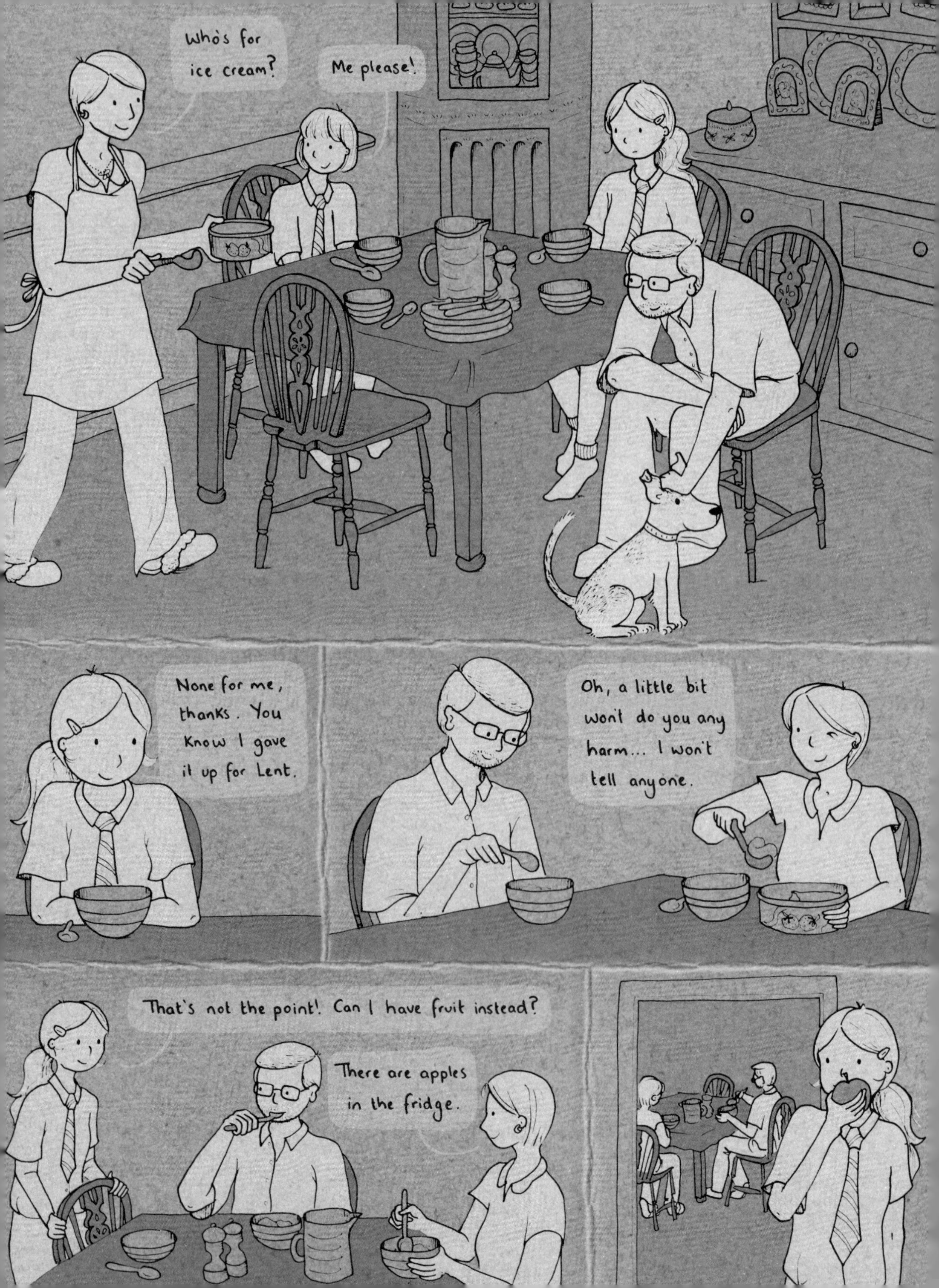
Who's for ice cream?
Me please!
None for me, thanks. You know I gave it up for Lent.
Oh, a little bit won't do you any harm... I won't tell anyone.
That's not the point! Can I have fruit instead?
There are apples in the fridge.

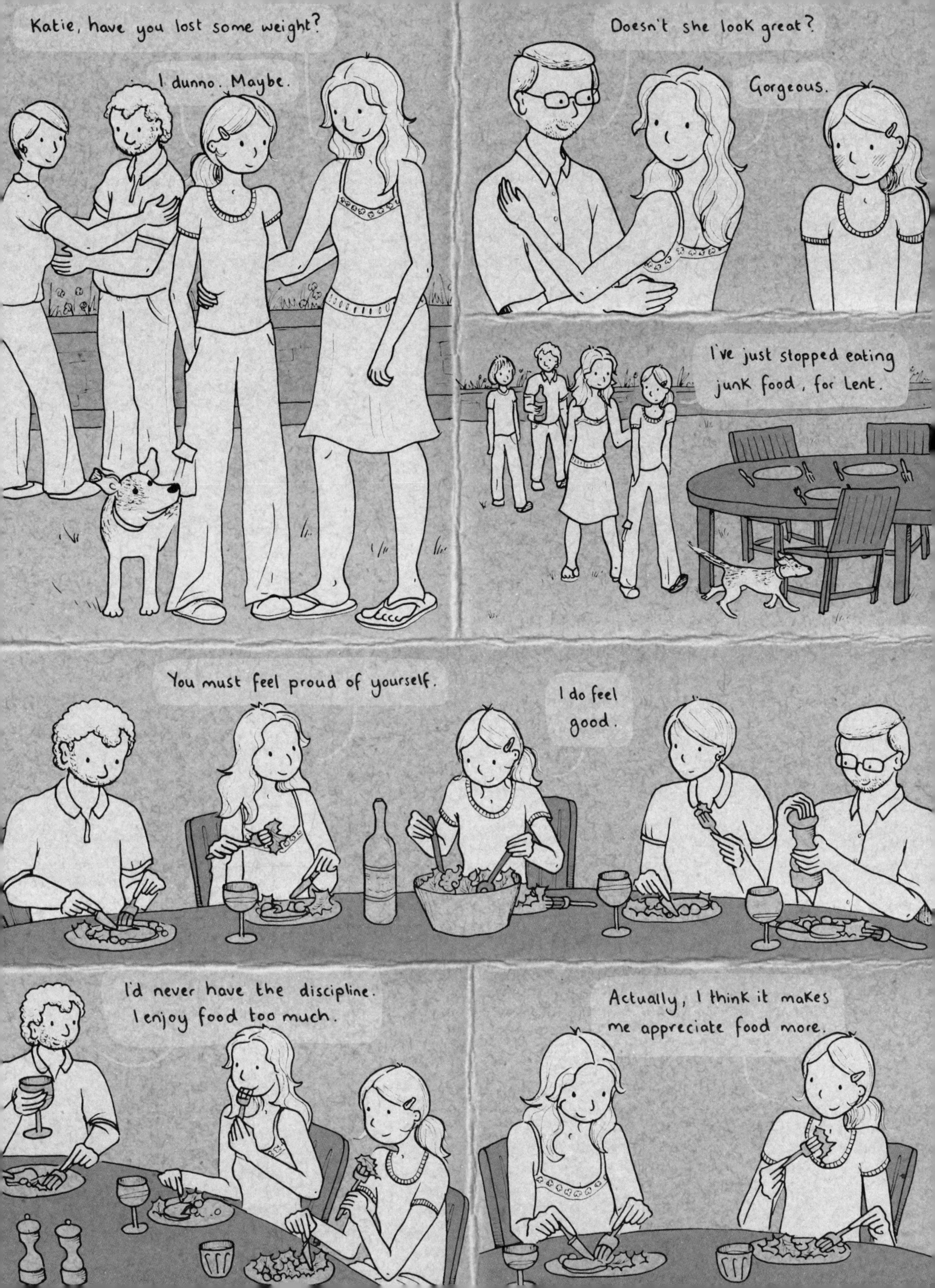
Katie, have you lost some weight?
I dunno. Maybe.
Doesn't she look great?
Gorgeous.
I've just stopped eating junk food, for Lent.
You must feel proud of yourself.
I do feel good.
I'd never have the discipline. I enjoy food too much.
Actually, I think it makes me appreciate food more.

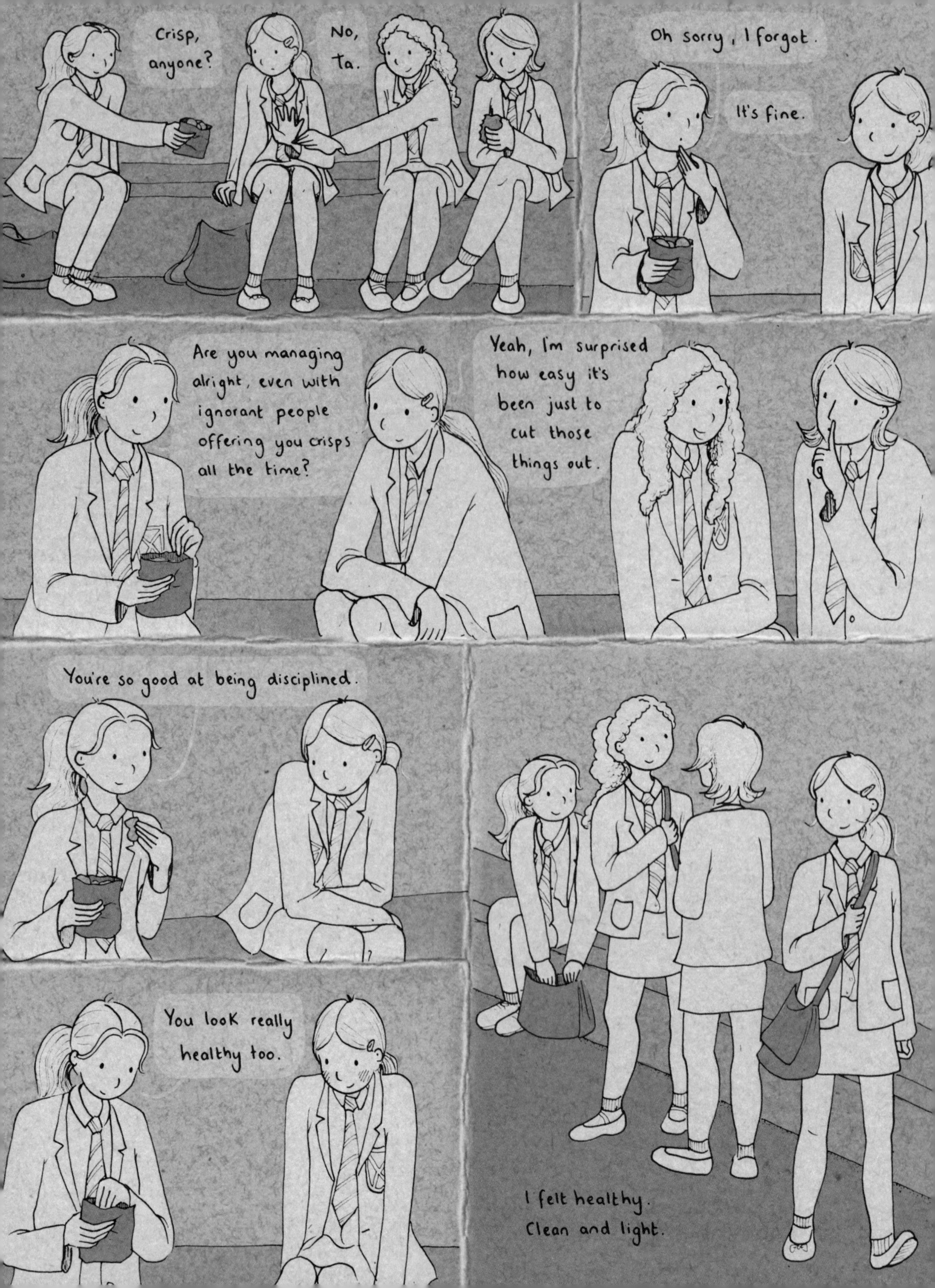

Crisp, anyone?
No, ta.
Oh sorry, I forgot.
It's fine.
Are you managing alright, even with ignorant people offering you crisps all the time?
Yeah, I'm surprised how easy it's been just to cut those things out.
You're so good at being disciplined.
You look really healthy too.
I felt healthy.
Clean and light.

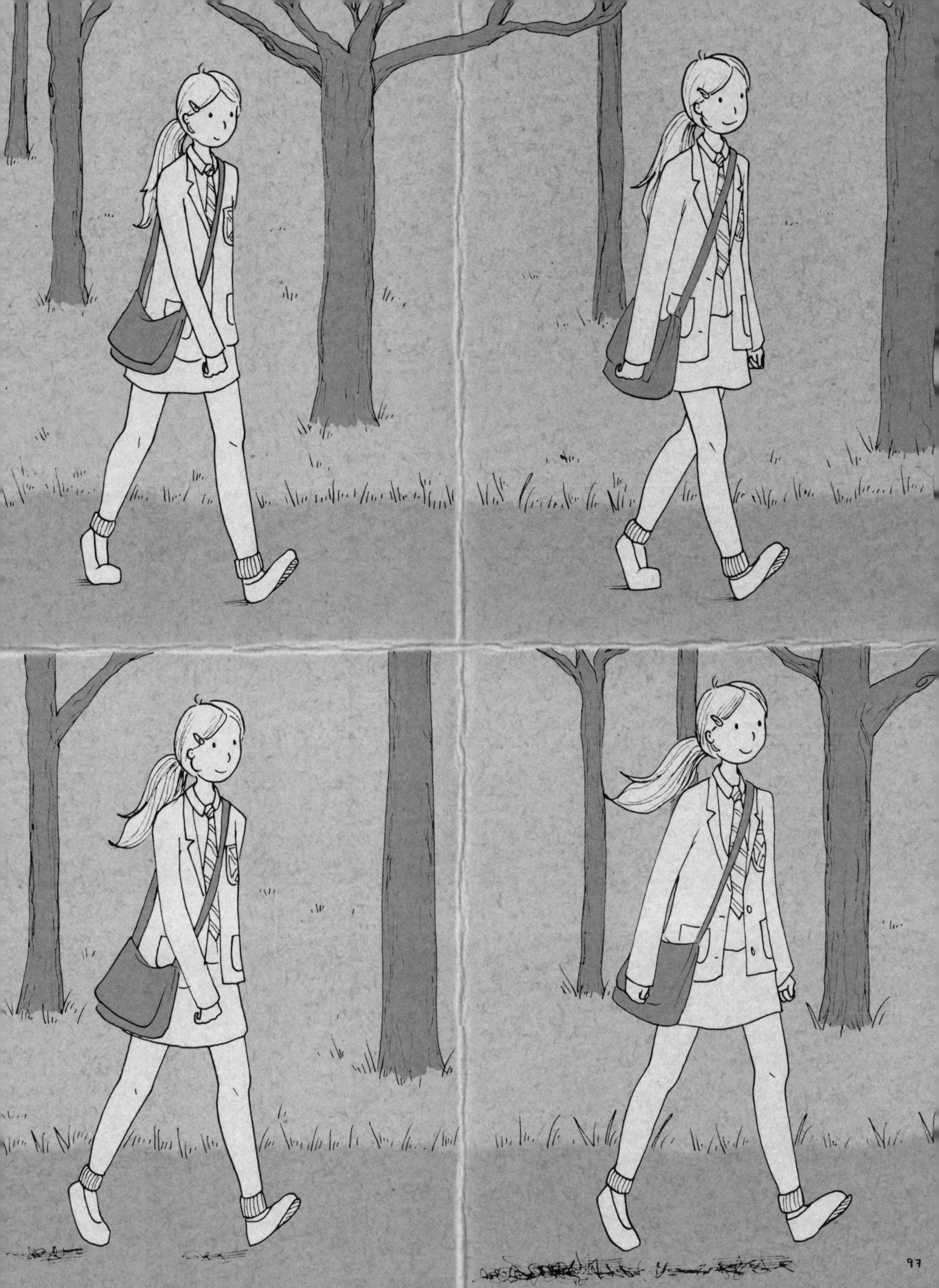

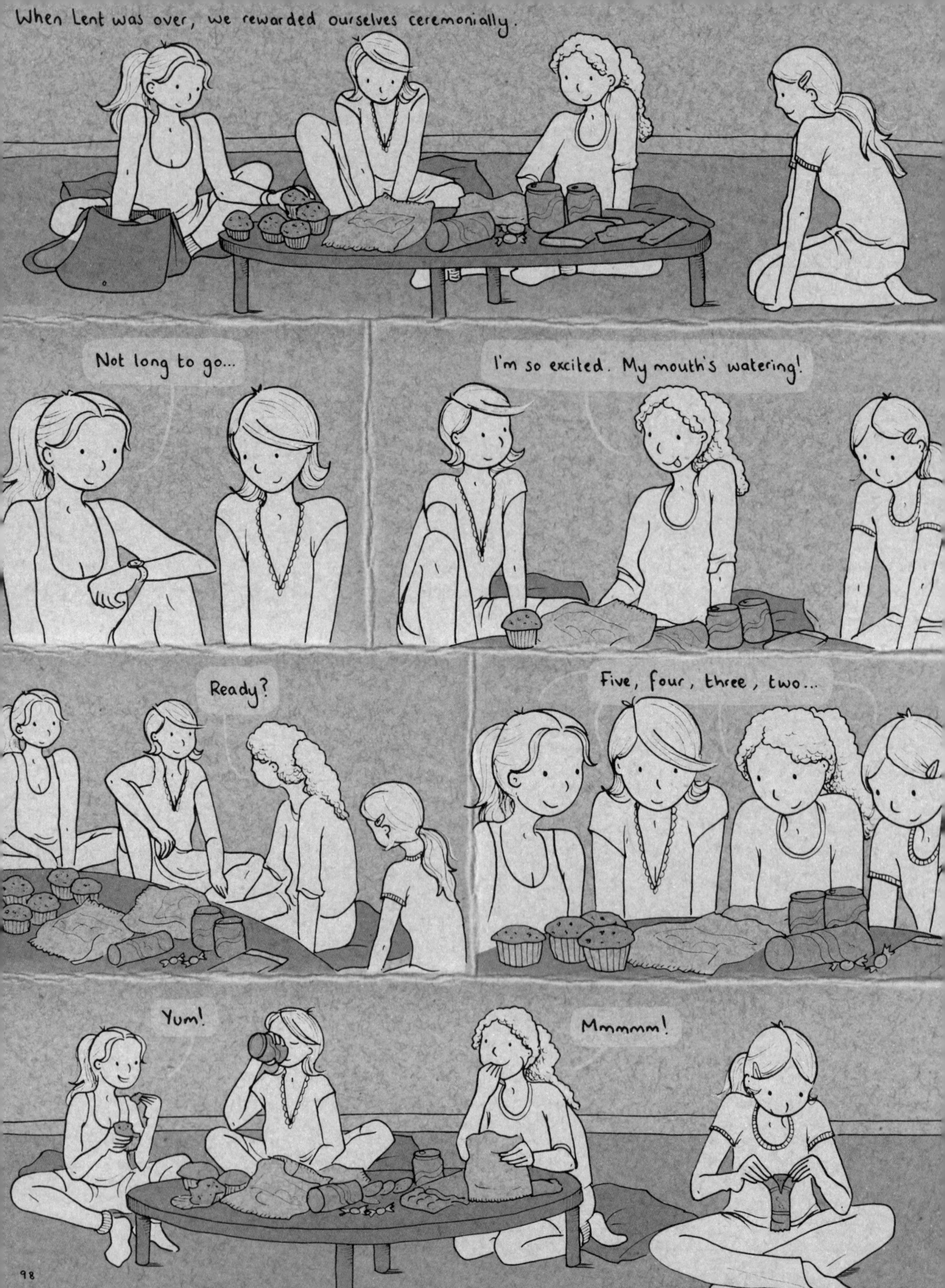
When Lent was over, we rewarded ourselves ceremonially.
Not long to go...
I'm so excited. My mouth's watering!
Ready?
Five, four, three, two...
Yum!
Mmmmm!

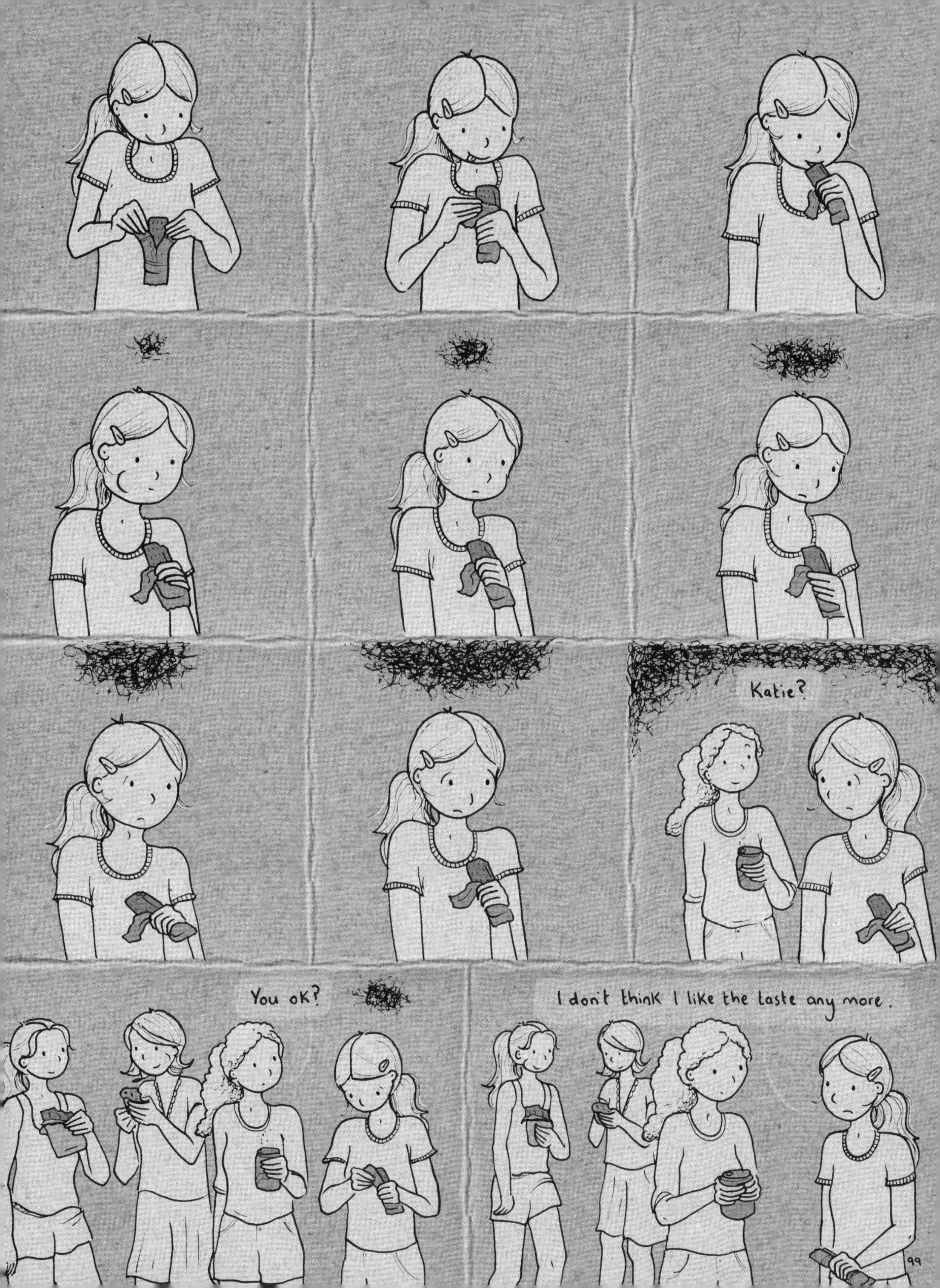
Katie?
You ok?
I don't think I like the taste any more.

But it wasn't
the taste, it was
the feeling.

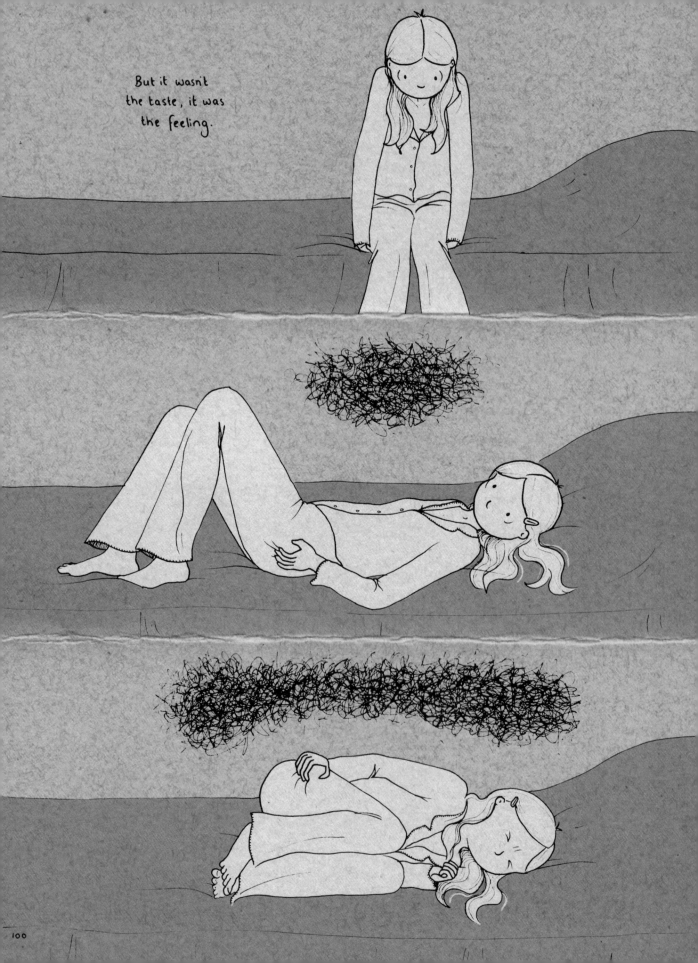

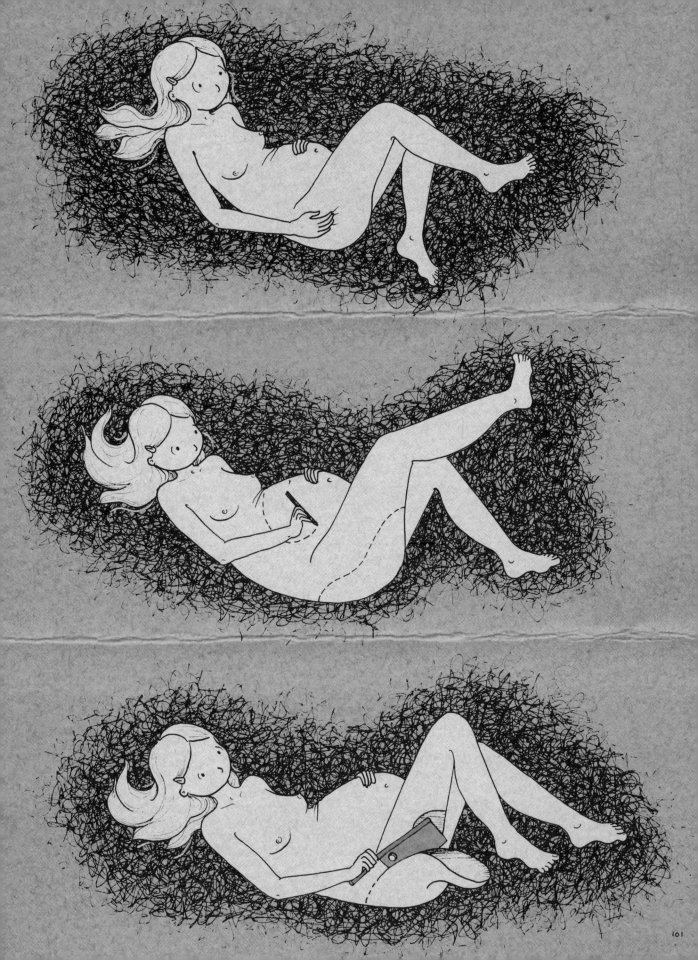

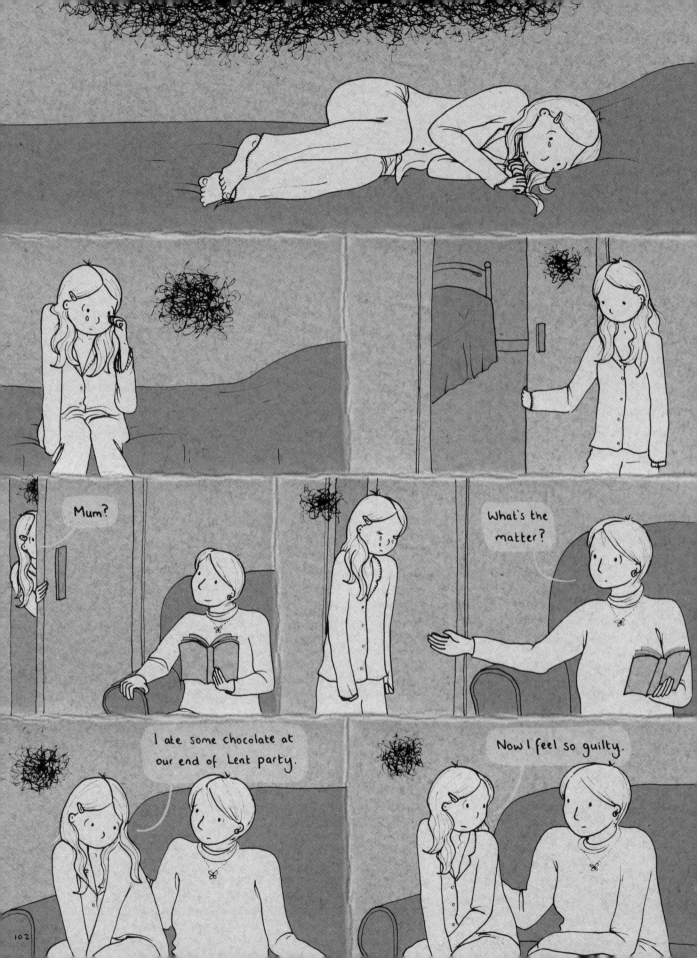

Mum?

What's the matter?

I ate some chocolate at our end of Lent party.

Now I feel so guilty.

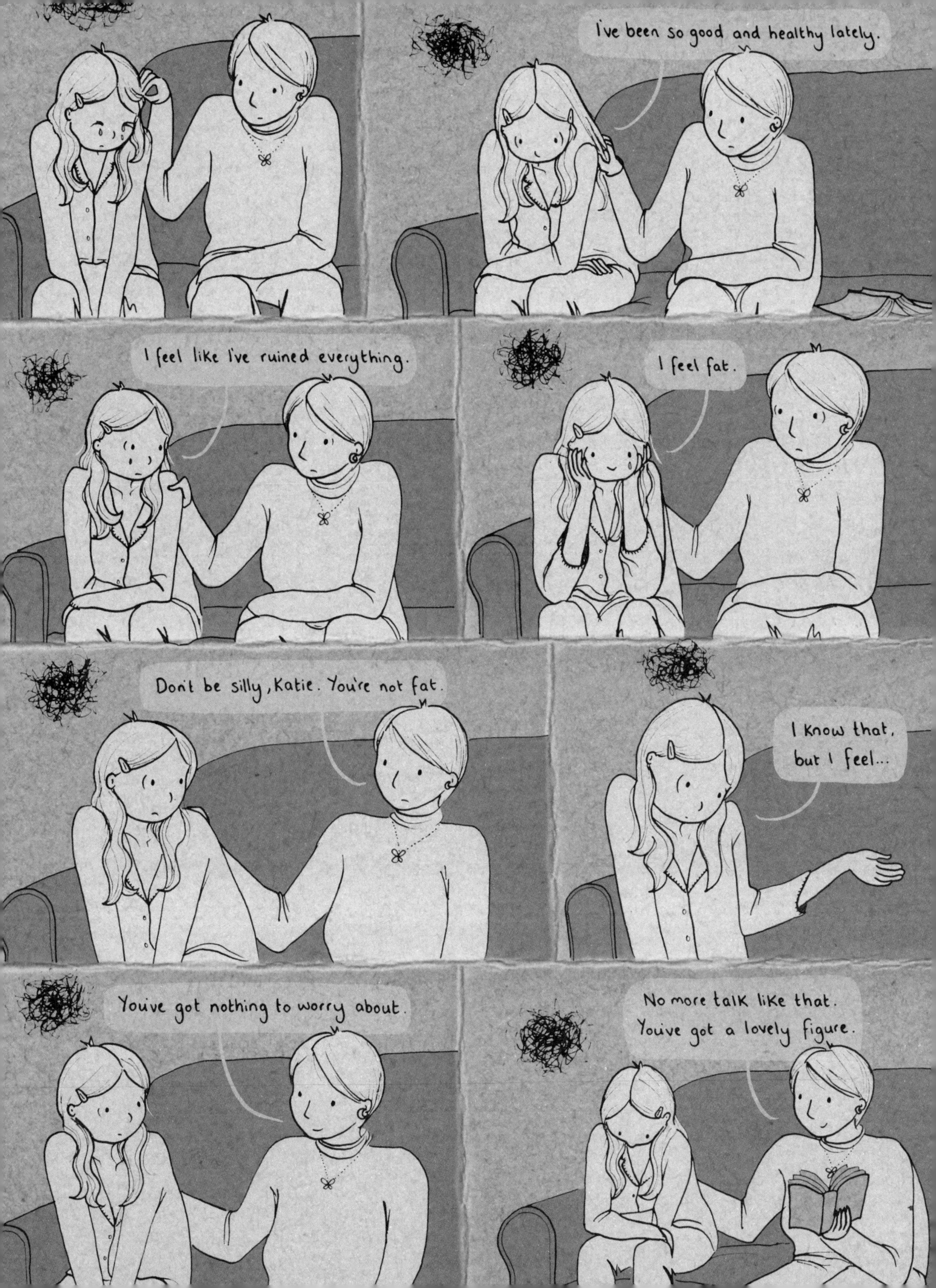
I've been so good and healthy lately.
I feel like I've ruined everything.
I feel fat.
Don't be silly, Katie. You're not fat.
I know that, but I feel...
You've got nothing to worry about.
No more talk like that. You've got a lovely figure.

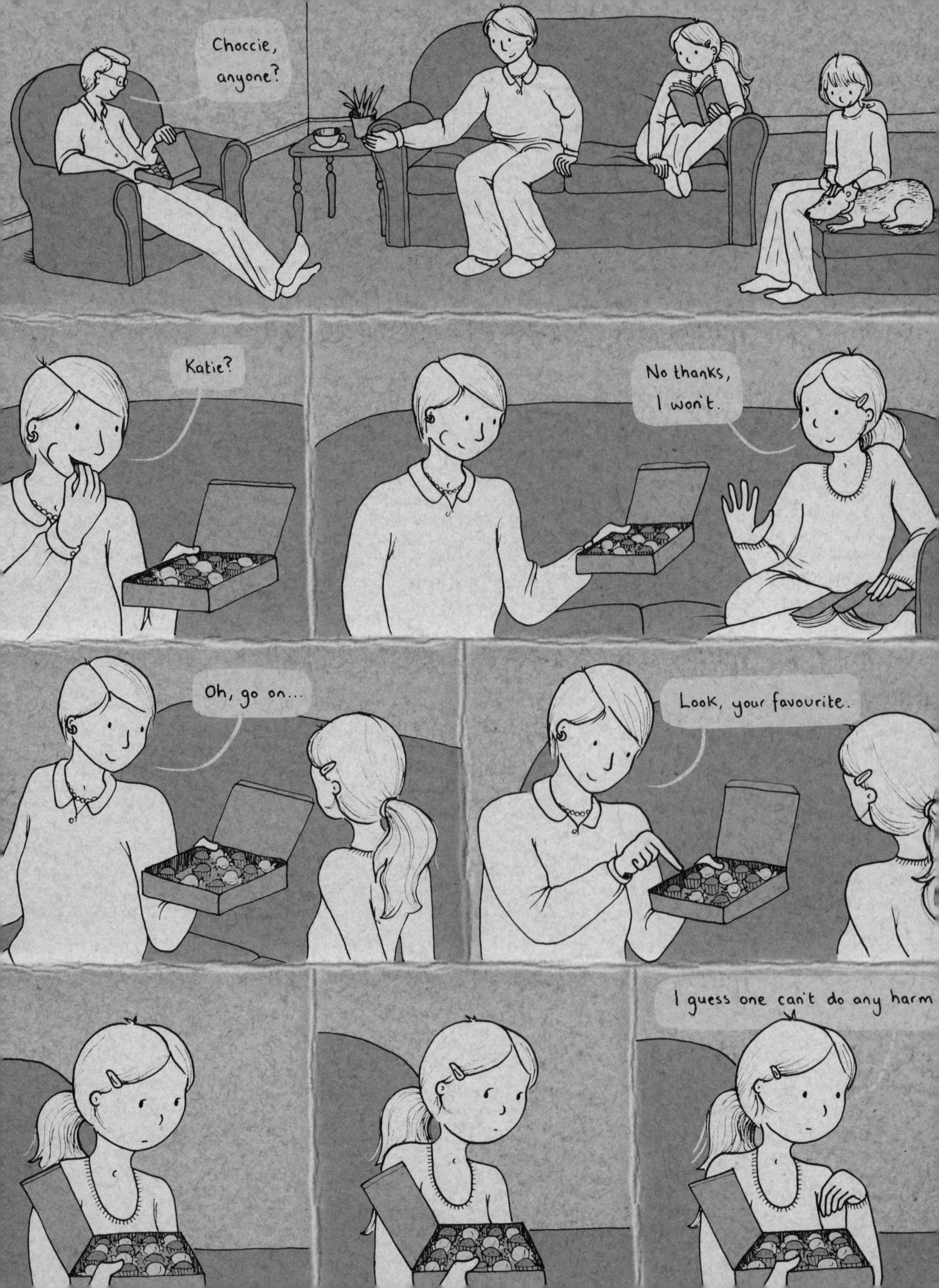
Choccie, anyone?
Katie?
No thanks, I won't.
Oh, go on...
Look, your favourite.
I guess one can't do any harm

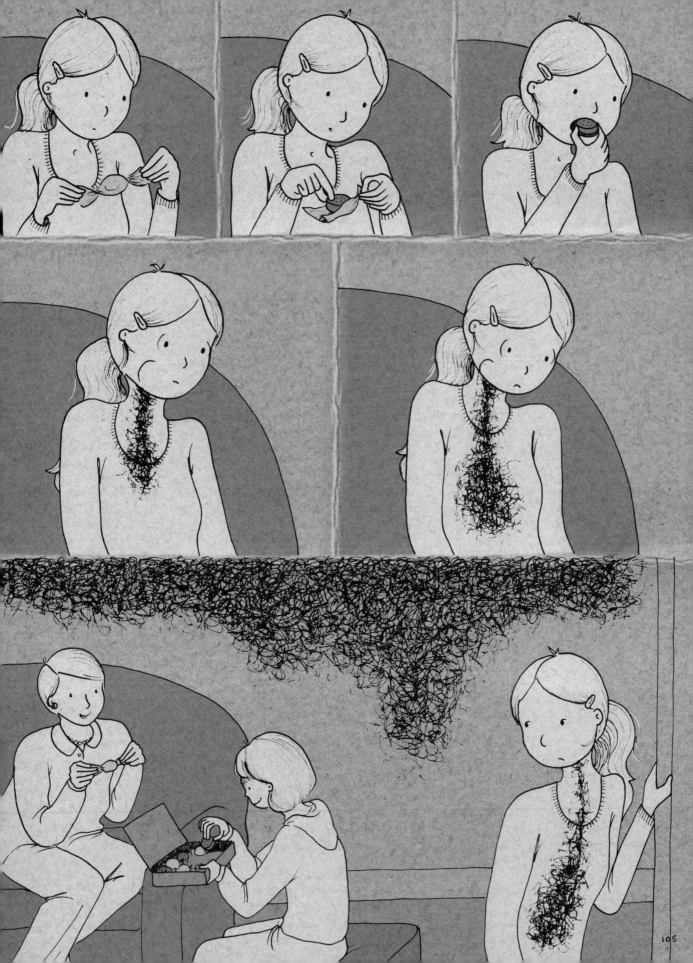

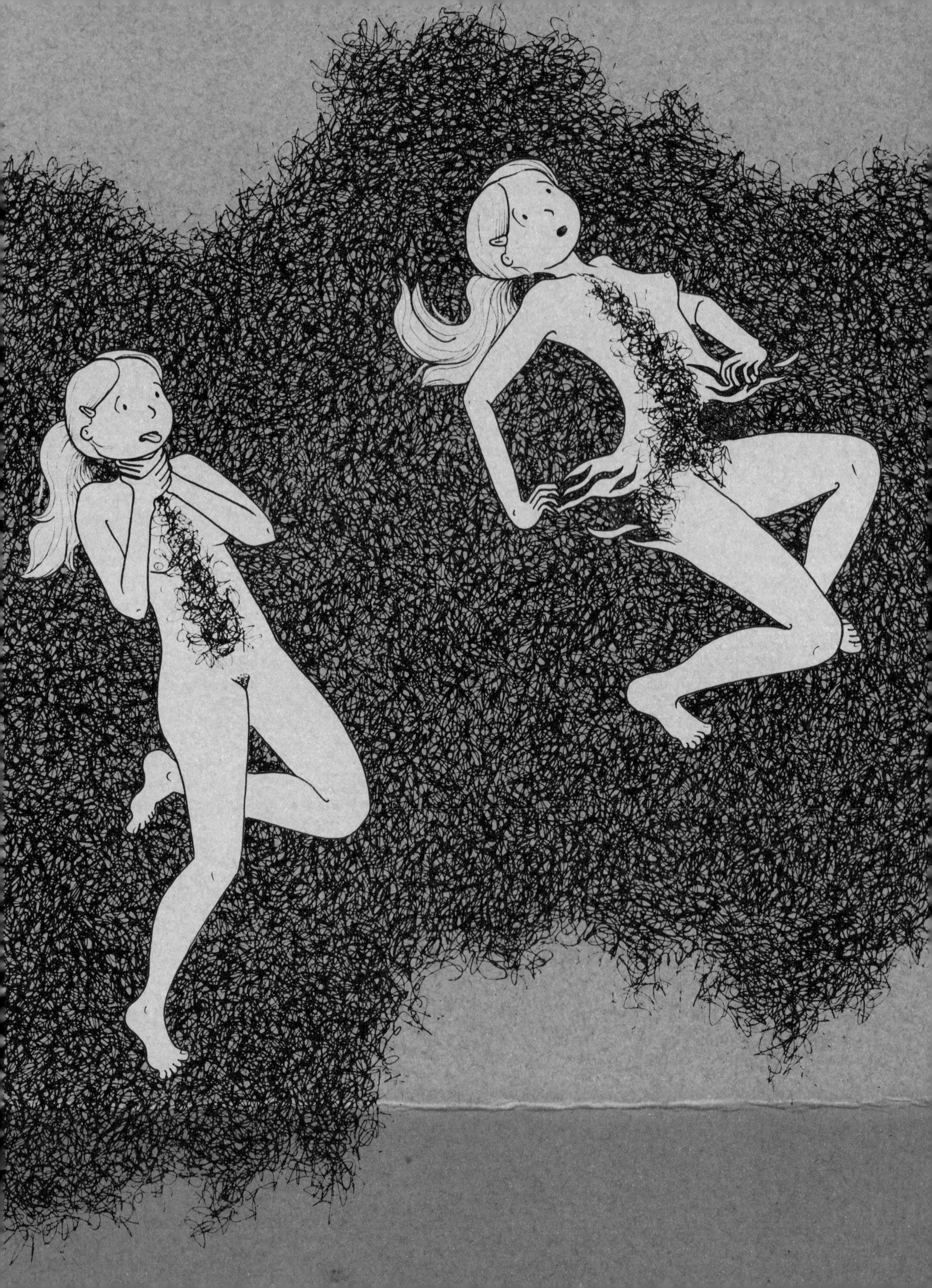

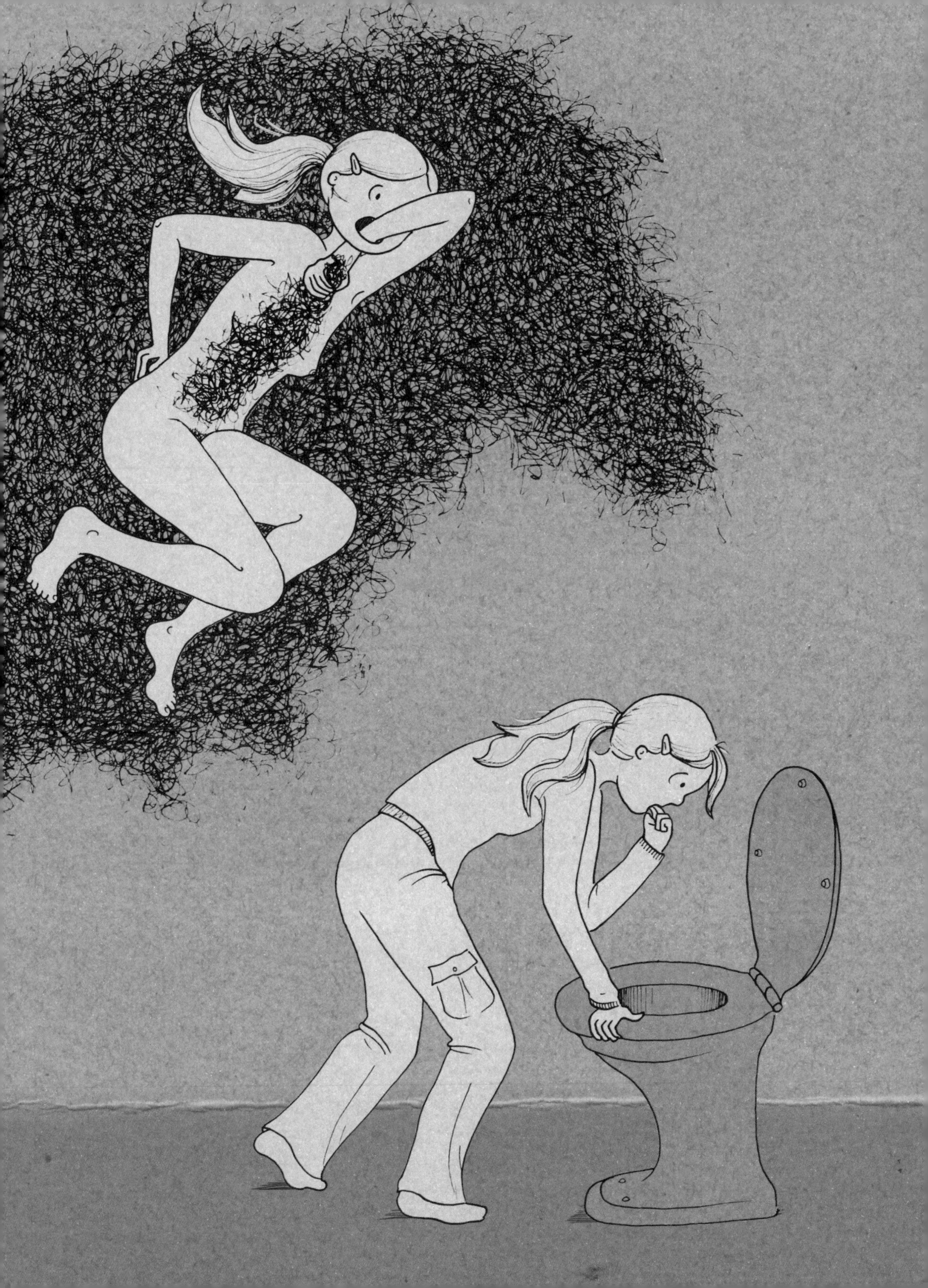

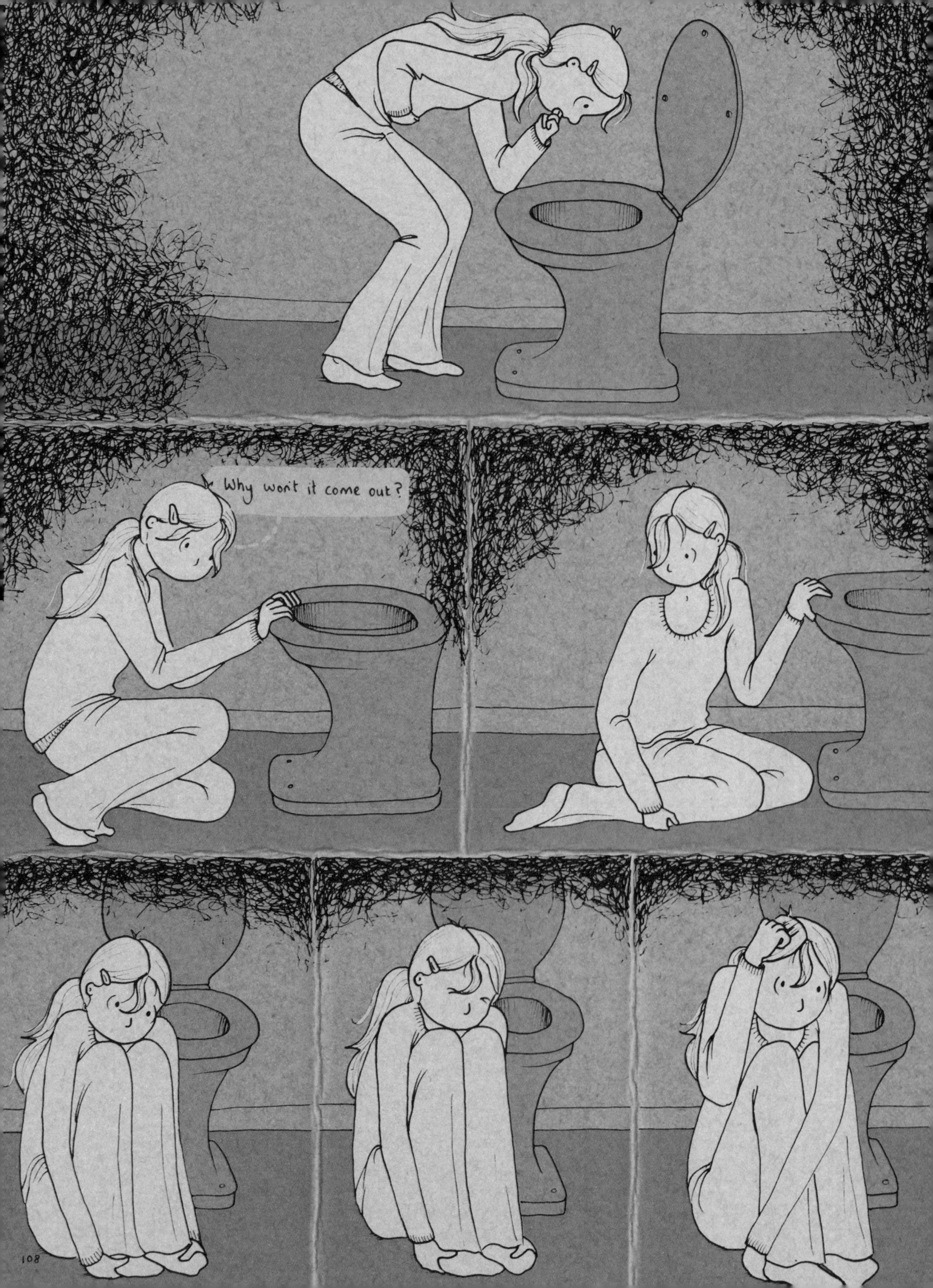
Why won't it come out?

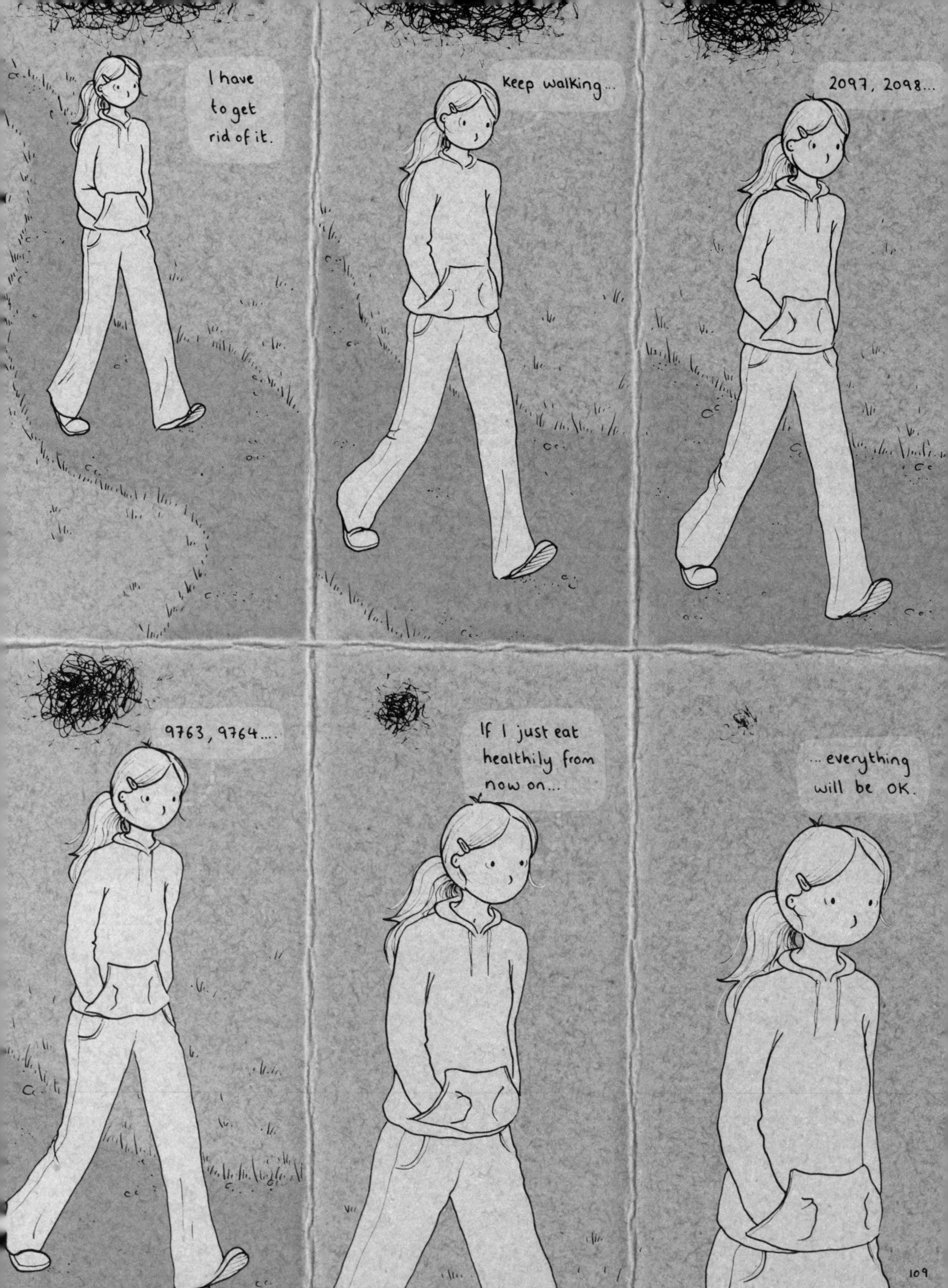
I have to get rid of it.
Keep walking...
2097, 2098...
9763, 9764....
If I just eat healthily from now on...
...everything will be OK.

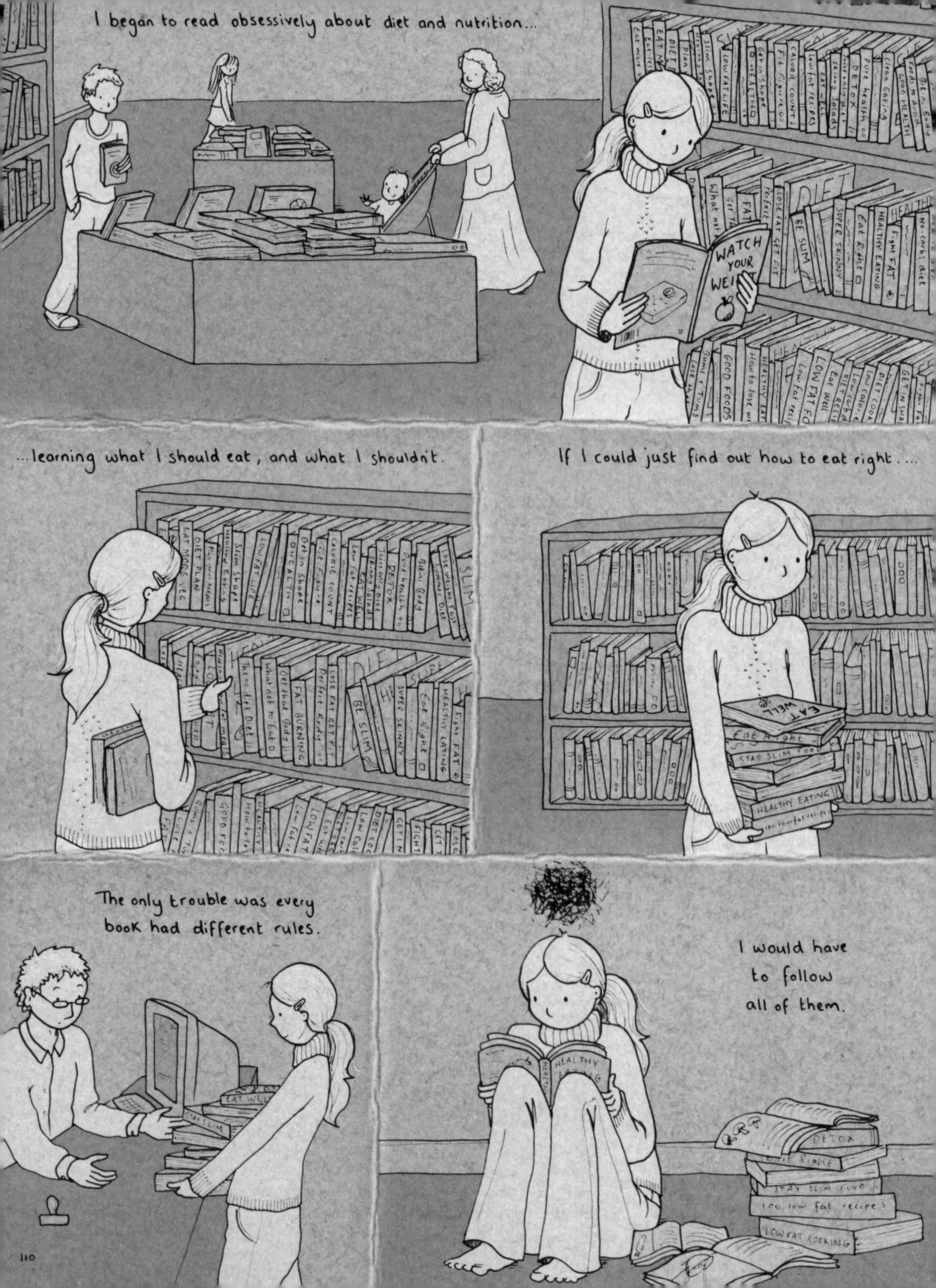
I began to read obsessively about diet and nutrition...
...learning what I should eat, and what I shouldn't.
If I could just find out how to eat right....
EAT WELL
STAY SLIM FOOD
HEALTHY EATING
The only trouble was every book had different rules.
I would have to follow all of them.
HEALTHY EATING
DETOX
STAY SLIM FOOD
100 low fat recipes
LOW FAT COOKING

That made feeding myself extremely complicated.

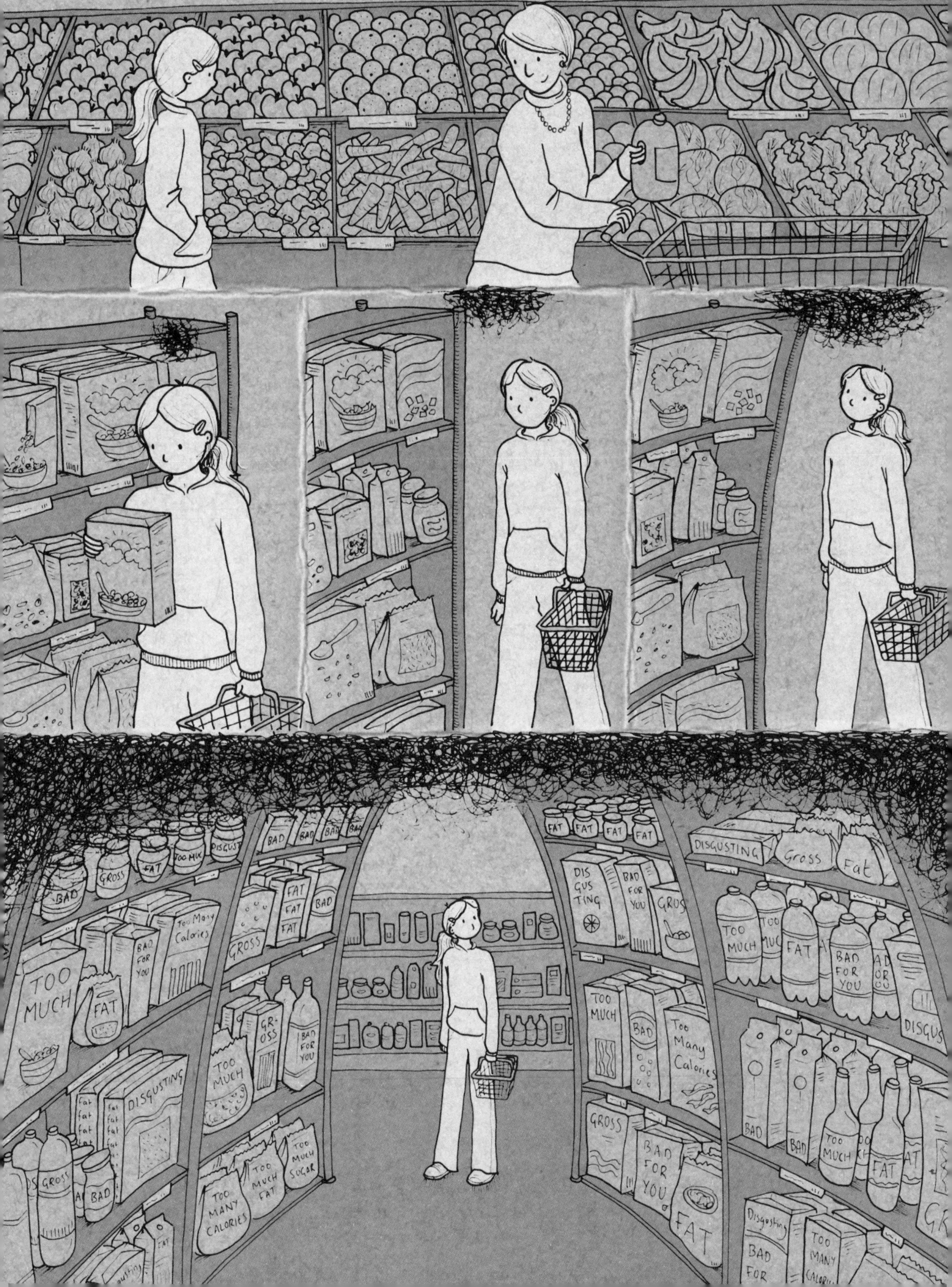

BAD
GROSS
FAT
TOO MUCH
DISGUST
BAD
FAT
FAT
FAT
BAD
GROSS
Too Many Calories
BAD FOR YOU
TOO MUCH
FAT
GR-OSS
BAD FOR YOU
fat fat fat fat
fat fat fat fat
DISGUSTING
TOO MUCH
TOO MUCH FAT
TOO MUCH SUGAR
TOO MANY CALORIES
GROSS
BAD
FAT
FAT
FAT
FAT
DISGUSTING
Gross
Fat
DIS GUS TING
BAD FOR YOU
GROSS
TOO MUCH
FAT
BAD FOR YOU
TOO MUCH
BAD
Too Many Calories
GROSS
BAD FOR YOU
FAT
BAD
BAD
TOO MUCH
FAT
Disgusting
BAD FOR
TOO MANY

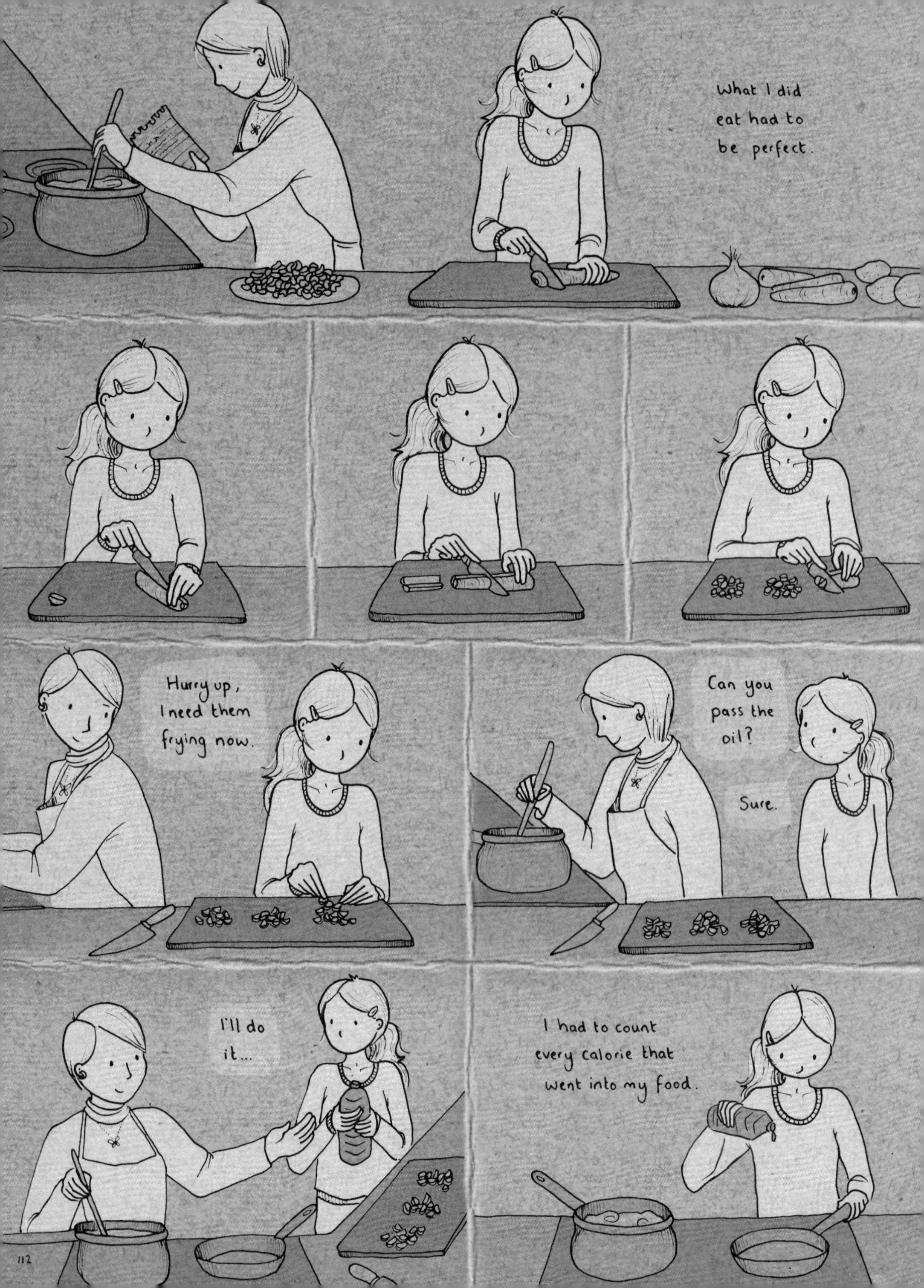
What I did
eat had to
be perfect.
Hurry up,
I need them
frying now.
Can you
pass the
oil?
Sure.
I'll do
it...
I had to count
every calorie that
went into my food.

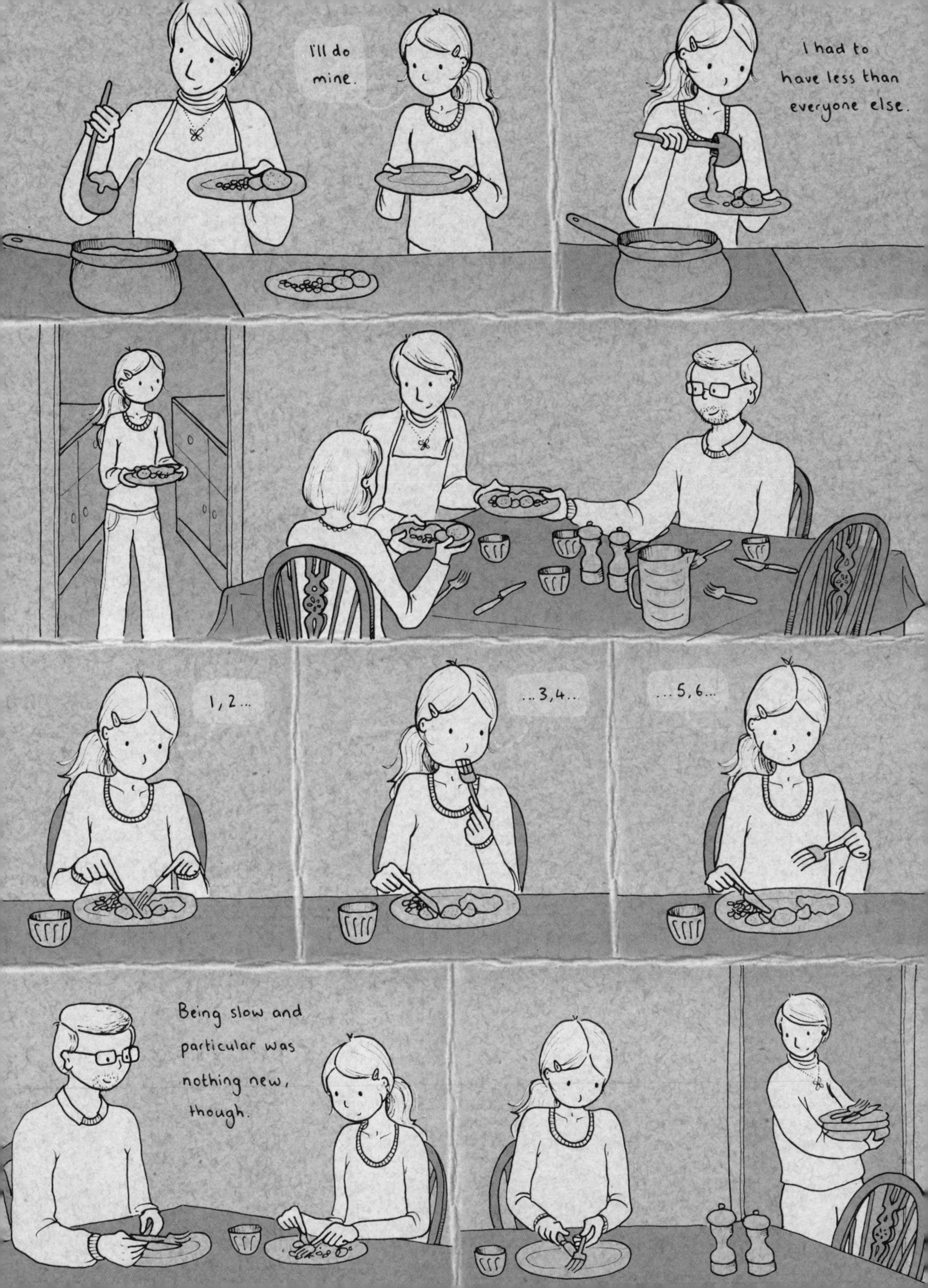
I'll do mine.
I had to have less than everyone else.
1, 2...
...3, 4...
...5, 6...
Being slow and particular was nothing new, though.

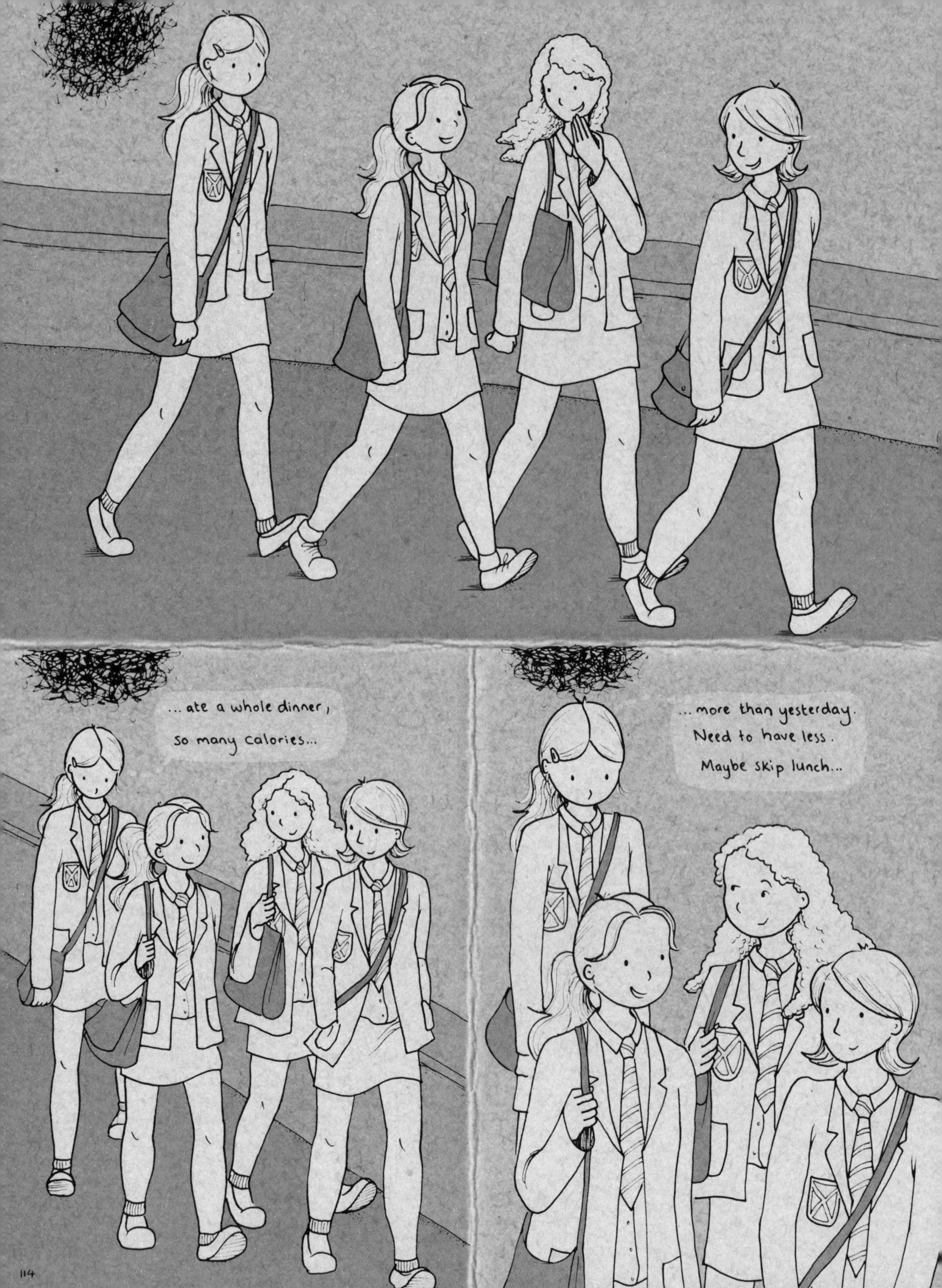
... ate a whole dinner,
so many calories...
... more than yesterday.
Need to have less.
Maybe skip lunch...

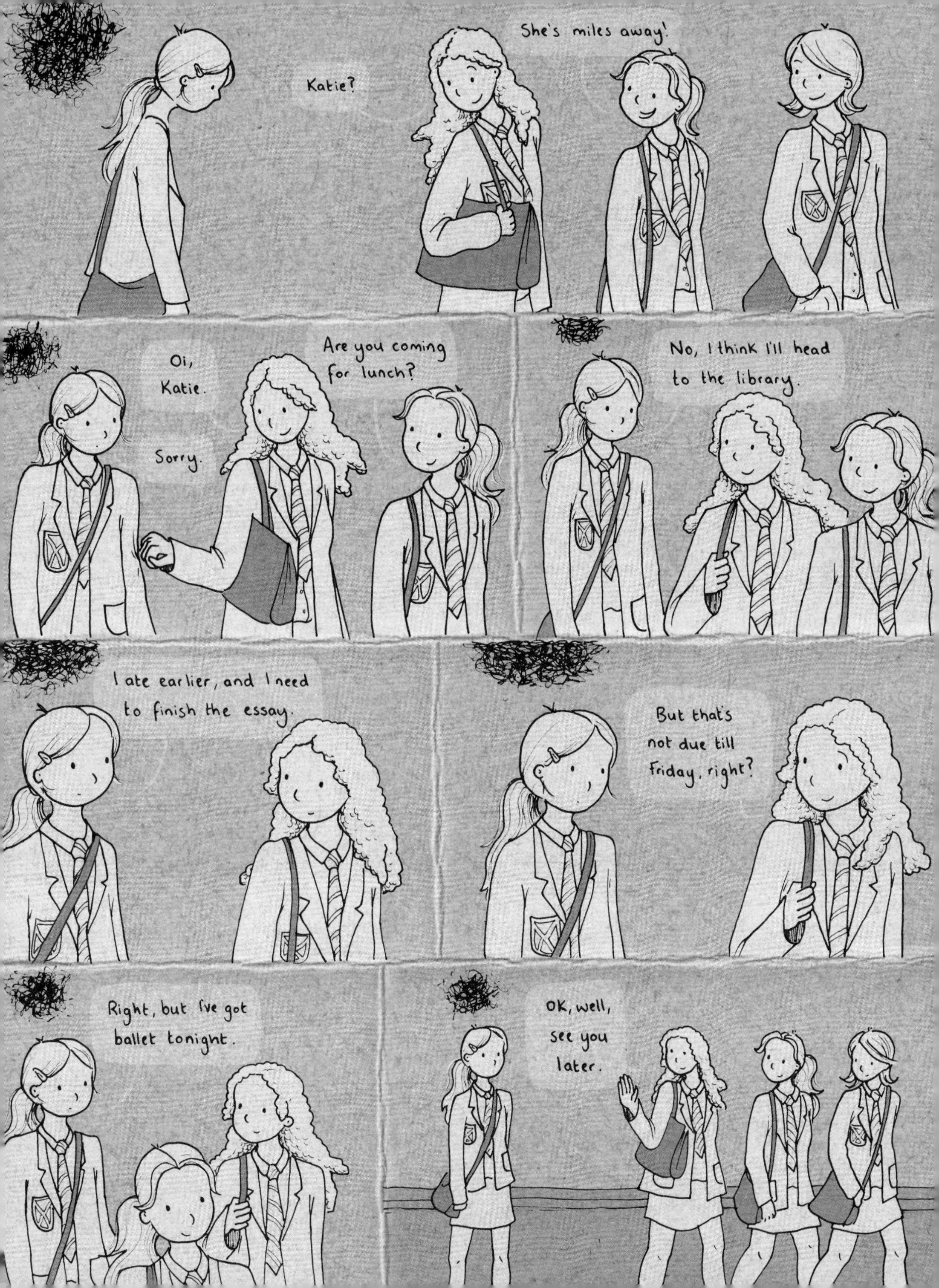
Katie?
She's miles away!
Oi, Katie.
Sorry.
Are you coming for lunch?
No, I think I'll head to the library.
I ate earlier, and I need to finish the essay.
But that's not due till Friday, right?
Right, but I've got ballet tonight.
OK, well, see you later.

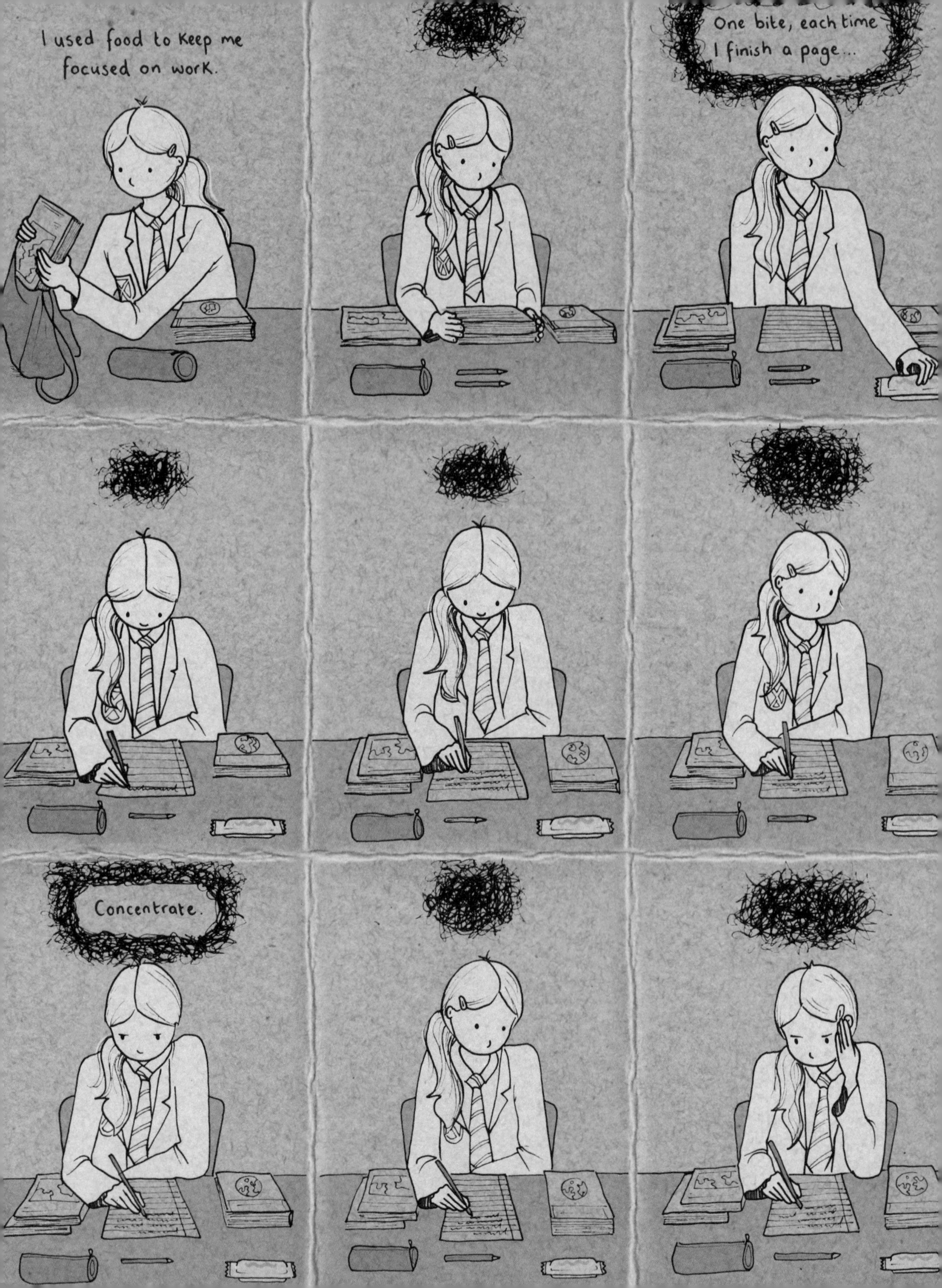
I used food to keep me focused on work.
One bite, each time I finish a page...
Concentrate.

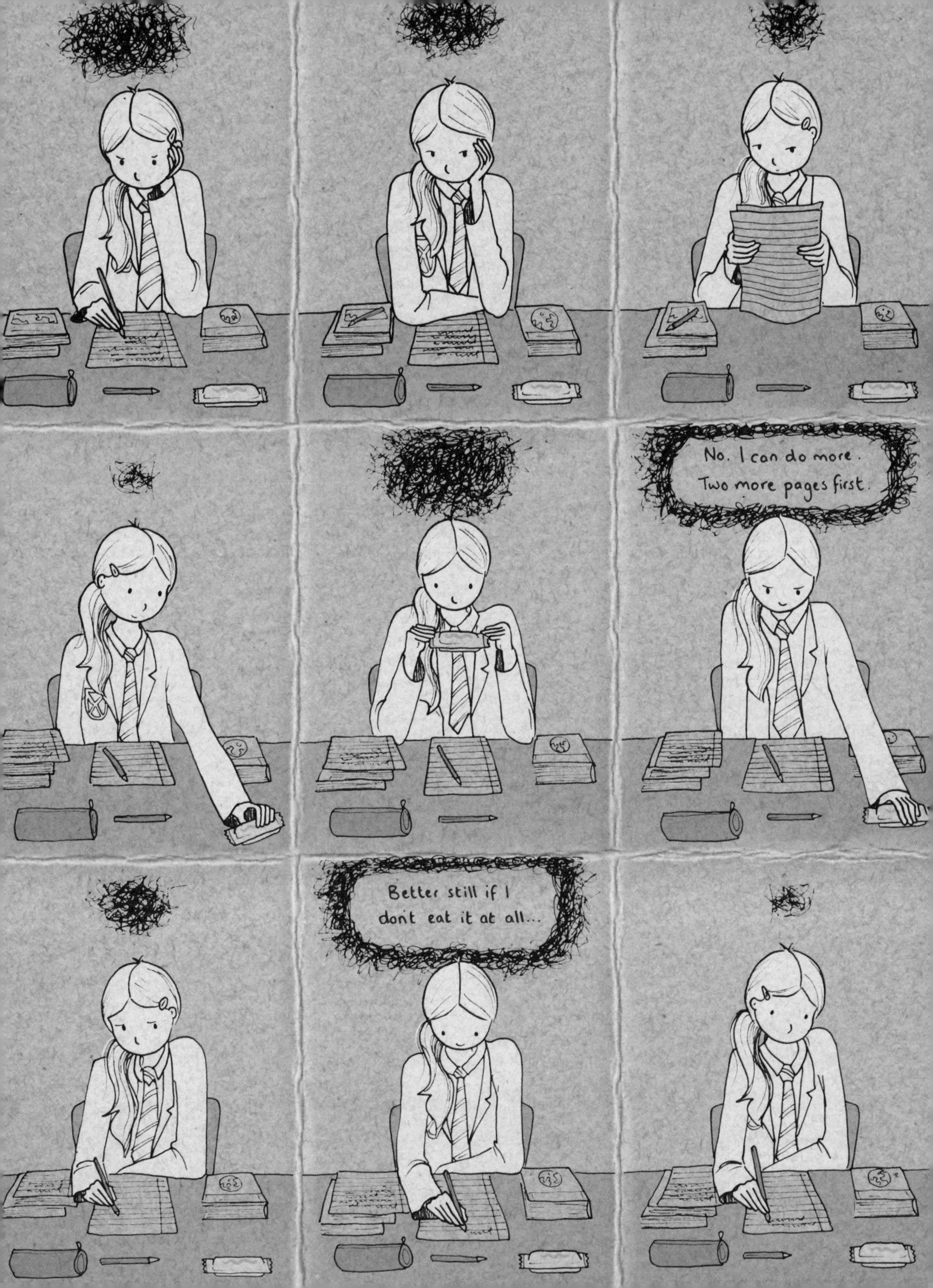
No. I can do more. Two more pages first.
Better still if I don't eat it at all...

I couldn't see my whole body in the mirror.

I only saw parts of myself. The parts I hated.

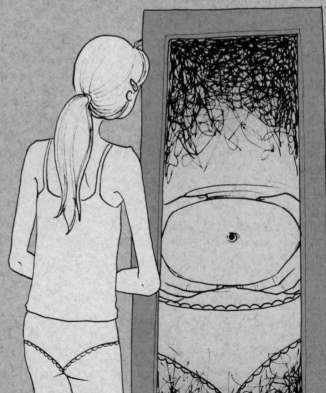

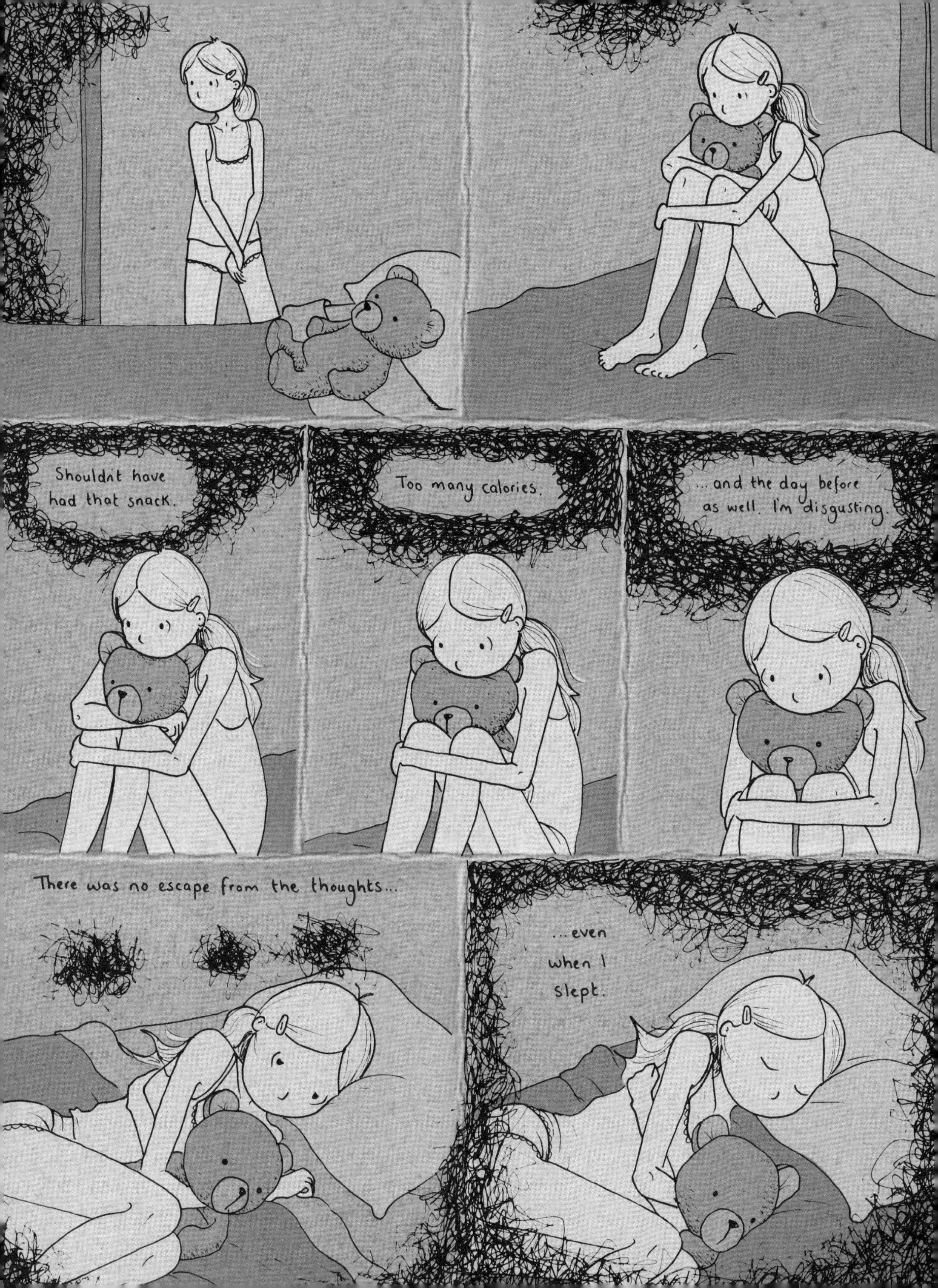
Shouldn't have had that snack.
Too many calories.
...and the day before as well. I'm disgusting.
There was no escape from the thoughts...
...even when I slept.

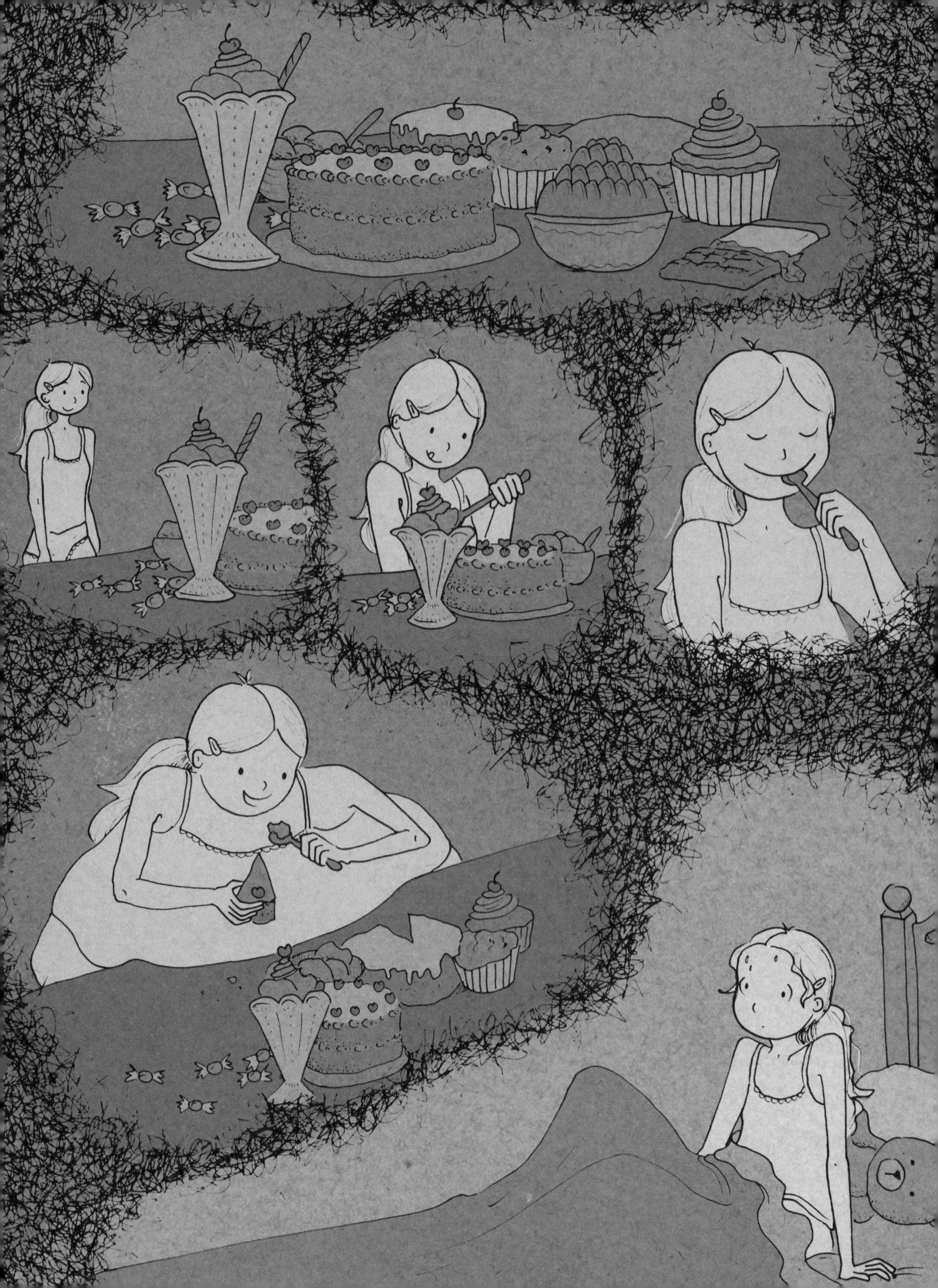

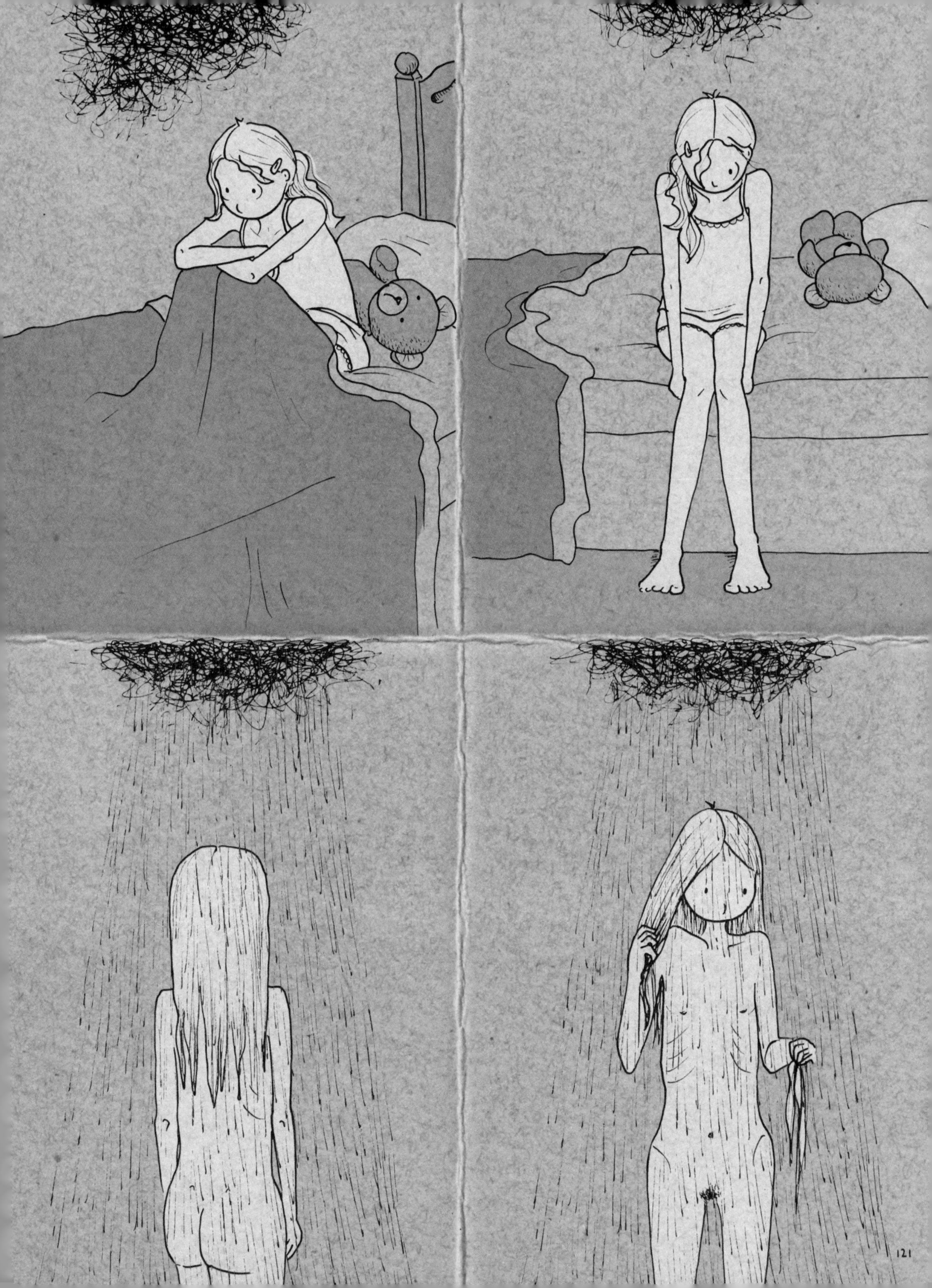

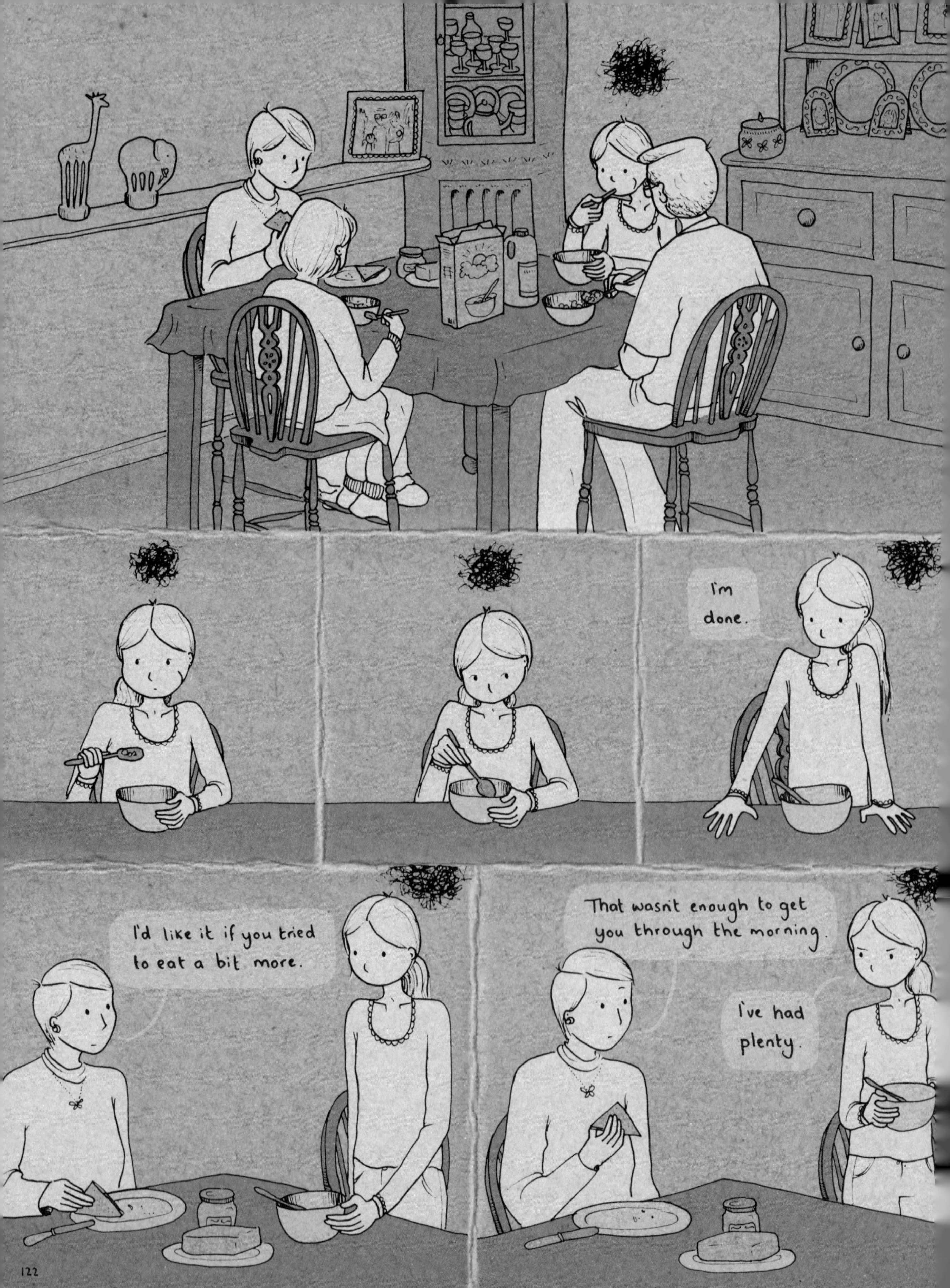
I'm done.
I'd like it if you tried to eat a bit more.
That wasn't enough to get you through the morning.
I've had plenty.

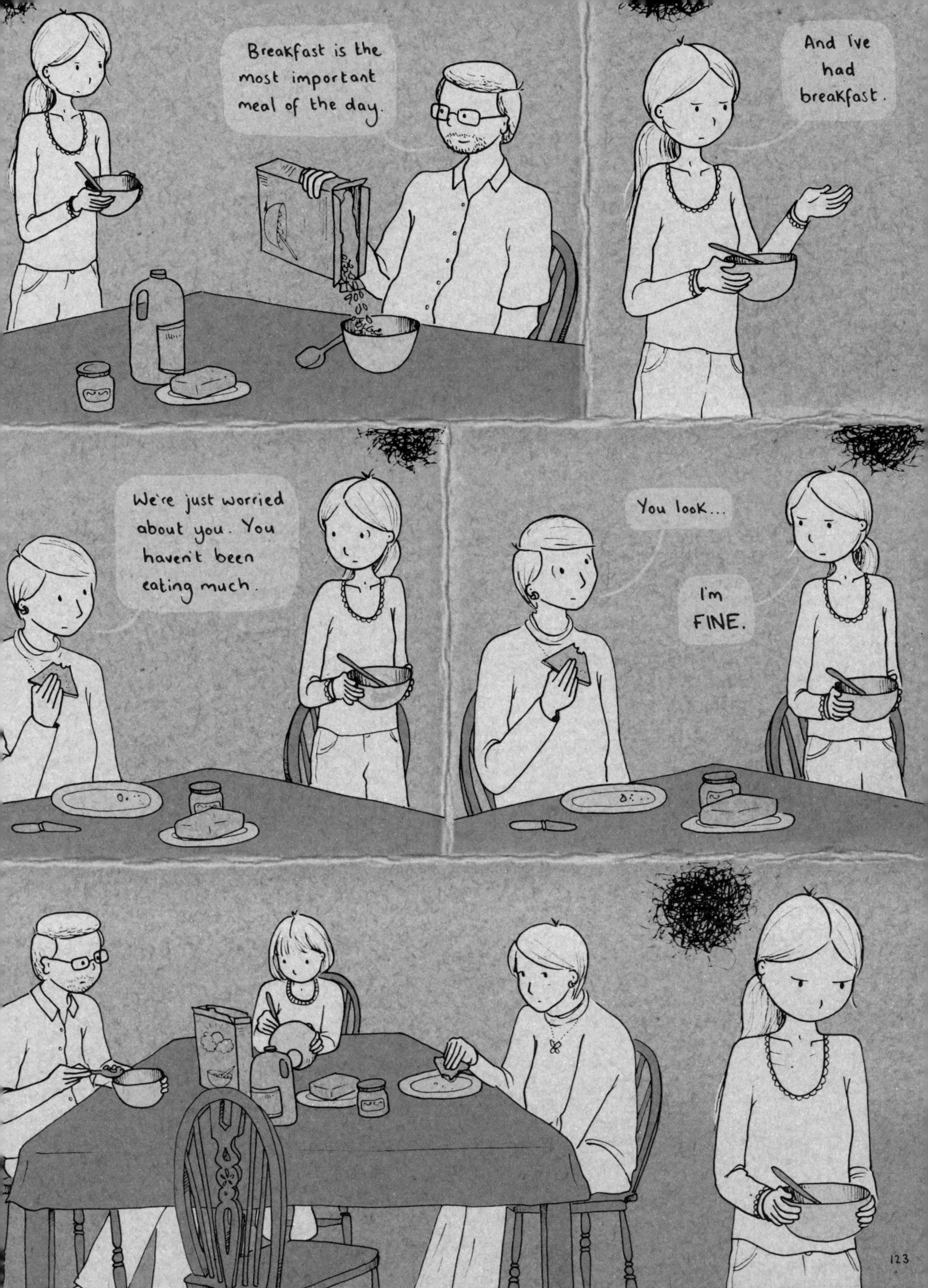
Breakfast is the most important meal of the day.
And I've had breakfast.
We're just worried about you. You haven't been eating much.
You look...
I'm FINE.

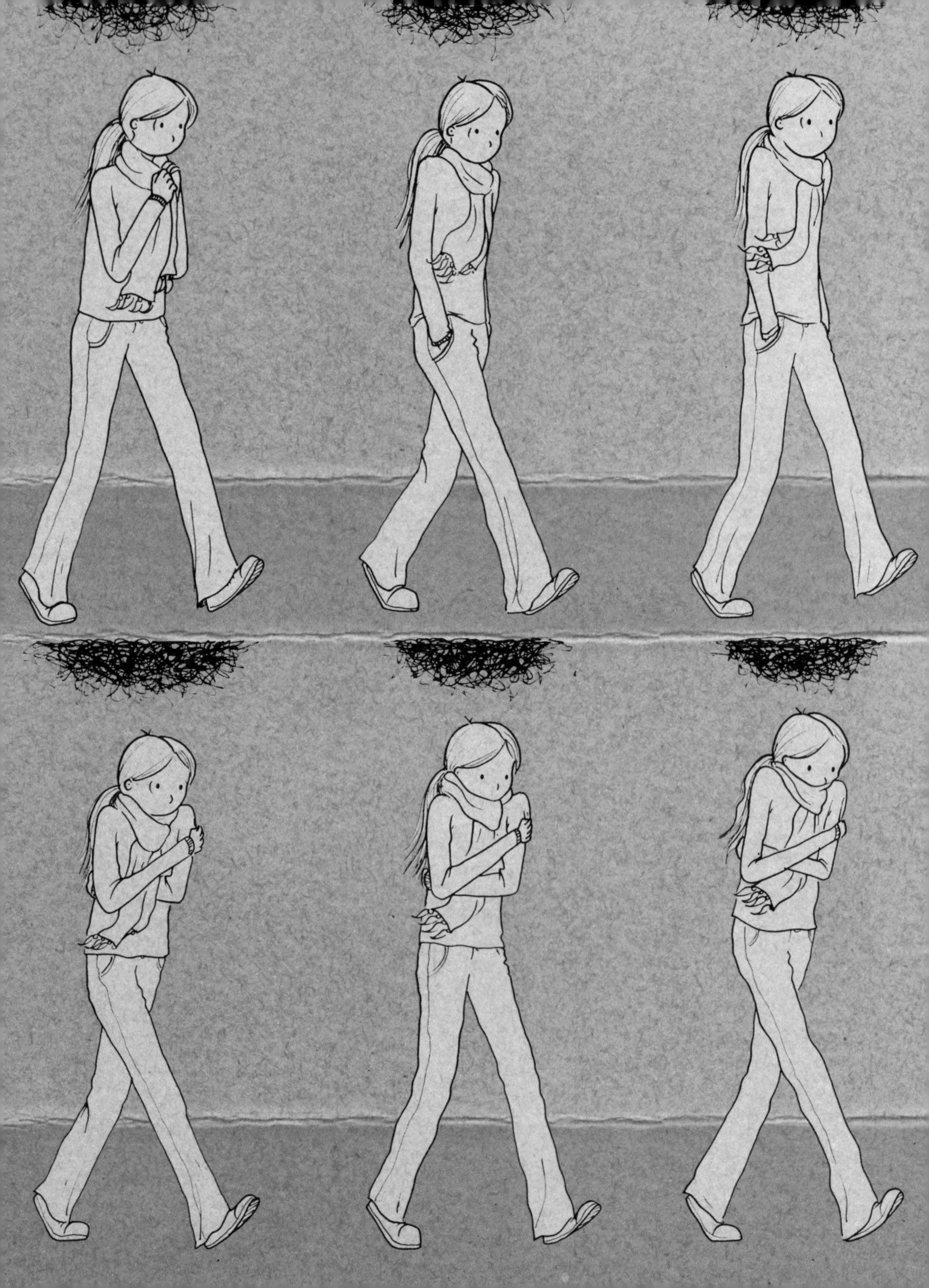

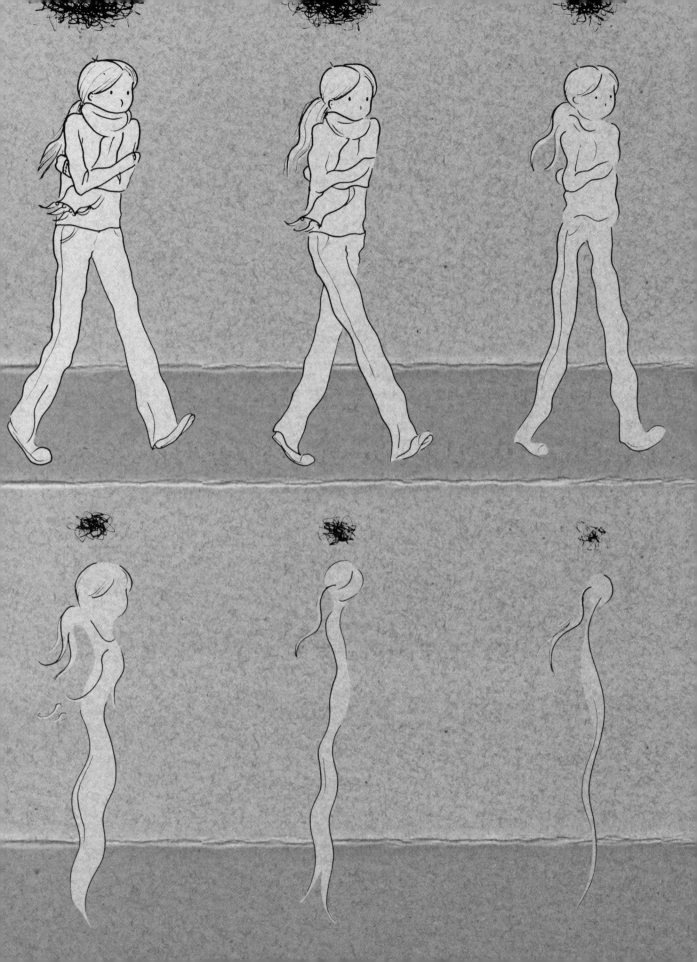

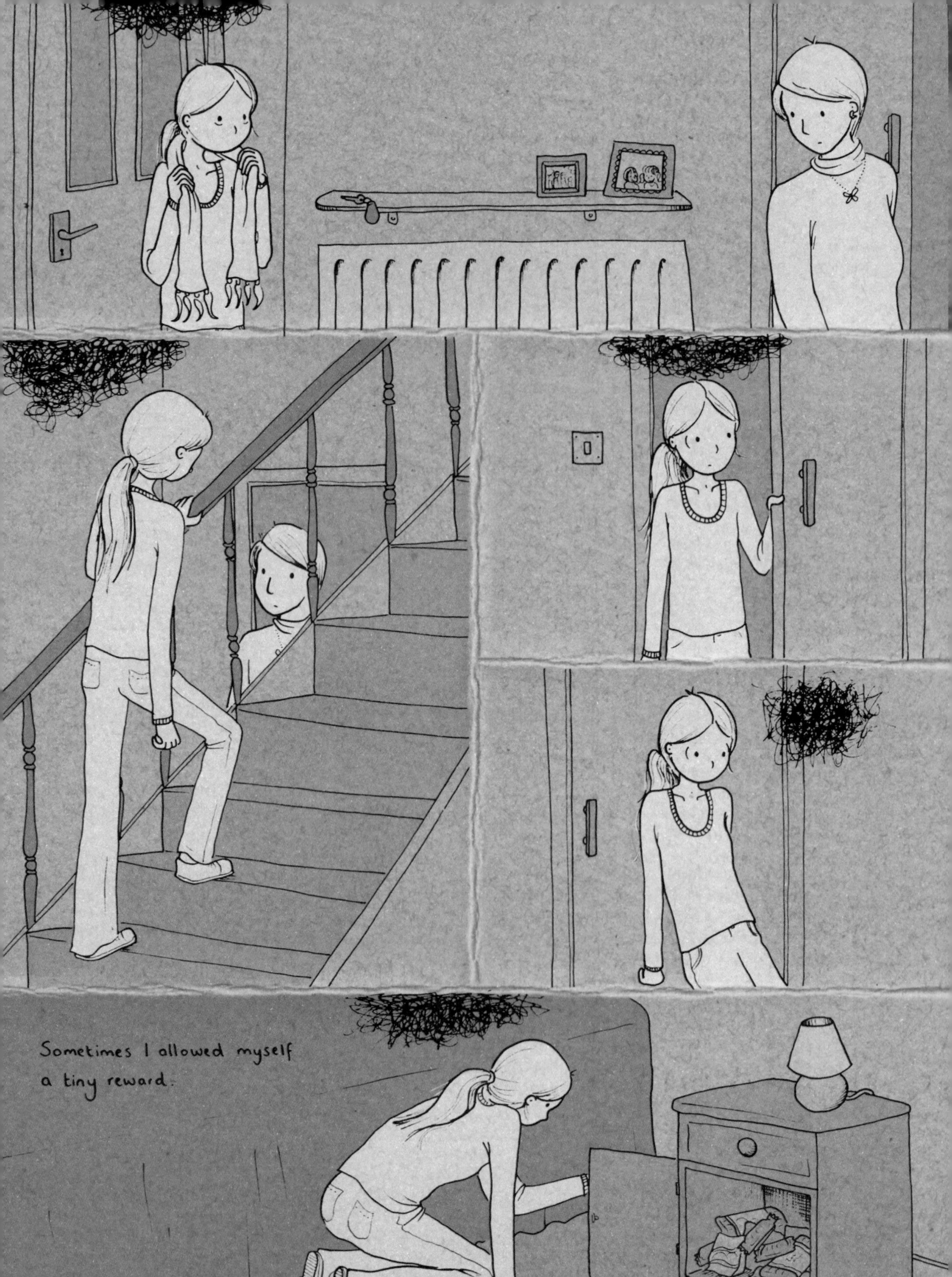
Sometimes I allowed myself
a tiny reward.

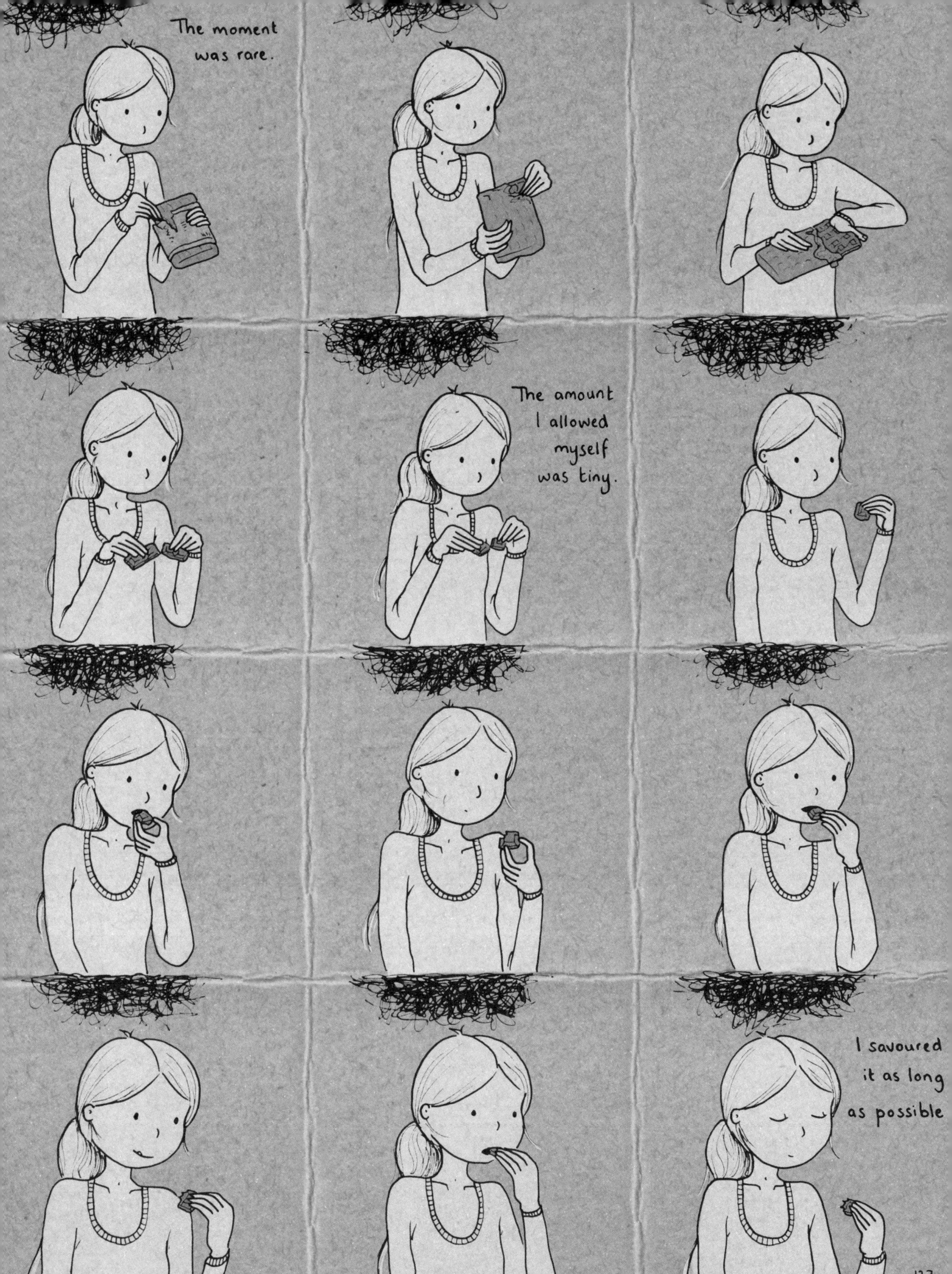
The moment
was rare.
The amount
I allowed
myself
was tiny.
I savoured
it as long
as possible

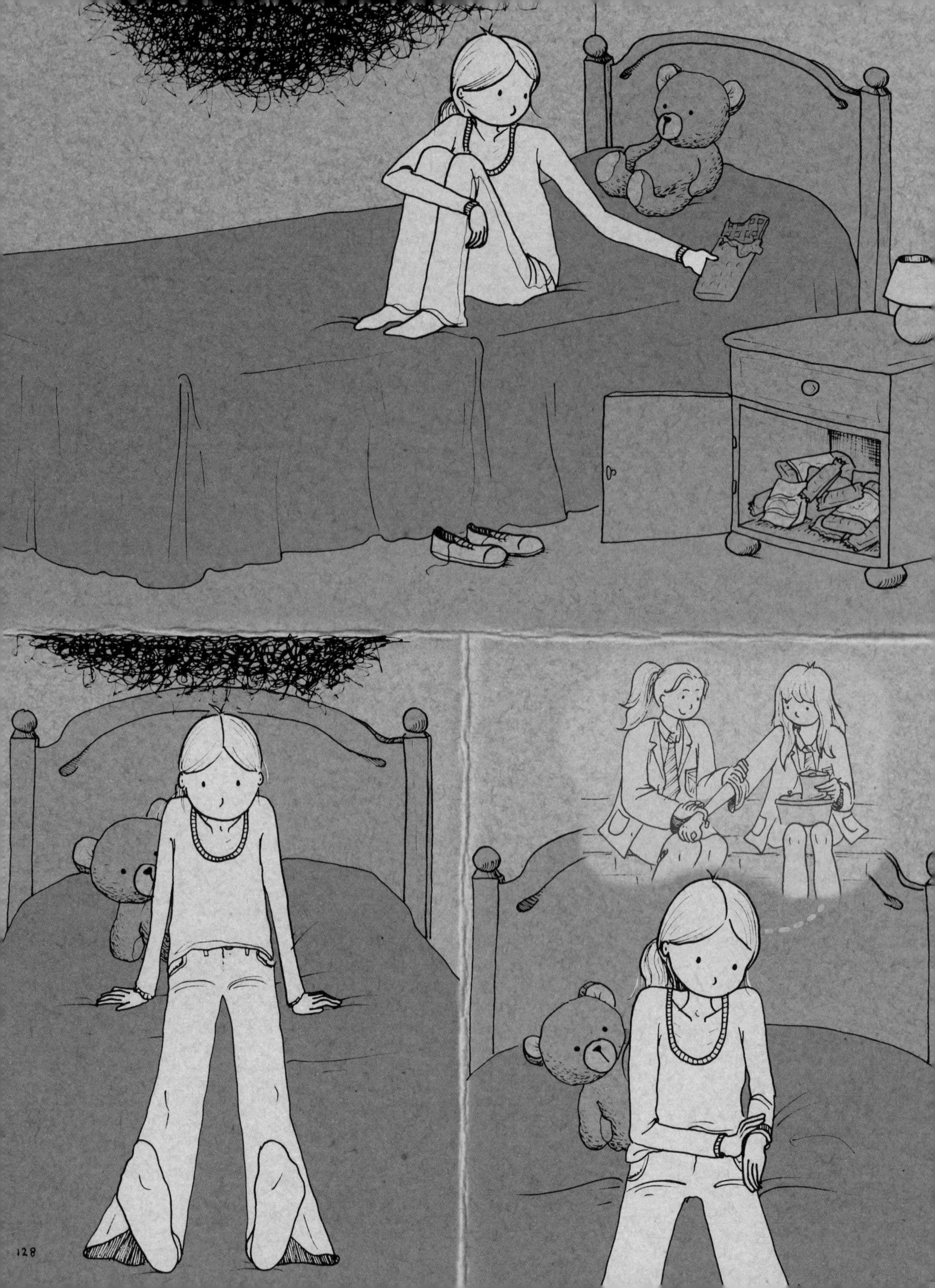

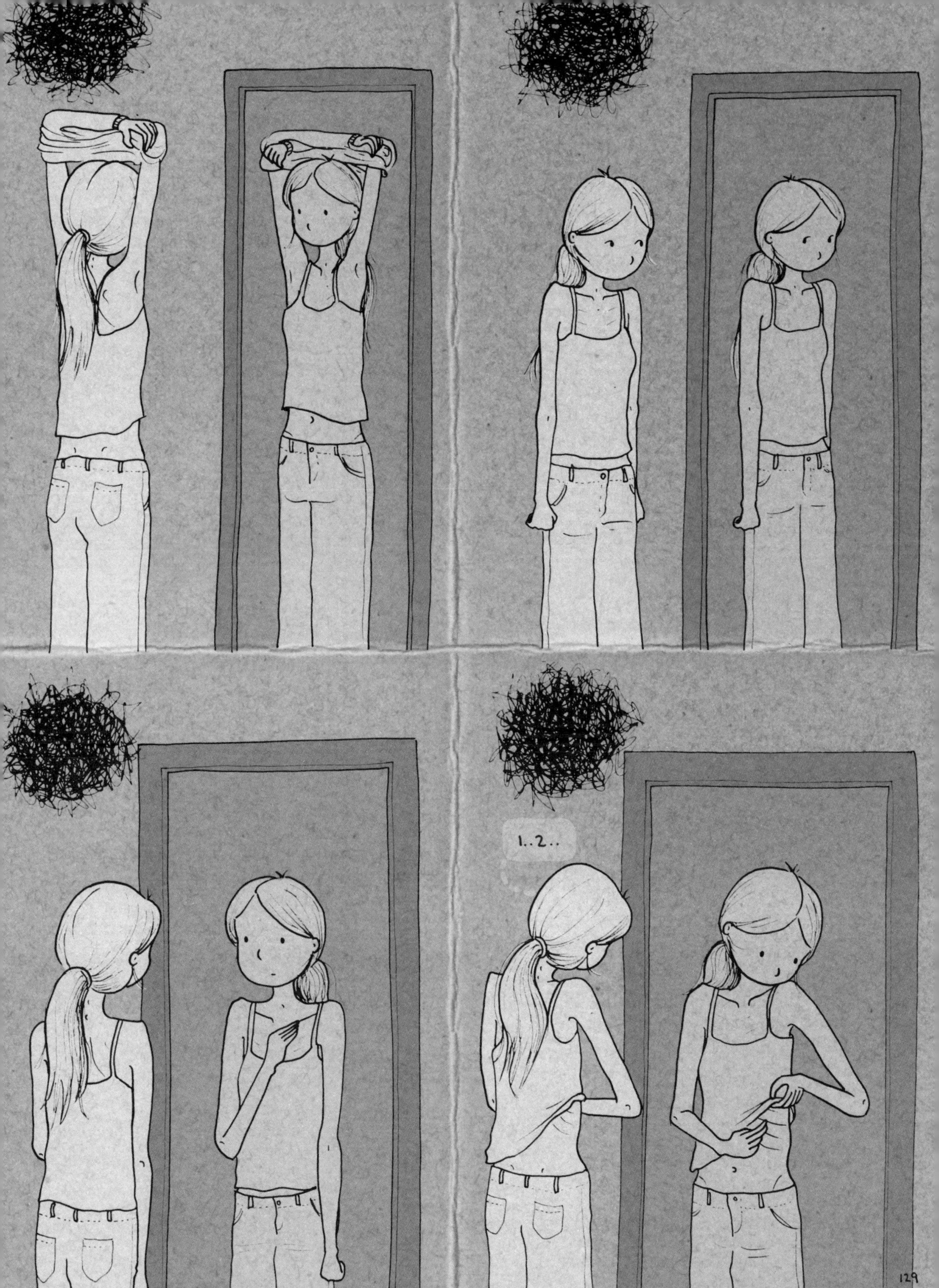
1..2..

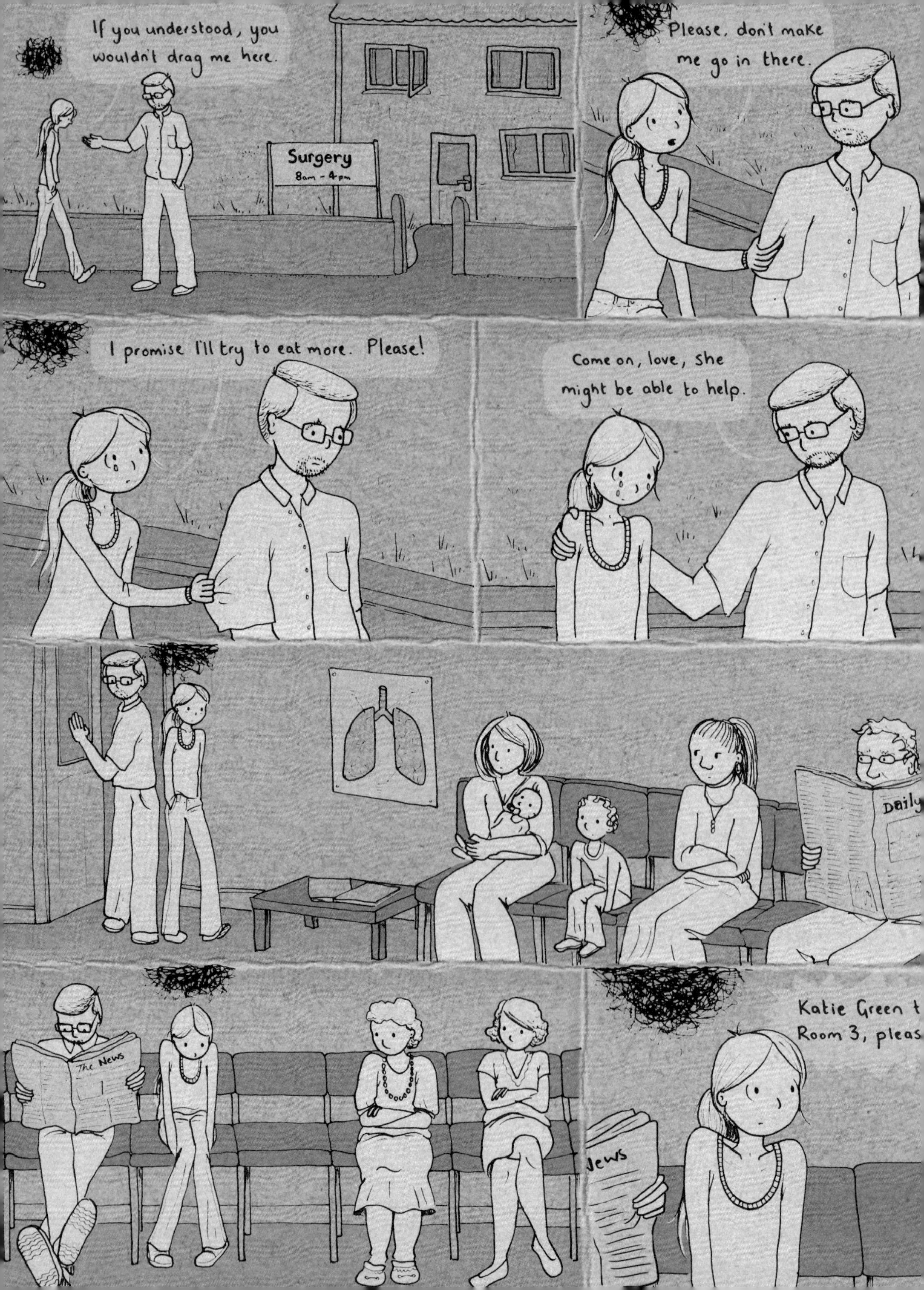
If you understood, you wouldn't drag me here.
Surgery
8am - 4pm
Please, don't make me go in there.
I promise I'll try to eat more. Please!
Come on, love, she might be able to help.
Daily
The News
News
Katie Green t
Room 3, pleas

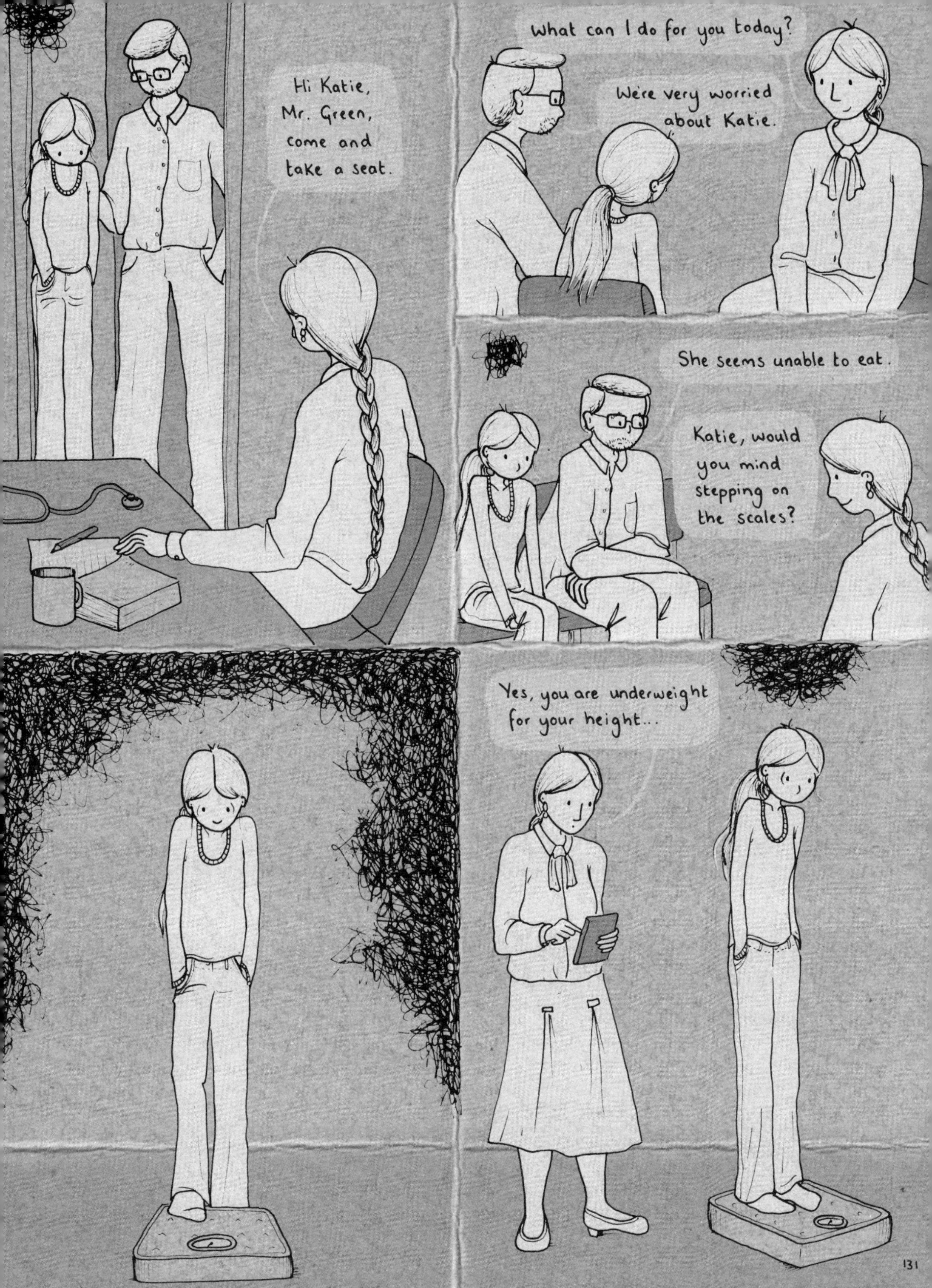
Hi Katie, Mr. Green, come and take a seat.
What can I do for you today?
We're very worried about Katie.
She seems unable to eat.
Katie, would you mind stepping on the scales?
Yes, you are underweight for your height...

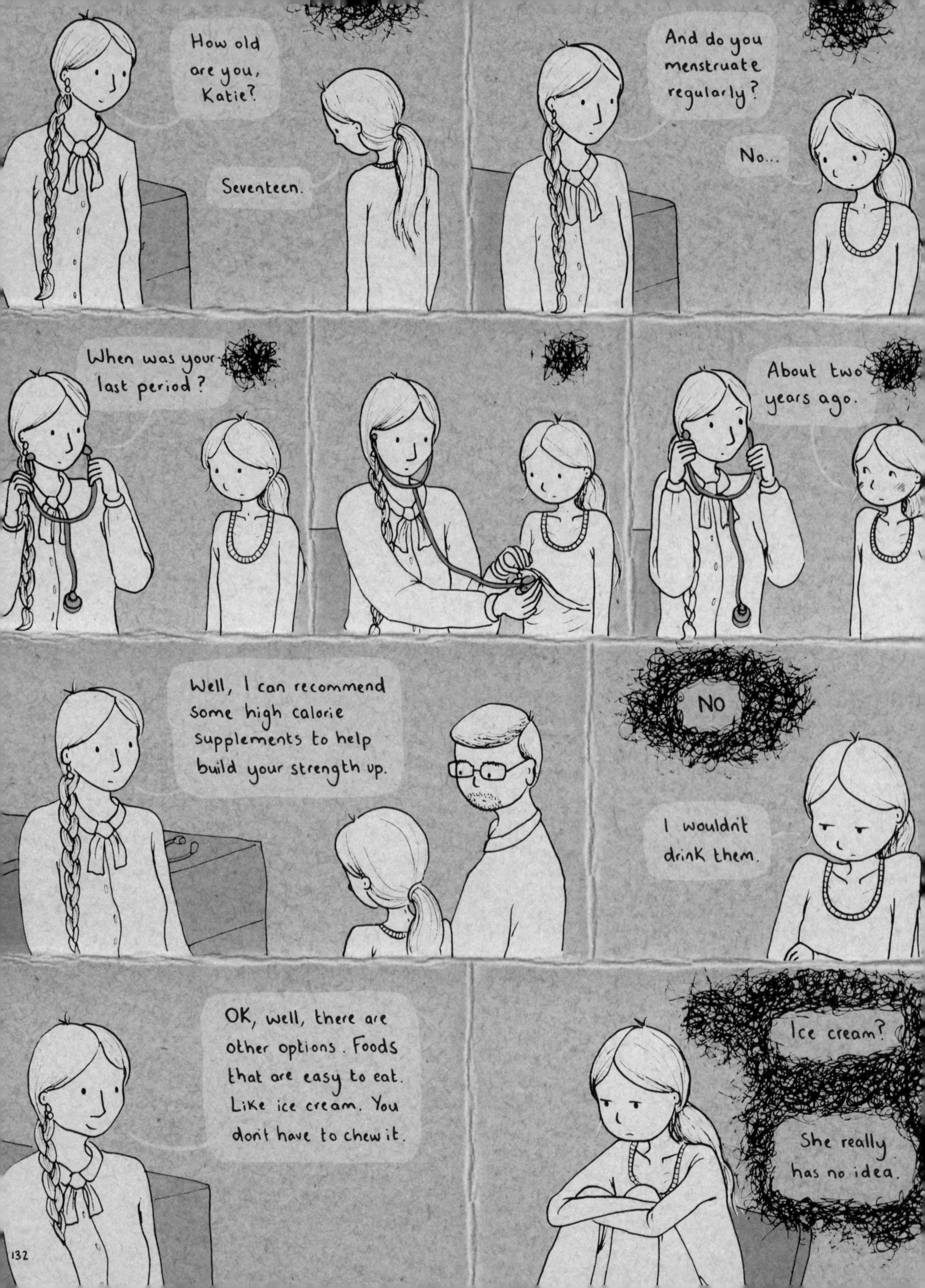
How old are you, Katie?
Seventeen.
And do you menstruate regularly?
No...
When was your last period?
About two years ago.
Well, I can recommend some high calorie supplements to help build your strength up.
NO
I wouldn't drink them.
OK, well, there are other options. Foods that are easy to eat. Like ice cream. You don't have to chew it.
Ice cream?
She really has no idea.

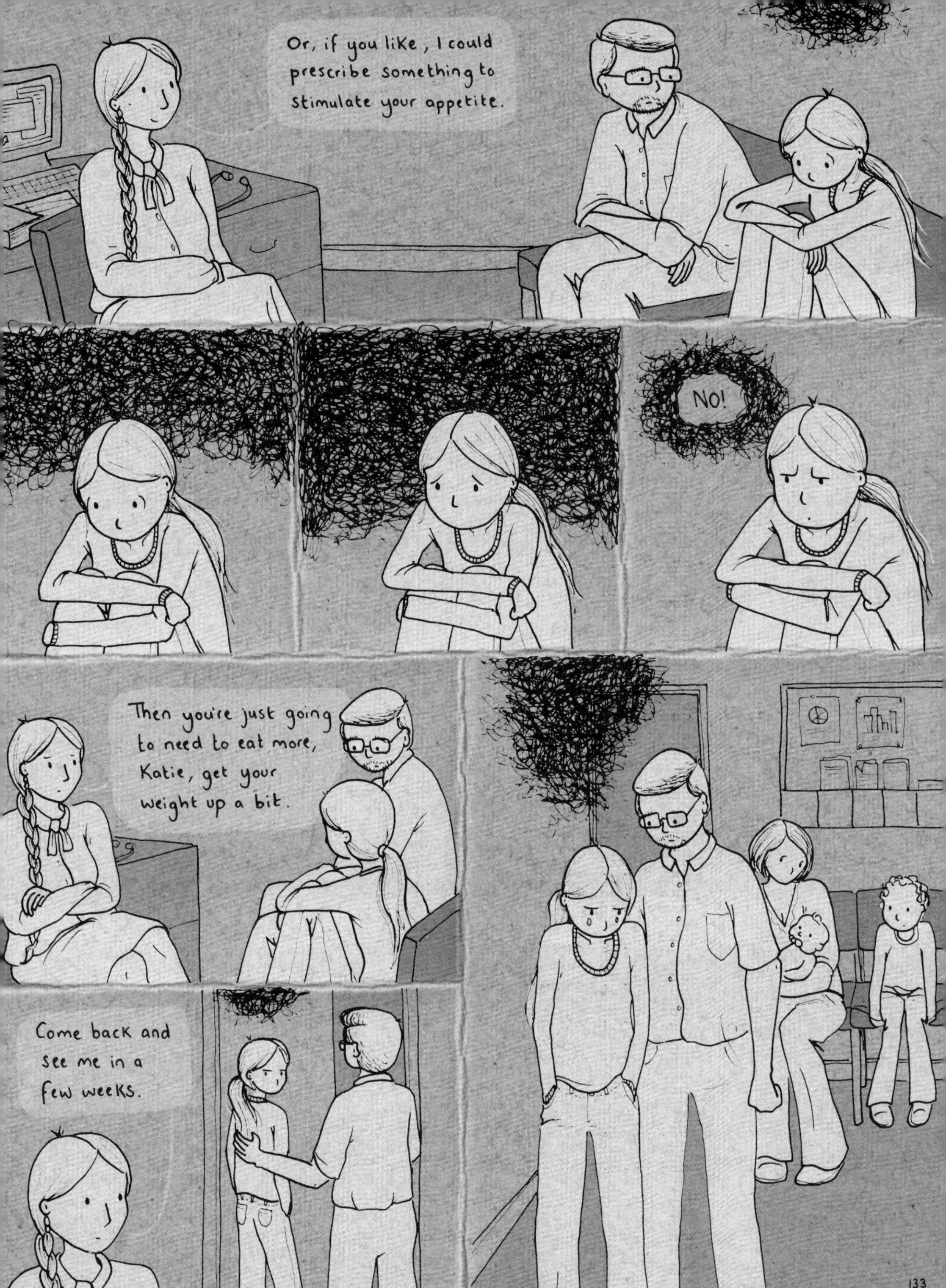
Or, if you like, I could prescribe something to stimulate your appetite.
No!
Then you're just going to need to eat more, Katie, get your weight up a bit.
Come back and see me in a few weeks.

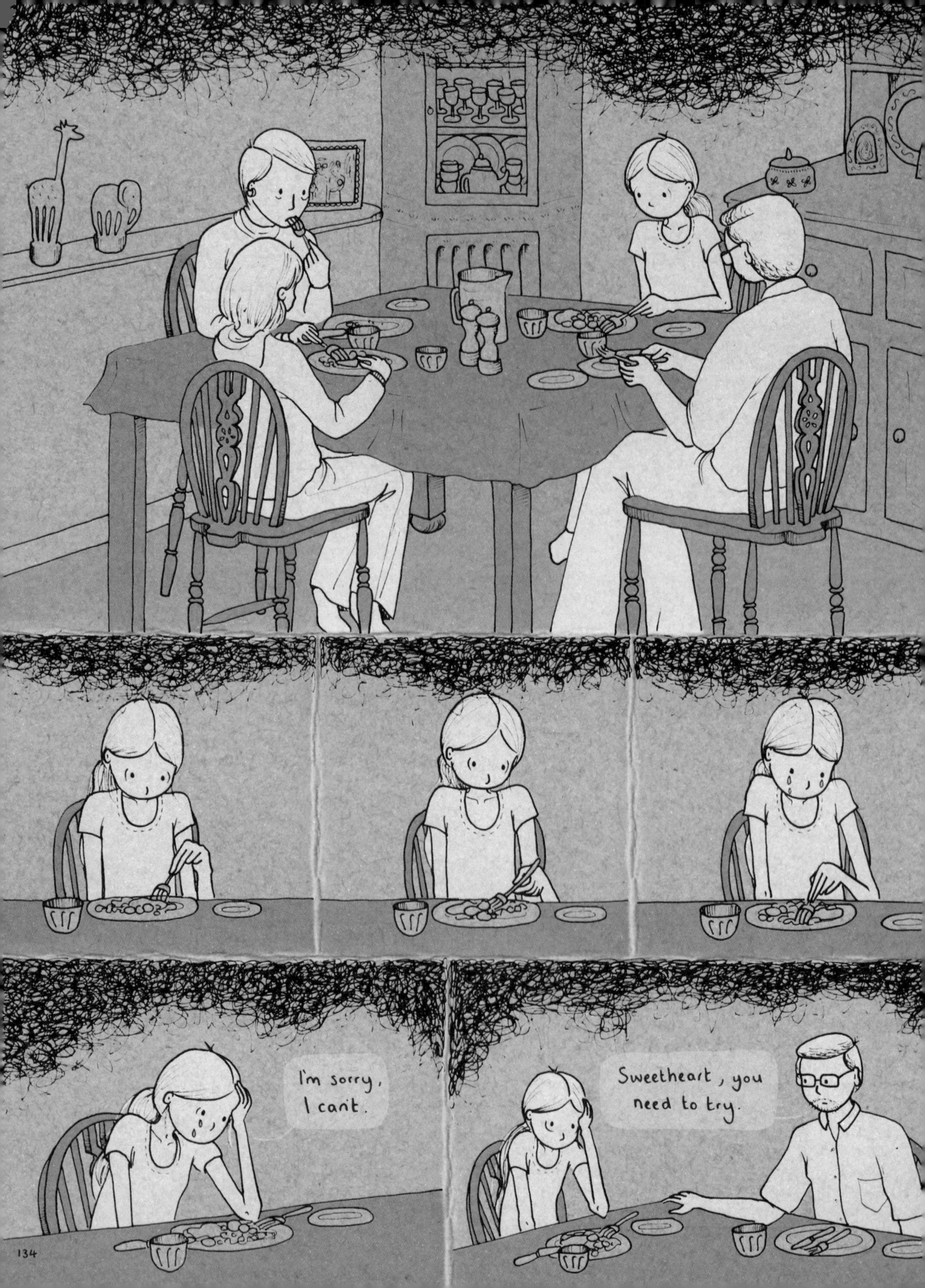
I'm sorry,
I can't.
Sweetheart, you
need to try.

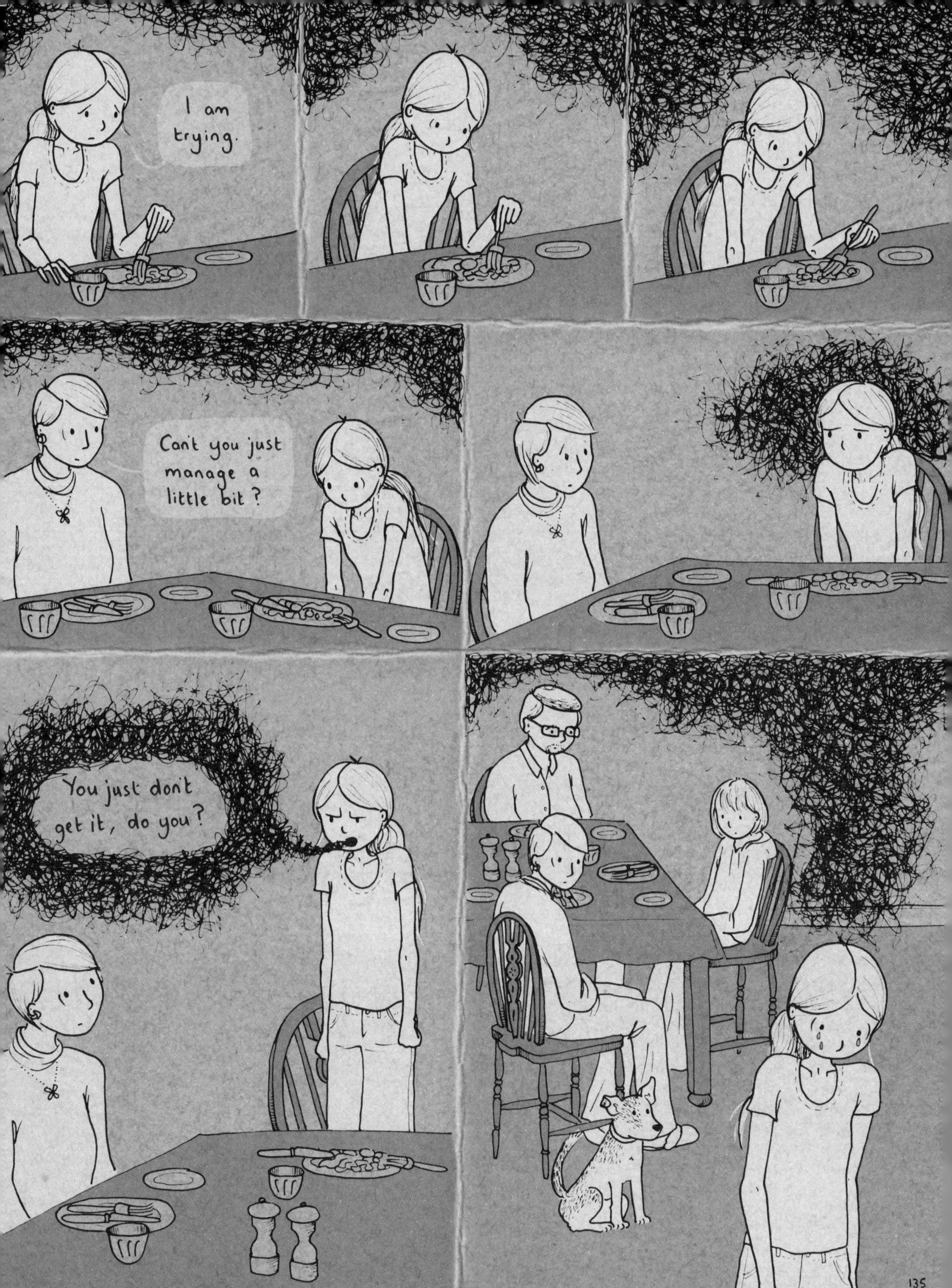
I am trying.
Can't you just manage a little bit?
You just don't get it, do you?

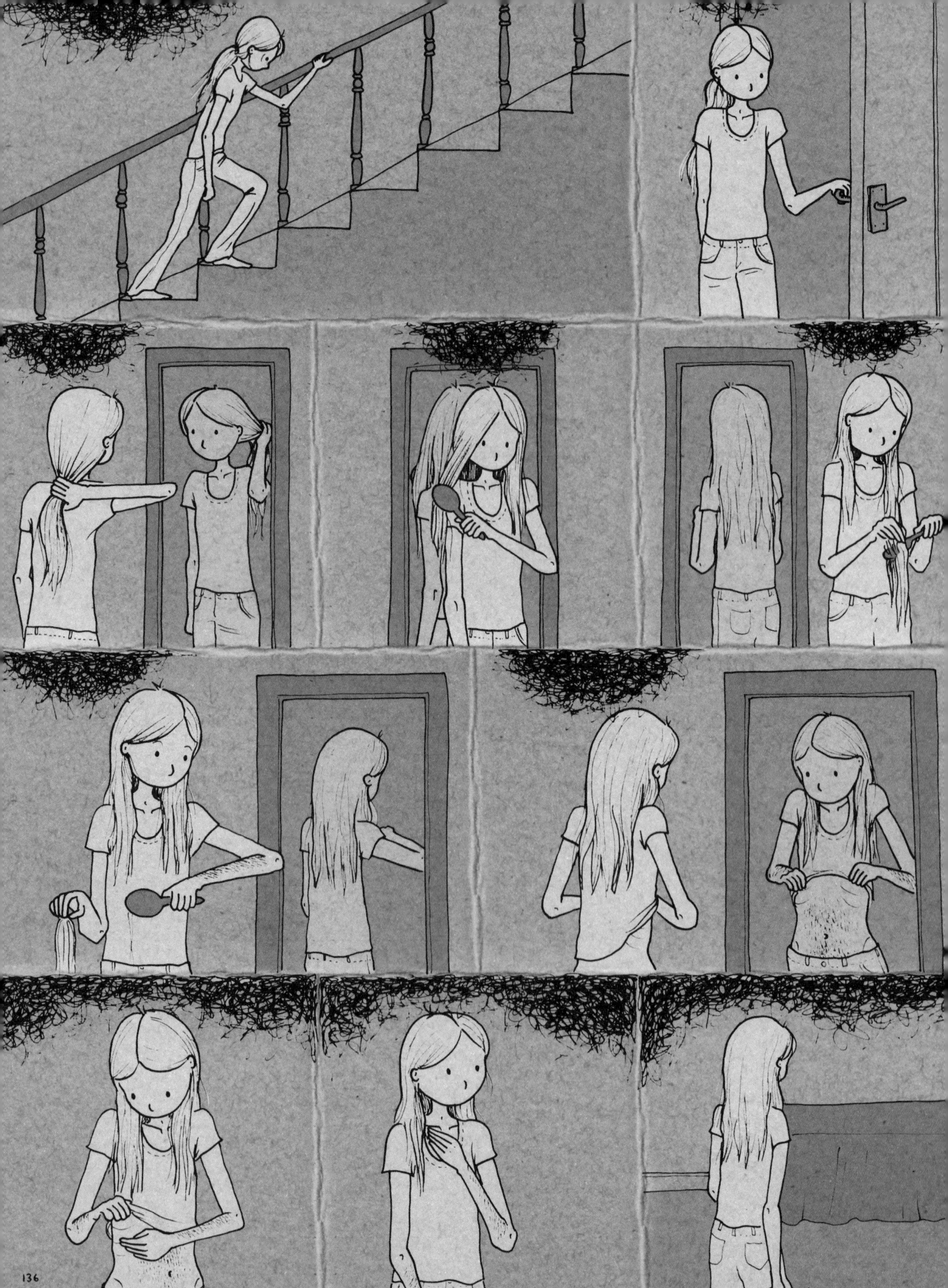

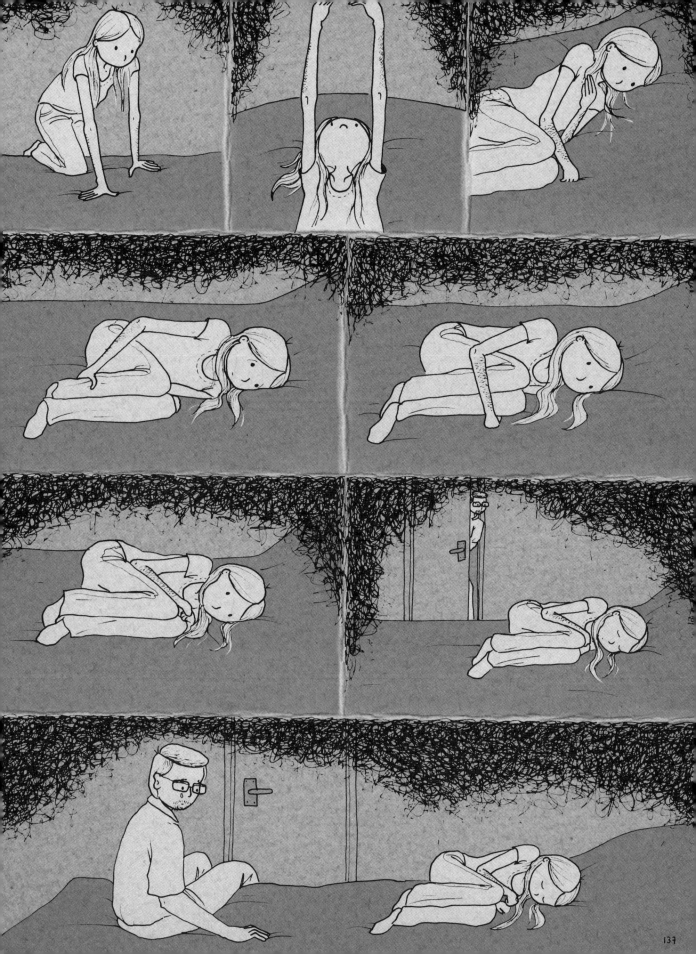

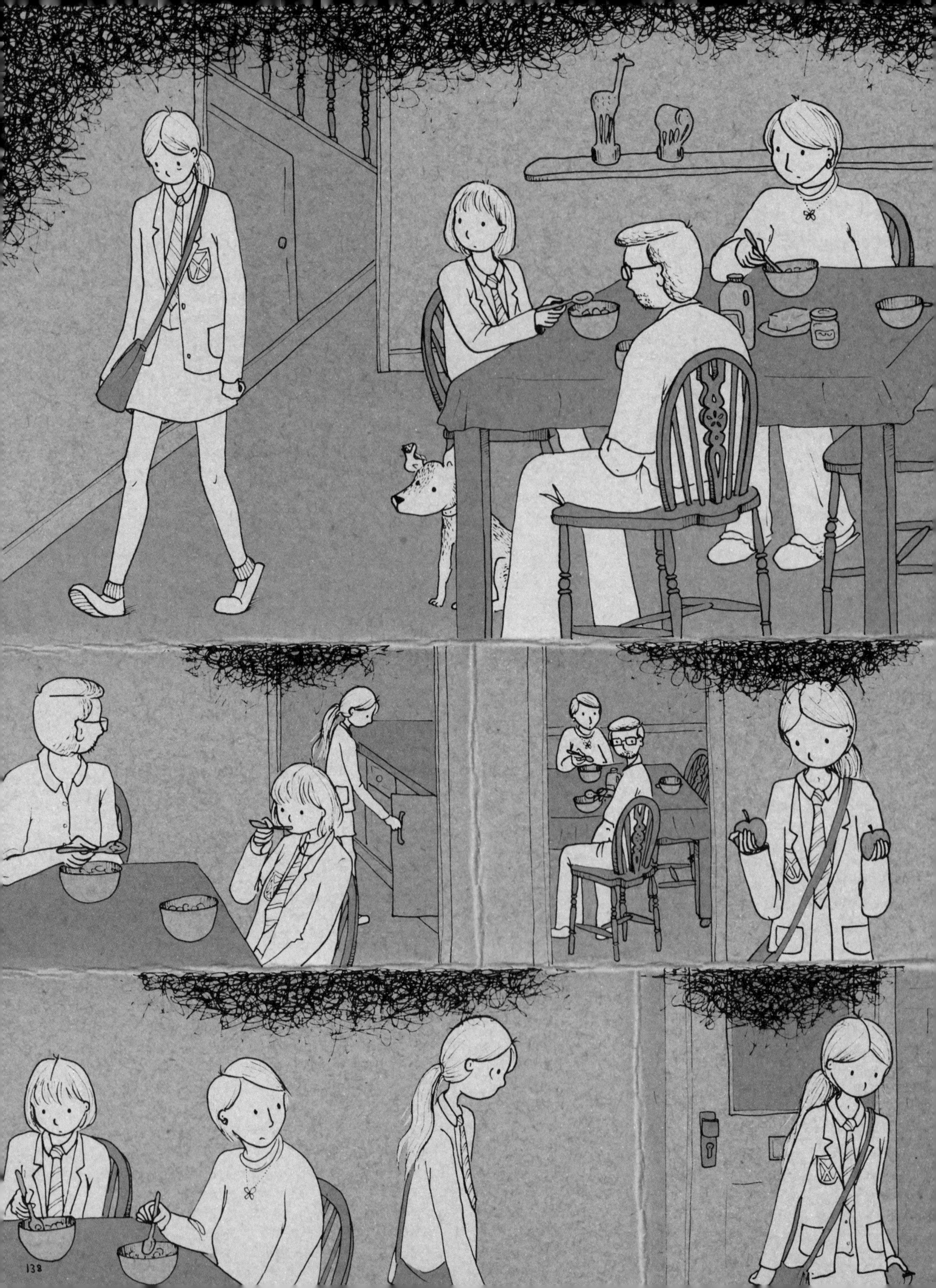

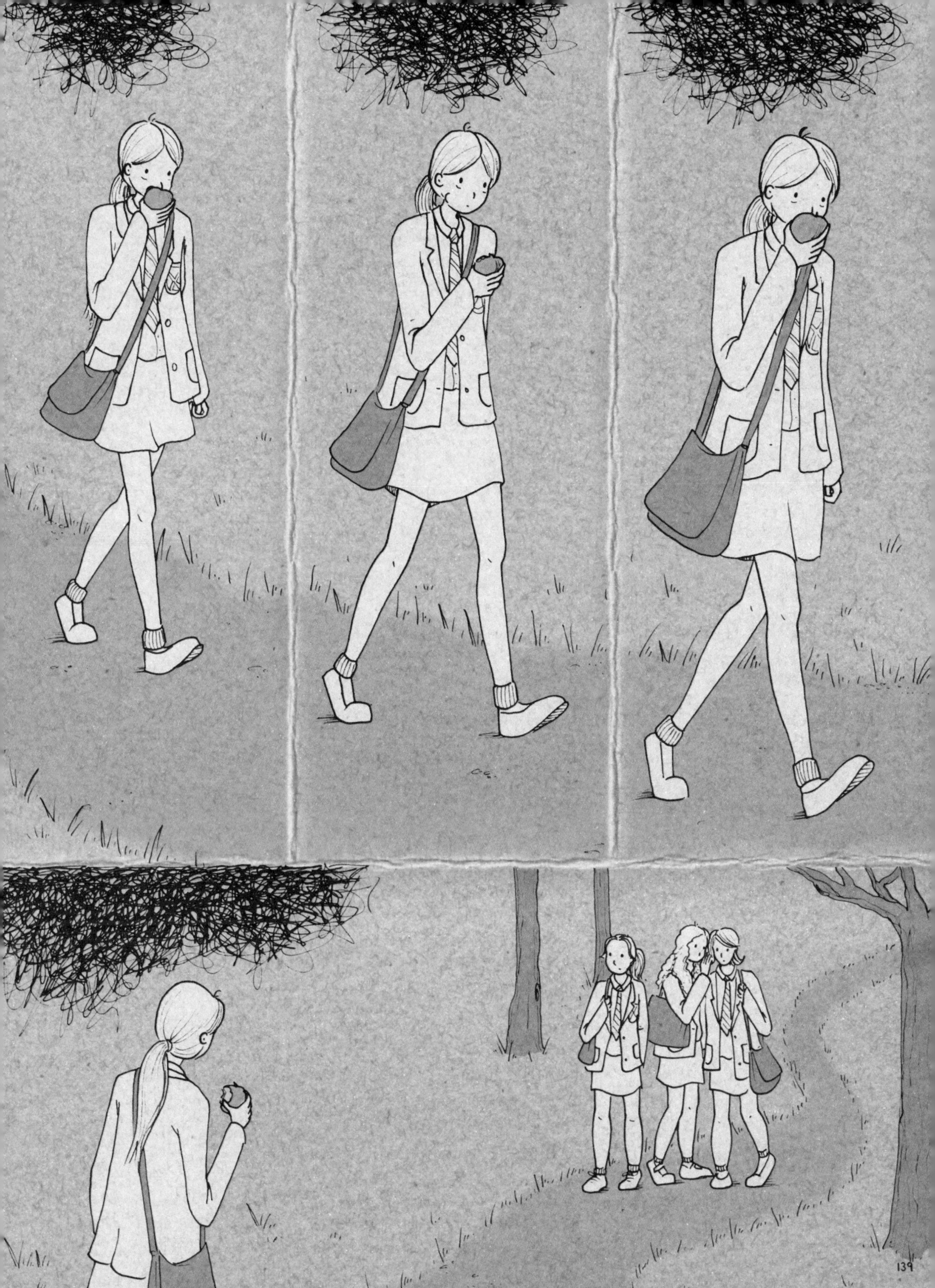

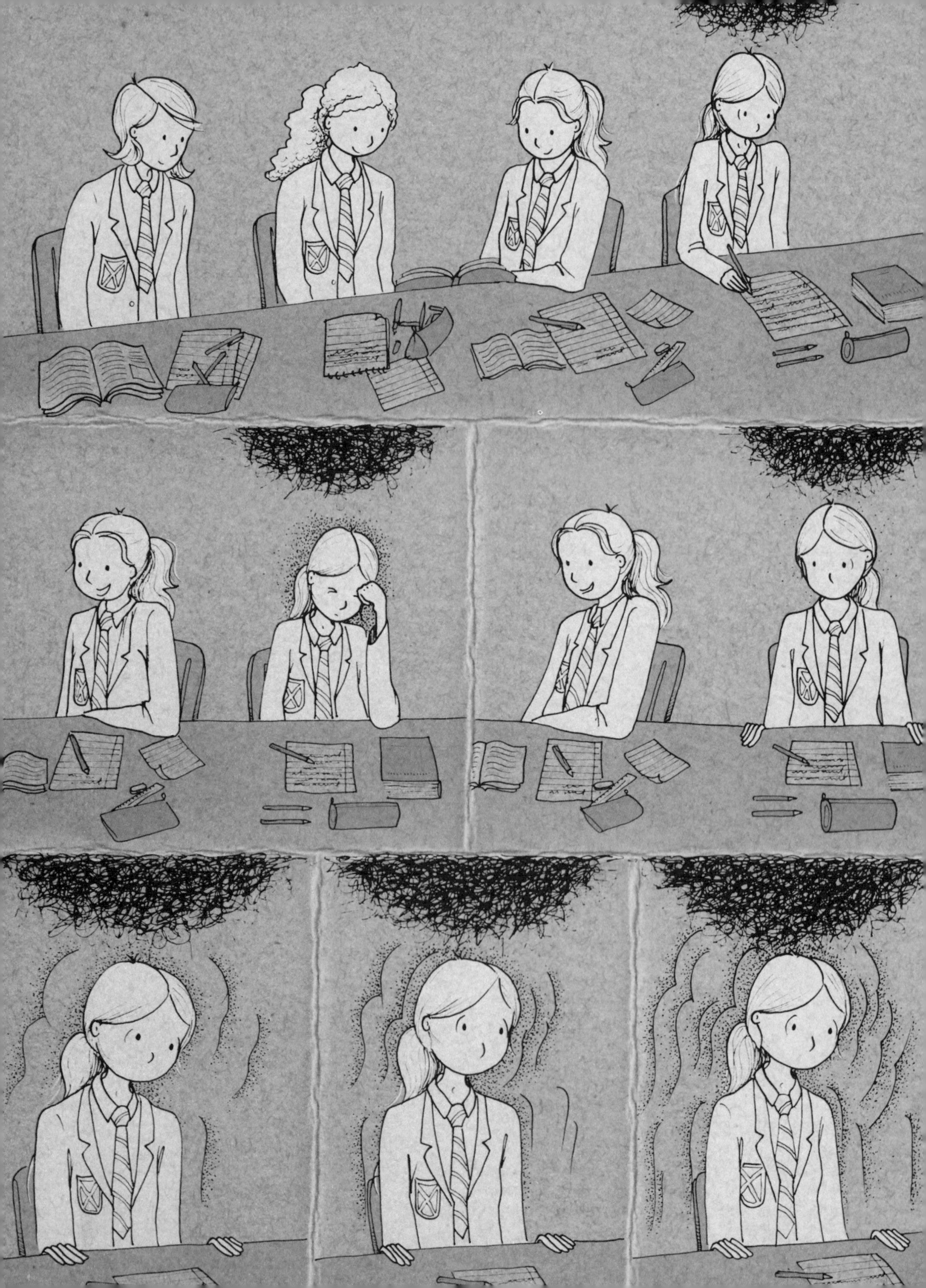

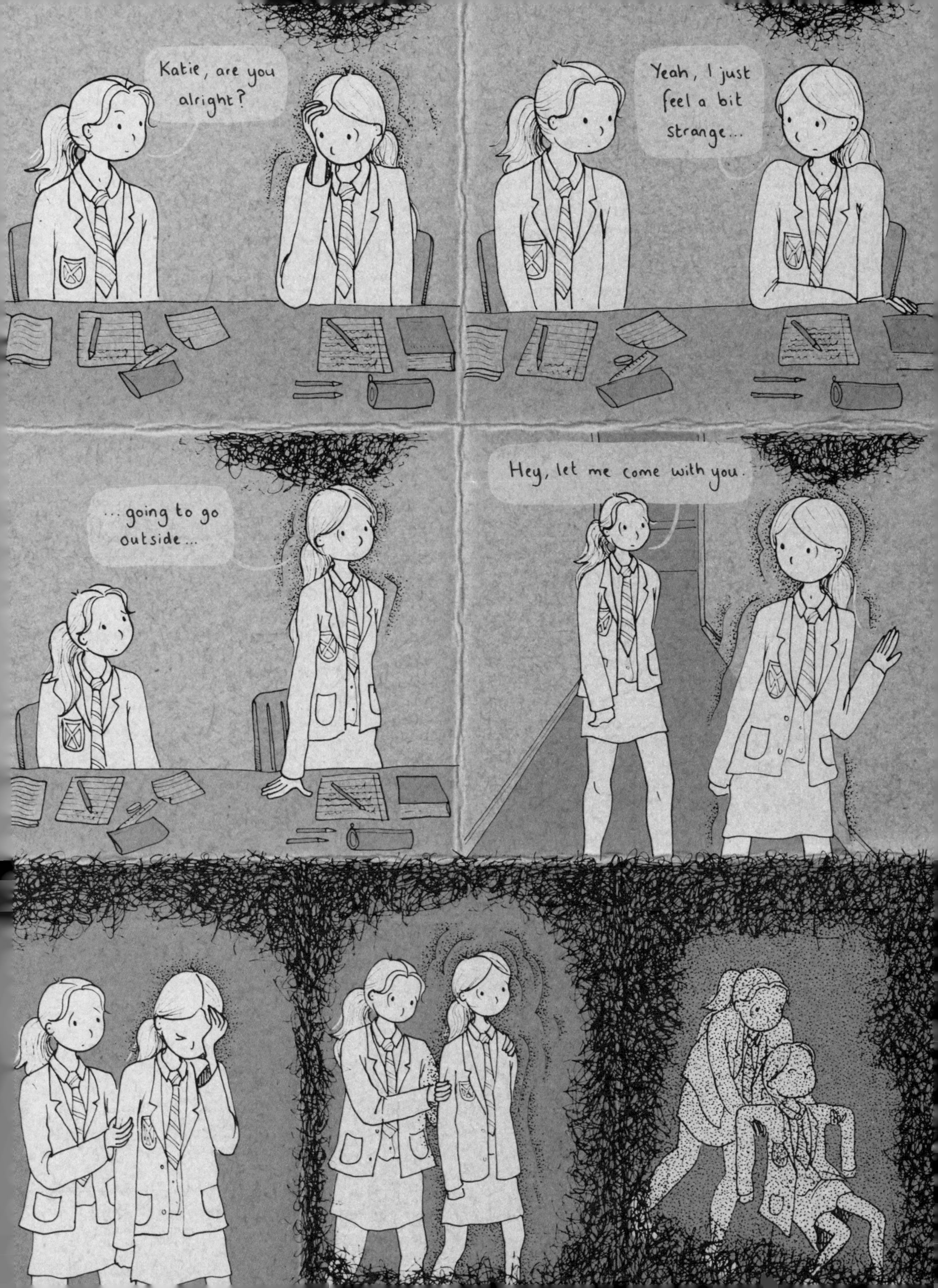
Katie, are you alright?
Yeah, I just feel a bit strange...
...going to go outside...
Hey, let me come with you.

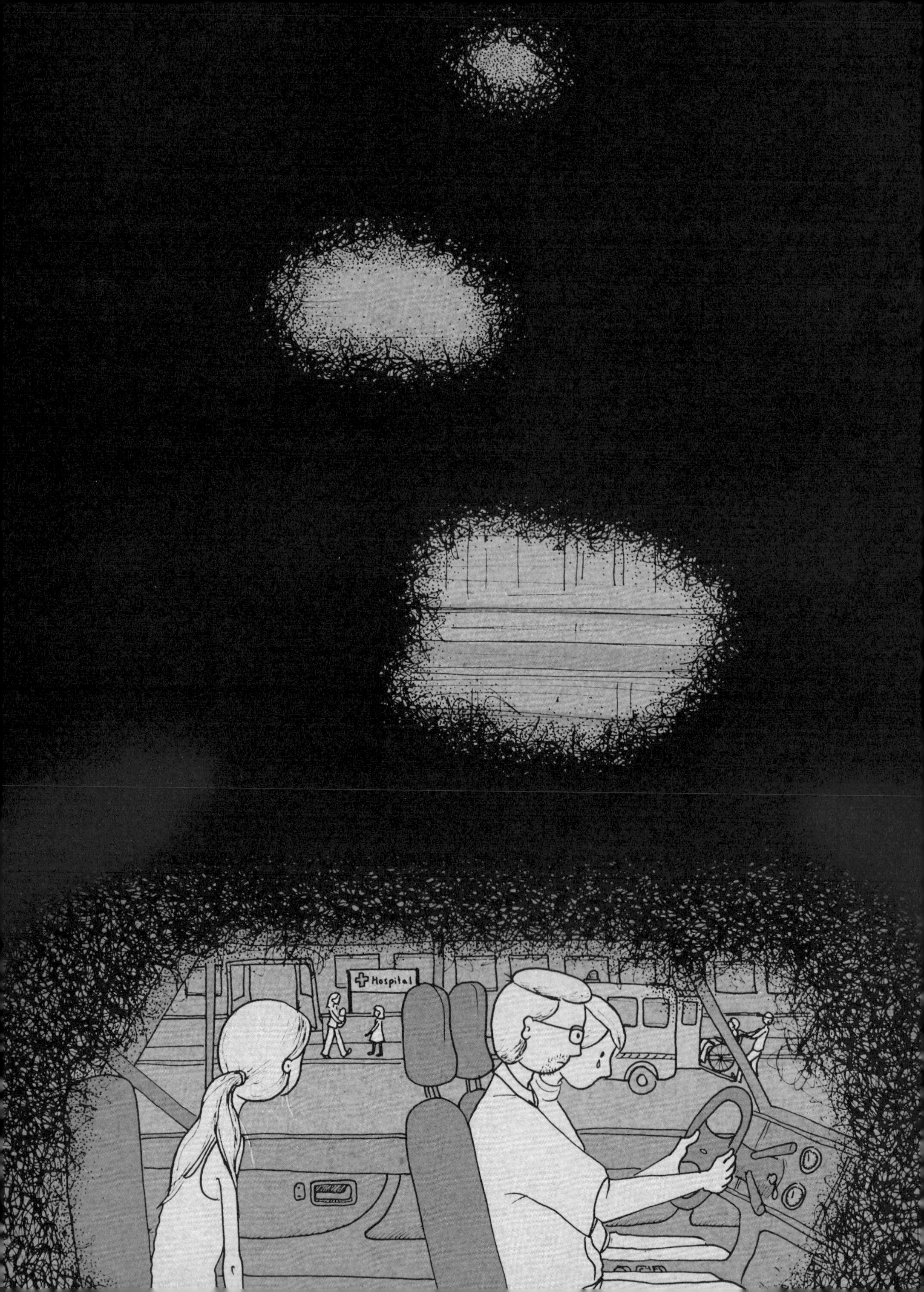
Hospital

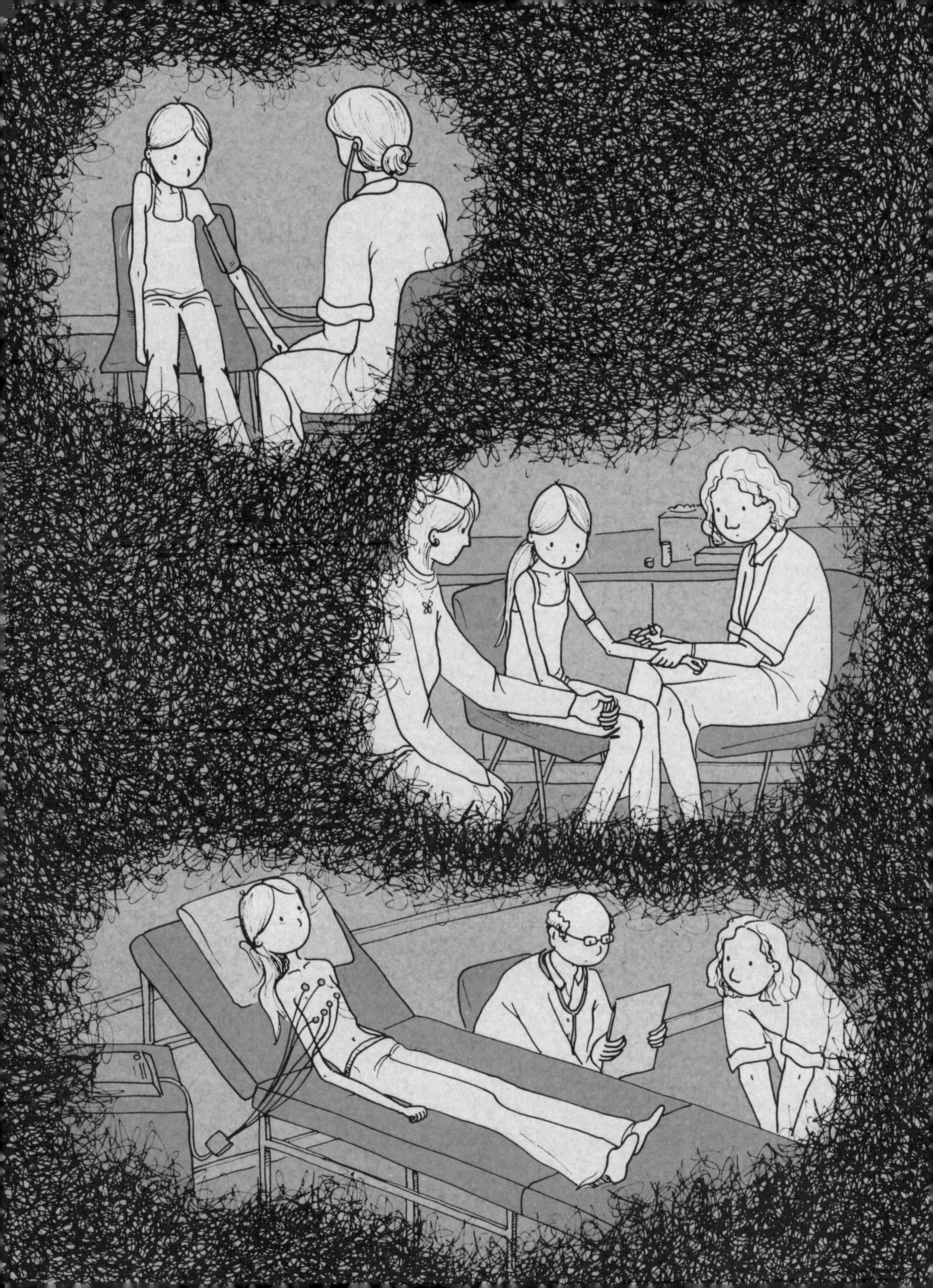

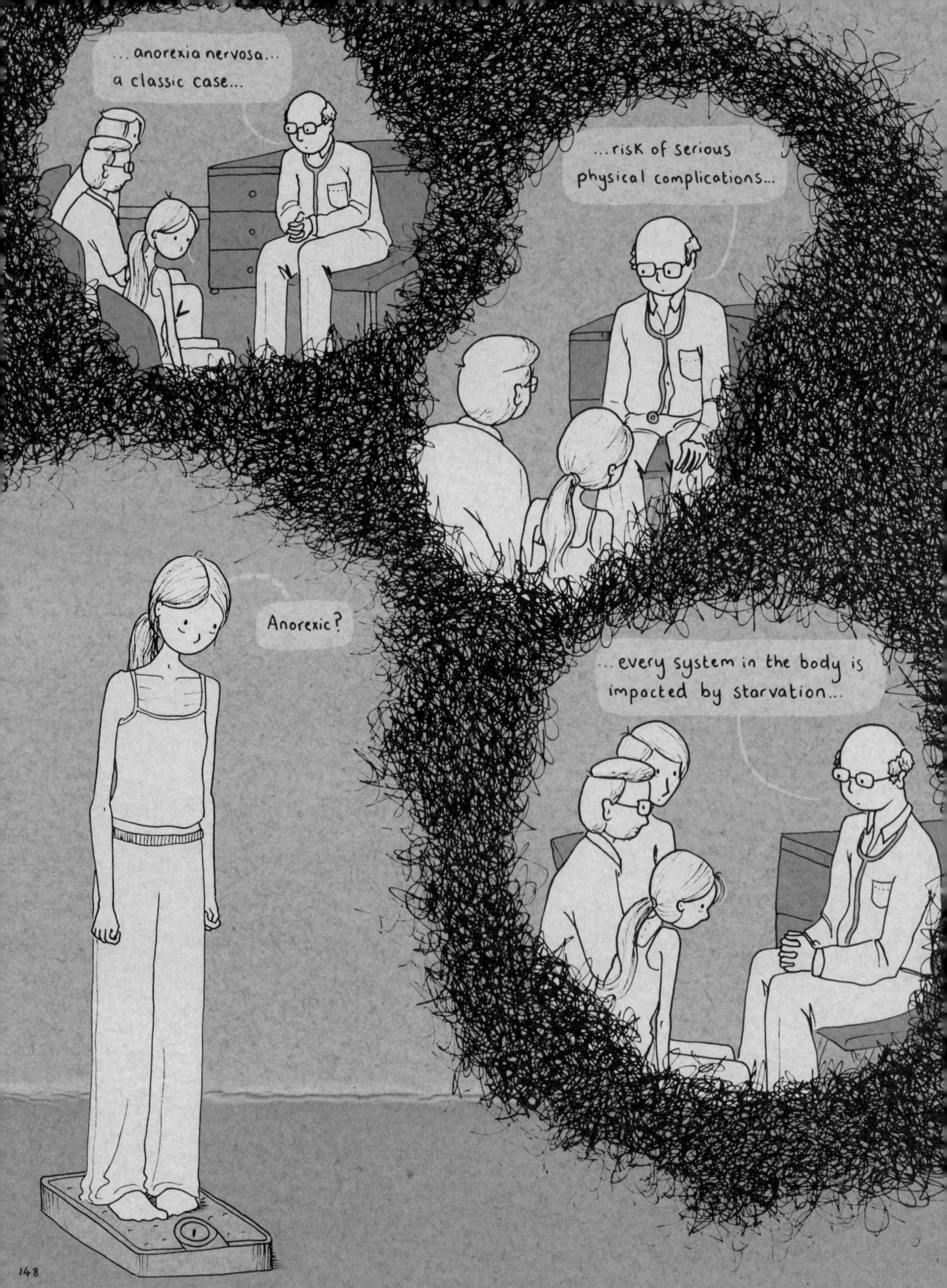
... anorexia nervosa...
a classic case...
... risk of serious
physical complications...
Anorexic?
... every system in the body is
impacted by starvation...

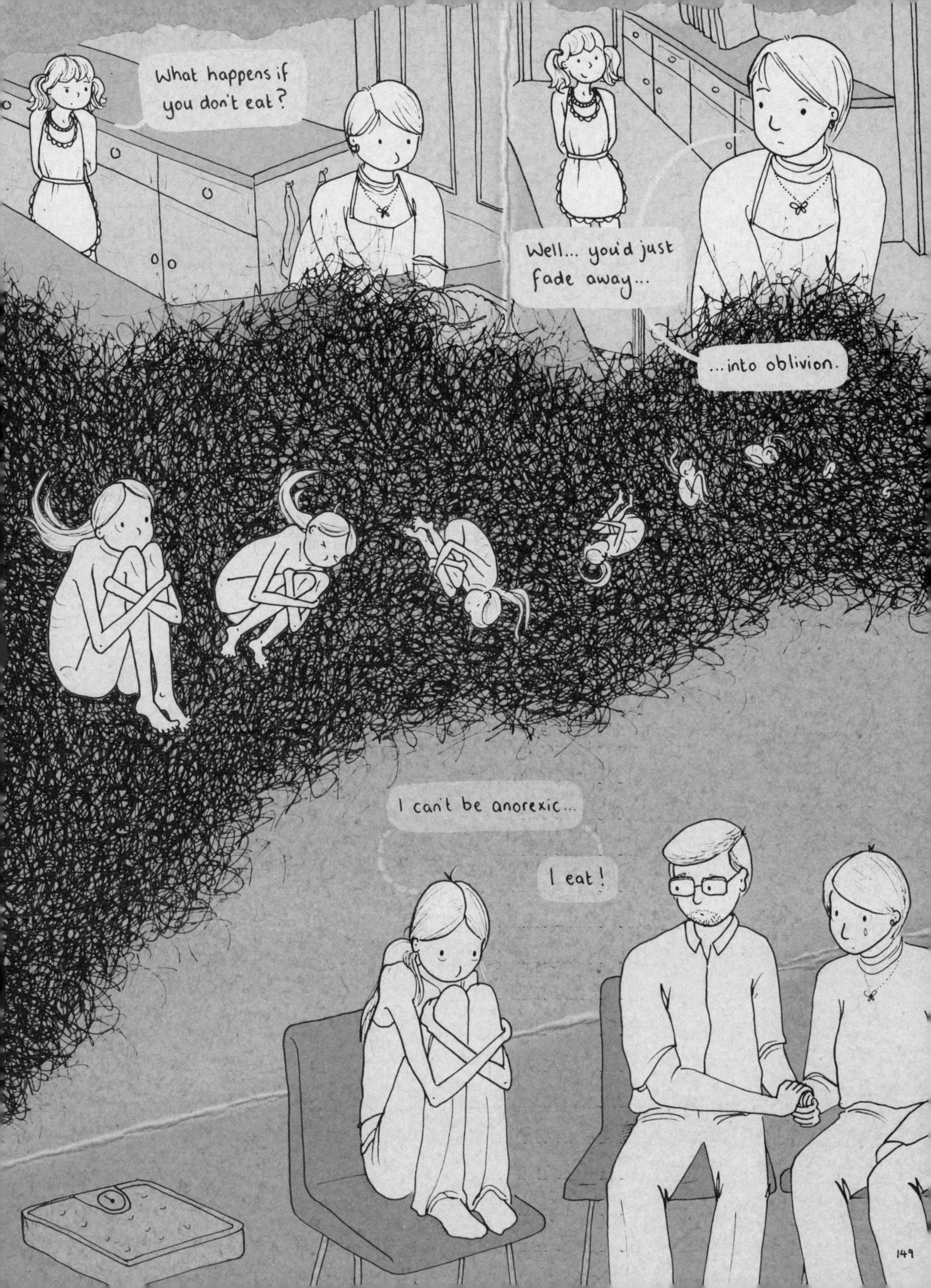
What happens if you don't eat?
Well... you'd just fade away...
...into oblivion.
I can't be anorexic...
I eat!

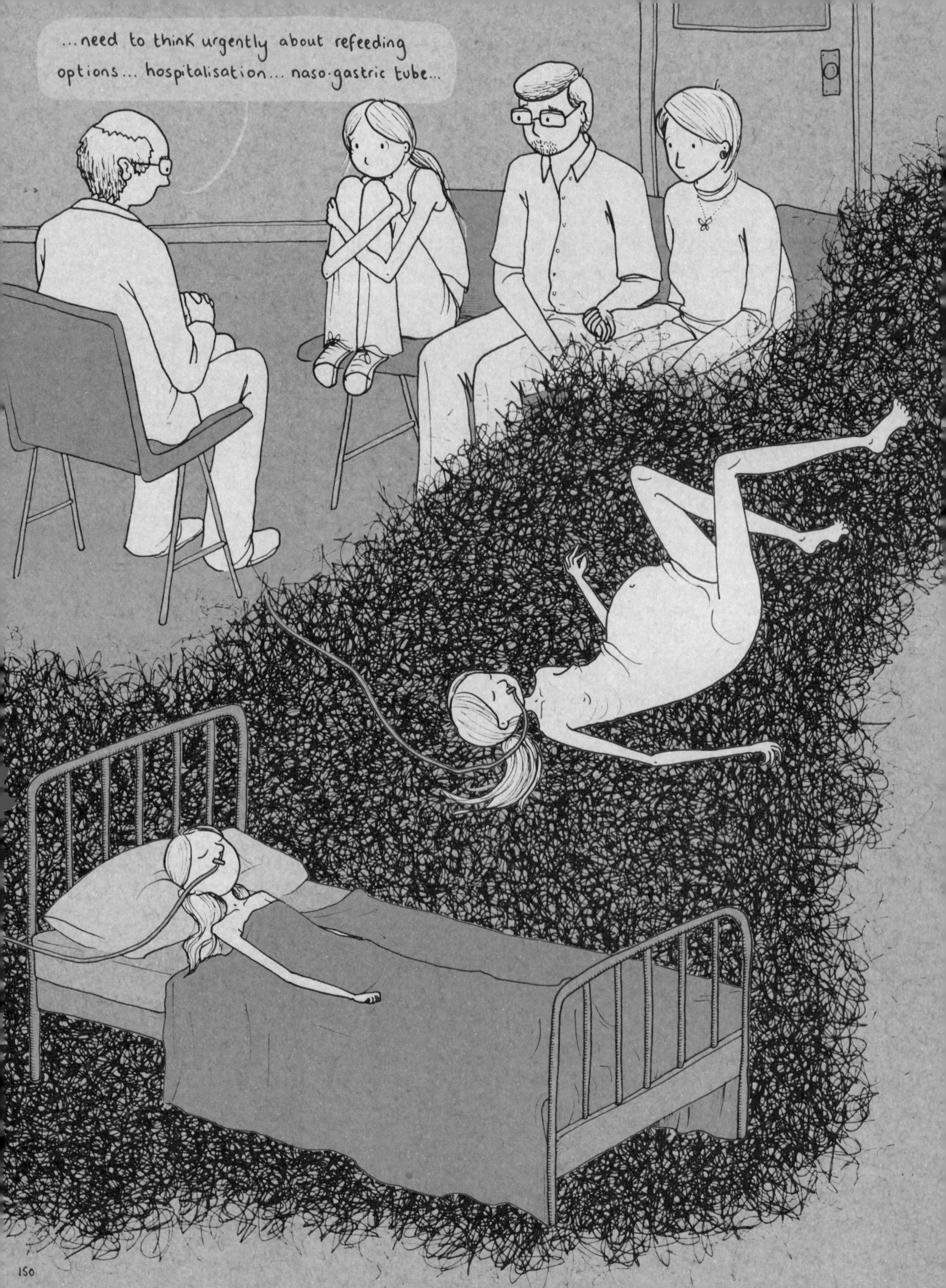
...need to think urgently about refeeding options... hospitalisation... naso-gastric tube...

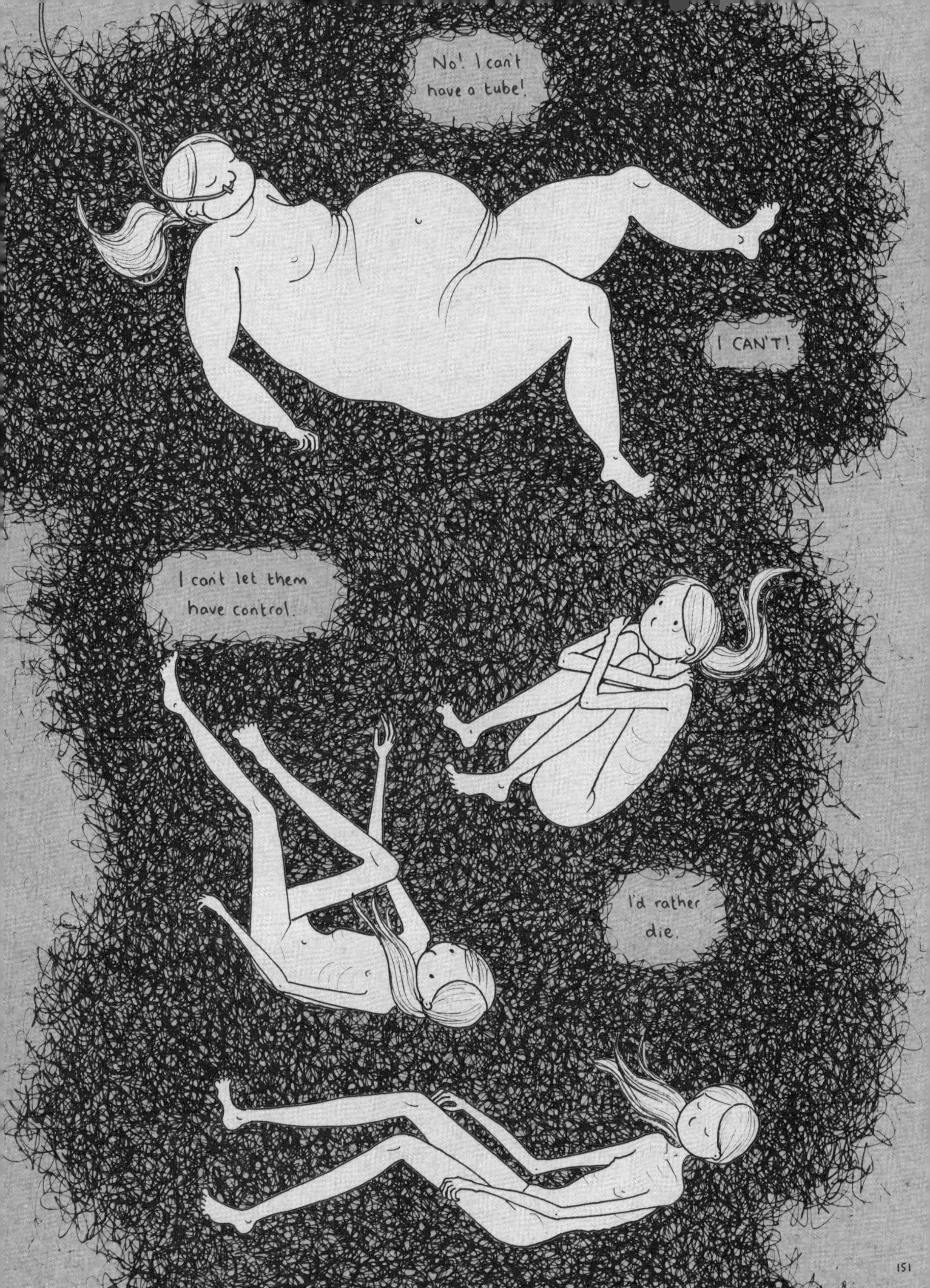
No! I can't
have a tube!
I CAN'T!
I can't let them
have control.
I'd rather
die.

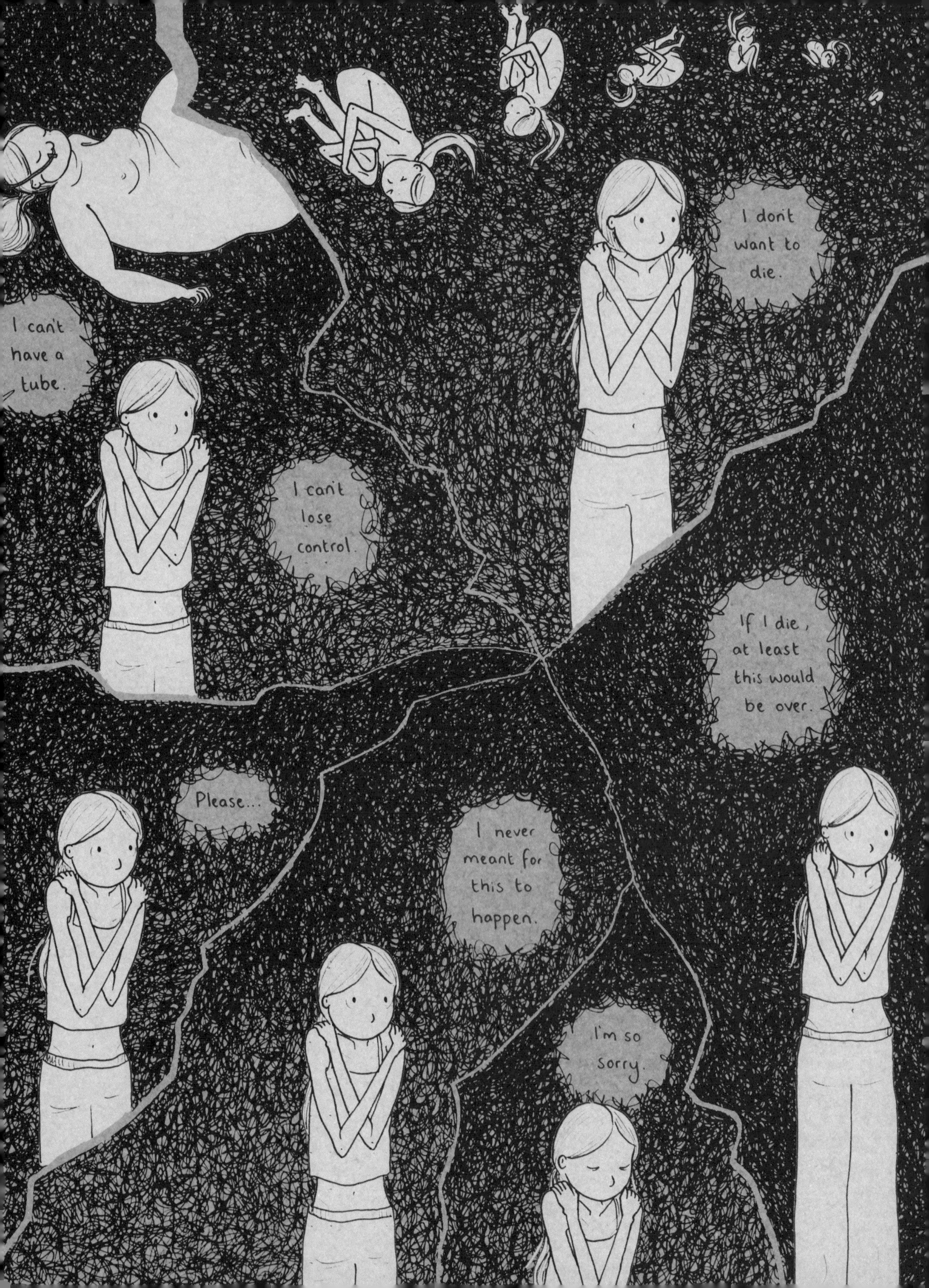
I can't have a tube.
I can't lose control.
I don't want to die.
If I die, at least this would be over.
Please...
I never meant for this to happen.
I'm so sorry.

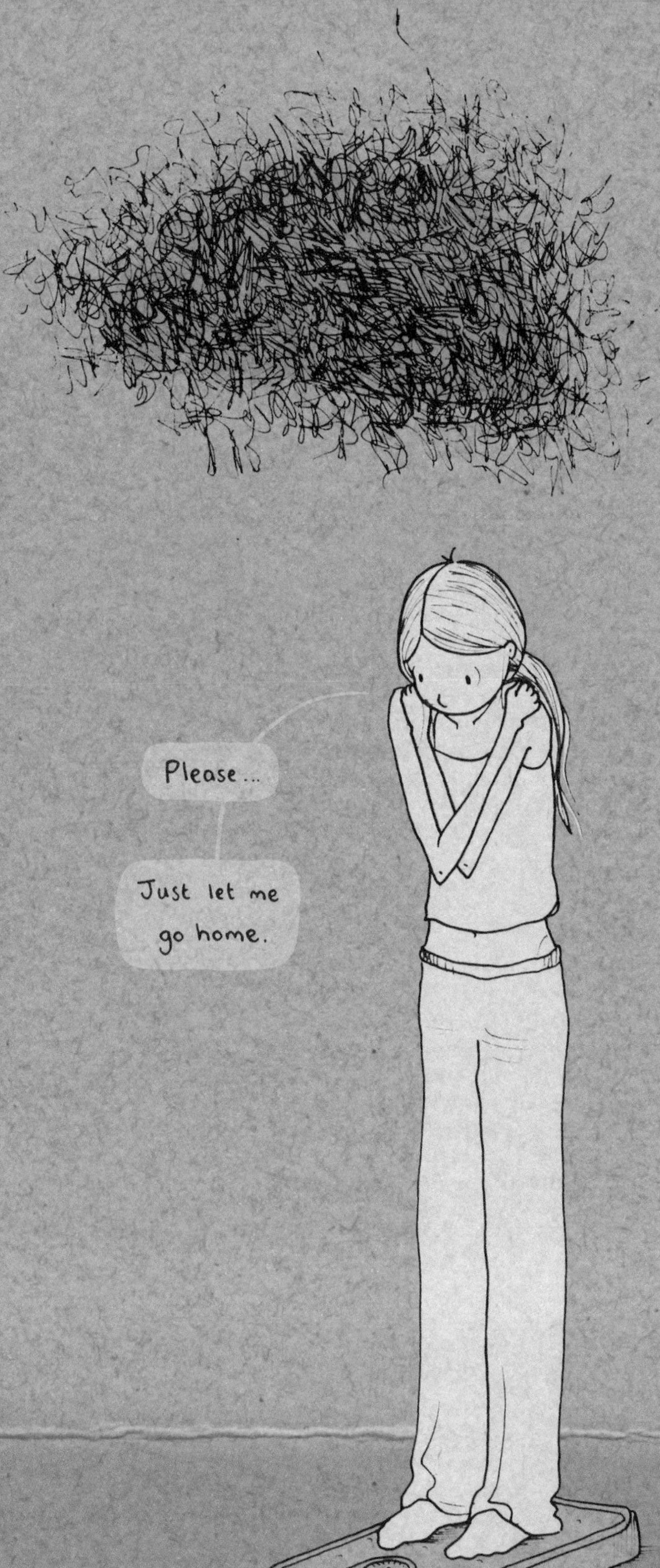
Please...
Just let me go home.

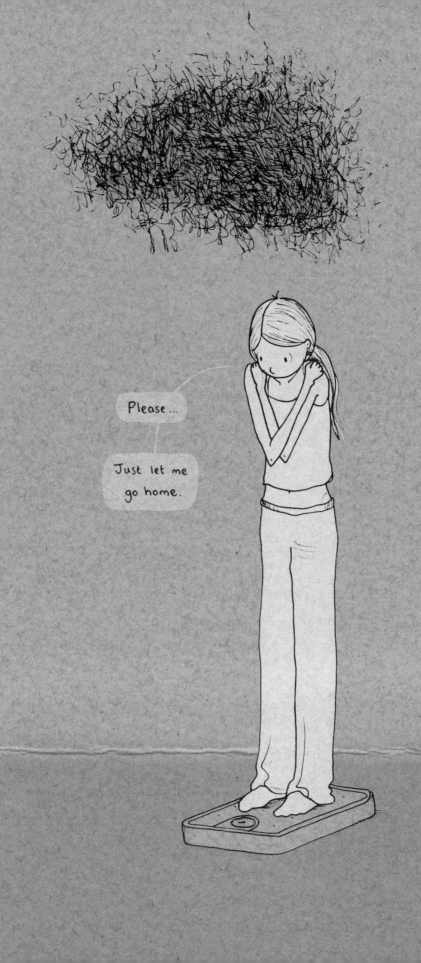

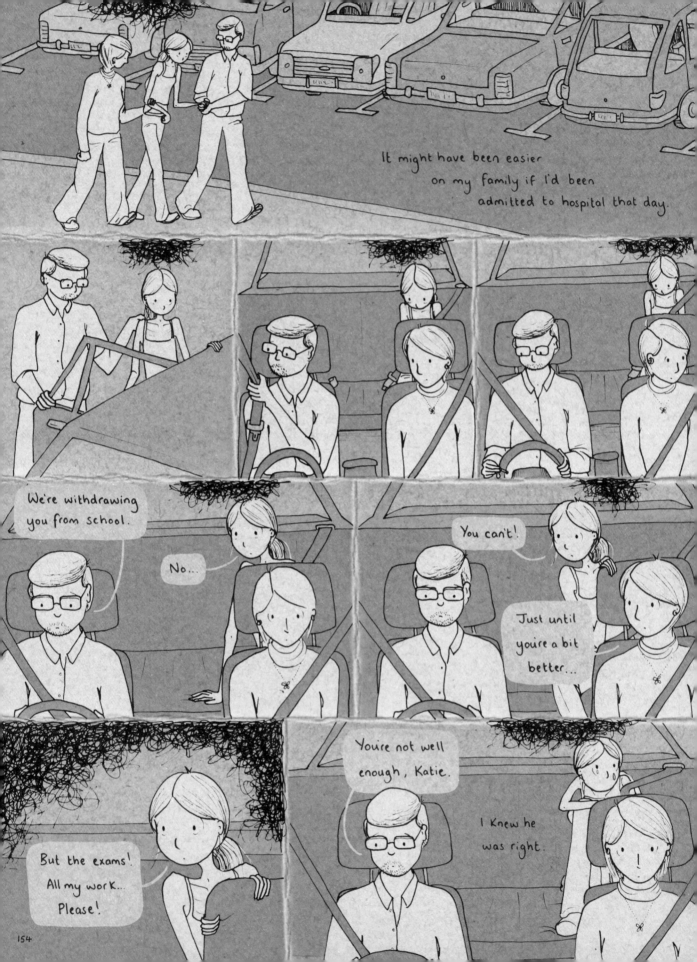

It might have been easier on my family if I'd been admitted to hospital that day.

We're withdrawing you from school.

No...

You can't!

Just until you're a bit better...

But the exams! All my work... Please!

You're not well enough, Katie.

I knew he was right.

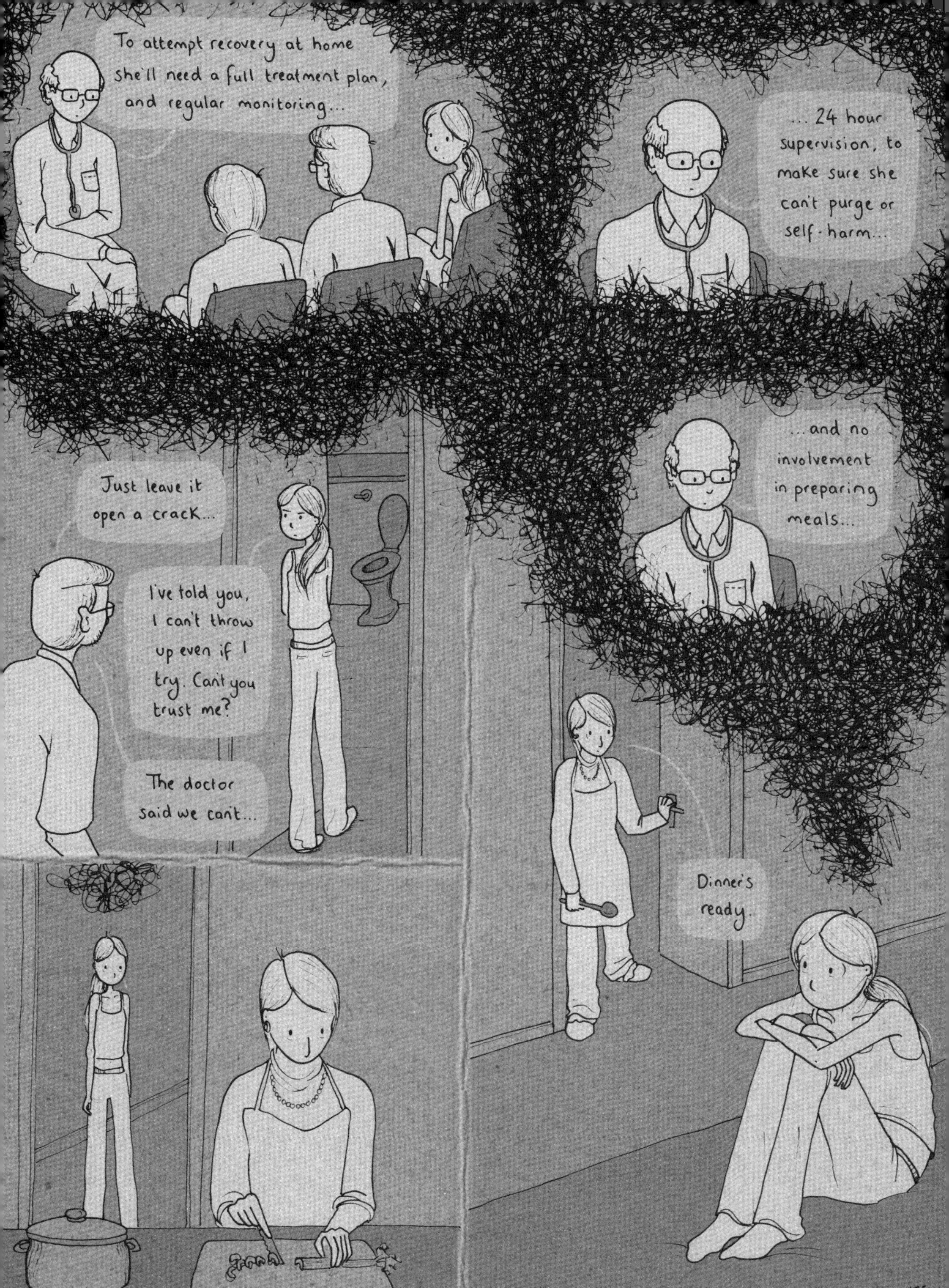

To attempt recovery at home she'll need a full treatment plan, and regular monitoring...
... 24 hour supervision, to make sure she can't purge or self-harm...
...and no involvement in preparing meals...
Just leave it open a crack...
I've told you, I can't throw up even if I try. Can't you trust me?
The doctor said we can't...
Dinner's ready.

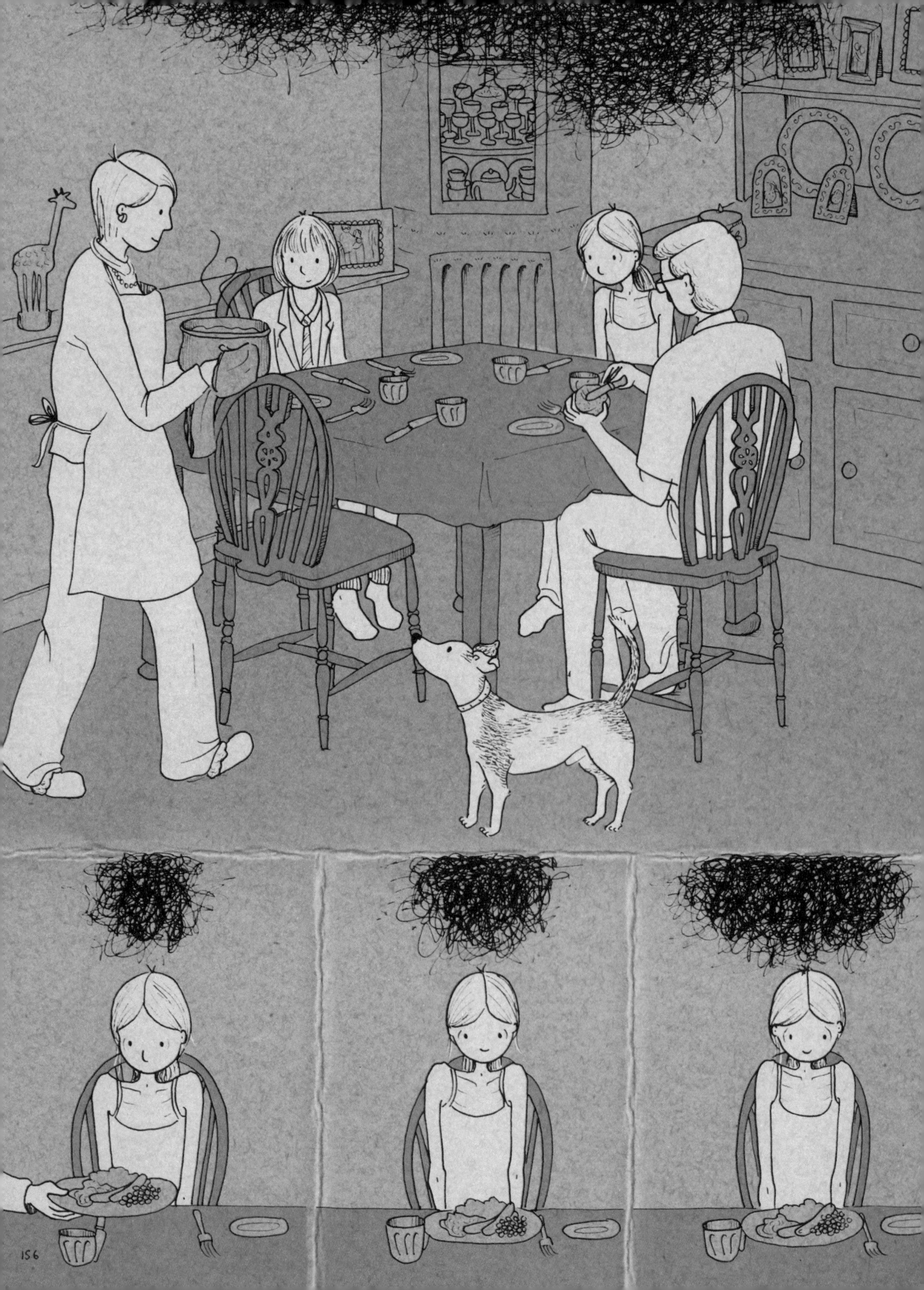

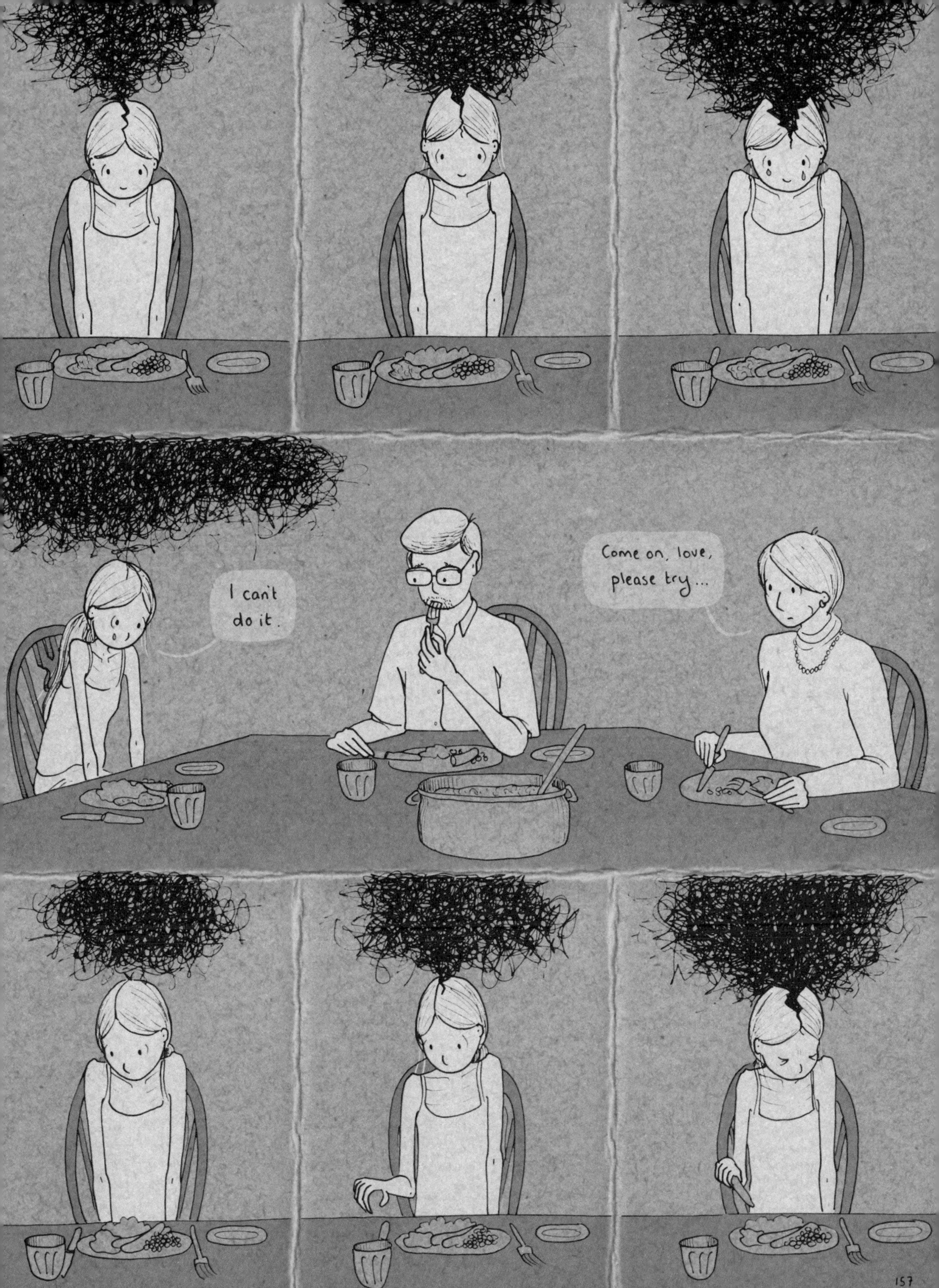
I can't do it.
Come on, love, please try...

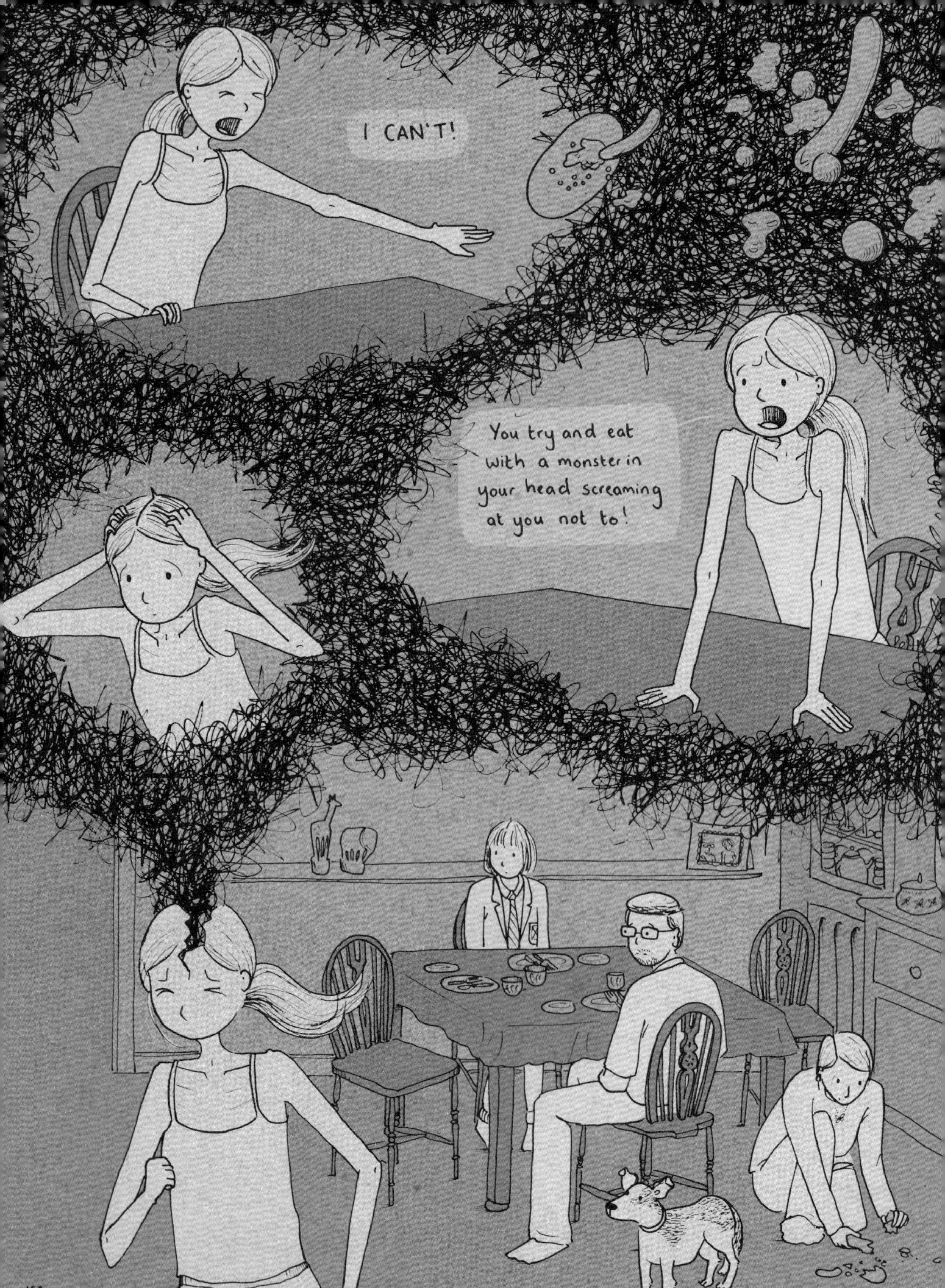
I CAN'T!
You try and eat with a monster in your head screaming at you not to!

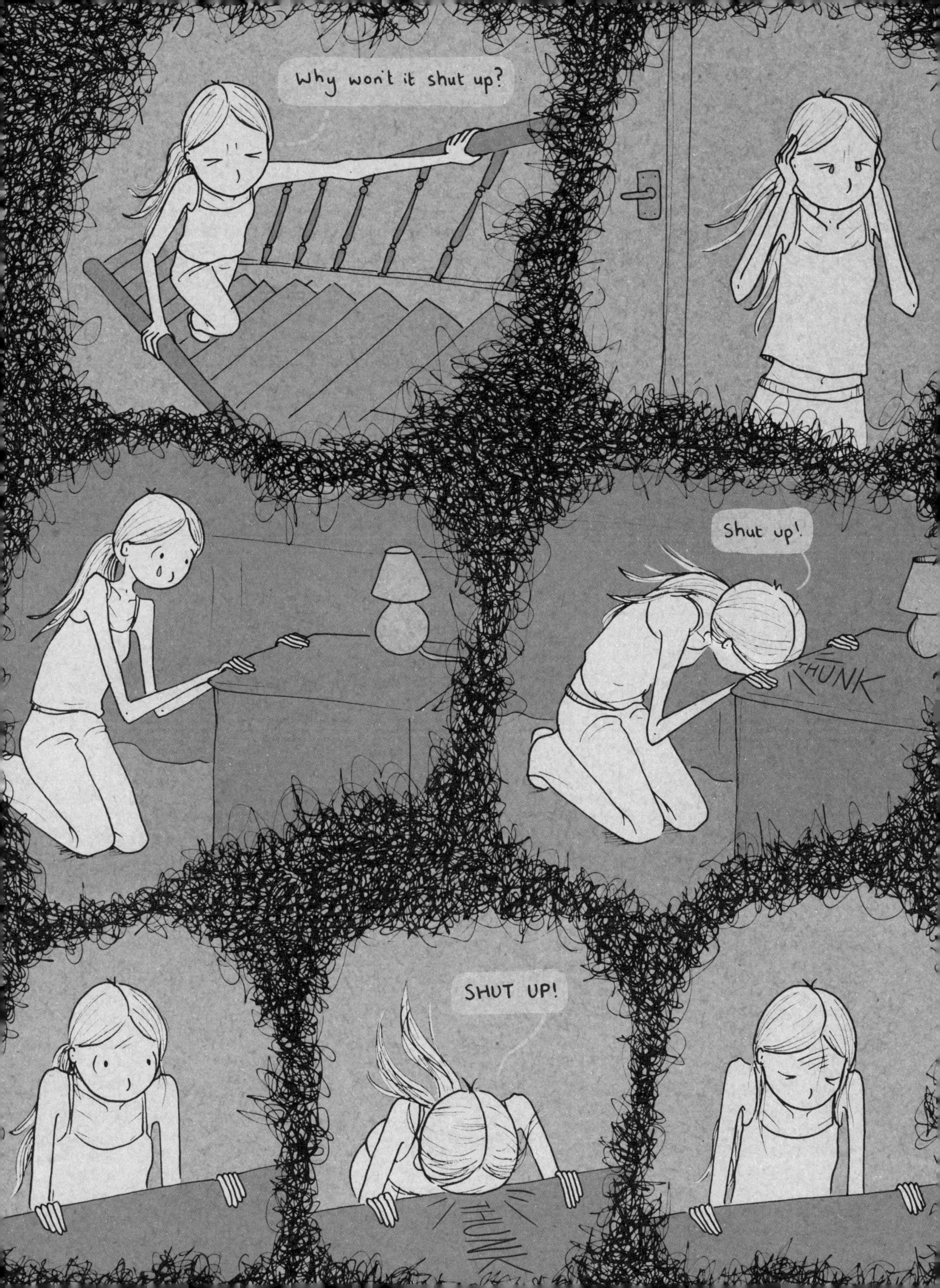
Why won't it shut up?
Shut up!
THUNK
SHUT UP!
THUNK

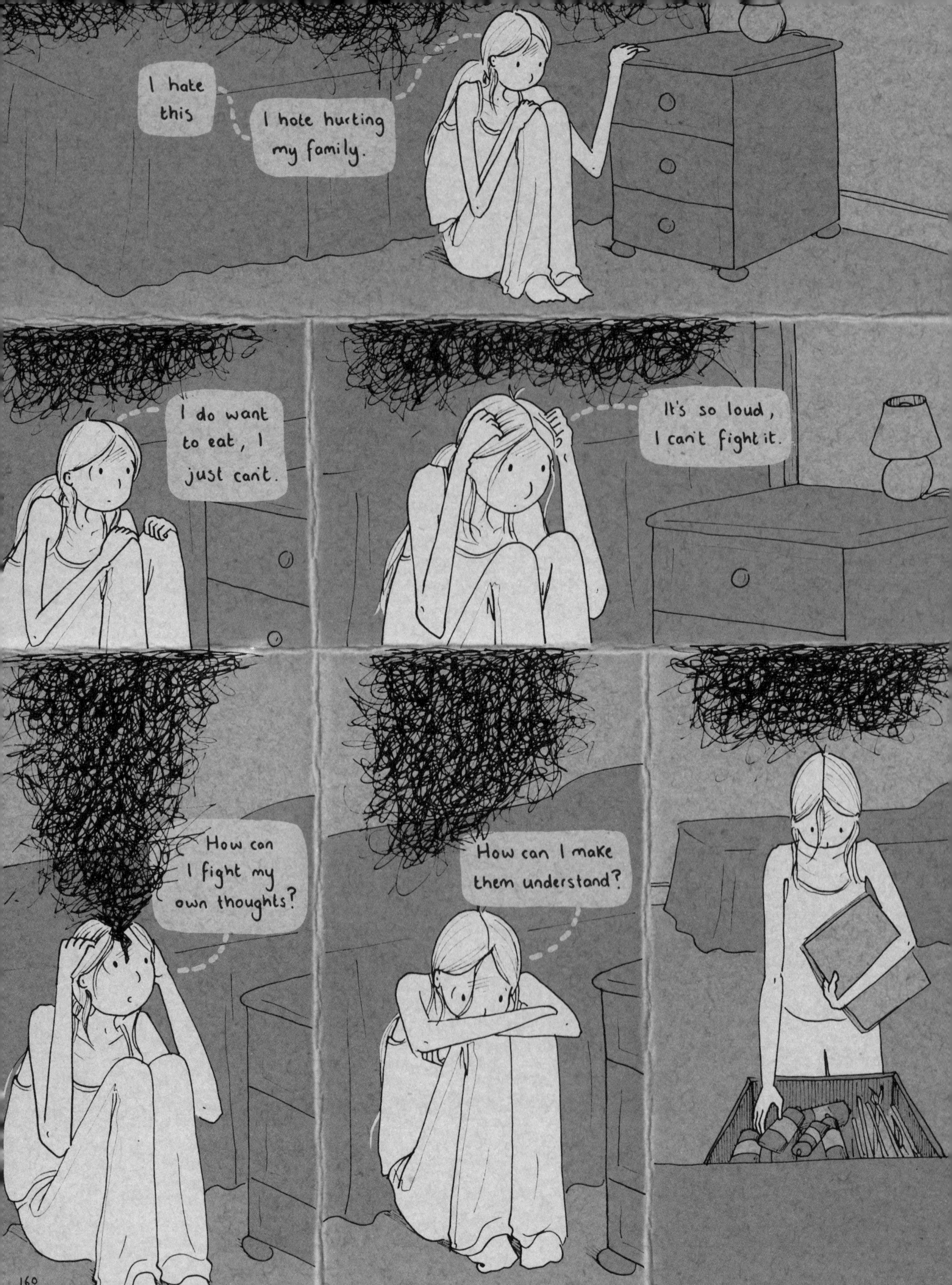
I hate this
I hate hurting my family.
I do want to eat, I just can't.
It's so loud, I can't fight it.
How can I fight my own thoughts?
How can I make them understand?

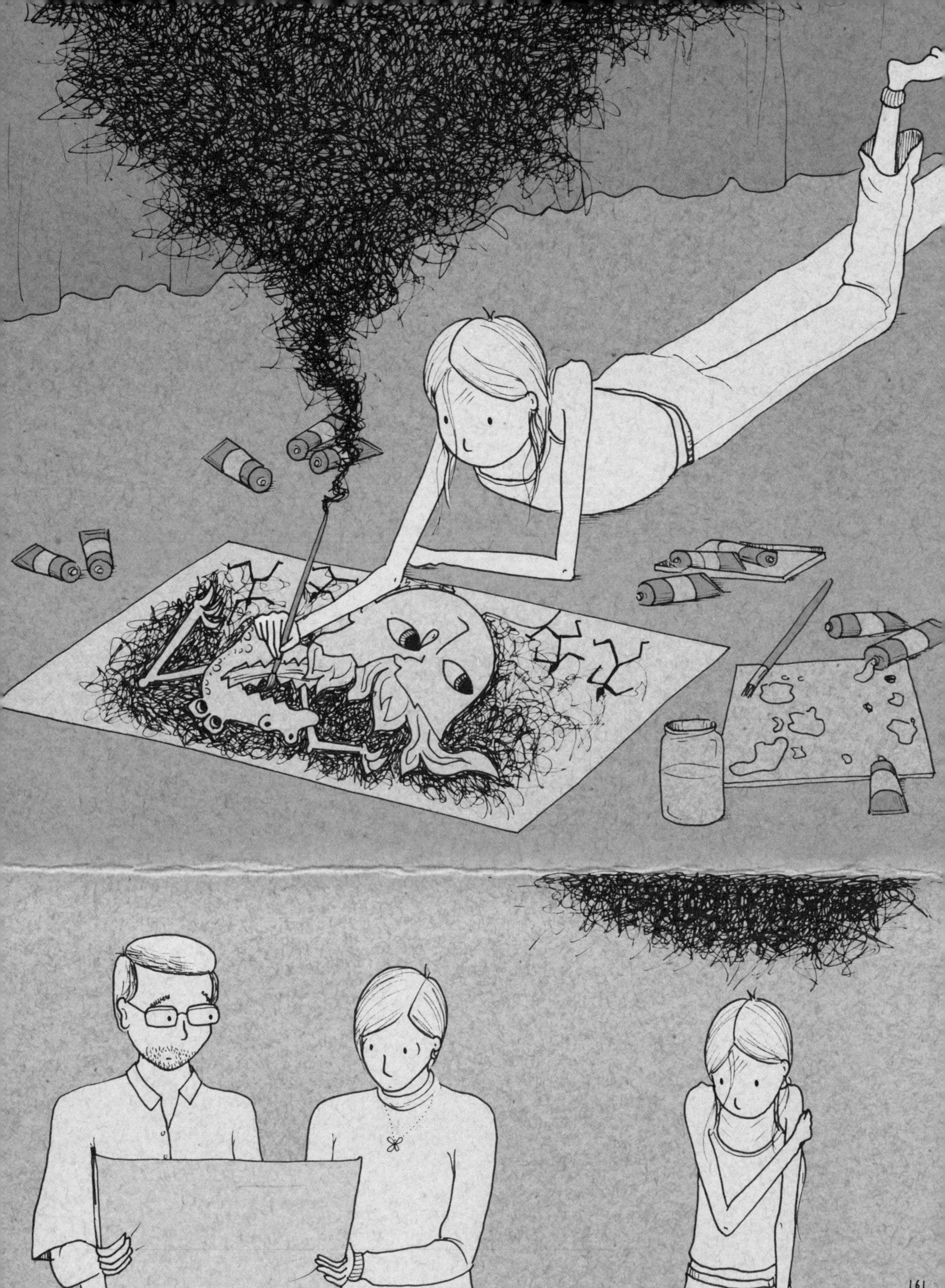

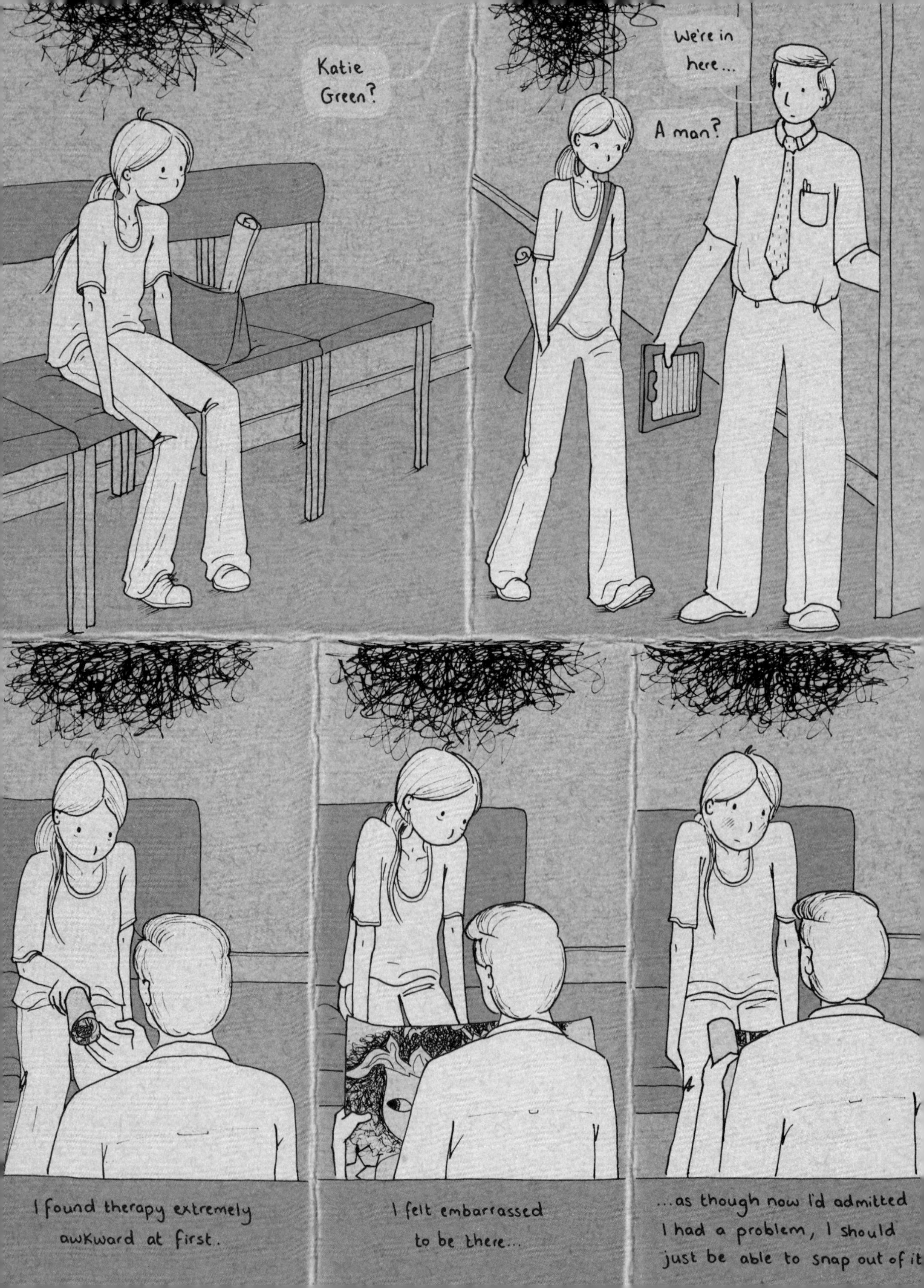
Katie
Green?
We're in
here...
A man?
I found therapy extremely
awkward at first.
I felt embarrassed
to be there...
...as though now I'd admitted
I had a problem, I should
just be able to snap out of it

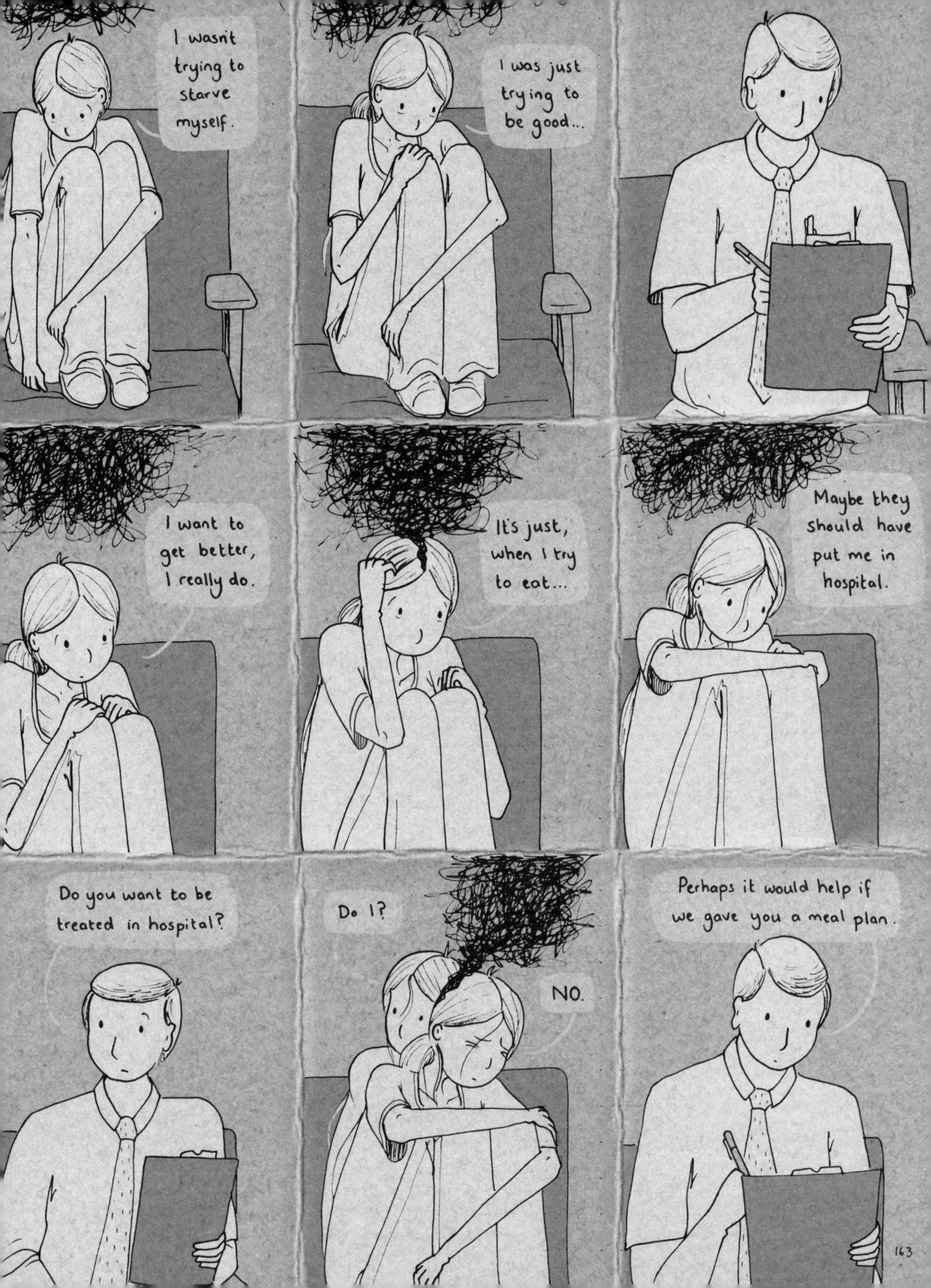
I wasn't trying to starve myself.
I was just trying to be good...
I want to get better, I really do.
It's just, when I try to eat...
Maybe they should have put me in hospital.
Do you want to be treated in hospital?
Do I?
NO.
Perhaps it would help if we gave you a meal plan.

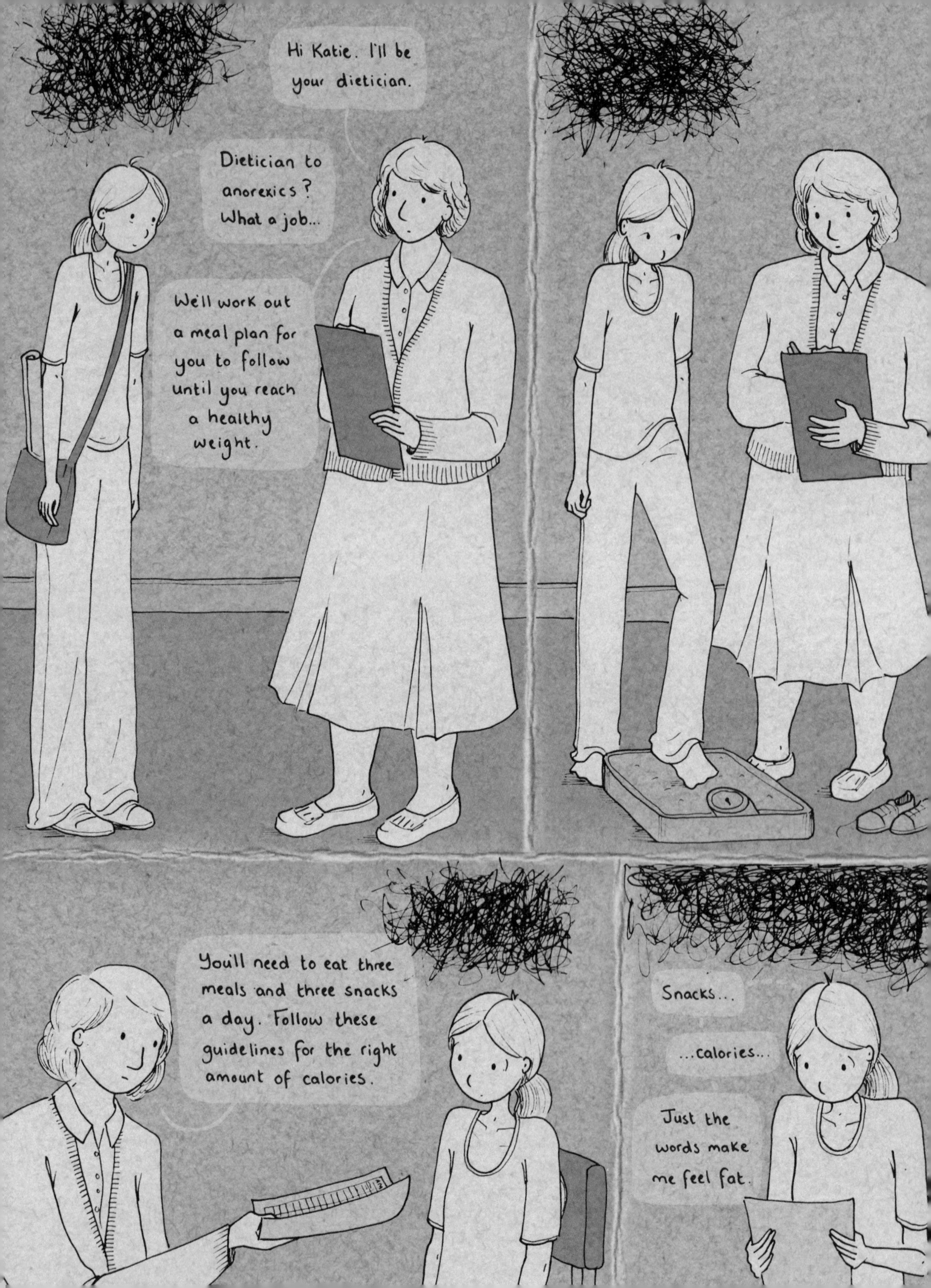
Hi Katie. I'll be your dietician.
Dietician to anorexics? What a job...
We'll work out a meal plan for you to follow until you reach a healthy weight.
You'll need to eat three meals and three snacks a day. Follow these guidelines for the right amount of calories.
Snacks...
...calories...
Just the words make me feel fat.

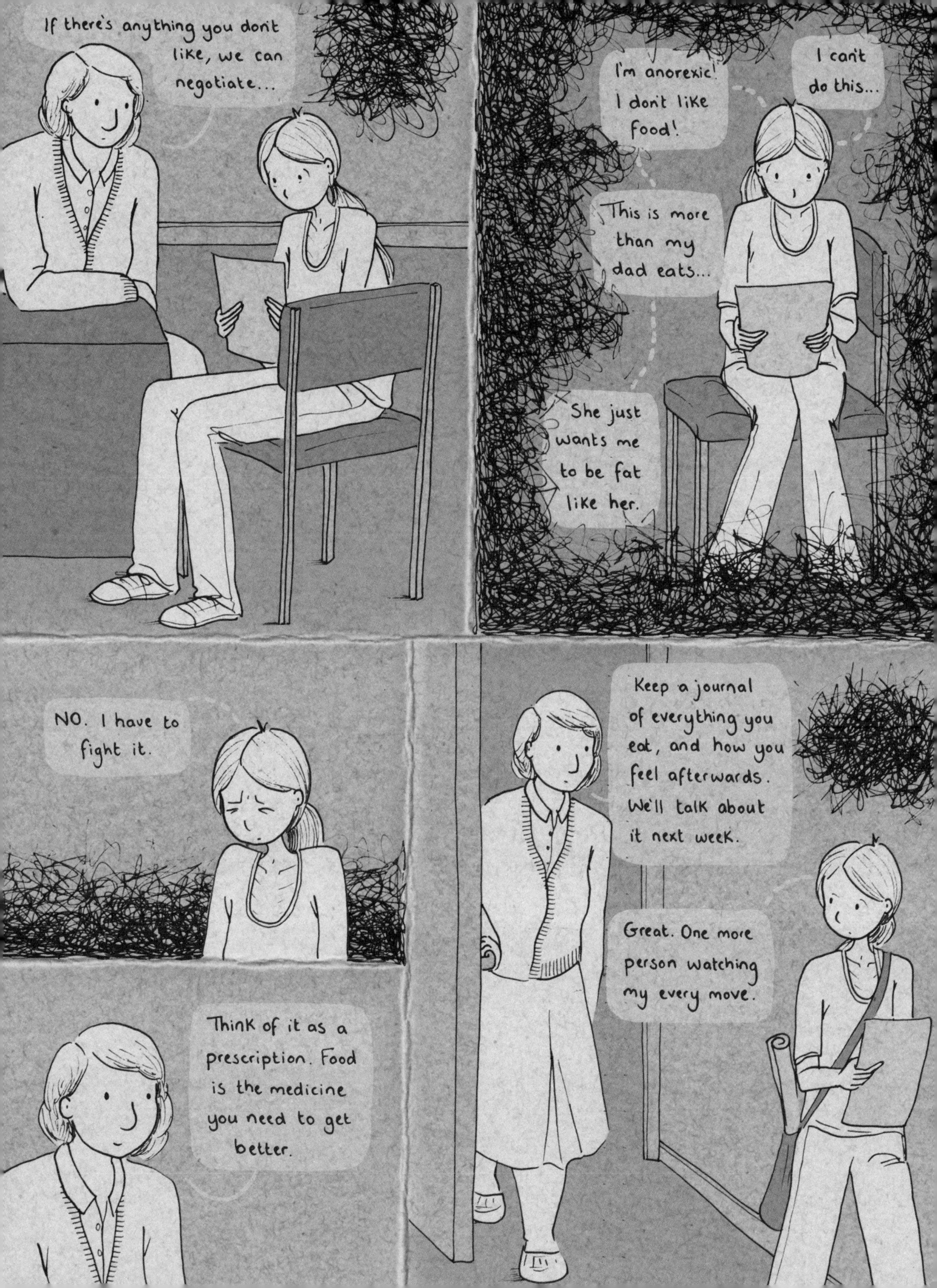
If there's anything you don't like, we can negotiate...
I'm anorexic! I don't like food!
I can't do this...
This is more than my dad eats...
She just wants me to be fat like her.
NO. I have to fight it.
Think of it as a prescription. Food is the medicine you need to get better.
Keep a journal of everything you eat, and how you feel afterwards. We'll talk about it next week.
Great. One more person watching my every move.

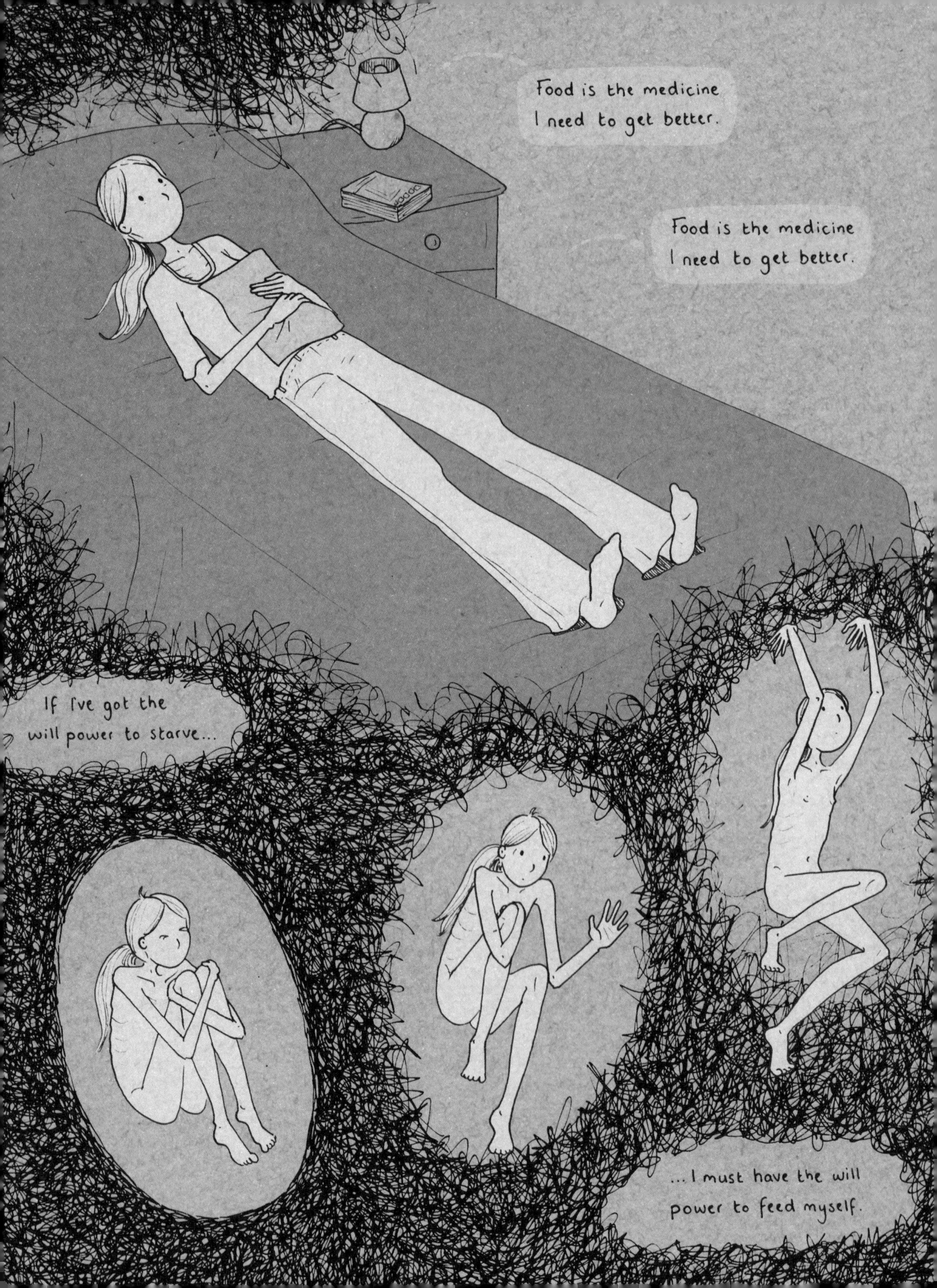

Food is the medicine
I need to get better.
Food is the medicine
I need to get better.
If I've got the
will power to starve...
... I must have the will
power to feed myself.

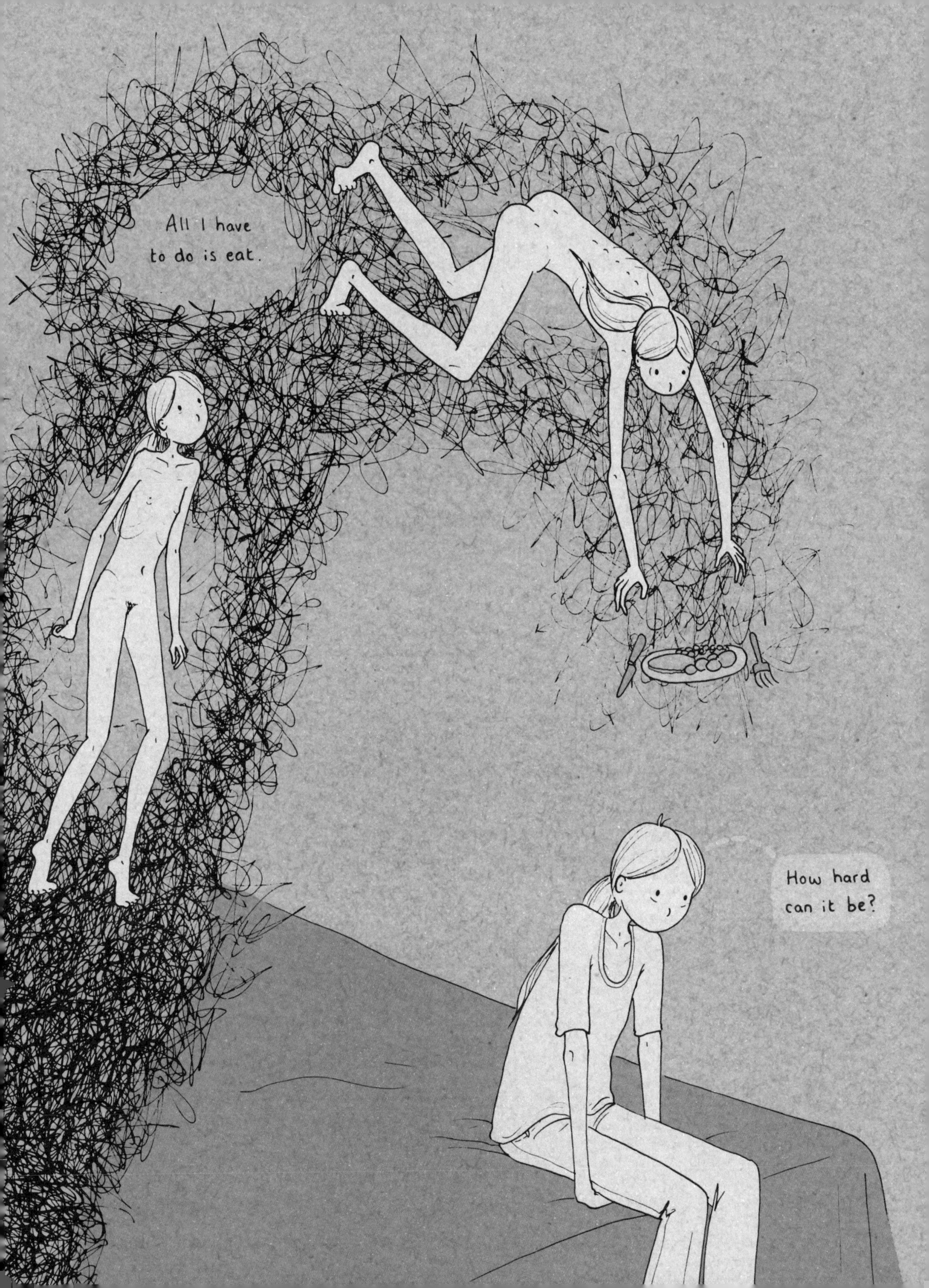
All I have to do is eat.
How hard can it be?

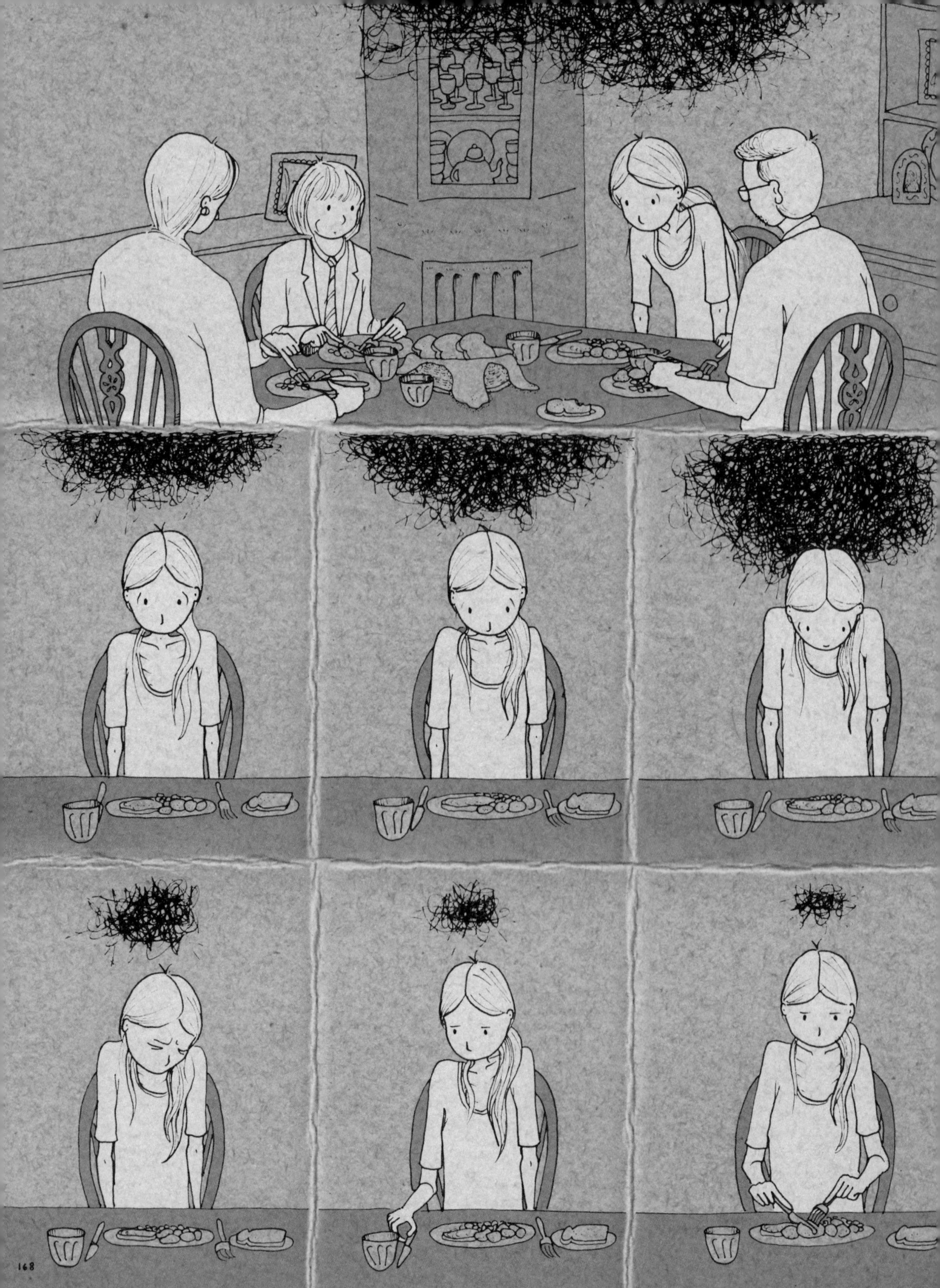

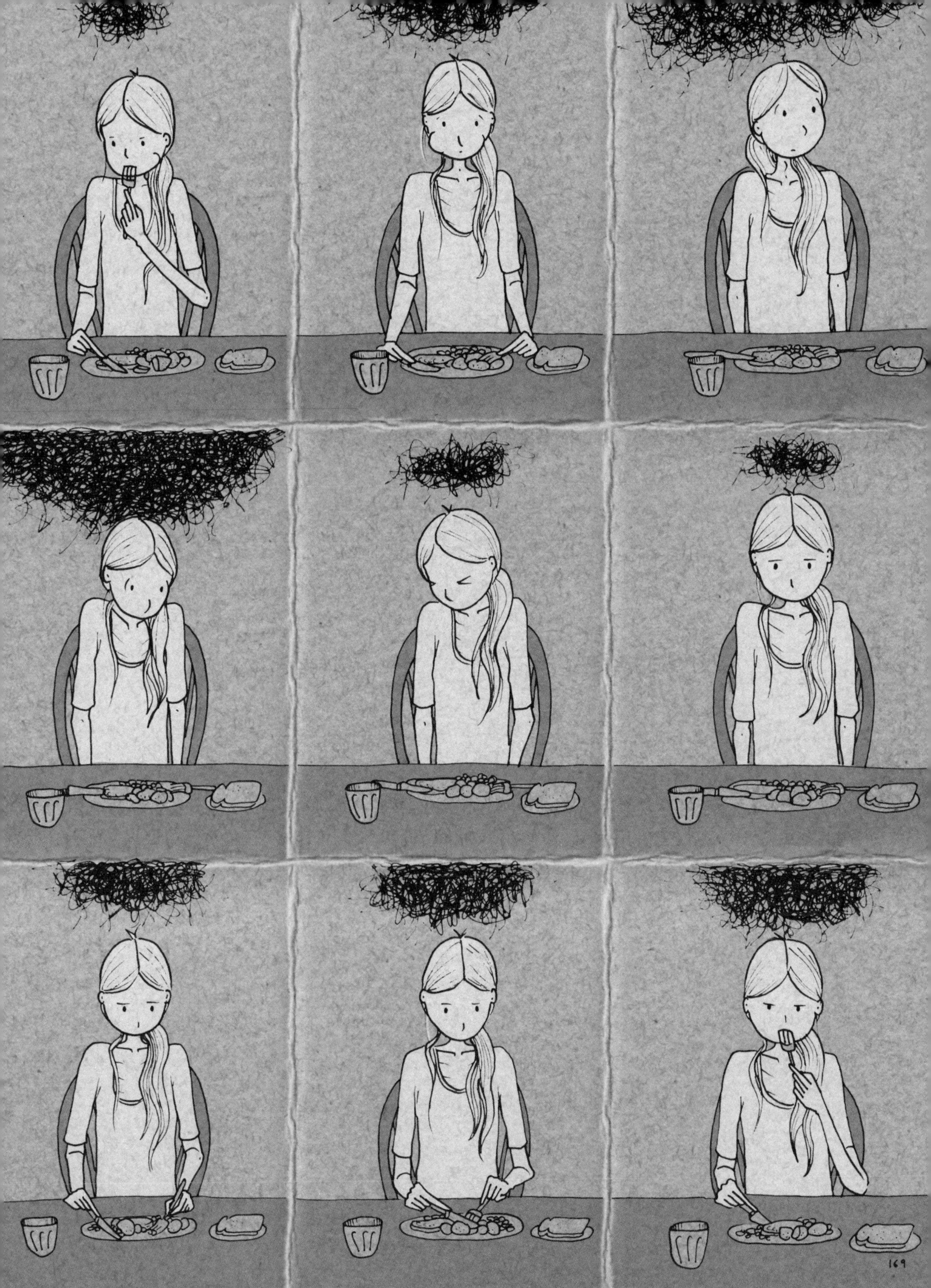

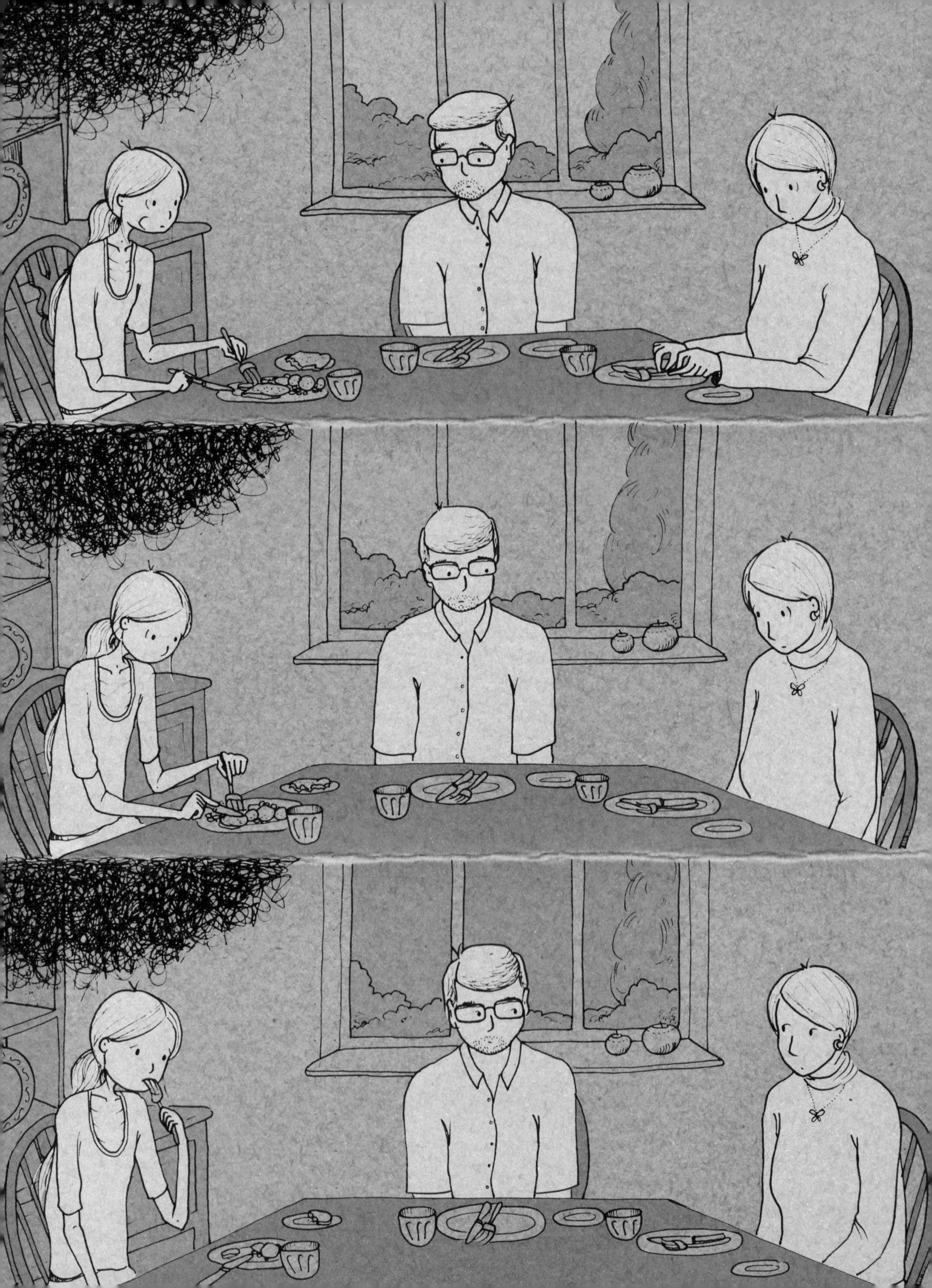

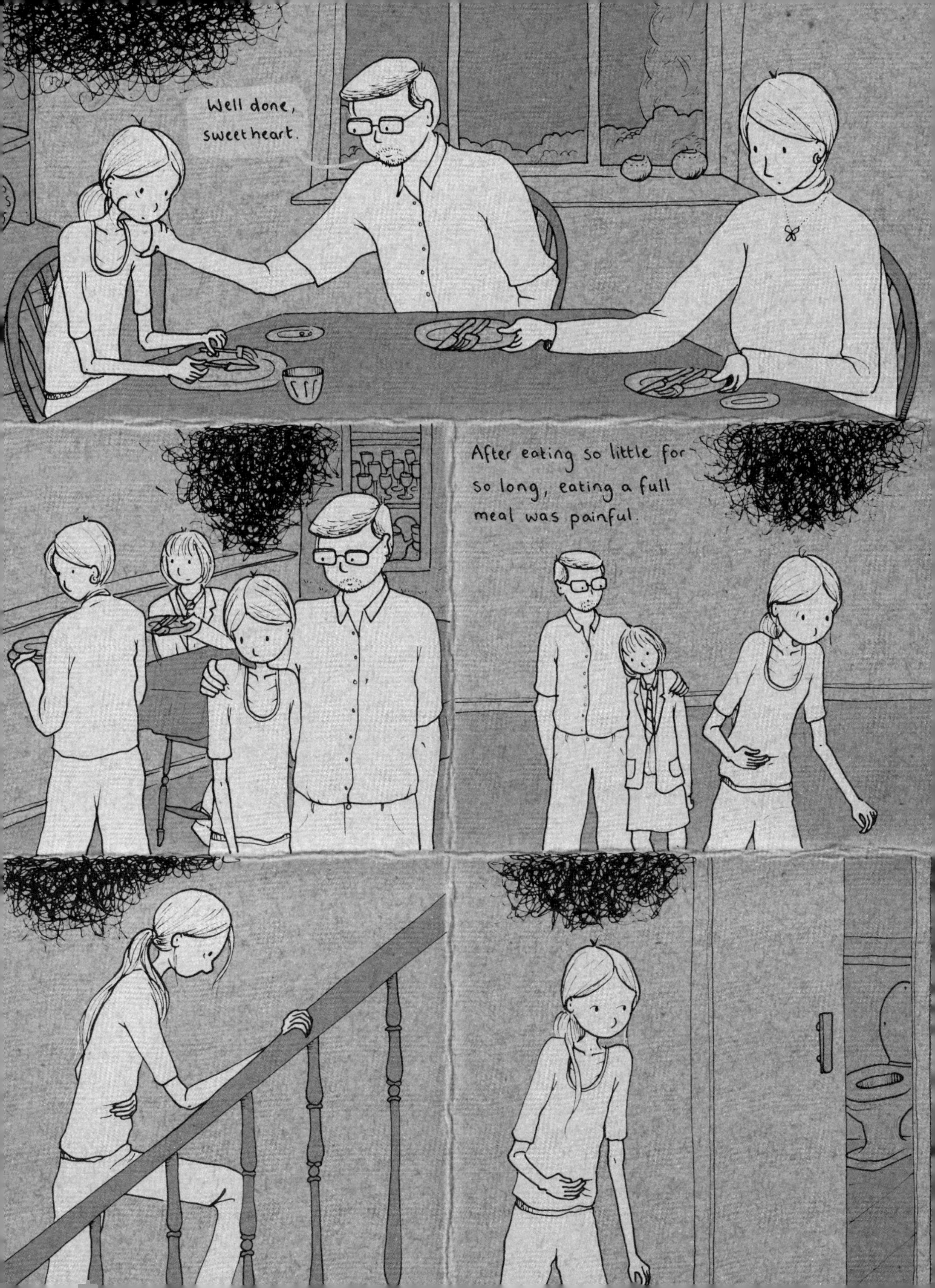
Well done, sweetheart.
After eating so little for so long, eating a full meal was painful.

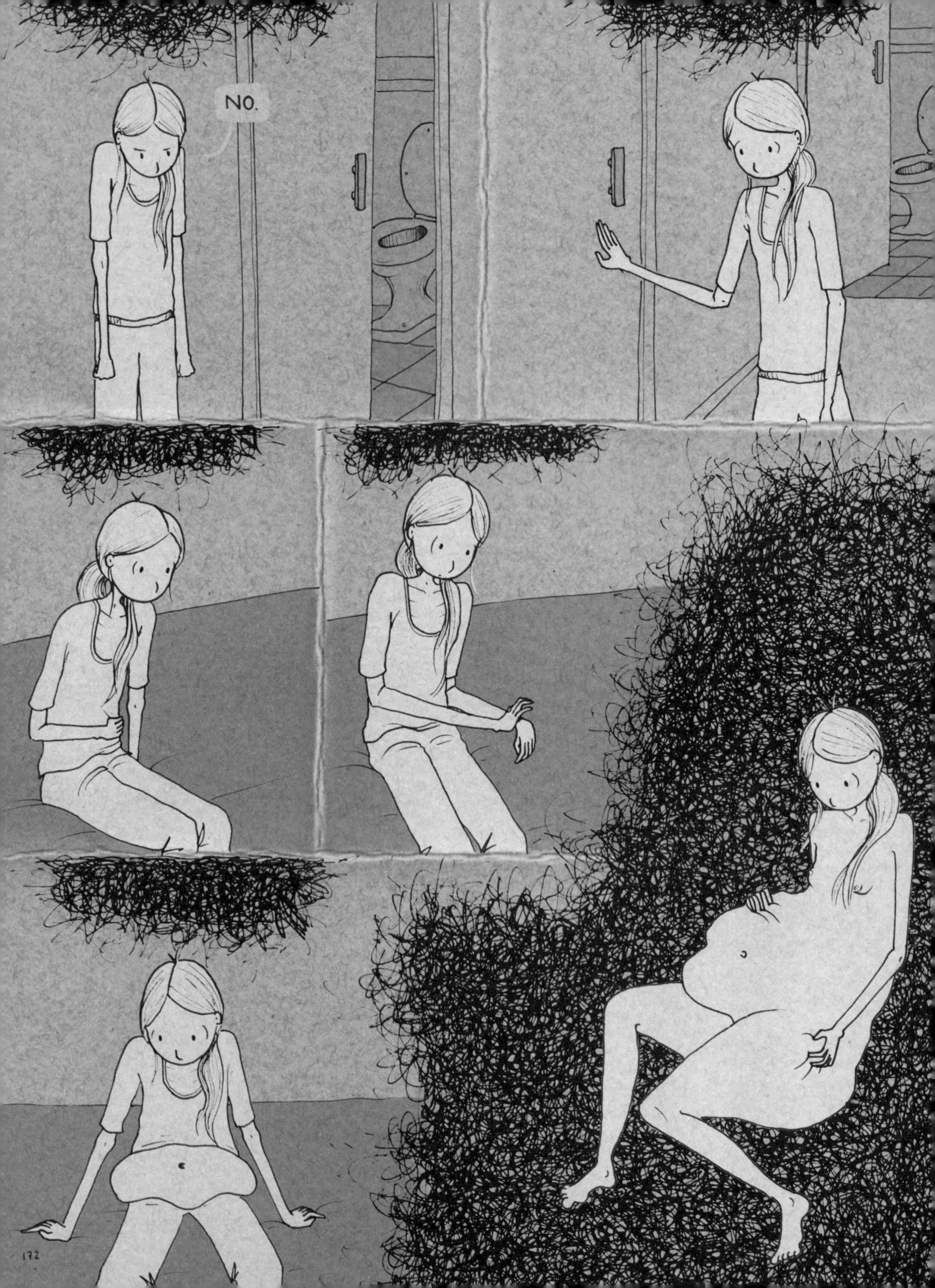
NO.

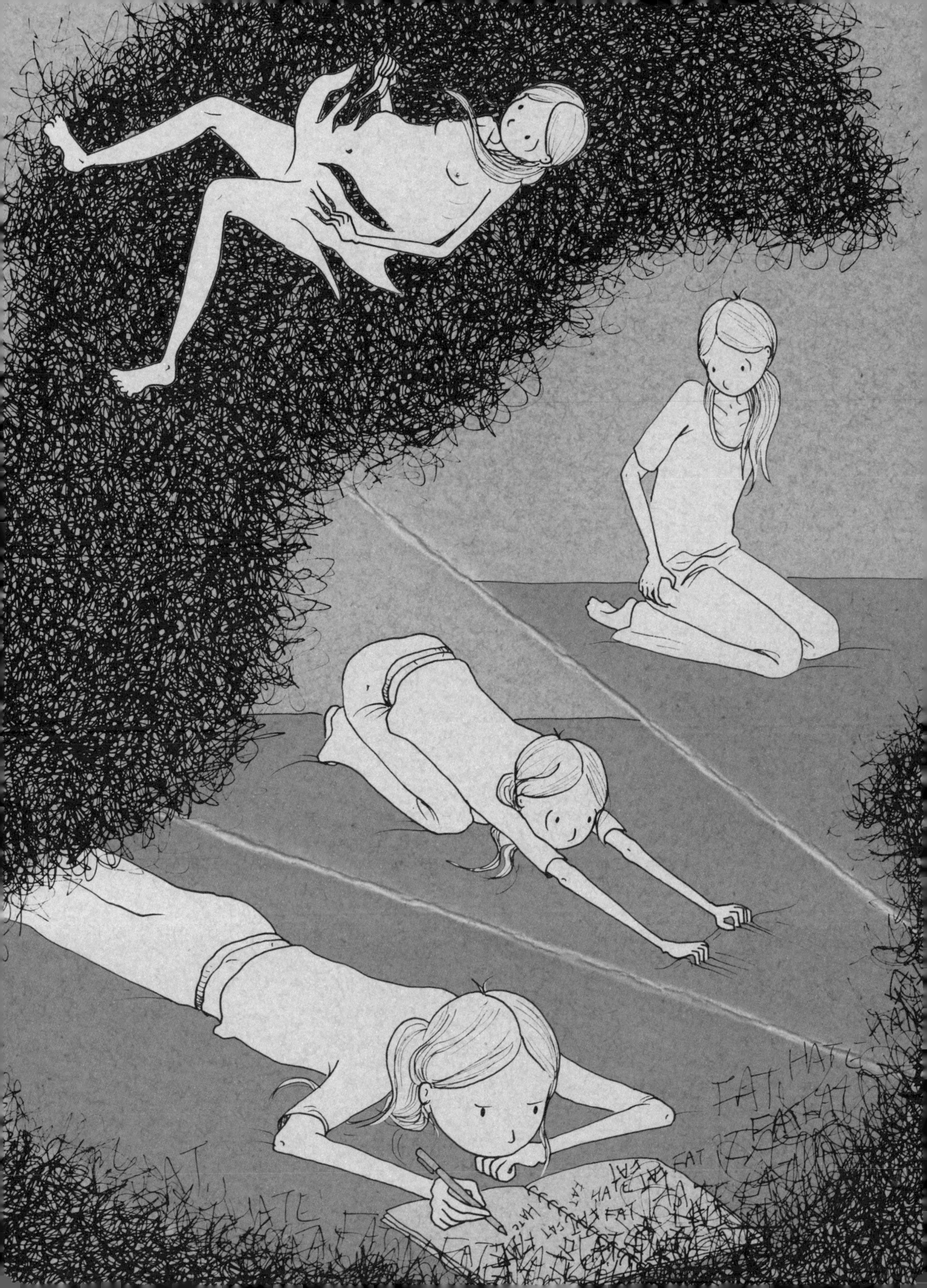
HATE
FAT
FAT
HATE
FAT

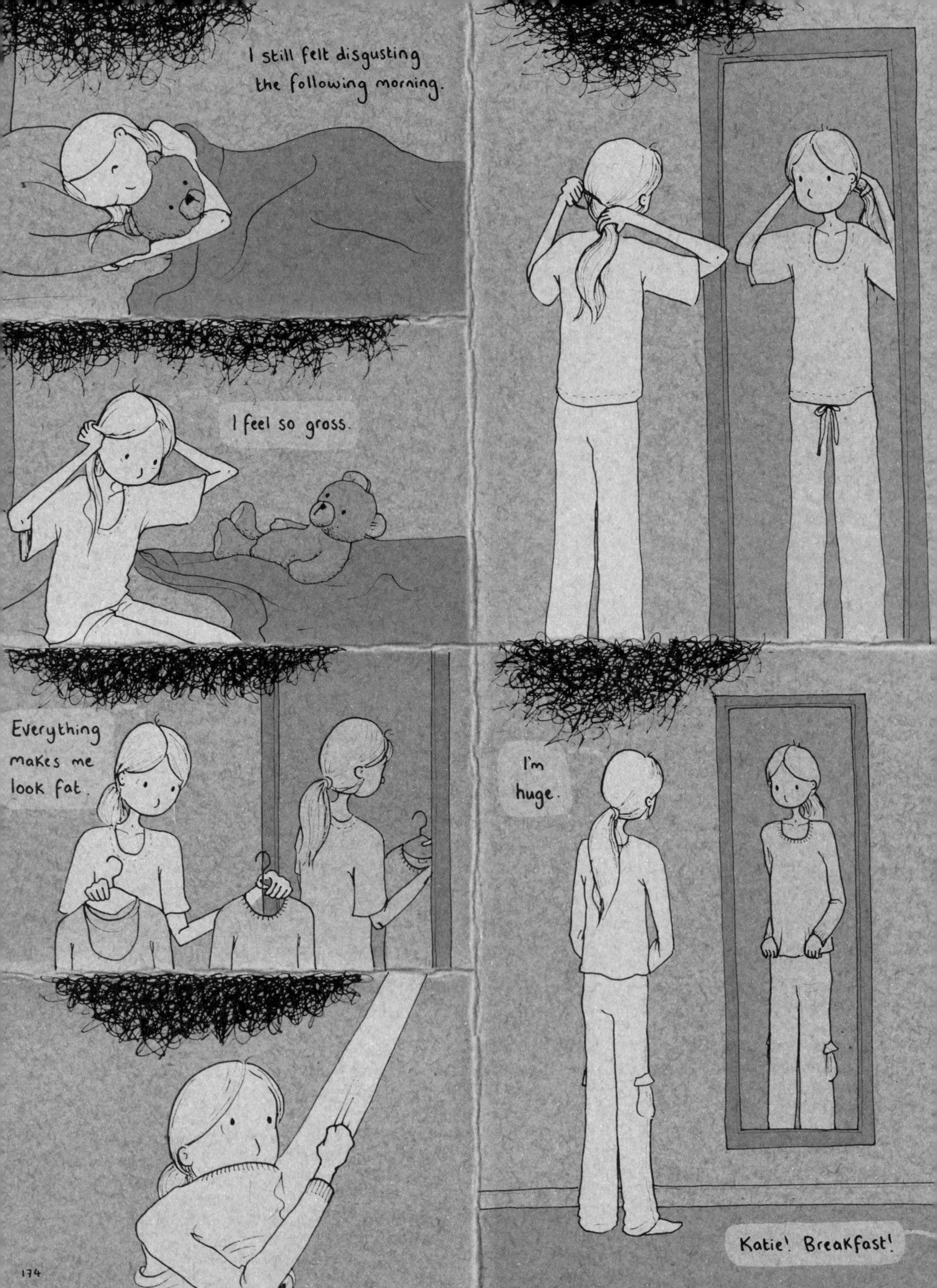
I still felt disgusting the following morning.
I feel so gross.
Everything makes me look fat.
I'm huge.
Katie! Breakfast!

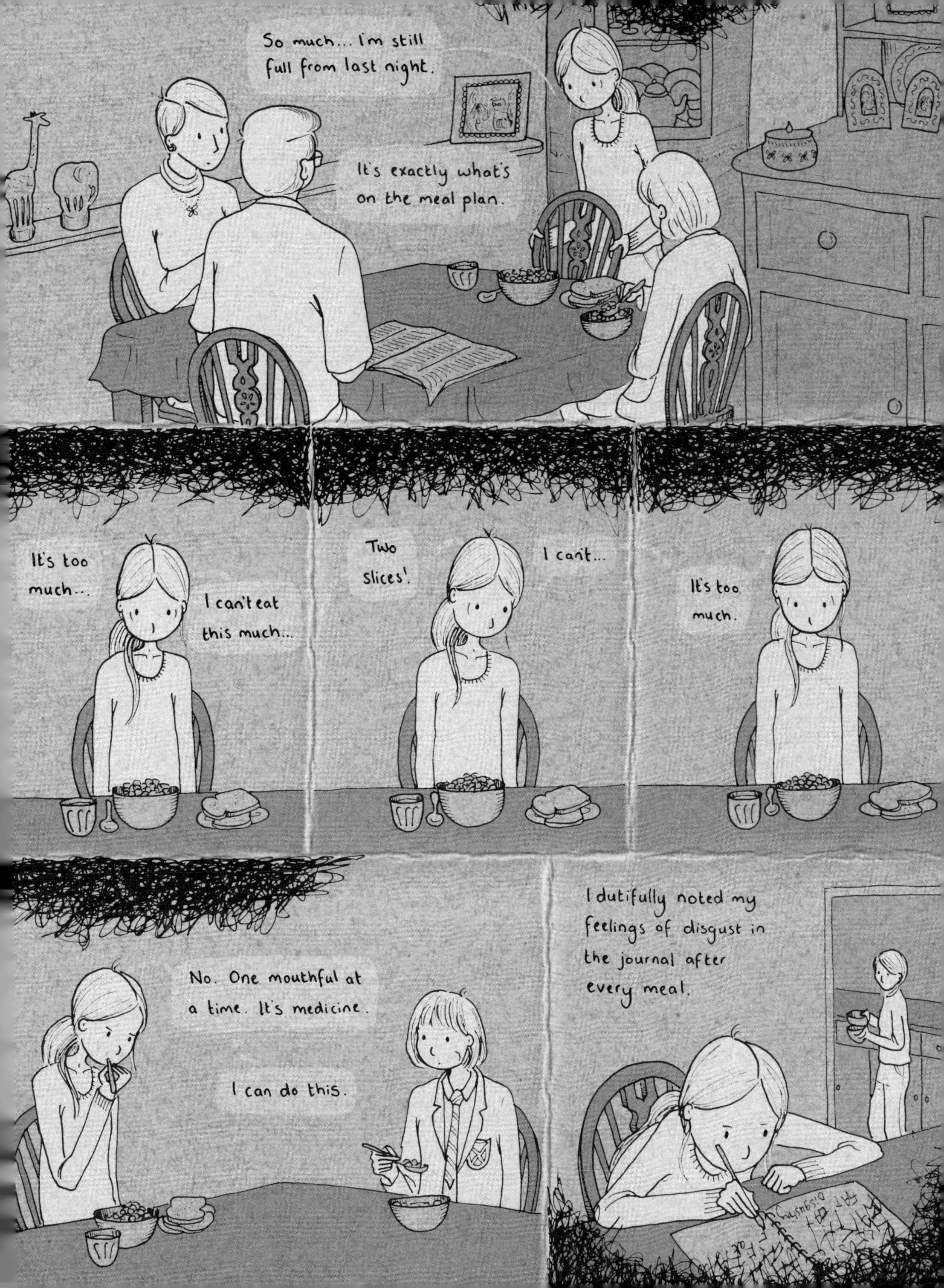
So much... I'm still full from last night.
It's exactly what's on the meal plan.
It's too much...
I can't eat this much...
Two slices!
I can't...
It's too much.
No. One mouthful at a time. It's medicine.
I can do this.
I dutifully noted my feelings of disgust in the journal after every meal.

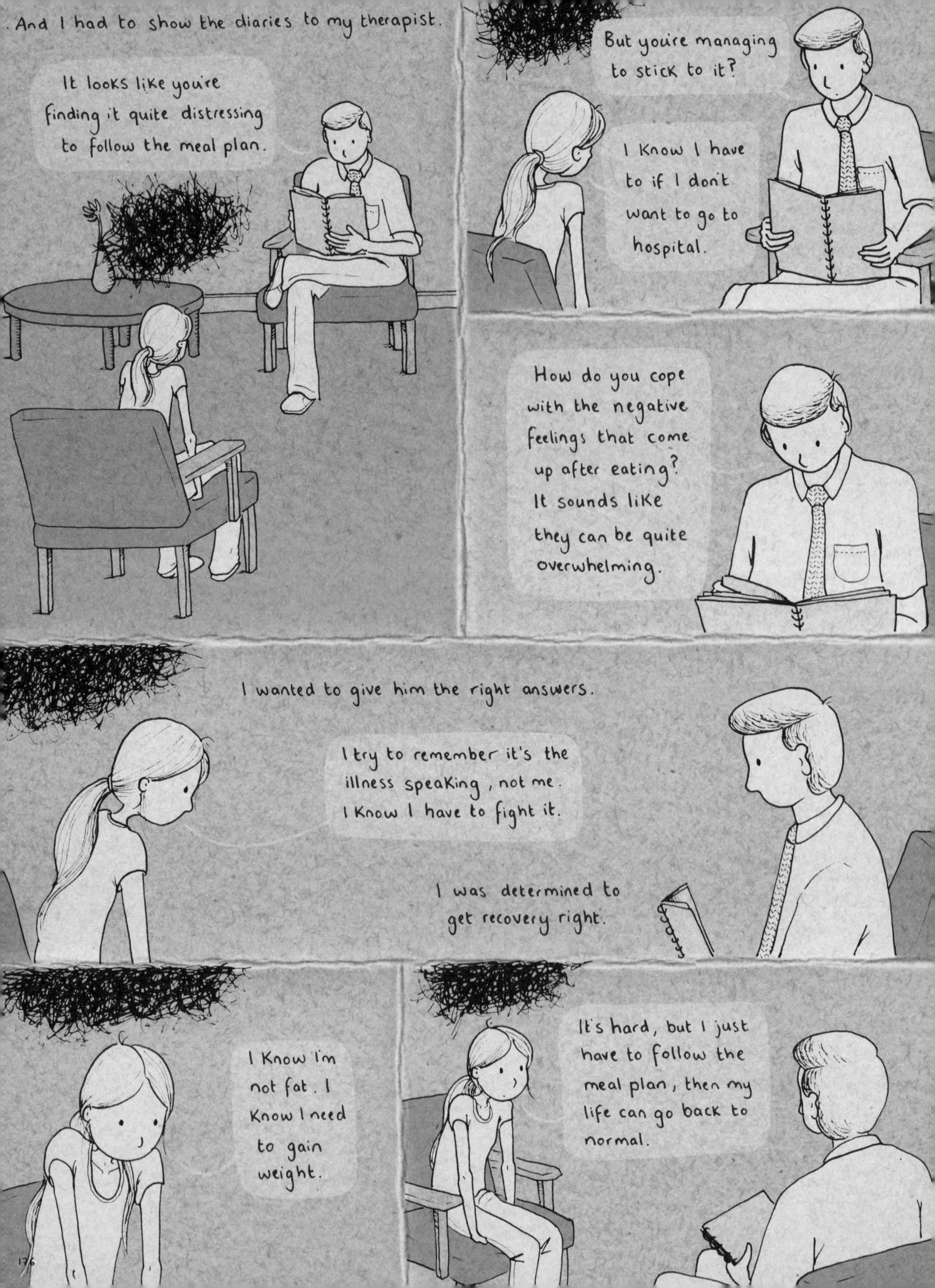

. And I had to show the diaries to my therapist.
It looks like you're finding it quite distressing to follow the meal plan.
But you're managing to stick to it?
I know I have to if I don't want to go to hospital.
How do you cope with the negative feelings that come up after eating? It sounds like they can be quite overwhelming.
I wanted to give him the right answers.
I try to remember it's the illness speaking, not me. I know I have to fight it.
I was determined to get recovery right.
I know I'm not fat. I know I need to gain weight.
It's hard, but I just have to follow the meal plan, then my life can go back to normal.

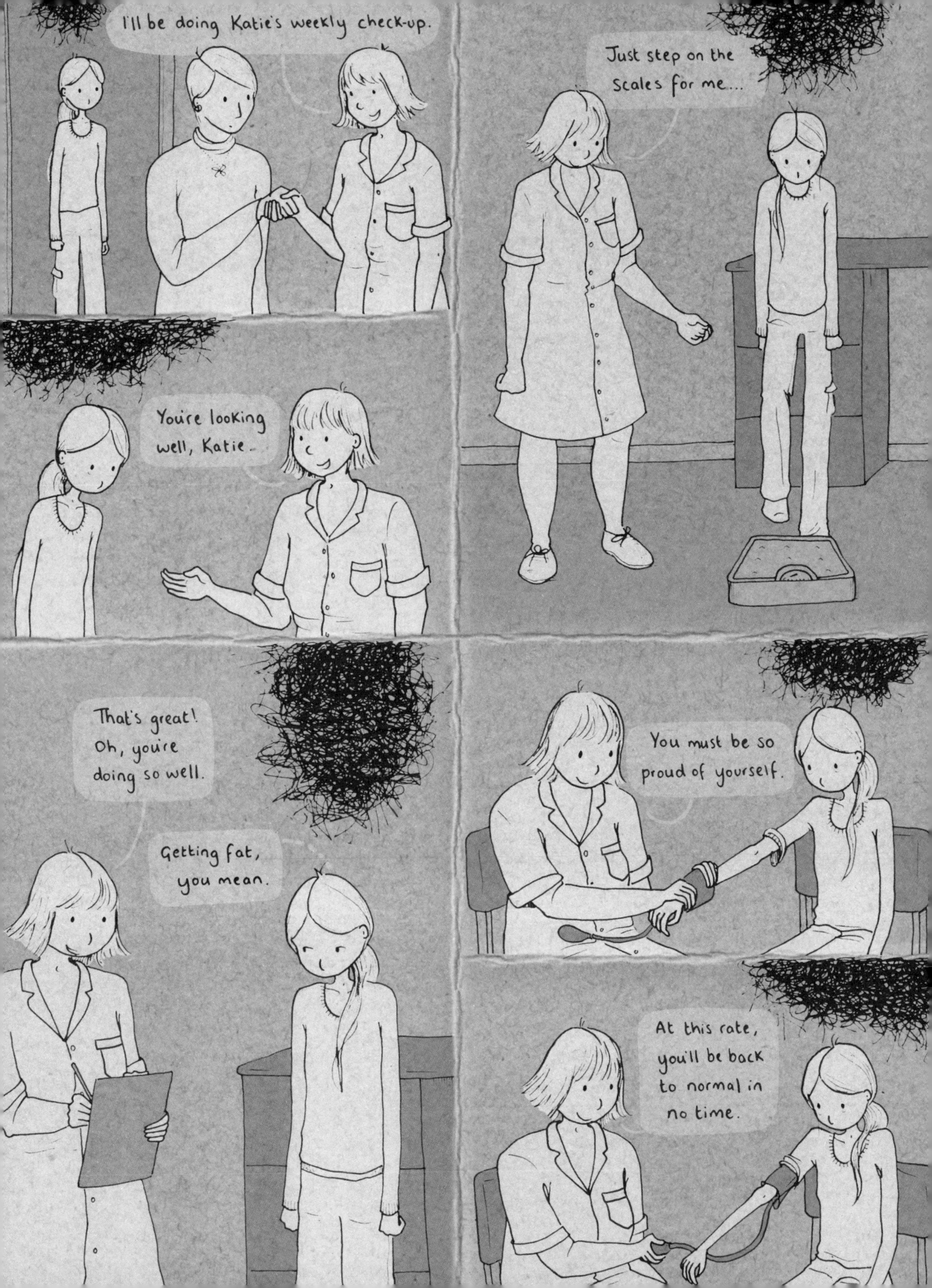
I'll be doing Katie's weekly check-up.
Just step on the scales for me...
You're looking well, Katie.
That's great! Oh, you're doing so well.
Getting fat, you mean.
You must be so proud of yourself.
At this rate, you'll be back to normal in no time.

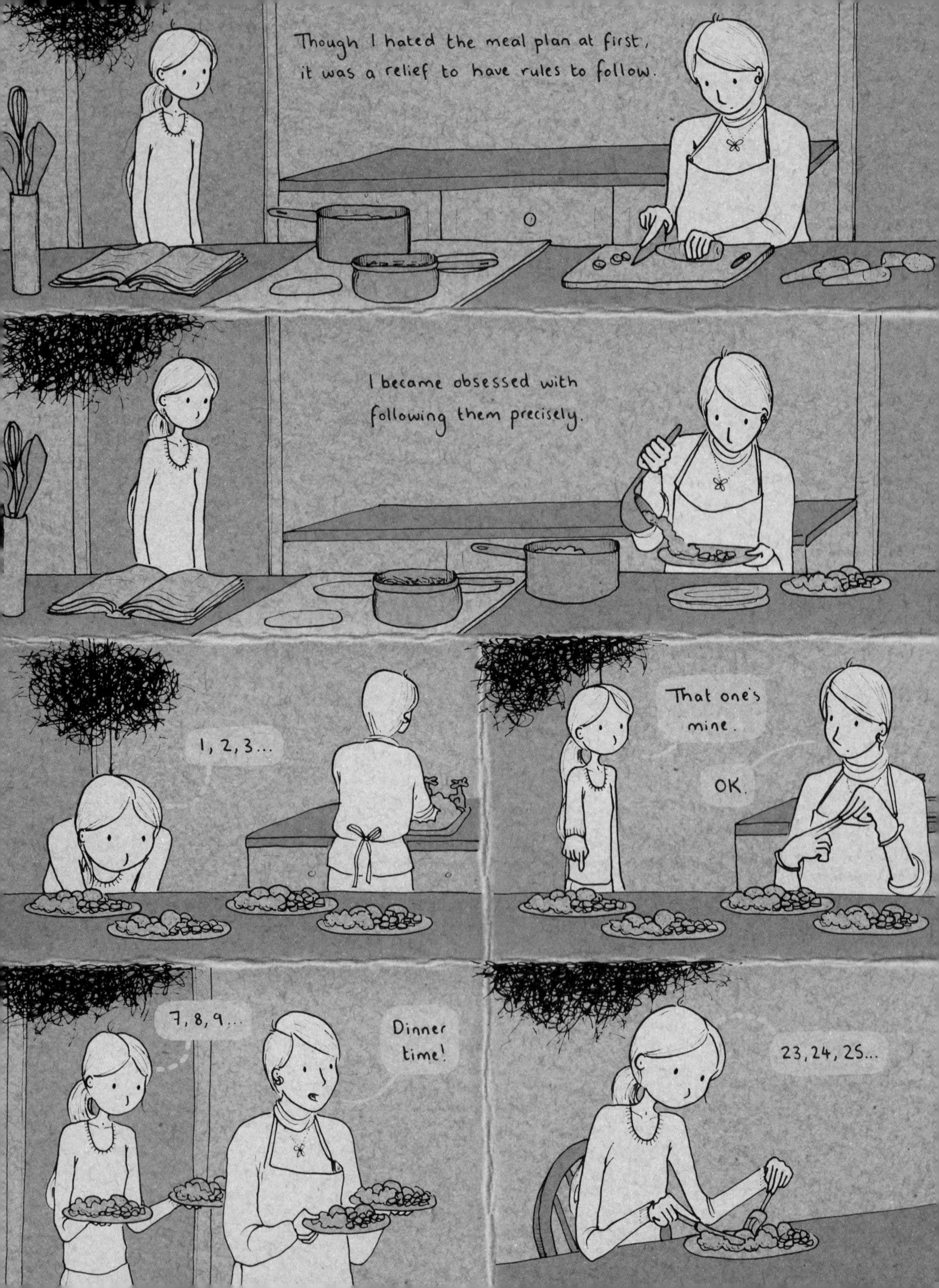

Though I hated the meal plan at first, it was a relief to have rules to follow.
I became obsessed with following them precisely.
1, 2, 3...
That one's mine.
OK.
7, 8, 9...
Dinner time!
23, 24, 25...

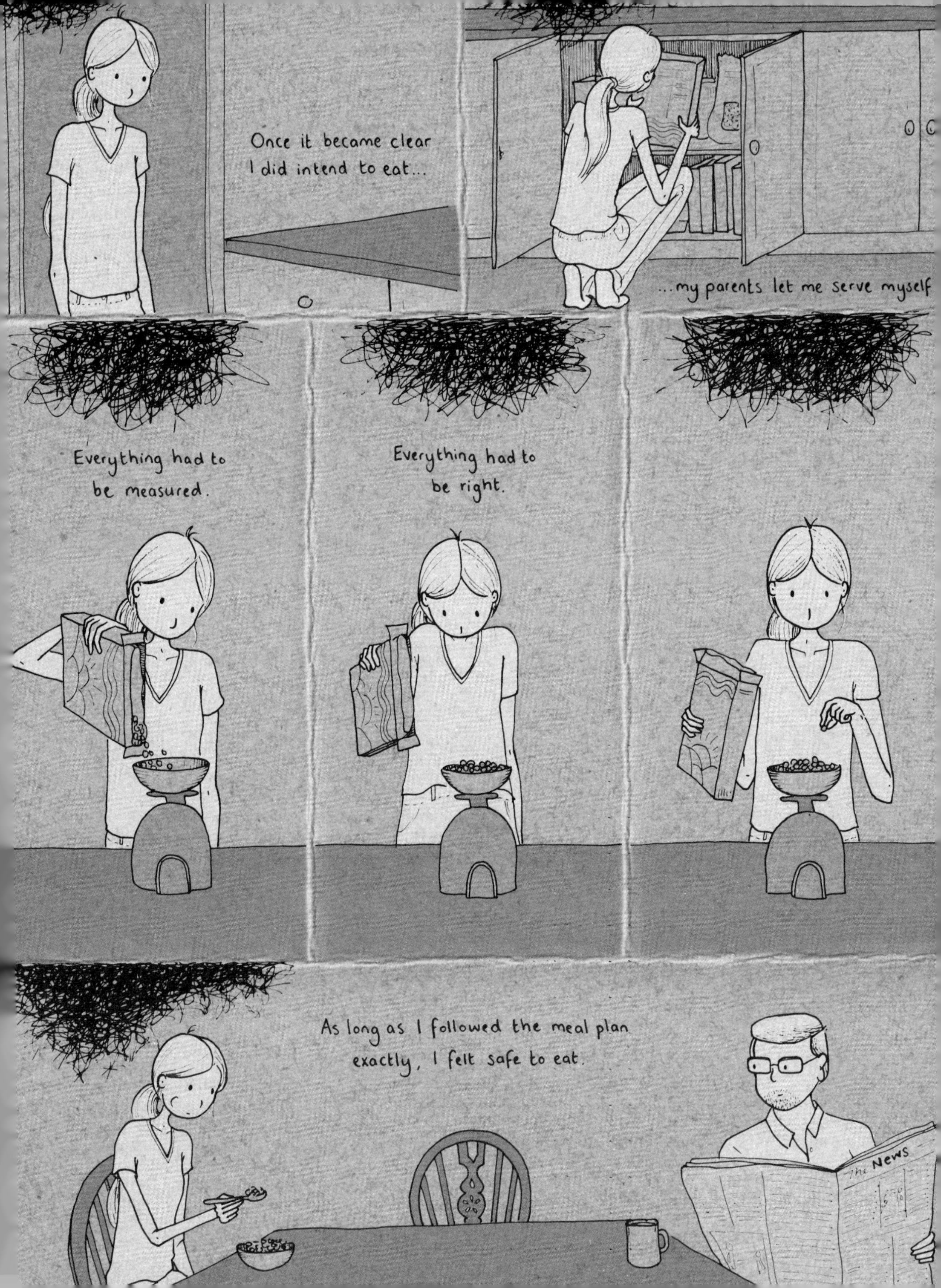
Once it became clear
I did intend to eat...
...my parents let me serve myself
Everything had to
be measured.
Everything had to
be right.
As long as I followed the meal plan
exactly, I felt safe to eat.
The News

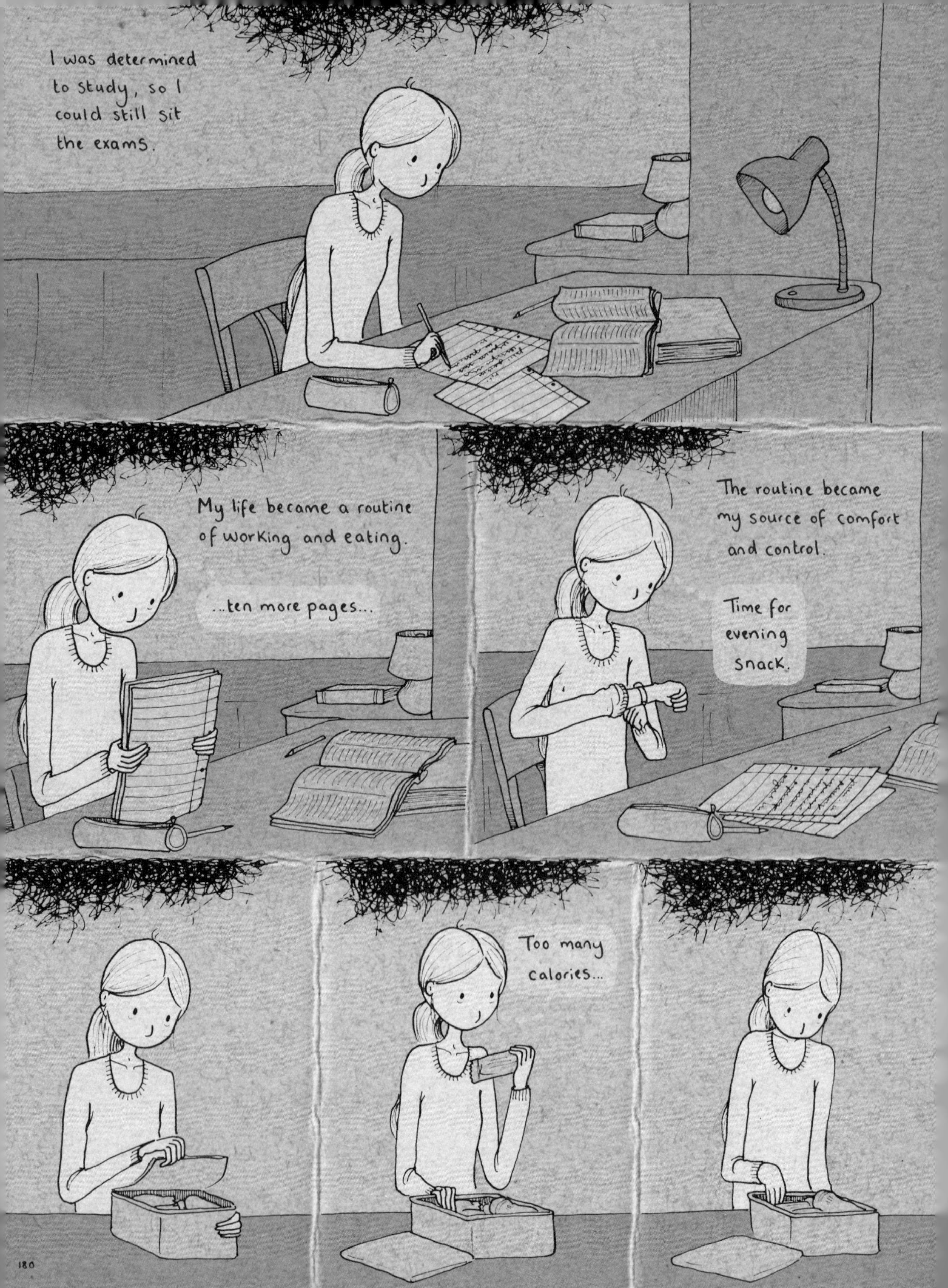
I was determined to study, so I could still sit the exams.
My life became a routine of working and eating.
...ten more pages...
The routine became my source of comfort and control.
Time for evening snack.
Too many calories...

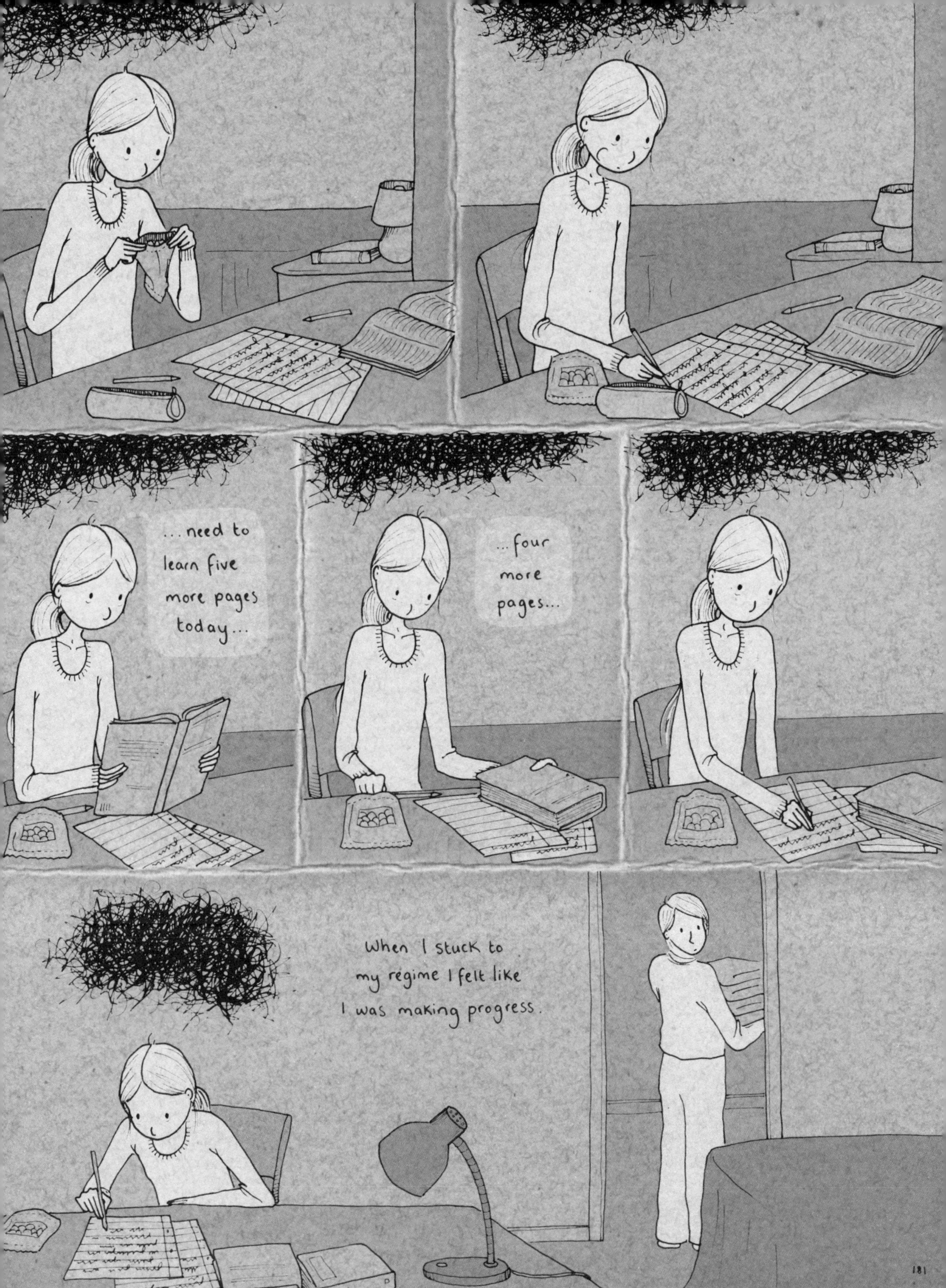
...need to learn five more pages today...
...four more pages...
When I stuck to my regime I felt like I was making progress.

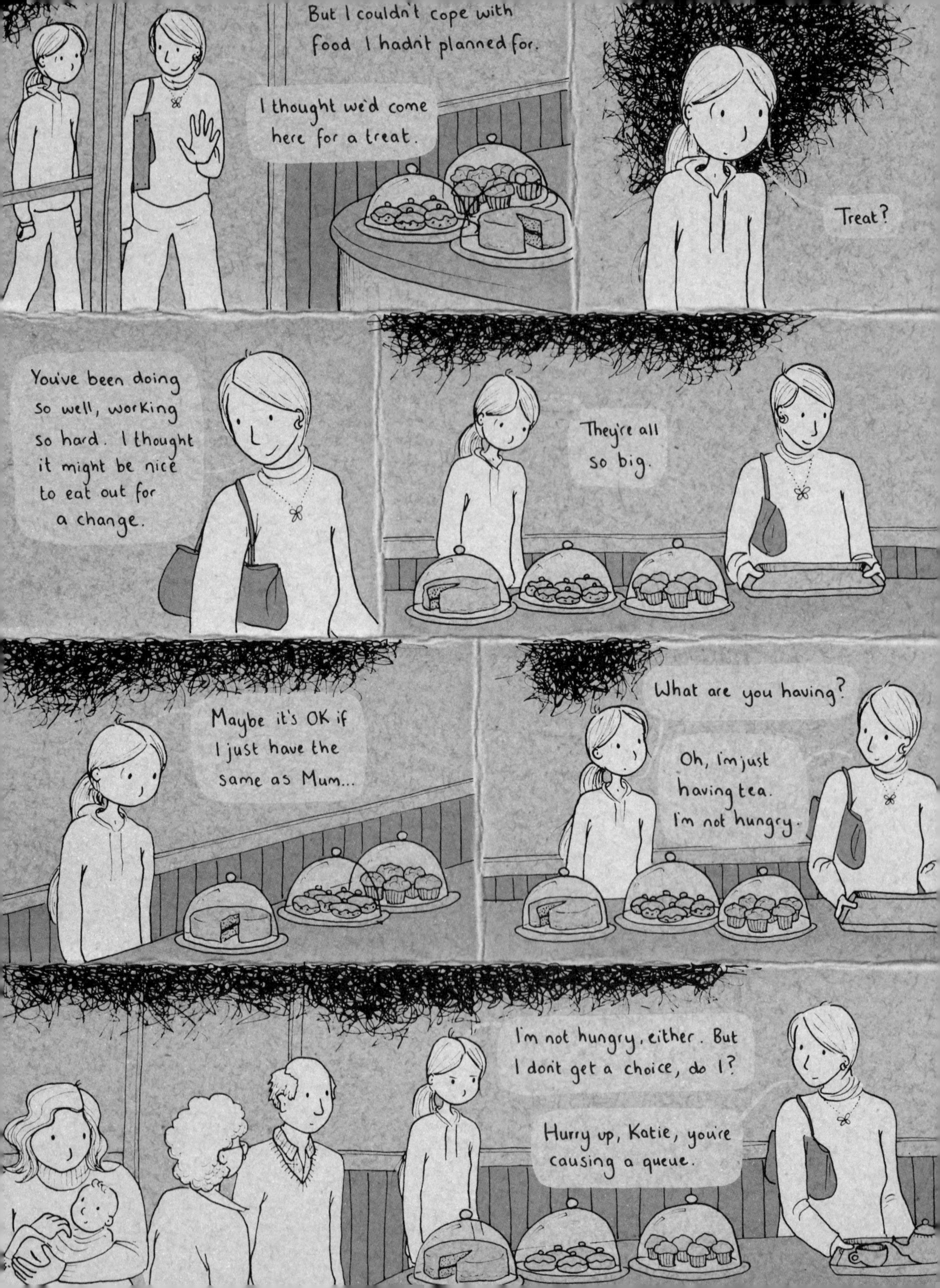
But I couldn't cope with food I hadn't planned for.
I thought we'd come here for a treat.
Treat?
You've been doing so well, working so hard. I thought it might be nice to eat out for a change.
They're all so big.
Maybe it's OK if I just have the same as Mum...
What are you having?
Oh, I'm just having tea. I'm not hungry.
I'm not hungry, either. But I don't get a choice, do I?
Hurry up, Katie, you're causing a queue.

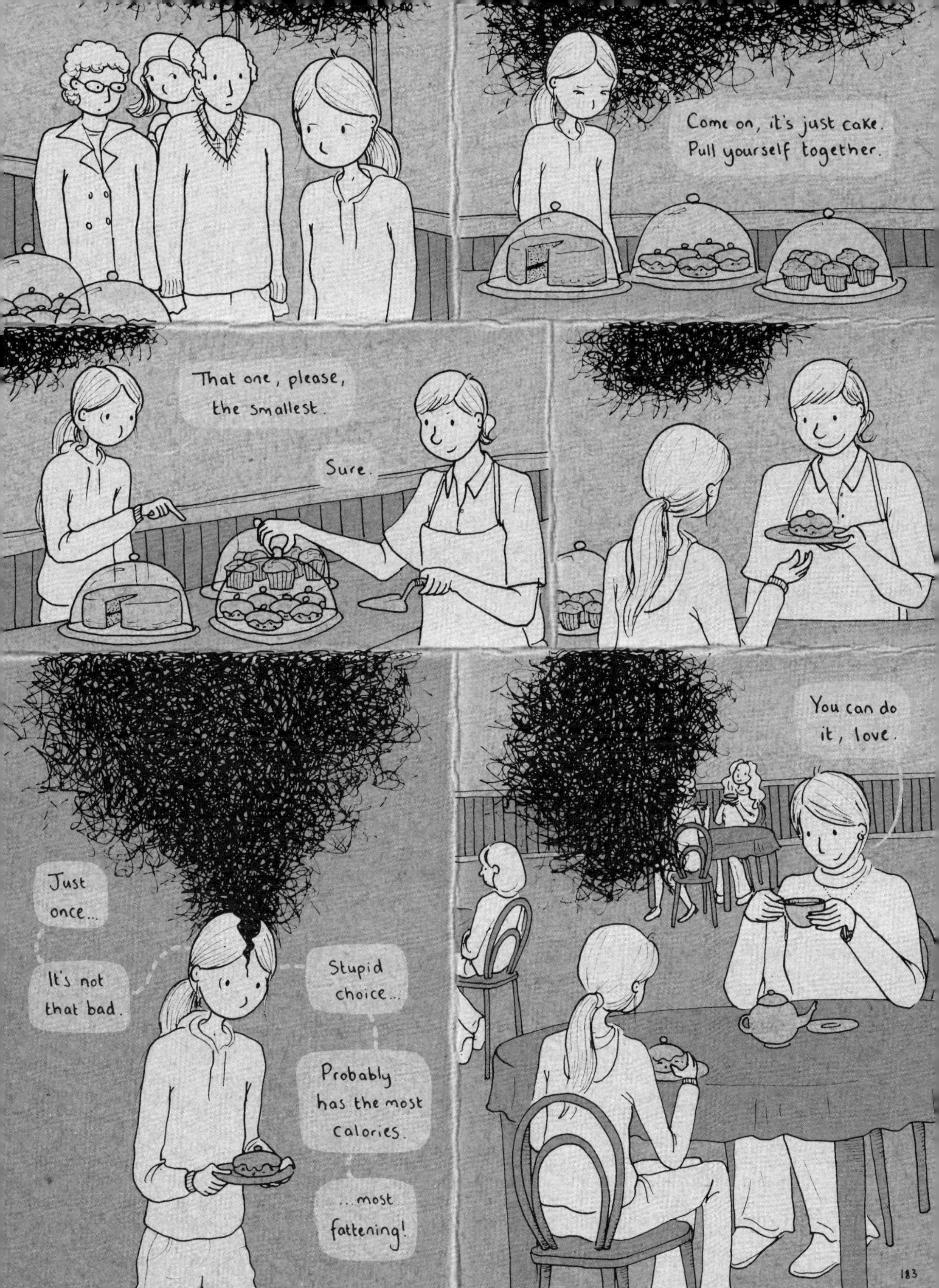
Come on, it's just cake. Pull yourself together.
That one, please, the smallest.
Sure.
Just once...
It's not that bad.
Stupid choice...
Probably has the most calories.
...most fattening!
You can do it, love.

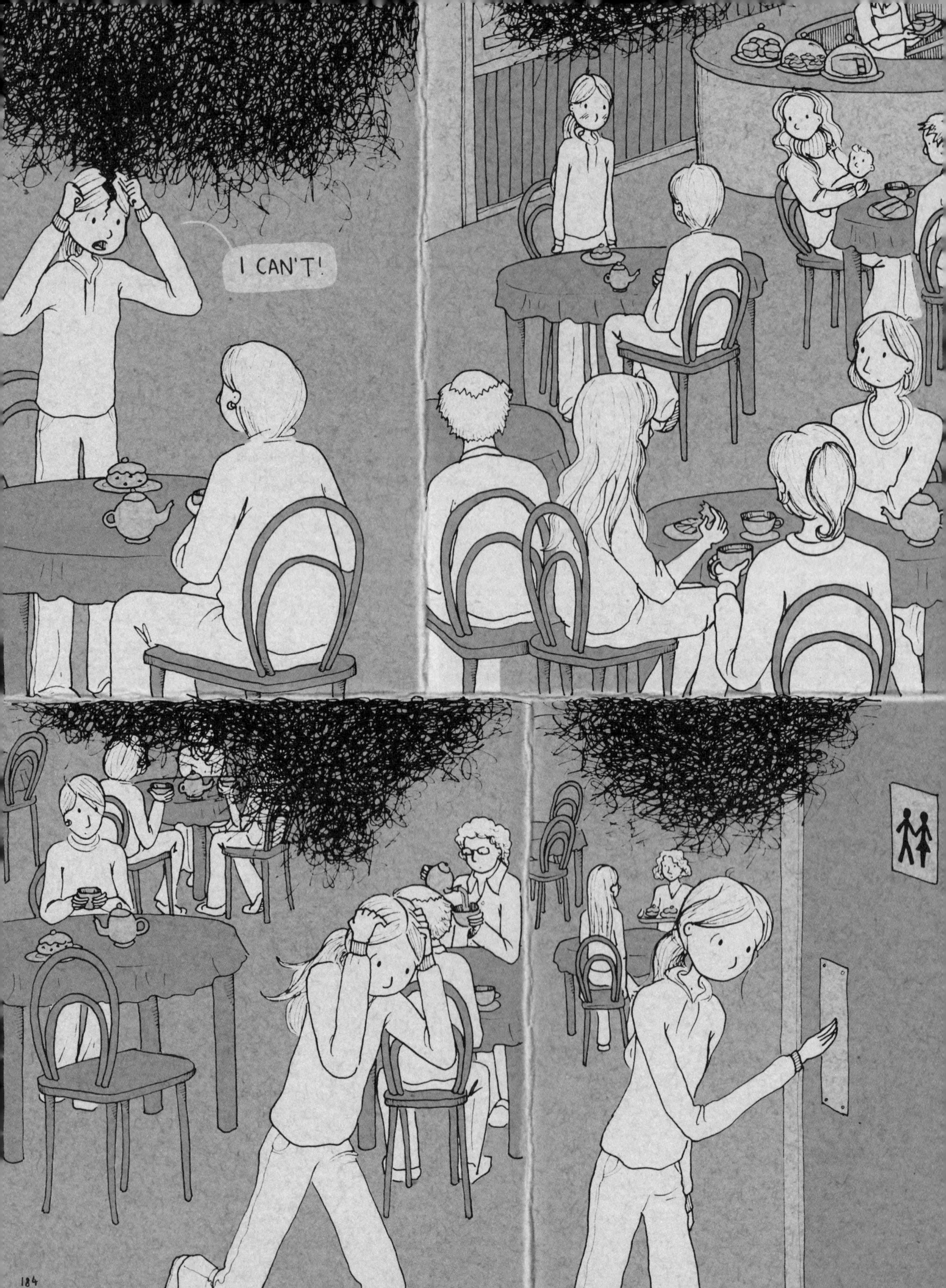
I CAN'T!

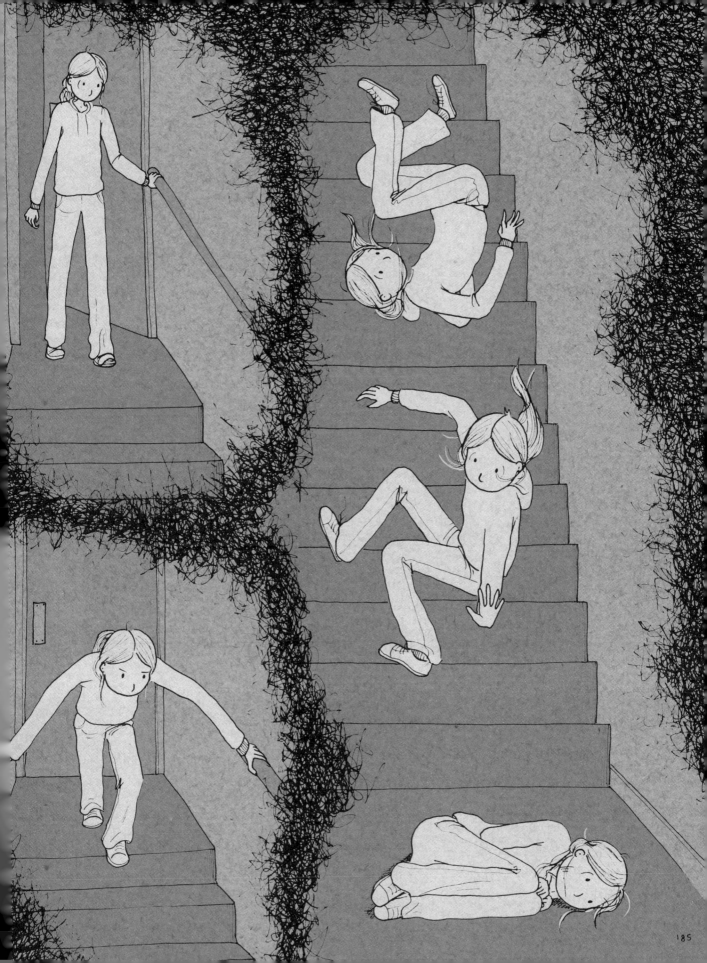

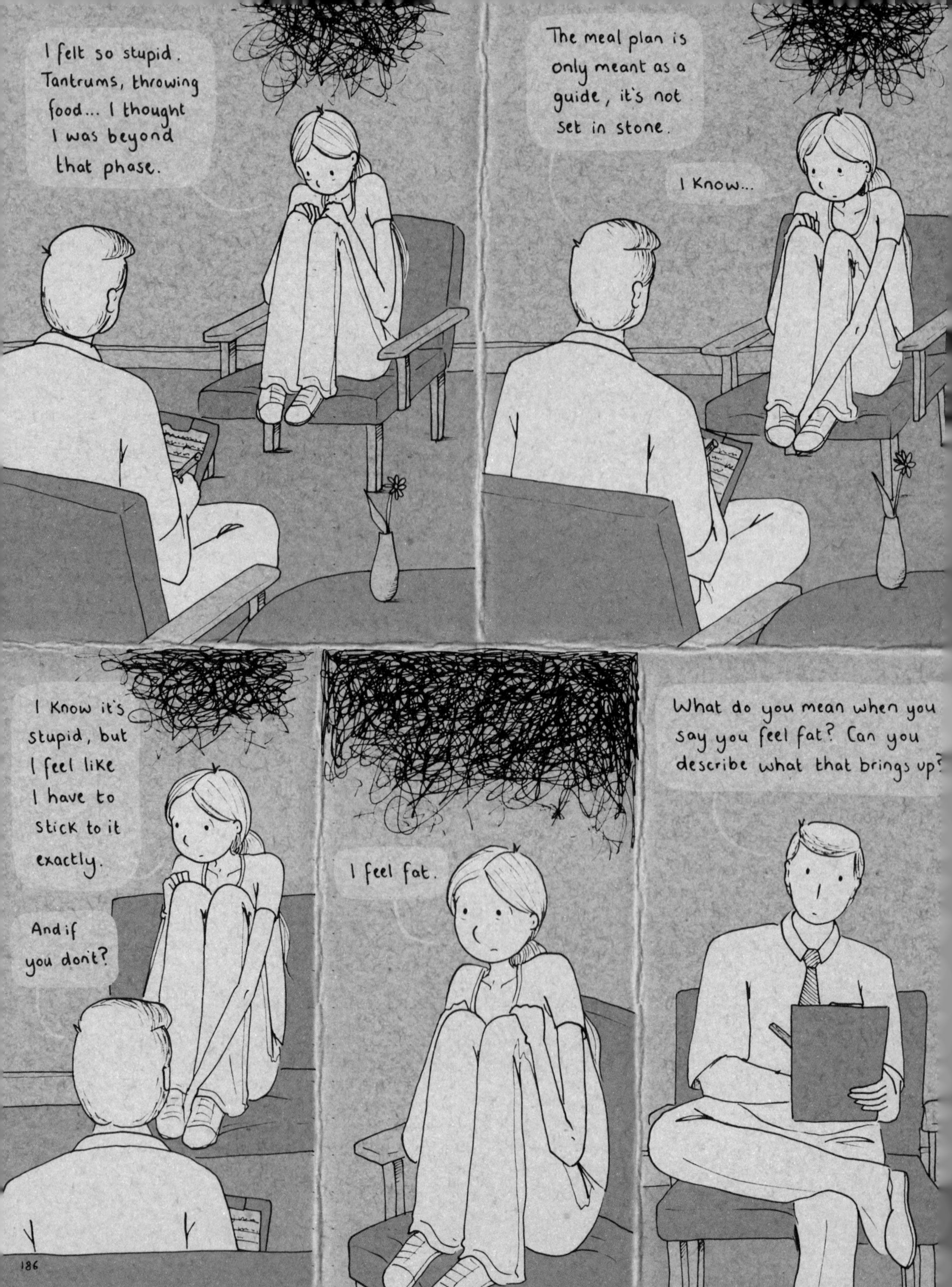
I felt so stupid. Tantrums, throwing food... I thought I was beyond that phase.
The meal plan is only meant as a guide, it's not set in stone.
I know...
I know it's stupid, but I feel like I have to stick to it exactly.
And if you don't?
I feel fat.
What do you mean when you say you feel fat? Can you describe what that brings up?

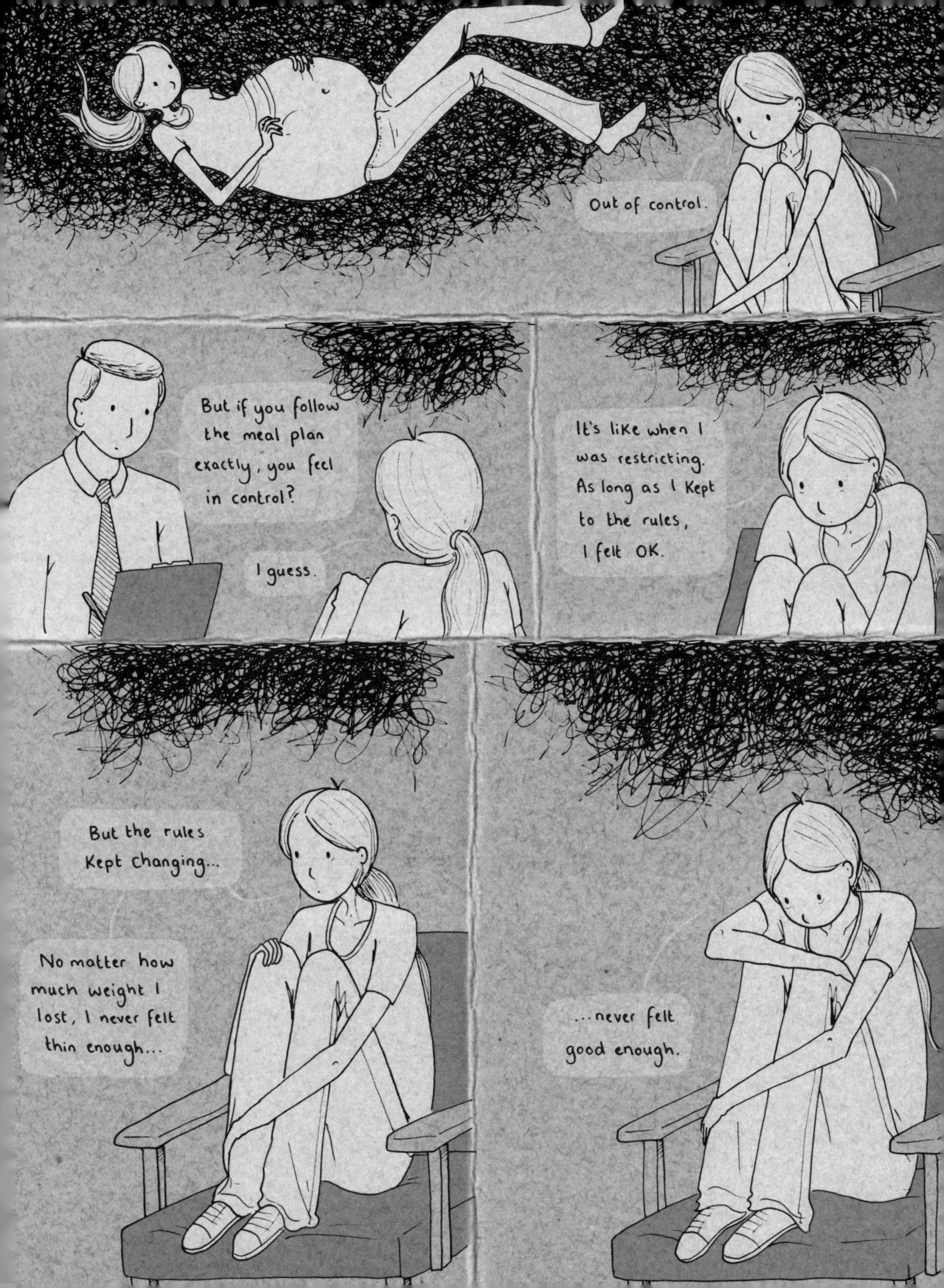
Out of control.
But if you follow the meal plan exactly, you feel in control?
I guess.
It's like when I was restricting. As long as I kept to the rules, I felt OK.
But the rules kept changing...
No matter how much weight I lost, I never felt thin enough...
...never felt good enough.

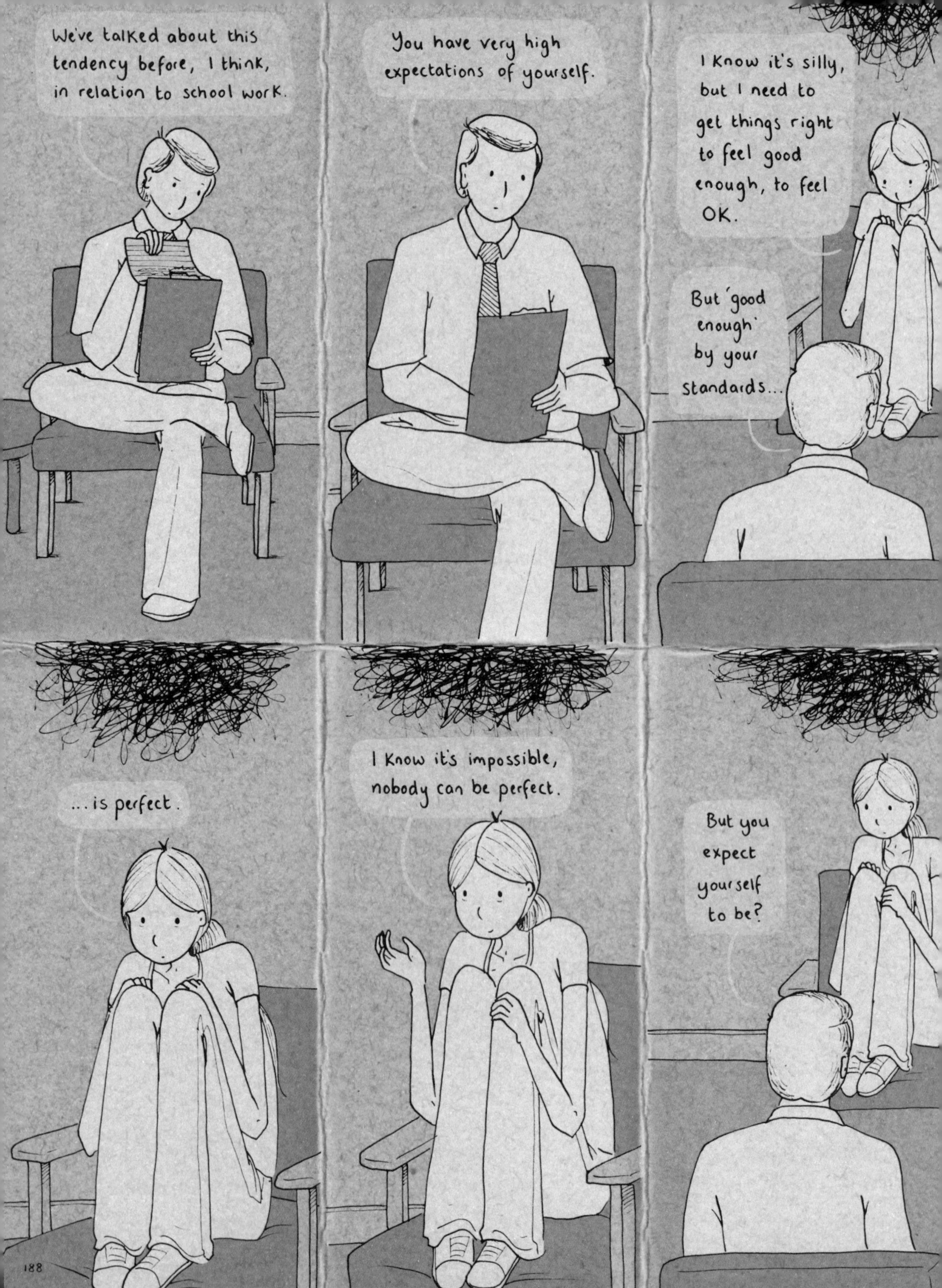

We've talked about this tendency before, I think, in relation to school work.
You have very high expectations of yourself.
I know it's silly, but I need to get things right to feel good enough, to feel OK.
But 'good enough' by your standards...
... is perfect.
I know it's impossible, nobody can be perfect.
But you expect yourself to be?

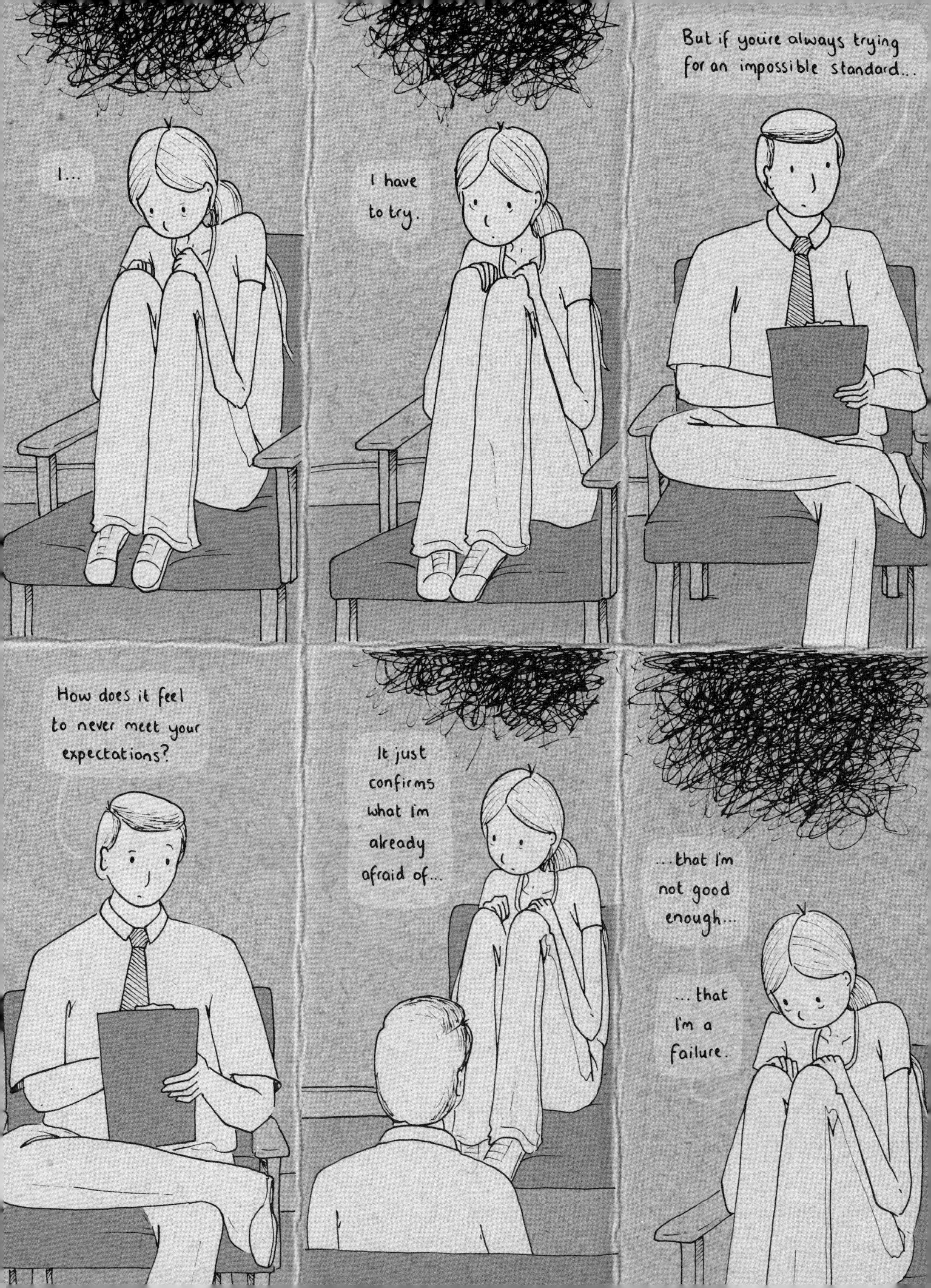
I...
I have to try.
But if youre always trying for an impossible standard...
How does it feel to never meet your expectations?
It just confirms what I'm already afraid of...
...that I'm not good enough...
...that I'm a failure.

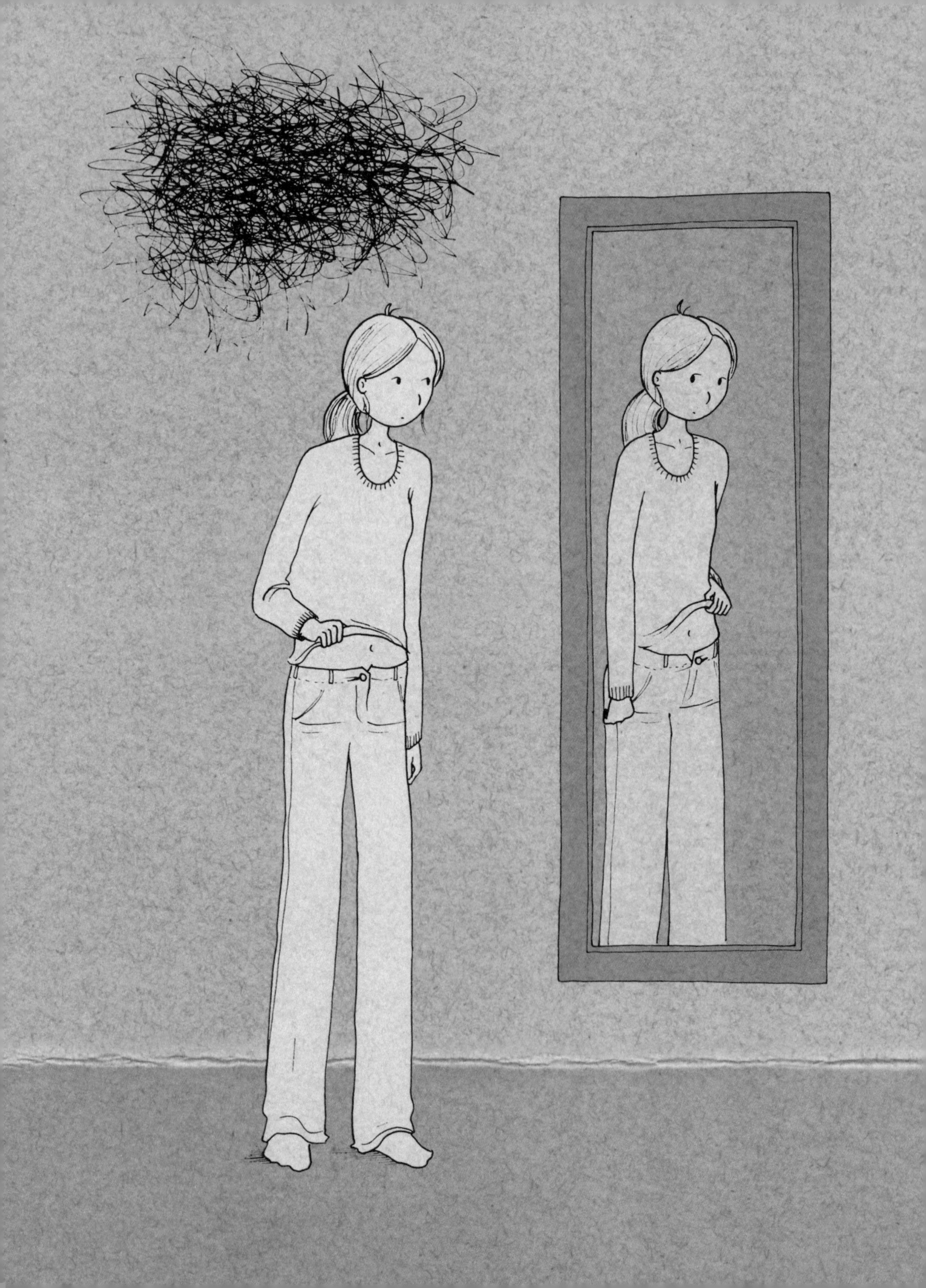

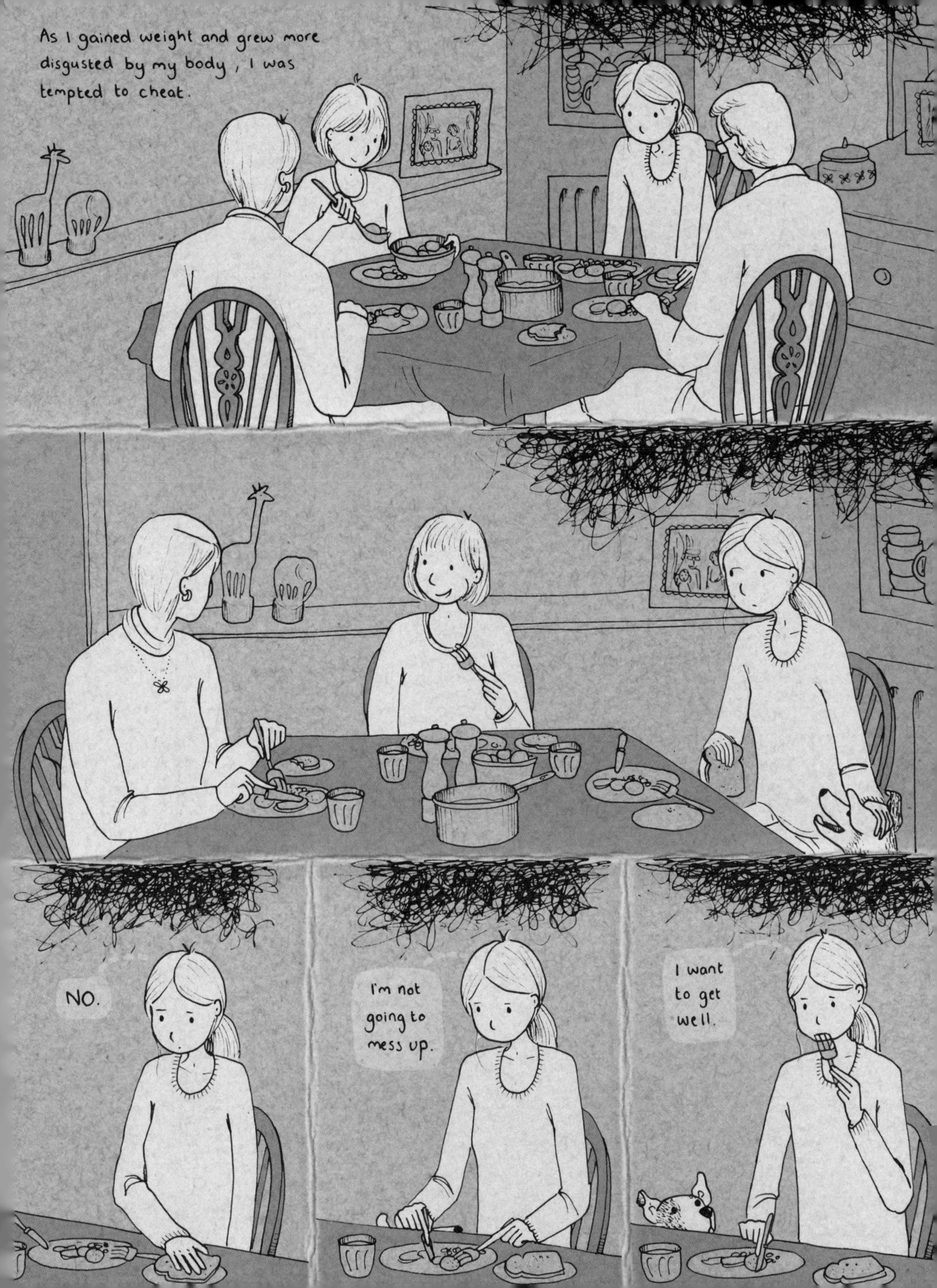
As I gained weight and grew more disgusted by my body, I was tempted to cheat.
NO.
I'm not going to mess up.
I want to get well.

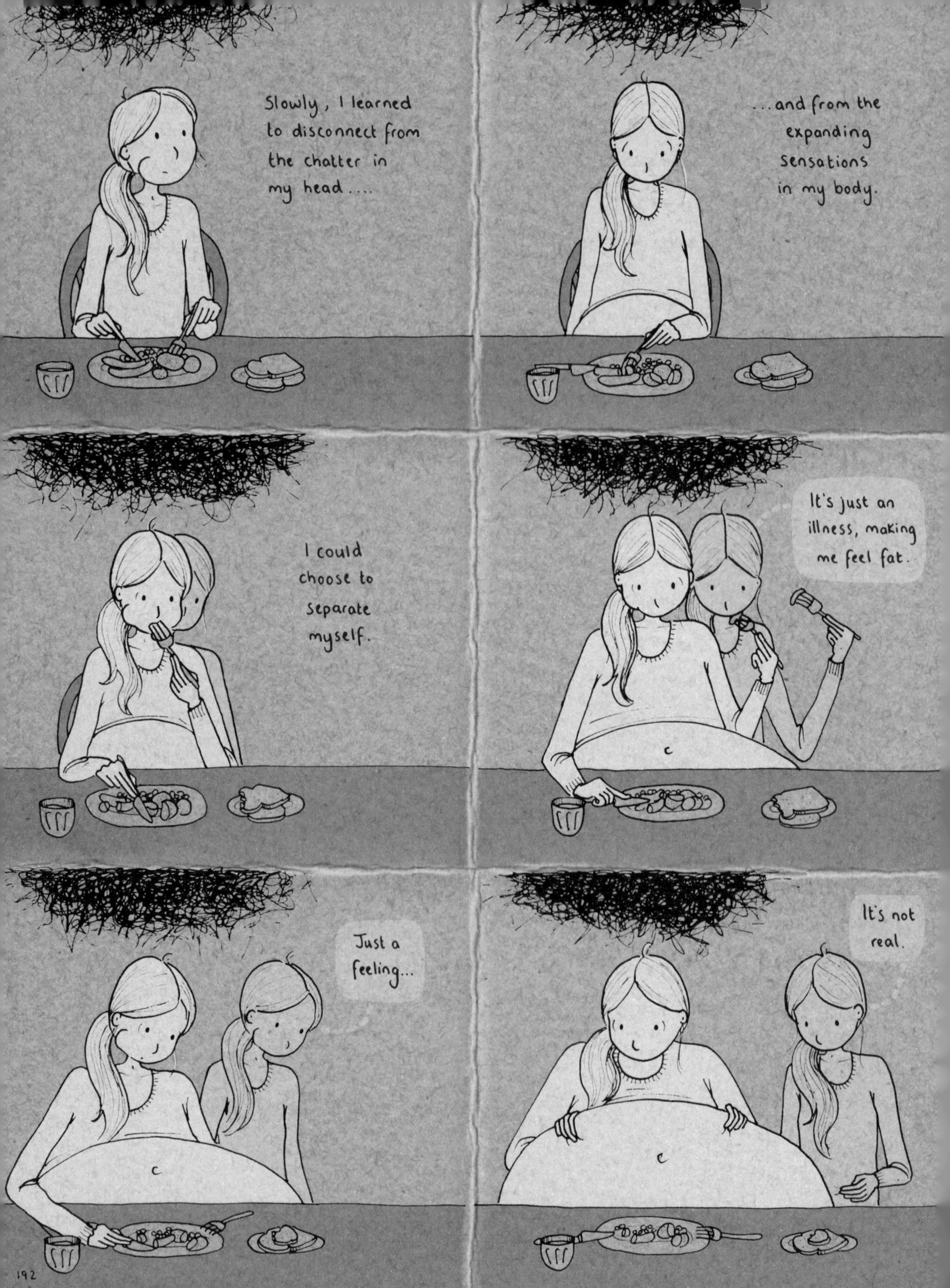
Slowly, I learned to disconnect from the chatter in my head....
...and from the expanding sensations in my body.
I could choose to separate myself.
It's just an illness, making me feel fat.
Just a feeling...
It's not real.

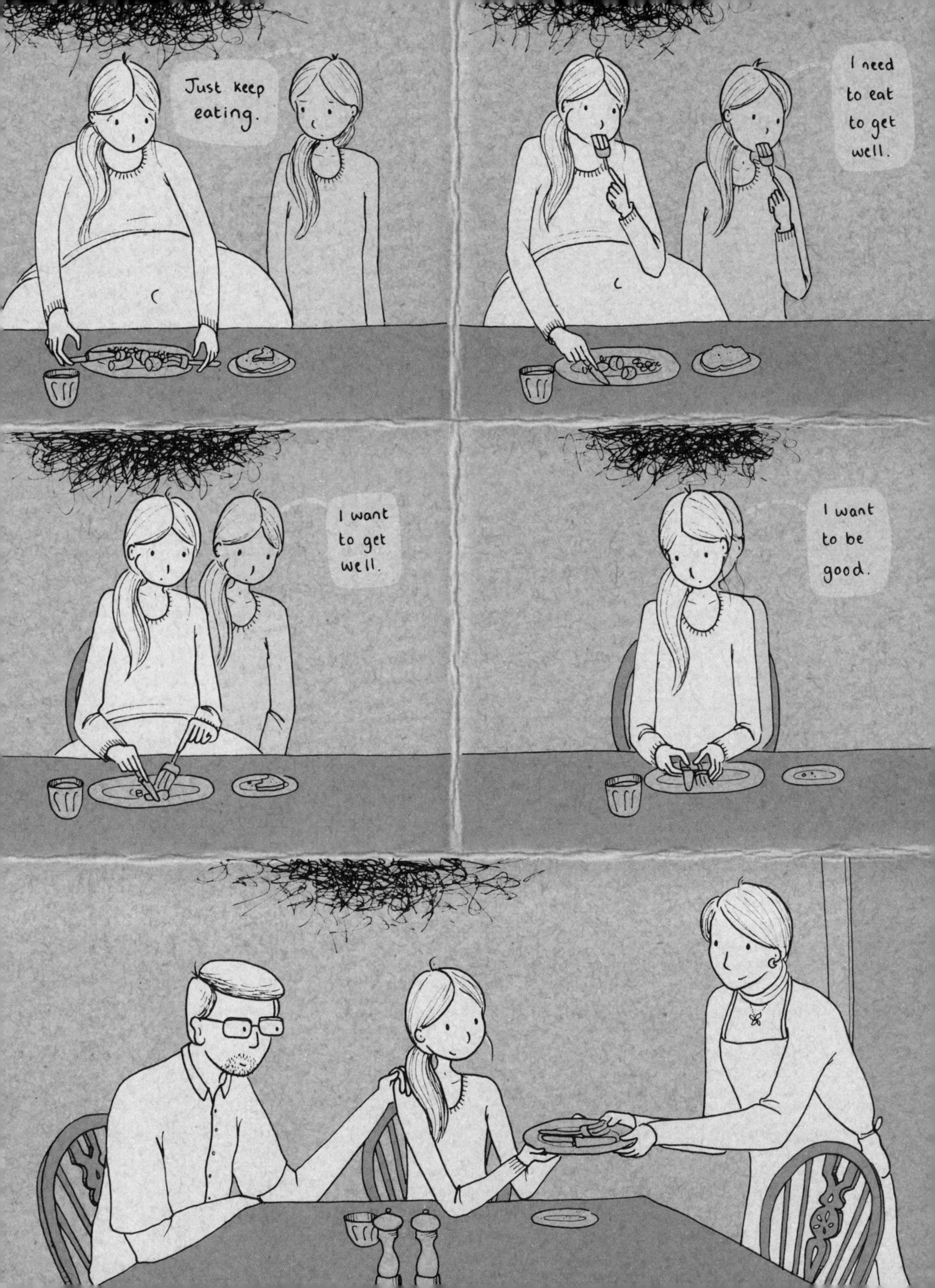
Just keep eating.
I need to eat to get well.
I want to get well.
I want to be good.

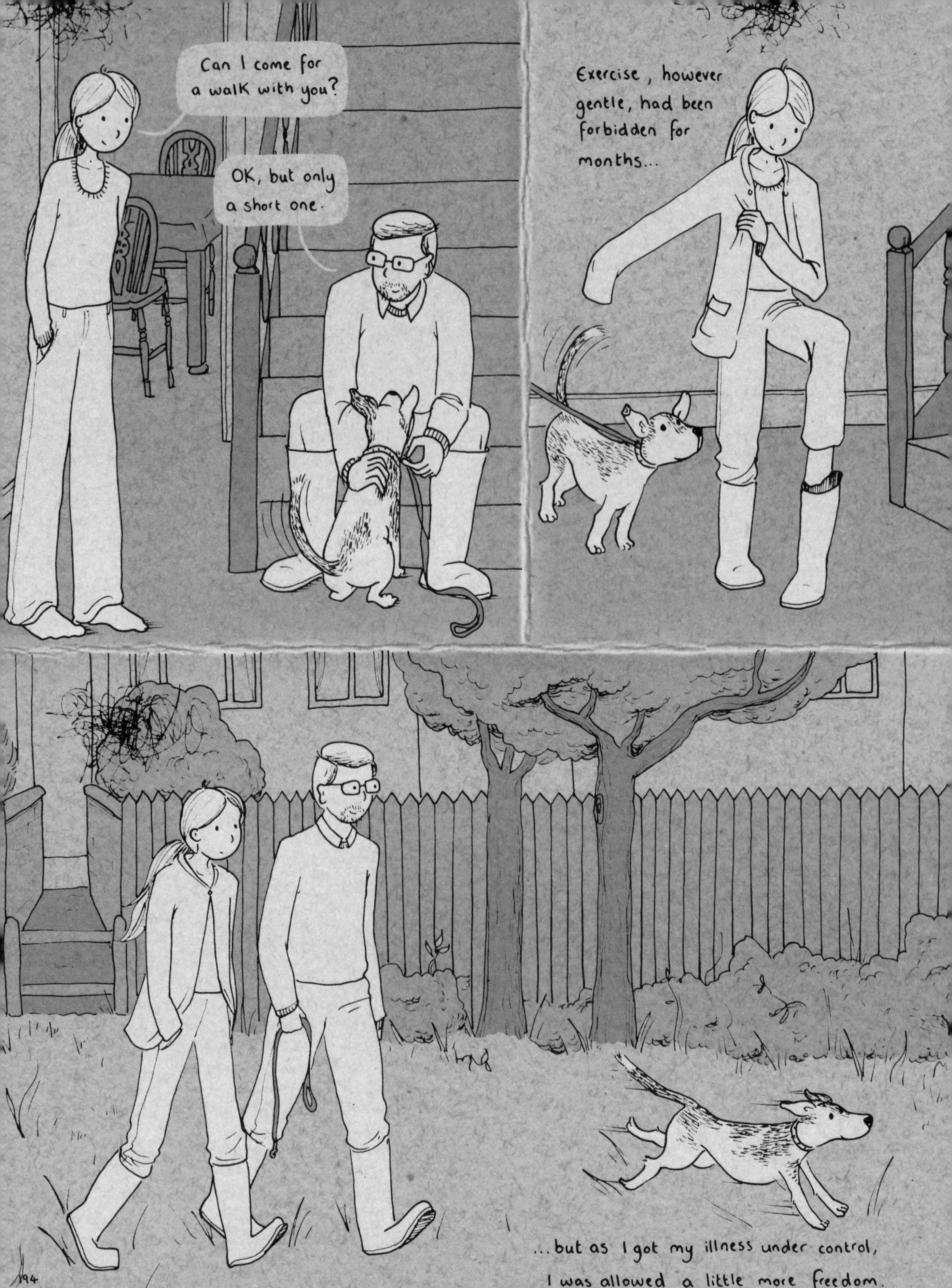
Can I come for a walk with you?
OK, but only a short one.
Exercise, however gentle, had been forbidden for months...
...but as I got my illness under control, I was allowed a little more freedom.

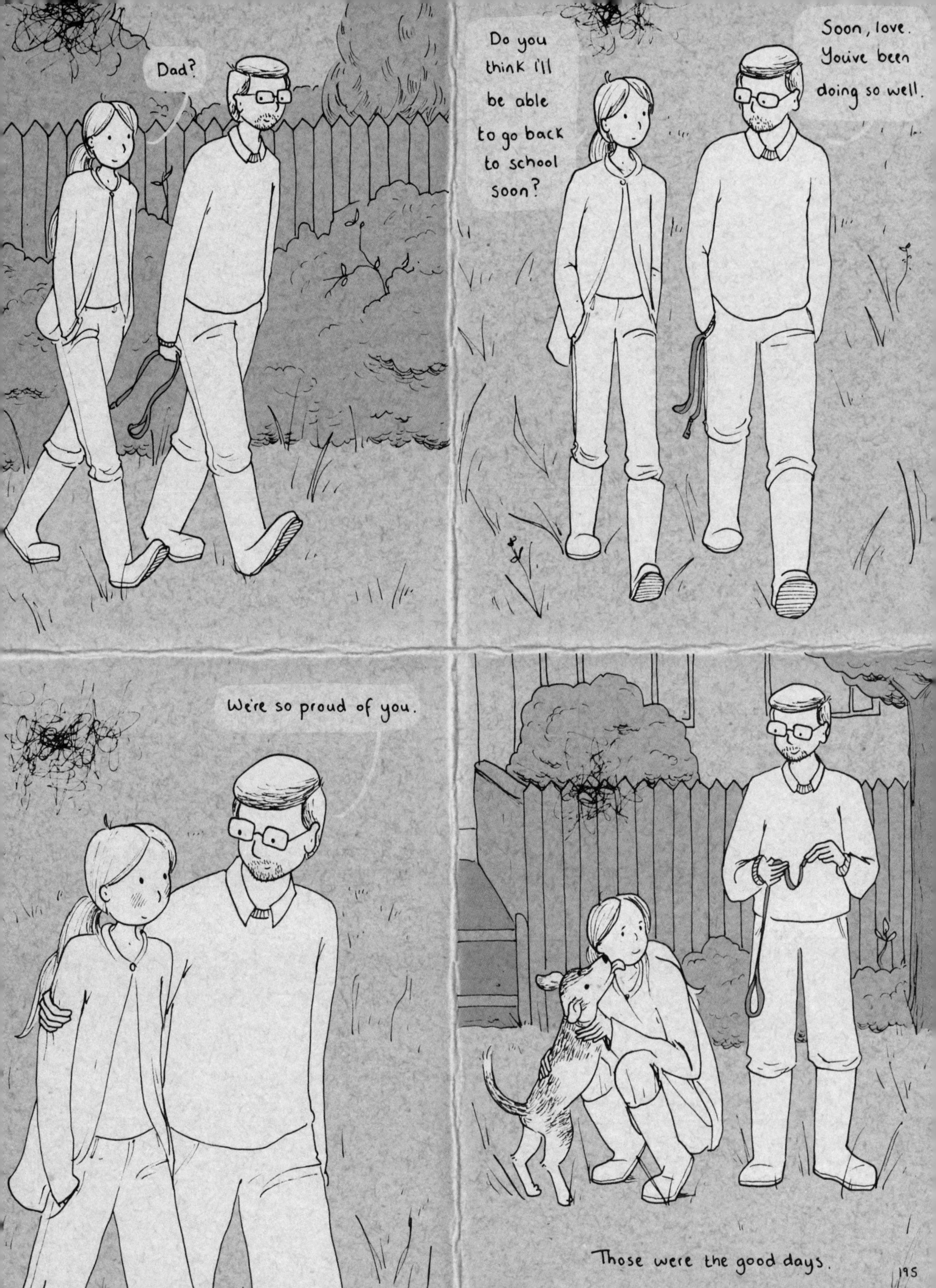
Dad?
Do you think I'll be able to go back to school soon?
Soon, love. You've been doing so well.
We're so proud of you.
Those were the good days.

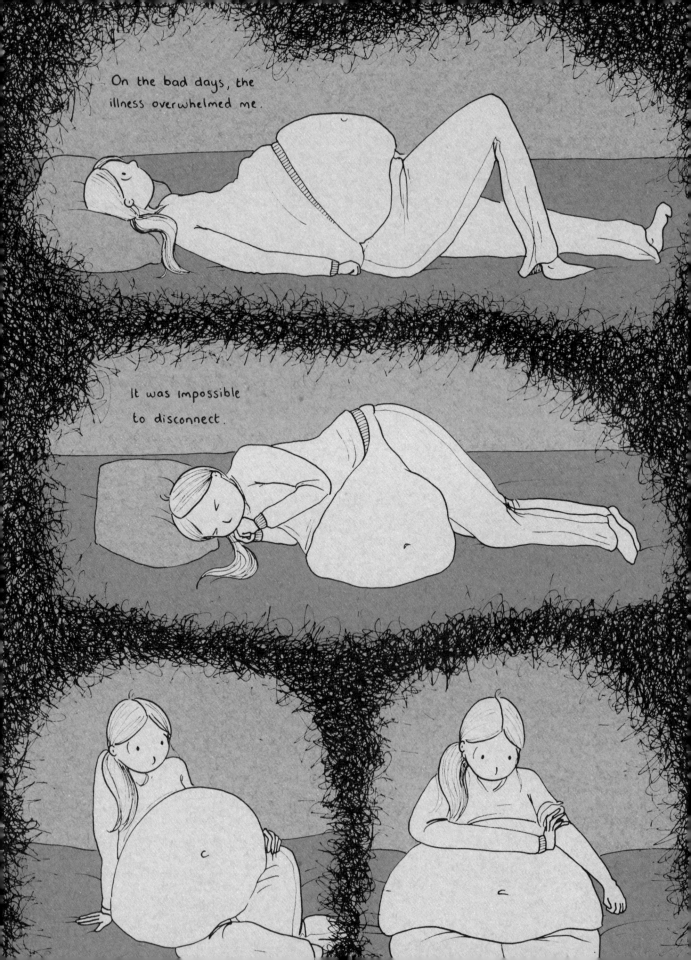

On the bad days, the illness overwhelmed me.

It was impossible to disconnect.

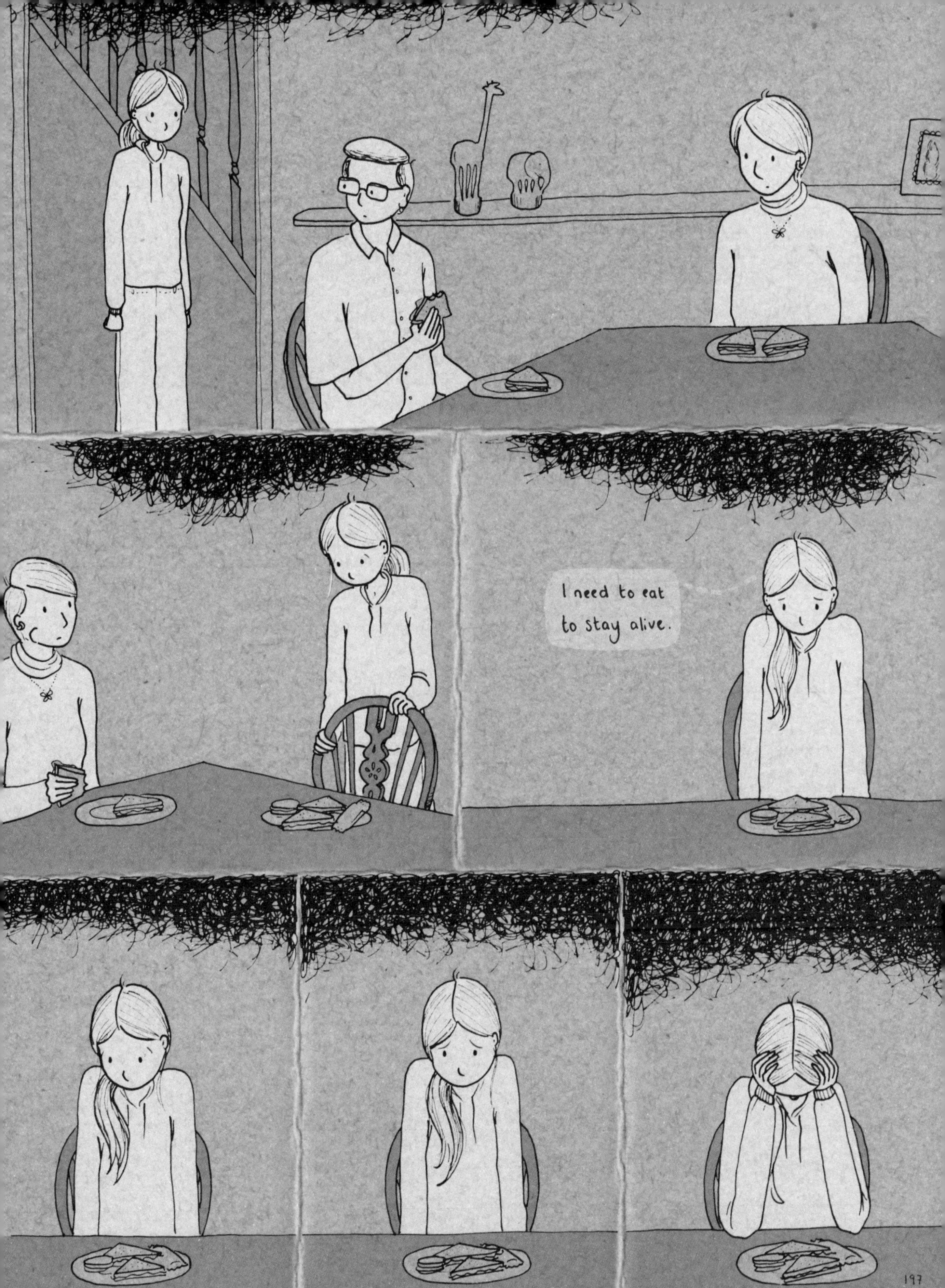
I need to eat to stay alive.

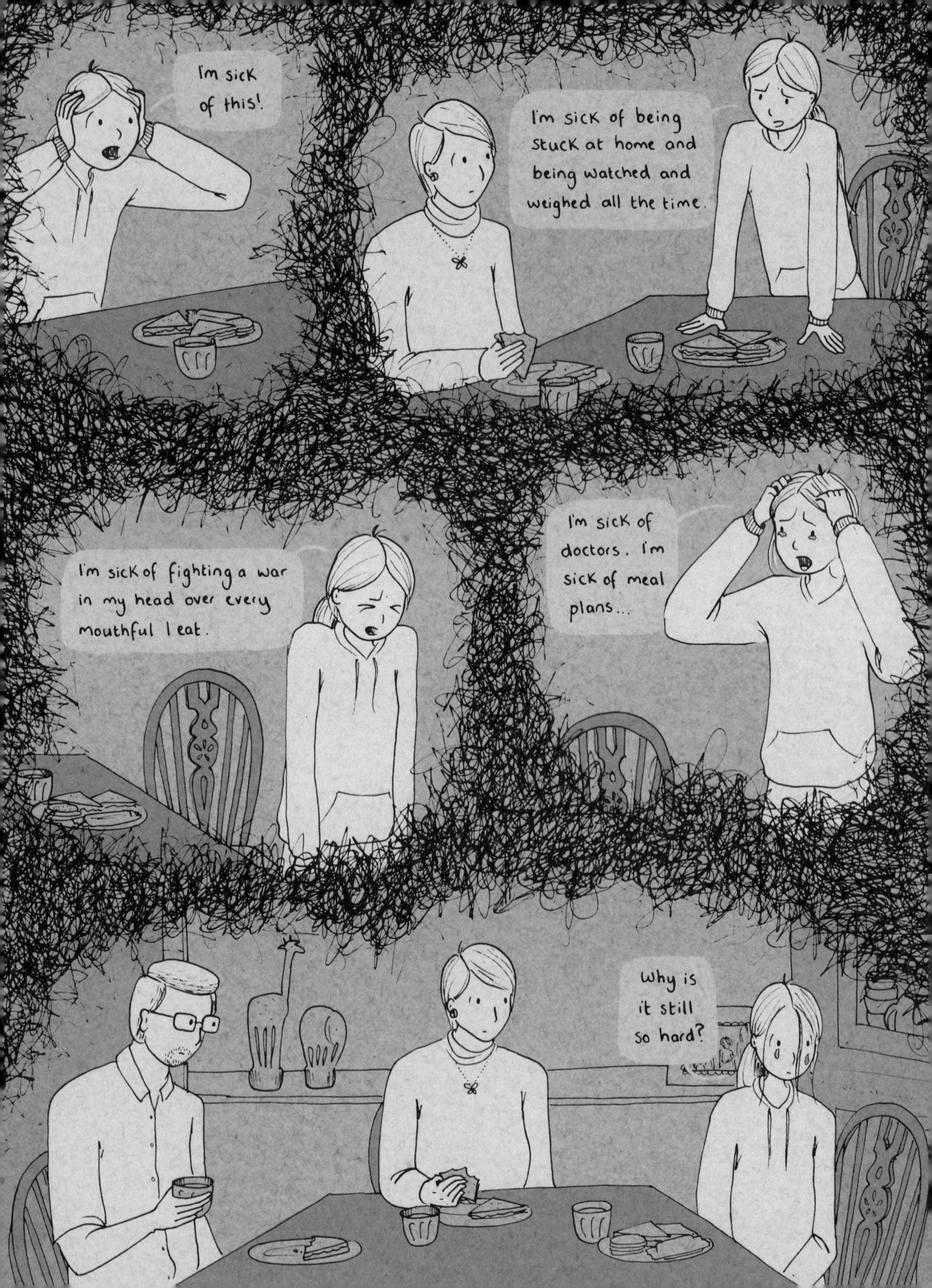
I'm sick of this!
I'm sick of being stuck at home and being watched and weighed all the time.
I'm sick of fighting a war in my head over every mouthful I eat.
I'm sick of doctors. I'm sick of meal plans...
Why is it still so hard?

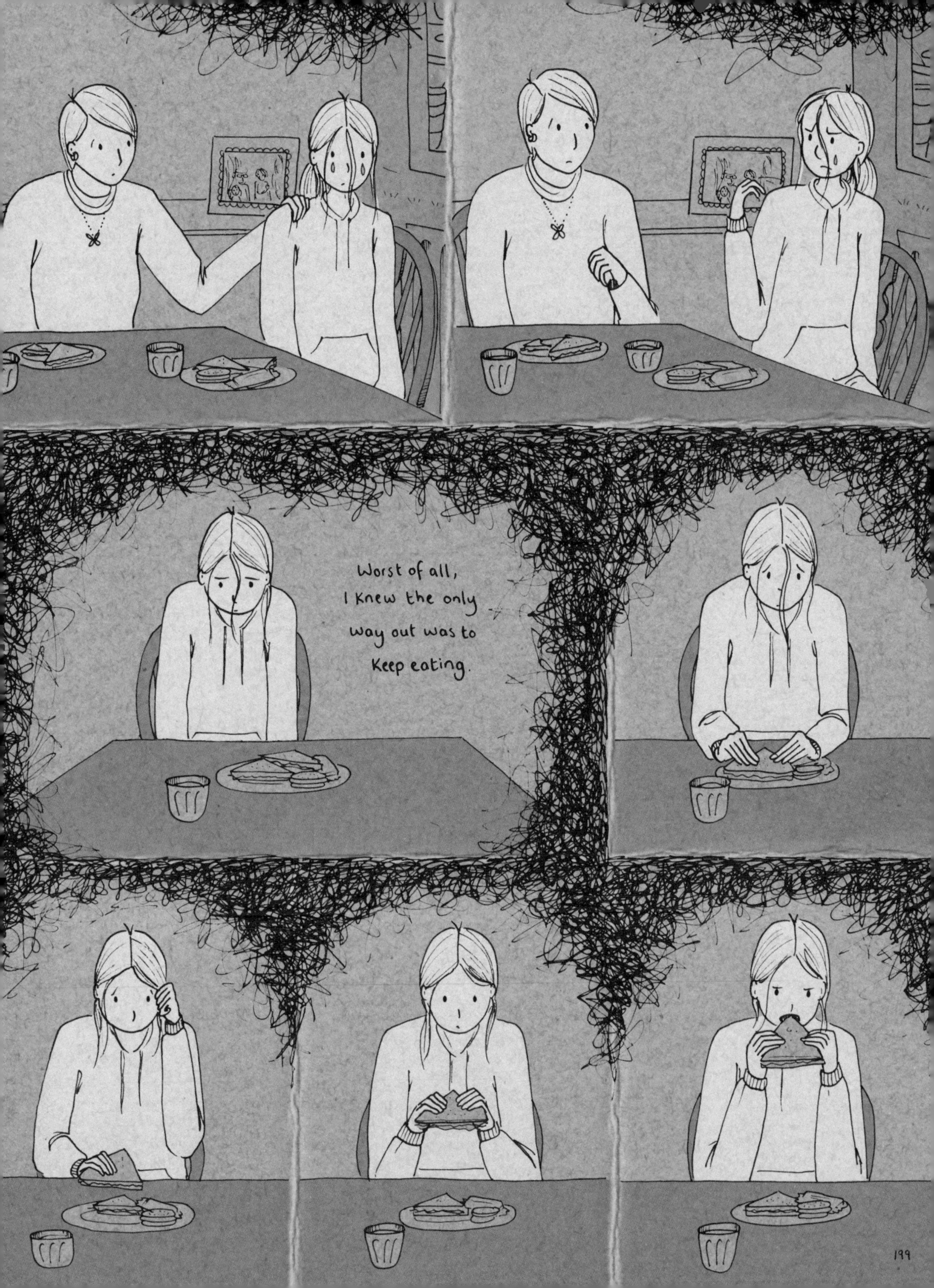
Worst of all,
I knew the only
way out was to
keep eating.

Eventually, after what seemed like a lifetime, the end was in sight.

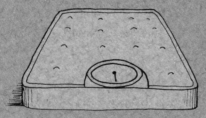

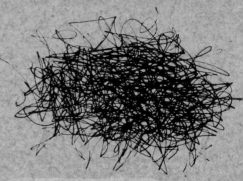

Great! Just a couple more weeks and you'll be at a healthy weight!

Come on, aren't you proud of yourself?
Am I supposed to be?

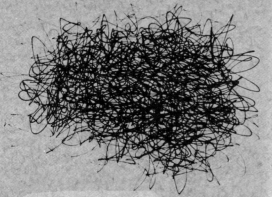

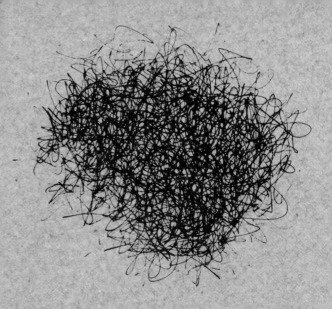

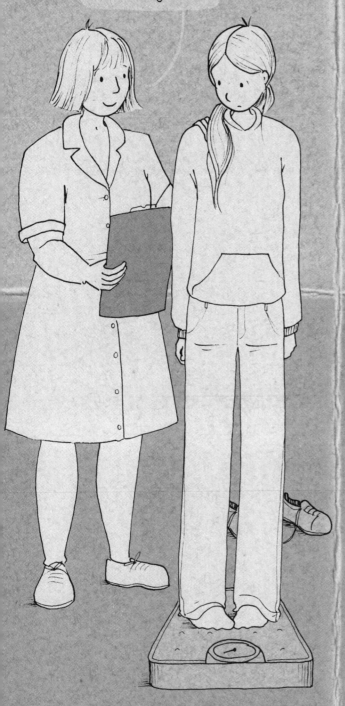

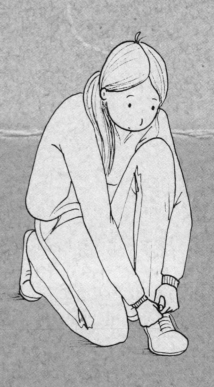

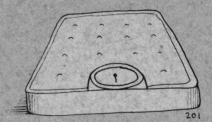

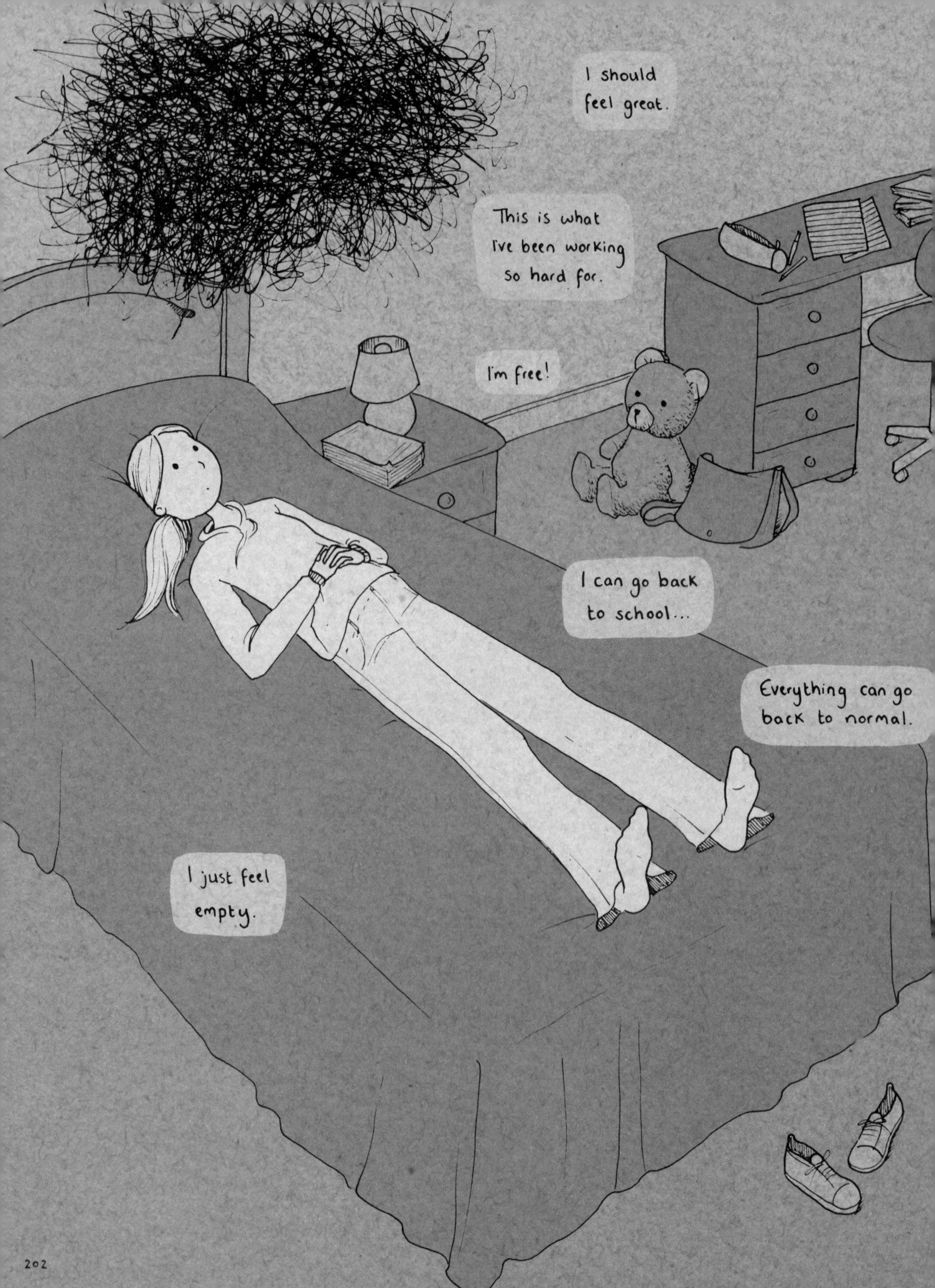
I should feel great.
This is what I've been working so hard for.
I'm free!
I can go back to school...
Everything can go back to normal.
I just feel empty.

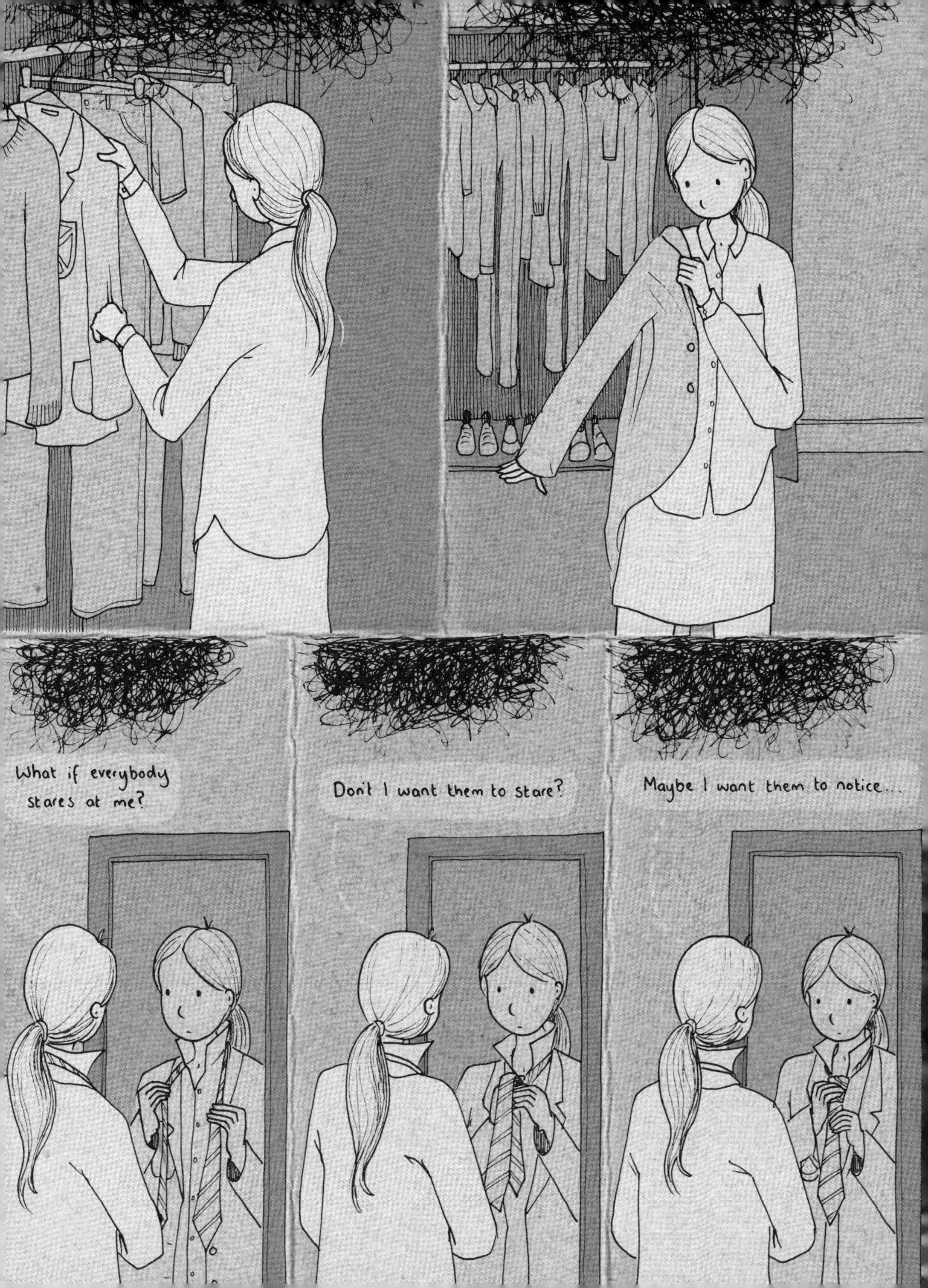
What if everybody stares at me?
Don't I want them to stare?
Maybe I want them to notice...

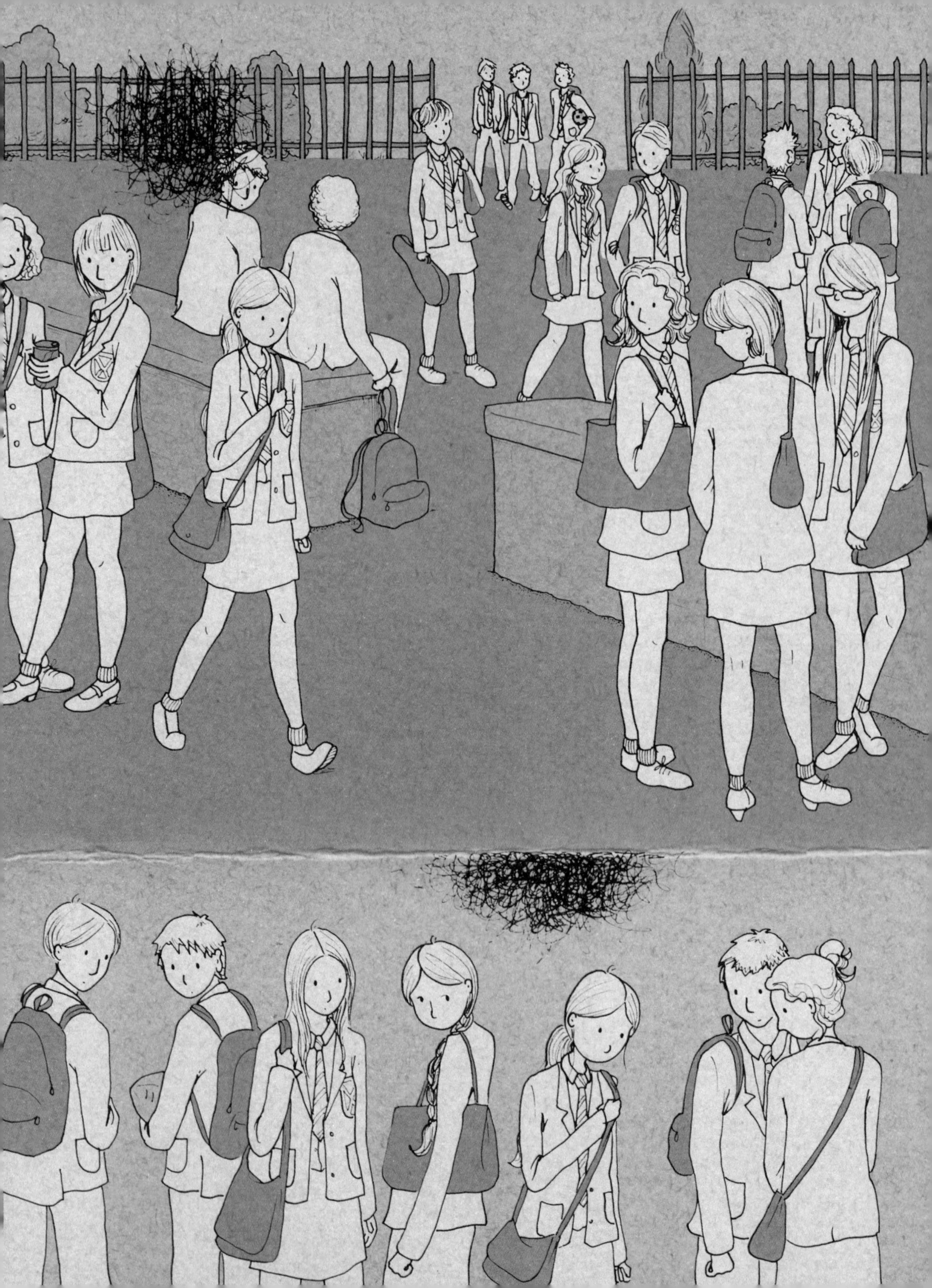

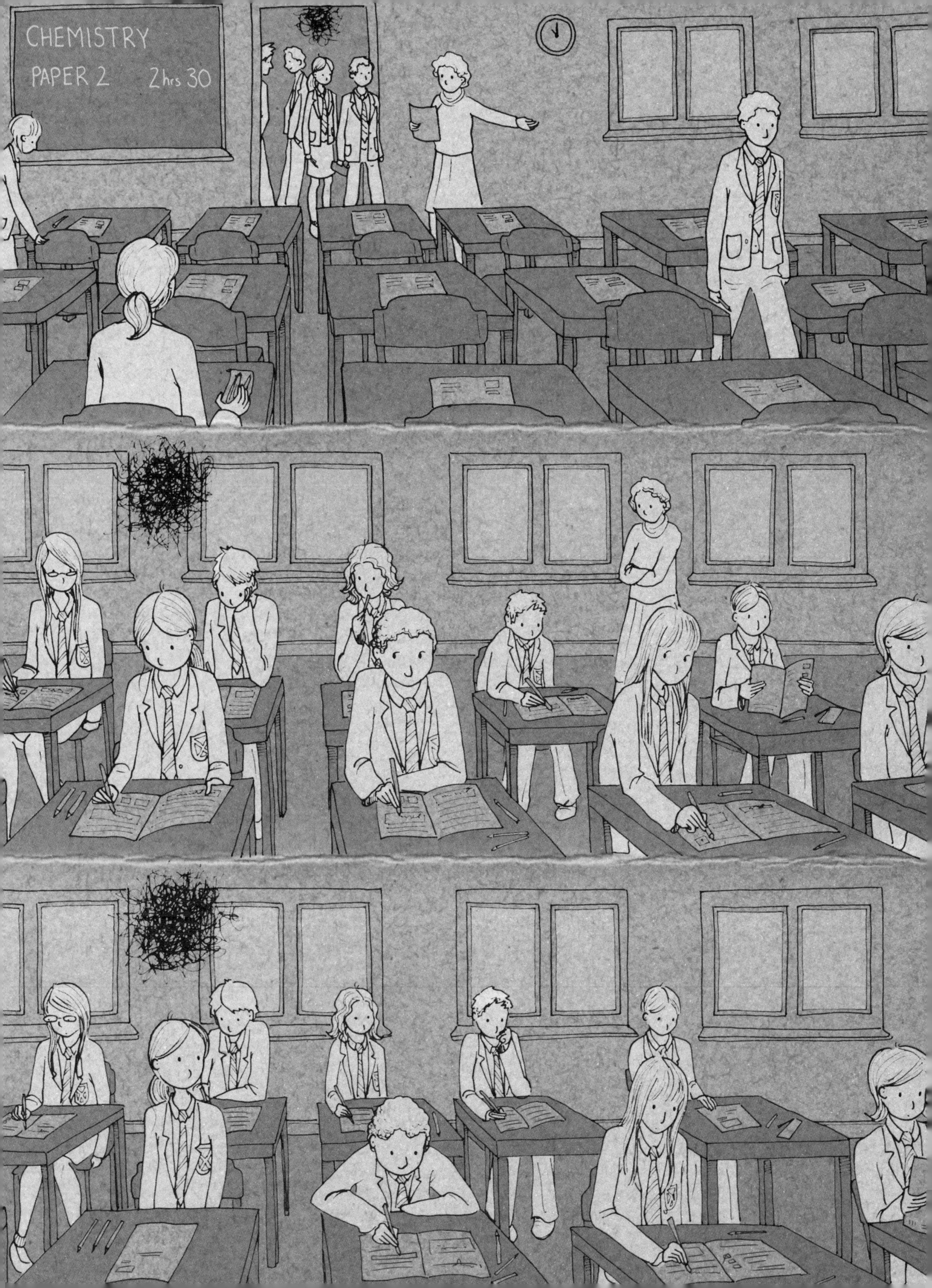
CHEMISTRY
PAPER 2
2 hrs 30

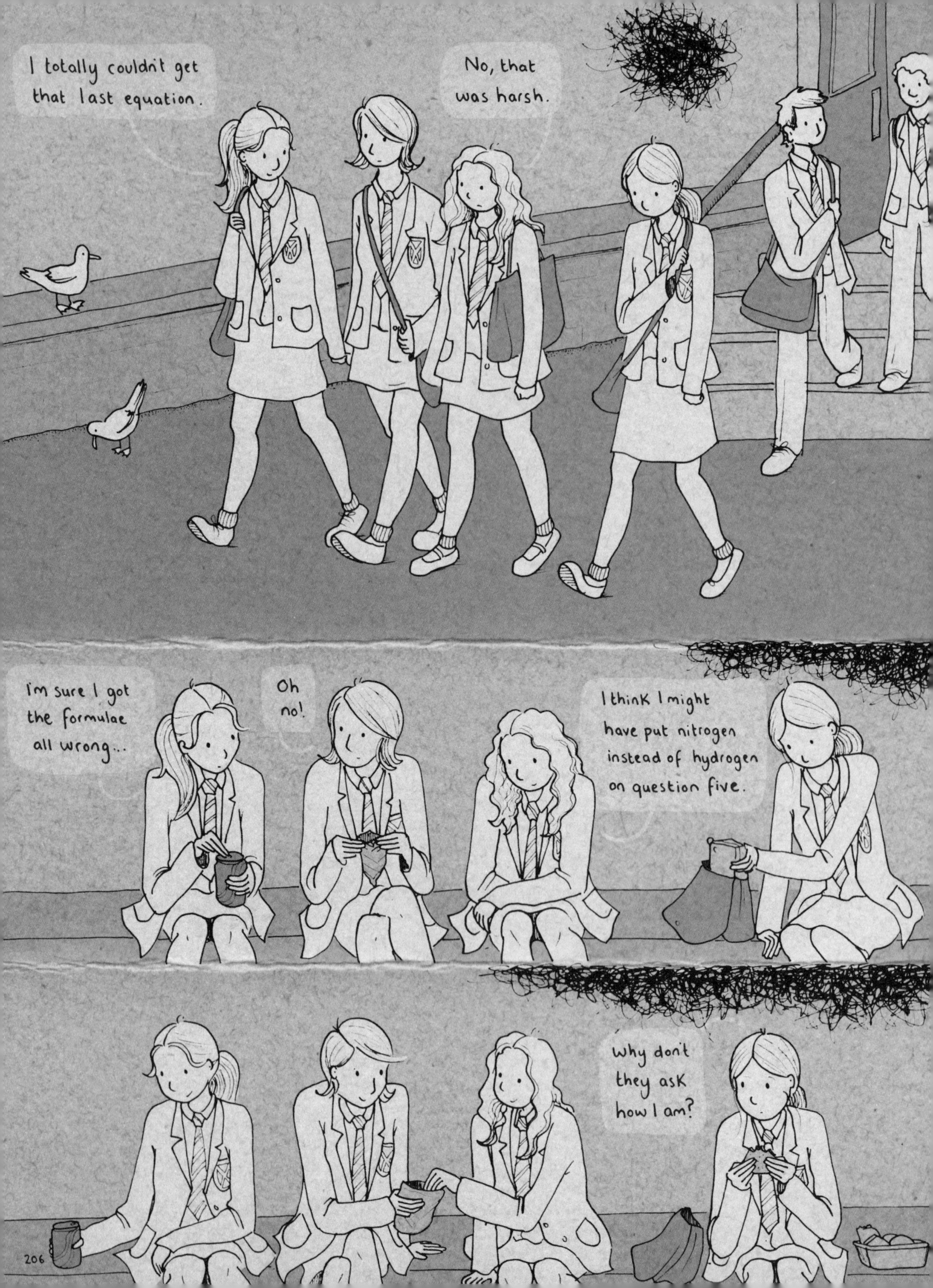
I totally couldn't get that last equation.
No, that was harsh.
I'm sure I got the formulae all wrong...
Oh no!
I think I might have put nitrogen instead of hydrogen on question five.
Why don't they ask how I am?

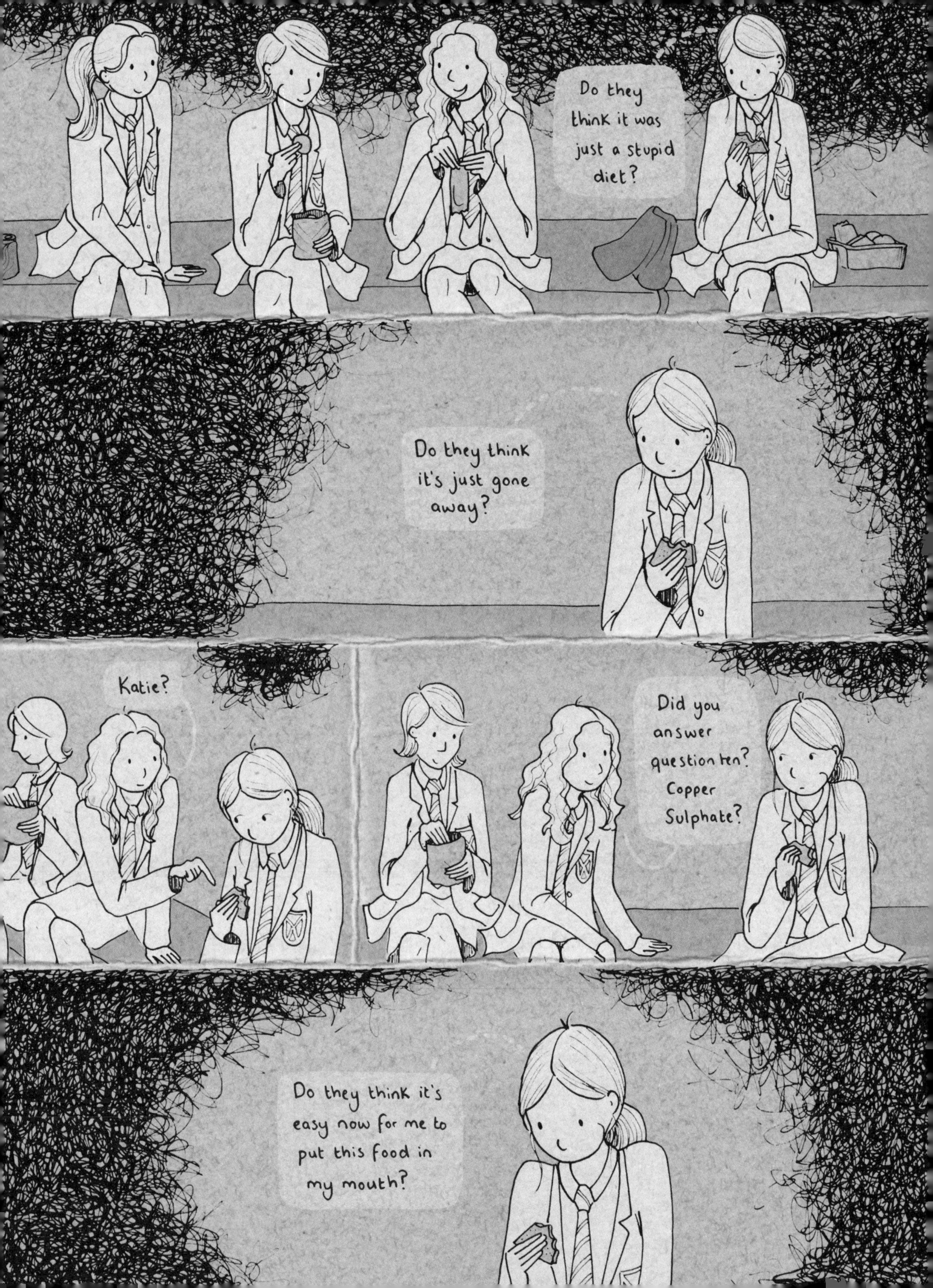
Do they think it was just a stupid diet?
Do they think it's just gone away?
Katie?
Did you answer question ten? Copper Sulphate?
Do they think it's easy now for me to put this food in my mouth?

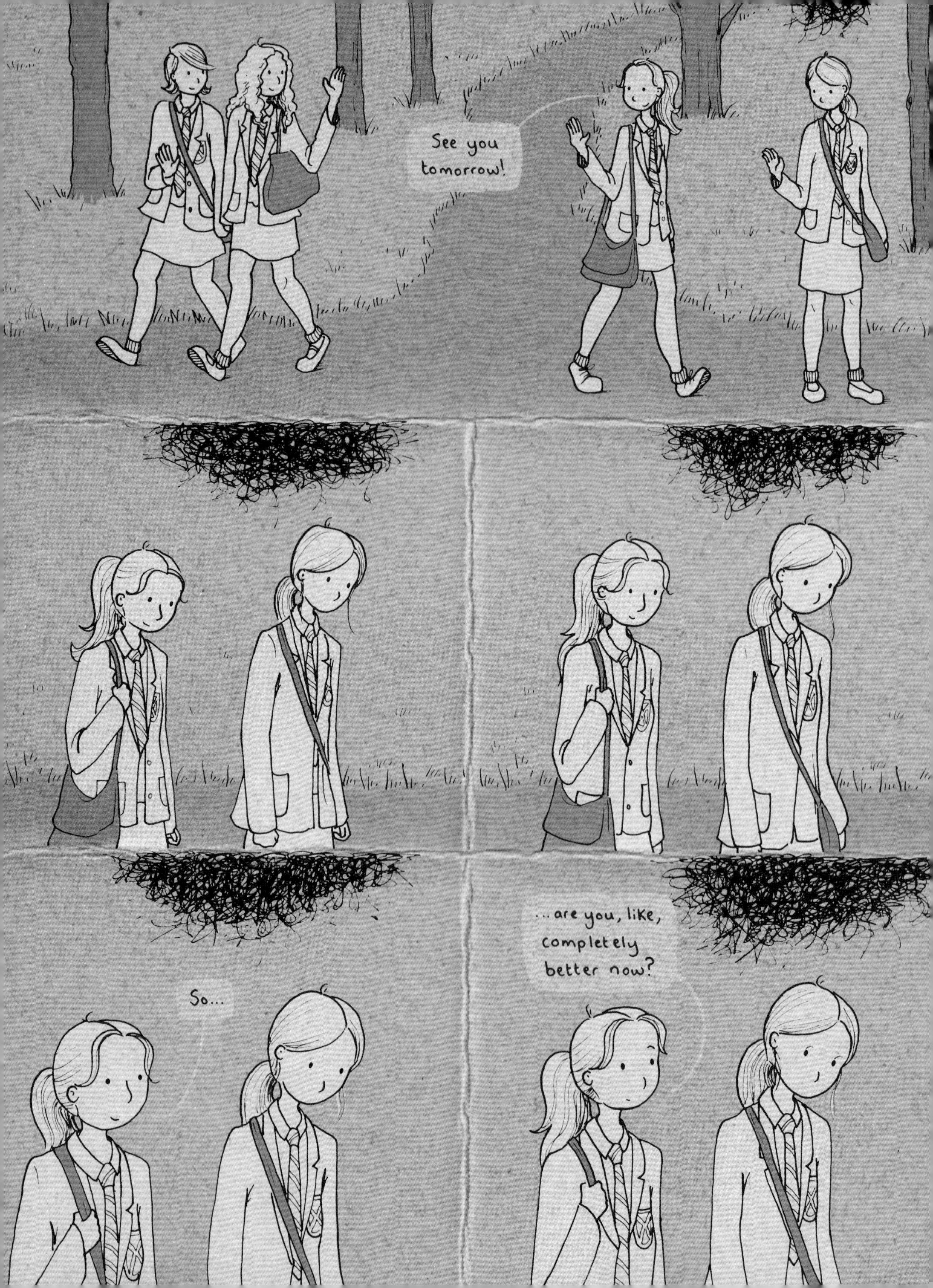
See you tomorrow!
So...
...are you, like, completely better now?

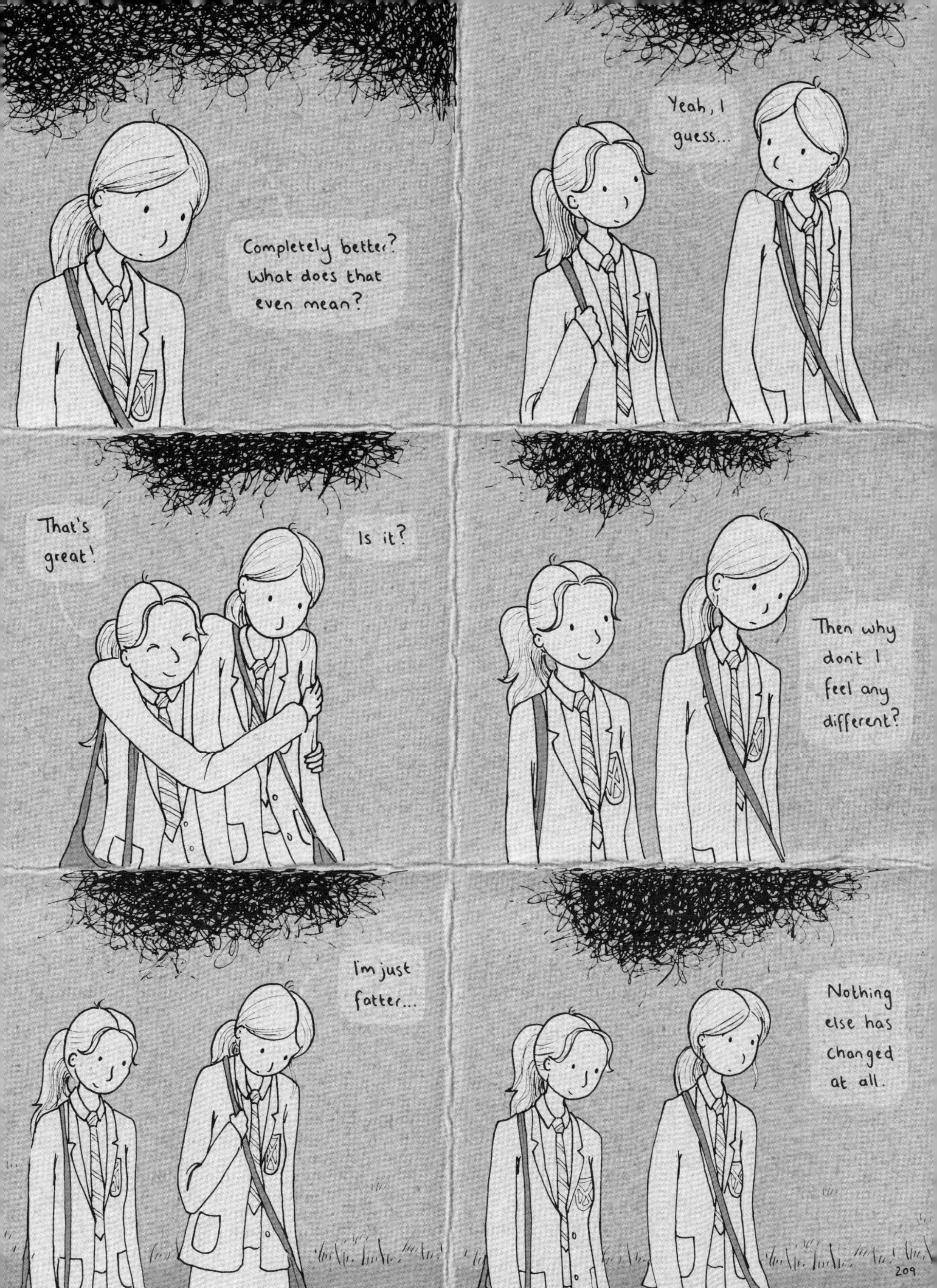
Completely better? What does that even mean?
Yeah, I guess...
That's great!
Is it?
Then why don't I feel any different?
I'm just fatter...
Nothing else has changed at all.

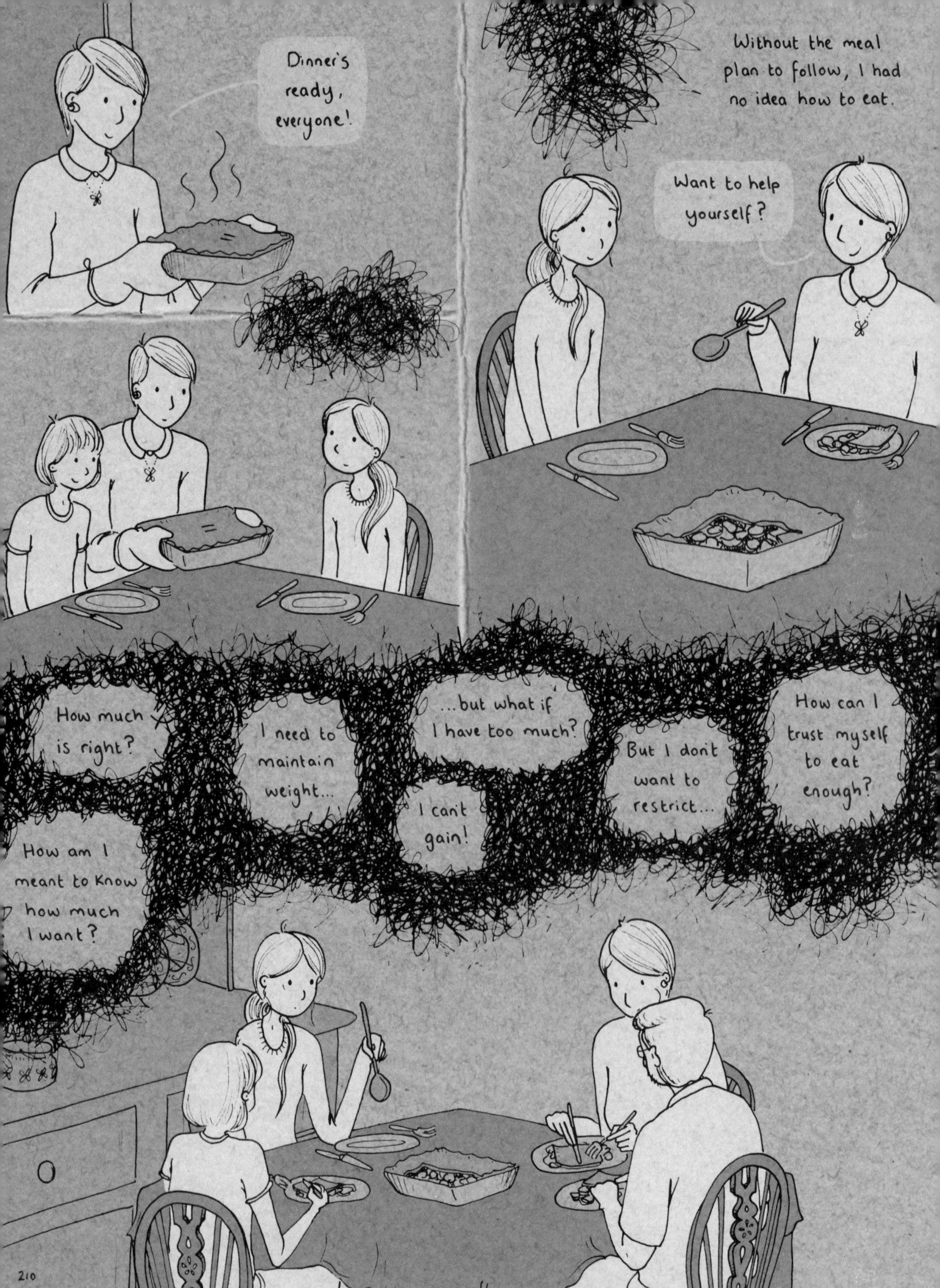
Dinner's ready, everyone!
Without the meal plan to follow, I had no idea how to eat.
Want to help yourself?
How much is right?
I need to maintain weight...
...but what if I have too much?
I can't gain!
But I don't want to restrict...
How can I trust myself to eat enough?
How am I meant to know how much I want?

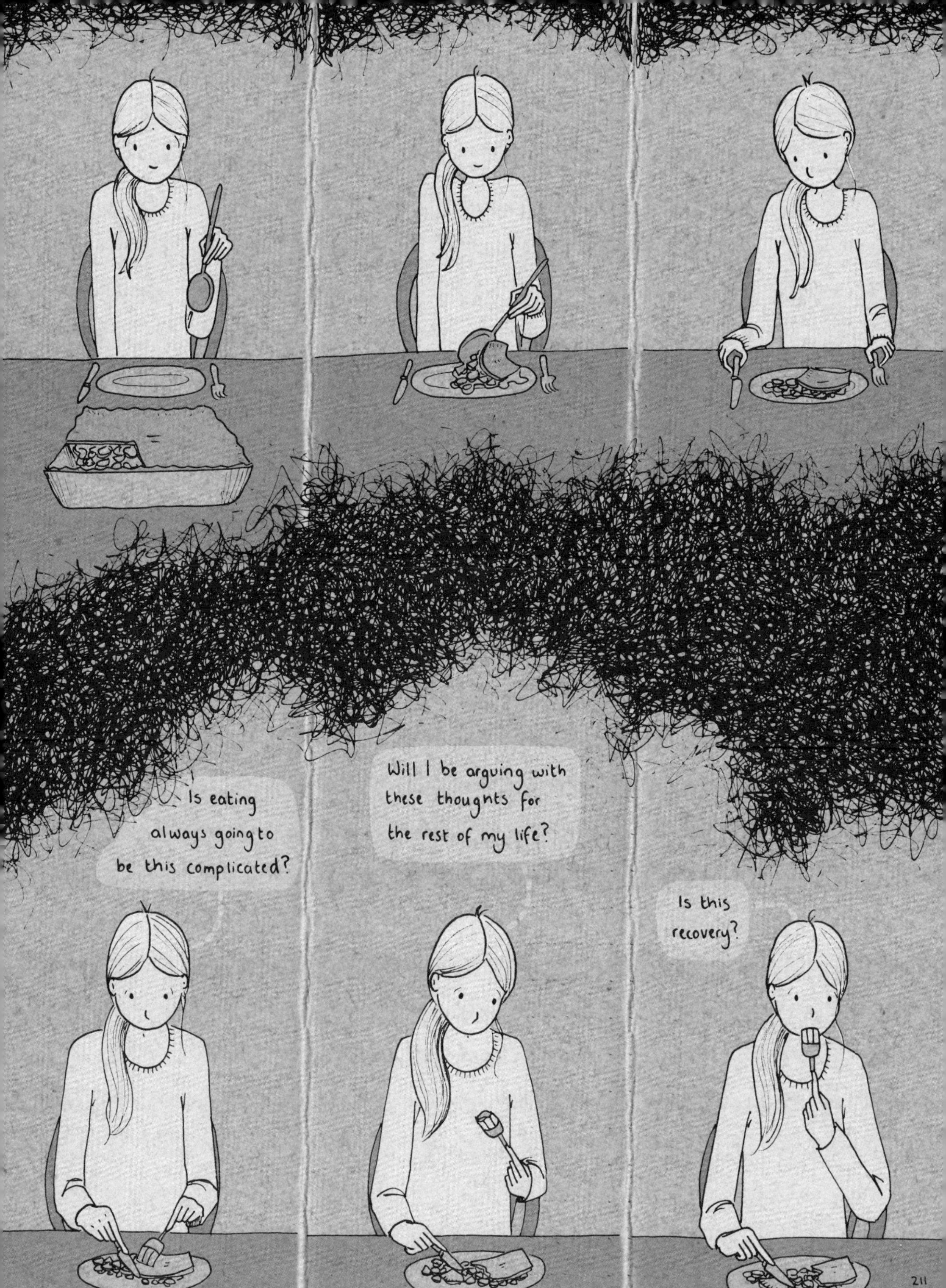
Is eating always going to be this complicated?
Will I be arguing with these thoughts for the rest of my life?
Is this recovery?

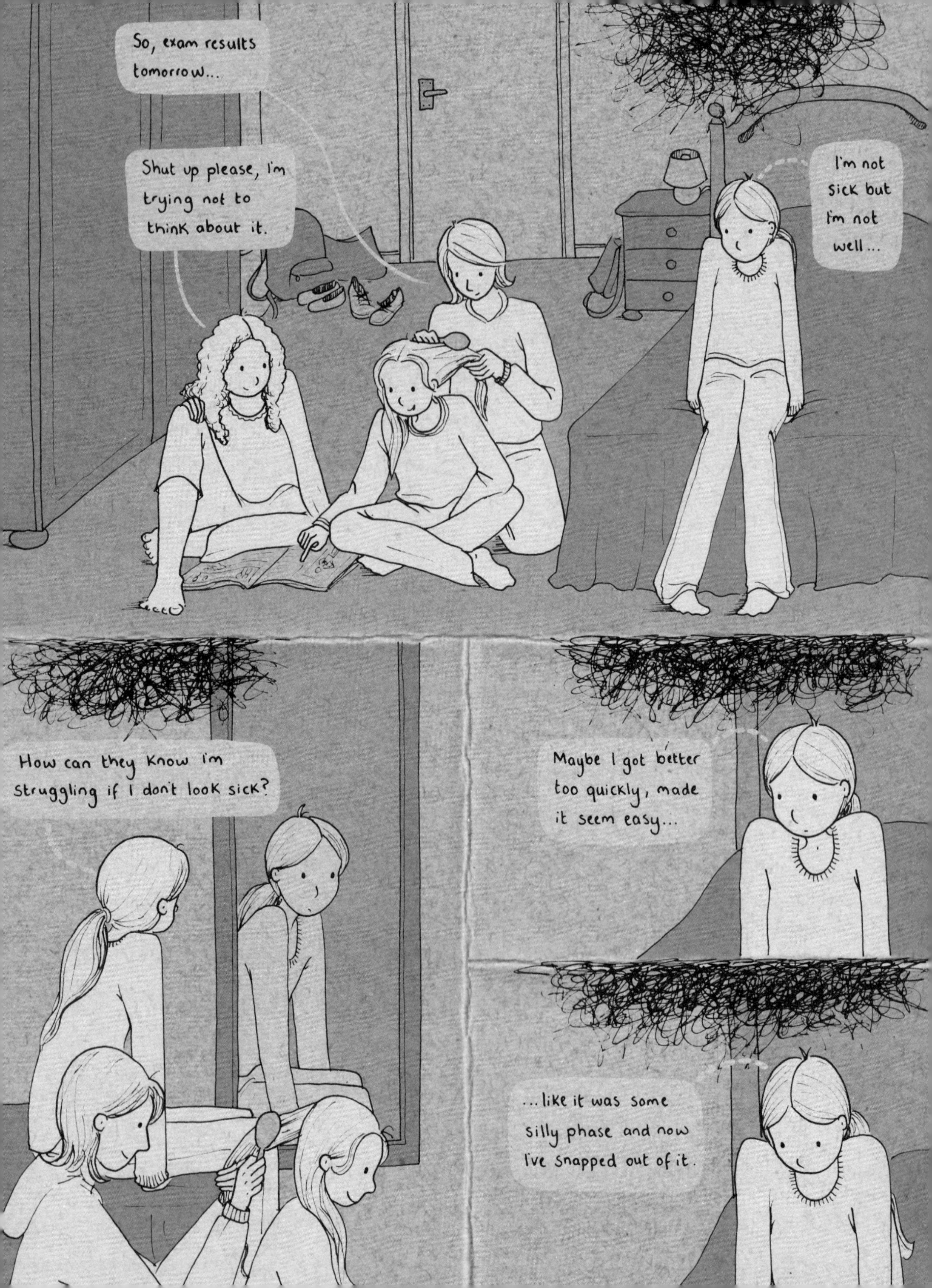
So, exam results tomorrow...
Shut up please, I'm trying not to think about it.
I'm not sick but I'm not well...
How can they know I'm struggling if I don't look sick?
Maybe I got better too quickly, made it seem easy...
...like it was some silly phase and now I've snapped out of it.

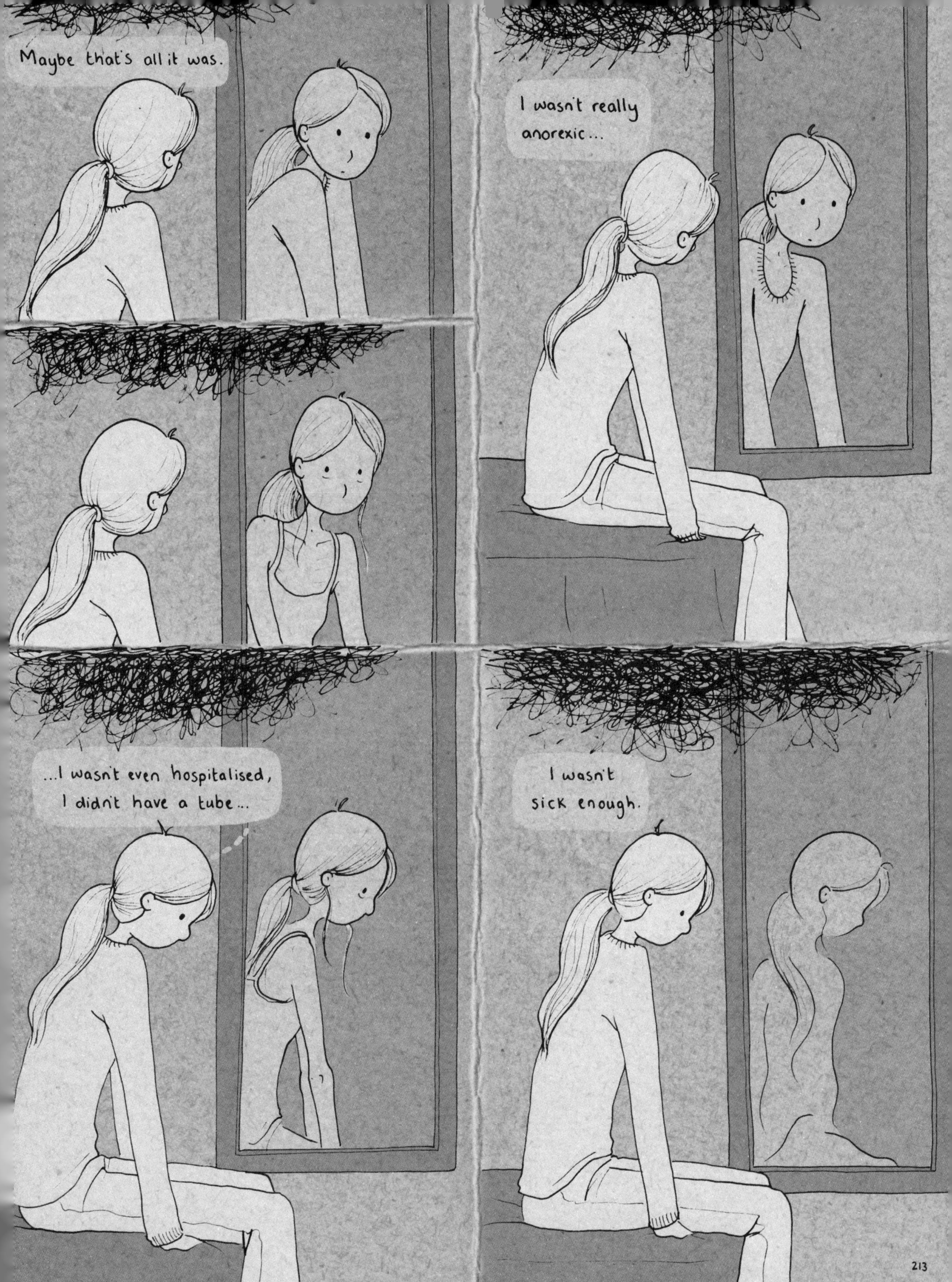
Maybe that's all it was.
I wasn't really anorexic...
...I wasn't even hospitalised, I didn't have a tube...
I wasn't sick enough.

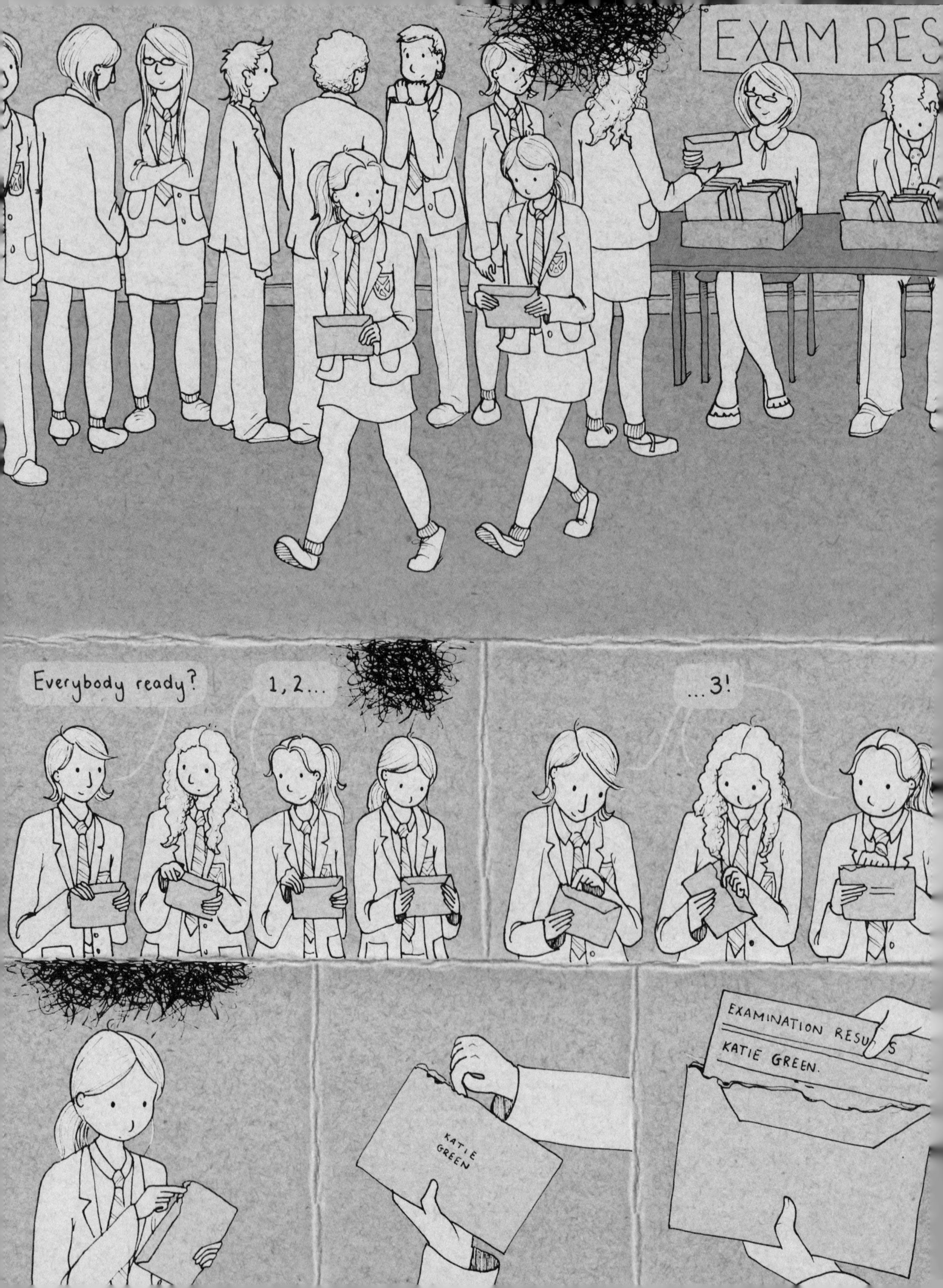
EXAM RES
Everybody ready?
1, 2...
...3!
KATIE GREEN
EXAMINATION RESULTS
KATIE GREEN.

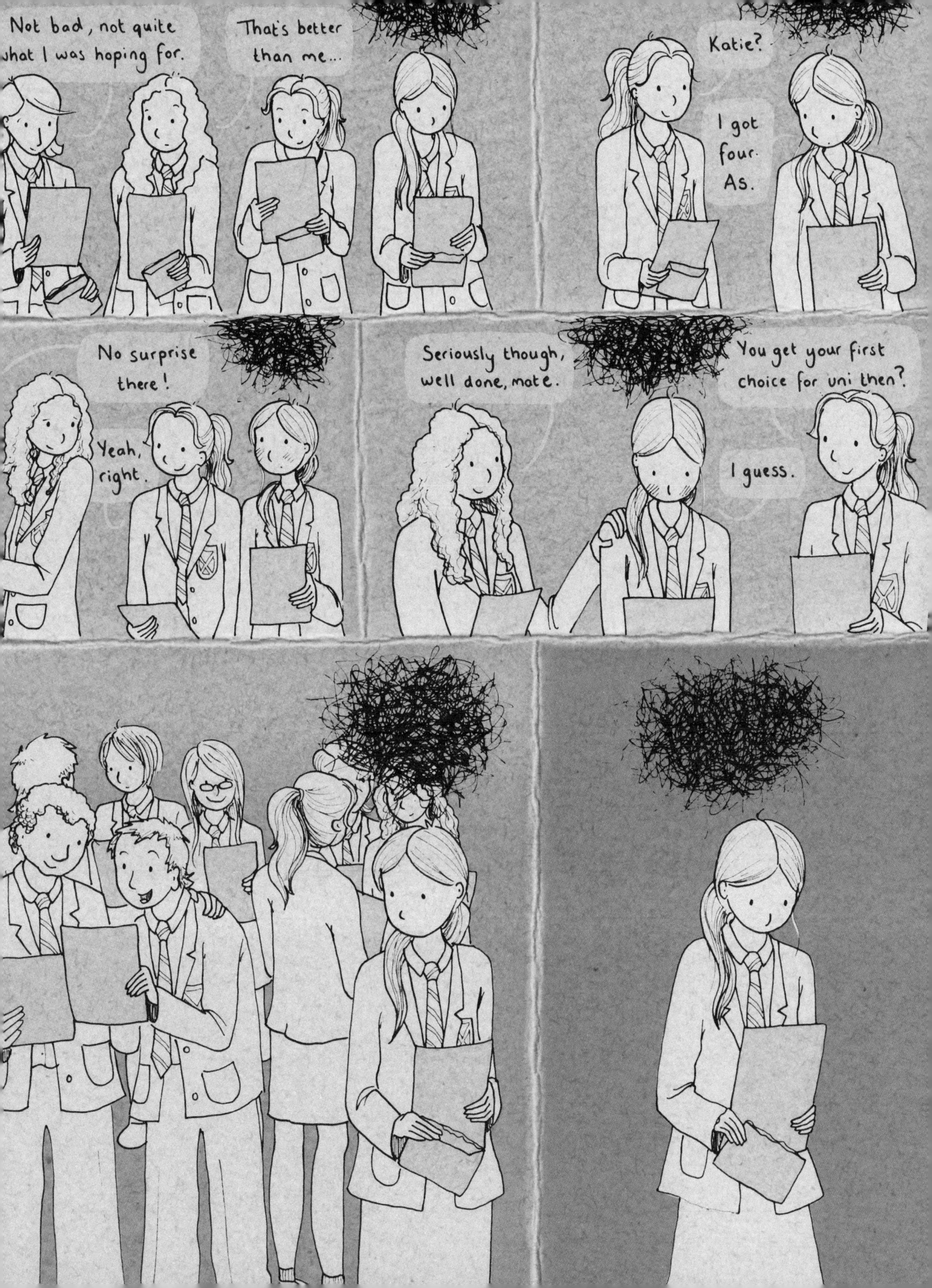
Not bad, not quite what I was hoping for.
That's better than me...
Katie?
I got four. As.
No surprise there!
Yeah, right.
Seriously though, well done, mate.
You get your first choice for uni then?
I guess.

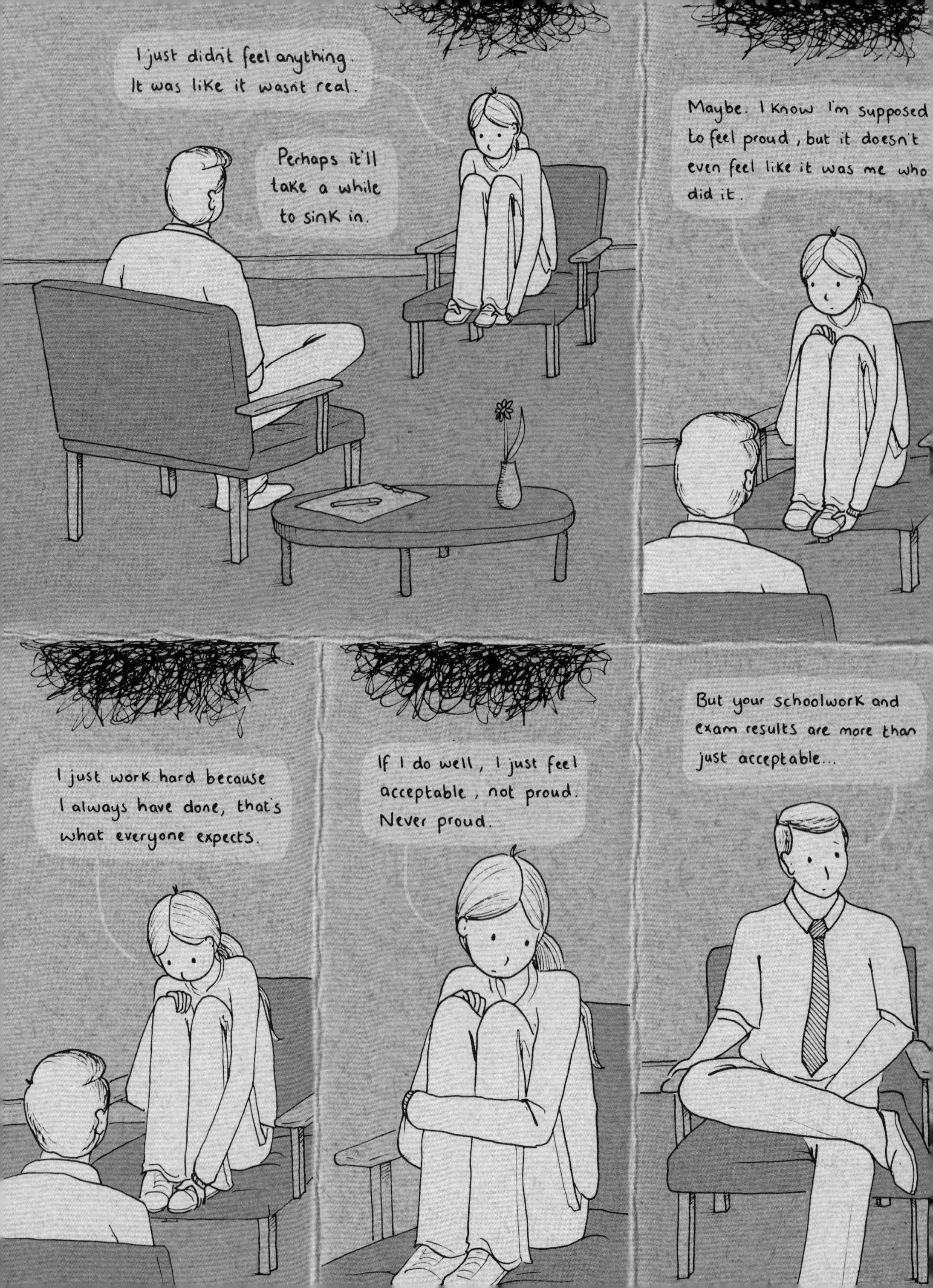
I just didn't feel anything. It was like it wasn't real.
Perhaps it'll take a while to sink in.
Maybe. I know I'm supposed to feel proud, but it doesn't even feel like it was me who did it.
I just work hard because I always have done, that's what everyone expects.
If I do well, I just feel acceptable, not proud. Never proud.
But your schoolwork and exam results are more than just acceptable...

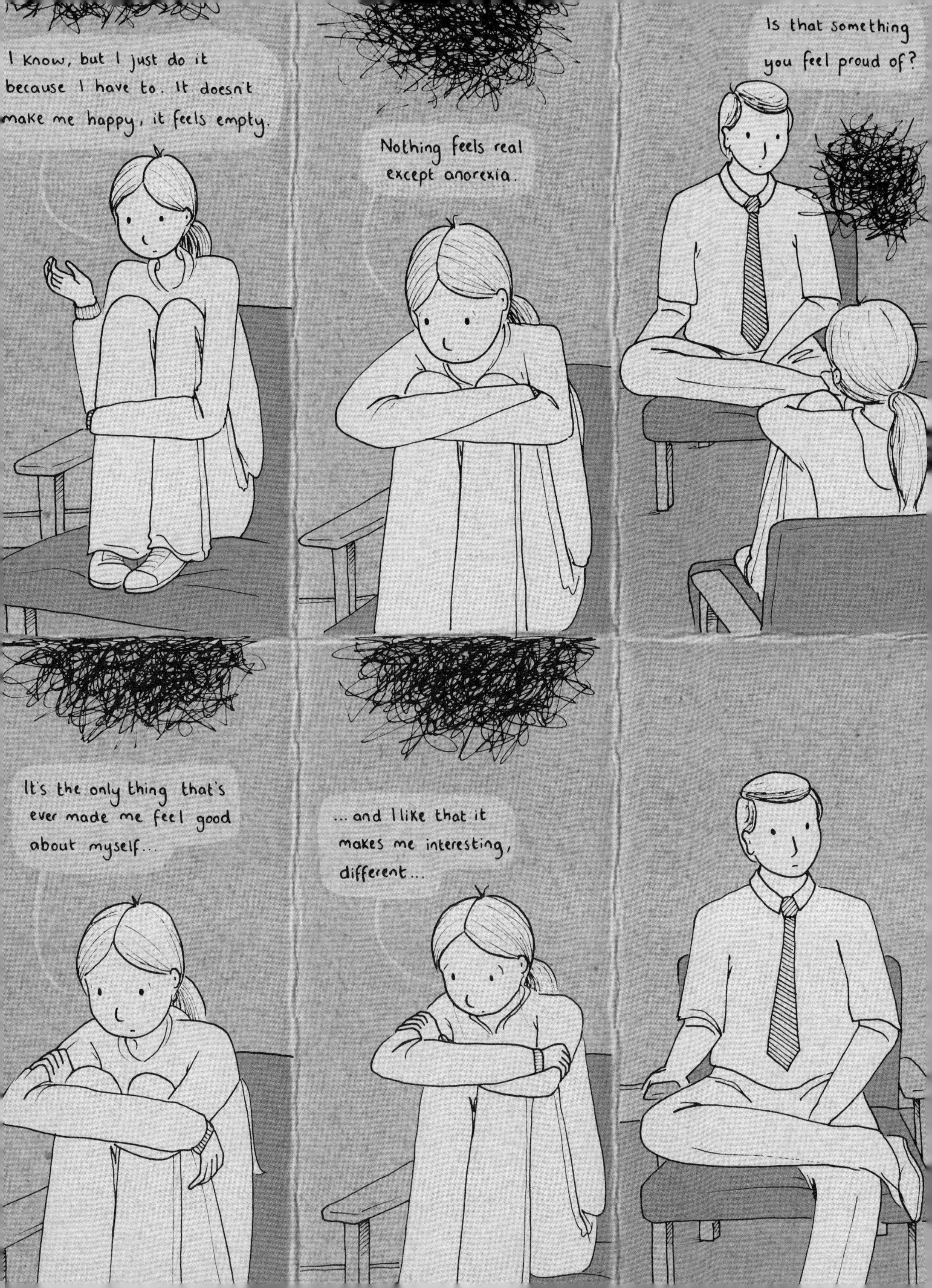
I know, but I just do it because I have to. It doesn't make me happy, it feels empty.
Nothing feels real except anorexia.
Is that something you feel proud of?
It's the only thing that's ever made me feel good about myself...
...and I like that it makes me interesting, different...

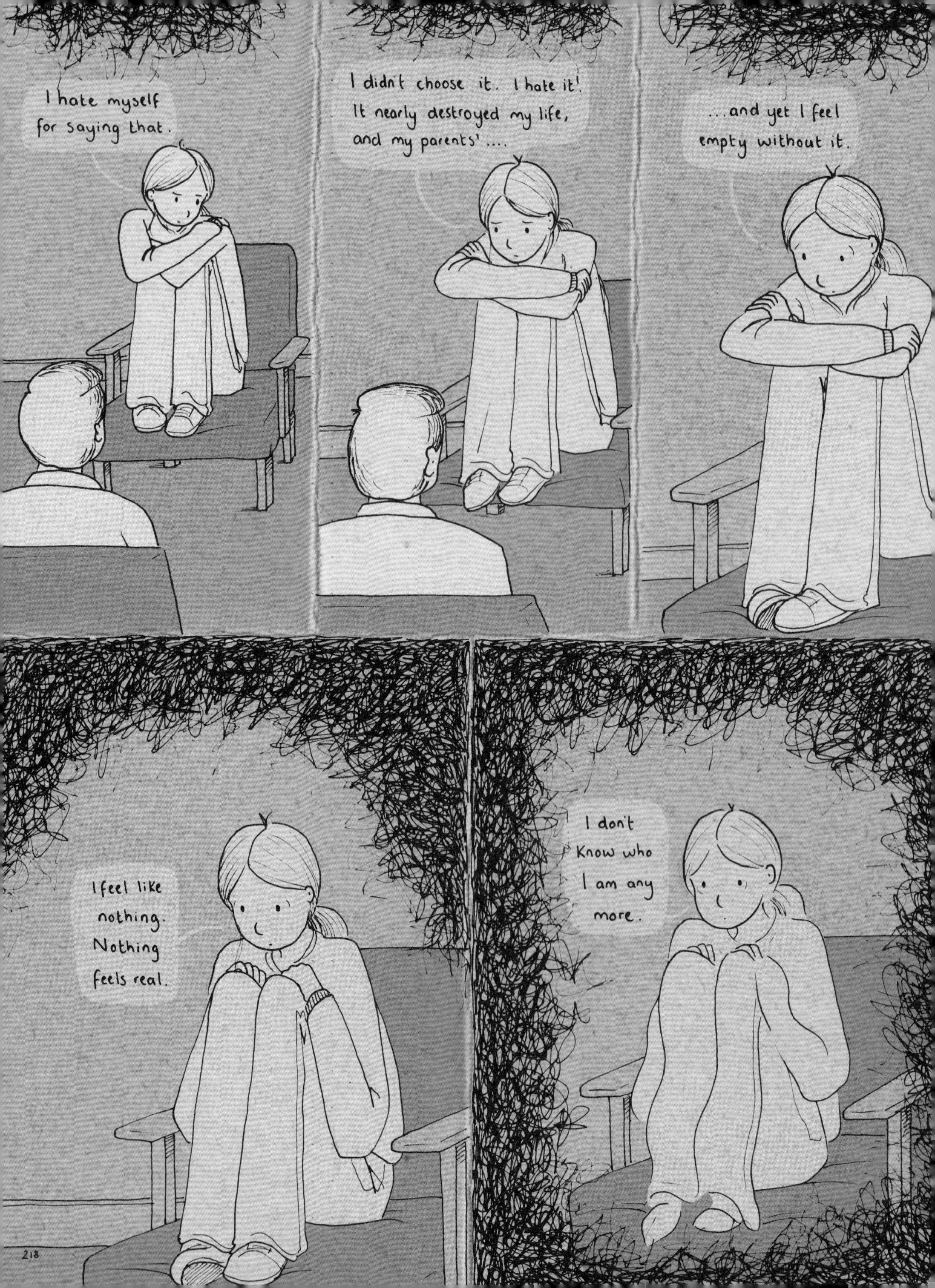
I hate myself for saying that.
I didn't choose it. I hate it! It nearly destroyed my life, and my parents'....
...and yet I feel empty without it.
I feel like nothing. Nothing feels real.
I don't know who I am any more.

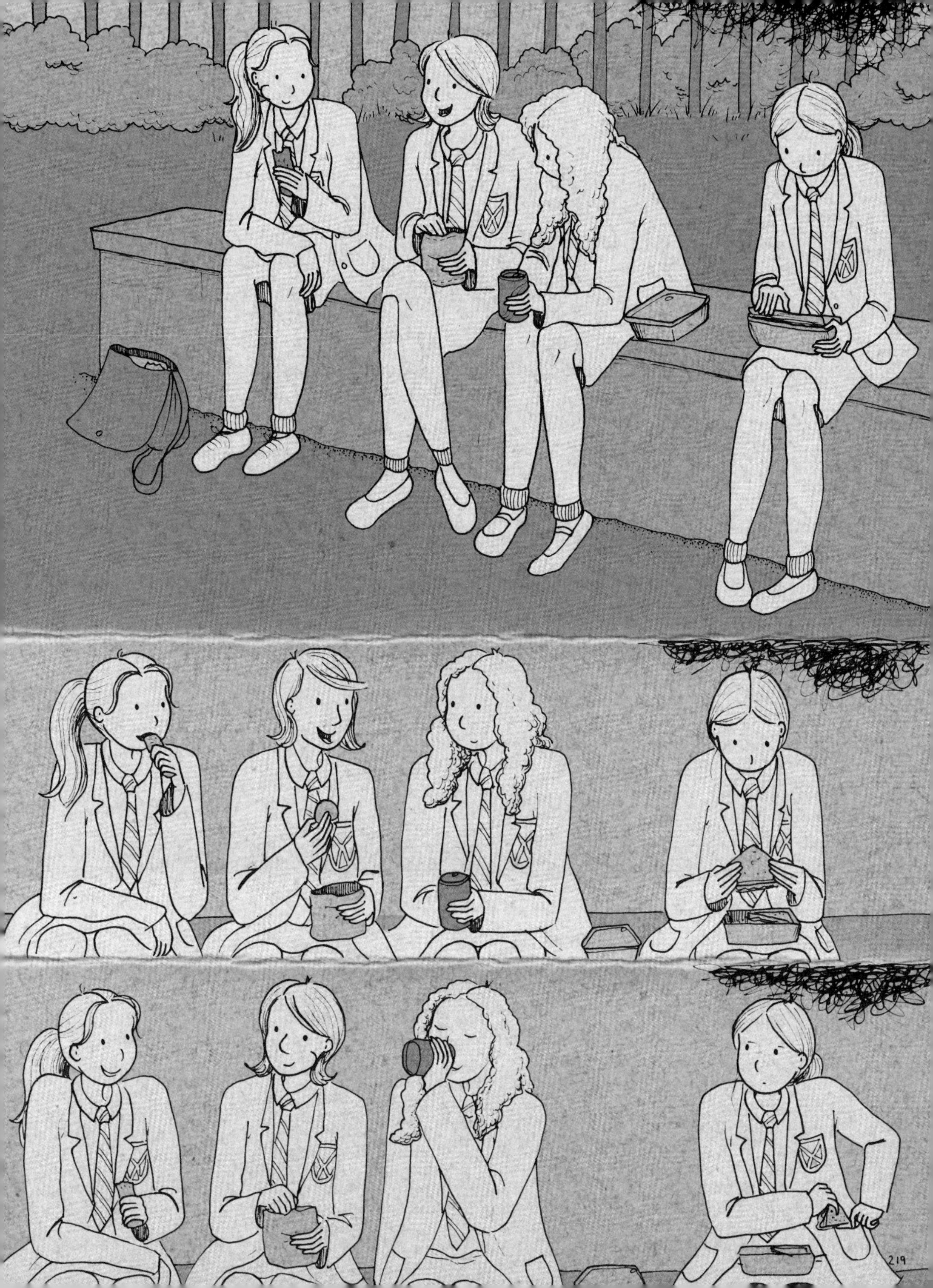

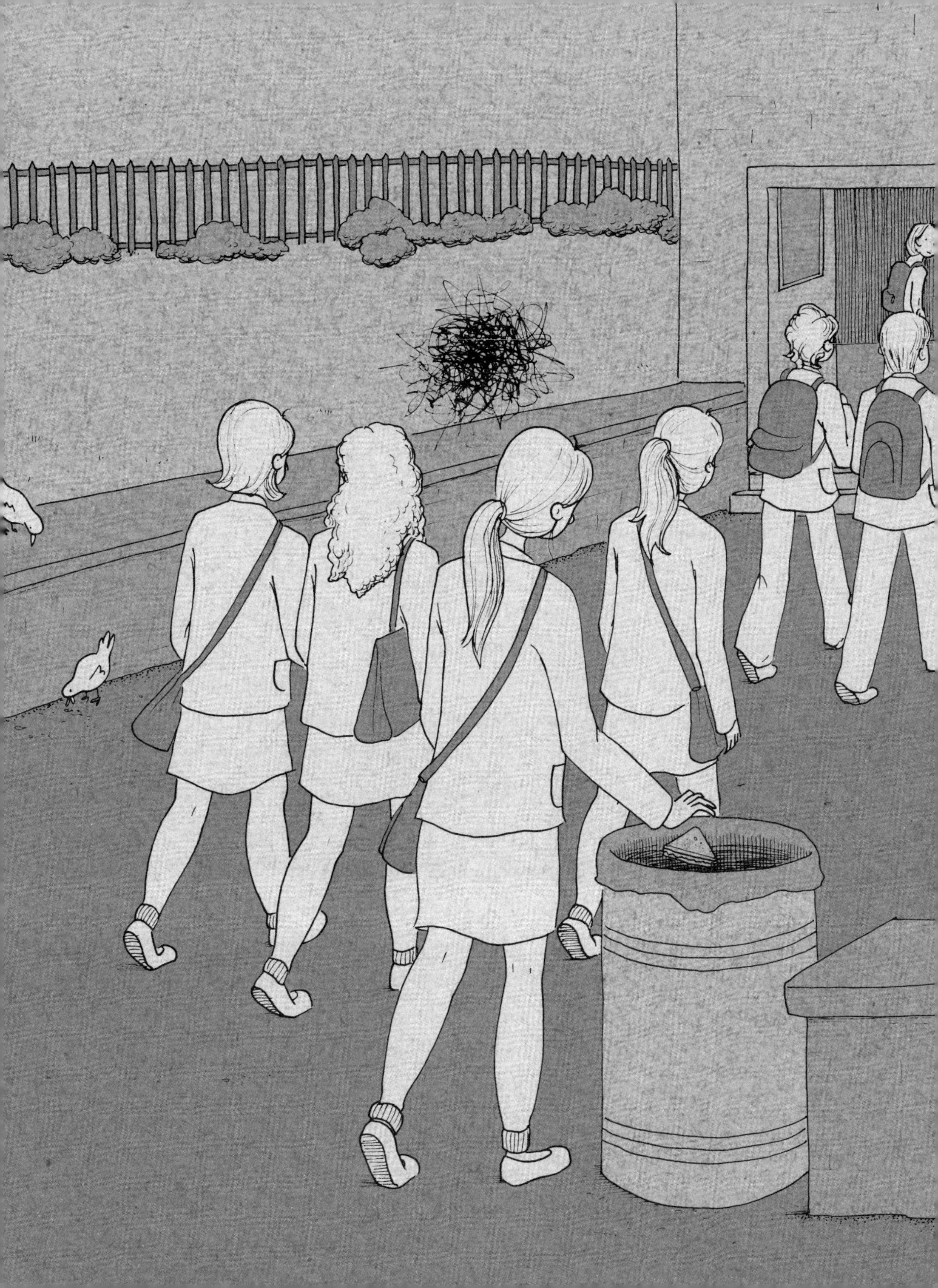

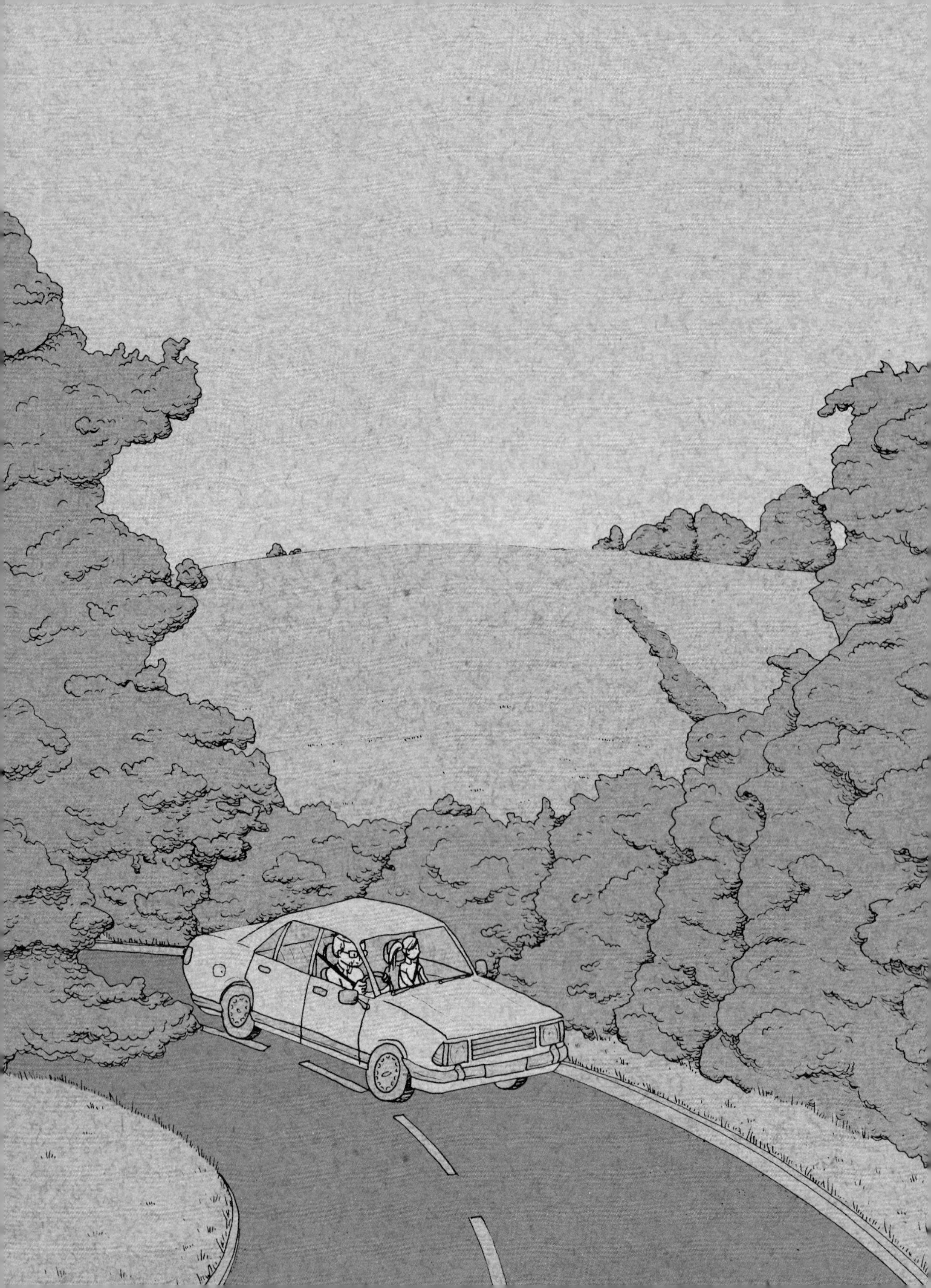

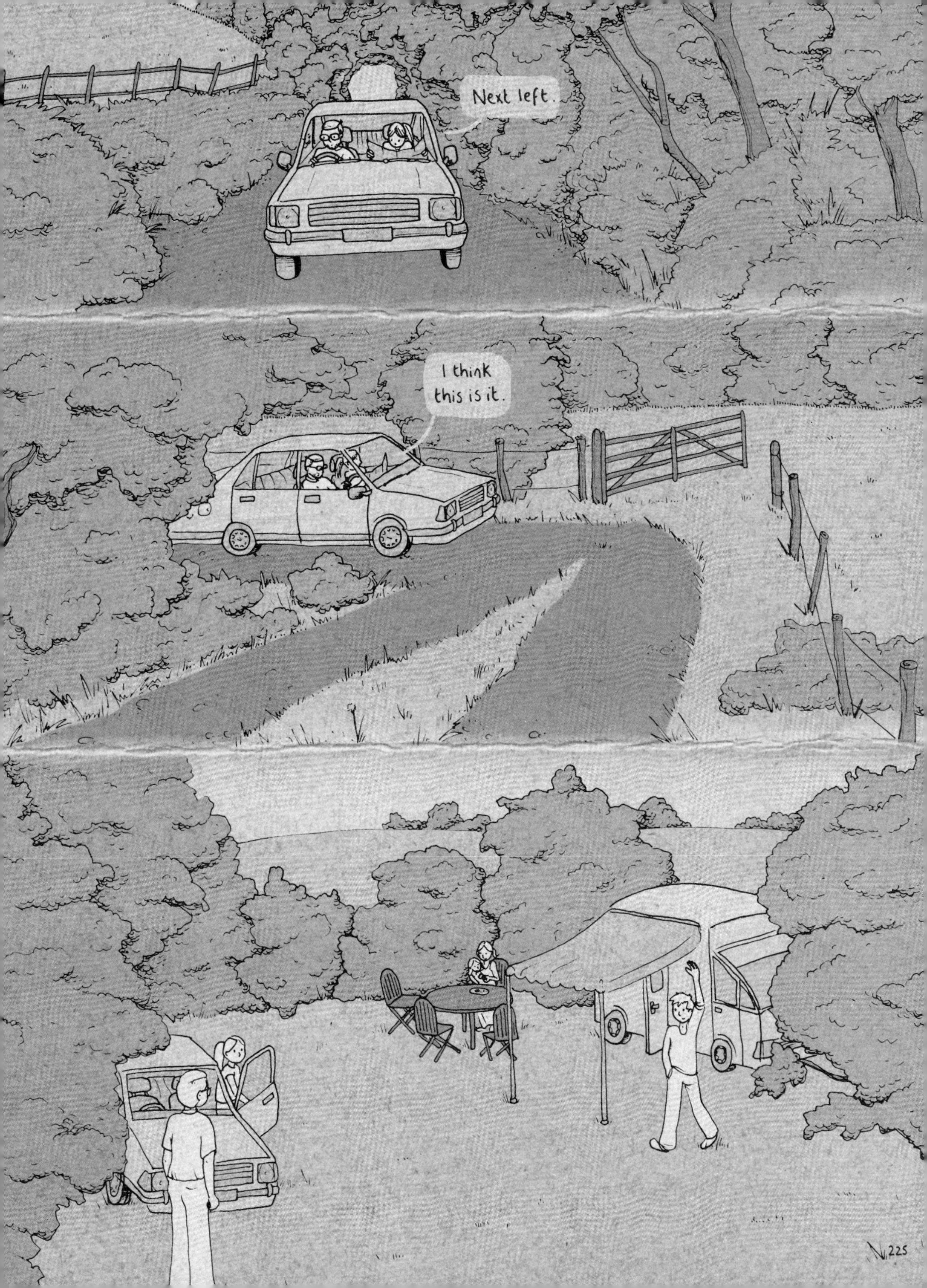
Next left.
I think this is it.

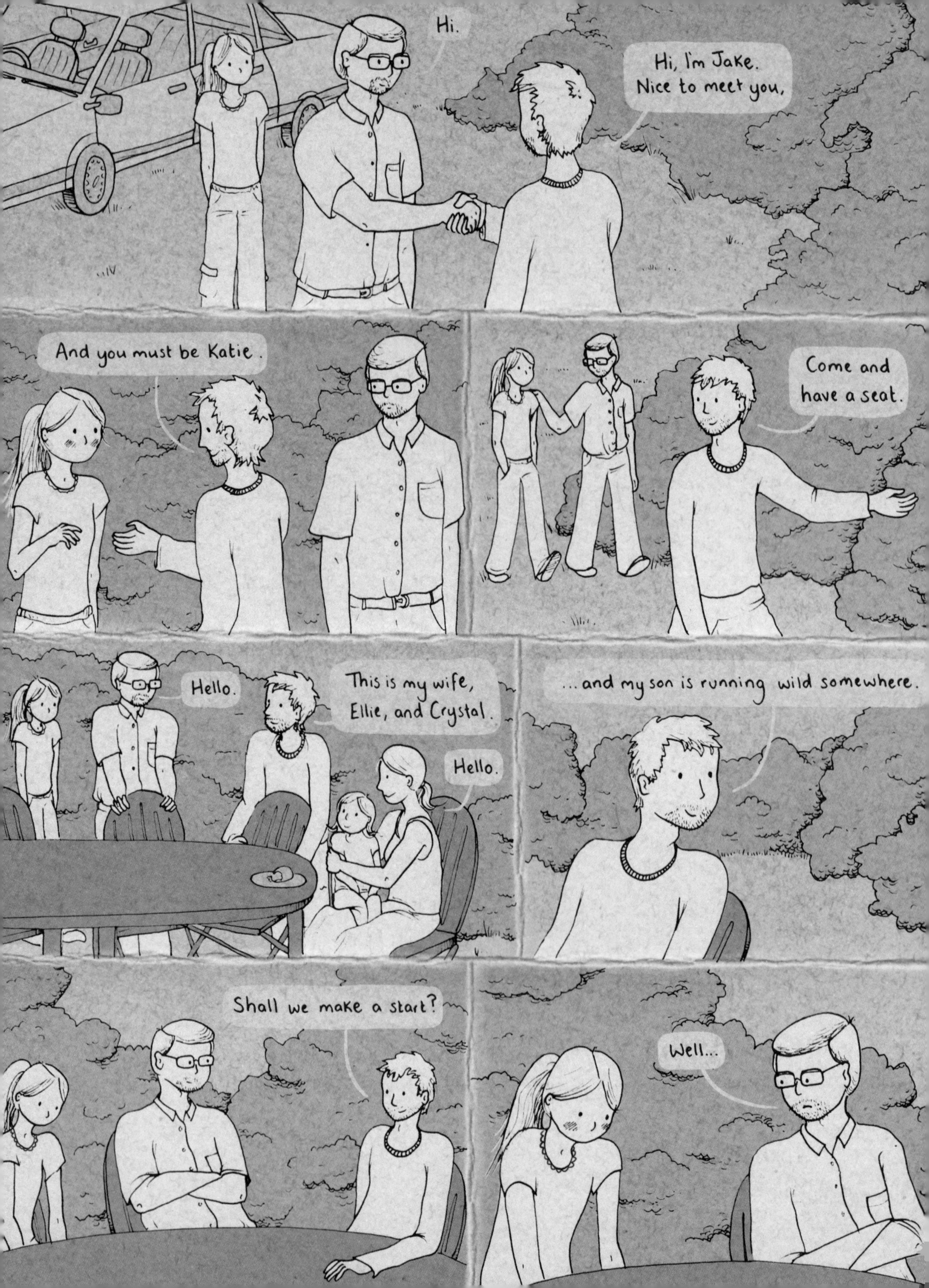
Hi.
Hi, I'm Jake. Nice to meet you,
And you must be Katie.
Come and have a seat.
Hello.
This is my wife, Ellie, and Crystal.
Hello.
...and my son is running wild somewhere.
Shall we make a start?
Well...

I'd heard the story a thousand times. I drifted, taking in my surroundings. It was beautiful.

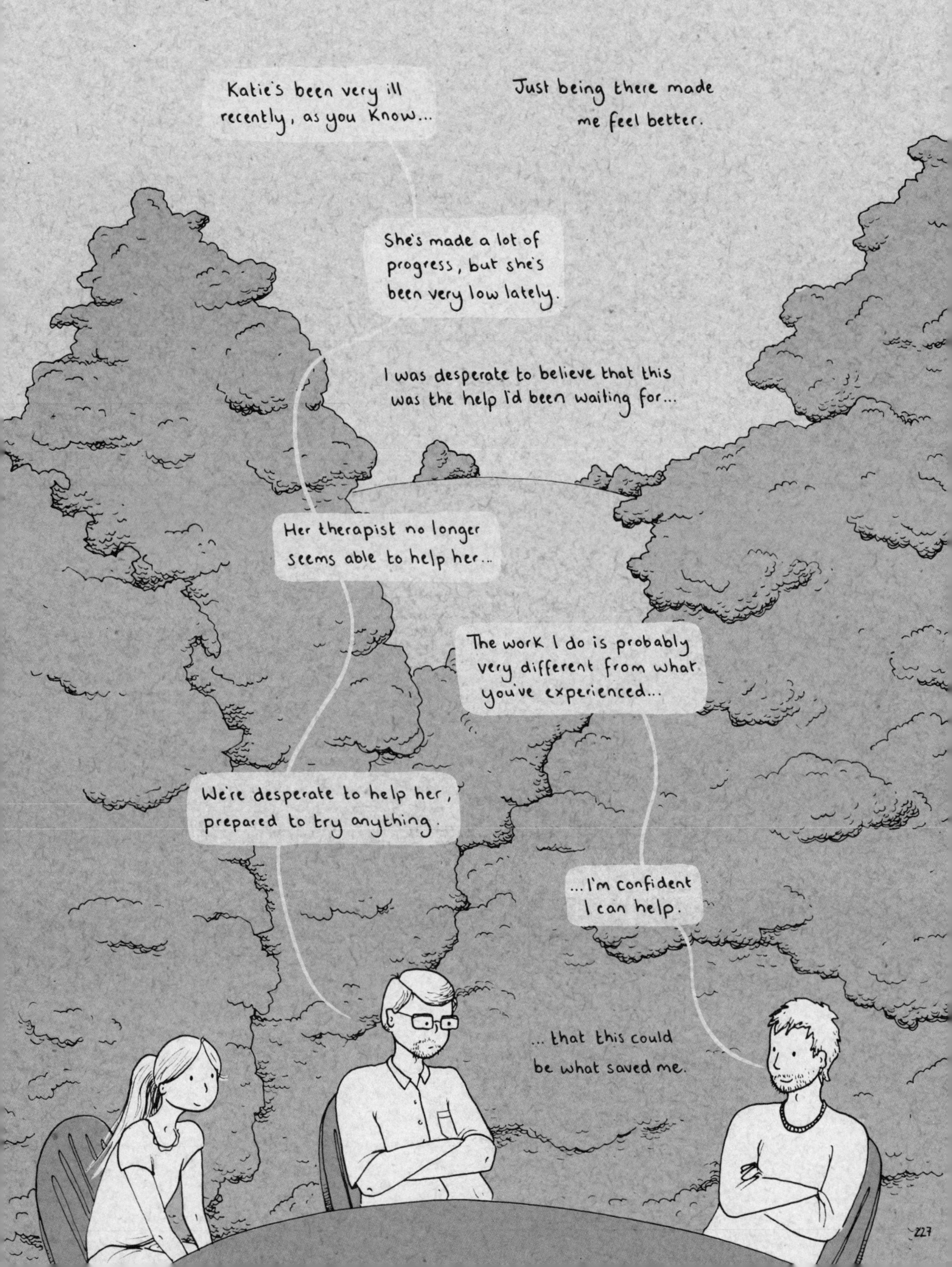

Katie's been very ill recently, as you know...
Just being there made me feel better.
She's made a lot of progress, but she's been very low lately.
I was desperate to believe that this was the help I'd been waiting for...
Her therapist no longer seems able to help her...
The work I do is probably very different from what you've experienced...
We're desperate to help her, prepared to try anything.
...I'm confident I can help.
... that this could be what saved me.

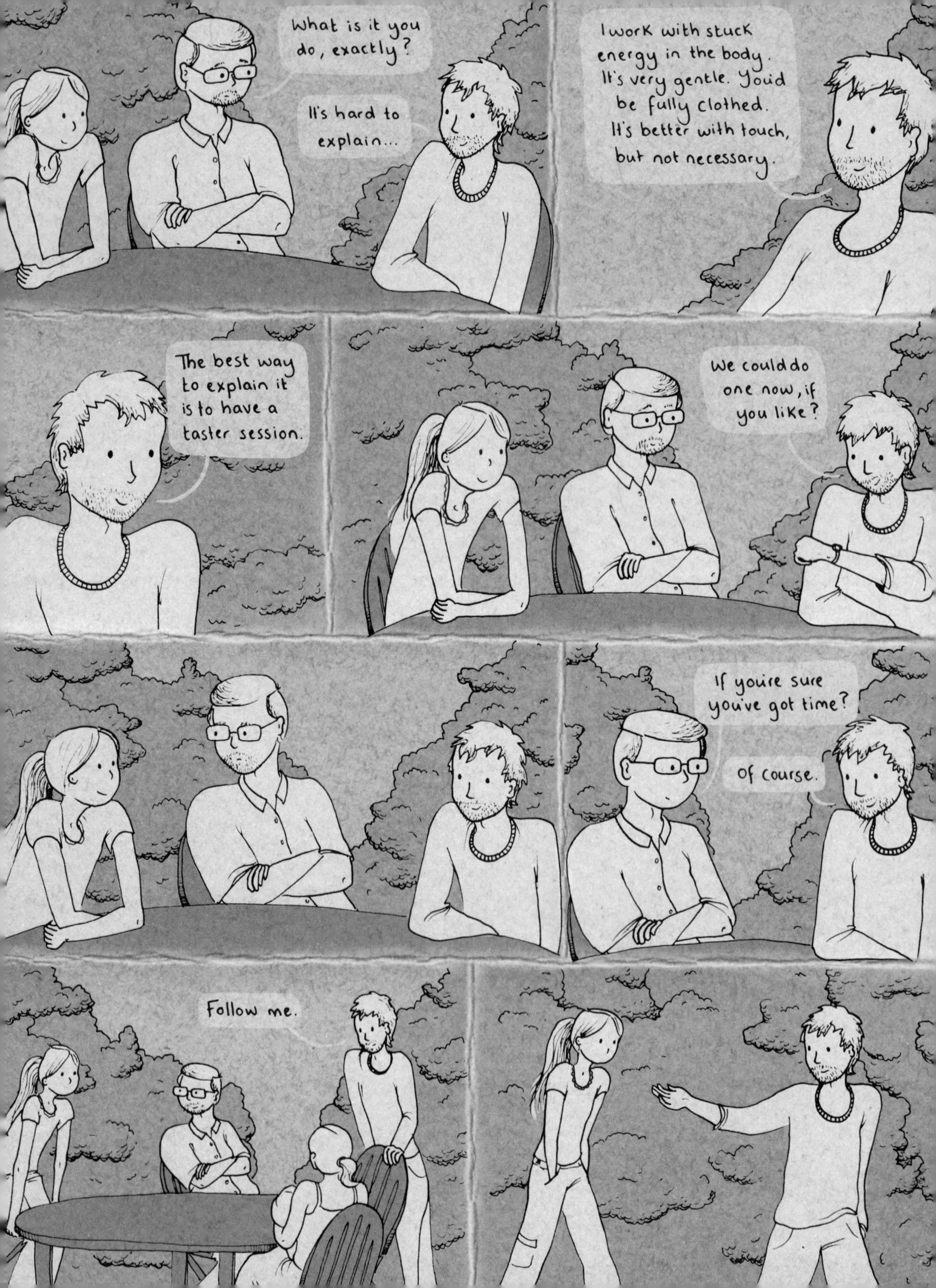
What is it you do, exactly?
It's hard to explain...
I work with stuck energy in the body. It's very gentle. You'd be fully clothed. It's better with touch, but not necessary.
The best way to explain it is to have a taster session.
We could do one now, if you like?
If you're sure you've got time?
Of course.
Follow me.

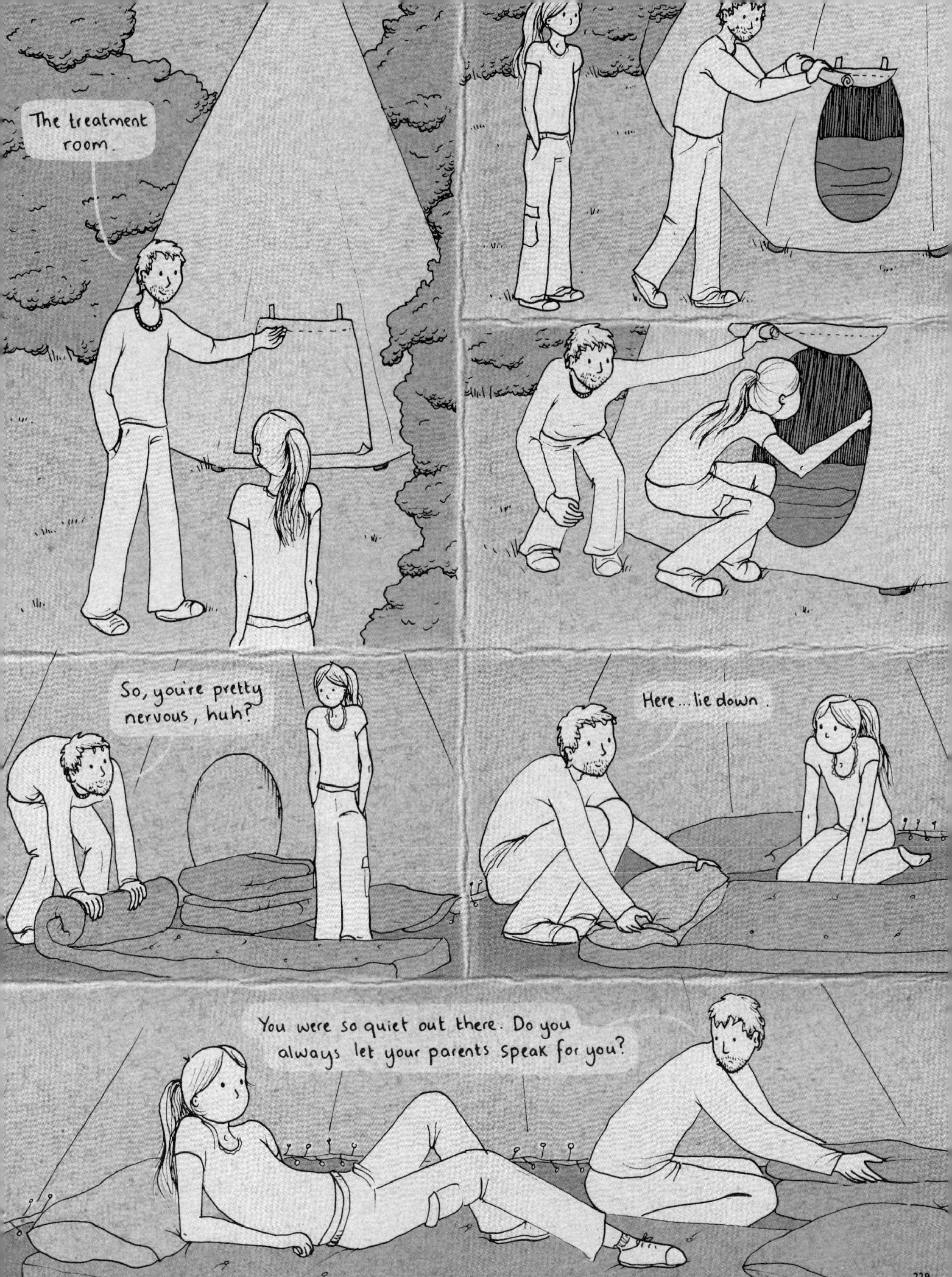
The treatment room.
So, you're pretty nervous, huh?
Here... lie down.
You were so quiet out there. Do you always let your parents speak for you?

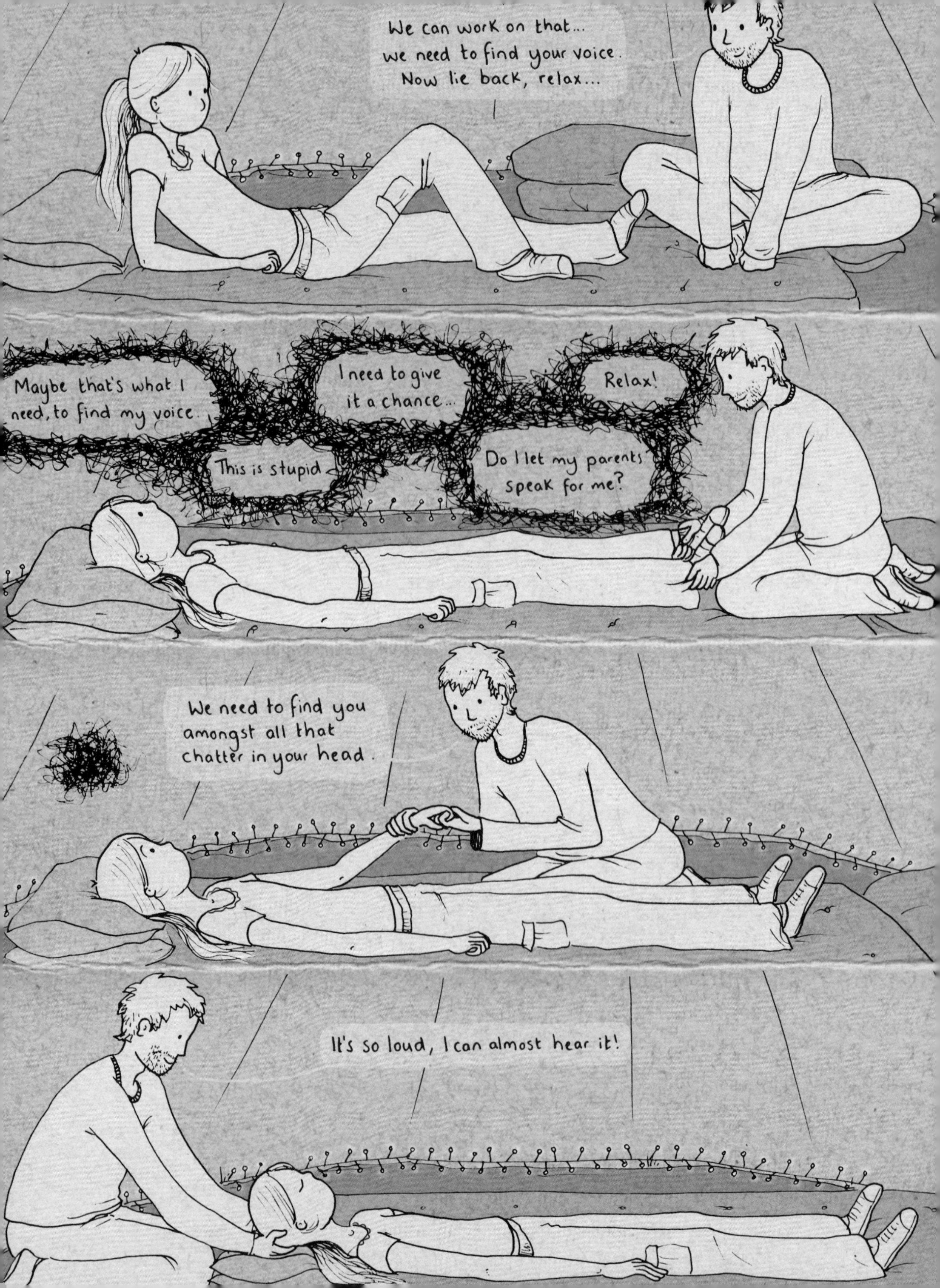
We can work on that... we need to find your voice. Now lie back, relax...
Maybe that's what I need, to find my voice.
I need to give it a chance...
Relax!
This is stupid
Do I let my parents speak for me?
We need to find you amongst all that chatter in your head.
It's so loud, I can almost hear it!

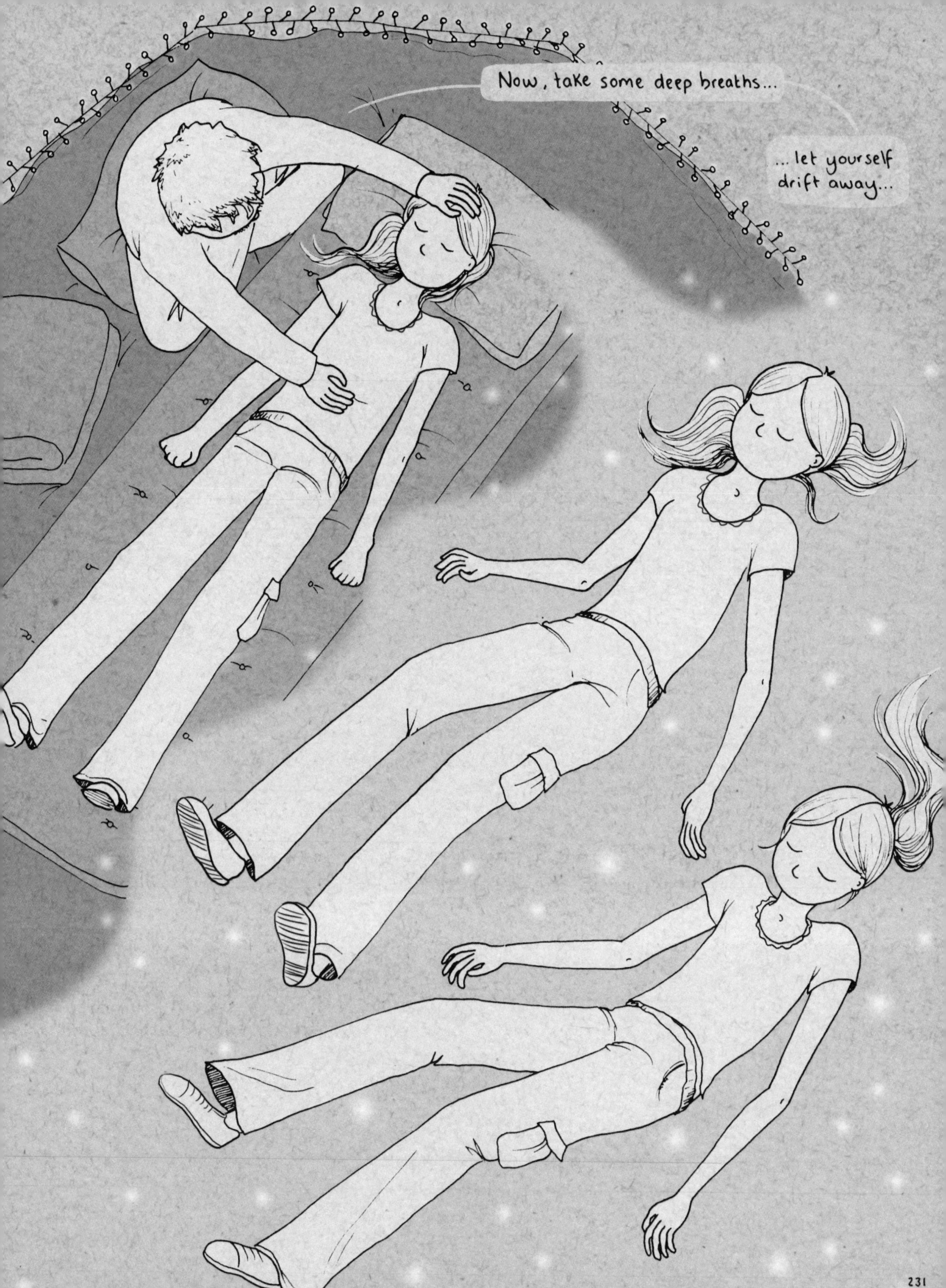
Now, take some deep breaths...
... let yourself drift away...

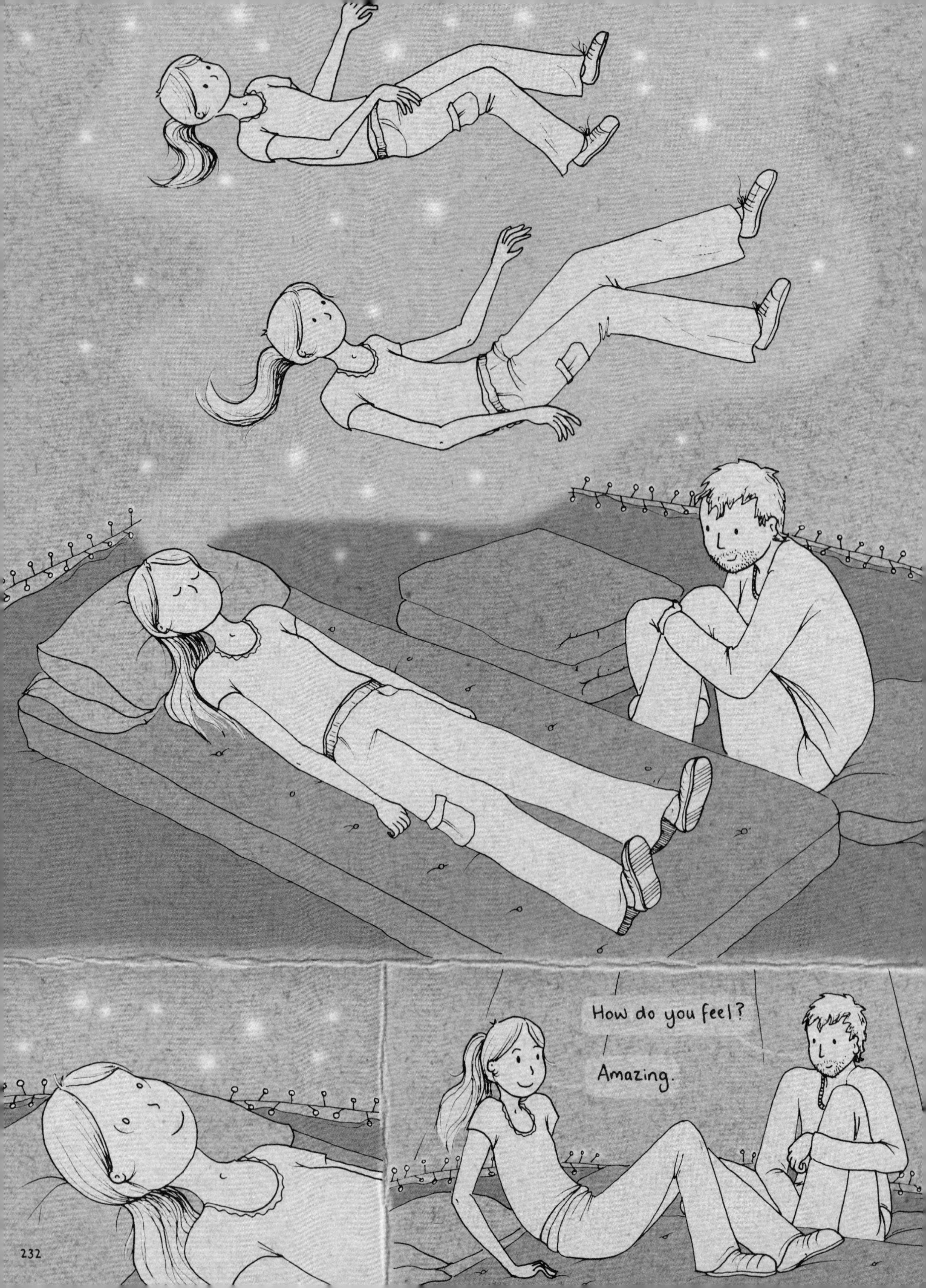
How do you feel?
Amazing.

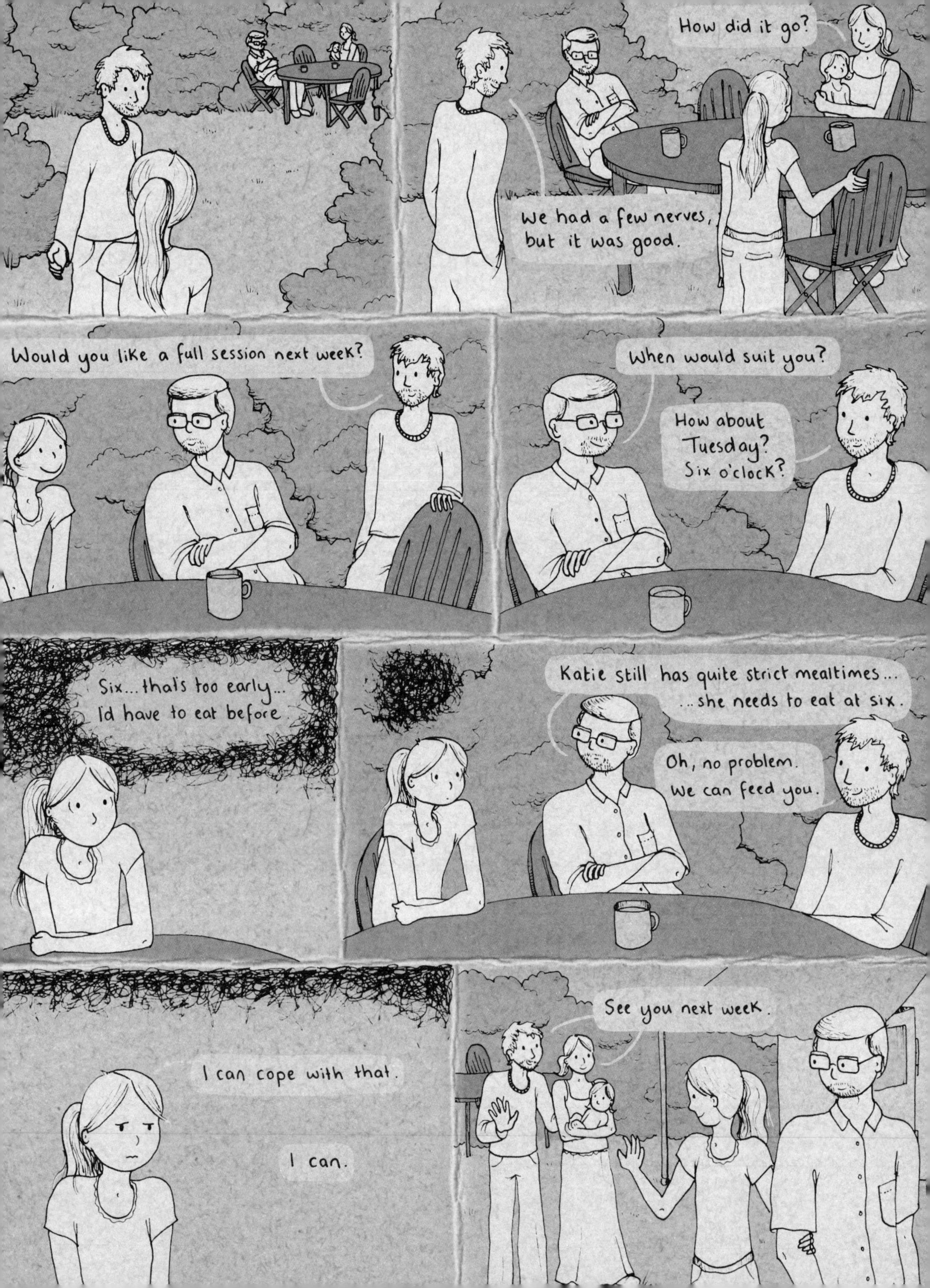
How did it go?
We had a few nerves, but it was good.
Would you like a full session next week?
When would suit you?
How about Tuesday? Six o'clock?
Six... that's too early... I'd have to eat before.
Katie still has quite strict mealtimes... ...she needs to eat at six.
Oh, no problem. We can feed you.
I can cope with that.
I can.
See you next week.

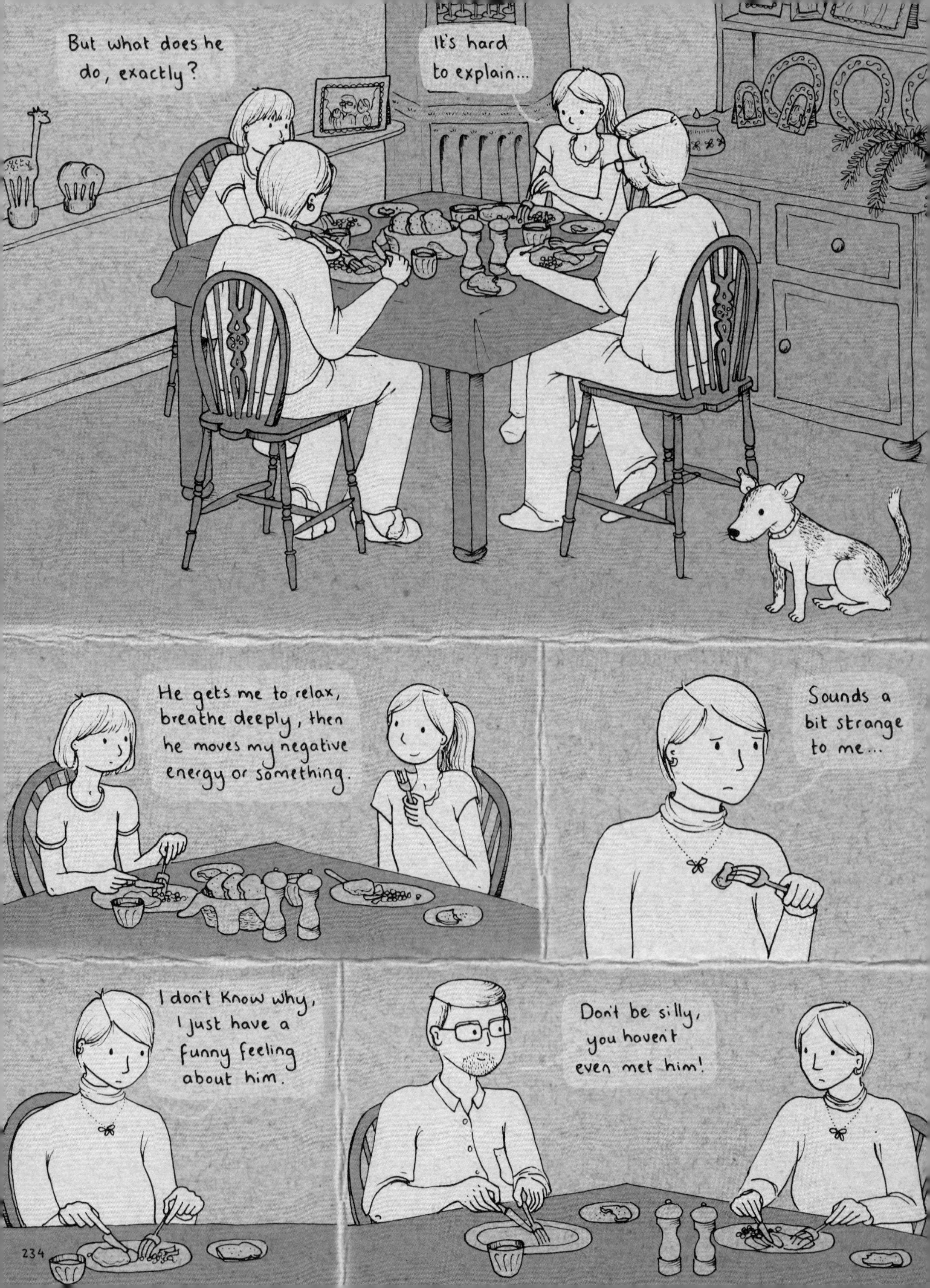
But what does he do, exactly?
It's hard to explain...
He gets me to relax, breathe deeply, then he moves my negative energy or something.
Sounds a bit strange to me...
I don't know why, I just have a funny feeling about him.
Don't be silly, you haven't even met him!

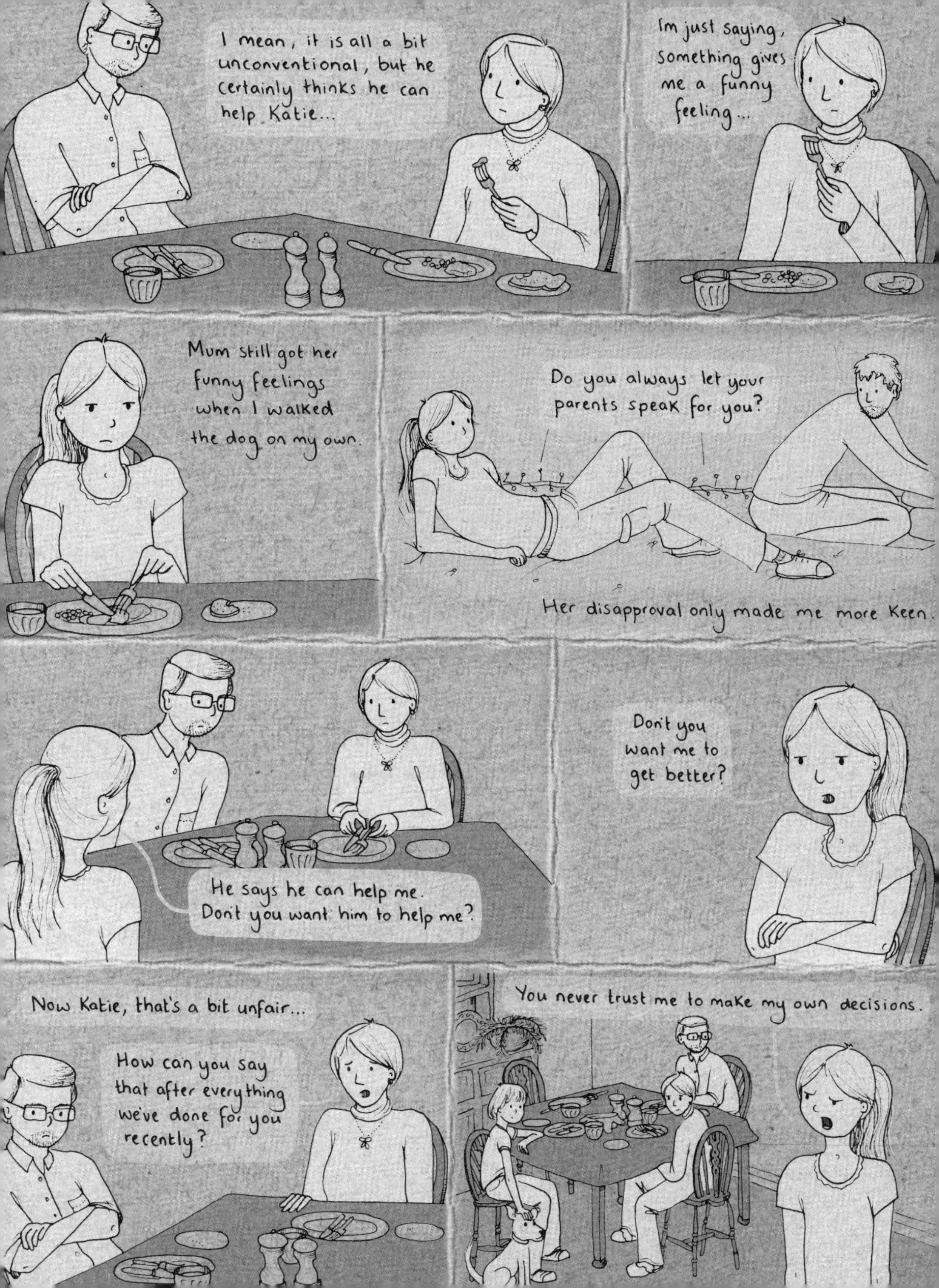
I mean, it is all a bit unconventional, but he certainly thinks he can help Katie...
I'm just saying, something gives me a funny feeling...
Mum still got her funny feelings when I walked the dog on my own.
Do you always let your parents speak for you?
Her disapproval only made me more keen.
He says he can help me. Don't you want him to help me?
Don't you want me to get better?
Now Katie, that's a bit unfair...
How can you say that after everything we've done for you recently?
You never trust me to make my own decisions.

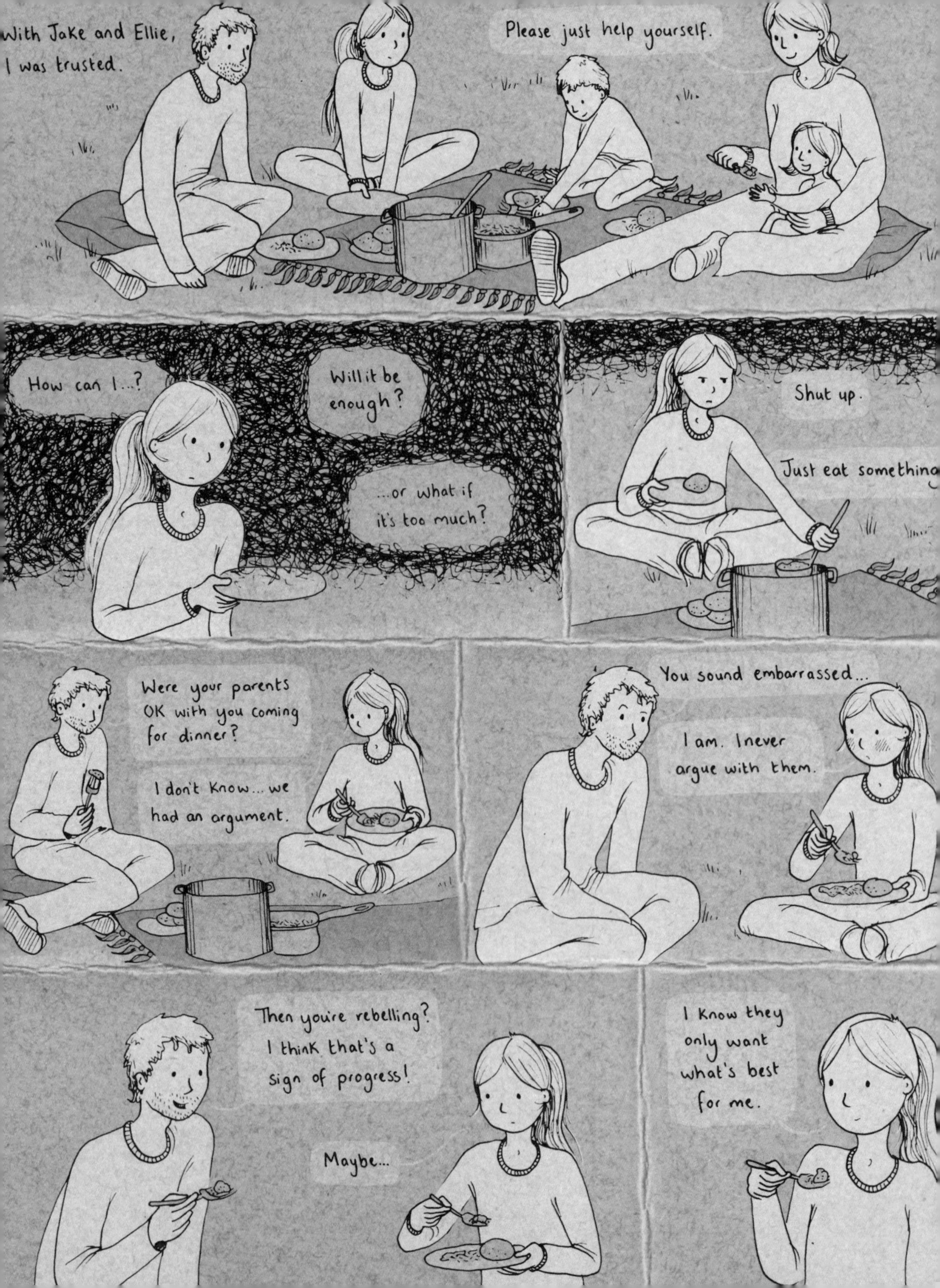
With Jake and Ellie, I was trusted.
Please just help yourself.
How can I...?
Will it be enough?
...or what if it's too much?
Shut up.
Just eat something
Were your parents OK with you coming for dinner?
I don't know... we had an argument.
You sound embarrassed...
I am. I never argue with them.
Then you're rebelling? I think that's a sign of progress!
Maybe...
I know they only want what's best for me.

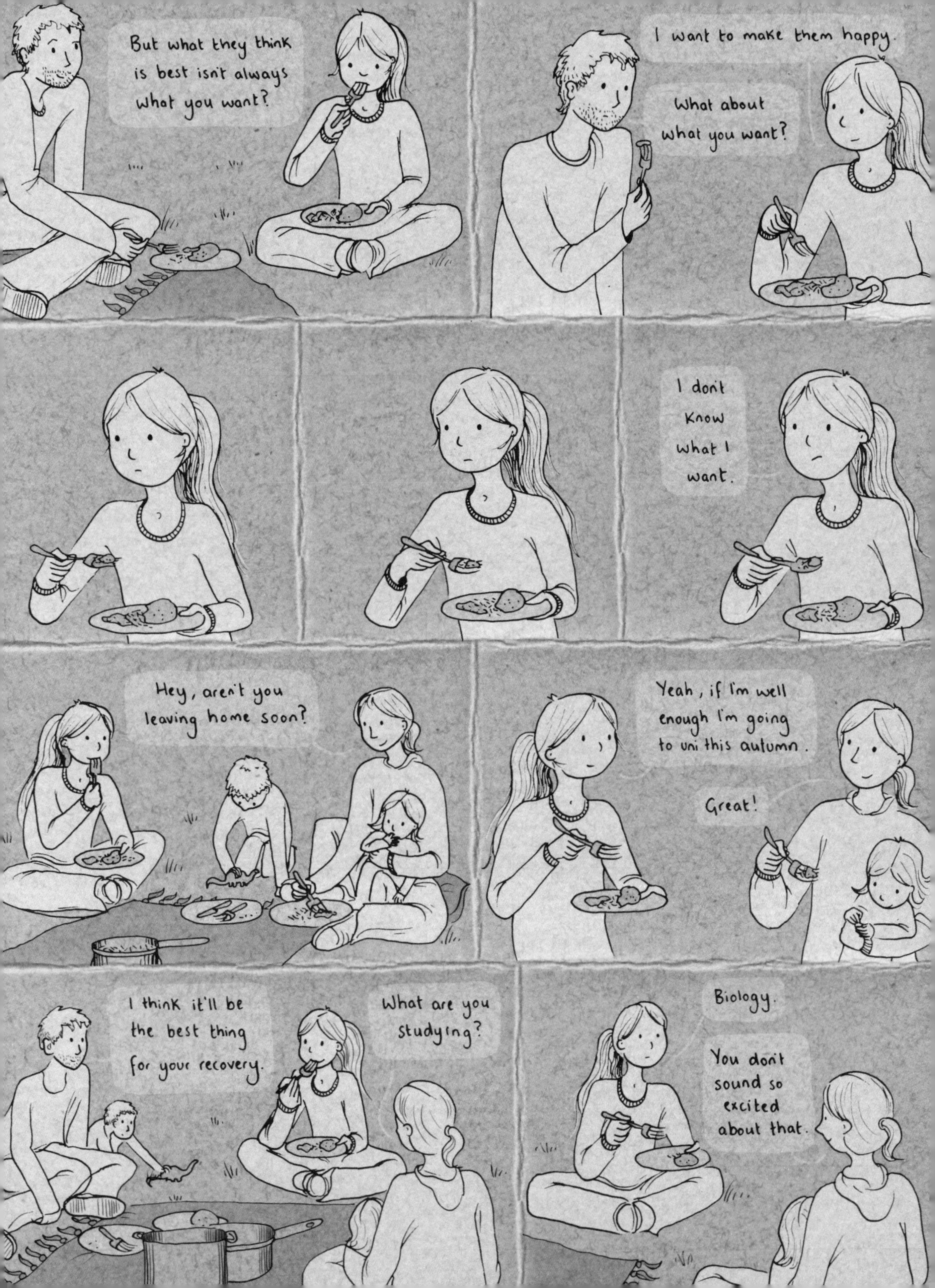

But what they think is best isn't always what you want?
I want to make them happy.
What about what you want?
I don't know what I want.
Hey, aren't you leaving home soon?
Yeah, if I'm well enough I'm going to uni this autumn.
Great!
I think it'll be the best thing for your recovery.
What are you studying?
Biology.
You don't sound so excited about that.

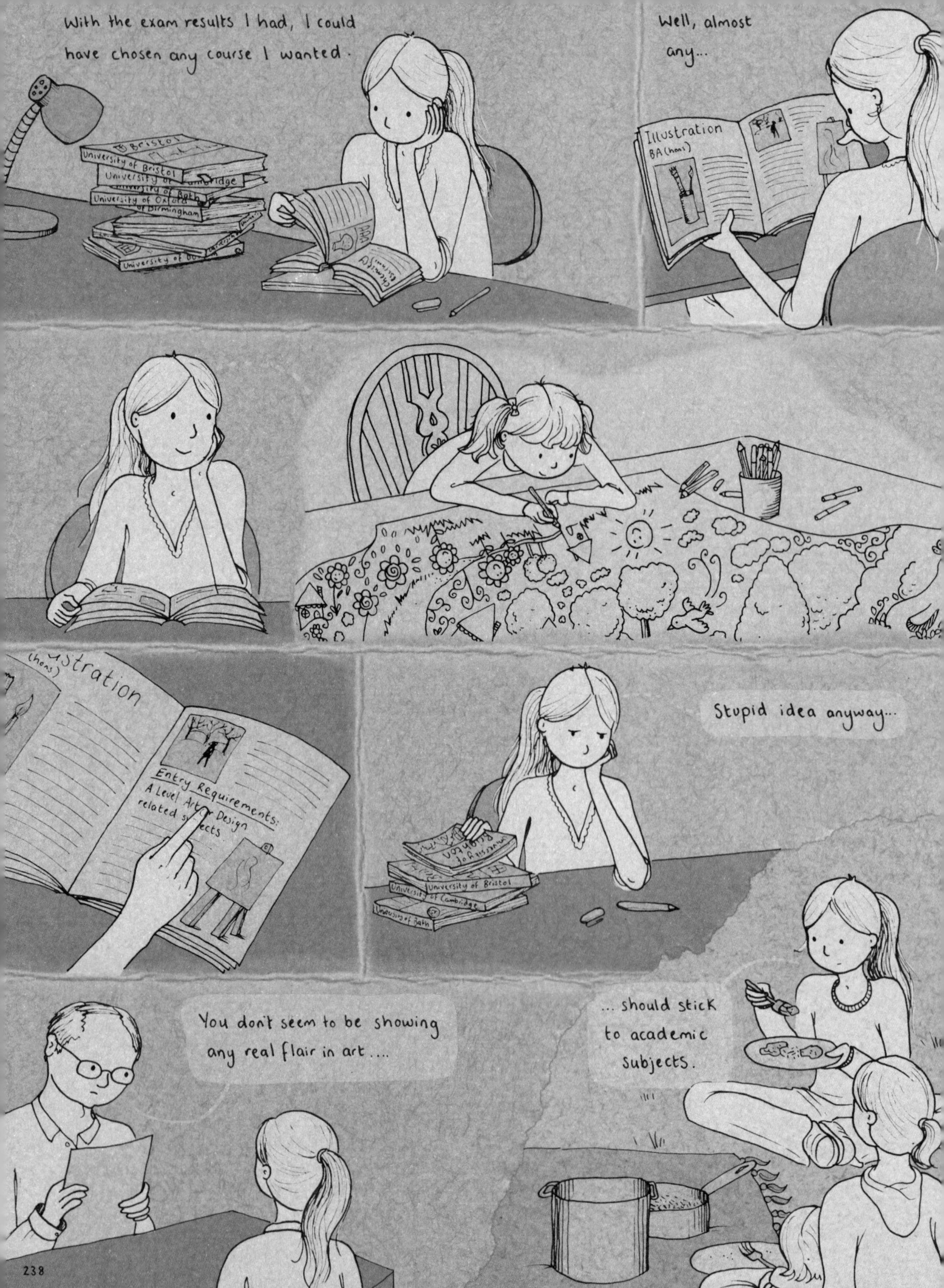

With the exam results I had, I could have chosen any course I wanted.
University of Bristol
University of Cambridge
University of Bath
University of Oxford
University of Birmingham
Well, almost any...
Illustration
BA (hons)
Entry Requirements:
Stupid idea anyway...
You don't seem to be showing any real flair in art....
... should stick to academic subjects.

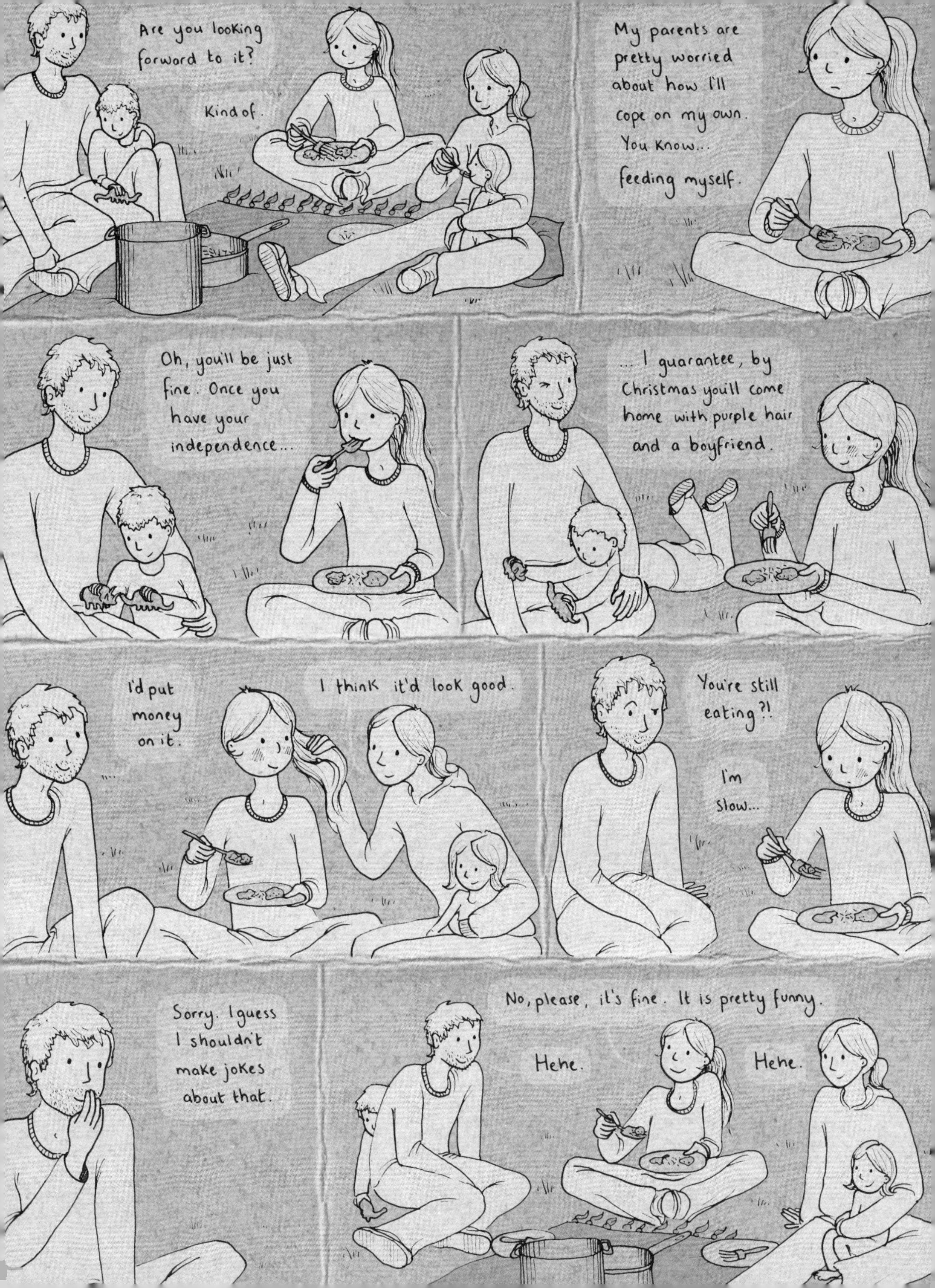
Are you looking forward to it?
Kind of.
My parents are pretty worried about how I'll cope on my own. You know... feeding myself.
Oh, you'll be just fine. Once you have your independence...
... I guarantee, by Christmas you'll come home with purple hair and a boyfriend.
I'd put money on it.
I think it'd look good.
You're still eating?!
I'm slow...
Sorry. I guess I shouldn't make jokes about that.
No, please, it's fine. It is pretty funny.
Hehe.
Hehe.

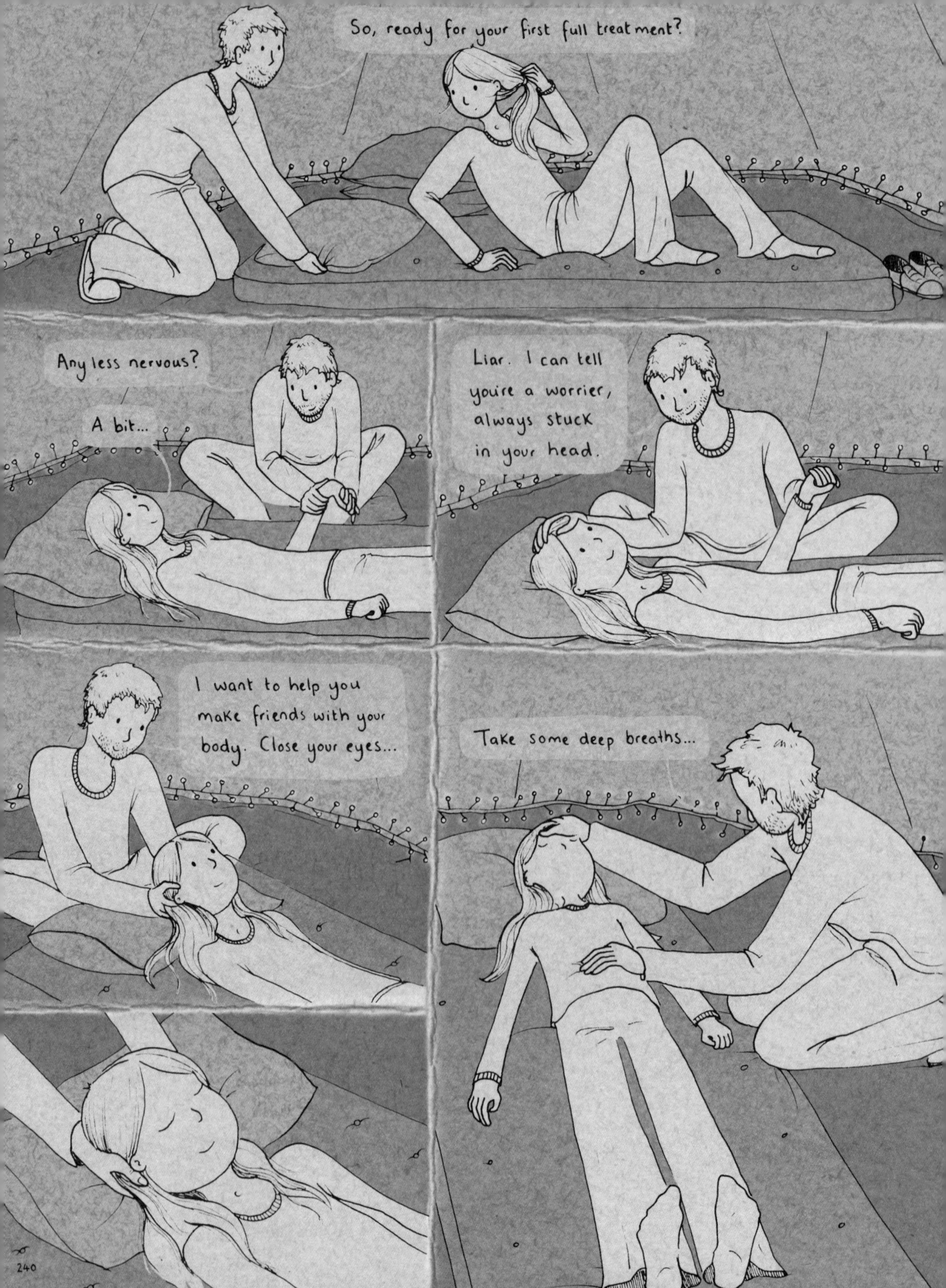
So, ready for your first full treatment?
Any less nervous?
A bit...
Liar. I can tell you're a worrier, always stuck in your head.
I want to help you make friends with your body. Close your eyes...
Take some deep breaths...

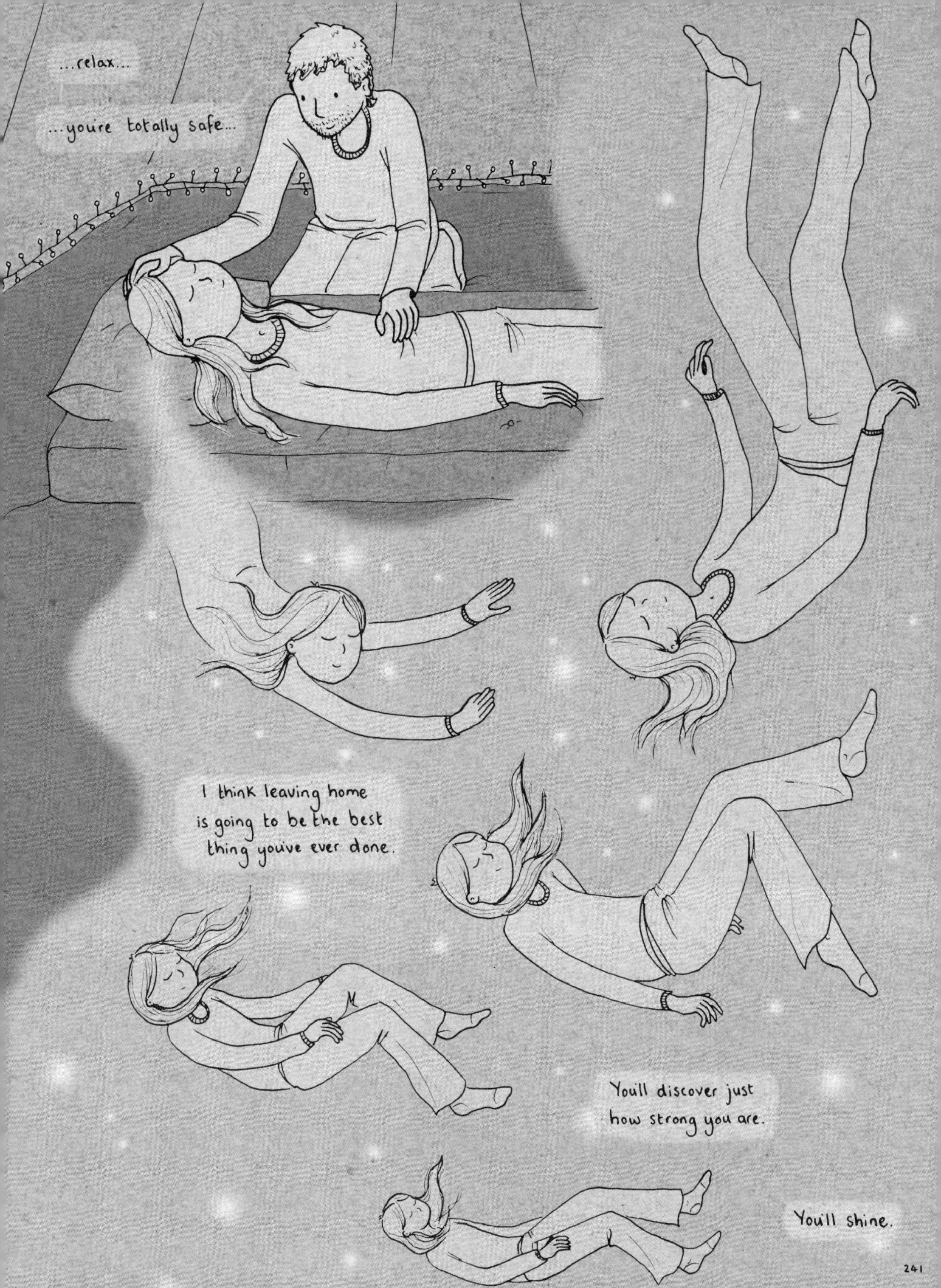

...relax...
...you're totally safe...
I think leaving home is going to be the best thing you've ever done.
You'll discover just how strong you are.
You'll shine.

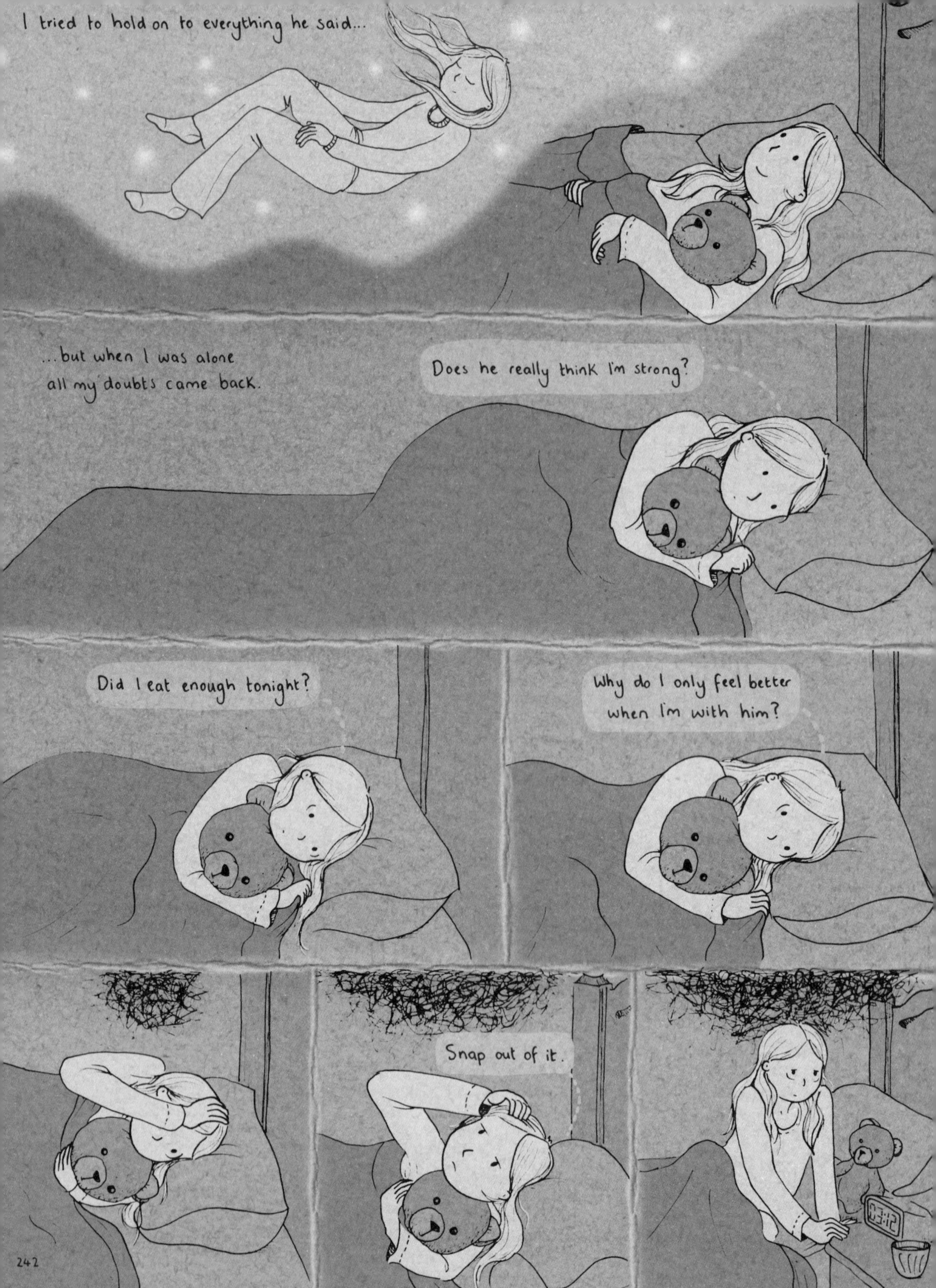
I tried to hold on to everything he said...
...but when I was alone all my doubts came back.
Does he really think I'm strong?
Did I eat enough tonight?
Why do I only feel better when I'm with him?
Snap out of it.

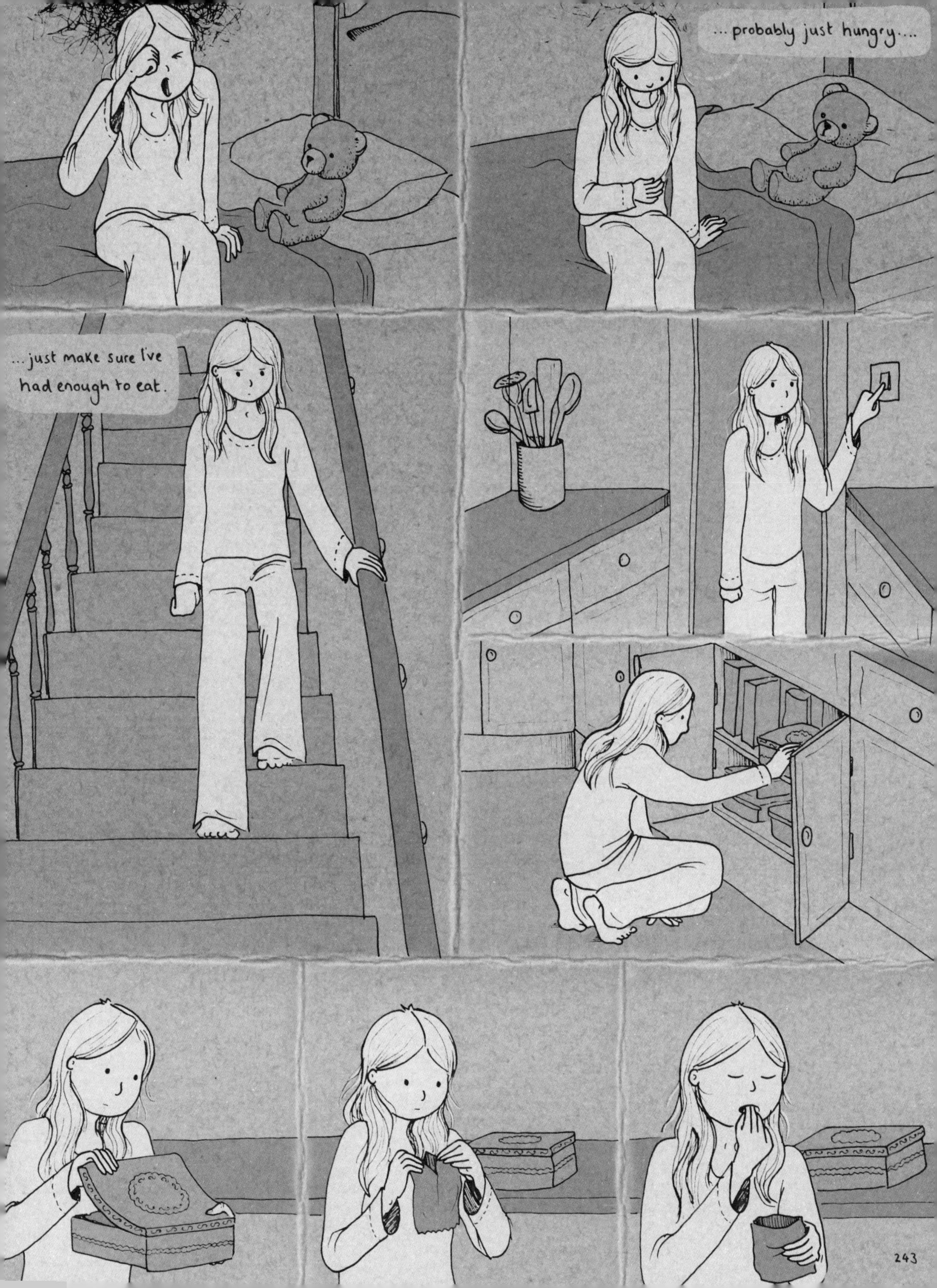
... probably just hungry....
... just make sure I've had enough to eat.

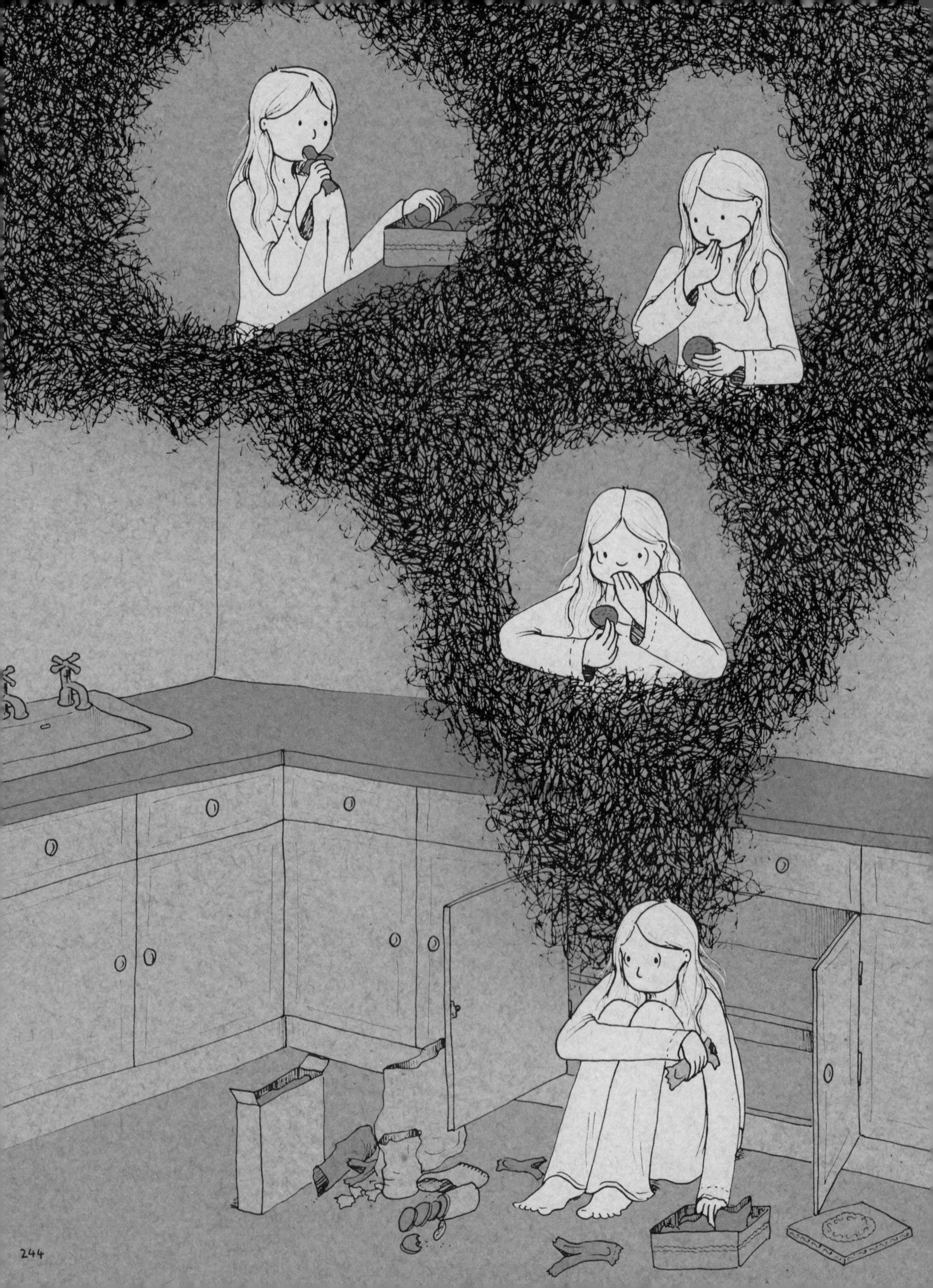

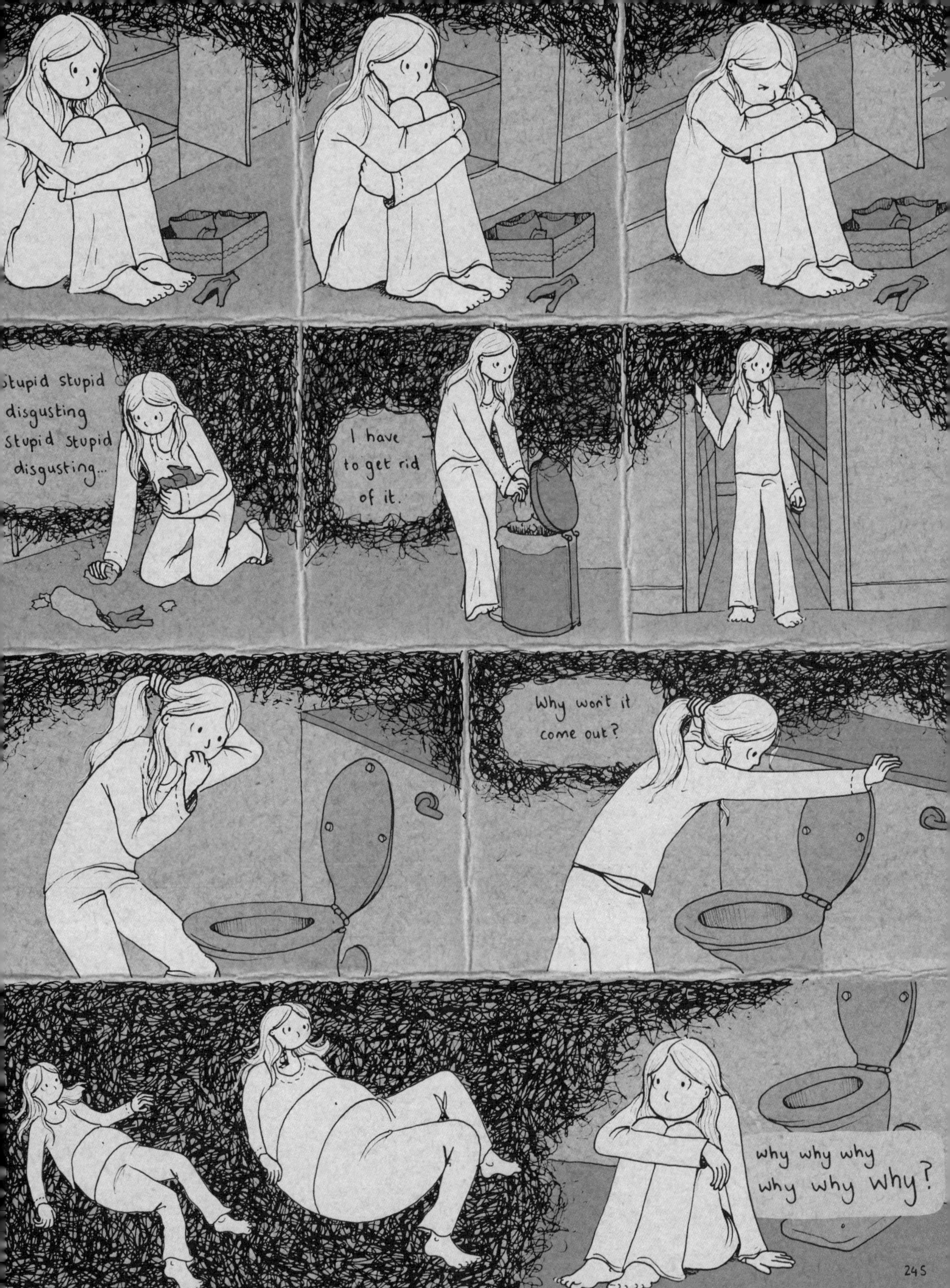
stupid stupid disgusting stupid stupid disgusting...
I have to get rid of it.
Why won't it come out?
why why why why why why?

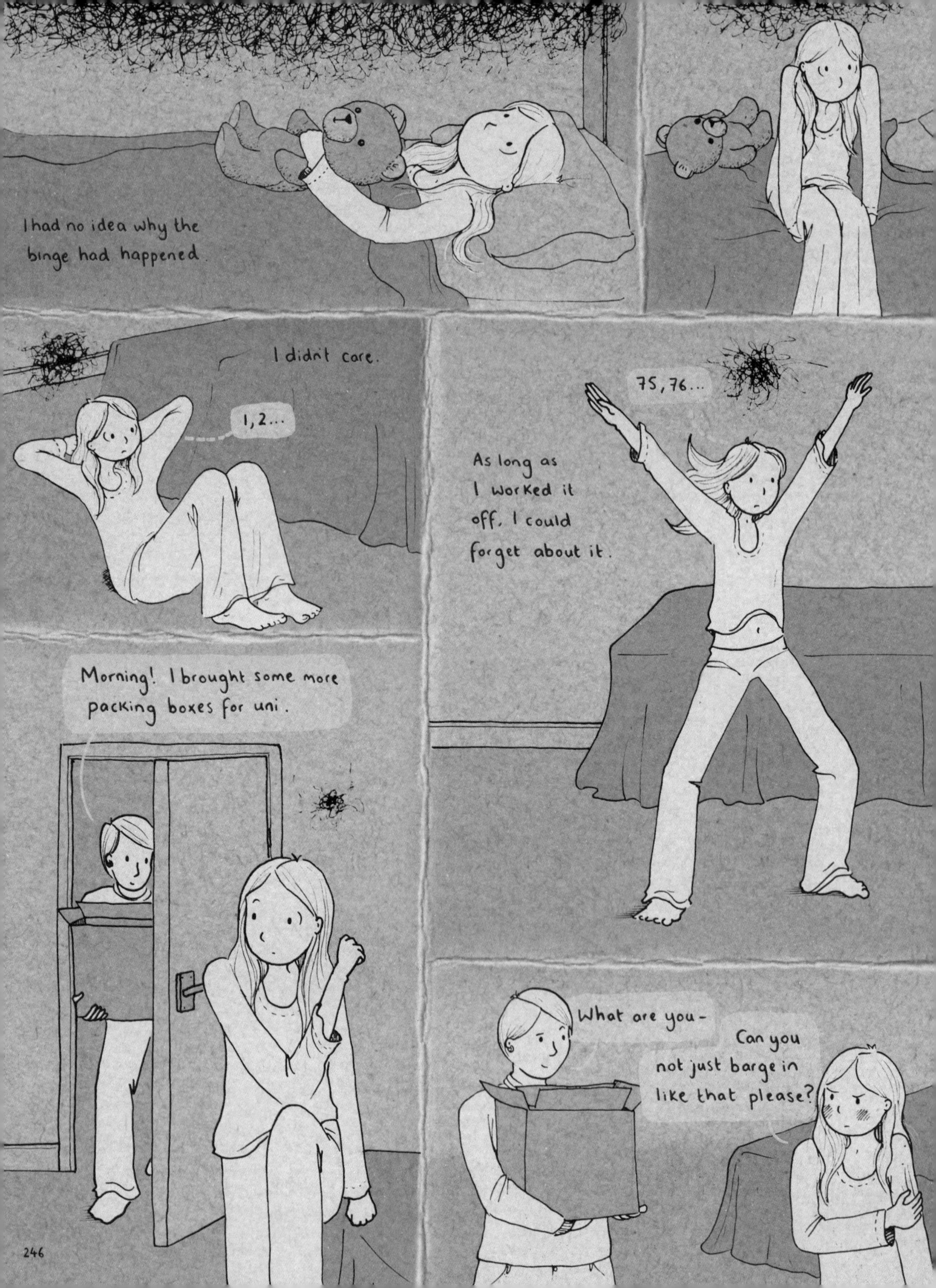
I had no idea why the binge had happened.
I didn't care.
1, 2...
75, 76...
As long as I worked it off, I could forget about it.
Morning! I brought some more packing boxes for uni.
What are you-
Can you not just barge in like that please?

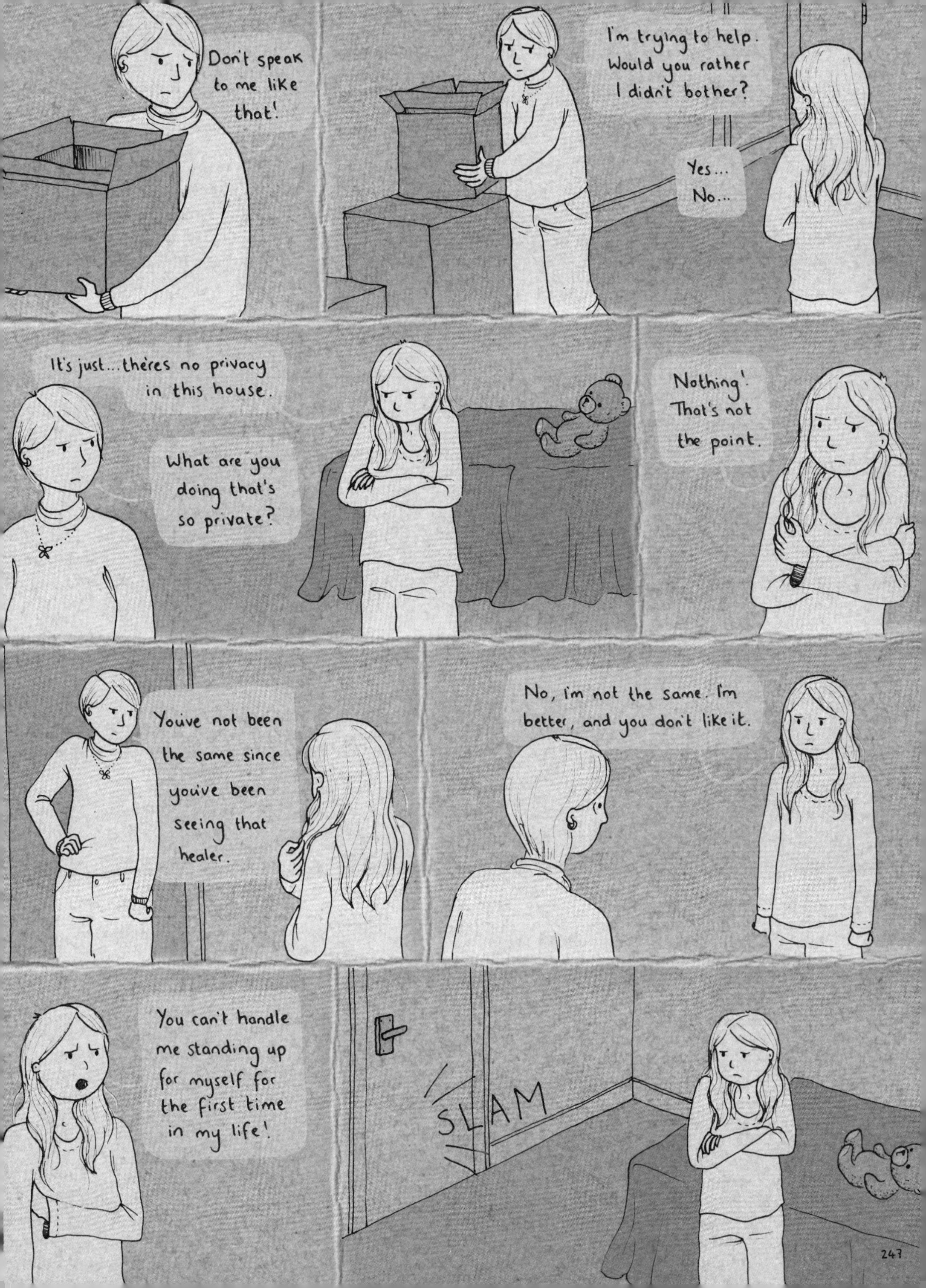
Don't speak to me like that!
I'm trying to help. Would you rather I didn't bother?
Yes... No...
It's just... there's no privacy in this house.
What are you doing that's so private?
Nothing! That's not the point.
You've not been the same since you've been seeing that healer.
No, I'm not the same. I'm better, and you don't like it.
You can't handle me standing up for myself for the first time in my life!
SLAM

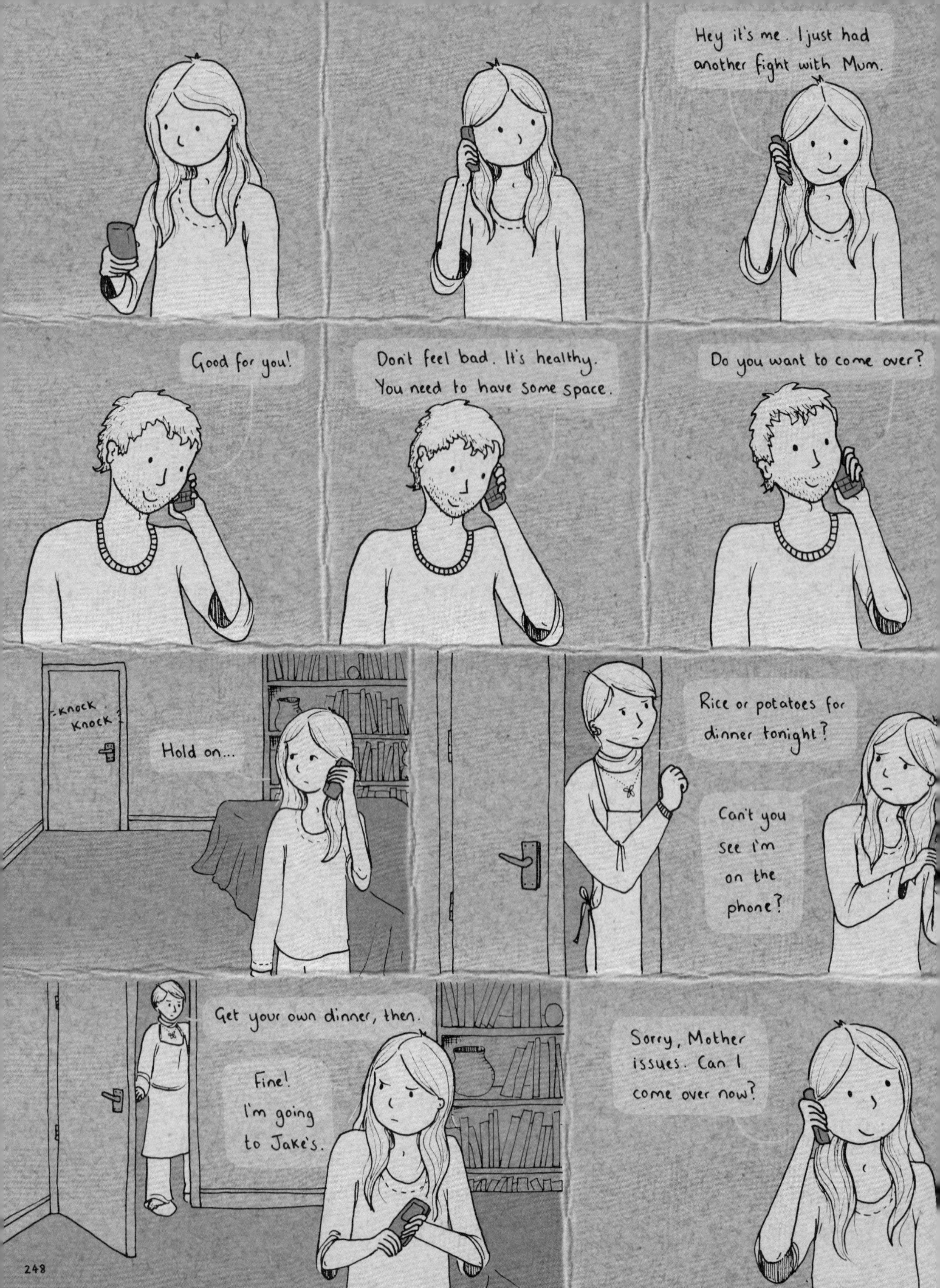
Hey it's me. I just had another fight with Mum.
Good for you!
Don't feel bad. It's healthy. You need to have some space.
Do you want to come over?
KNOCK KNOCK
Hold on...
Rice or potatoes for dinner tonight?
Can't you see I'm on the phone?
Get your own dinner, then.
Fine! I'm going to Jake's.
Sorry, Mother issues. Can I come over now?

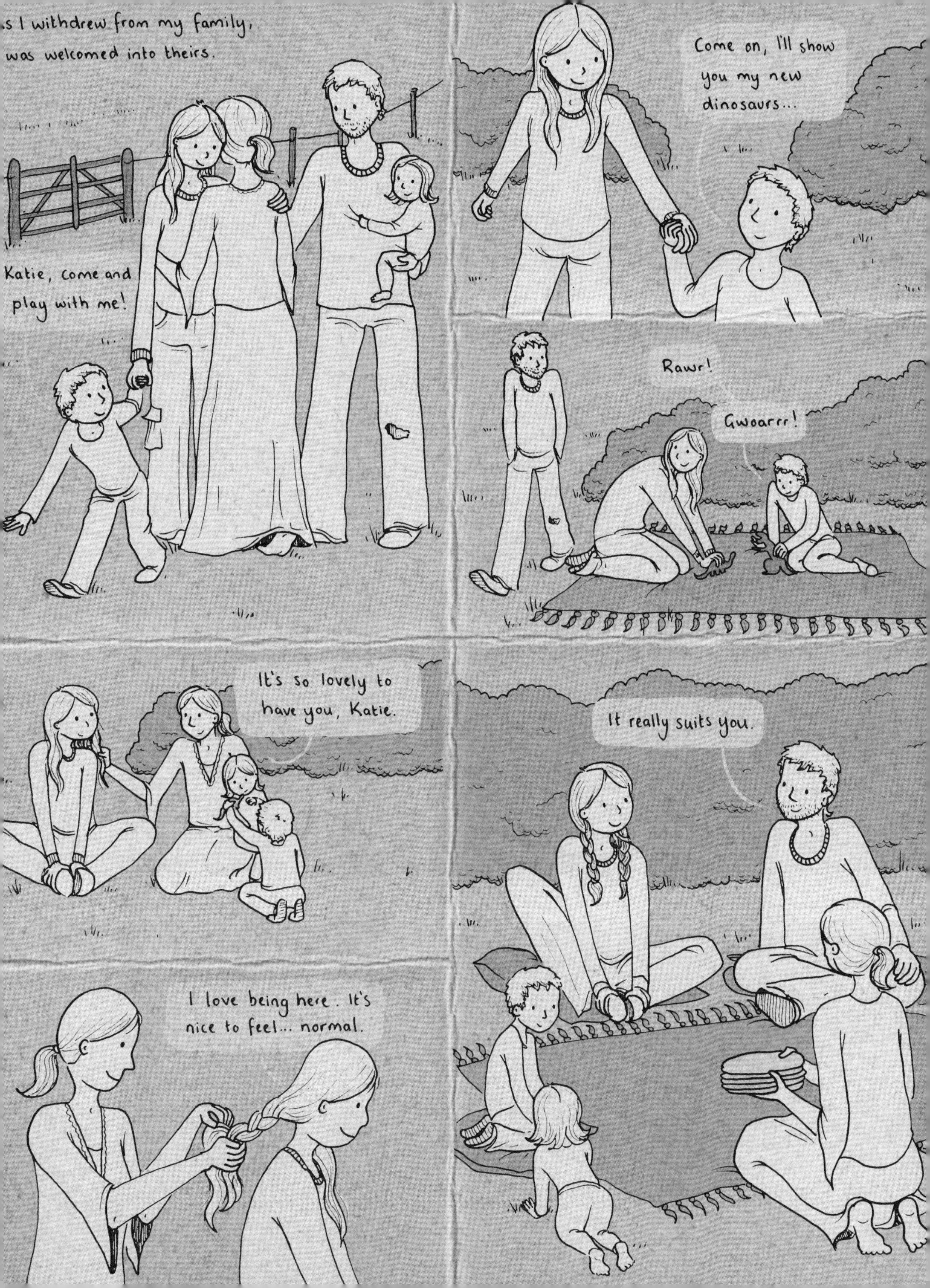
s I withdrew from my family,
was welcomed into theirs.
Katie, come and play with me!
Come on, I'll show you my new dinosaurs...
Rawr!
Gwoarrr!
It's so lovely to have you, Katie.
I love being here. It's nice to feel... normal.
It really suits you.

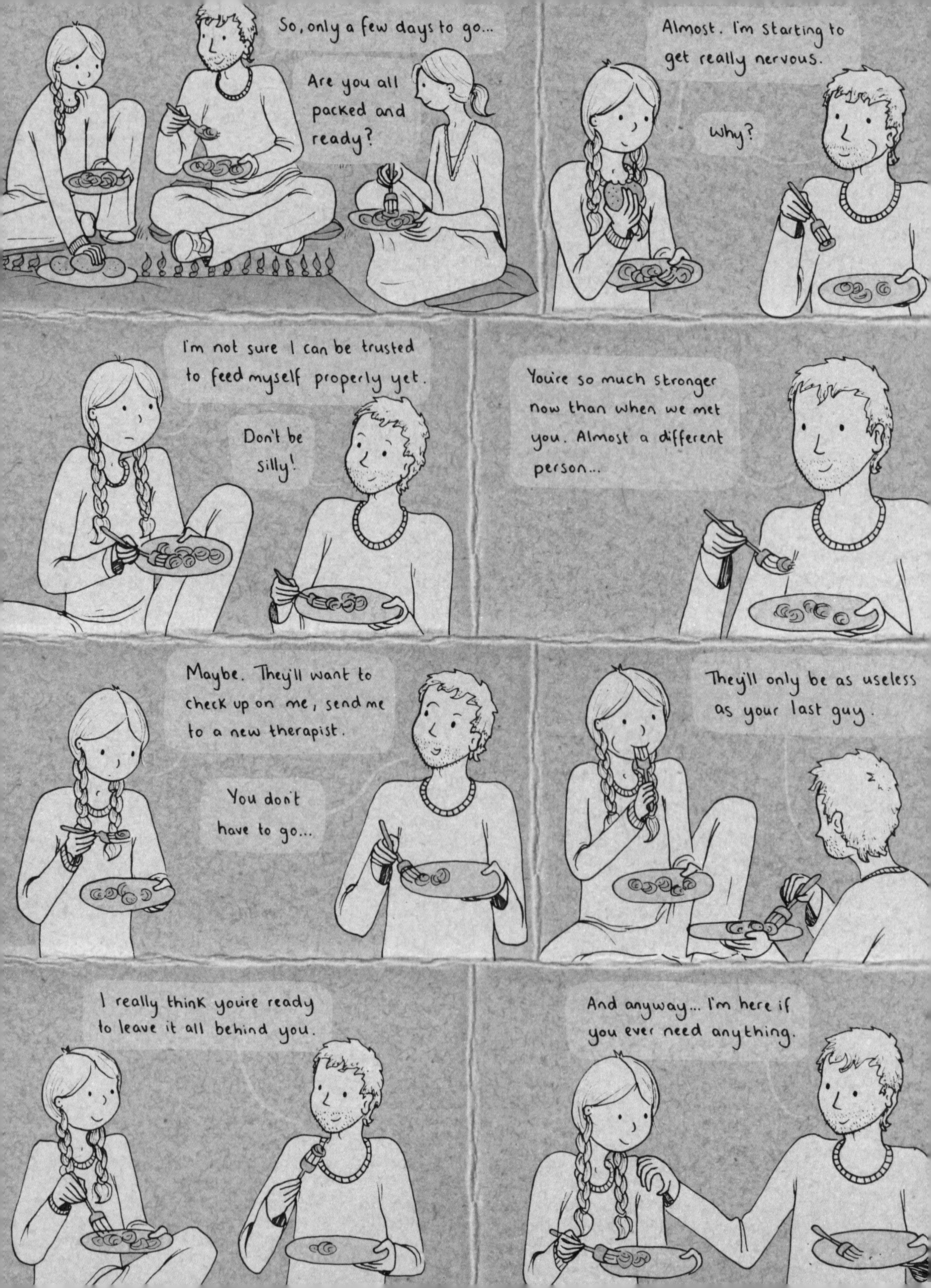
So, only a few days to go...
Are you all packed and ready?
Almost. I'm starting to get really nervous.
Why?
I'm not sure I can be trusted to feed myself properly yet.
Don't be silly!
You're so much stronger now than when we met you. Almost a different person...
Maybe. They'll want to check up on me, send me to a new therapist.
You don't have to go...
They'll only be as useless as your last guy.
I really think you're ready to leave it all behind you.
And anyway... I'm here if you ever need anything.

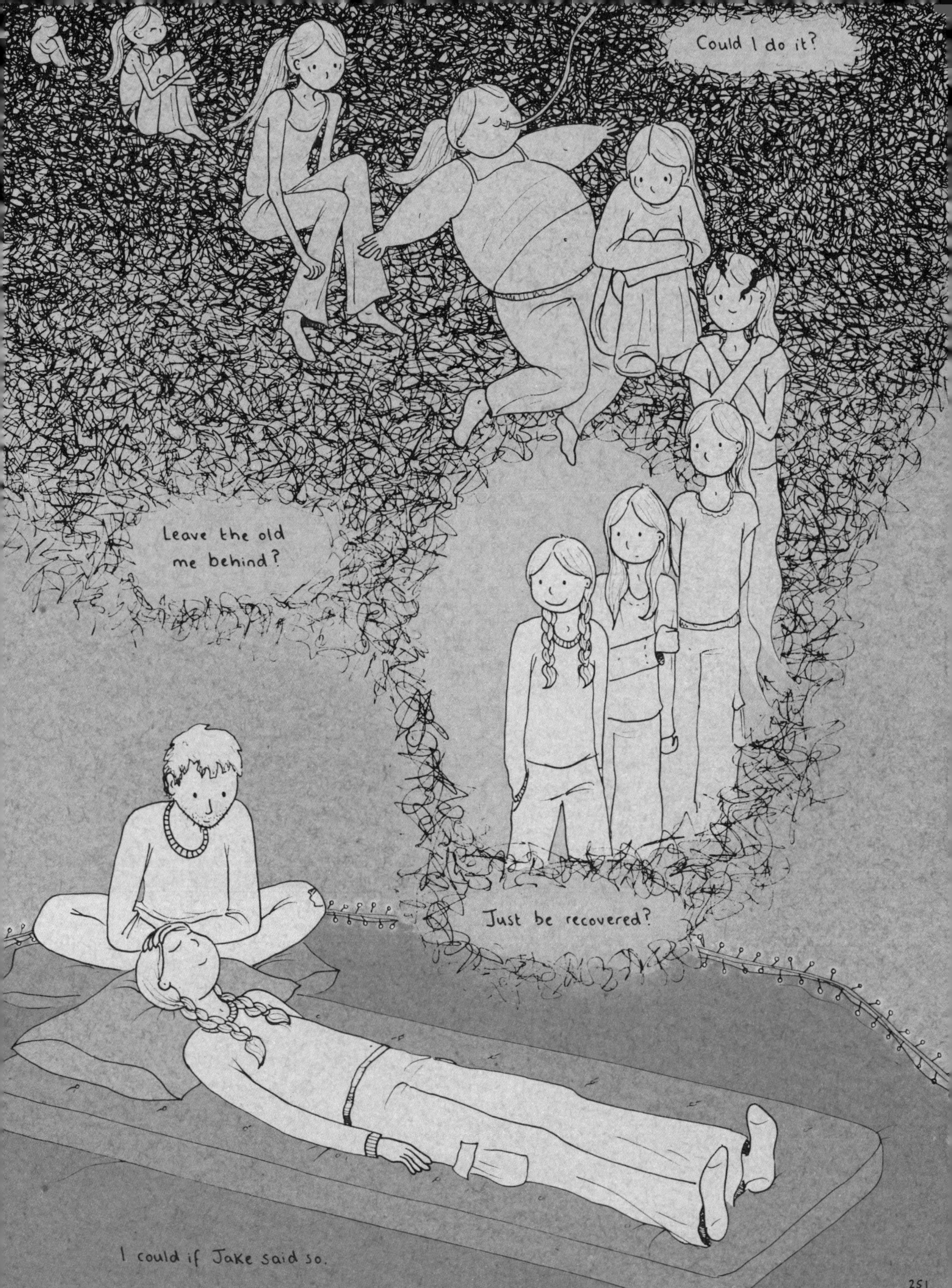

Could I do it?
Leave the old me behind?
Just be recovered?
I could if Jake said so.

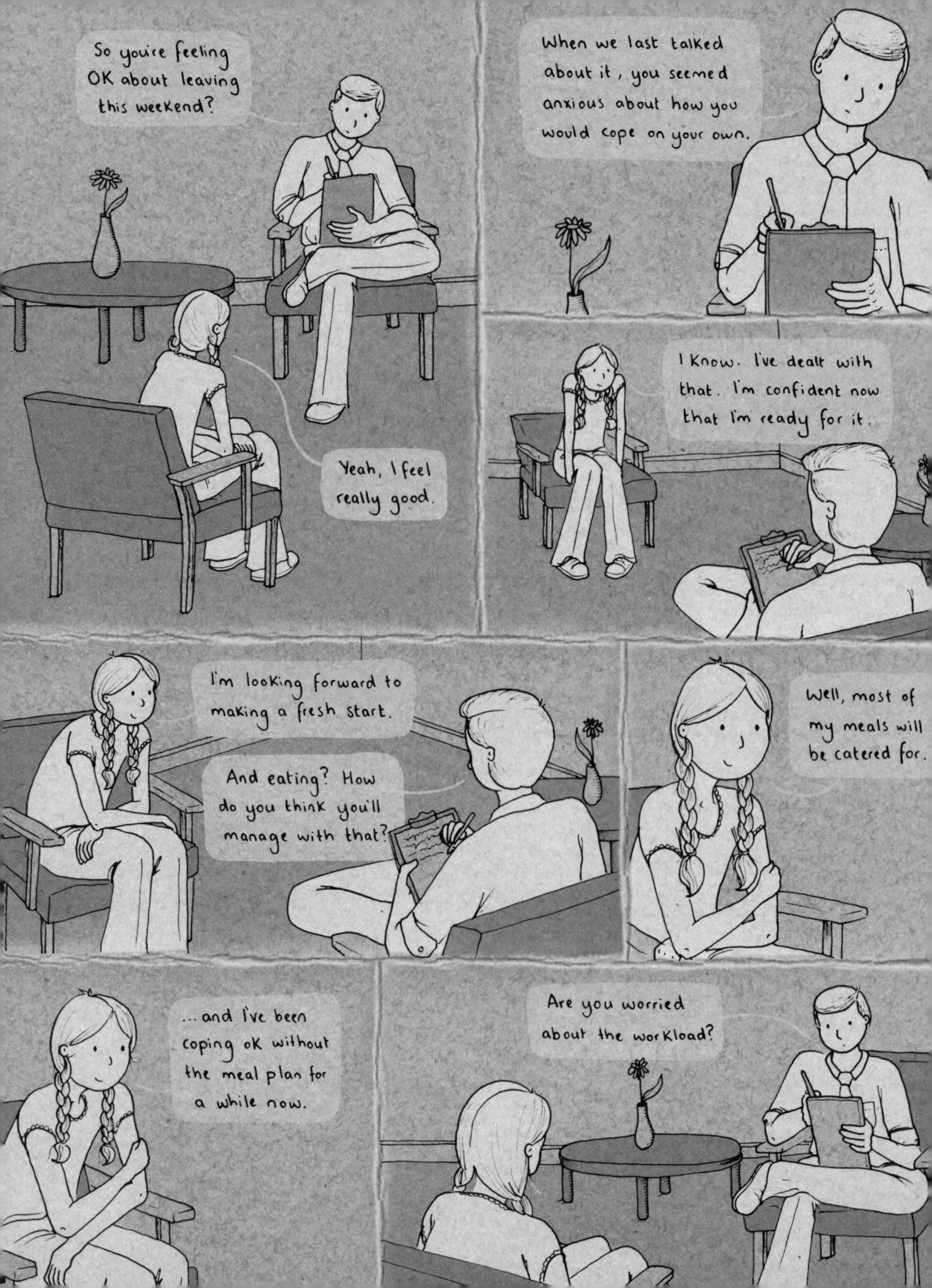
So you're feeling OK about leaving this weekend?
Yeah, I feel really good.
When we last talked about it, you seemed anxious about how you would cope on your own.
I know. I've dealt with that. I'm confident now that I'm ready for it.
I'm looking forward to making a fresh start.
And eating? How do you think you'll manage with that?
Well, most of my meals will be catered for.
...and I've been coping OK without the meal plan for a while now.
Are you worried about the workload?

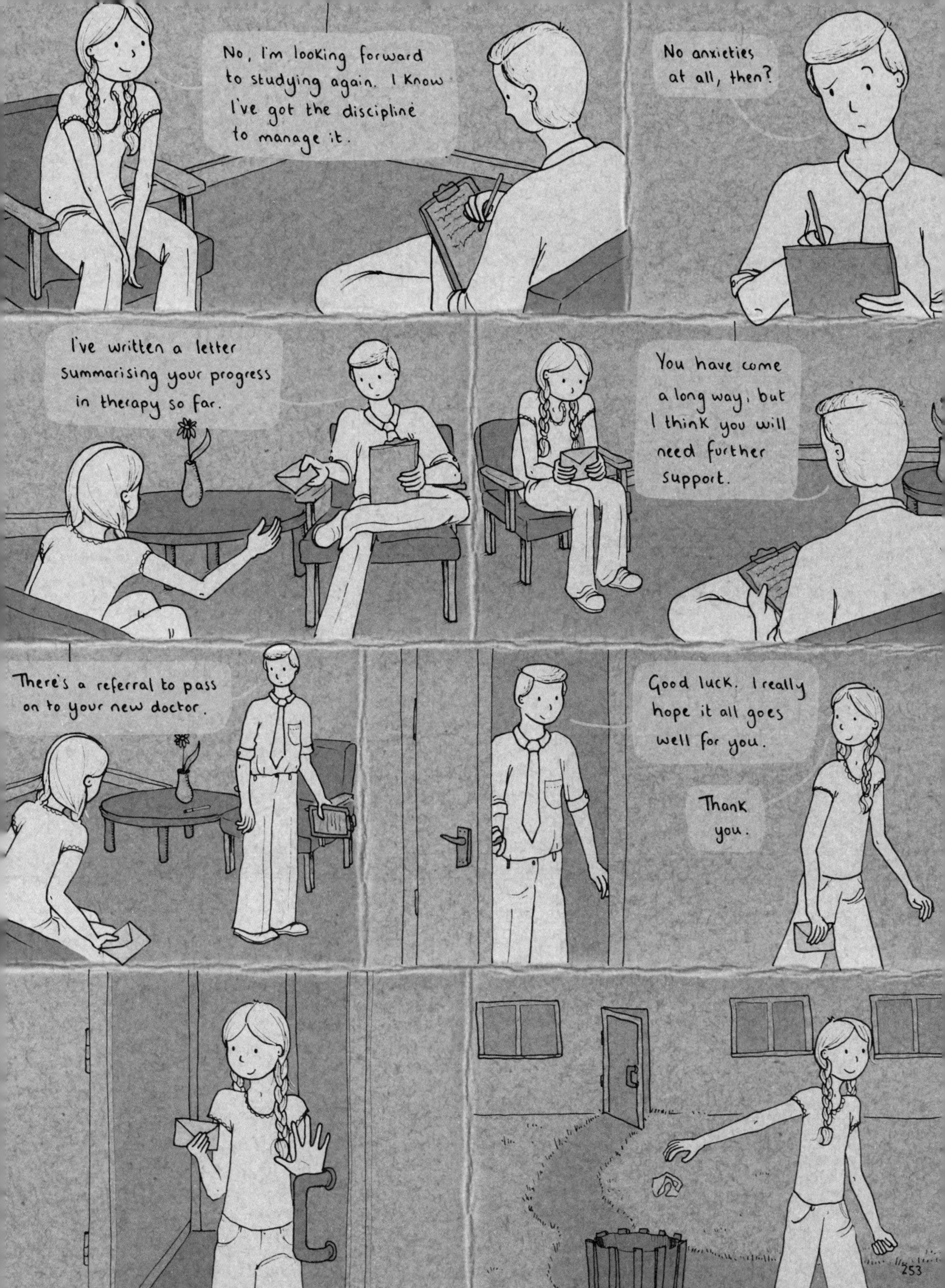
No, I'm looking forward to studying again. I know I've got the discipline to manage it.
No anxieties at all, then?
I've written a letter summarising your progress in therapy so far.
You have come a long way, but I think you will need further support.
There's a referral to pass on to your new doctor.
Good luck. I really hope it all goes well for you.
Thank you.

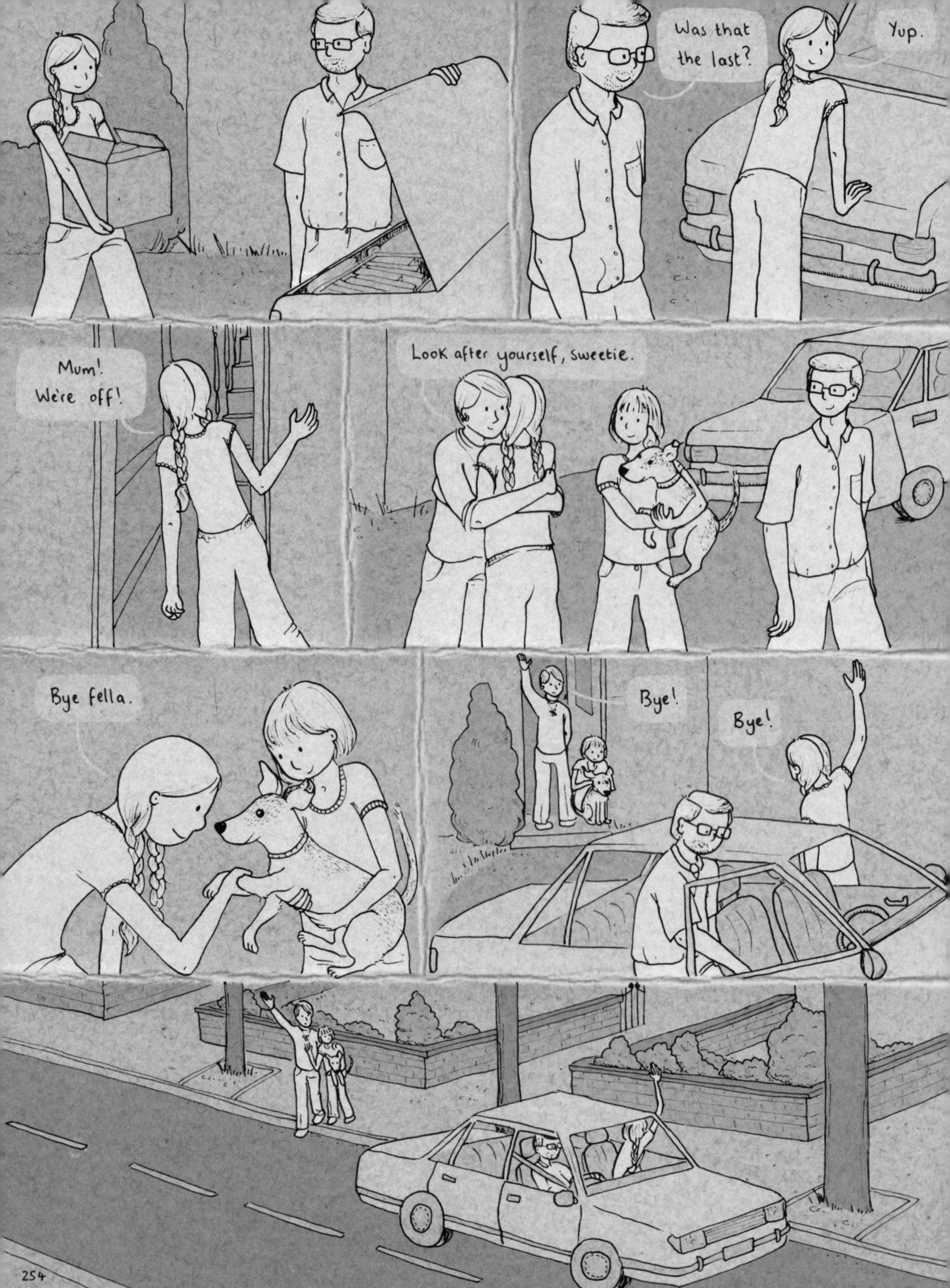
Was that the last?
Yup.
Mum! We're off!
Look after yourself, sweetie.
Bye fella.
Bye!
Bye!

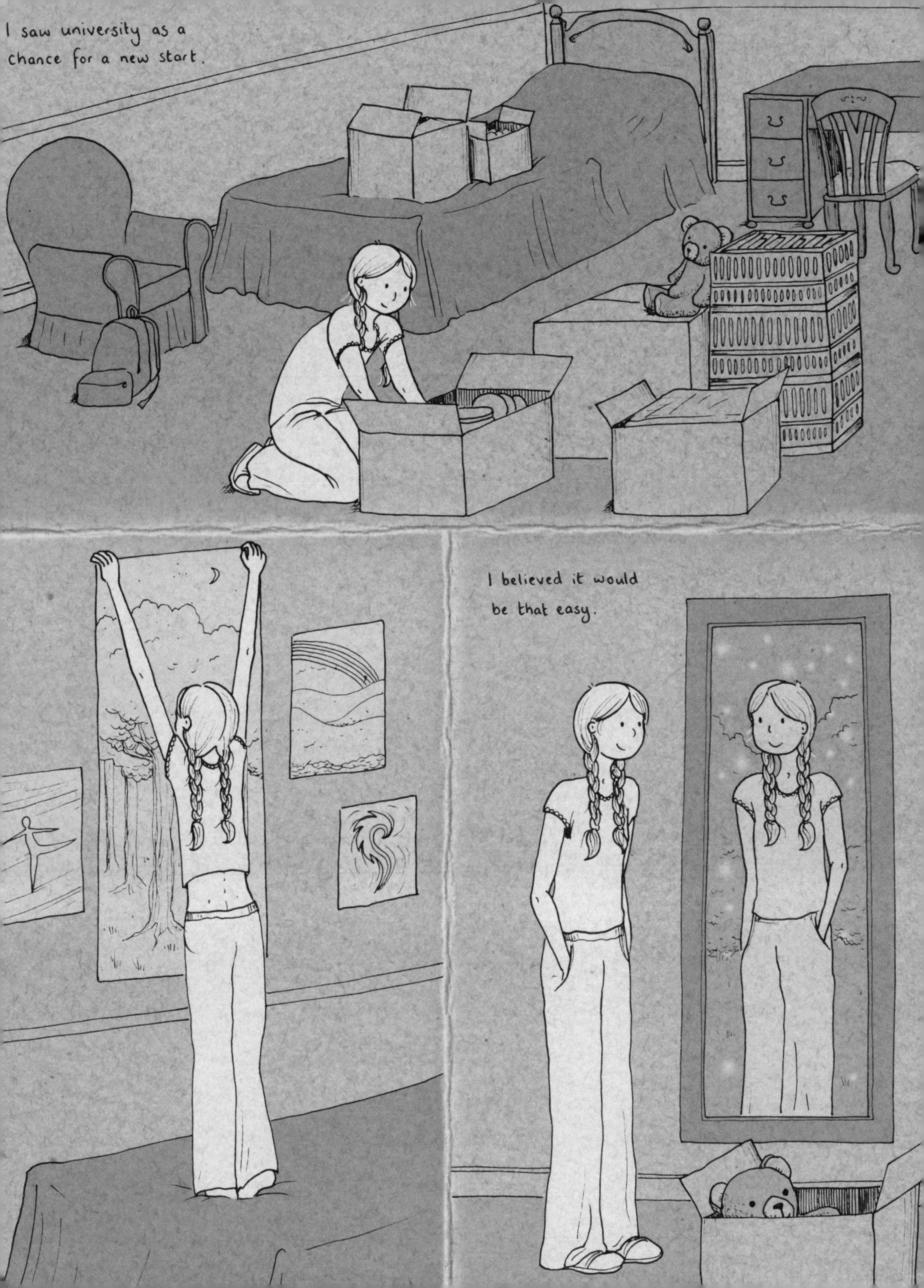
I saw university as a chance for a new start.
I believed it would be that easy.

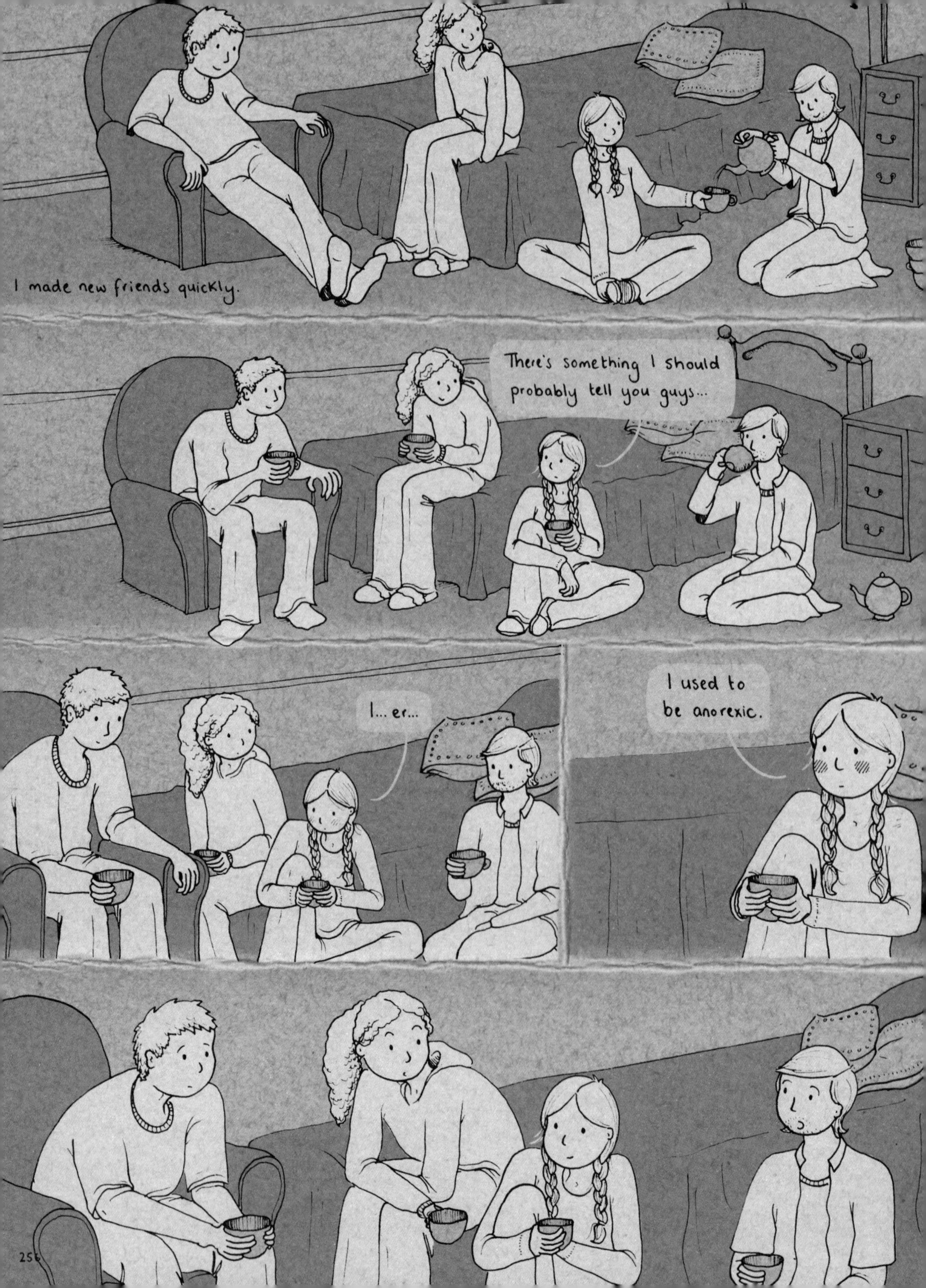
I made new friends quickly.
There's something I should probably tell you guys...
I... er...
I used to be anorexic.

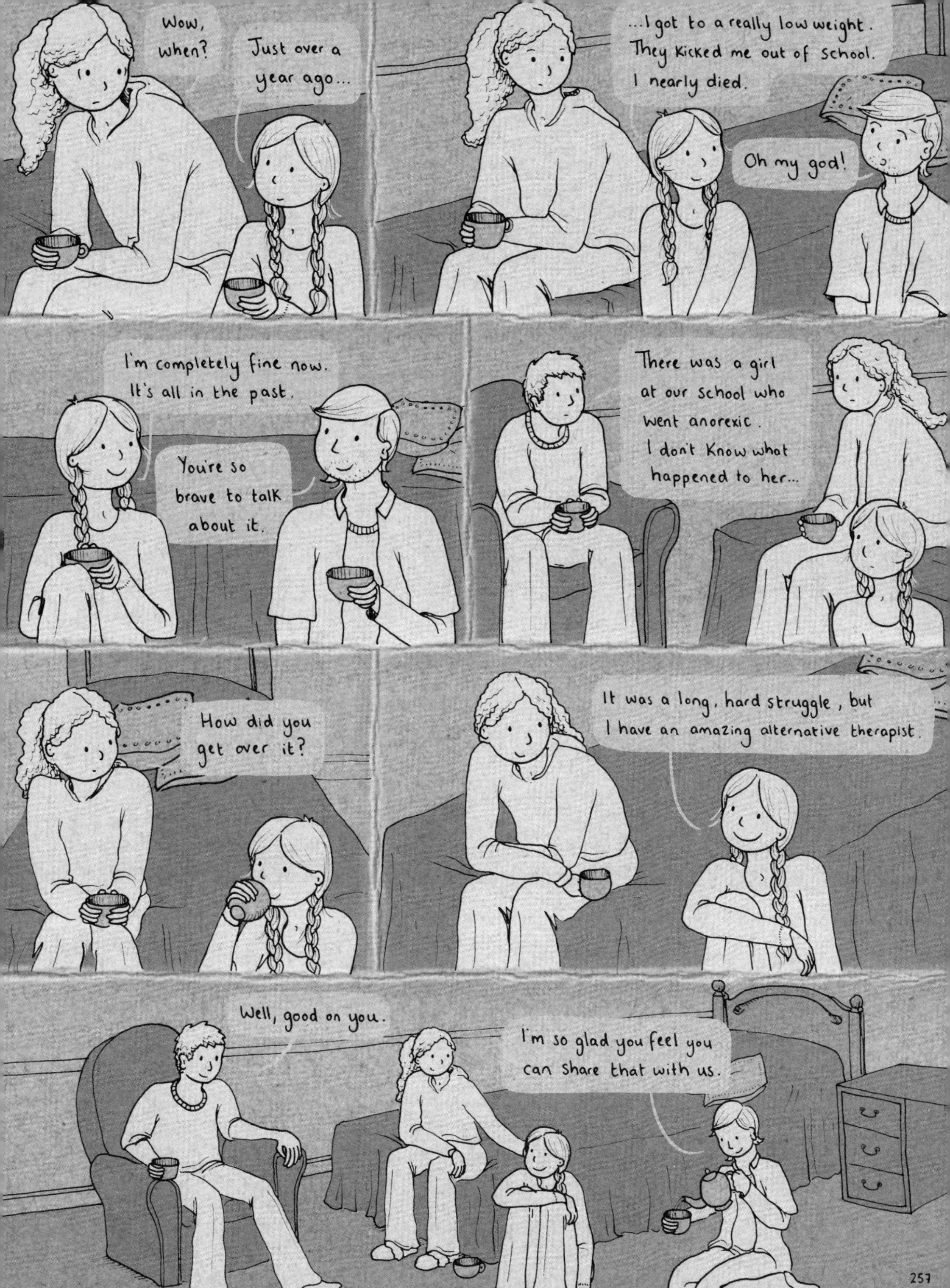
Wow, when?
Just over a year ago...
...I got to a really low weight. They kicked me out of school. I nearly died.
Oh my god!
I'm completely fine now. It's all in the past.
You're so brave to talk about it.
There was a girl at our school who went anorexic. I don't know what happened to her...
How did you get over it?
It was a long, hard struggle, but I have an amazing alternative therapist.
Well, good on you.
I'm so glad you feel you can share that with us.

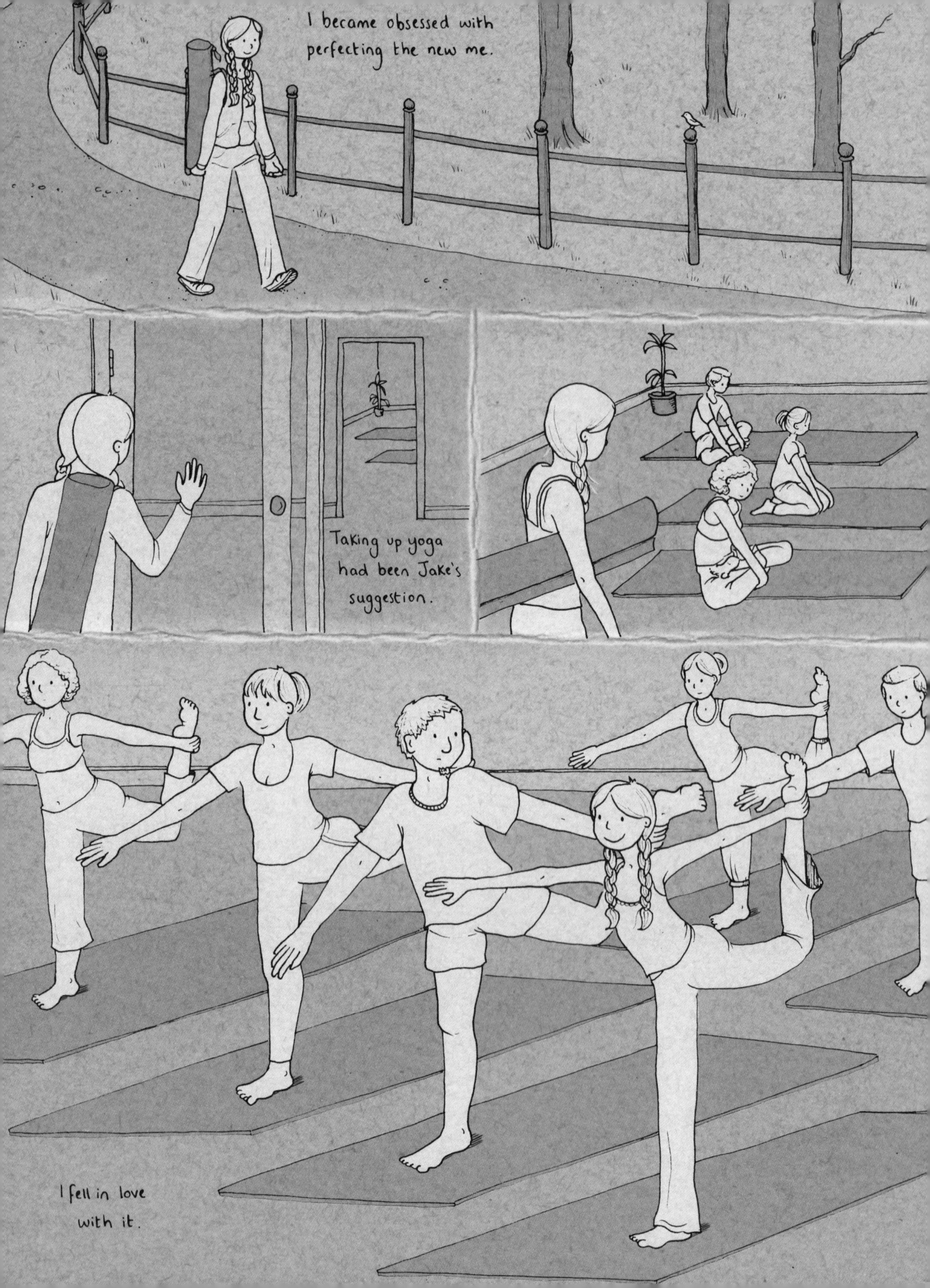
I became obsessed with perfecting the new me.
Taking up yoga had been Jake's suggestion.
I fell in love with it.

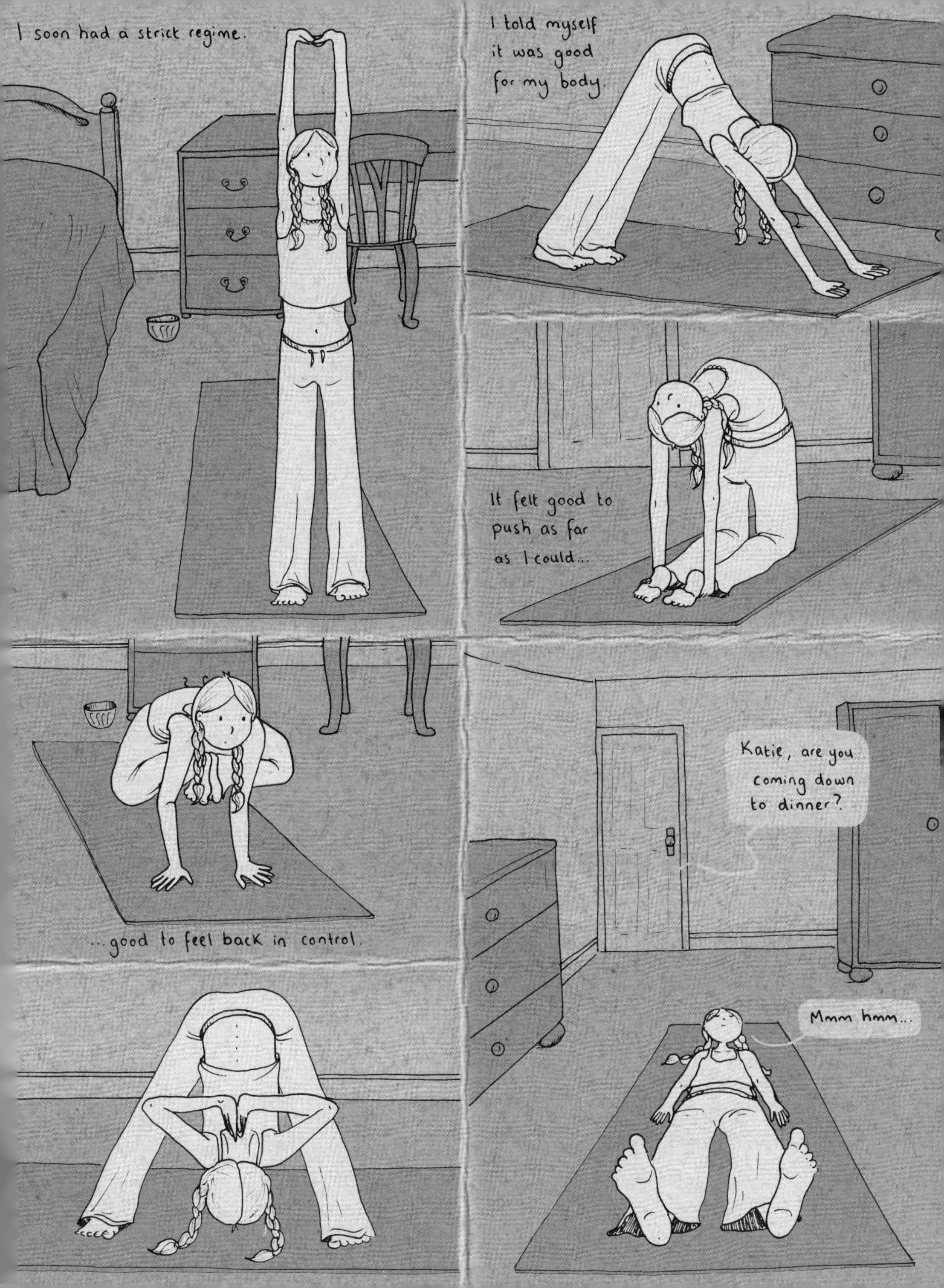
I soon had a strict regime.
I told myself it was good for my body.
It felt good to push as far as I could...
...good to feel back in control.
Katie, are you coming down to dinner?
Mmm hmm...

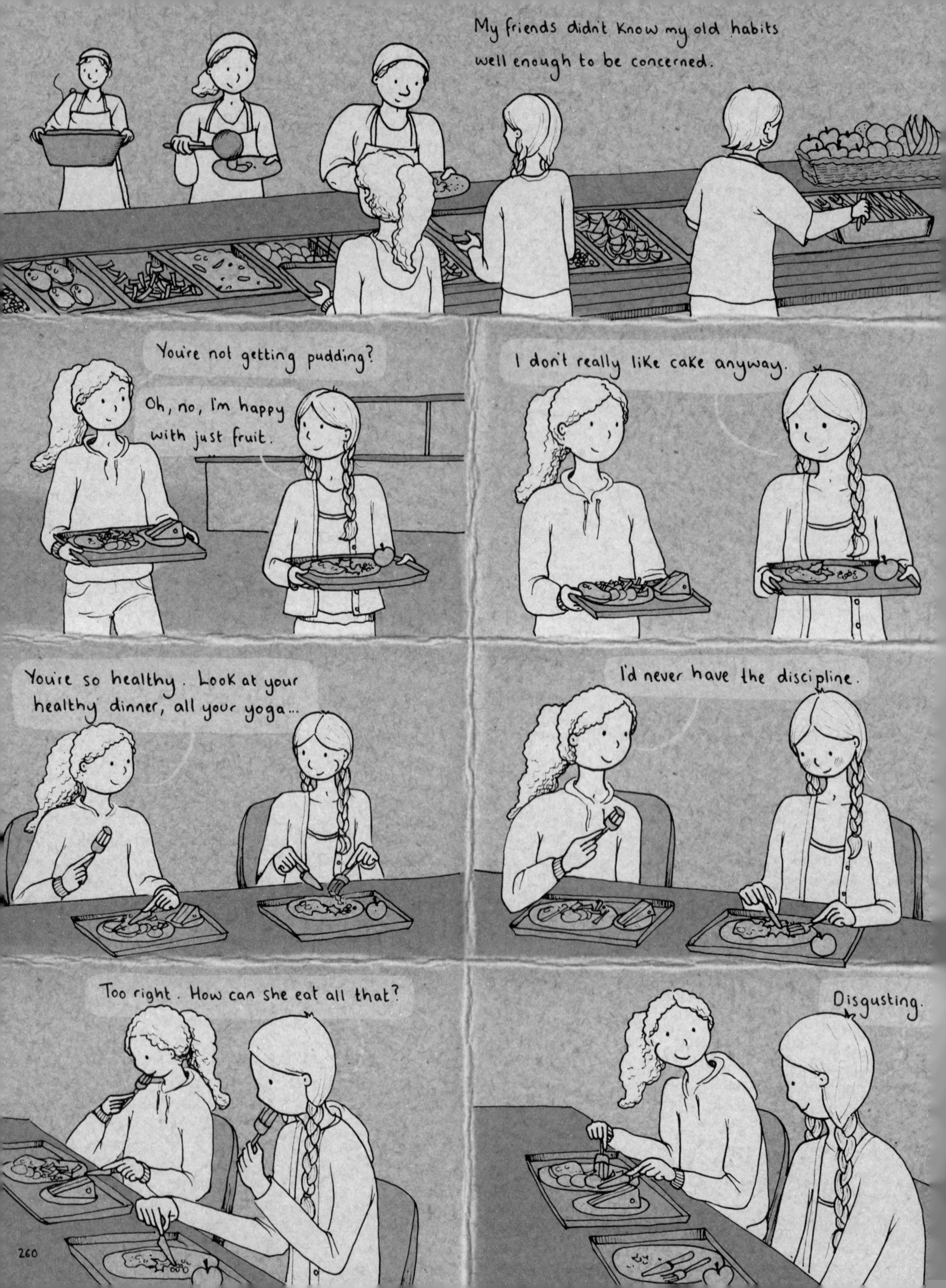

My friends didn't know my old habits well enough to be concerned.
You're not getting pudding?
Oh, no, I'm happy with just fruit.
I don't really like cake anyway.
You're so healthy. Look at your healthy dinner, all your yoga...
I'd never have the discipline.
Too right. How can she eat all that?
Disgusting.

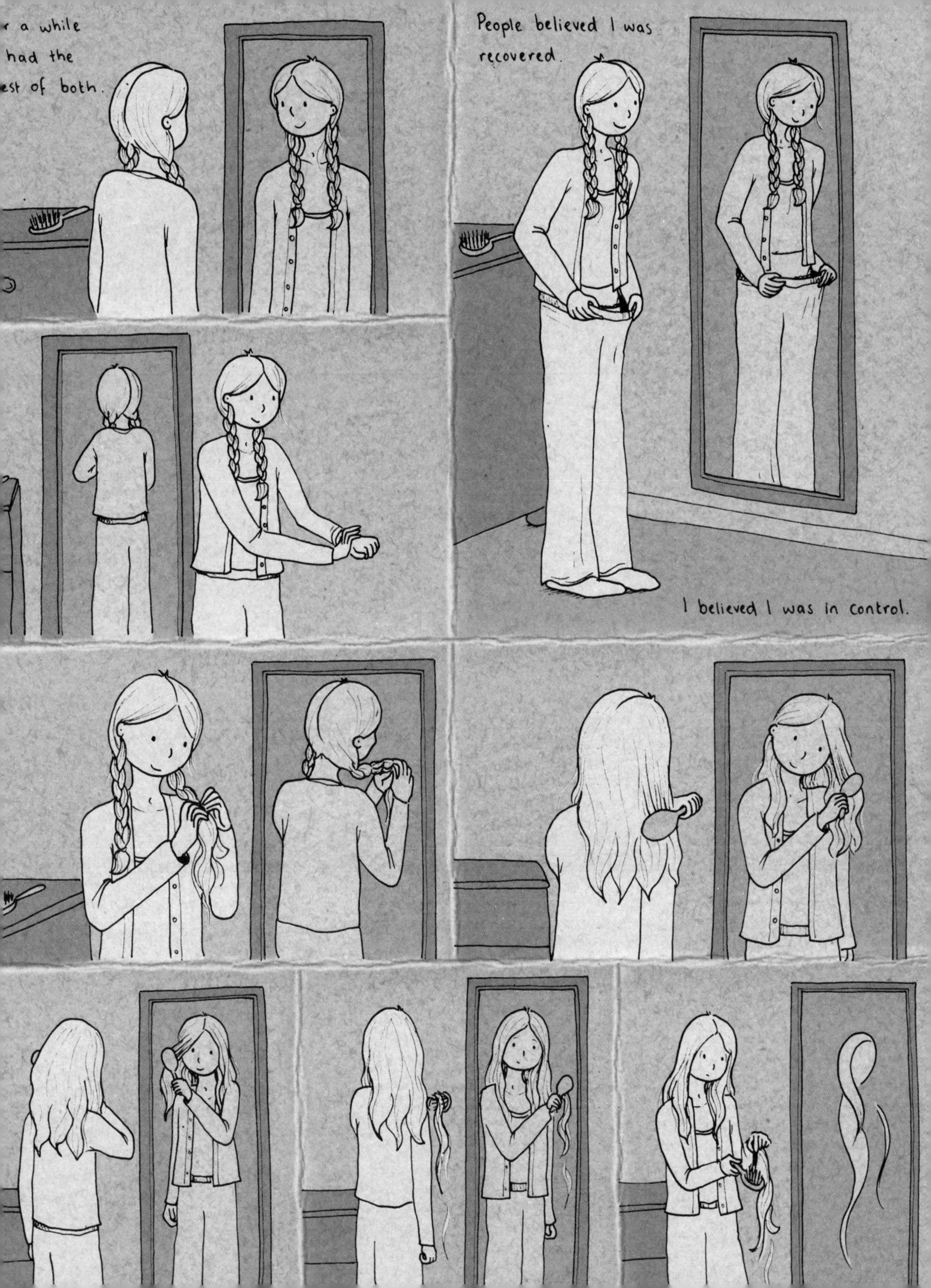
r a while
had the
est of both.
People believed I was
recovered.
I believed I was in control.

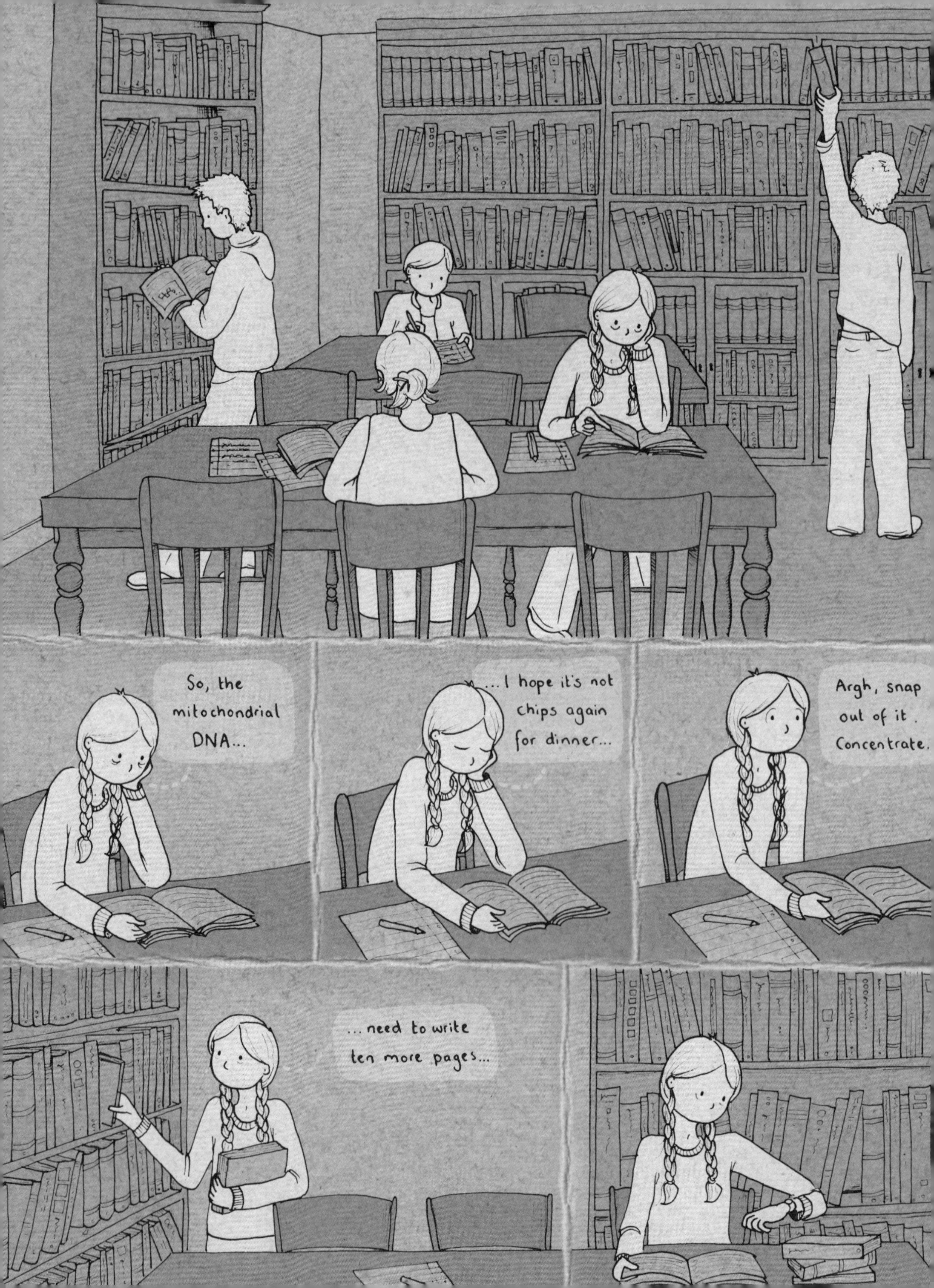
So, the mitochondrial DNA...
...I hope it's not chips again for dinner...
Argh, snap out of it. Concentrate.
...need to write ten more pages...

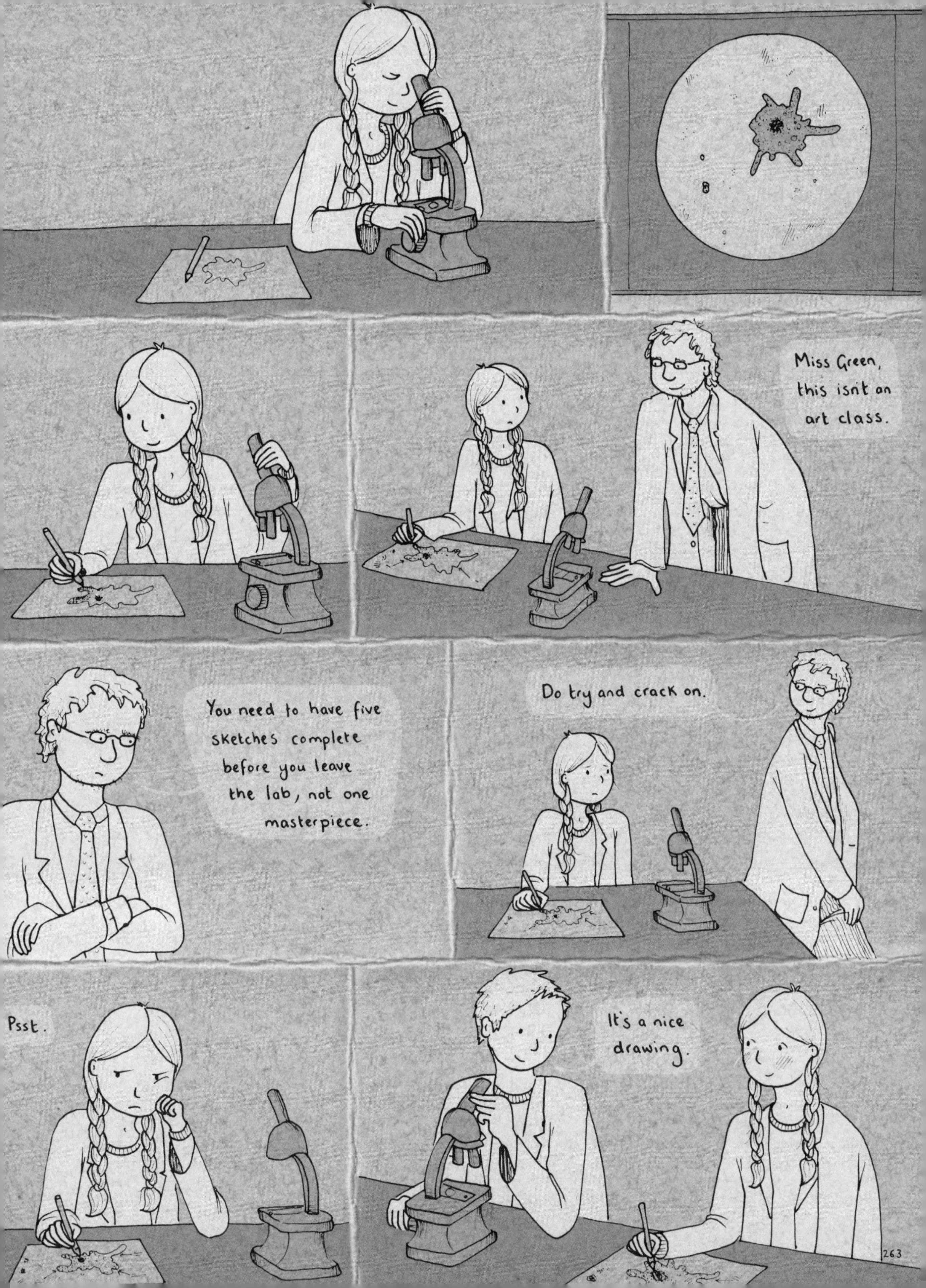
Miss Green, this isn't an art class.
You need to have five sketches complete before you leave the lab, not one masterpiece.
Do try and crack on.
Psst.
It's a nice drawing.

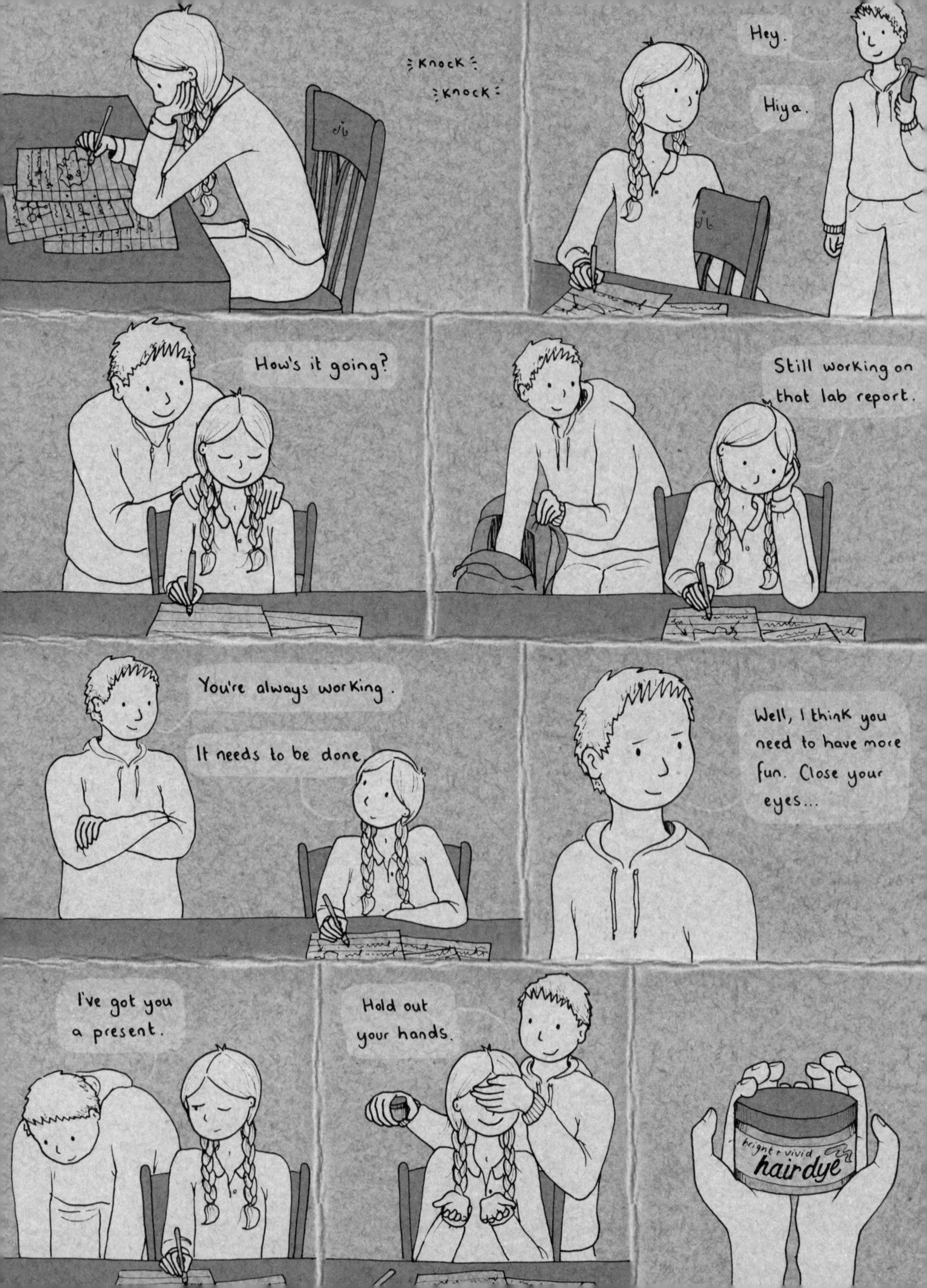
knock
knock
Hey.
Hiya.
How's it going?
Still working on that lab report.
You're always working.
It needs to be done.
Well, I think you need to have more fun. Close your eyes...
I've got you a present.
Hold out your hands.
bright + vivid
hairdye

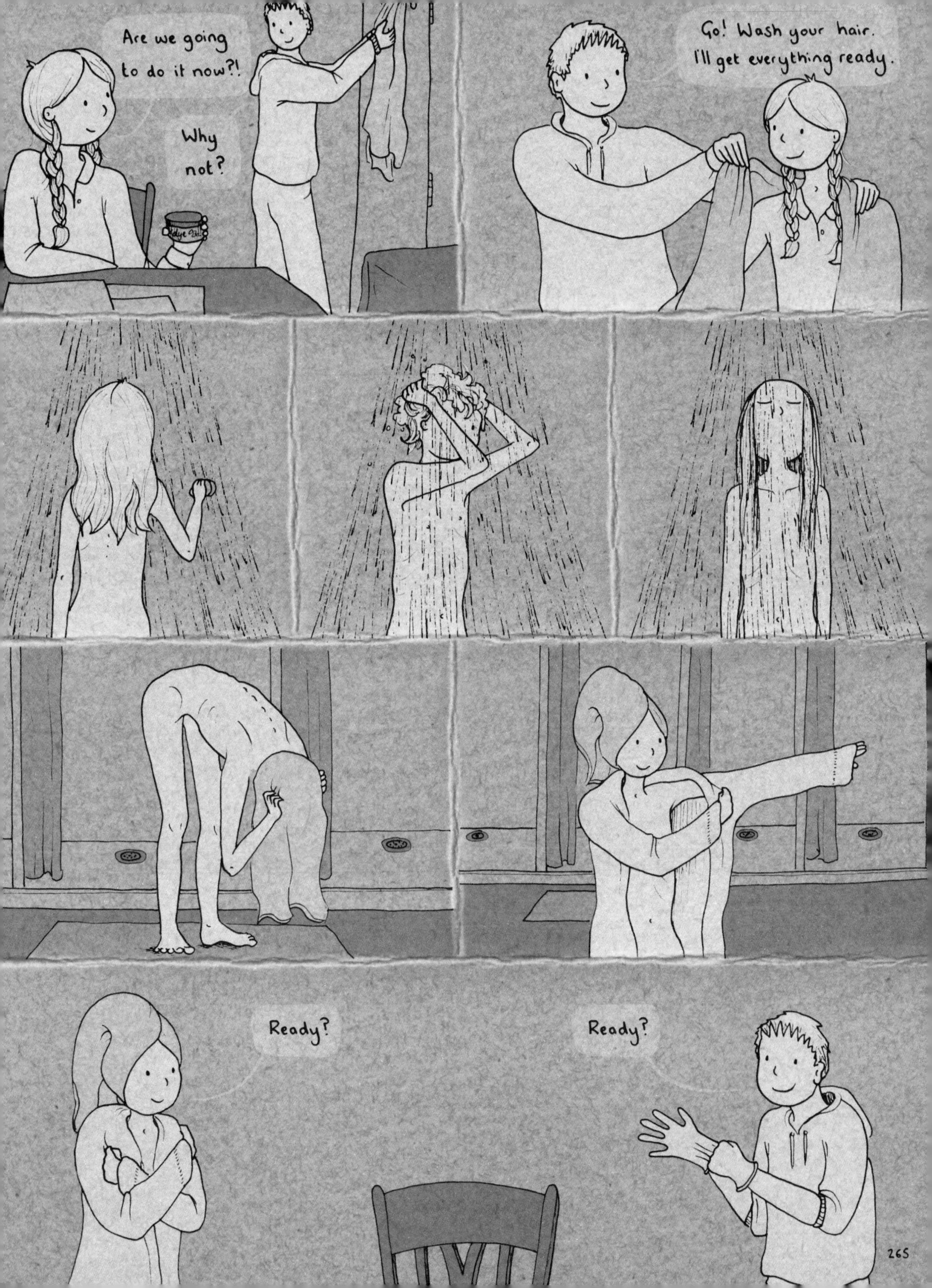

Are we going to do it now?!
Why not?
Go! Wash your hair. I'll get everything ready.
Ready?
Ready?

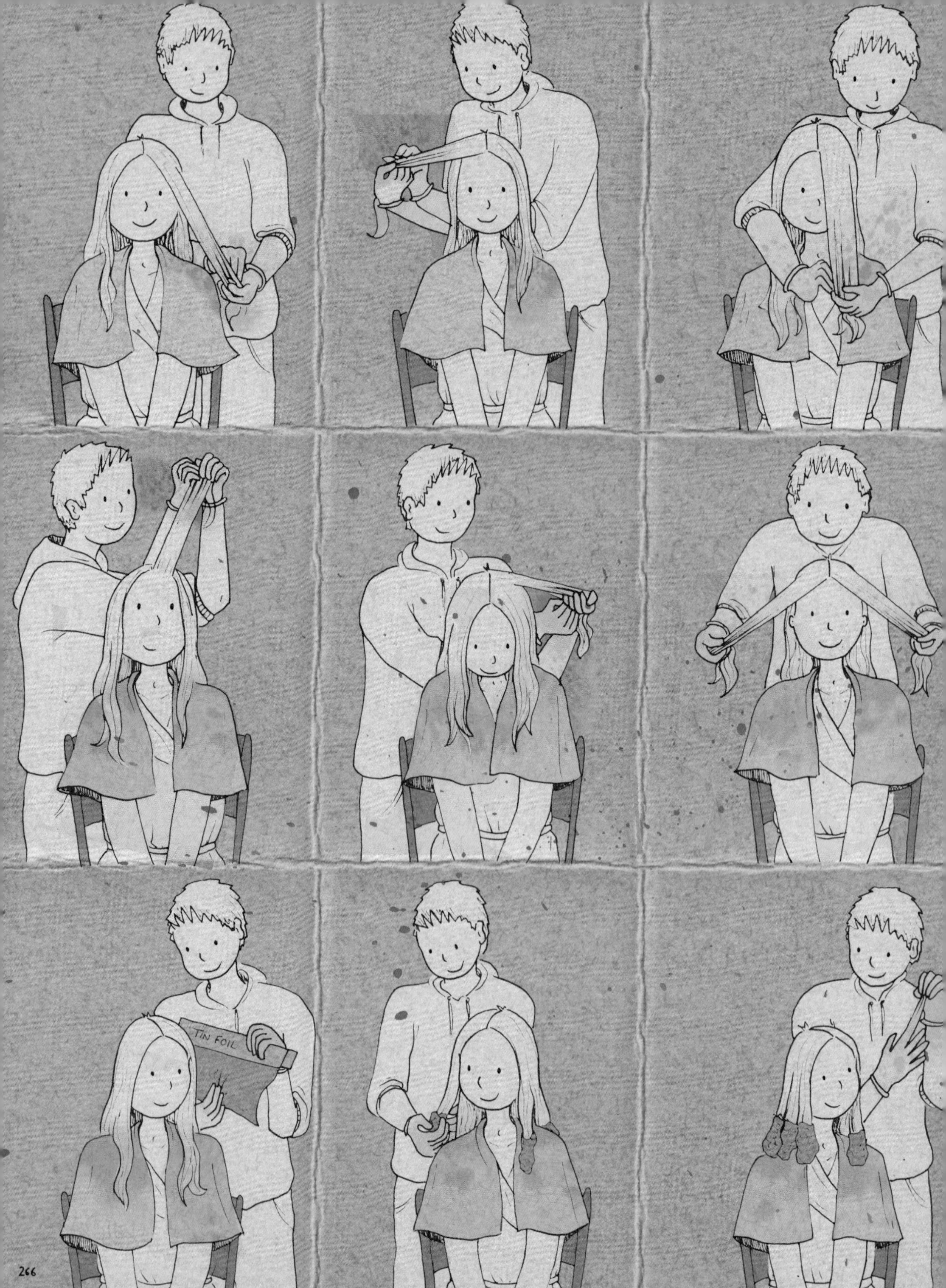
TIN FOIL

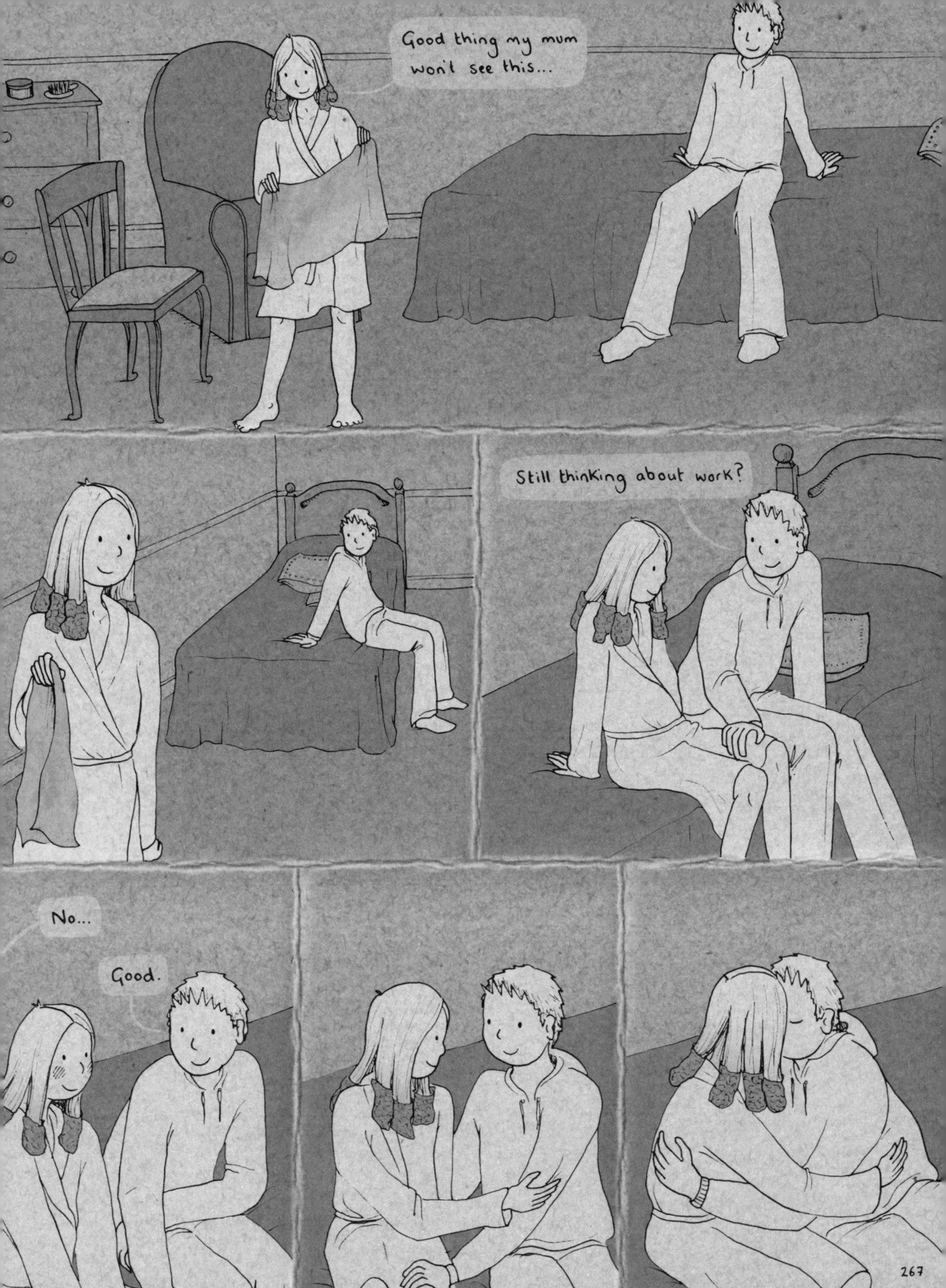
Good thing my mum won't see this...
Still thinking about work?
No...
Good.

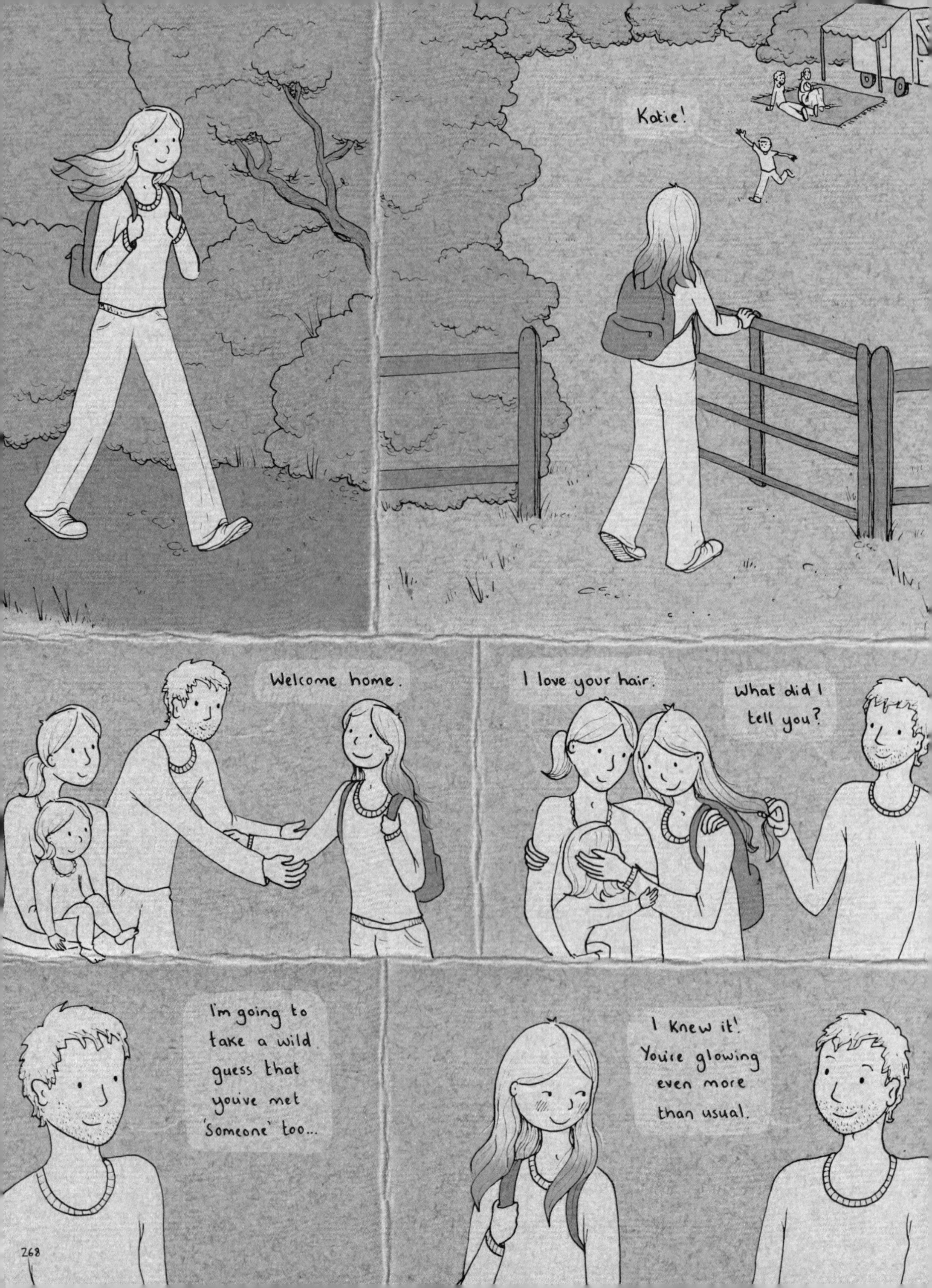
Katie!
Welcome home.
I love your hair.
What did I tell you?
I'm going to take a wild guess that you've met 'Someone' too...
I knew it! You're glowing even more than usual.

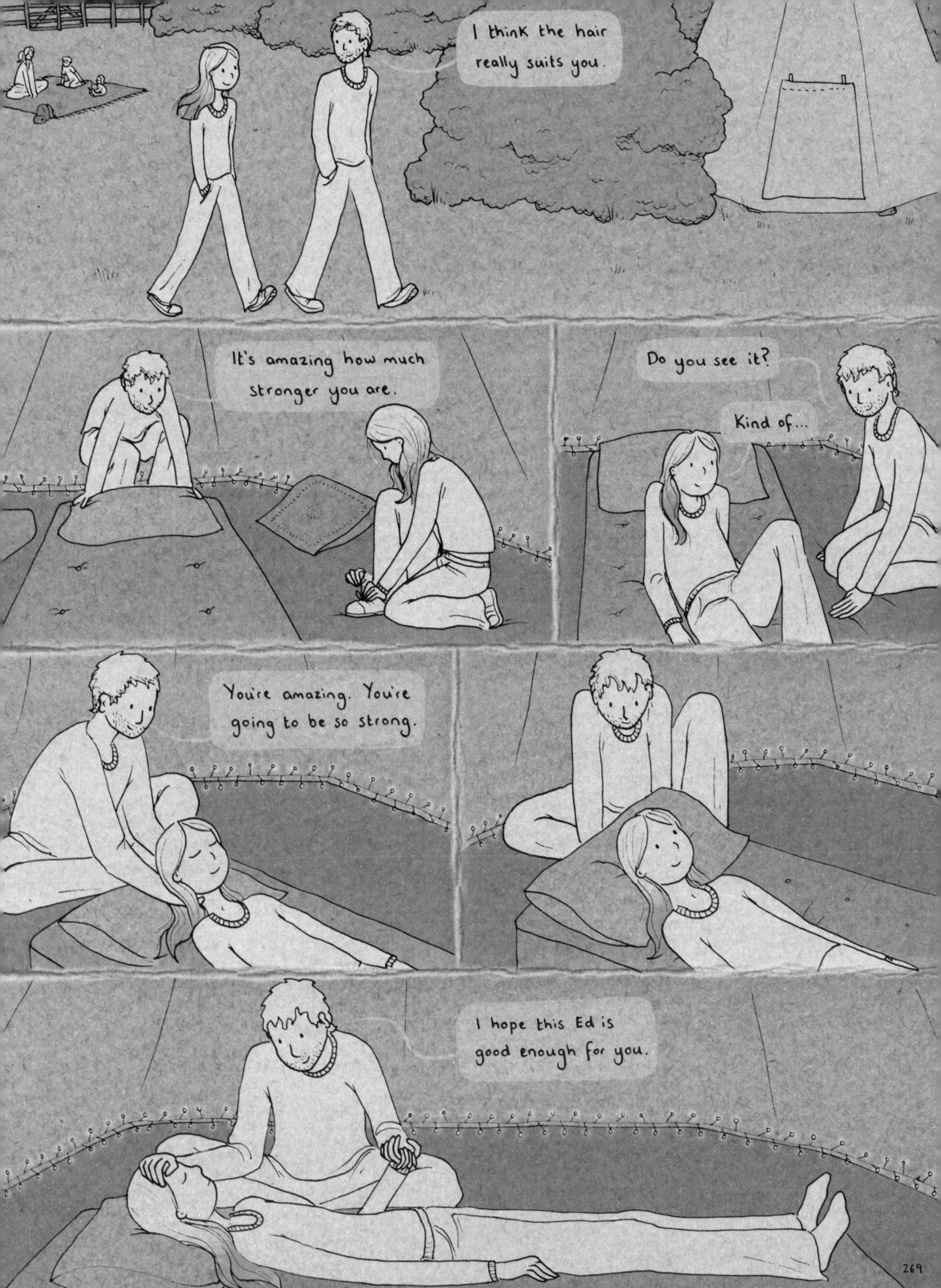
I think the hair really suits you.
It's amazing how much stronger you are.
Do you see it?
Kind of...
You're amazing. You're going to be so strong.
I hope this Ed is good enough for you.

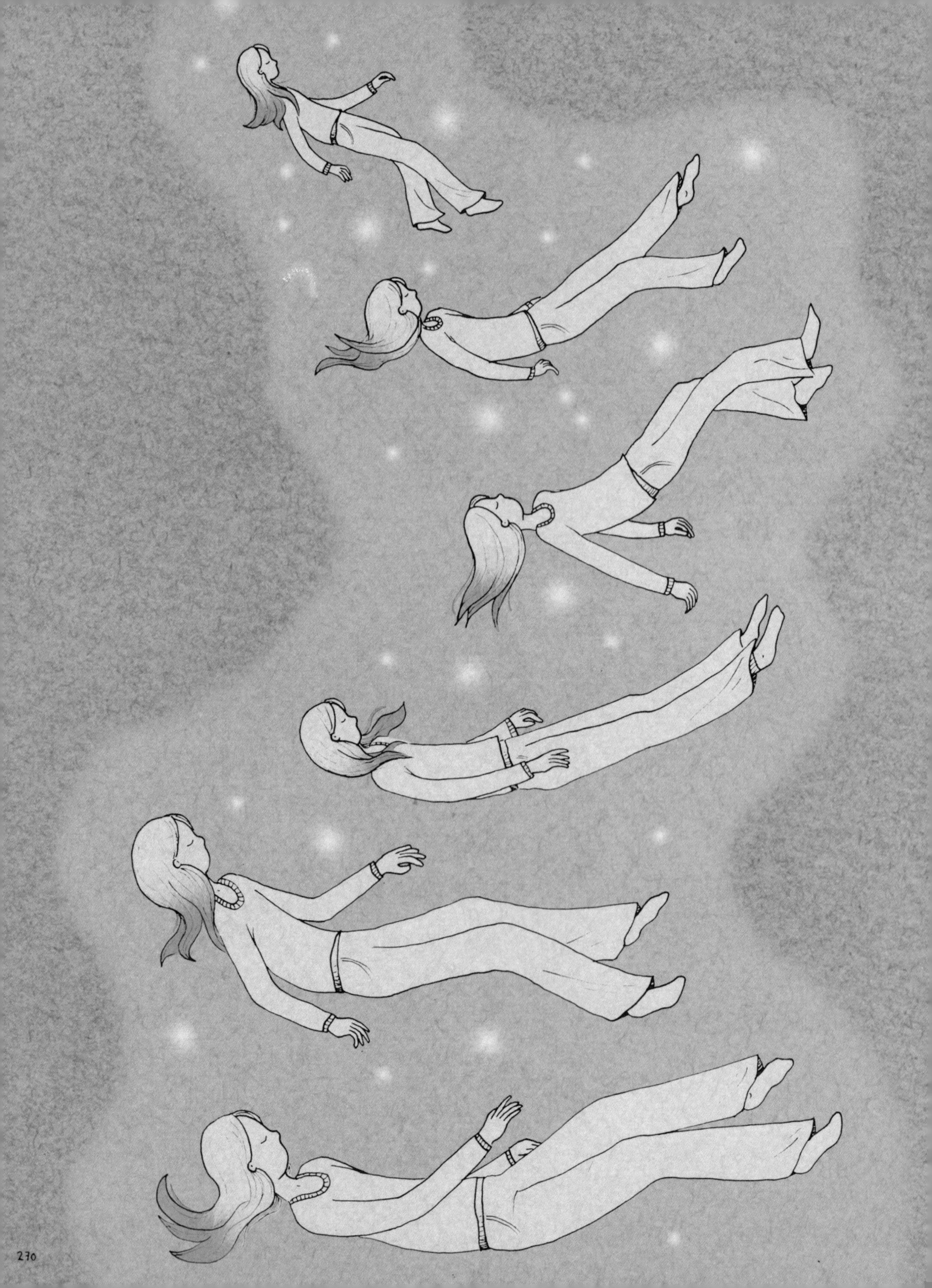

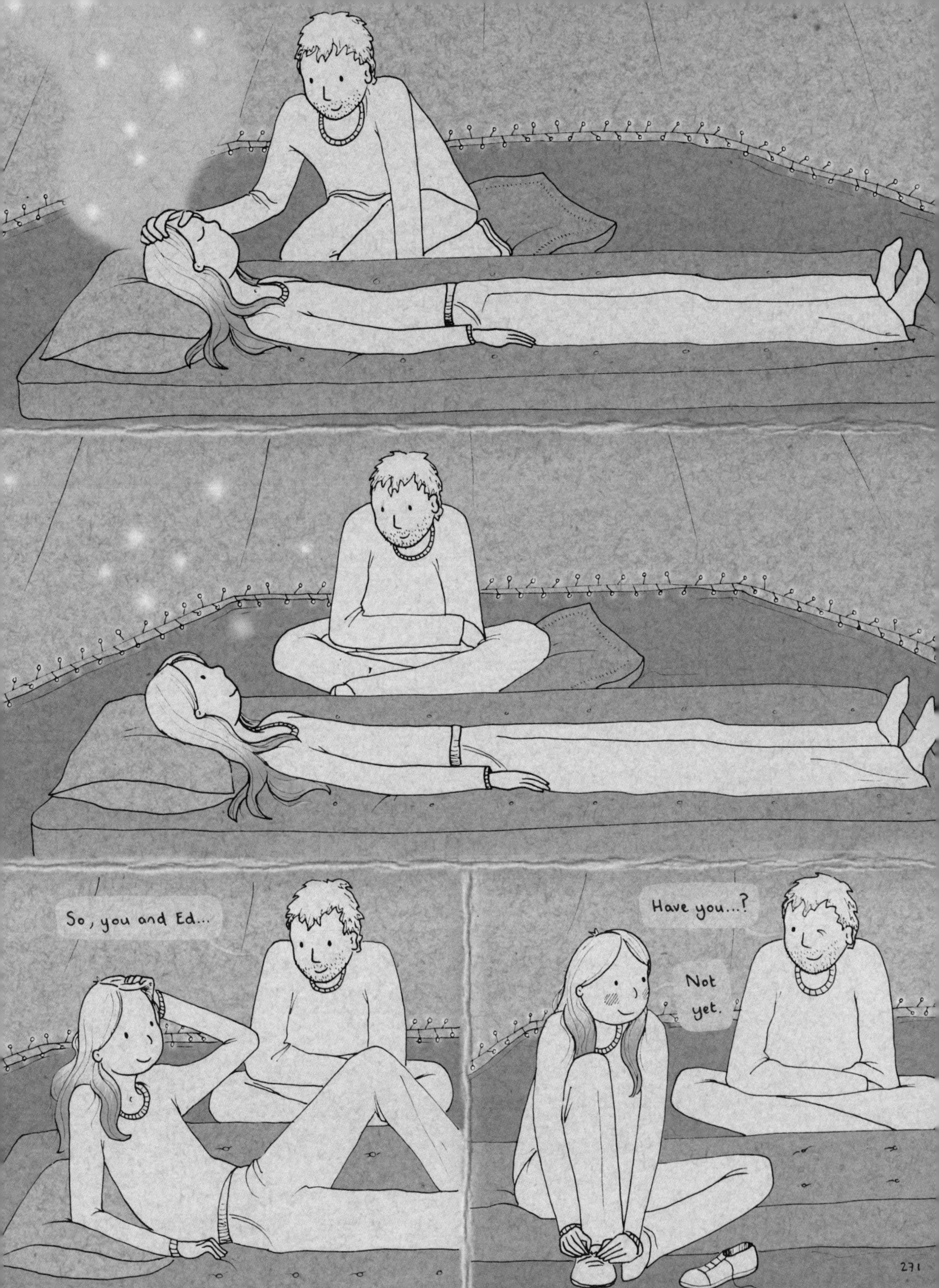
So, you and Ed...
Have you...?
Not yet.

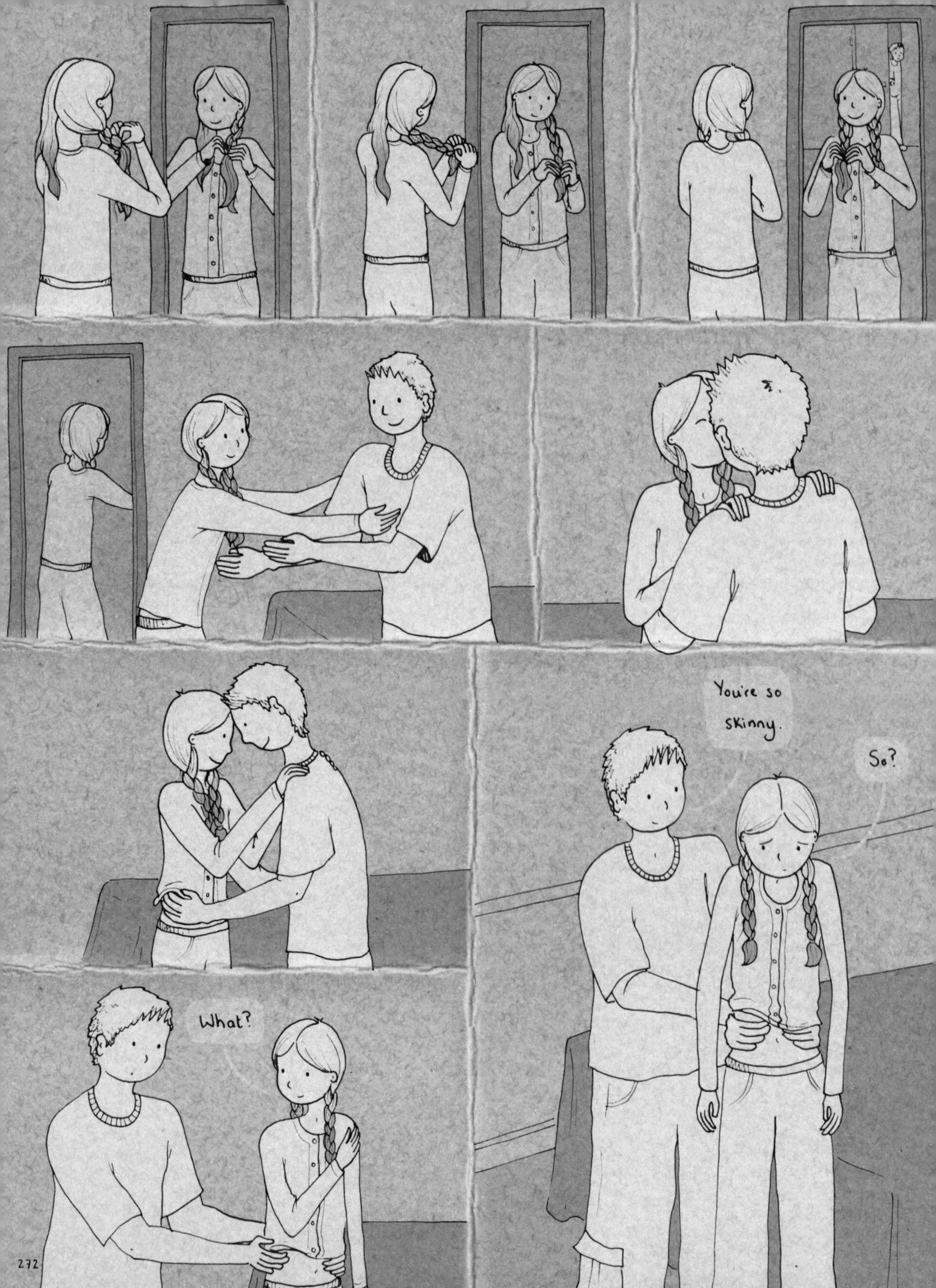
What?
You're so skinny.
So?

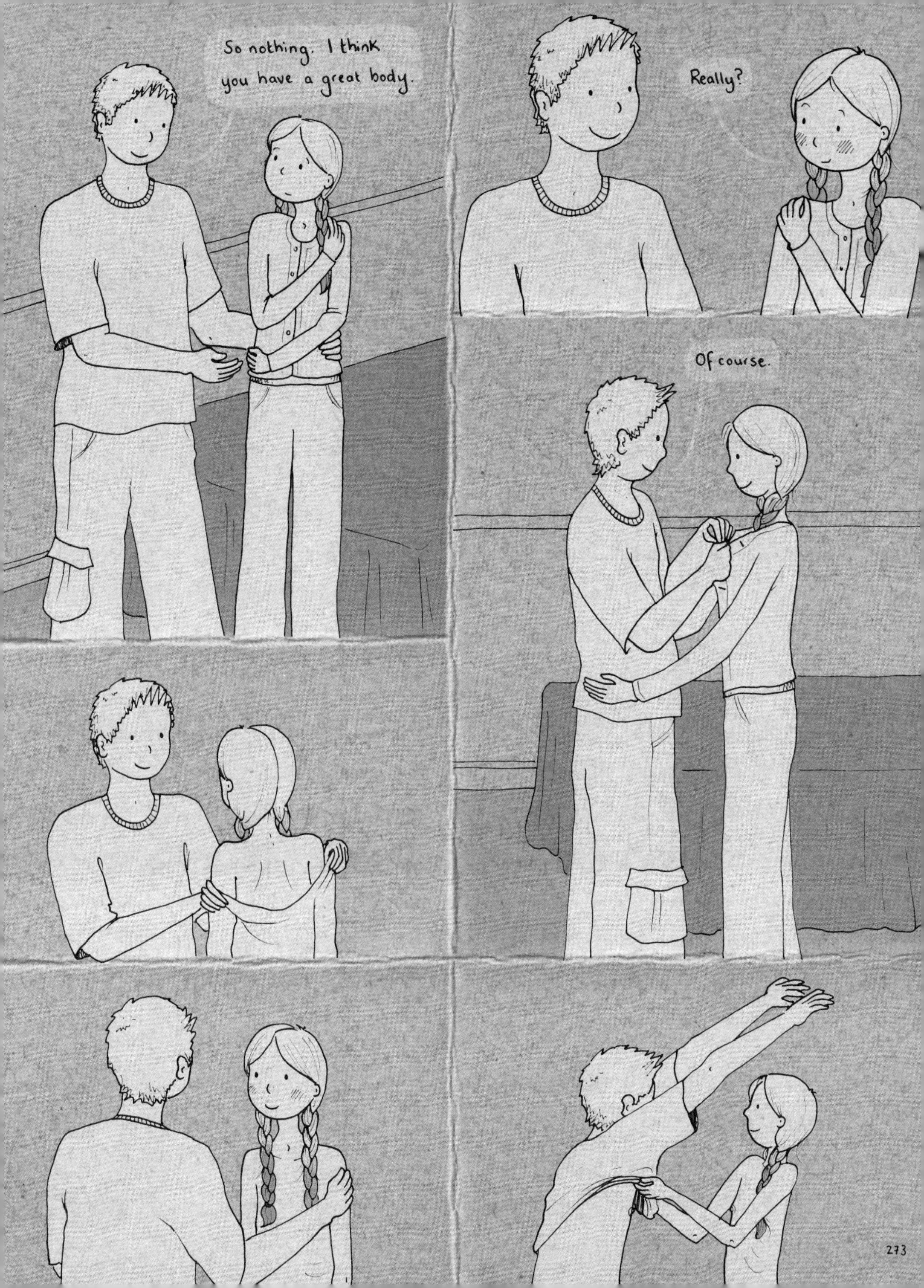
So nothing. I think you have a great body.
Really?
Of course.

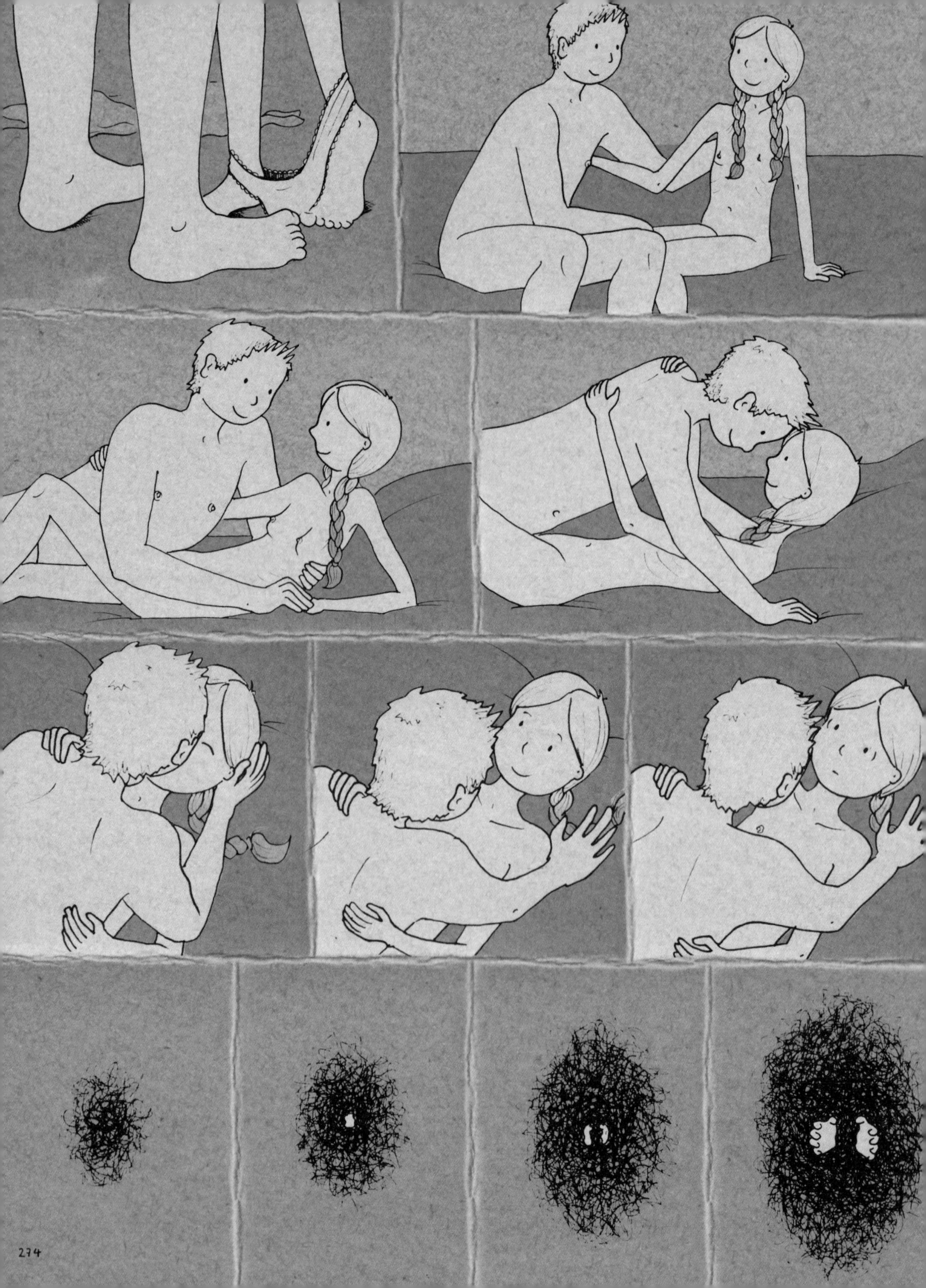

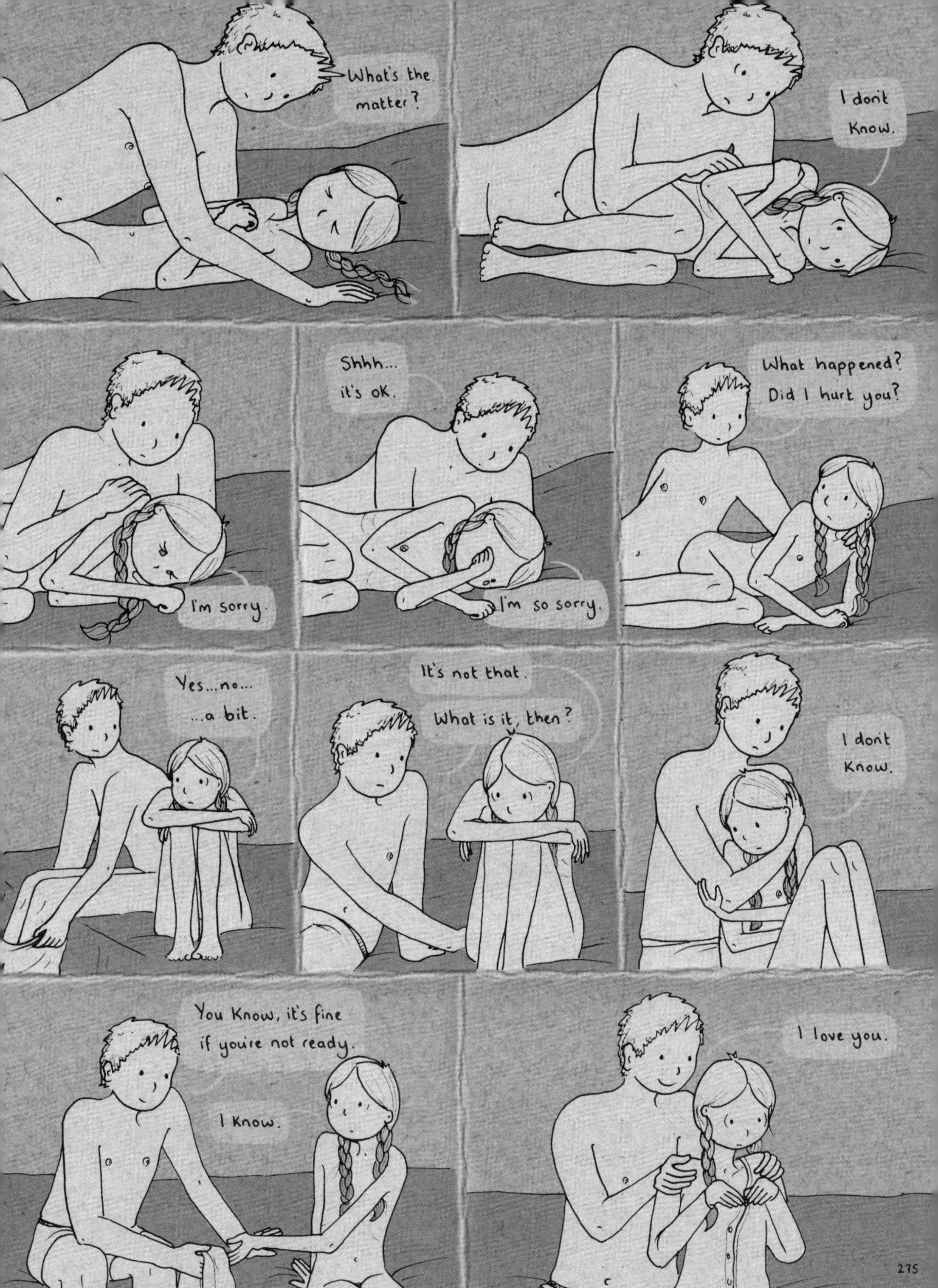
What's the matter?
I don't know.
I'm sorry.
Shhh... it's OK.
I'm so sorry.
What happened? Did I hurt you?
Yes...no... ...a bit.
It's not that.
What is it, then?
I don't know.
You know, it's fine if you're not ready.
I know.
I love you.

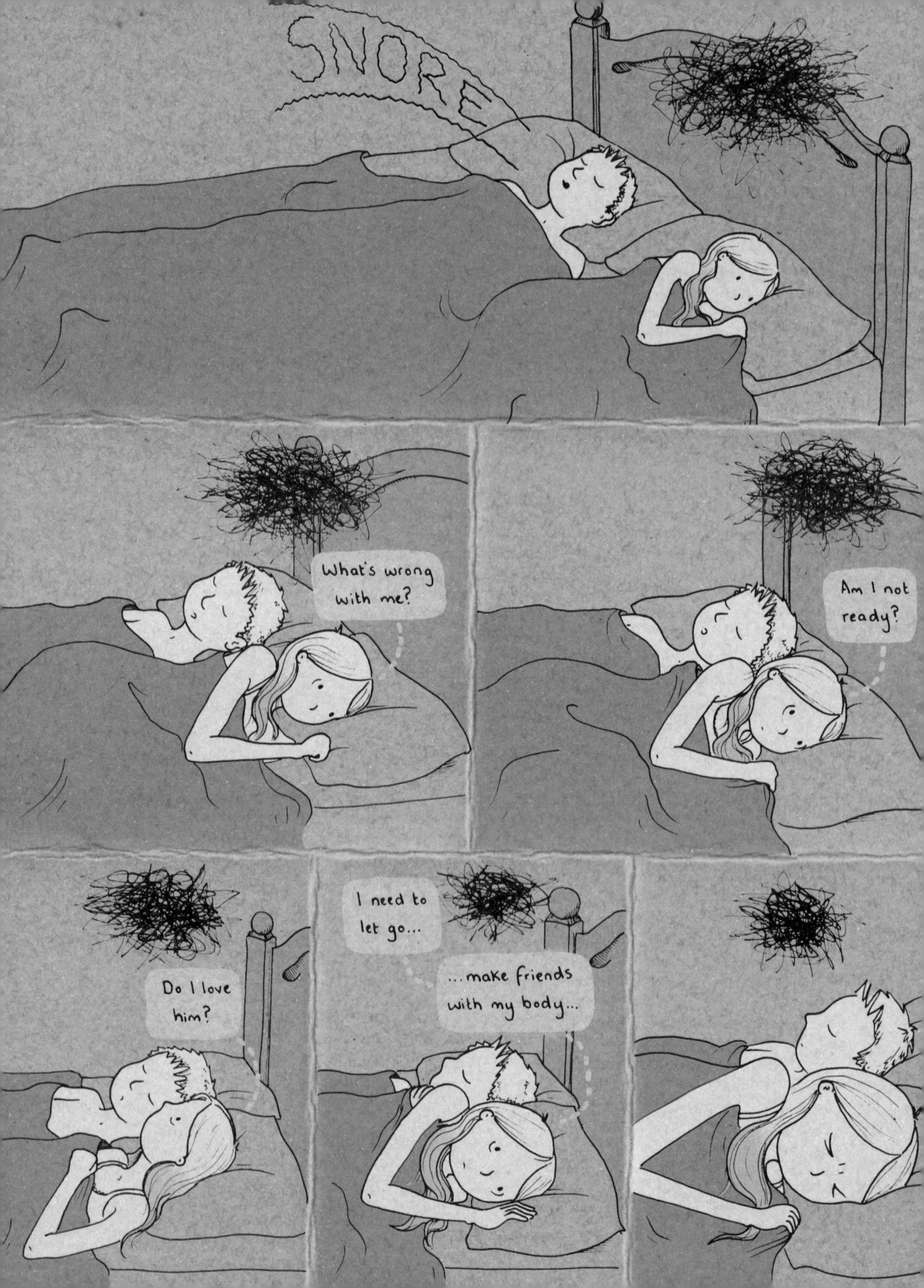
SNORE
What's wrong with me?
Am I not ready?
Do I love him?
I need to let go...
...make friends with my body...

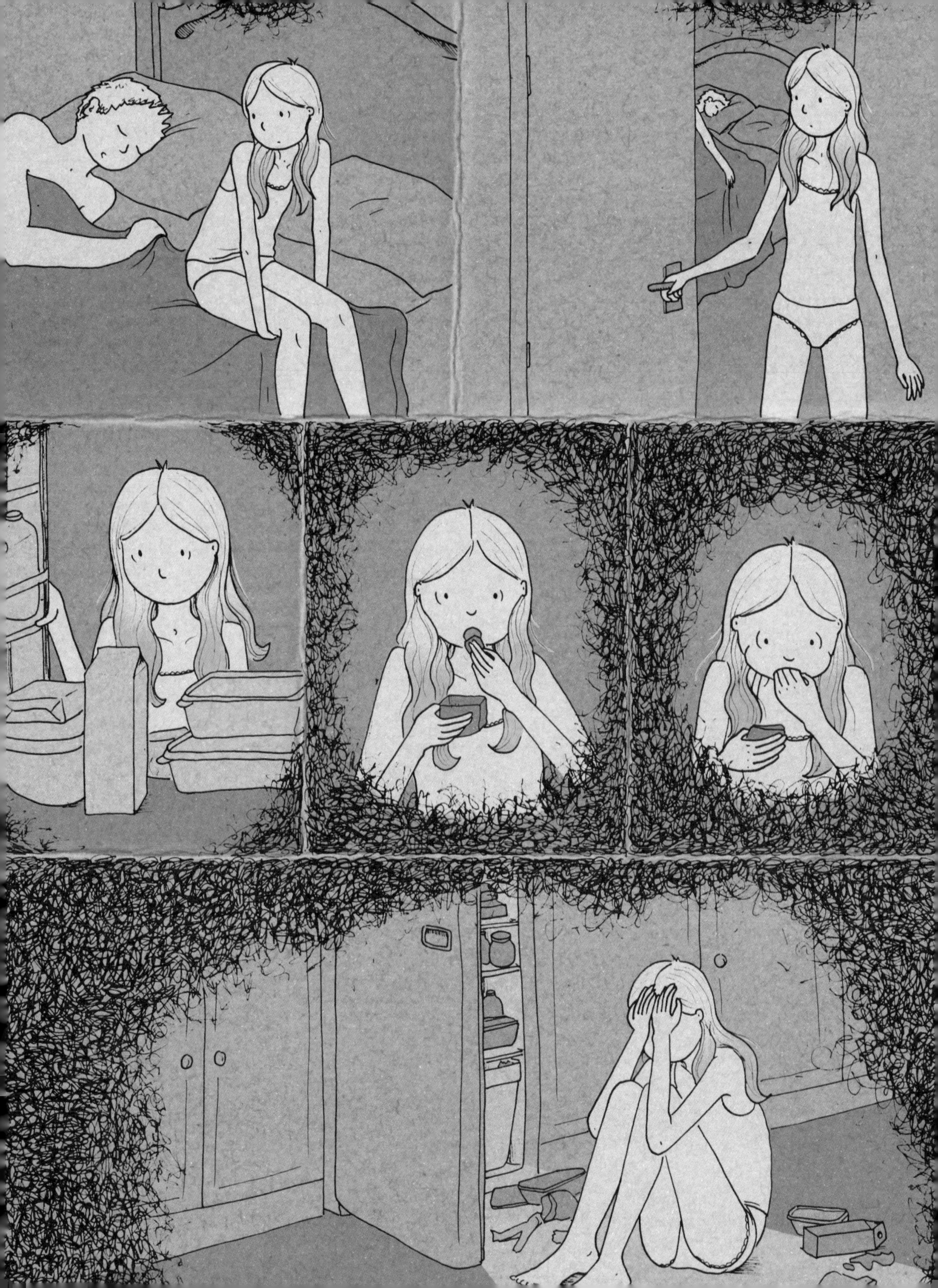

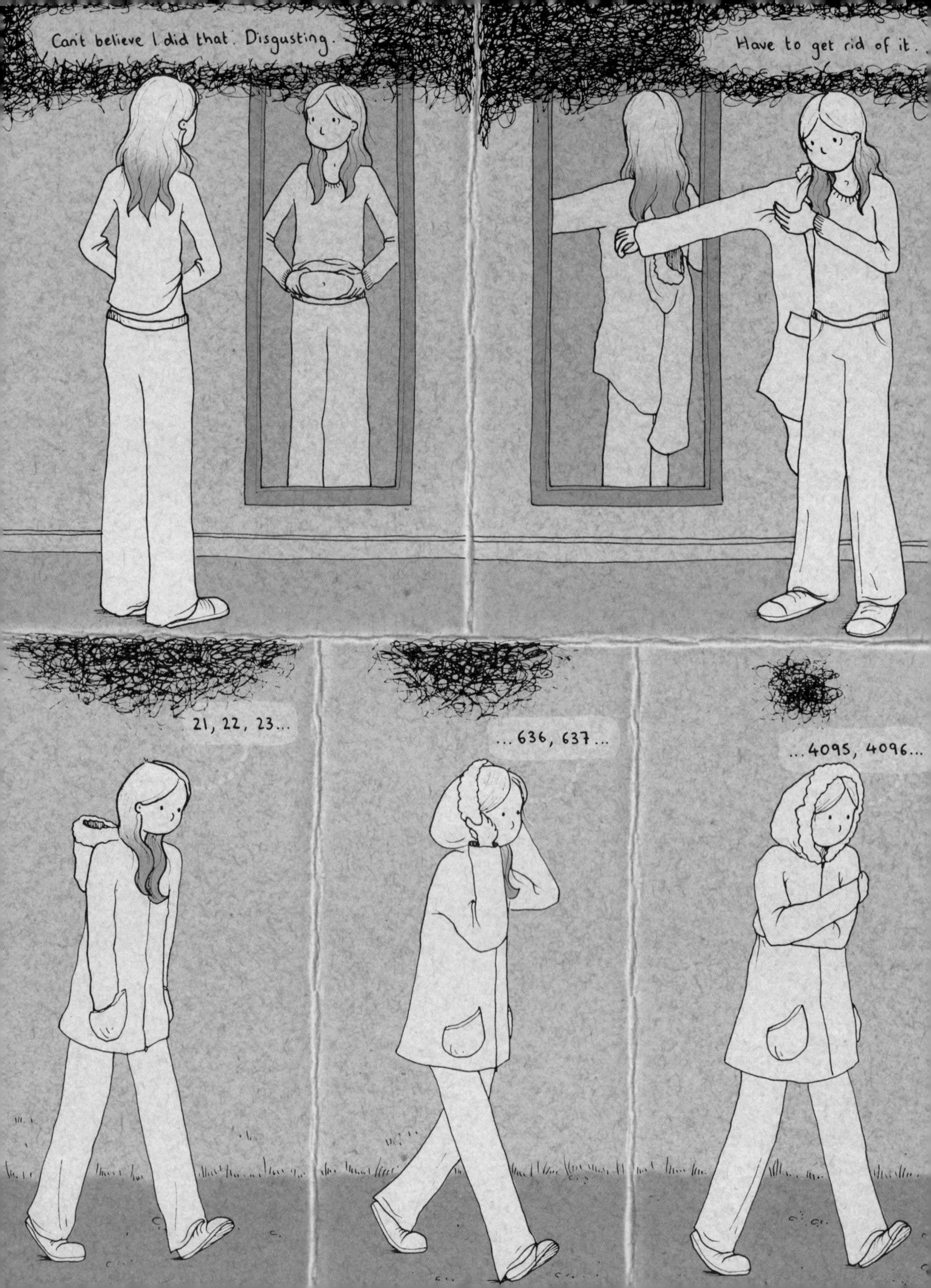
Can't believe I did that. Disgusting.
Have to get rid of it.
21, 22, 23...
...636, 637...
...4095, 4096...

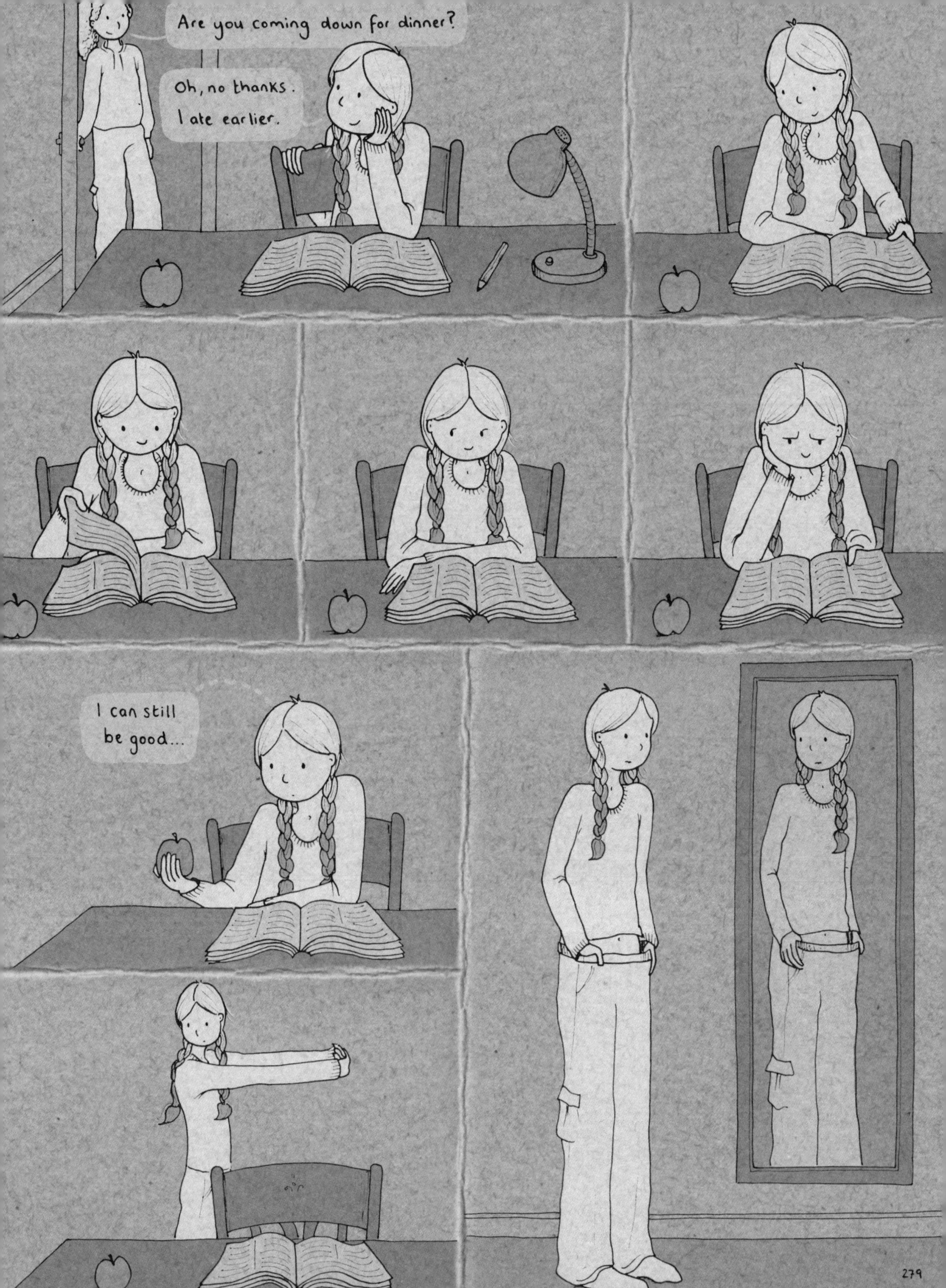
Are you coming down for dinner?
Oh, no thanks.
I ate earlier.
I can still be good...

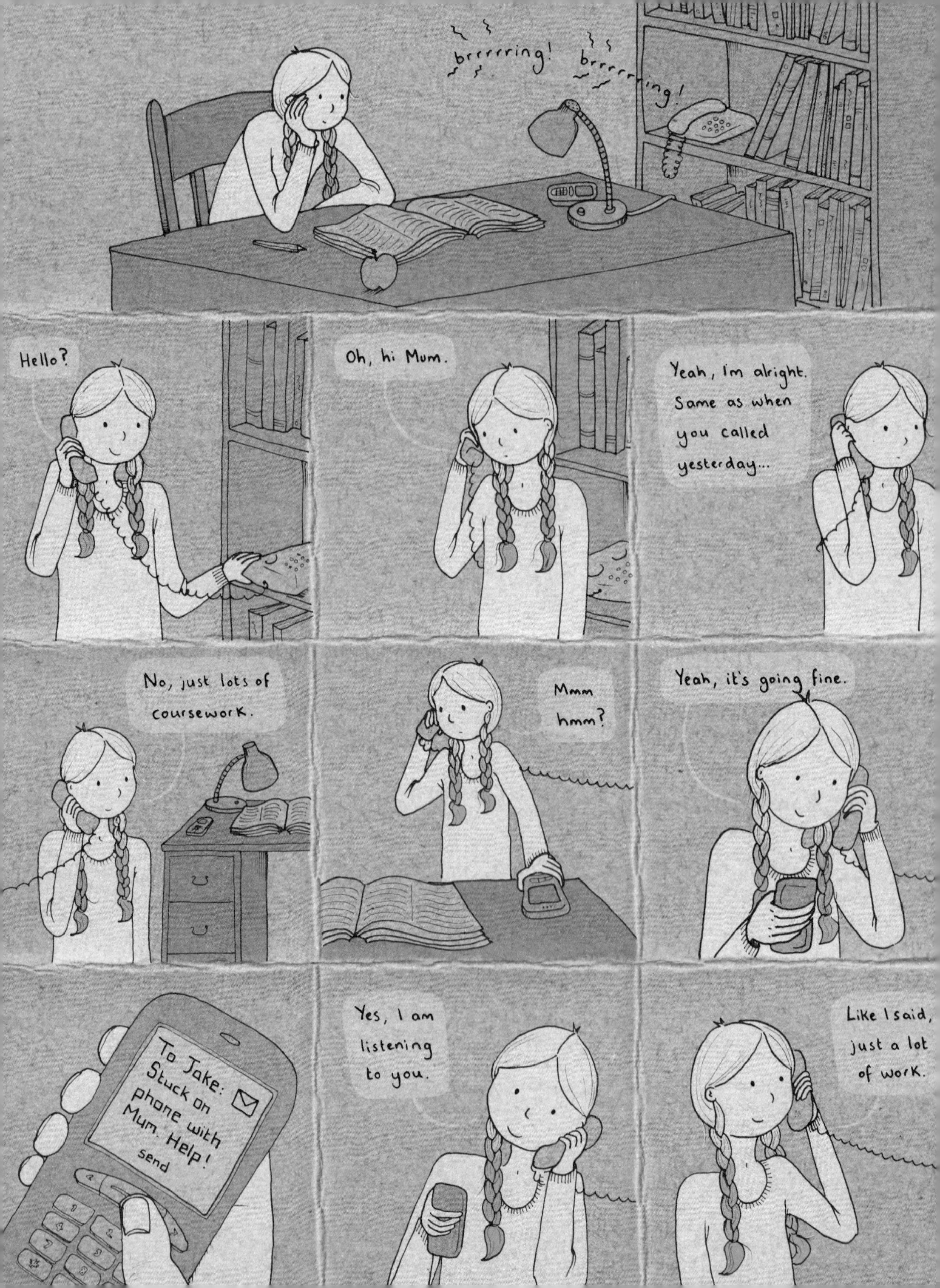
brrrrring!
brrrrrring!
Hello?
Oh, hi Mum.
Yeah, I'm alright. Same as when you called yesterday...
No, just lots of coursework.
Mmm hmm?
Yeah, it's going fine.
To Jake: Stuck on phone with Mum. Help!
send
Yes, I am listening to you.
Like I said, just a lot of work.

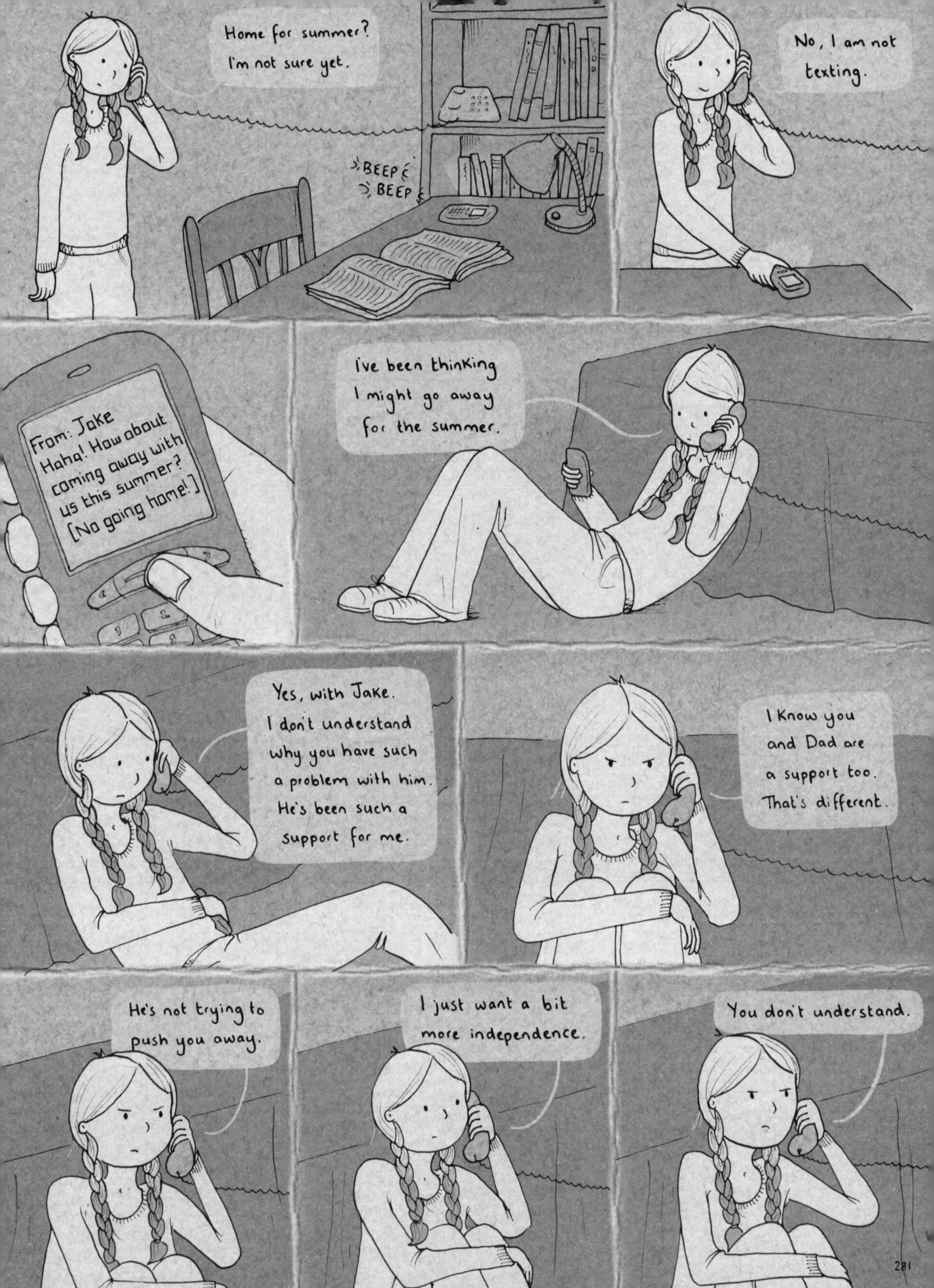
Home for summer? I'm not sure yet.
BEEP BEEP
No, I am not texting.
From: Jake Haha! How about coming away with us this summer? [No going home!]
I've been thinking I might go away for the summer.
Yes, with Jake. I don't understand why you have such a problem with him. He's been such a support for me.
I know you and Dad are a support too. That's different.
He's not trying to push you away.
I just want a bit more independence.
You don't understand.

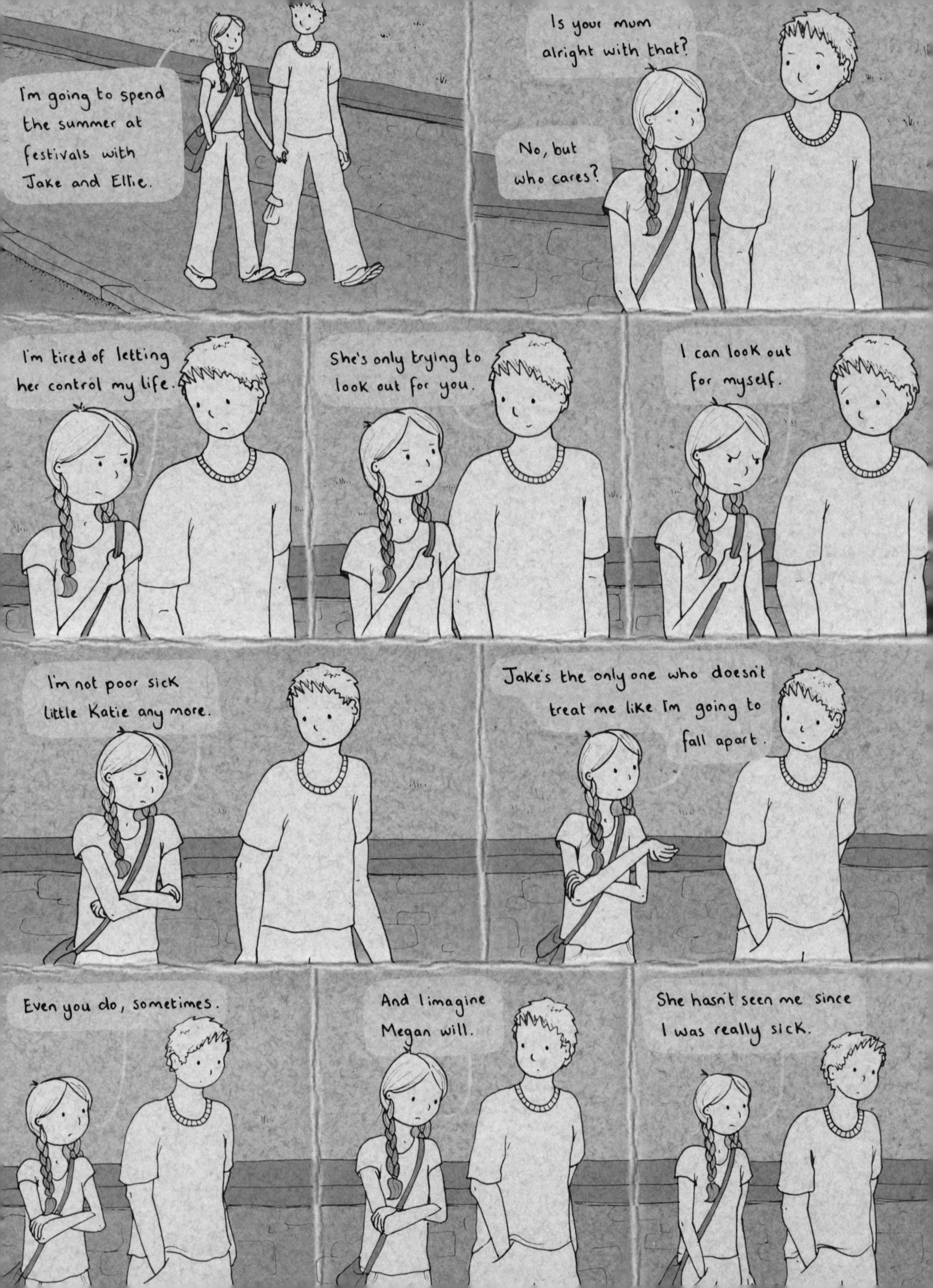
I'm going to spend the summer at festivals with Jake and Ellie.
Is your mum alright with that?
No, but who cares?
I'm tired of letting her control my life.
She's only trying to look out for you.
I can look out for myself.
I'm not poor sick little Katie any more.
Jake's the only one who doesn't treat me like I'm going to fall apart.
Even you do, sometimes.
And I imagine Megan will.
She hasn't seen me since I was really sick.

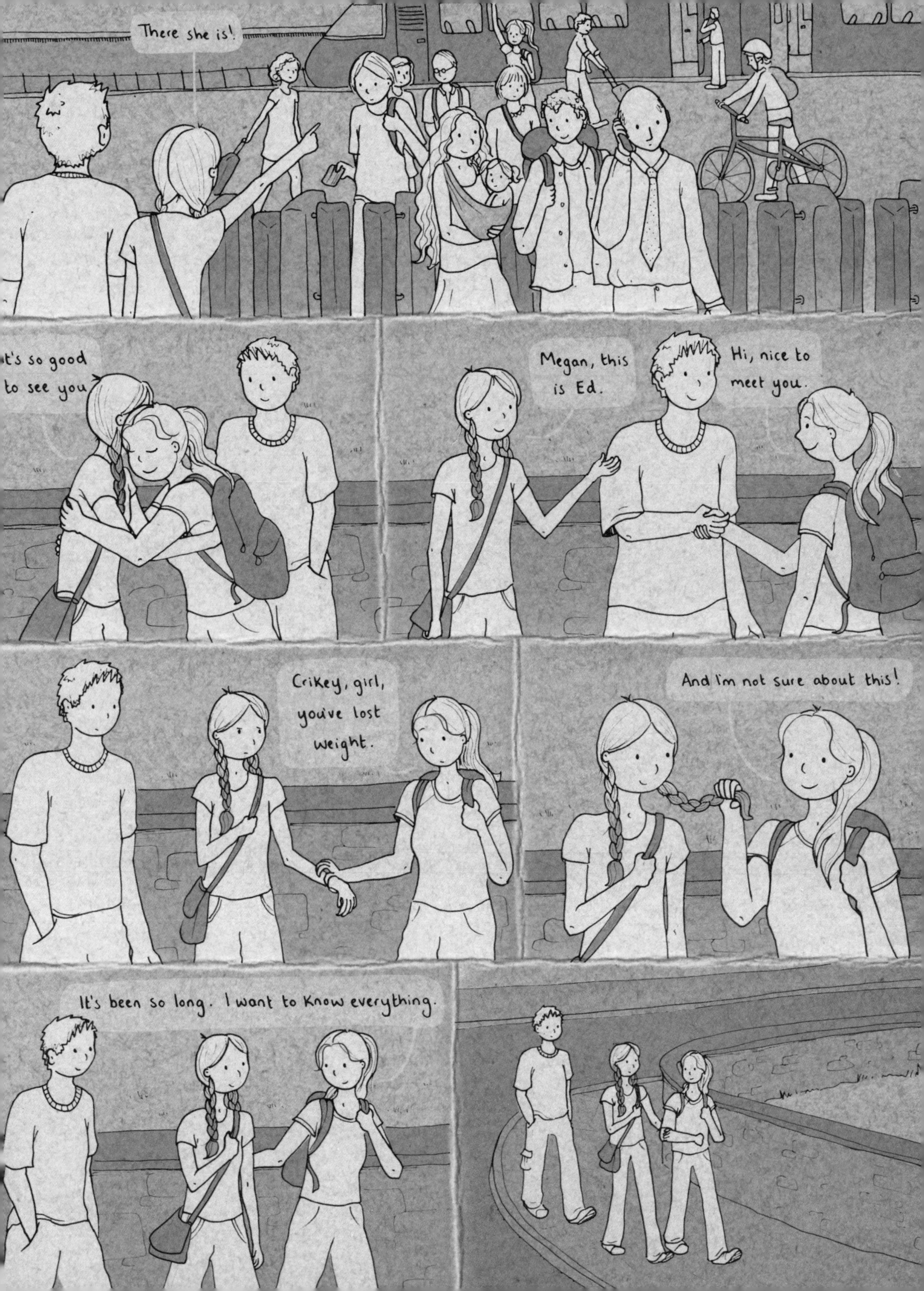
There she is!
It's so good to see you
Megan, this is Ed.
Hi, nice to meet you.
Crikey, girl, you've lost weight.
And I'm not sure about this!
It's been so long. I want to know everything.

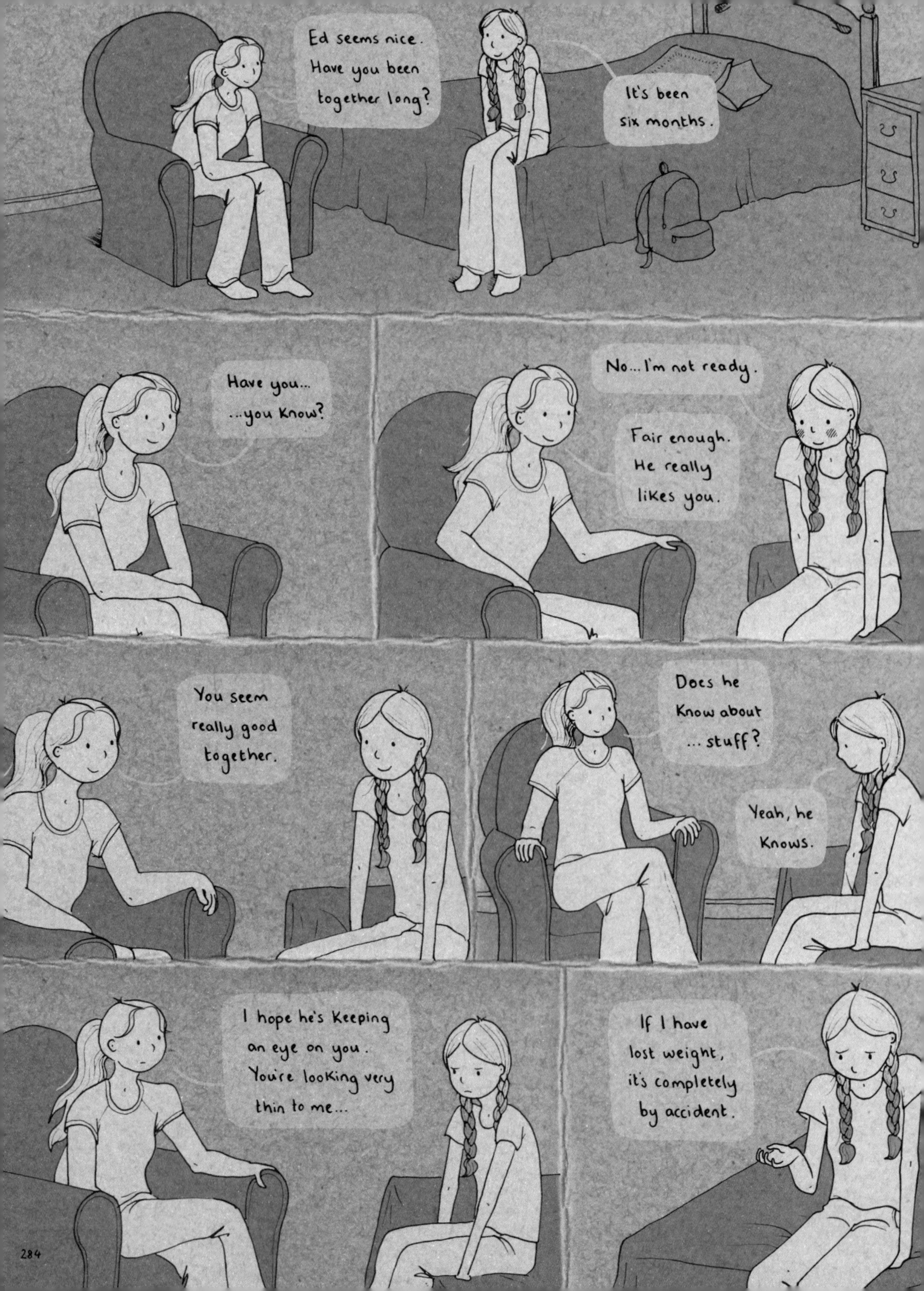
Ed seems nice. Have you been together long?
It's been six months.
Have you... ...you know?
No... I'm not ready.
Fair enough. He really likes you.
You seem really good together.
Does he know about ...stuff?
Yeah, he knows.
I hope he's keeping an eye on you. You're looking very thin to me...
If I have lost weight, it's completely by accident.

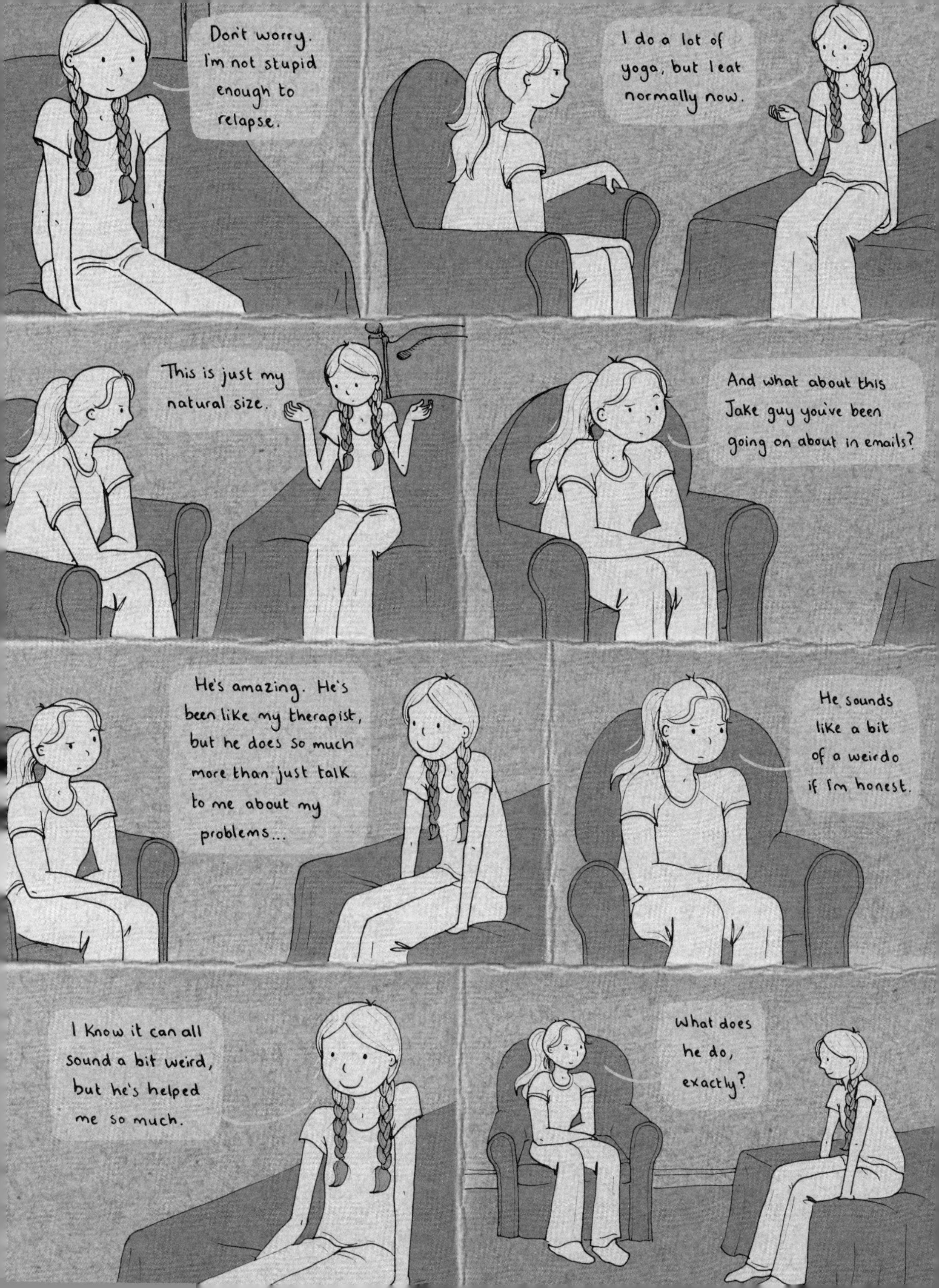
Don't worry. I'm not stupid enough to relapse.
I do a lot of yoga, but I eat normally now.
This is just my natural size.
And what about this Jake guy you've been going on about in emails?
He's amazing. He's been like my therapist, but he does so much more than just talk to me about my problems...
He sounds like a bit of a weirdo if I'm honest.
I know it can all sound a bit weird, but he's helped me so much.
What does he do, exactly?

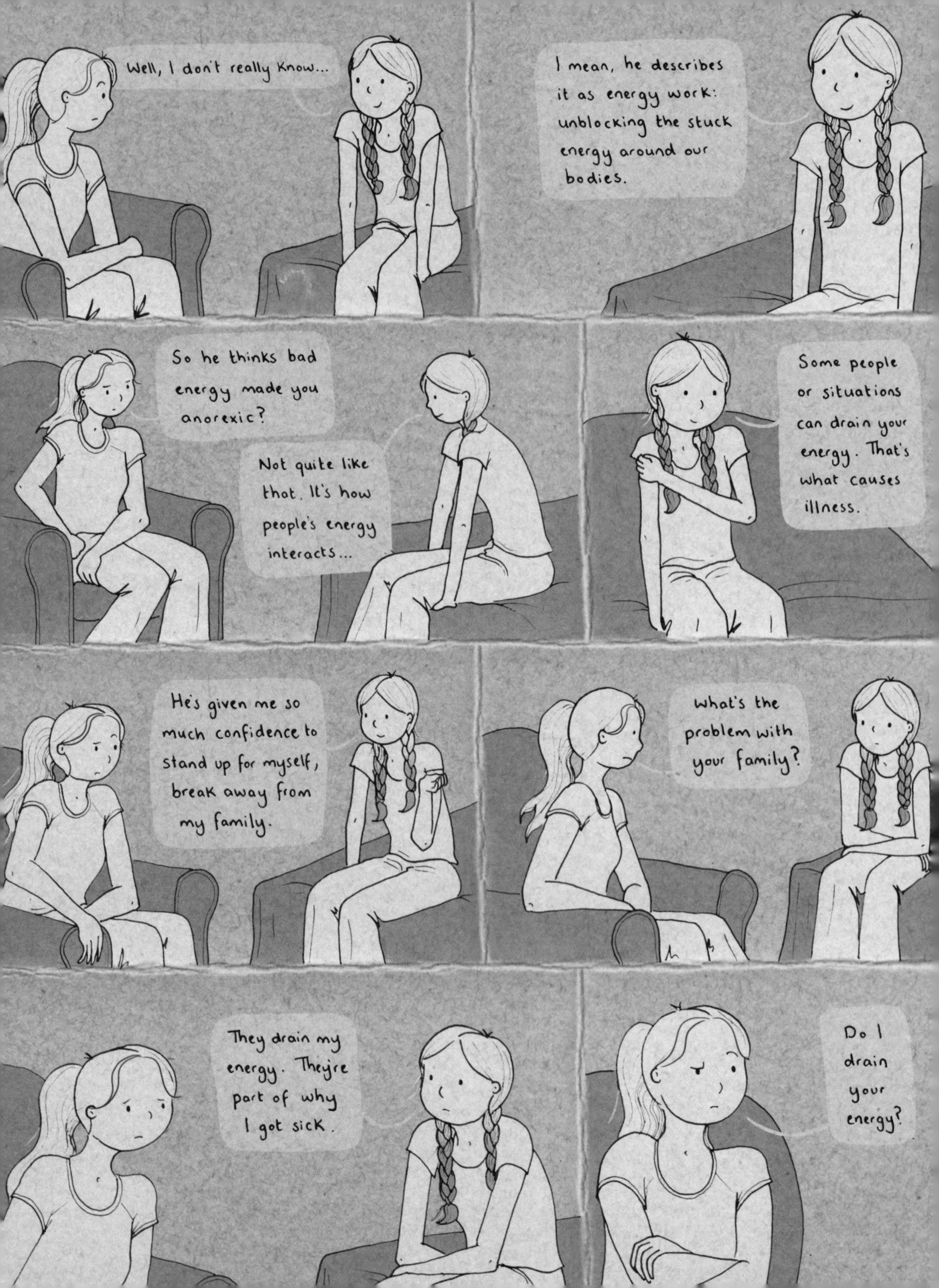
Well, I don't really know...
I mean, he describes it as energy work: unblocking the stuck energy around our bodies.
So he thinks bad energy made you anorexic?
Not quite like that. It's how people's energy interacts...
Some people or situations can drain your energy. That's what causes illness.
He's given me so much confidence to stand up for myself, break away from my family.
What's the problem with your family?
They drain my energy. They're part of why I got sick.
Do I drain your energy?

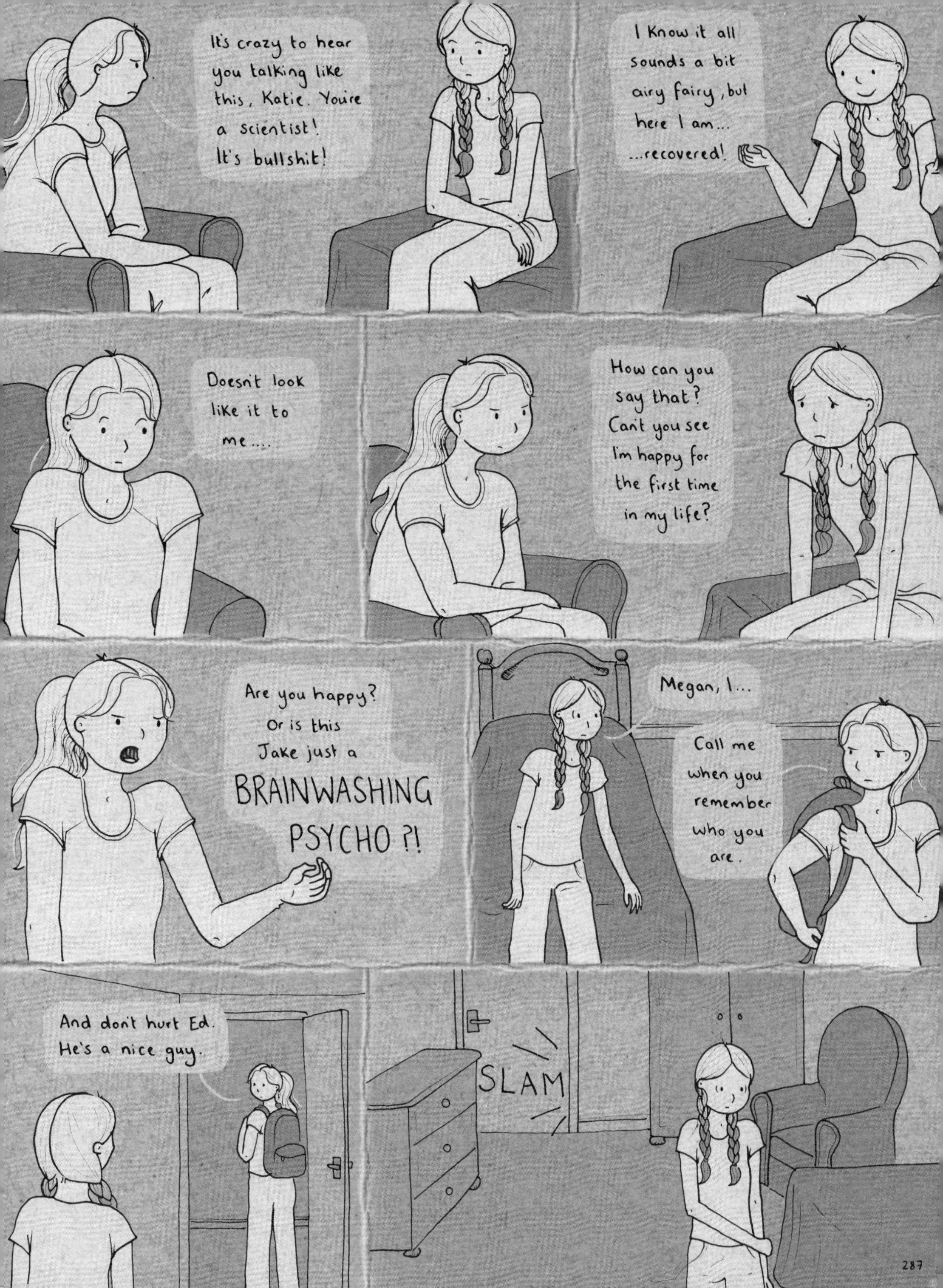
It's crazy to hear you talking like this, Katie. You're a scientist! It's bullshit!
I know it all sounds a bit airy fairy, but here I am... ...recovered!
Doesn't look like it to me....
How can you say that? Can't you see I'm happy for the first time in my life?
Are you happy? Or is this Jake just a BRAINWASHING PSYCHO?!
Megan, I...
Call me when you remember who you are.
And don't hurt Ed. He's a nice guy.
SLAM

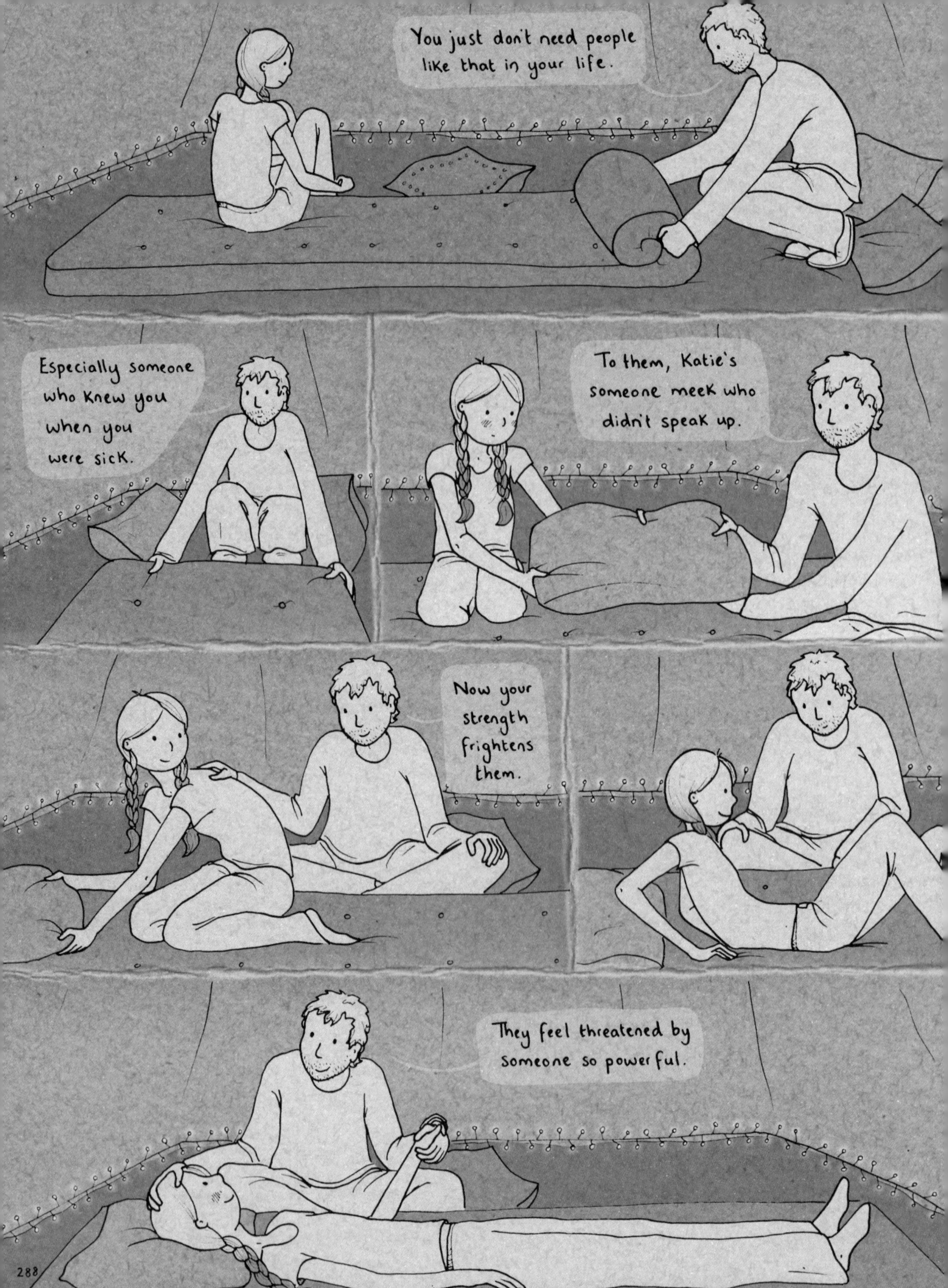
You just don't need people like that in your life.
Especially someone who knew you when you were sick.
To them, Katie's someone meek who didn't speak up.
Now your strength frightens them.
They feel threatened by someone so powerful.

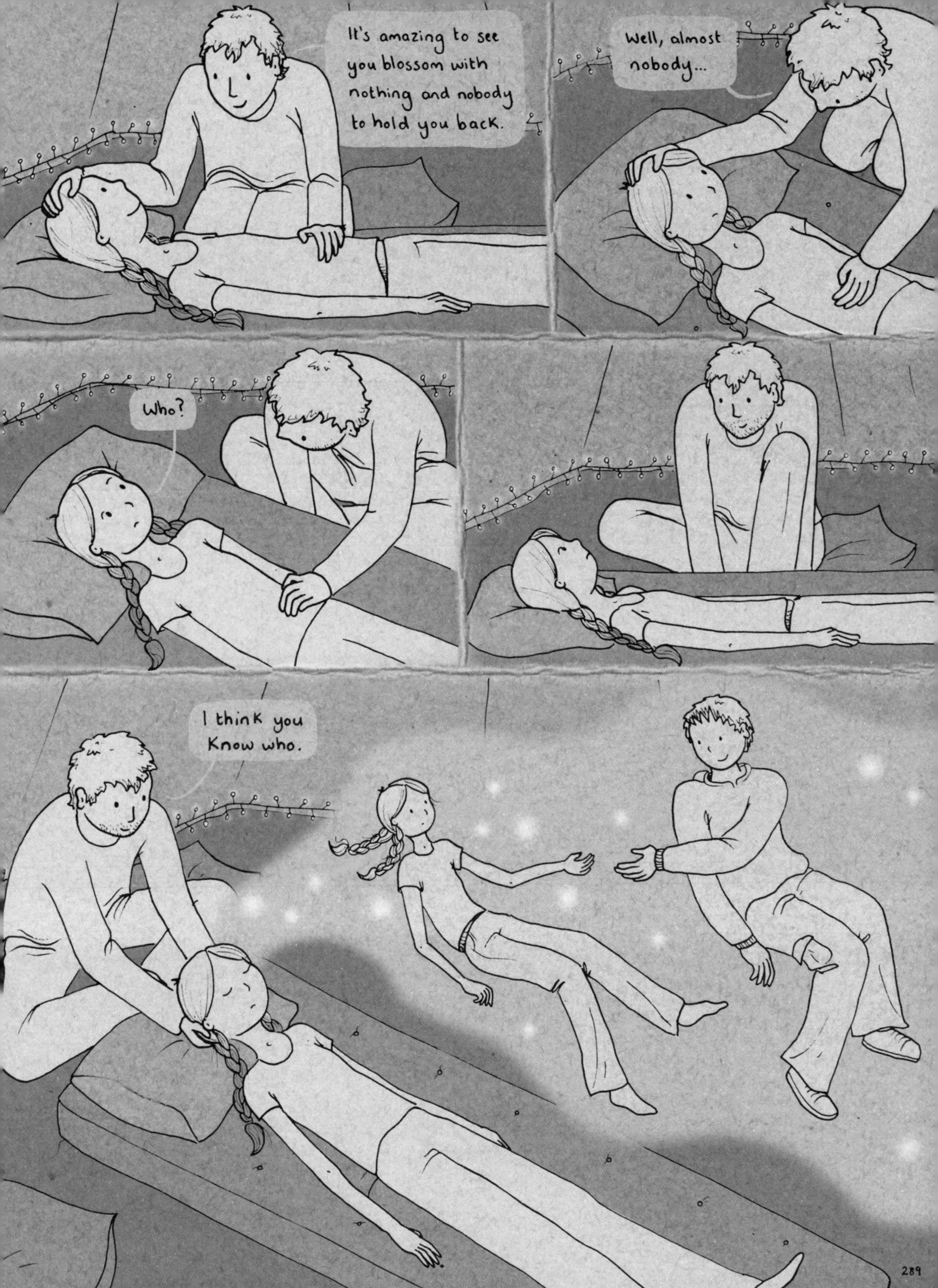
It's amazing to see you blossom with nothing and nobody to hold you back.
Well, almost nobody...
Who?
I think you Know who.

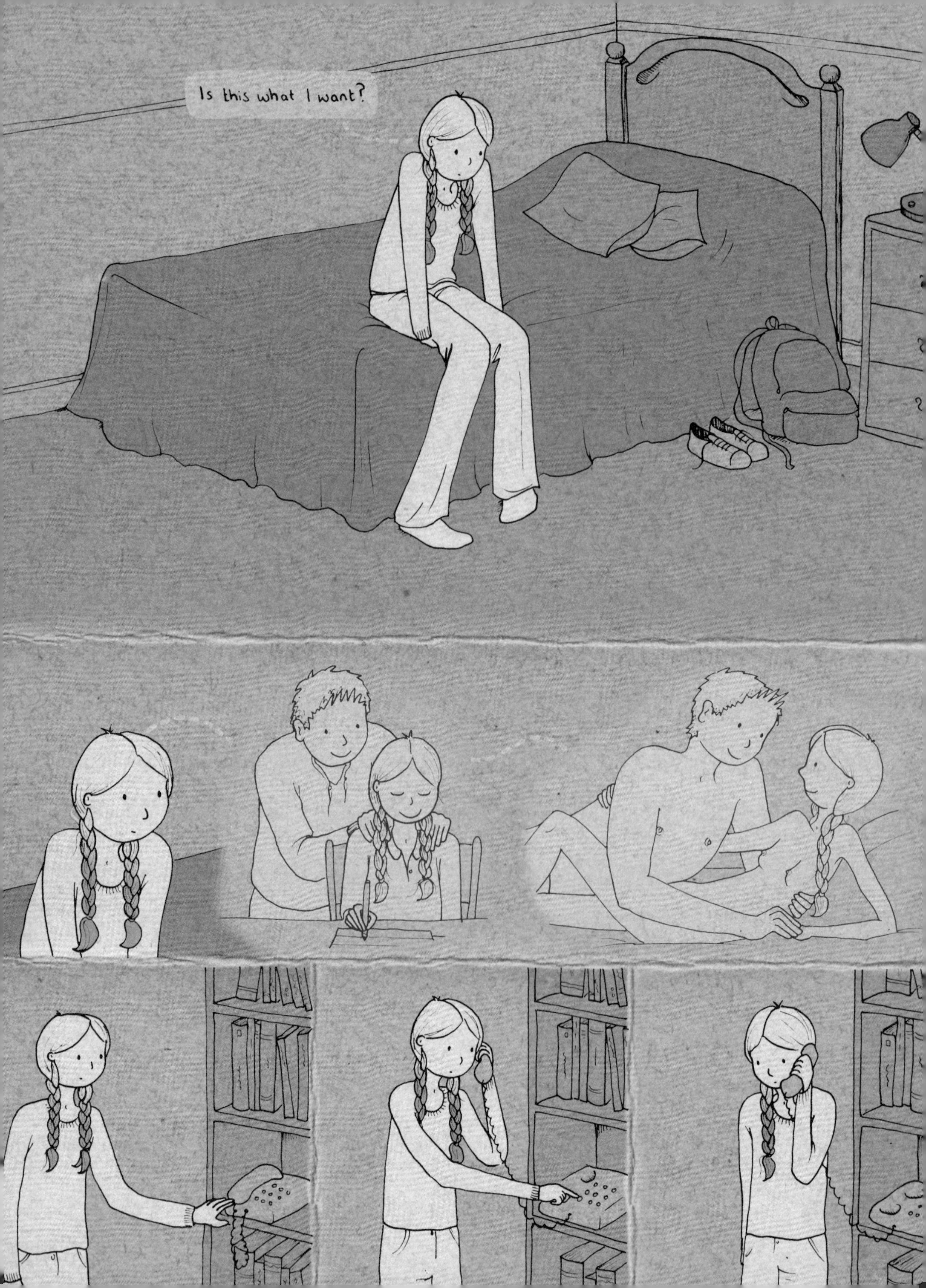
Is this what I want?

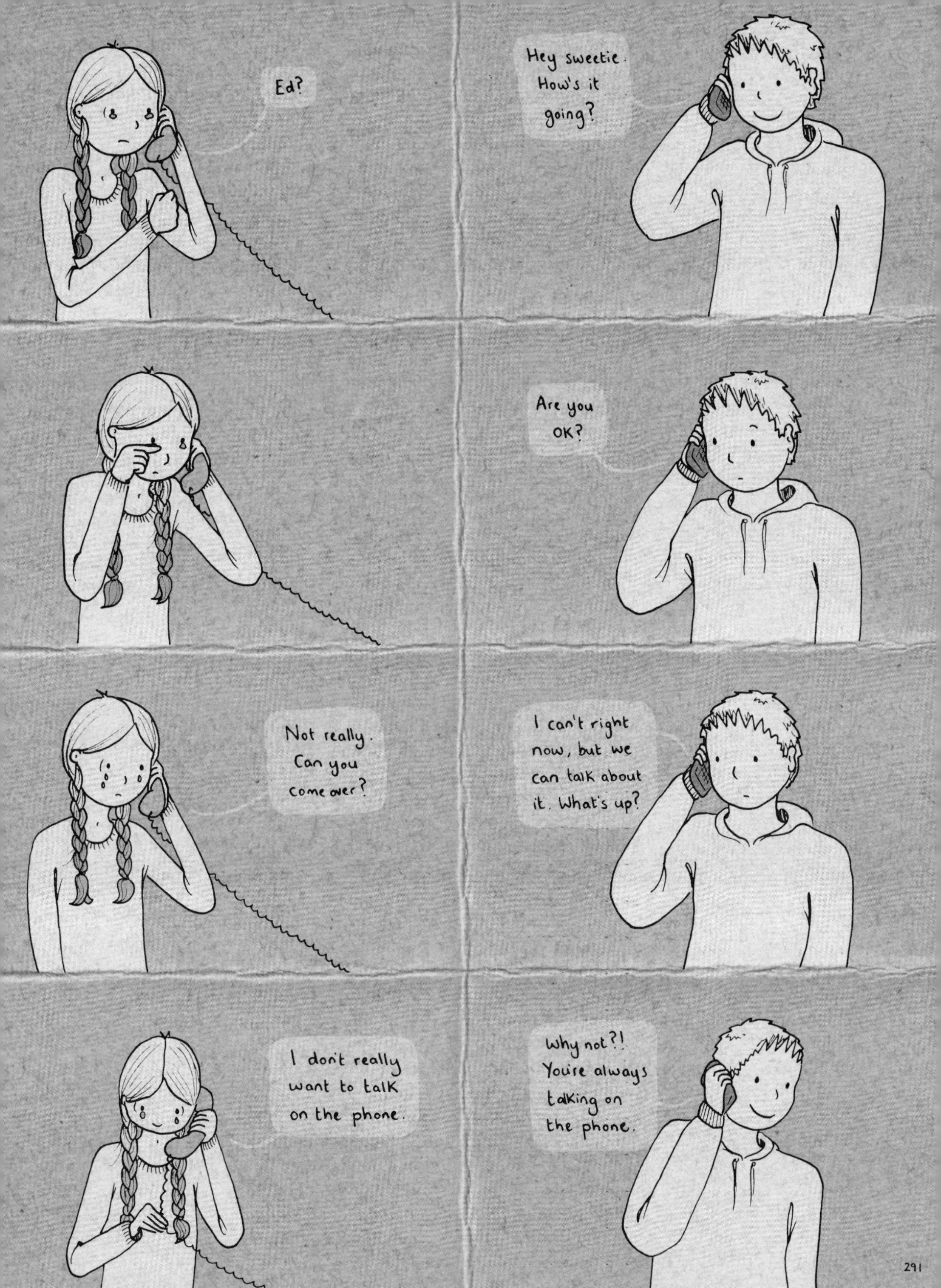
Ed?
Hey sweetie. How's it going?
Are you OK?
Not really. Can you come over?
I can't right now, but we can talk about it. What's up?
I don't really want to talk on the phone.
Why not?! You're always talking on the phone.

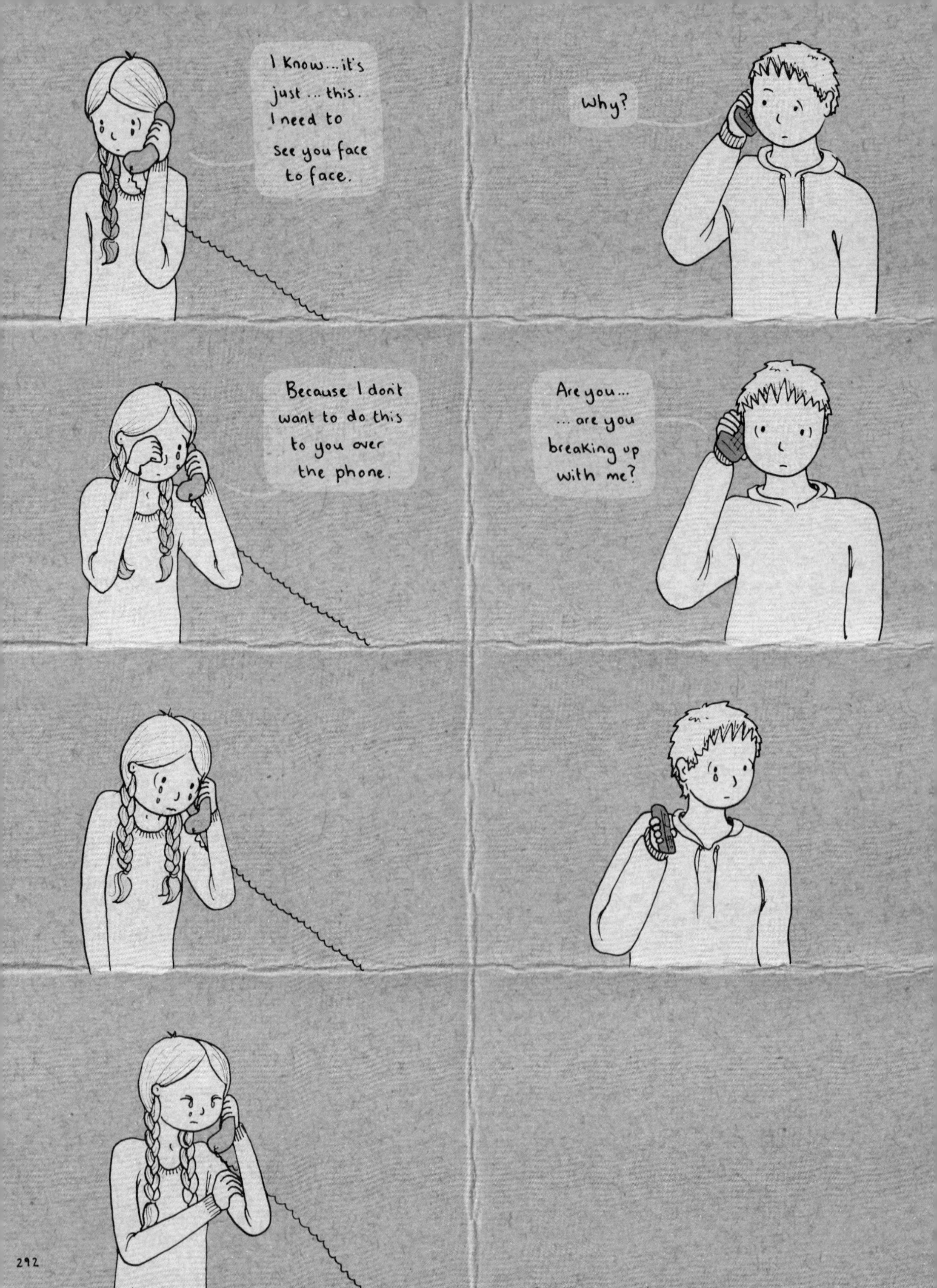
I know... it's just ... this. I need to see you face to face.
Why?
Because I don't want to do this to you over the phone.
Are you...
... are you breaking up with me?

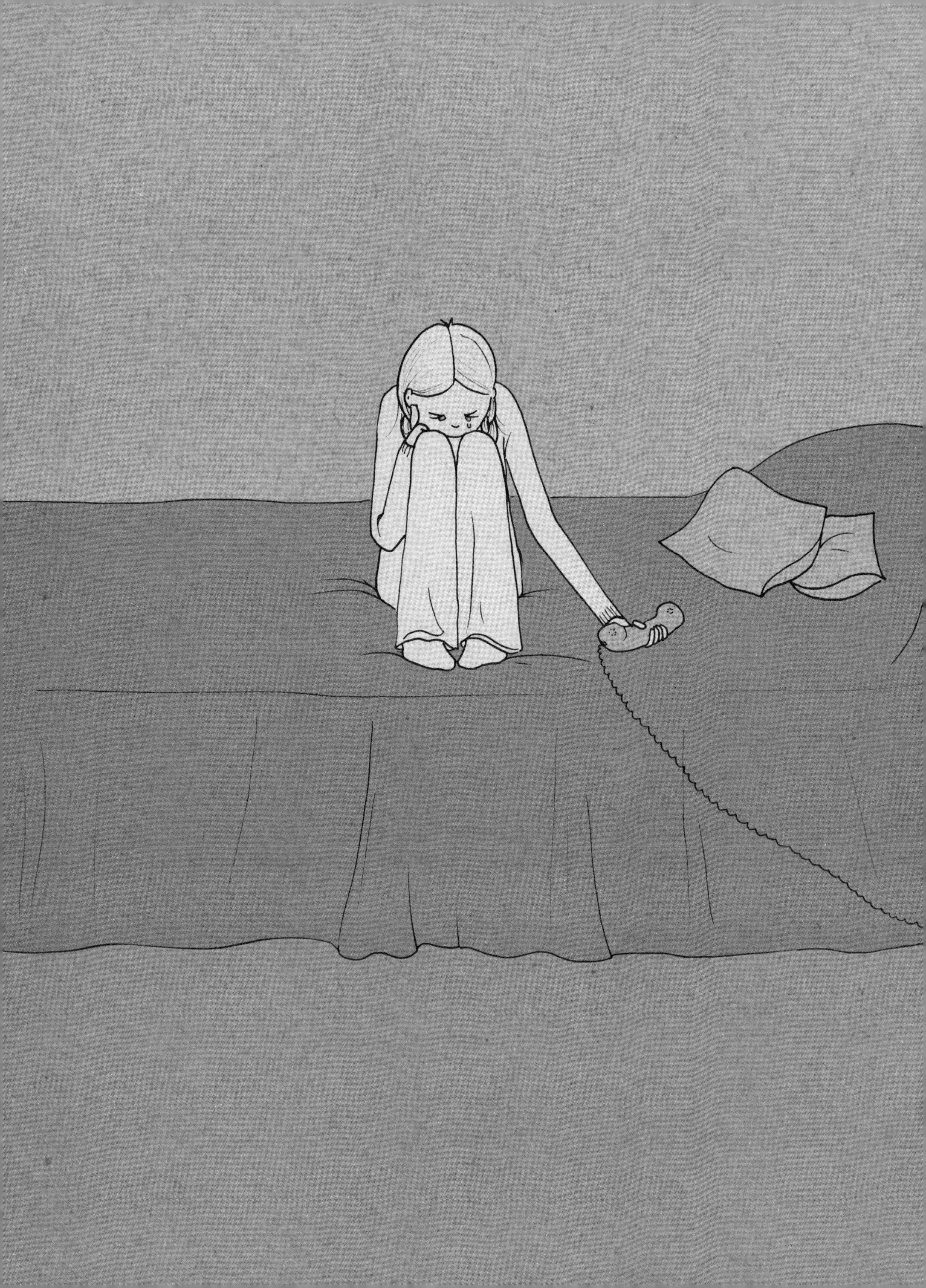

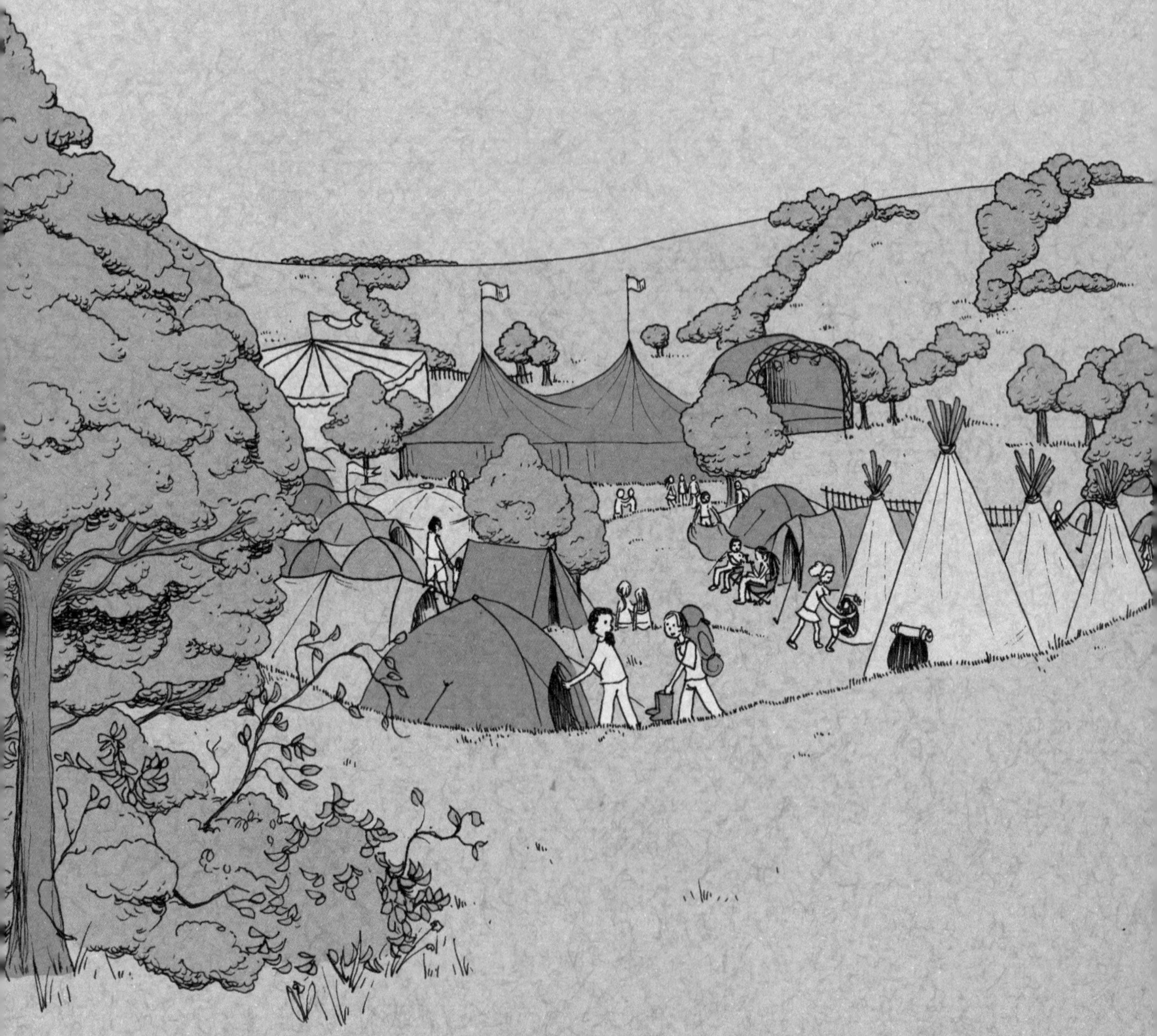

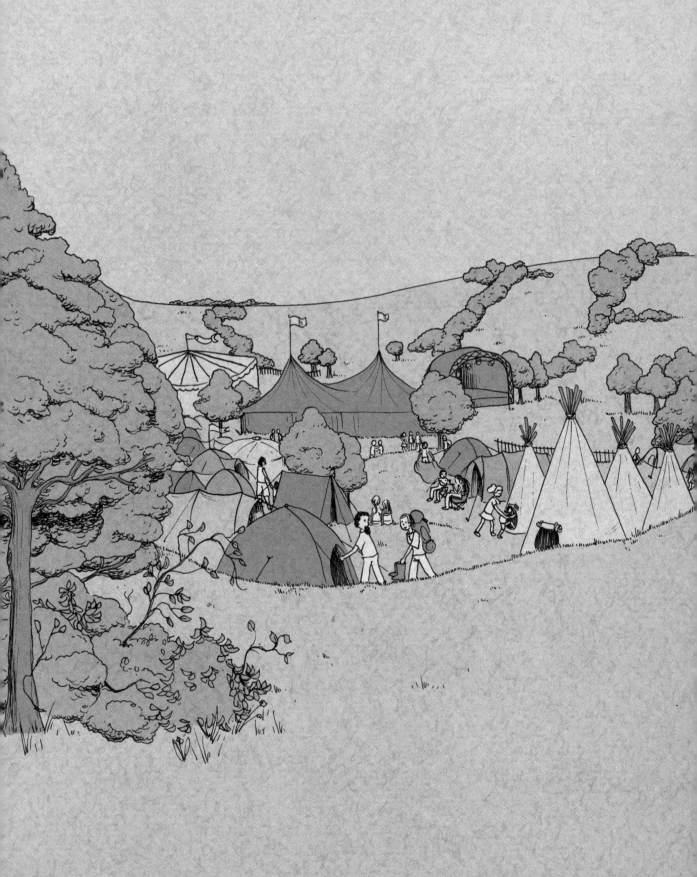

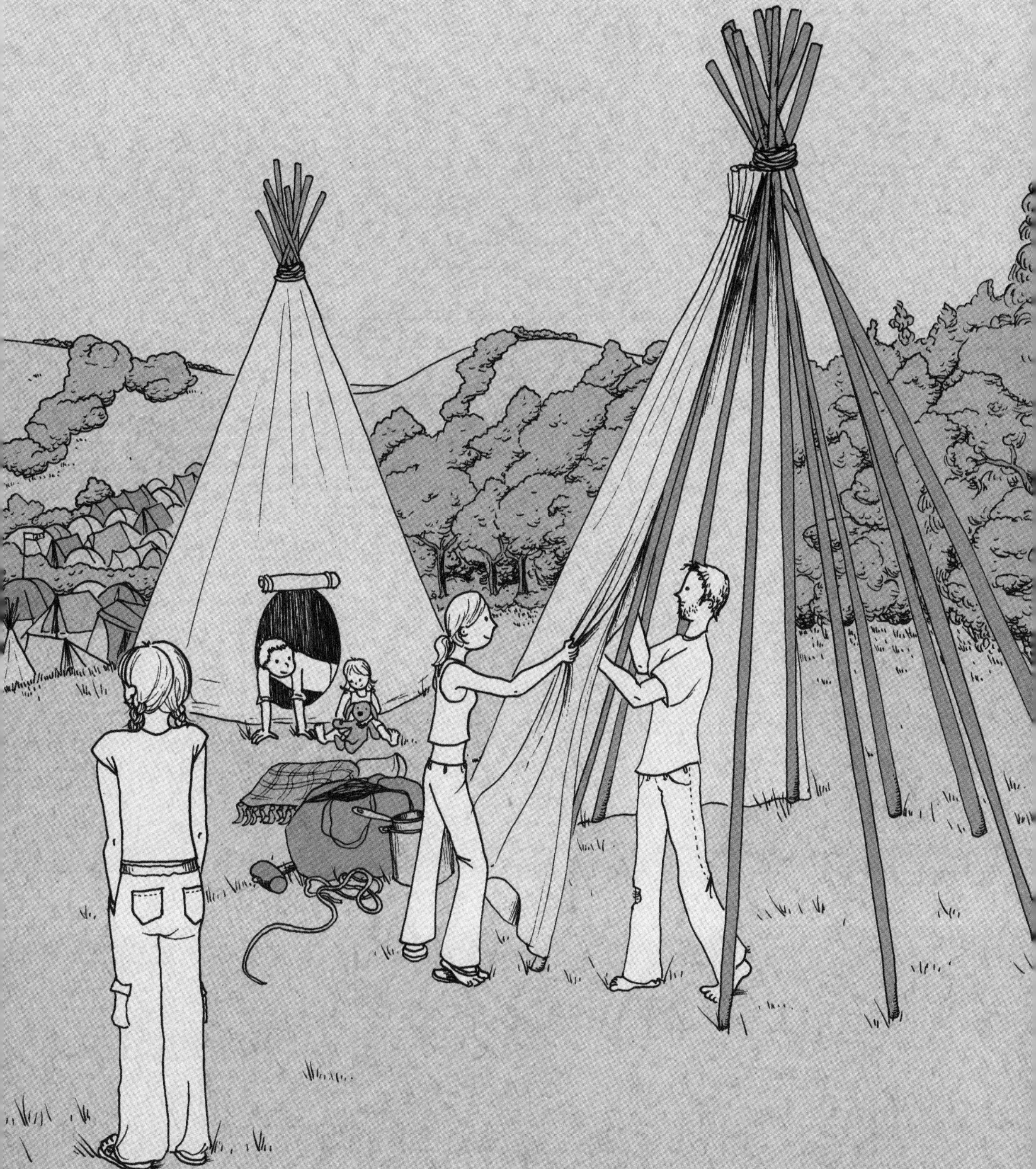

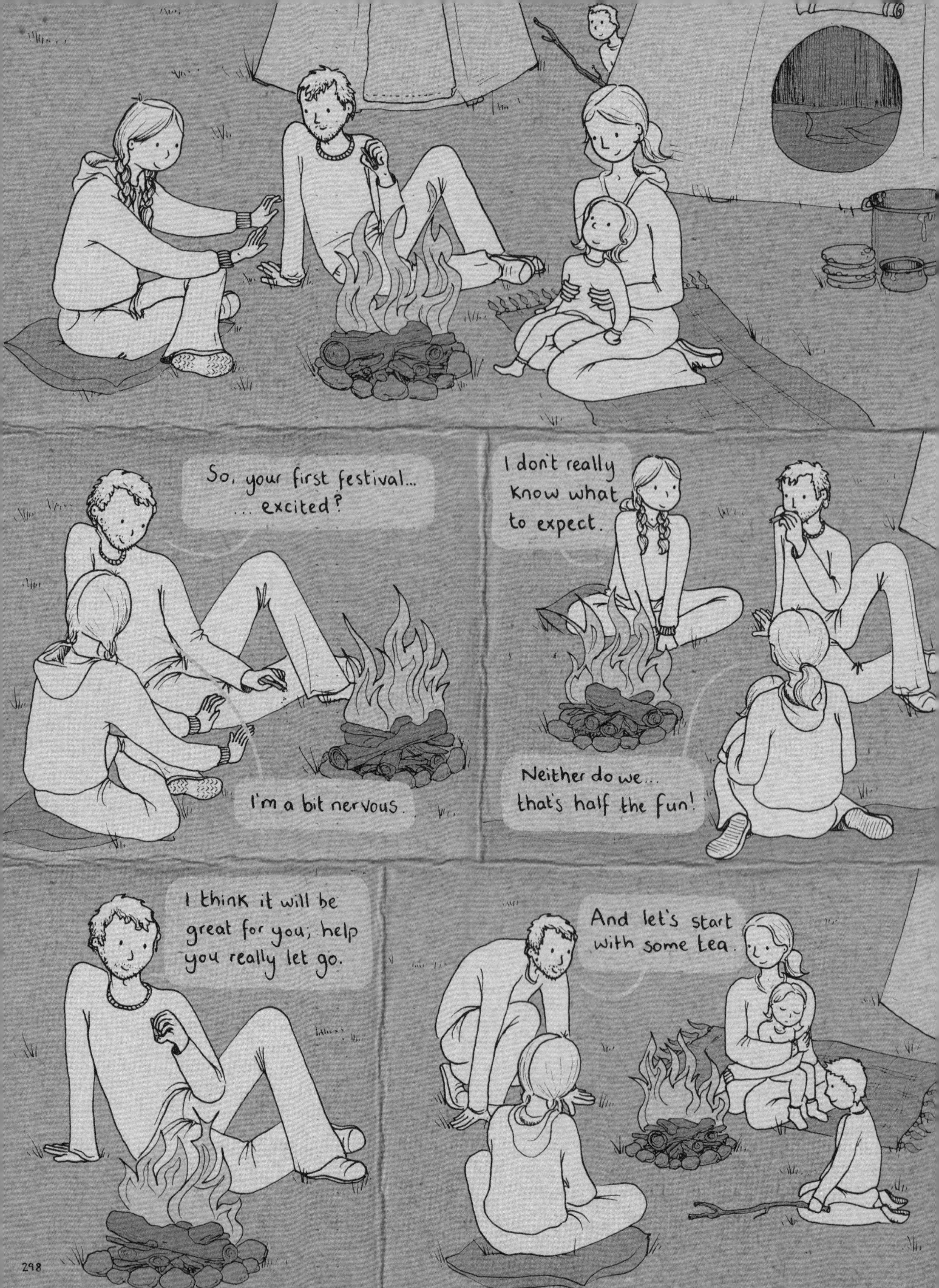
So, your first festival... ... excited?
I'm a bit nervous.
I don't really know what to expect.
Neither do we... that's half the fun!
I think it will be great for you; help you really let go.
And let's start with some tea.

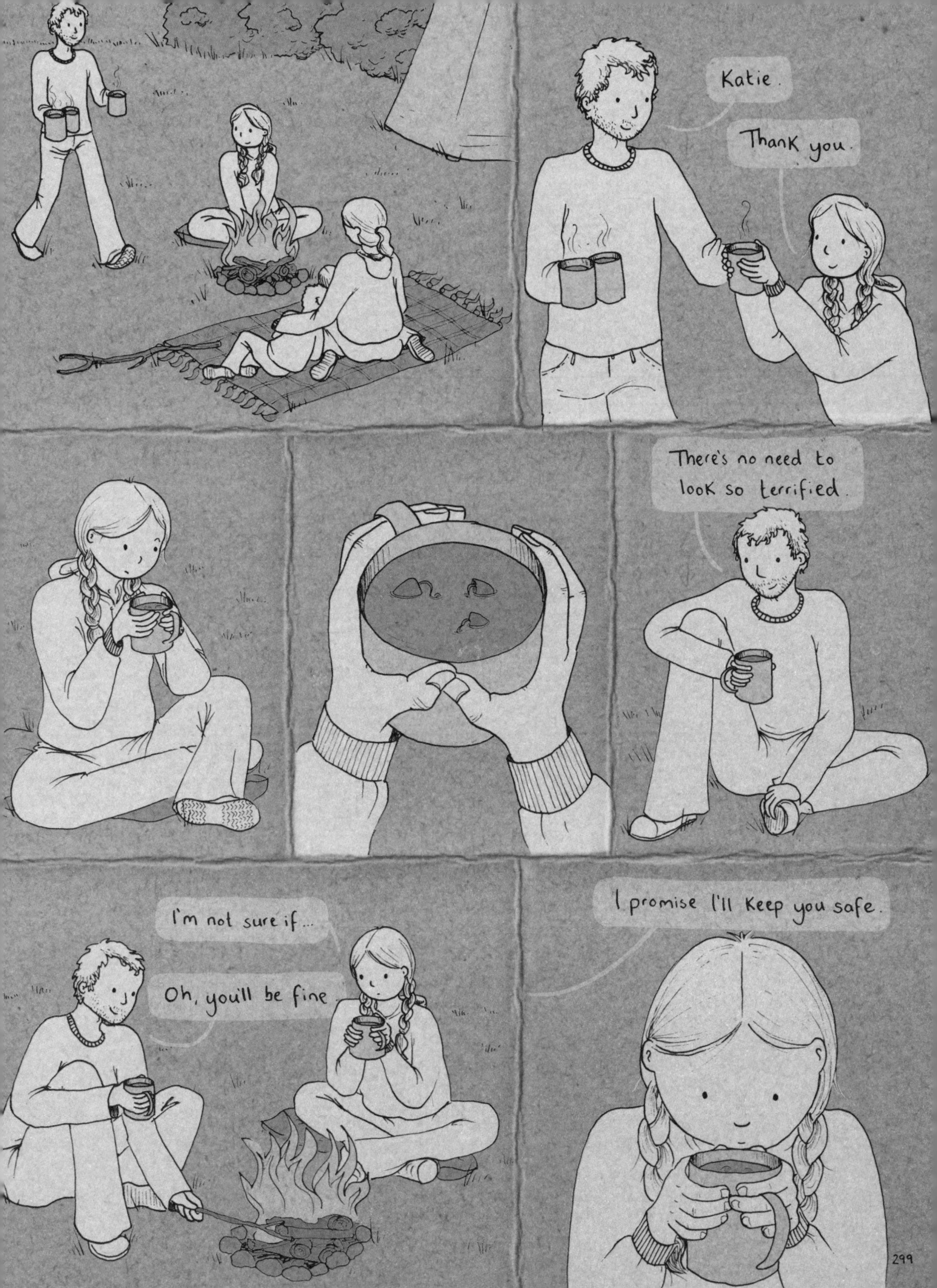

Katie.
Thank you.
There's no need to look so terrified.
I'm not sure if...
Oh, you'll be fine.
I promise I'll keep you safe.

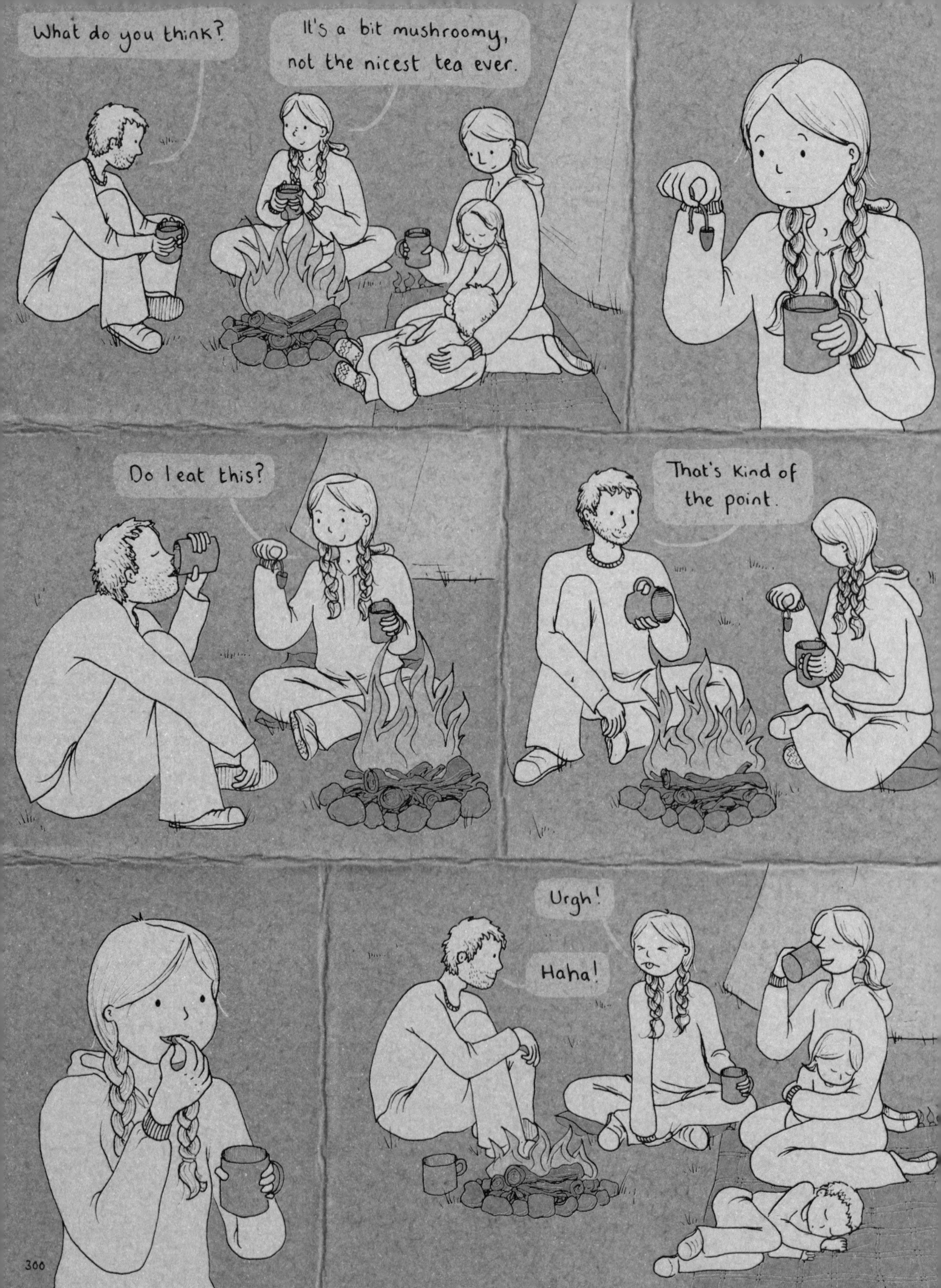
What do you think?
It's a bit mushroomy, not the nicest tea ever.
Do I eat this?
That's kind of the point.
Urgh!
Haha!

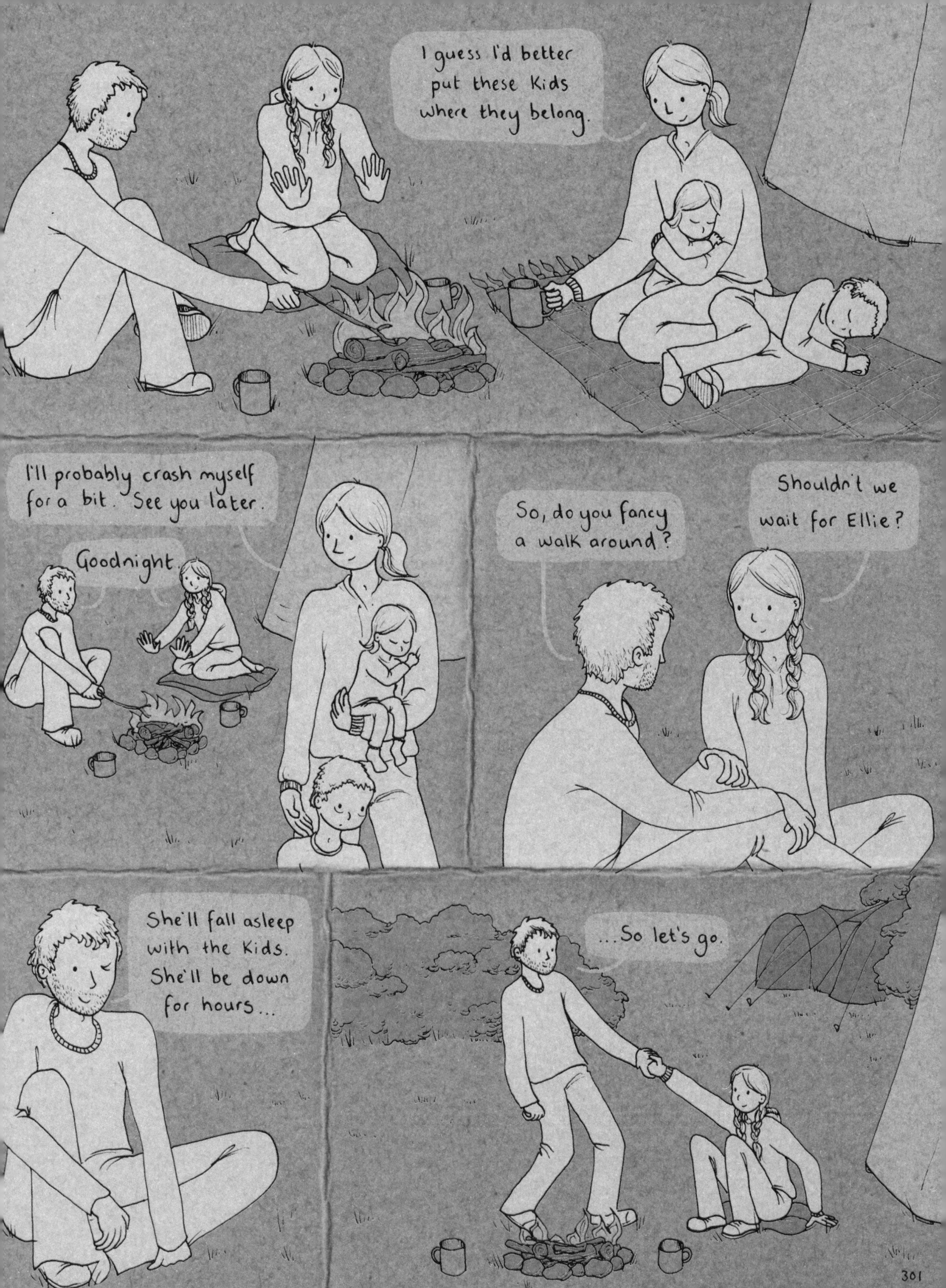
I guess I'd better put these Kids where they belong.
I'll probably crash myself for a bit. See you later.
Goodnight.
So, do you fancy a walk around?
Shouldn't we wait for Ellie?
She'll fall asleep with the Kids. She'll be down for hours...
...So let's go.

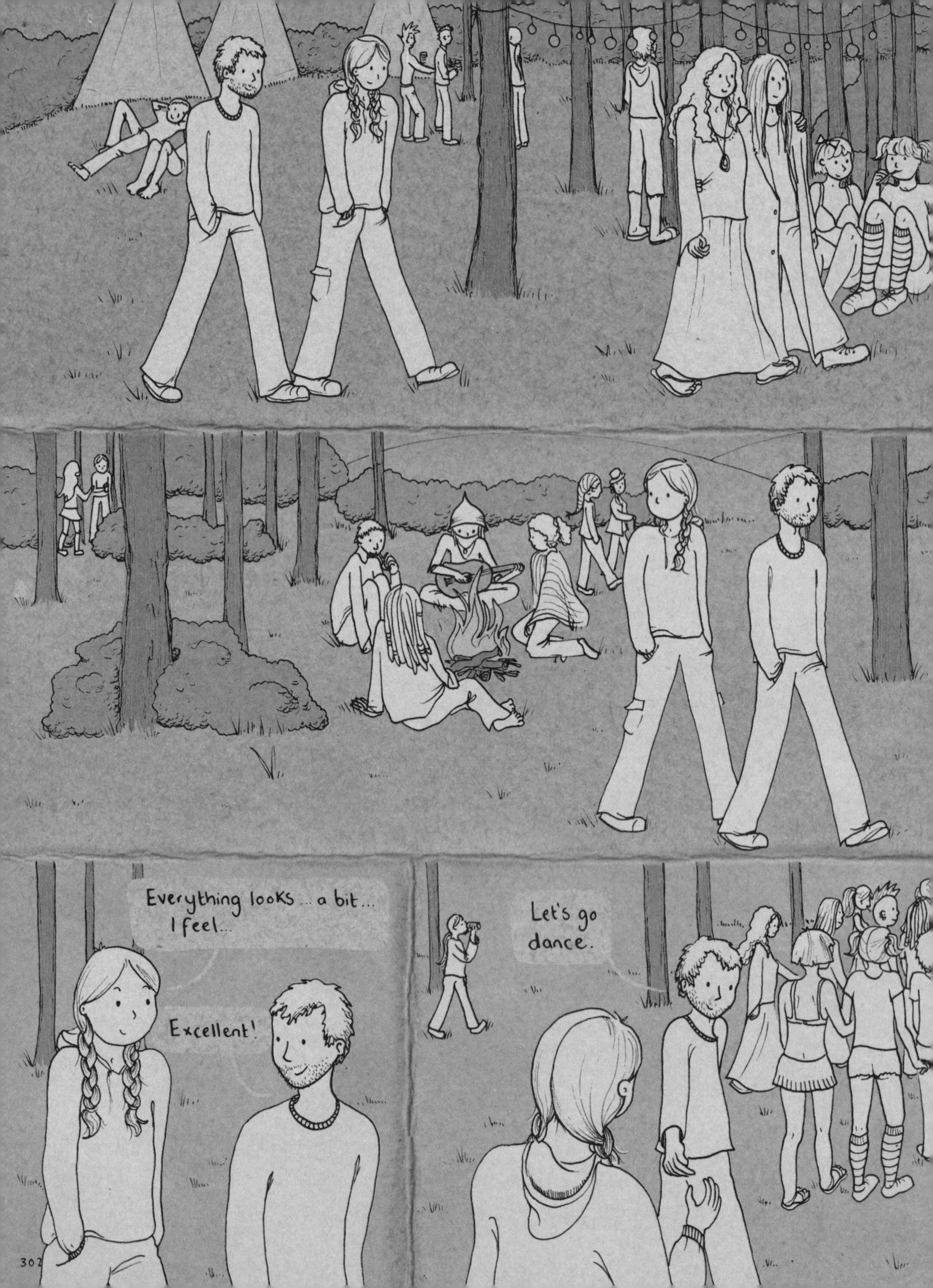
Everything looks ... a bit ...
I feel...
Excellent!
Let's go
dance.

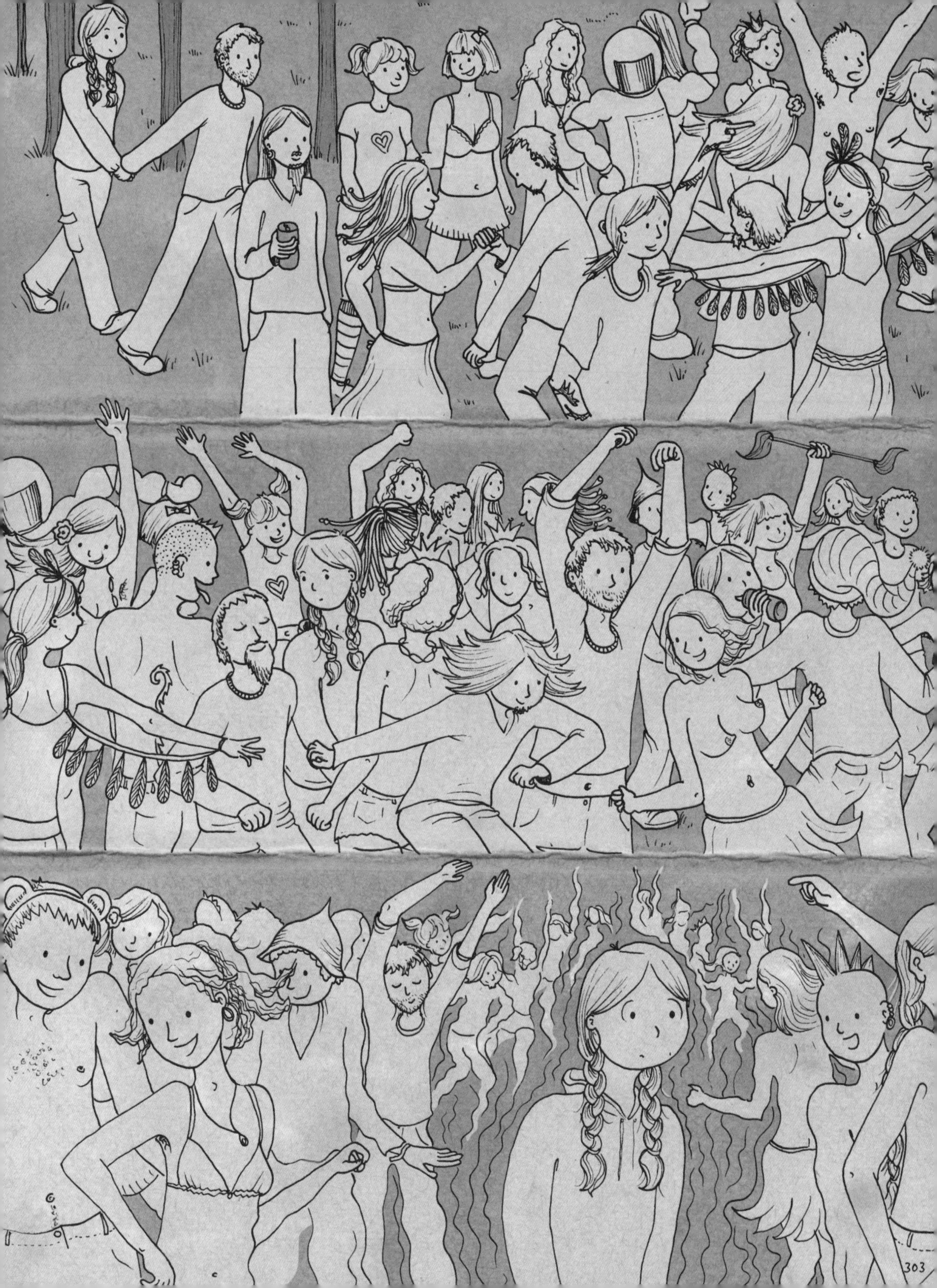

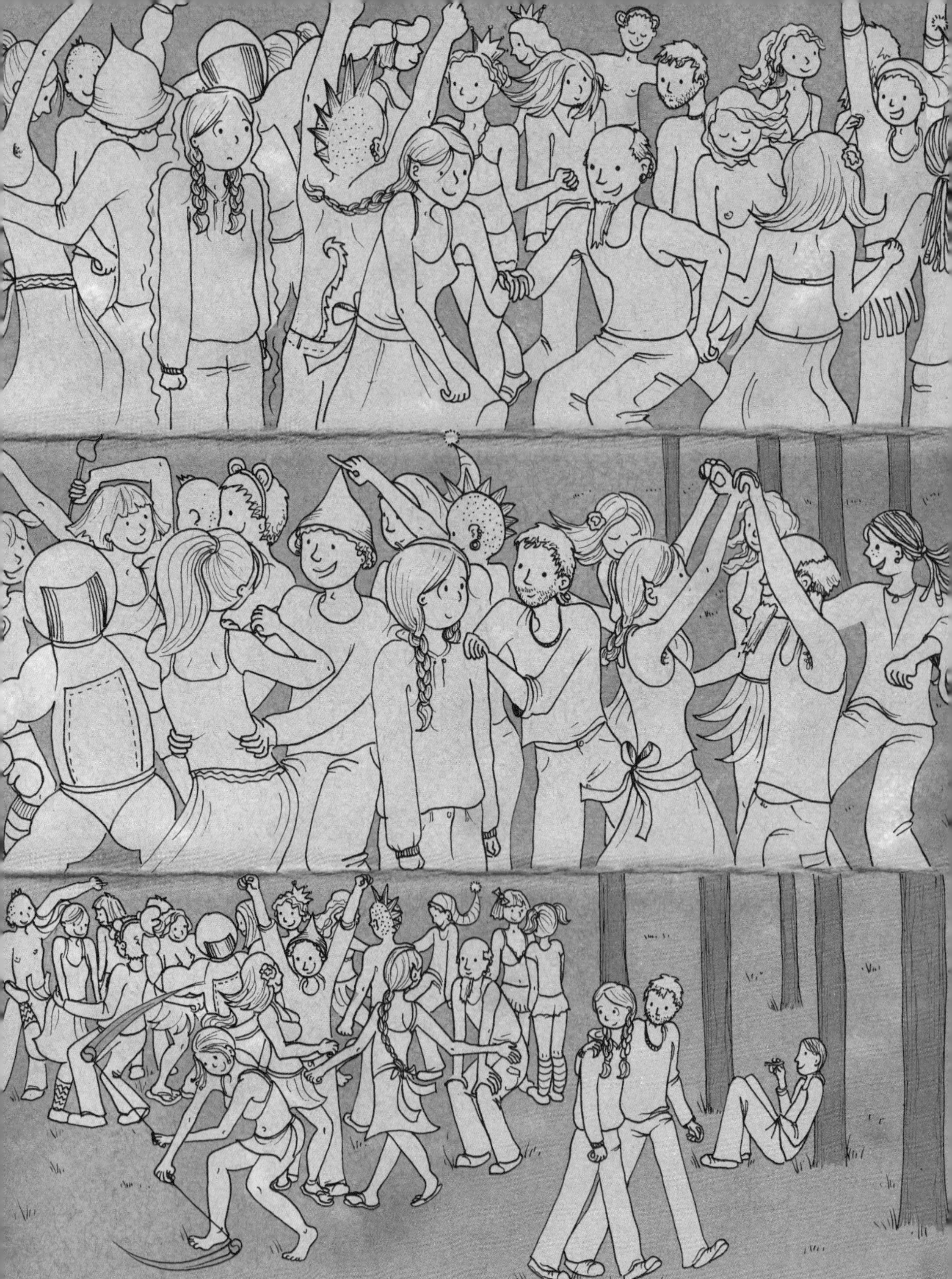

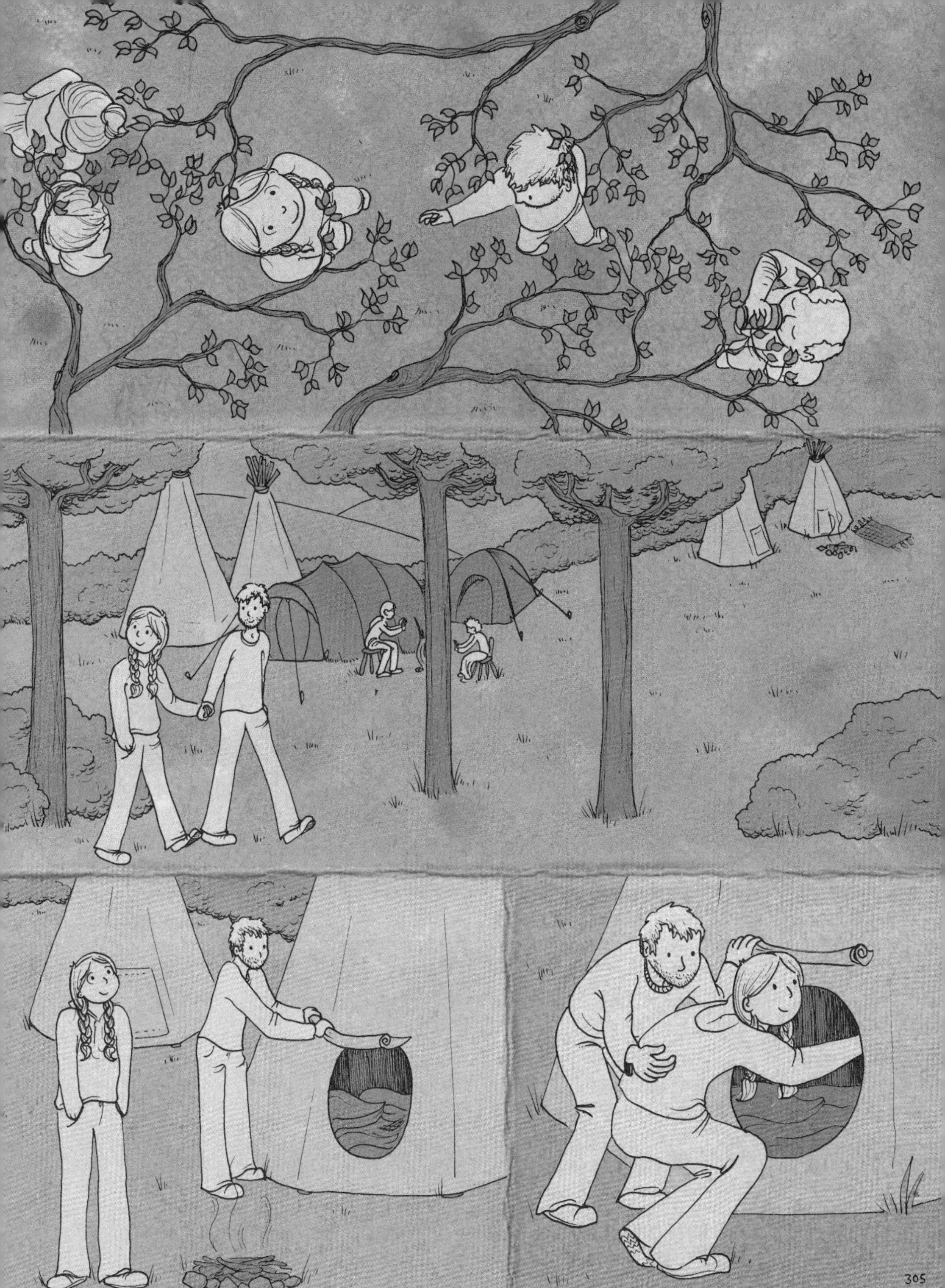

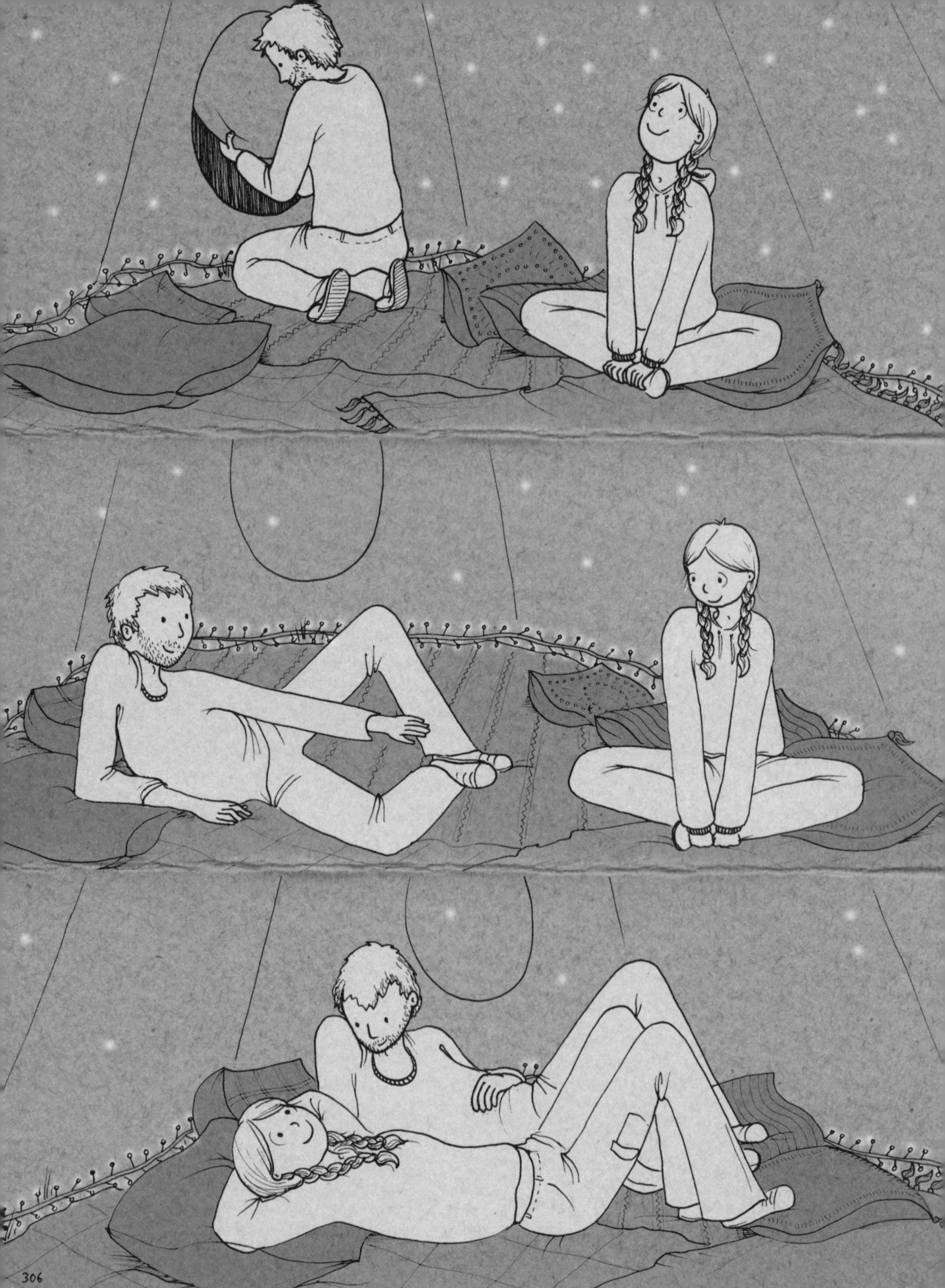

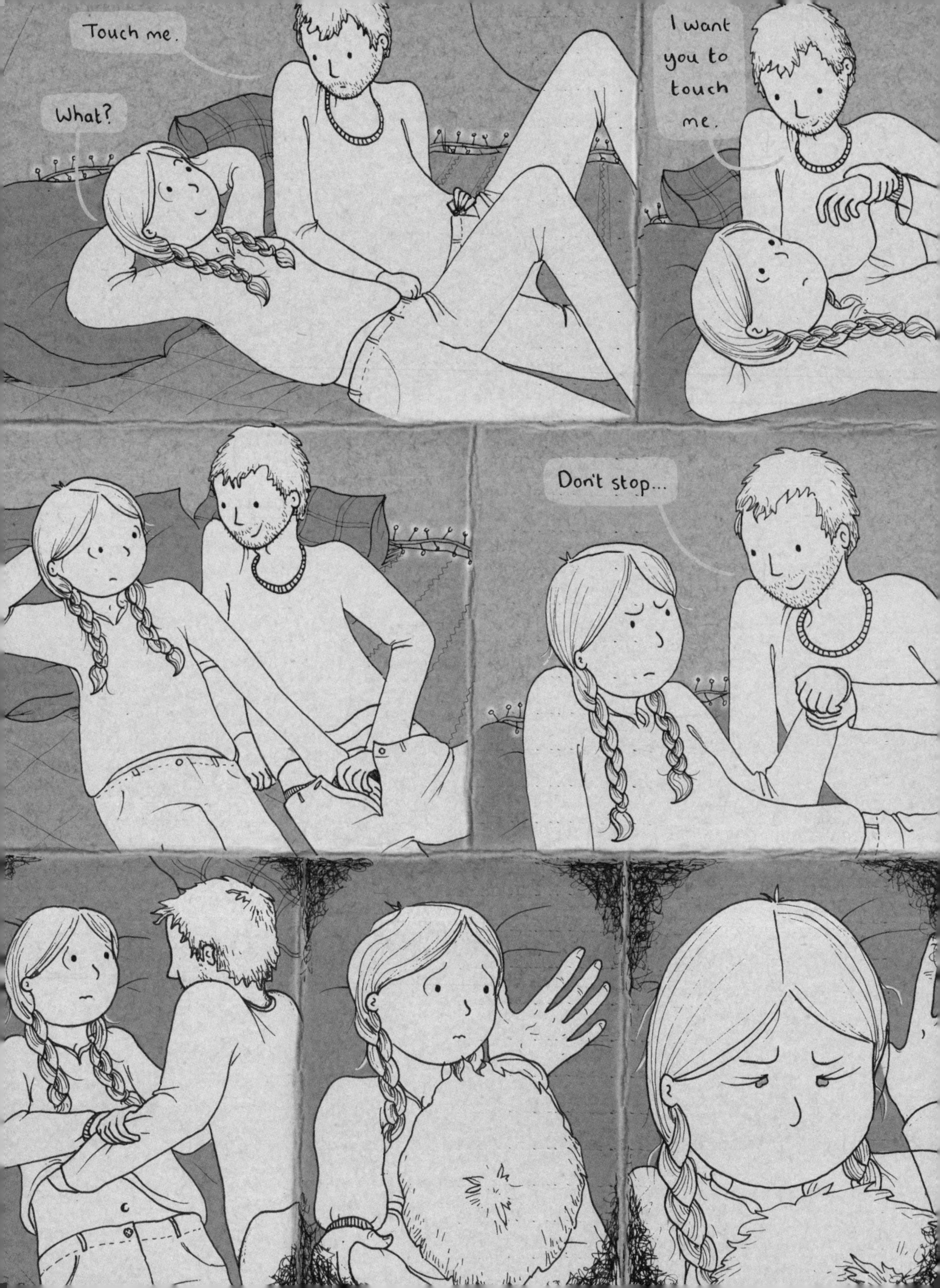
Touch me.
What?
I want you to touch me.
Don't stop...

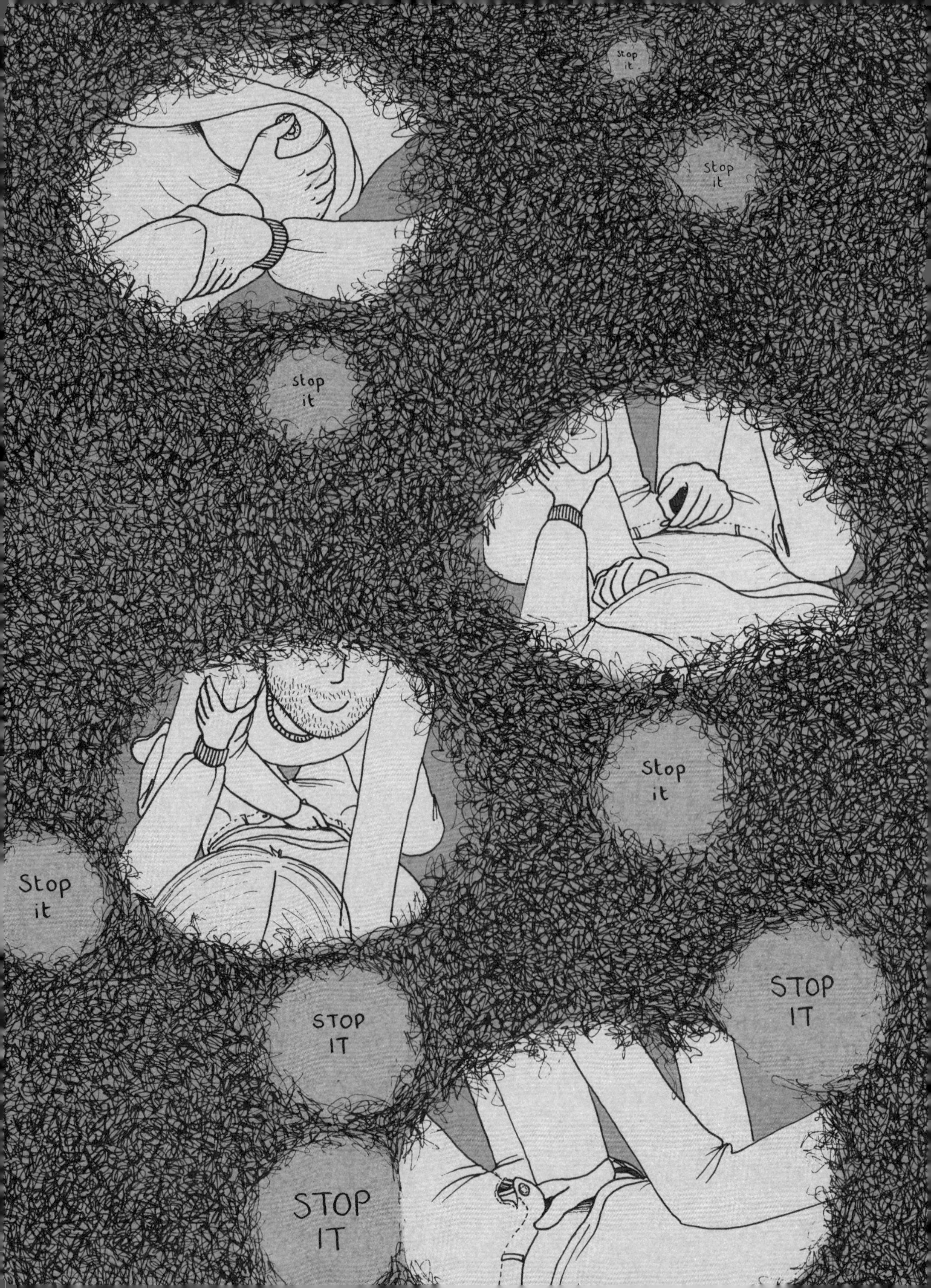
Stop it
Stop it
Stop it
Stop it
Stop it
STOP IT
STOP IT
STOP IT

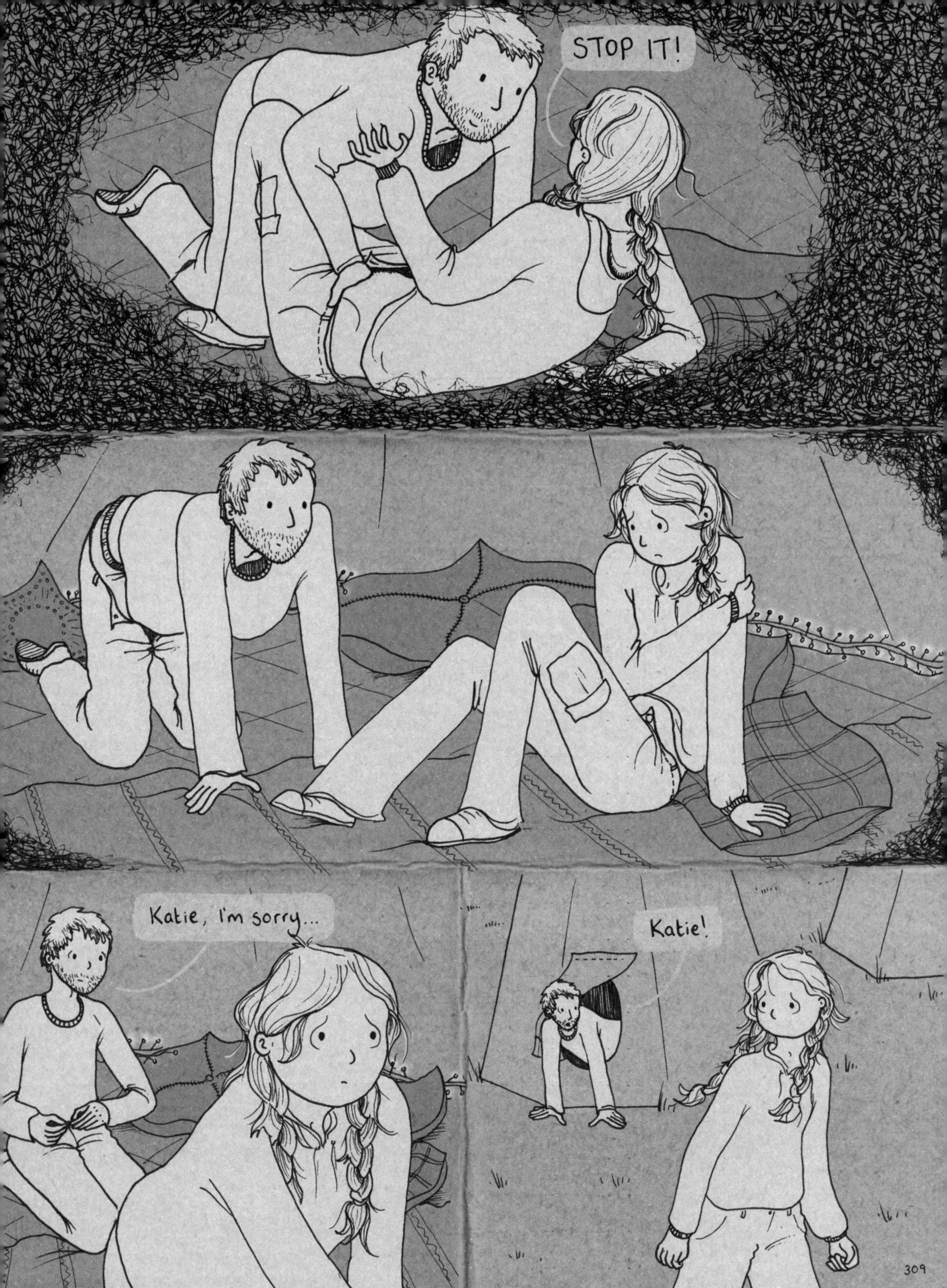
STOP IT!
Katie, I'm sorry...
Katie!

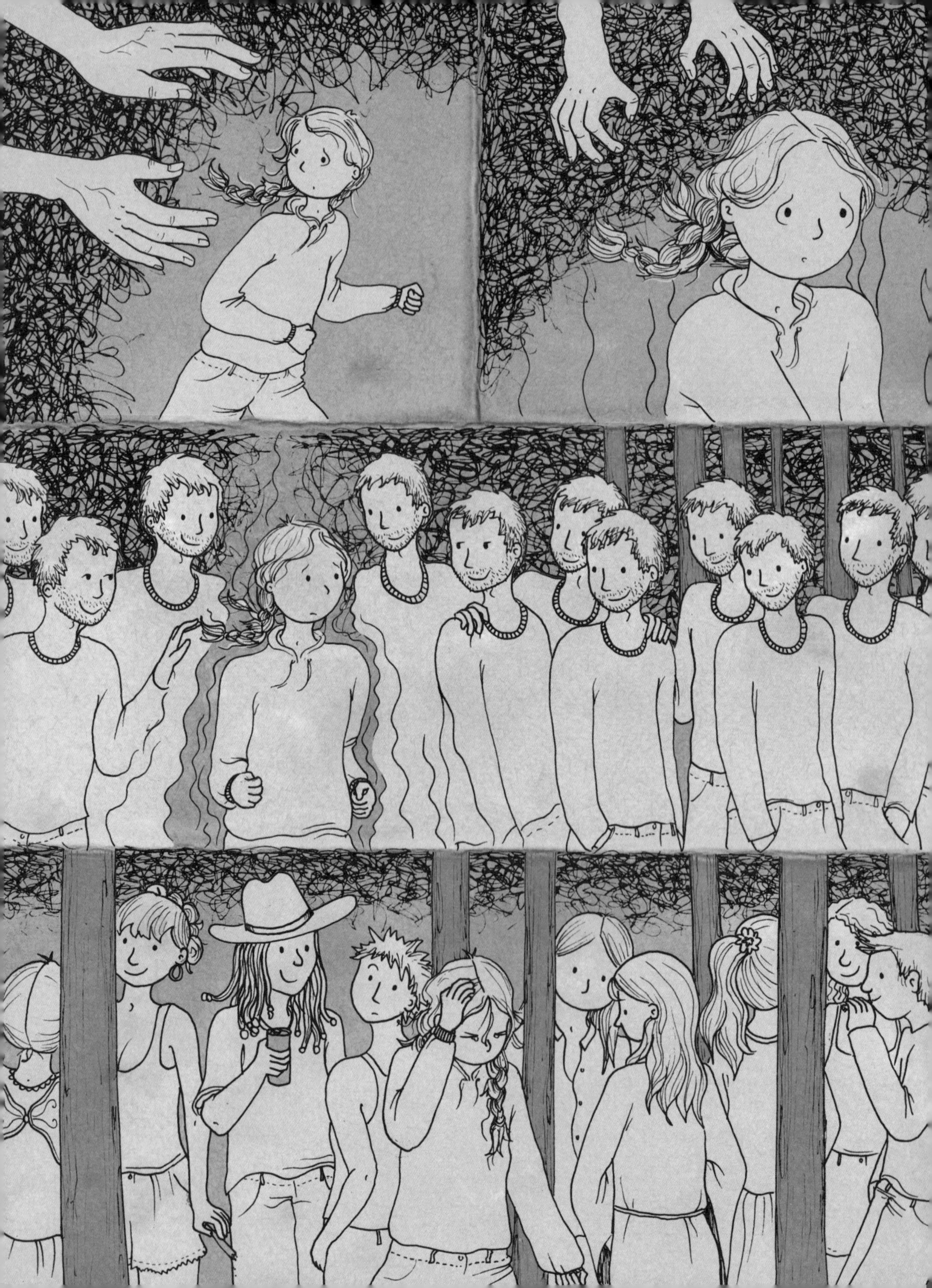

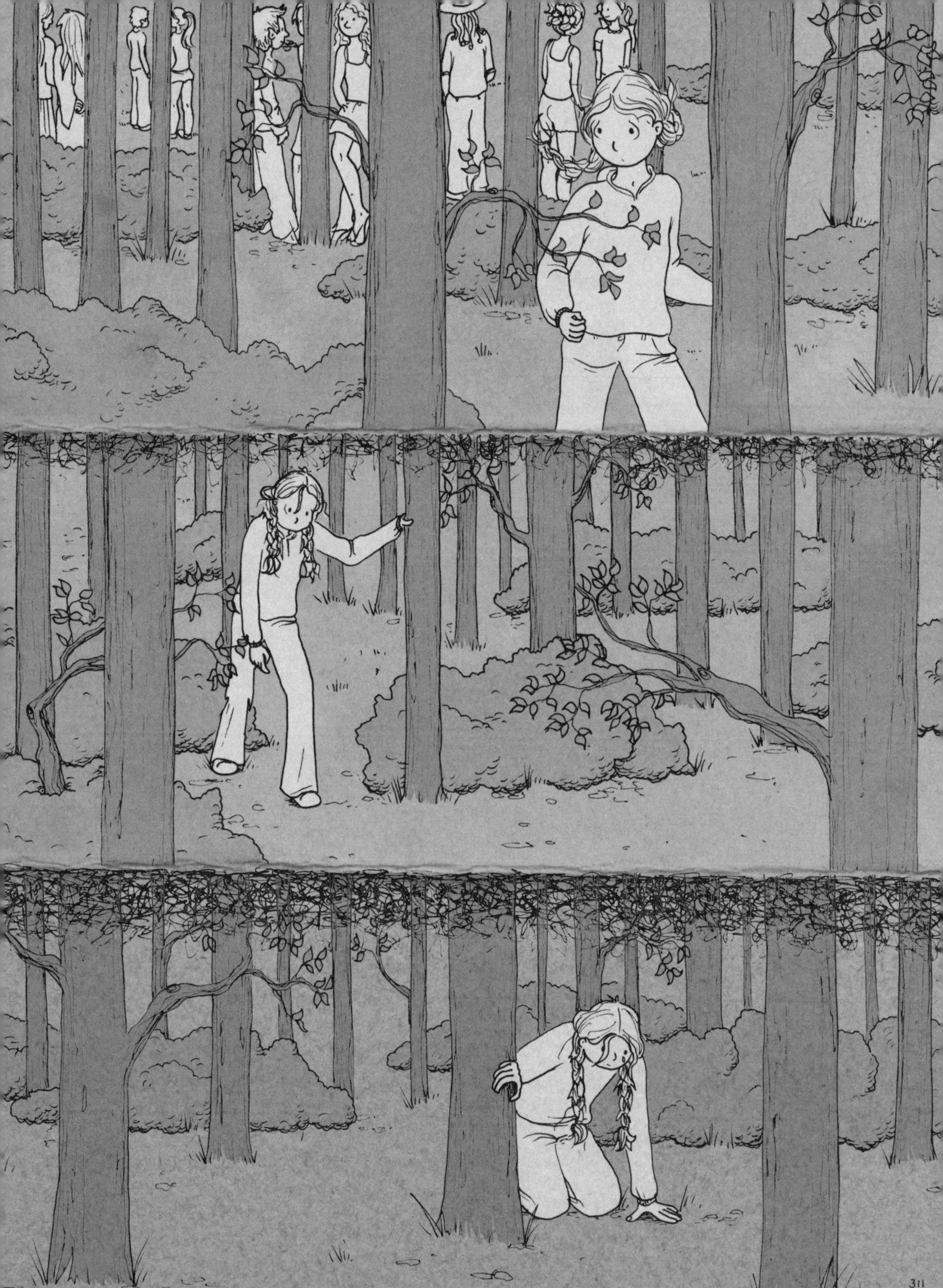

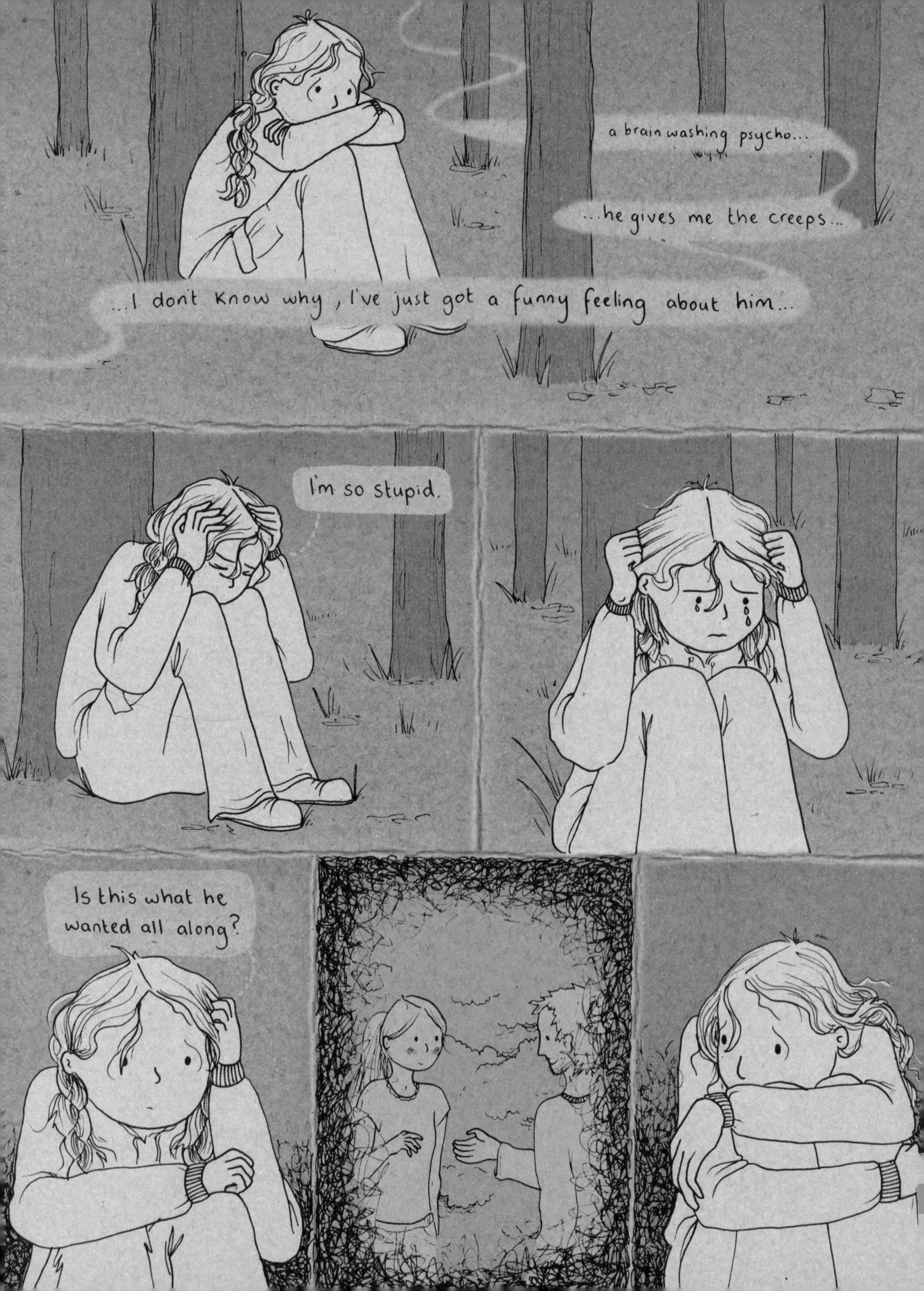
a brain washing psycho...
...he gives me the creeps...
...I don't know why, I've just got a funny feeling about him...
I'm so stupid.
Is this what he wanted all along?

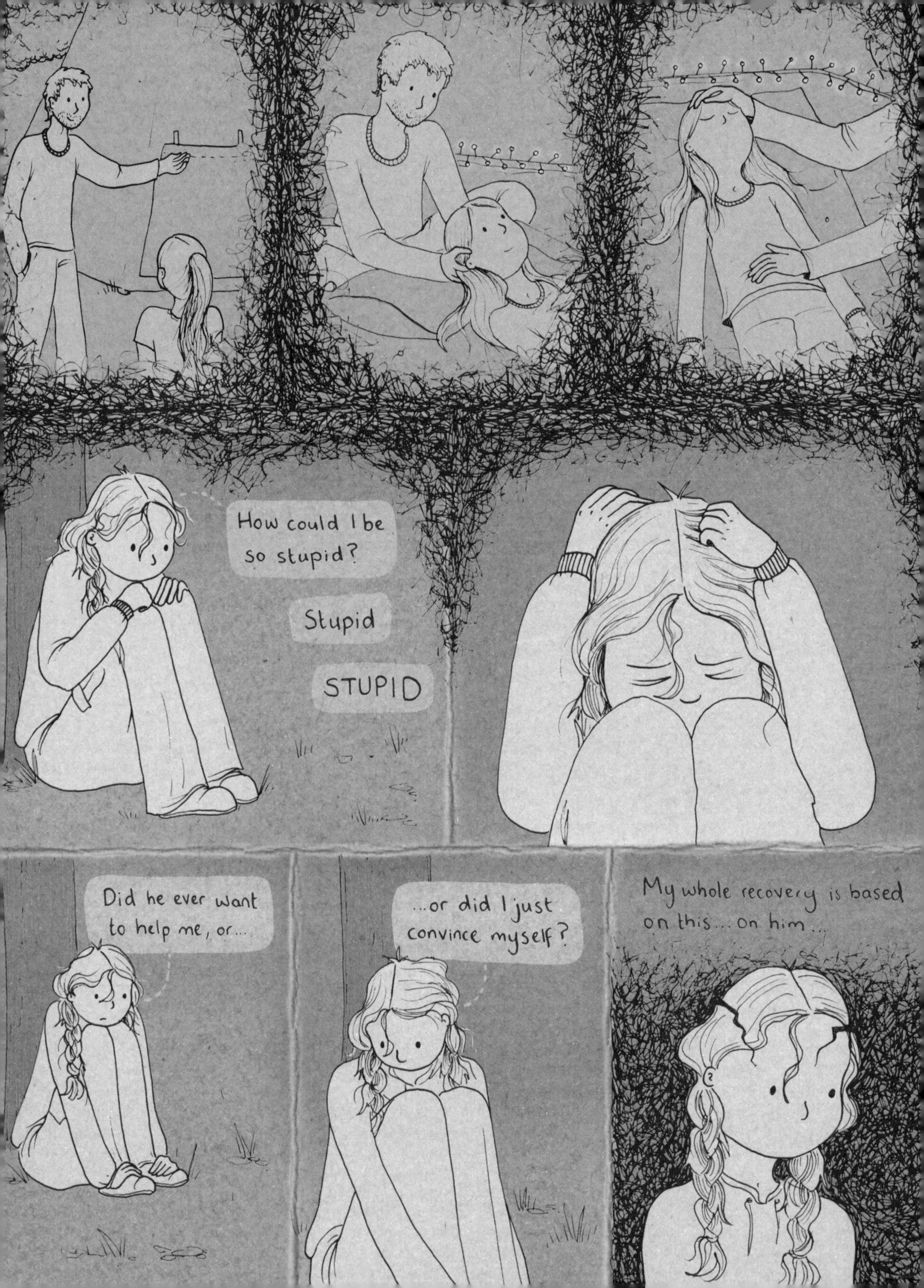
How could I be so stupid?
Stupid
STUPID
Did he ever want to help me, or...
...or did I just convince myself?
My whole recovery is based on this... on him...

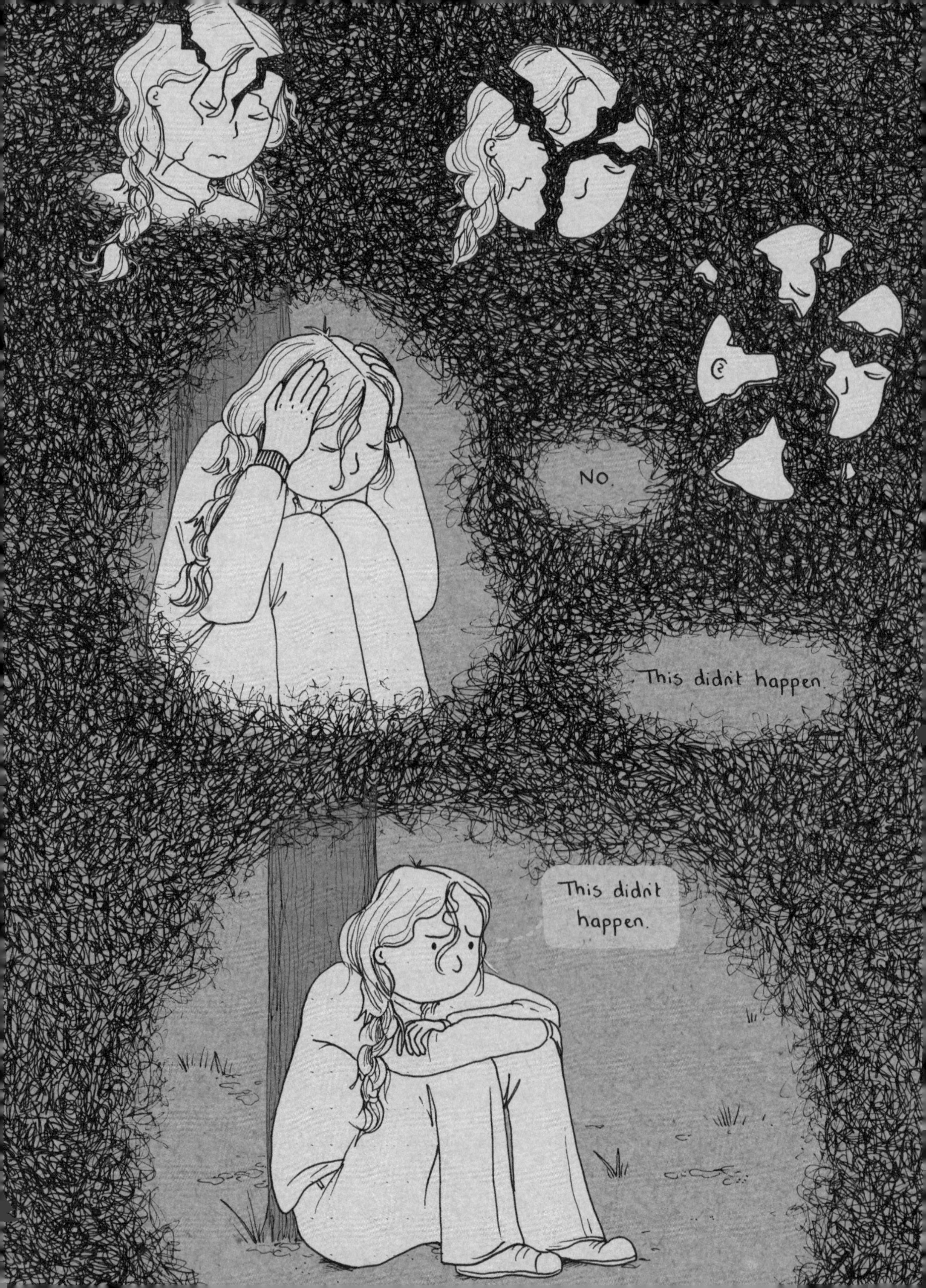
No.
This didn't happen.
This didn't happen.

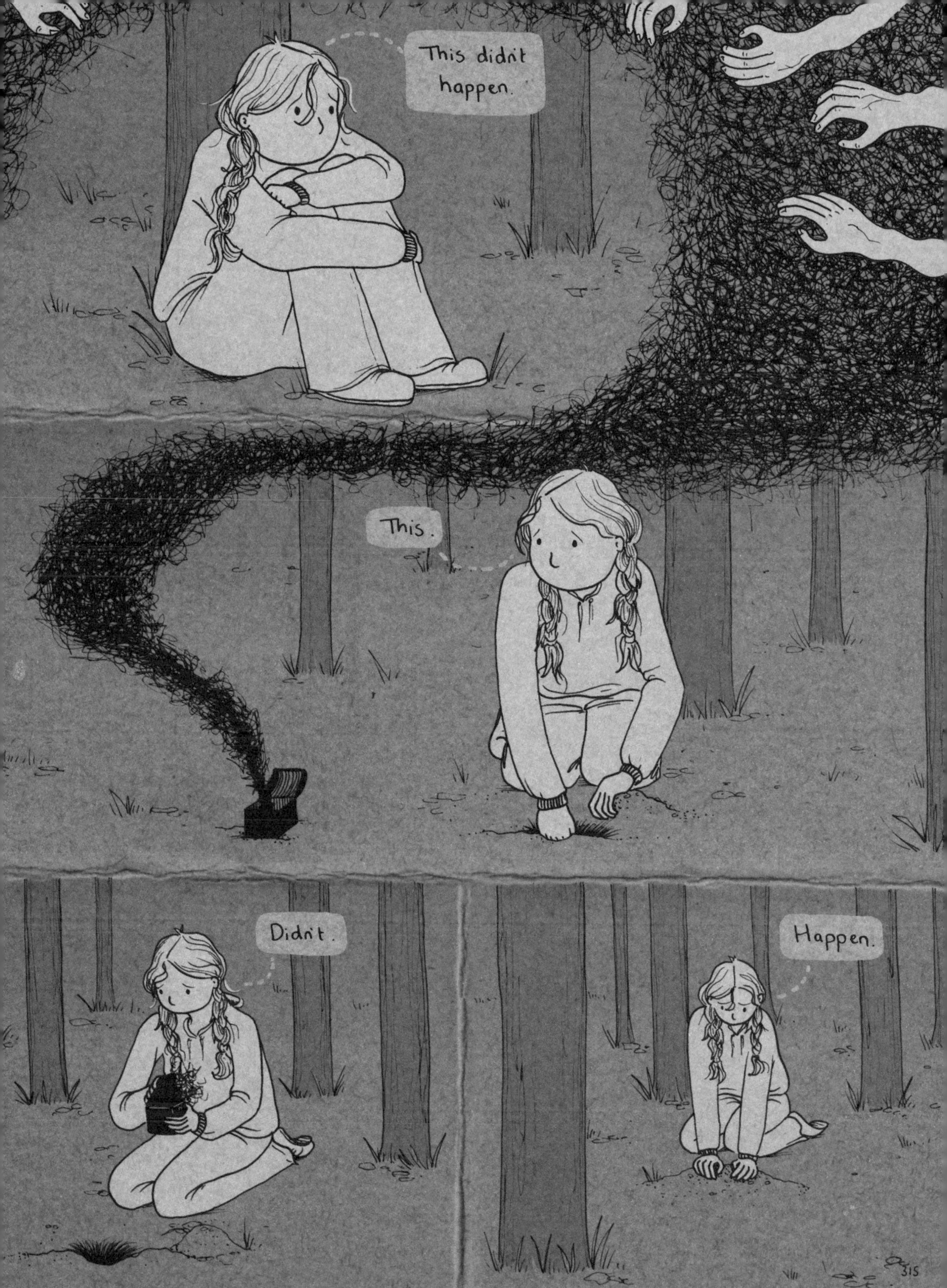
This didn't happen.
This.
Didn't.
Happen.

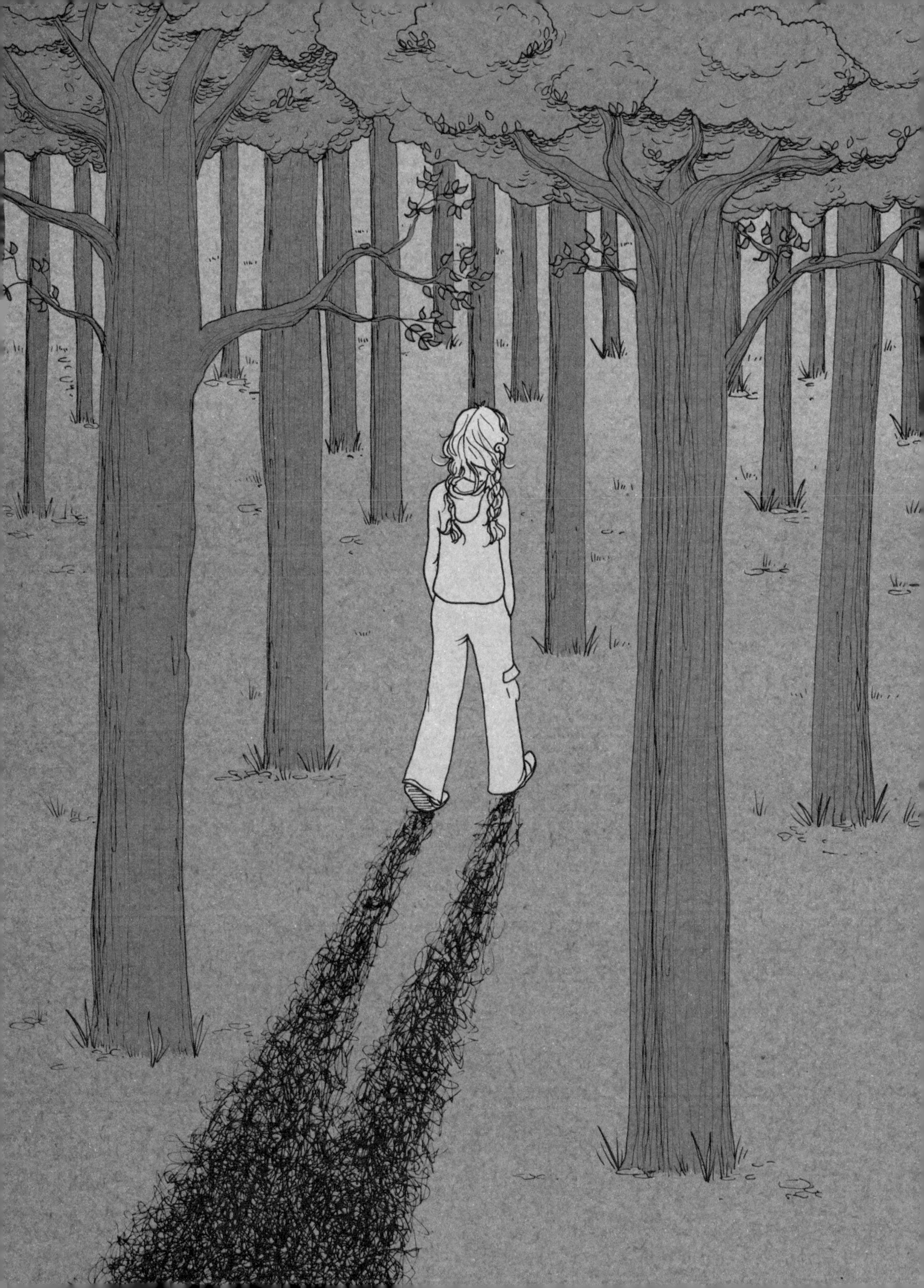

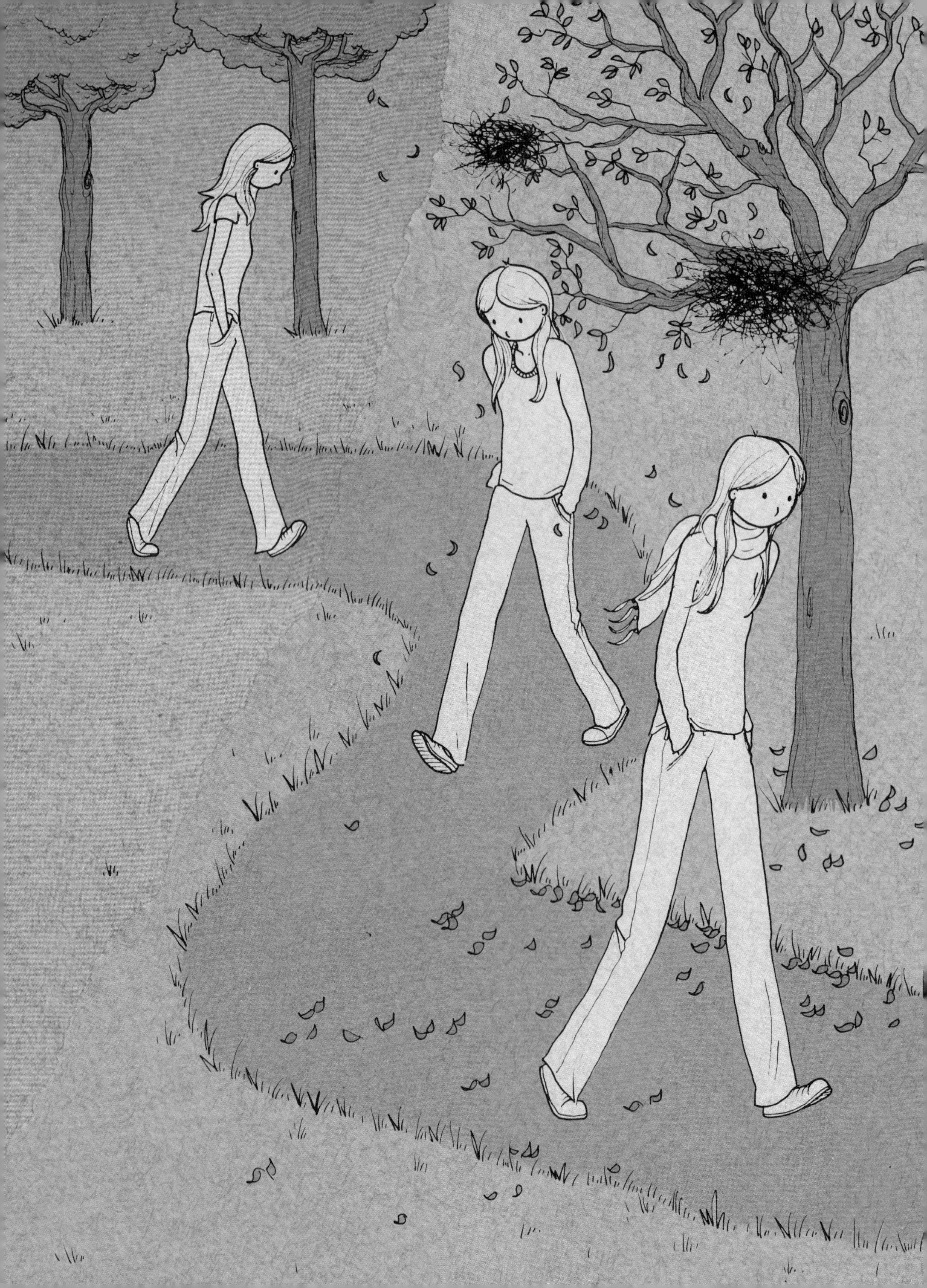

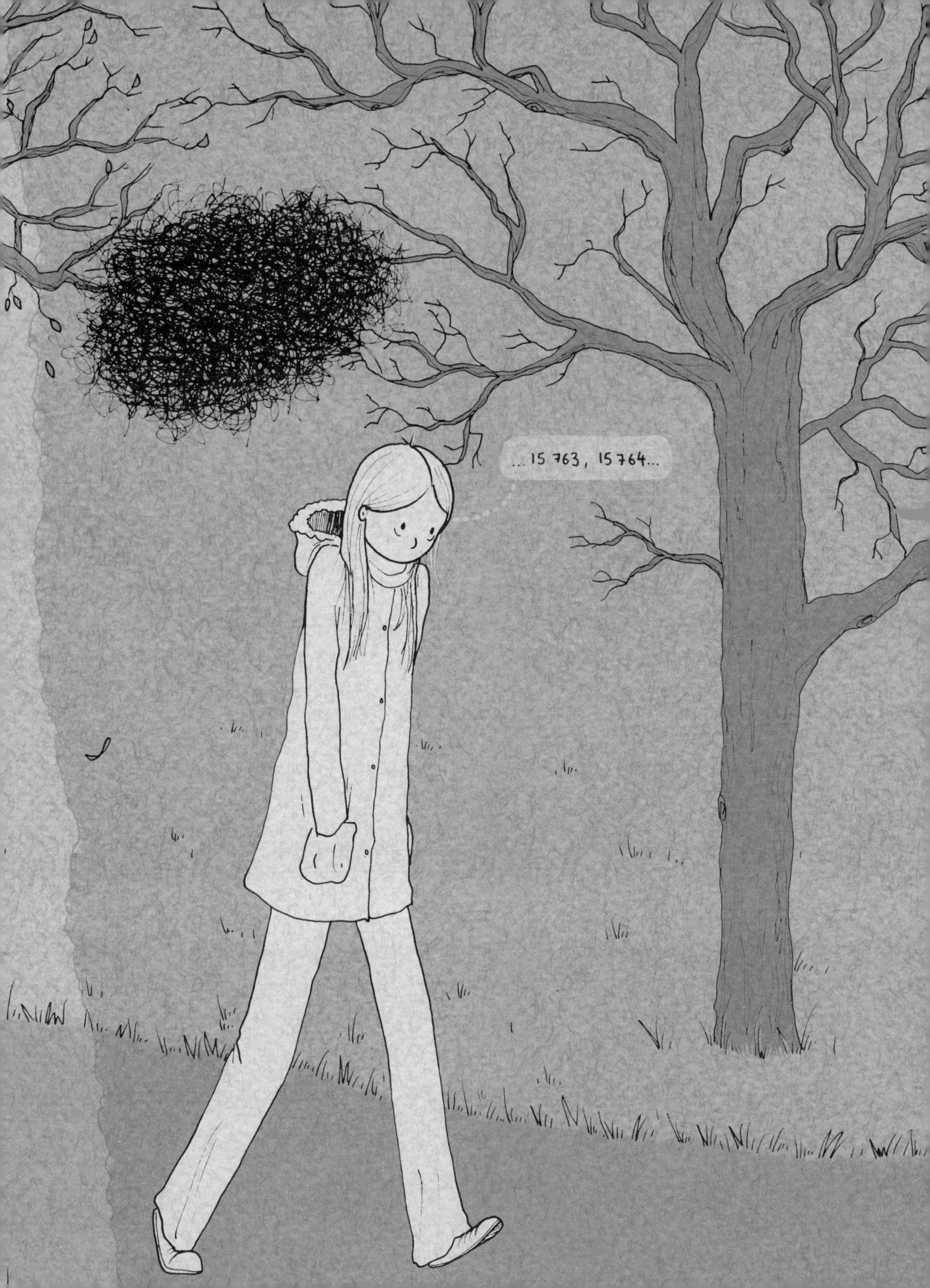
...15 763, 15 764...

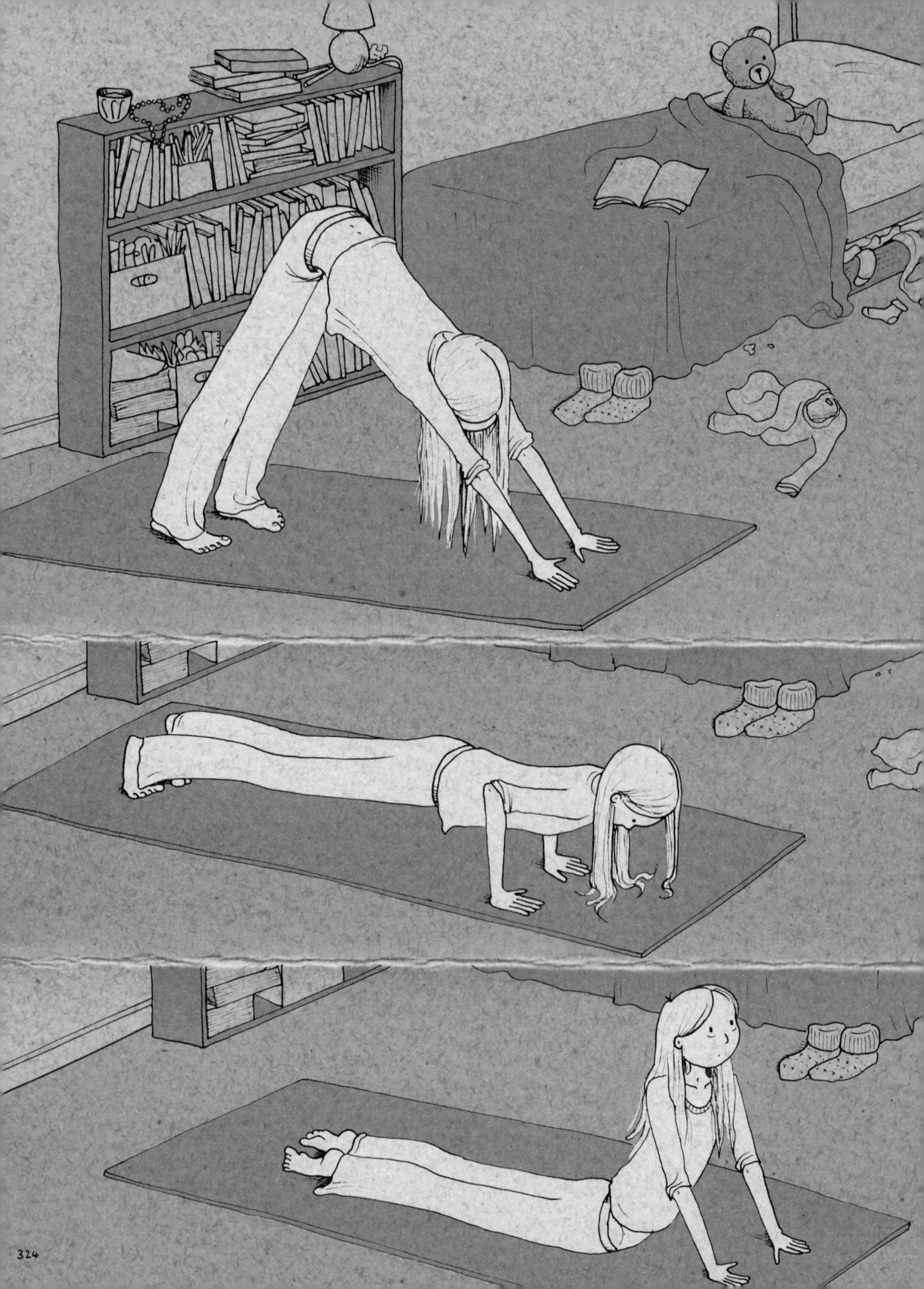

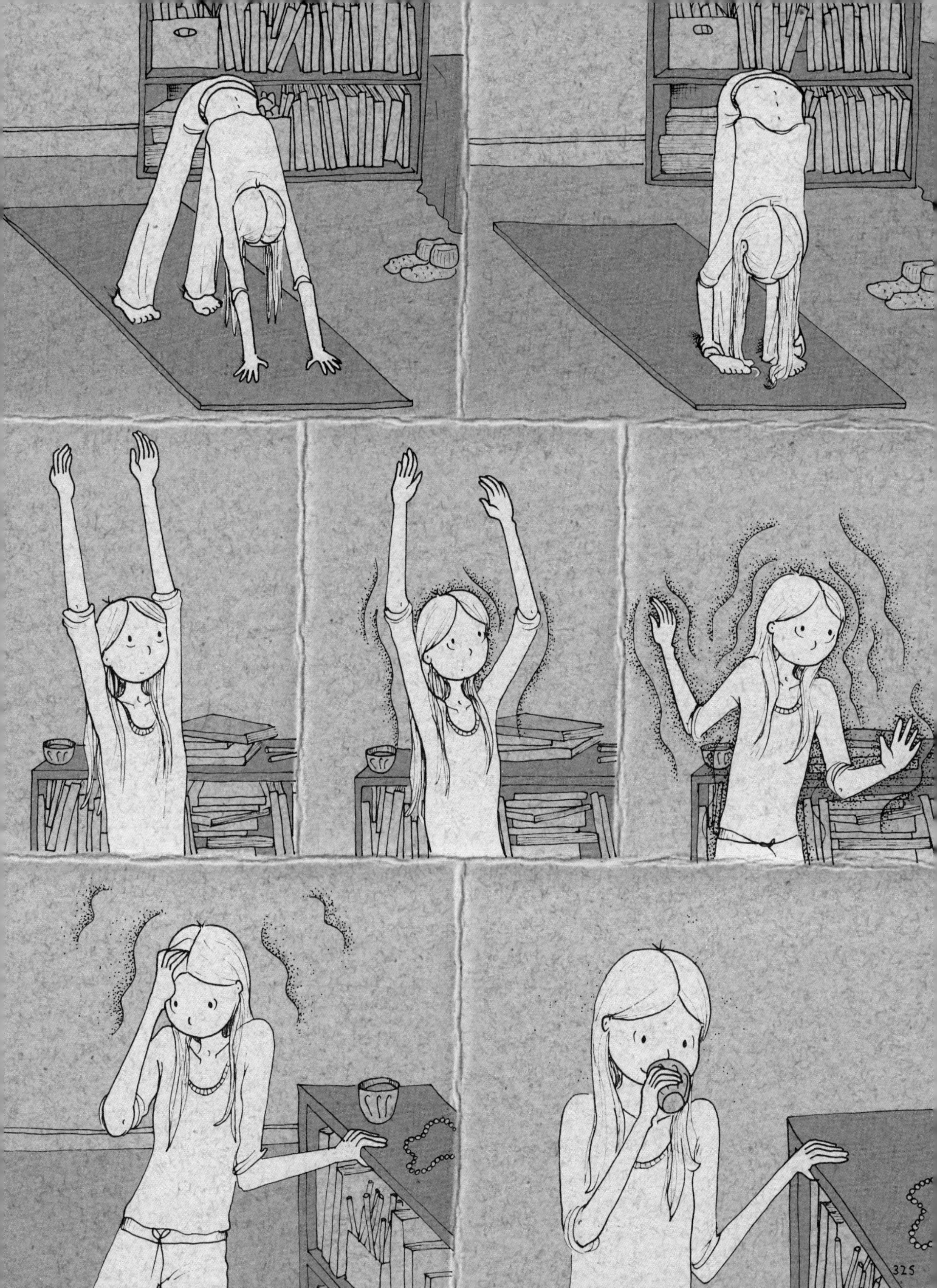

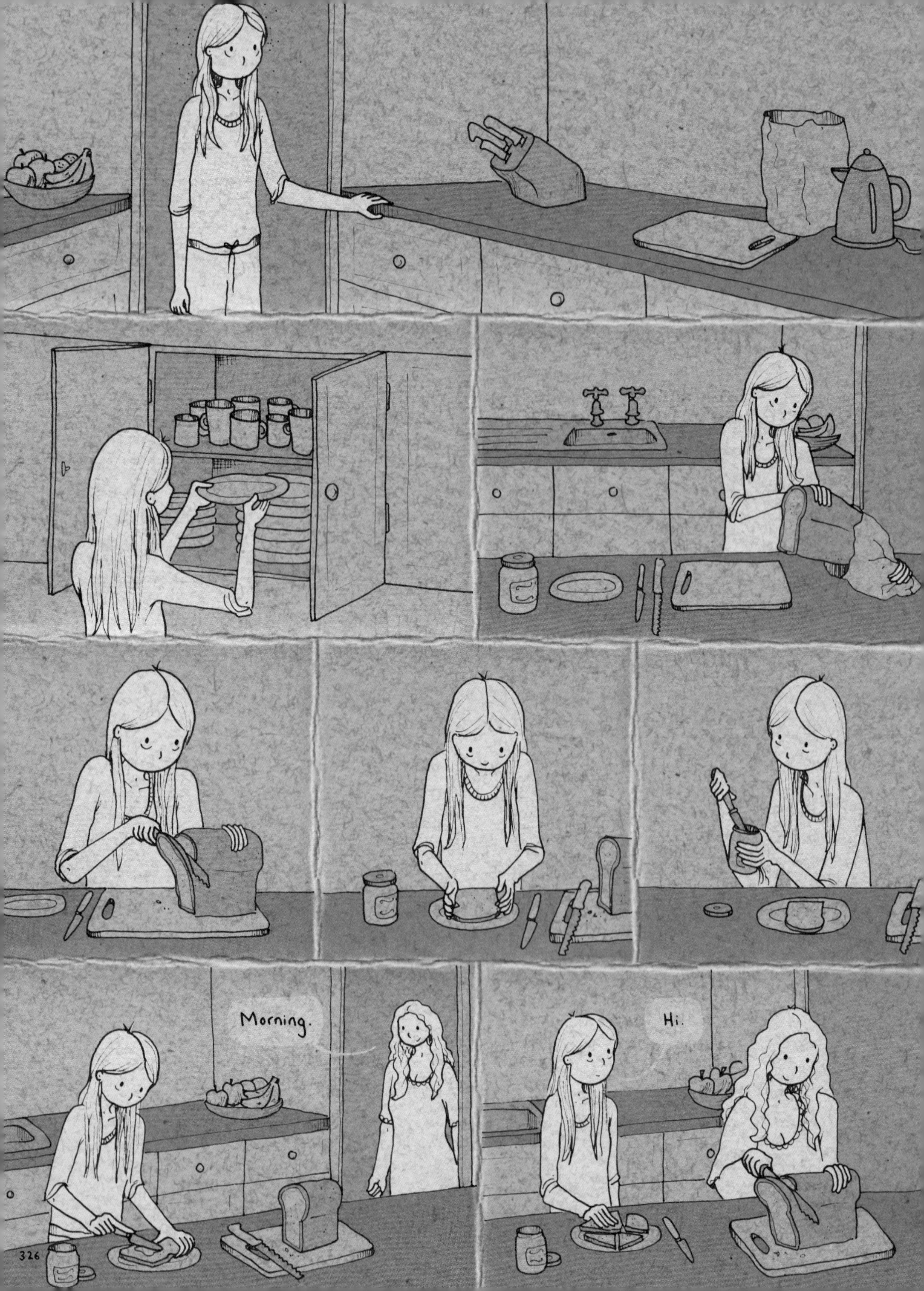
Morning.
Hi.

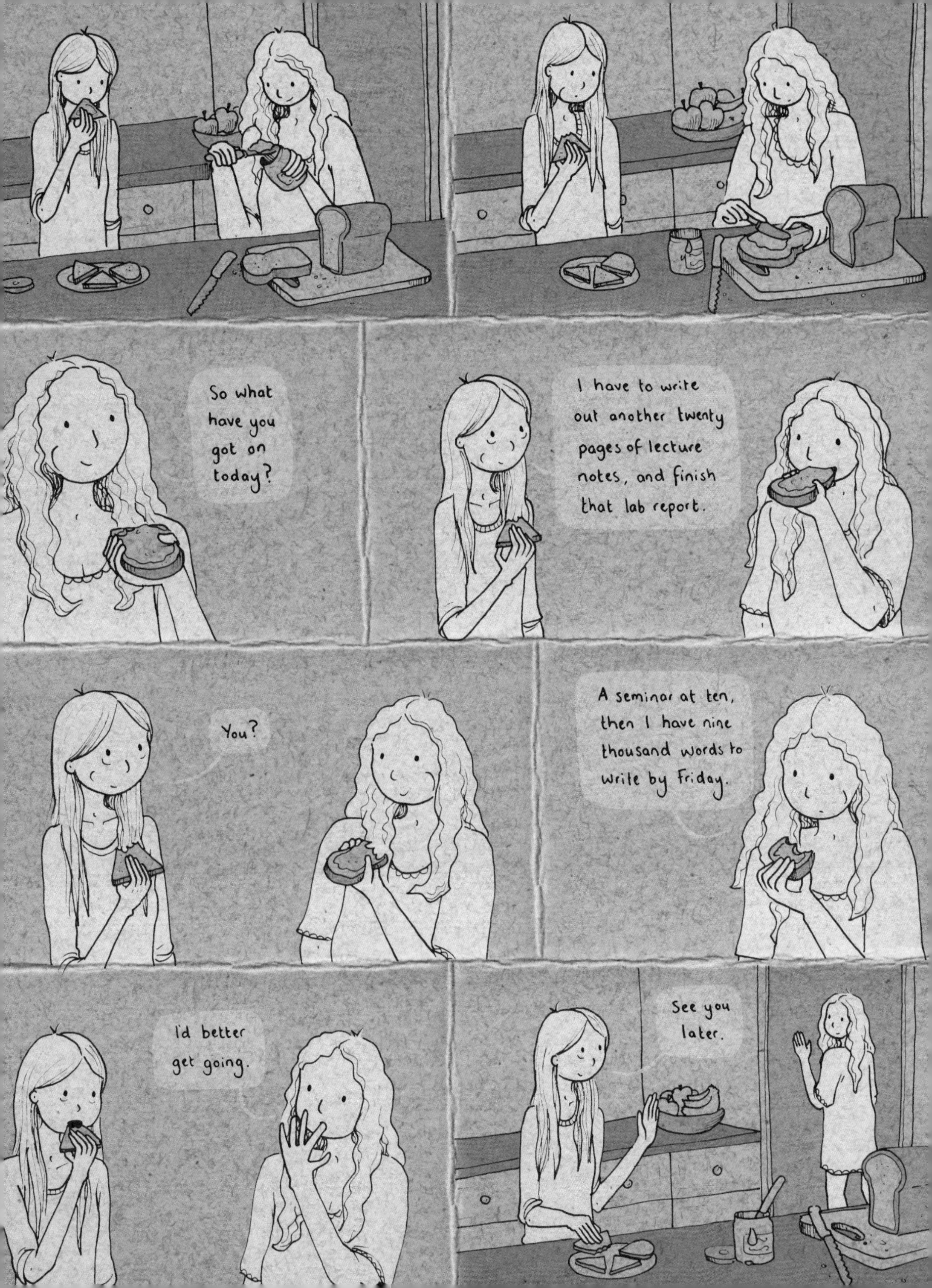
So what have you got on today?
I have to write out another twenty pages of lecture notes, and finish that lab report.
You?
A seminar at ten, then I have nine thousand words to write by Friday.
I'd better get going.
See you later.

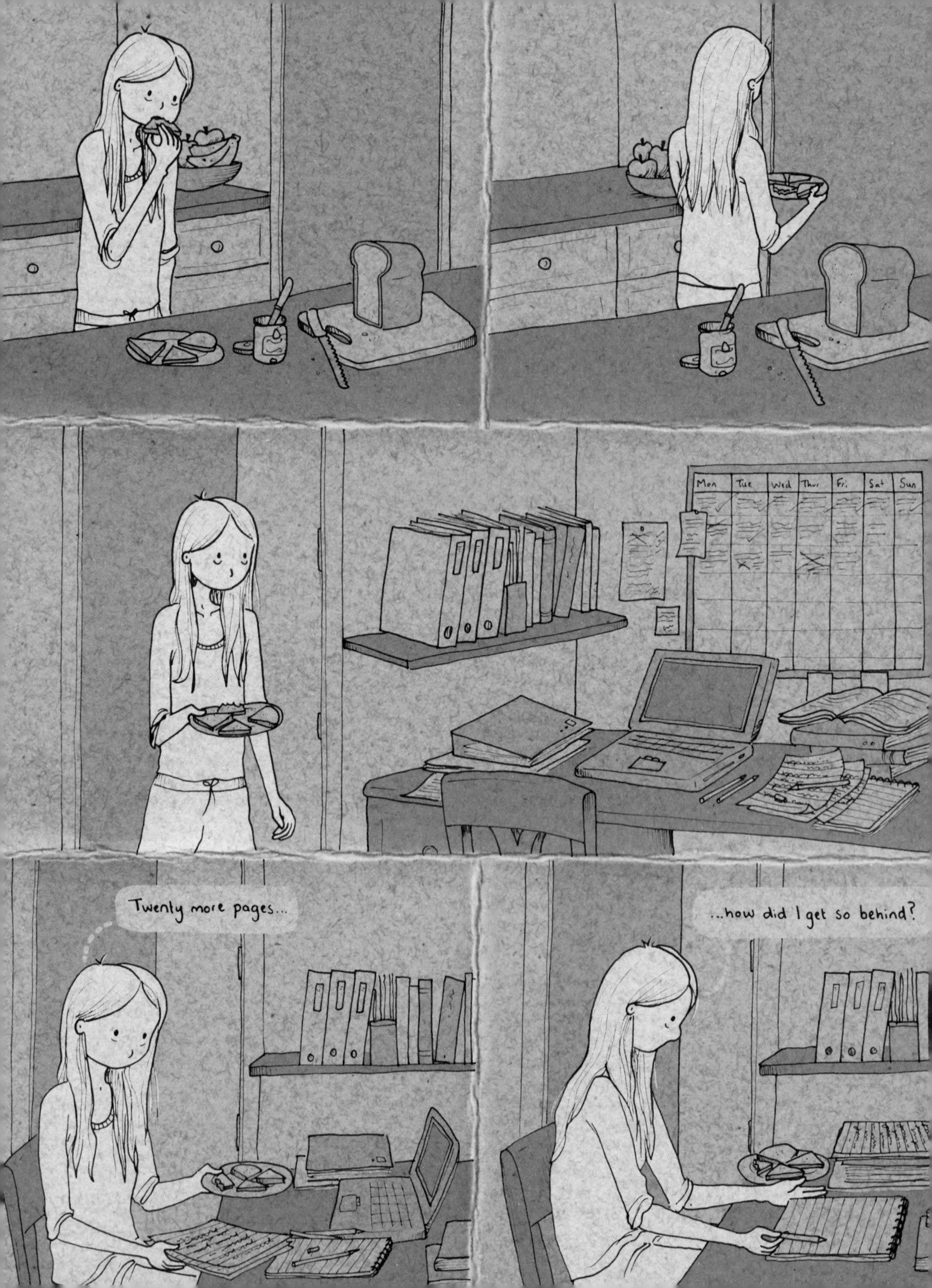
Mon
Tue
Wed
Thur
Fri
Sat
Sun
Twenty more pages...
...how did I get so behind?

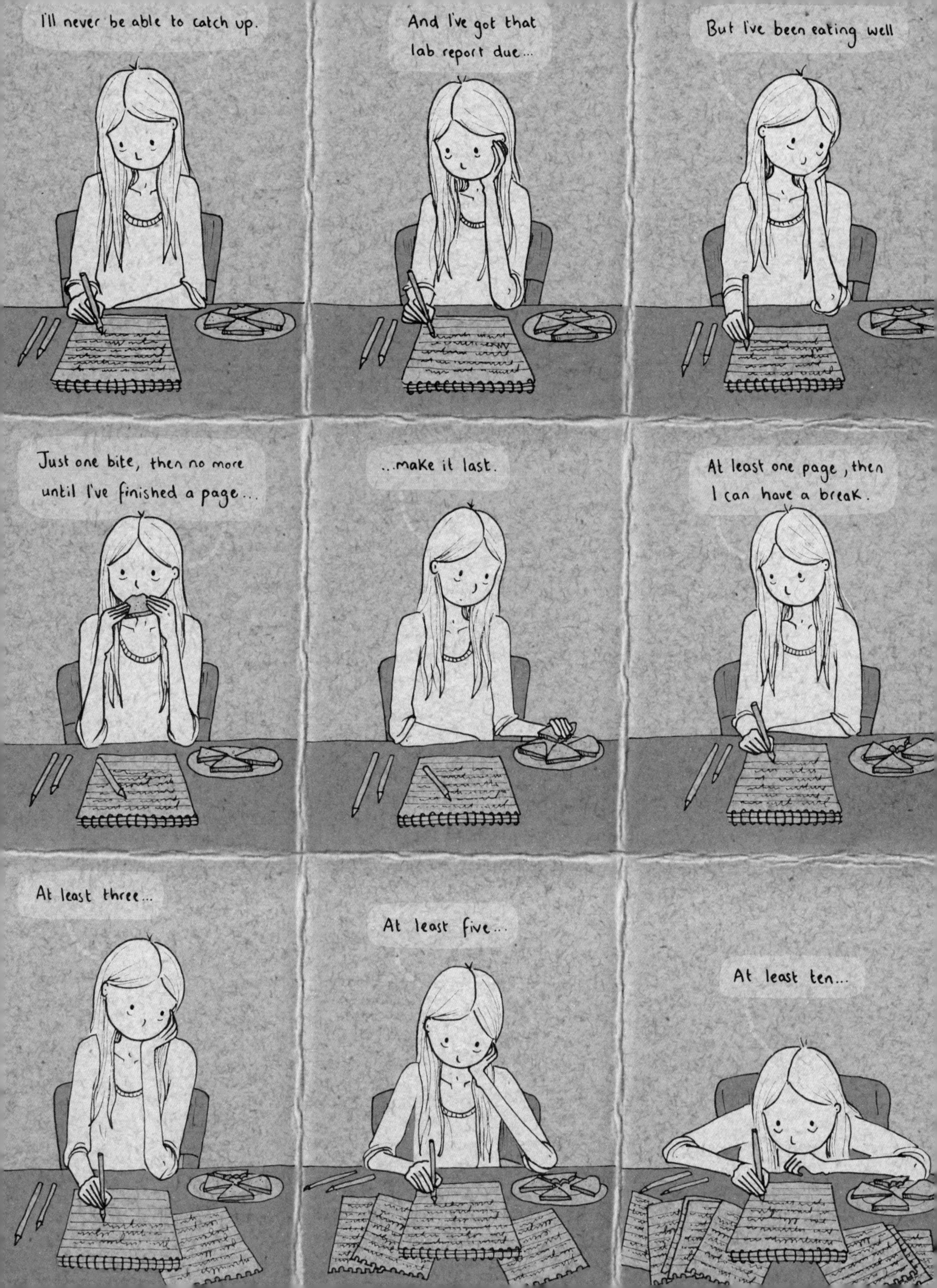
I'll never be able to catch up.
And I've got that lab report due...
But I've been eating well
Just one bite, then no more until I've finished a page...
...make it last.
At least one page, then I can have a break.
At least three...
At least five...
At least ten...

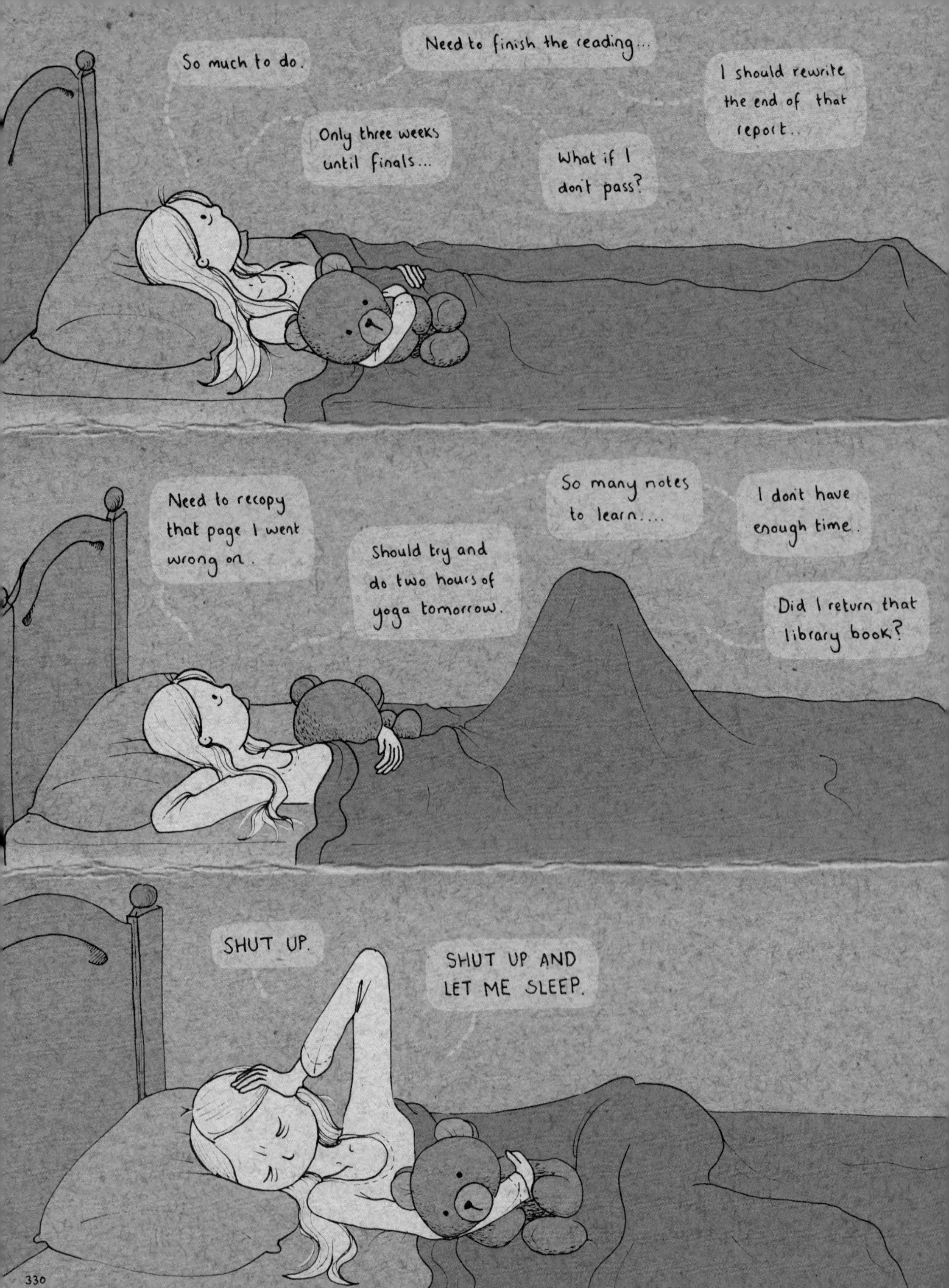
So much to do.
Need to finish the reading...
I should rewrite the end of that report.
Only three weeks until finals...
What if I don't pass?
Need to recopy that page I went wrong on.
Should try and do two hours of yoga tomorrow.
So many notes to learn....
I don't have enough time.
Did I return that library book?
SHUT UP.
SHUT UP AND LET ME SLEEP.

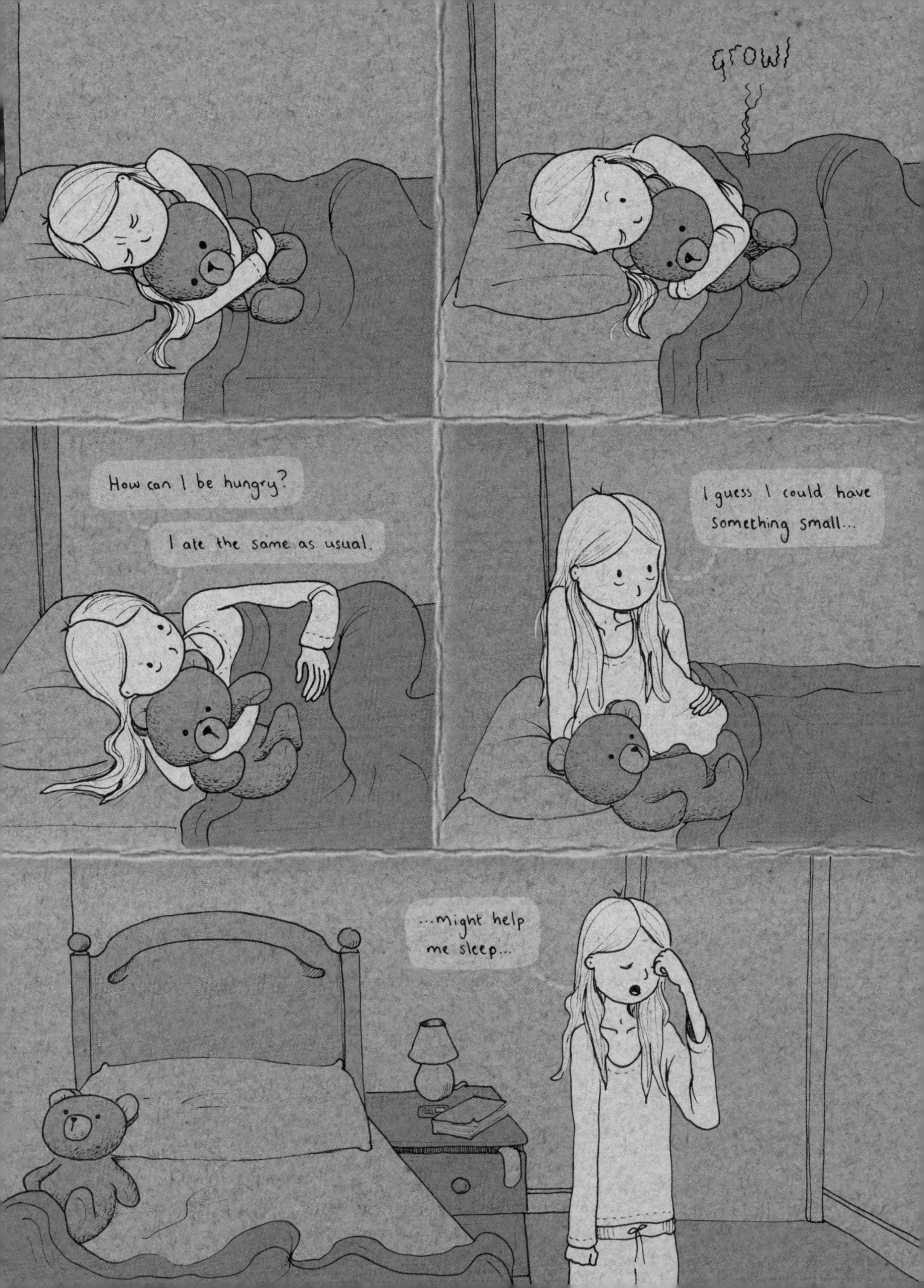
growl
How can I be hungry?
I ate the same as usual.
I guess I could have something small...
...might help me sleep...

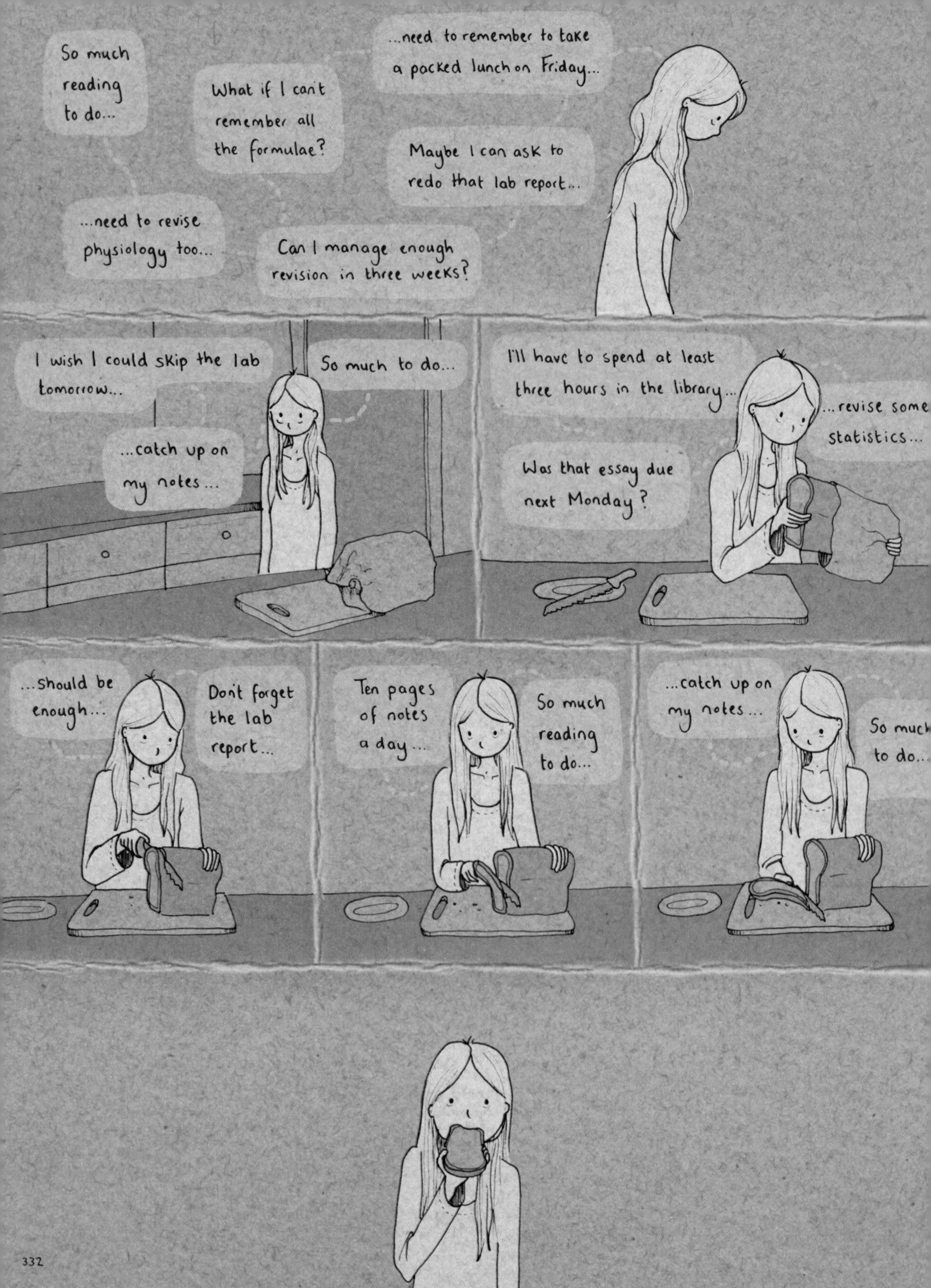
So much reading to do...
What if I can't remember all the formulae?
...need to remember to take a packed lunch on Friday...
Maybe I can ask to redo that lab report...
...need to revise physiology too...
Can I manage enough revision in three weeks?
I wish I could skip the lab tomorrow...
So much to do...
...catch up on my notes...
I'll have to spend at least three hours in the library...
...revise some statistics...
Was that essay due next Monday?
...should be enough...
Don't forget the lab report...
Ten pages of notes a day...
So much reading to do...
...catch up on my notes...
So much to do...

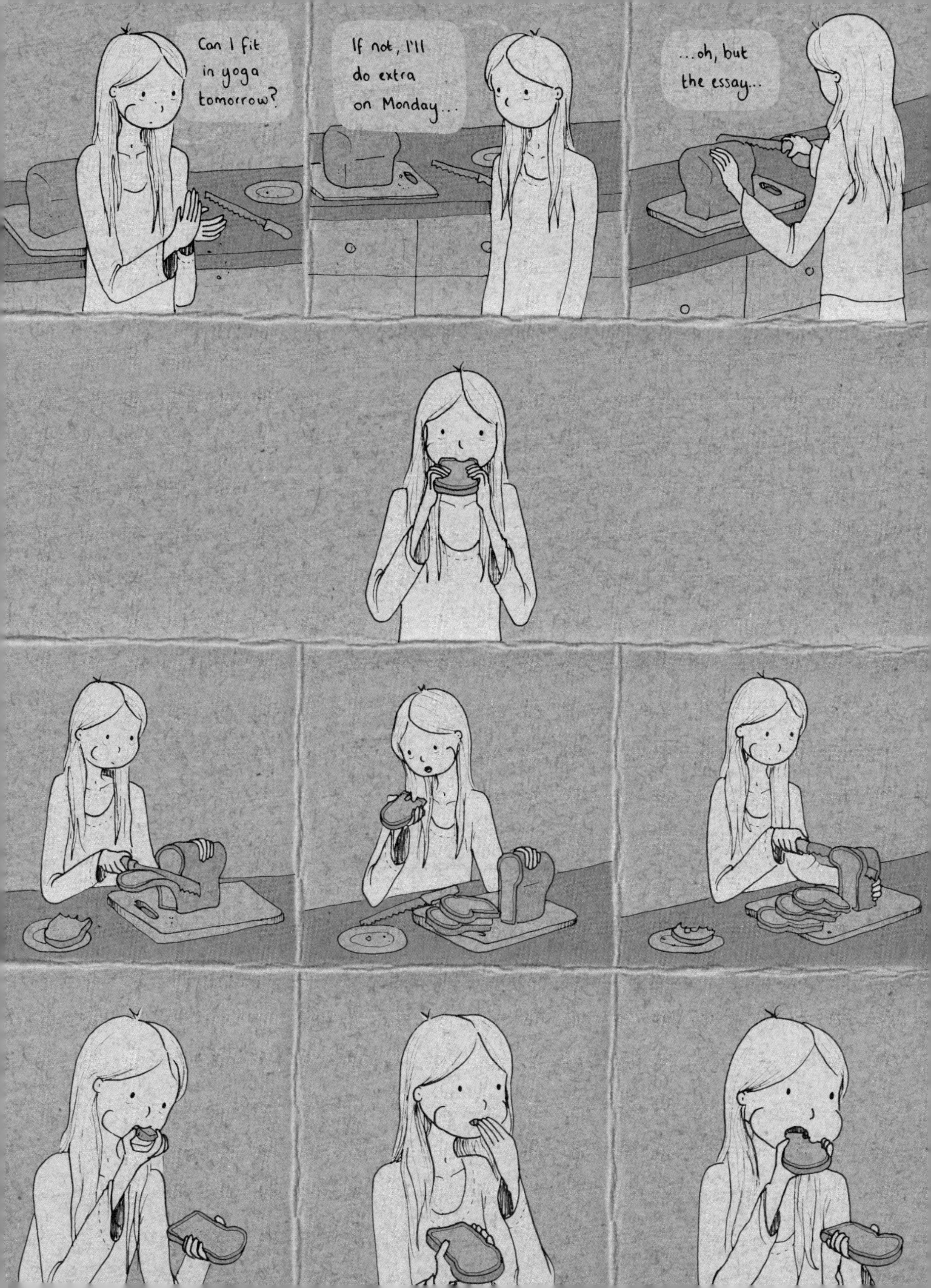

Can I fit in yoga tomorrow?
If not, I'll do extra on Monday...
...oh, but the essay...

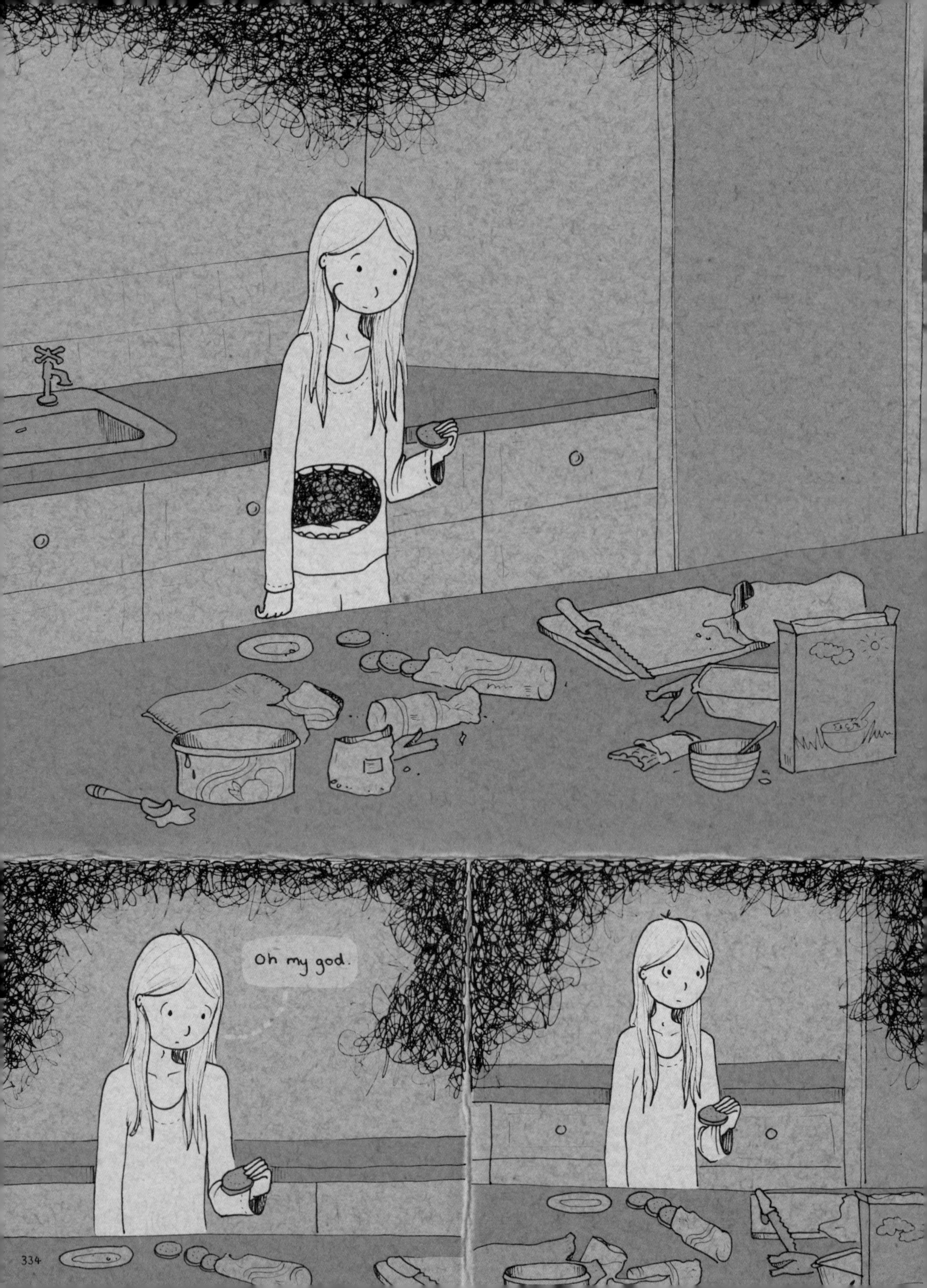
Oh my god.

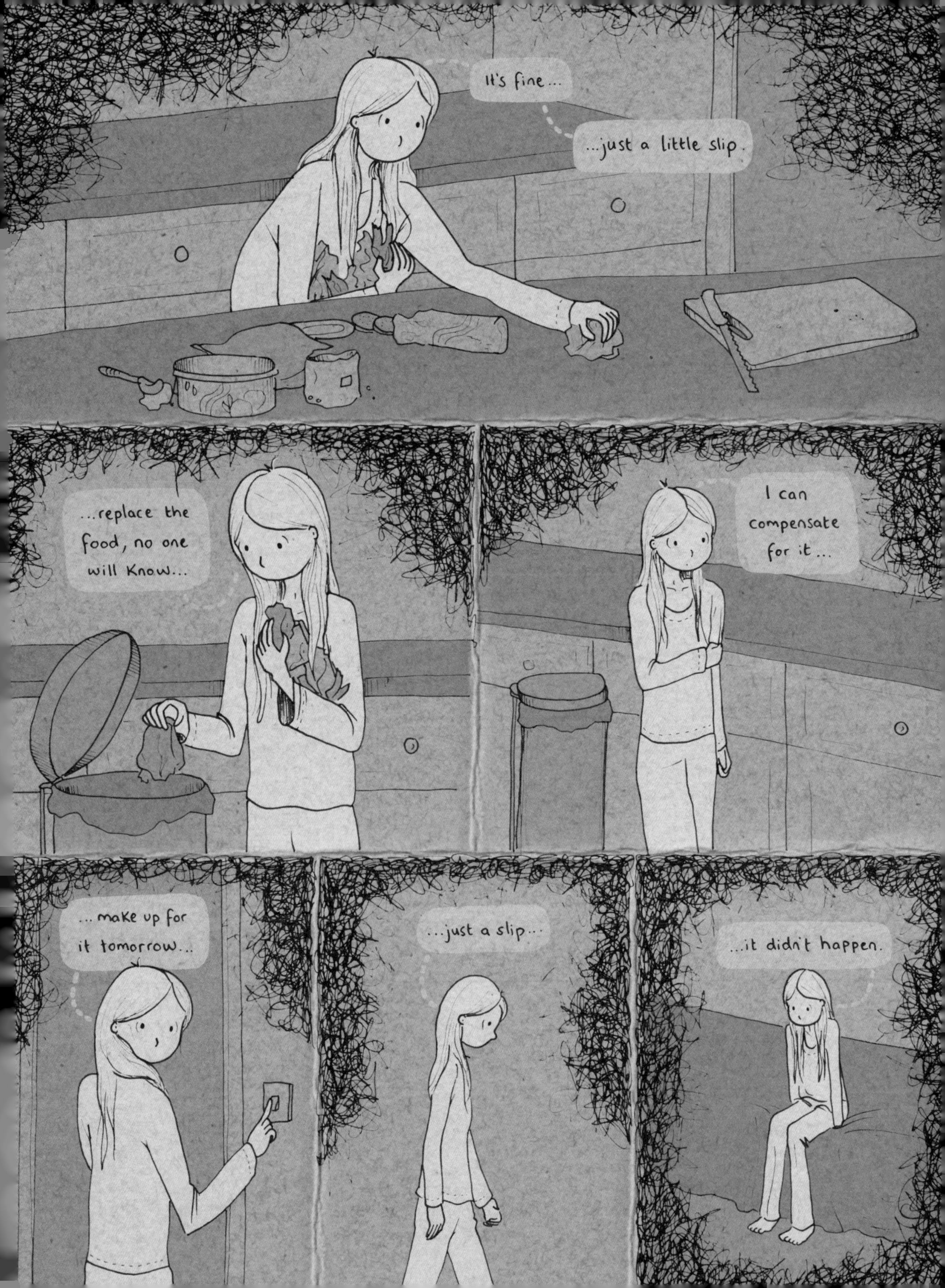
It's fine...
...just a little slip.
...replace the food, no one will know...
I can compensate for it...
...make up for it tomorrow...
...just a slip...
...it didn't happen.

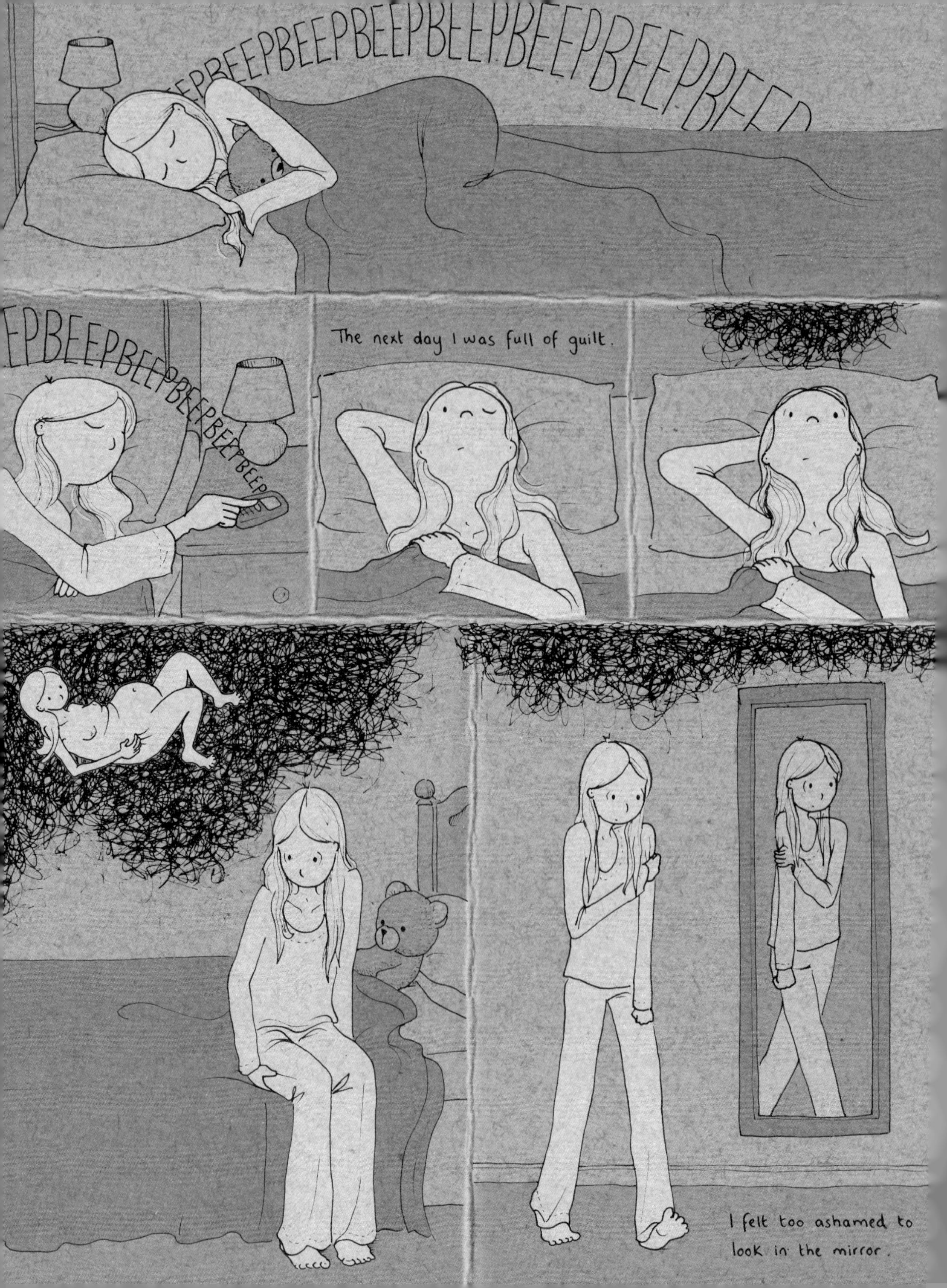
EPBEEPBEEPBEEPBEEPBEEPBEEP
EPBEEPBEEPBEEPBEEPBEEP
The next day I was full of guilt.
I felt too ashamed to look in the mirror.

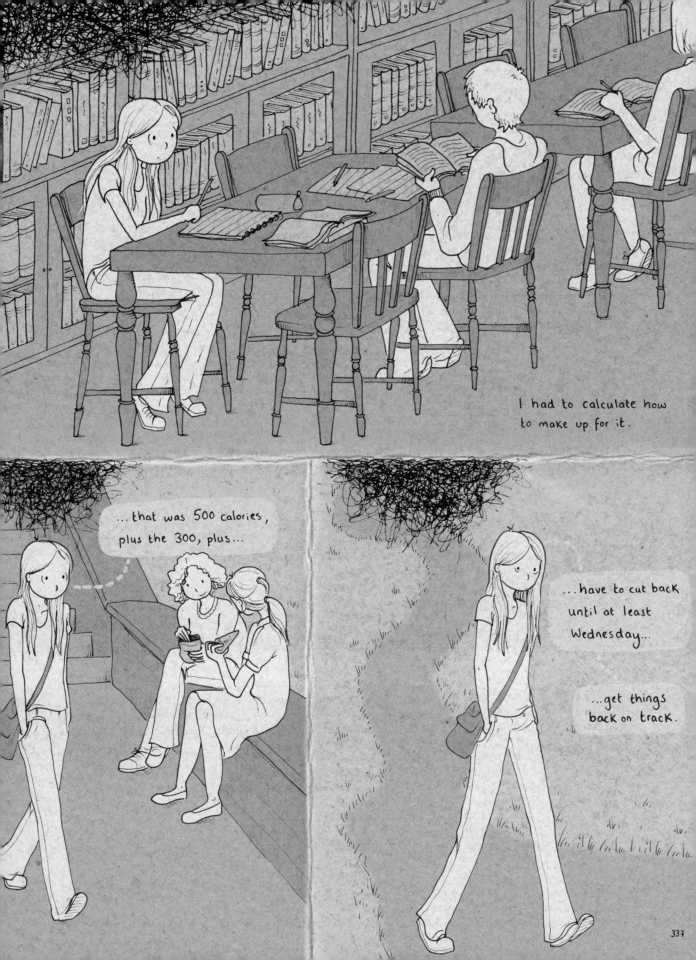

I had to calculate how to make up for it.

...that was 500 calories, plus the 300, plus...

...have to cut back until at least Wednesday...

...get things back on track.

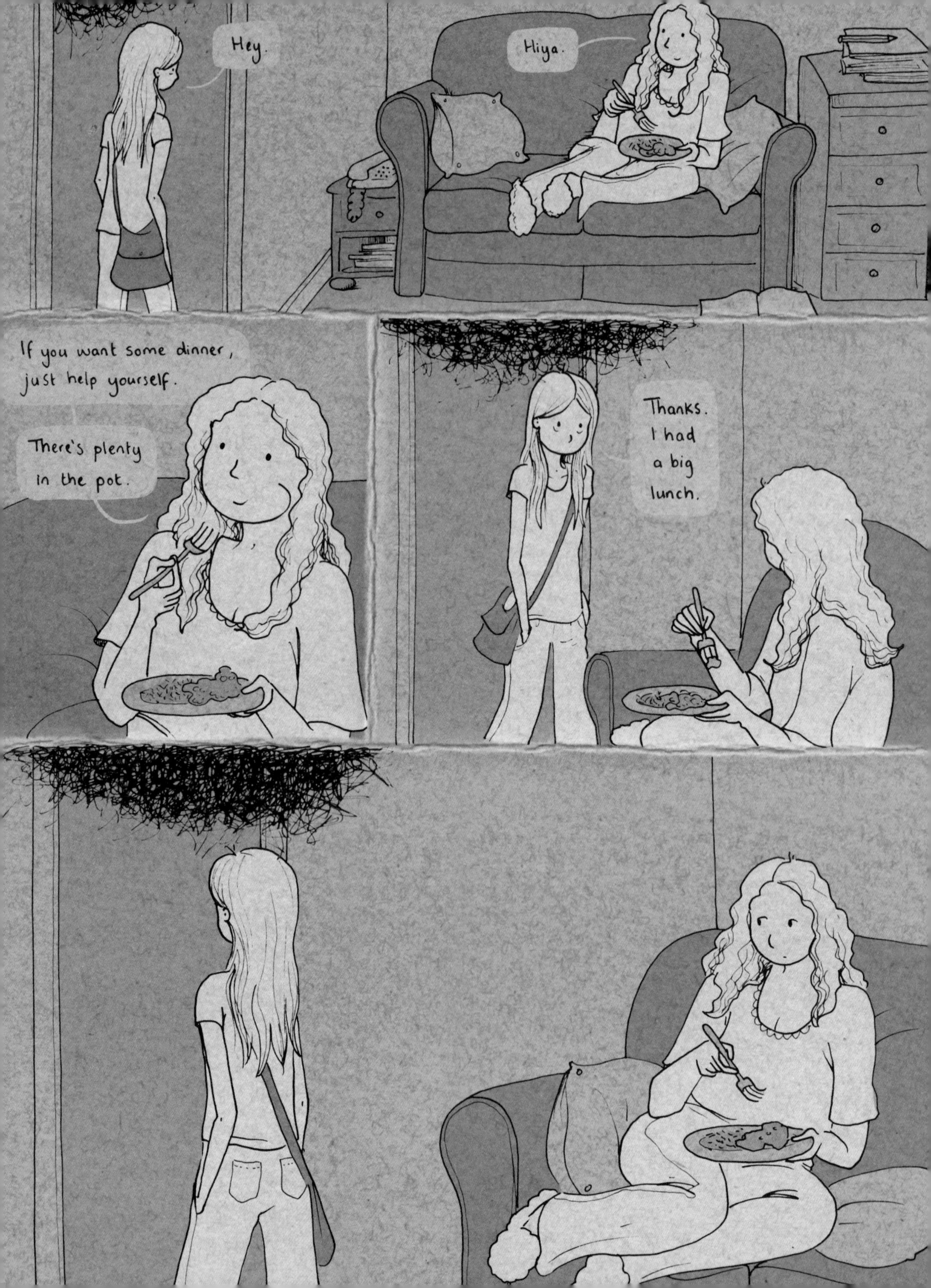
Hey.
Hiya.
If you want some dinner, just help yourself.
There's plenty in the pot.
Thanks. I had a big lunch.

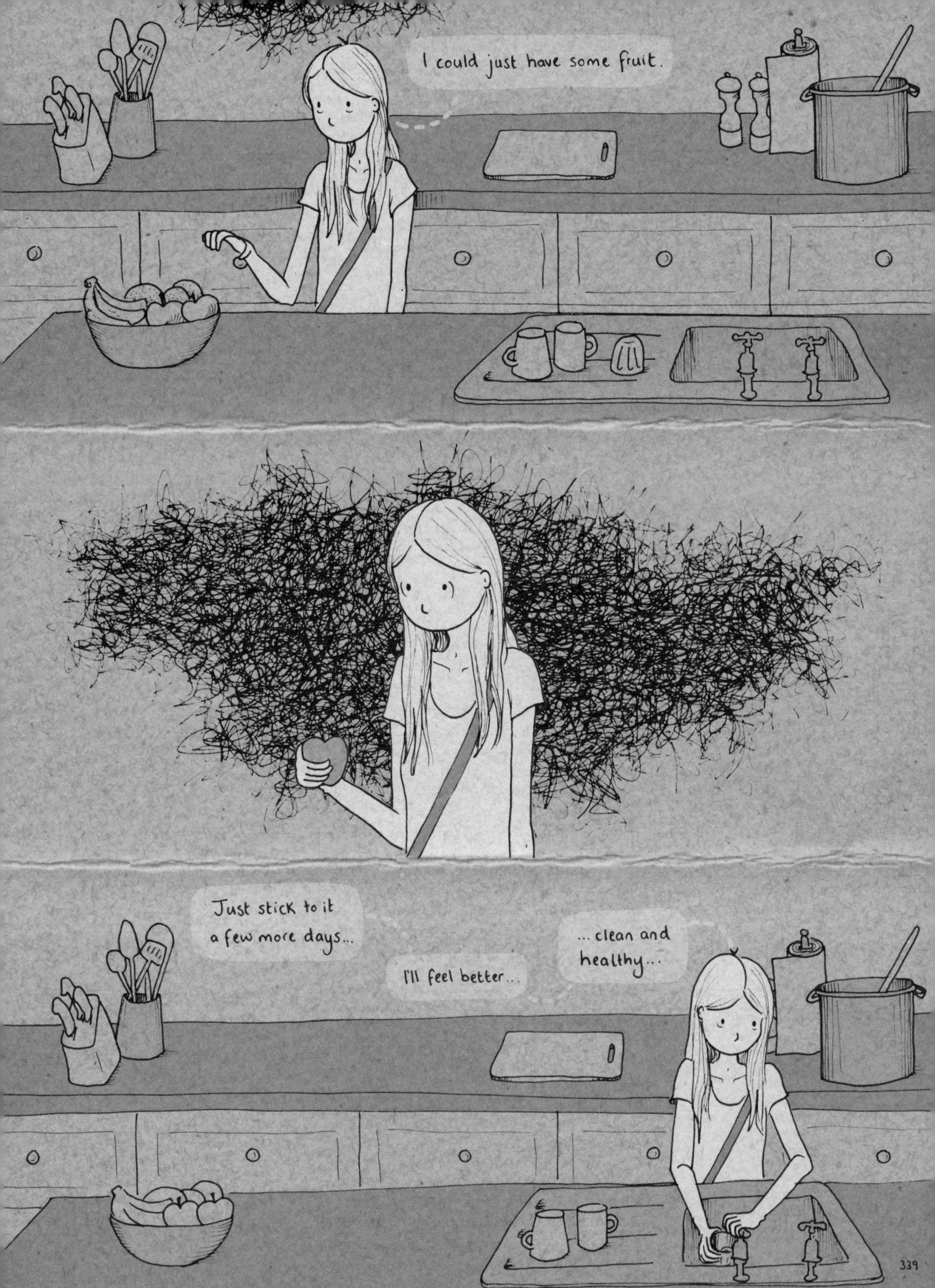
I could just have some fruit.
Just stick to it a few more days...
I'll feel better...
... clean and healthy...

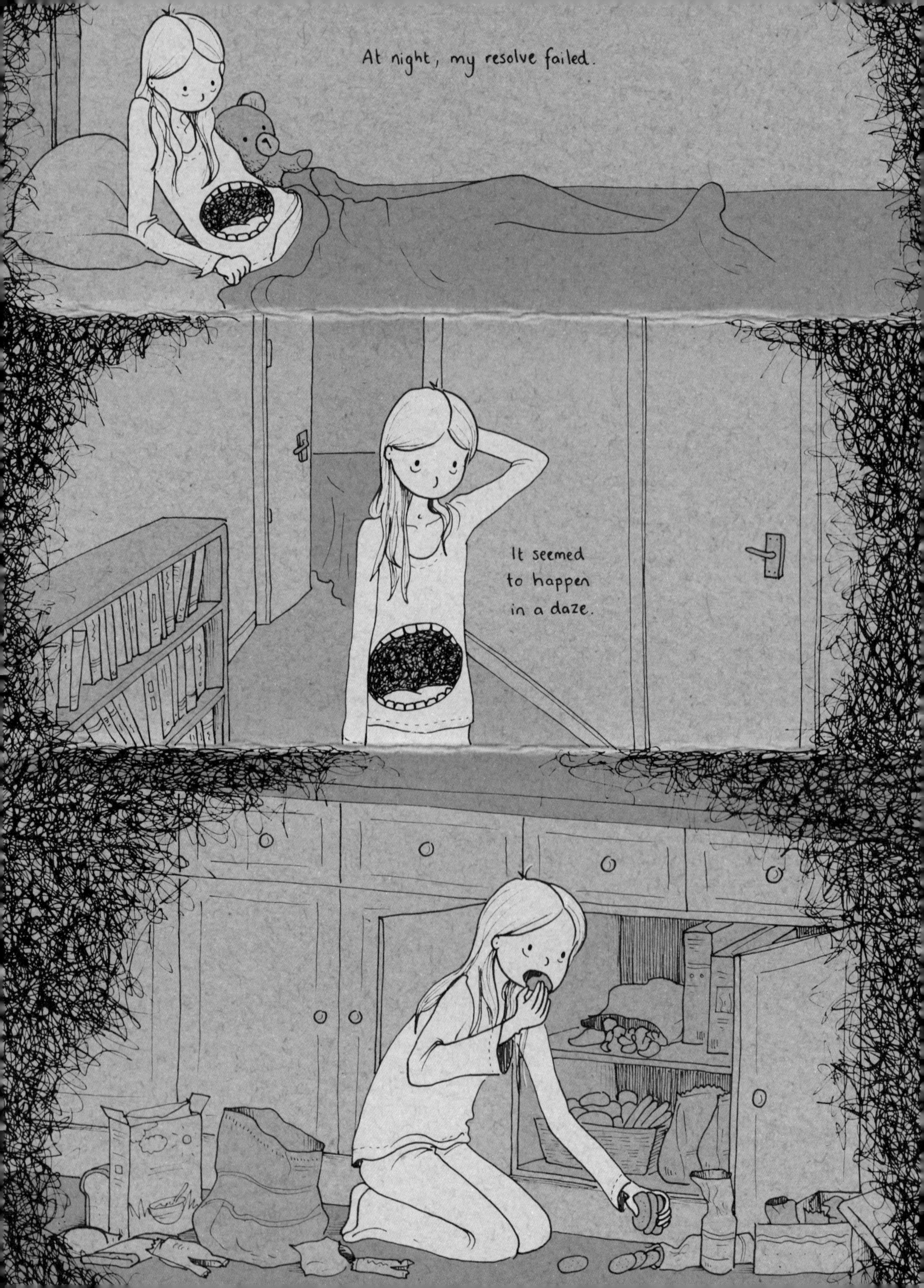
At night, my resolve failed.
It seemed to happen in a daze.

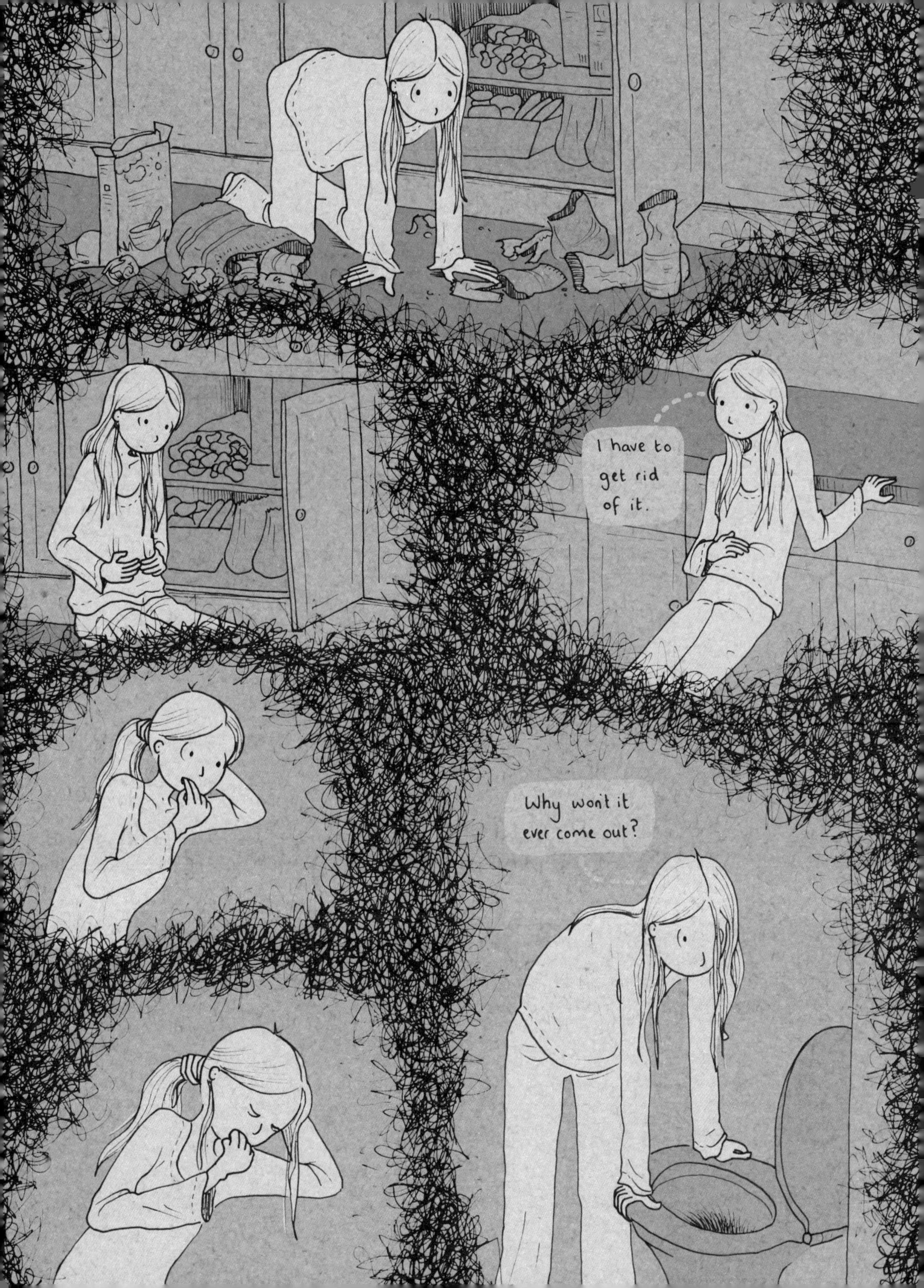
I have to get rid of it.
Why won't it ever come out?

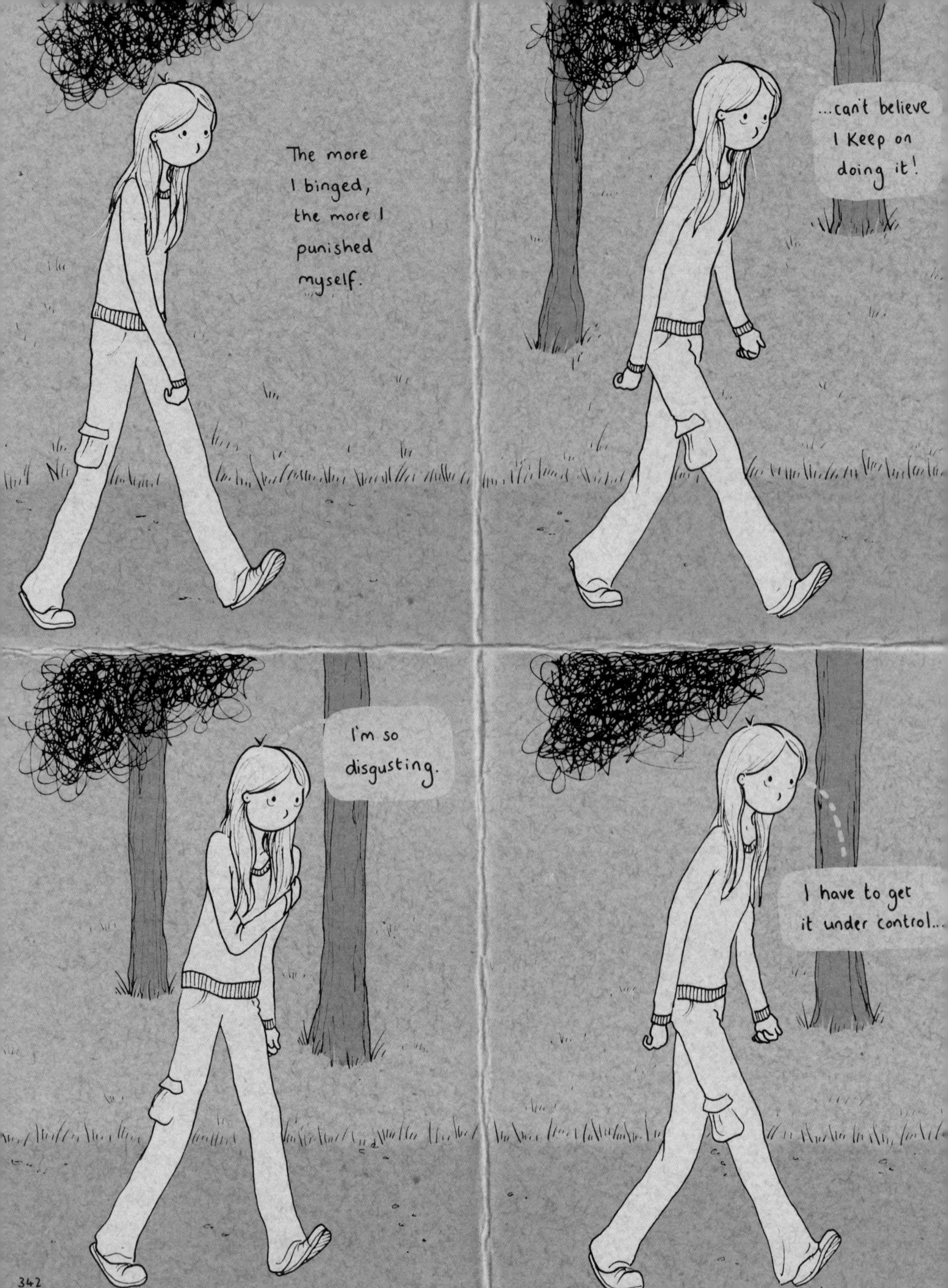
The more I binged, the more I punished myself.
...can't believe I Keep on doing it!
I'm so disgusting.
I have to get it under control...

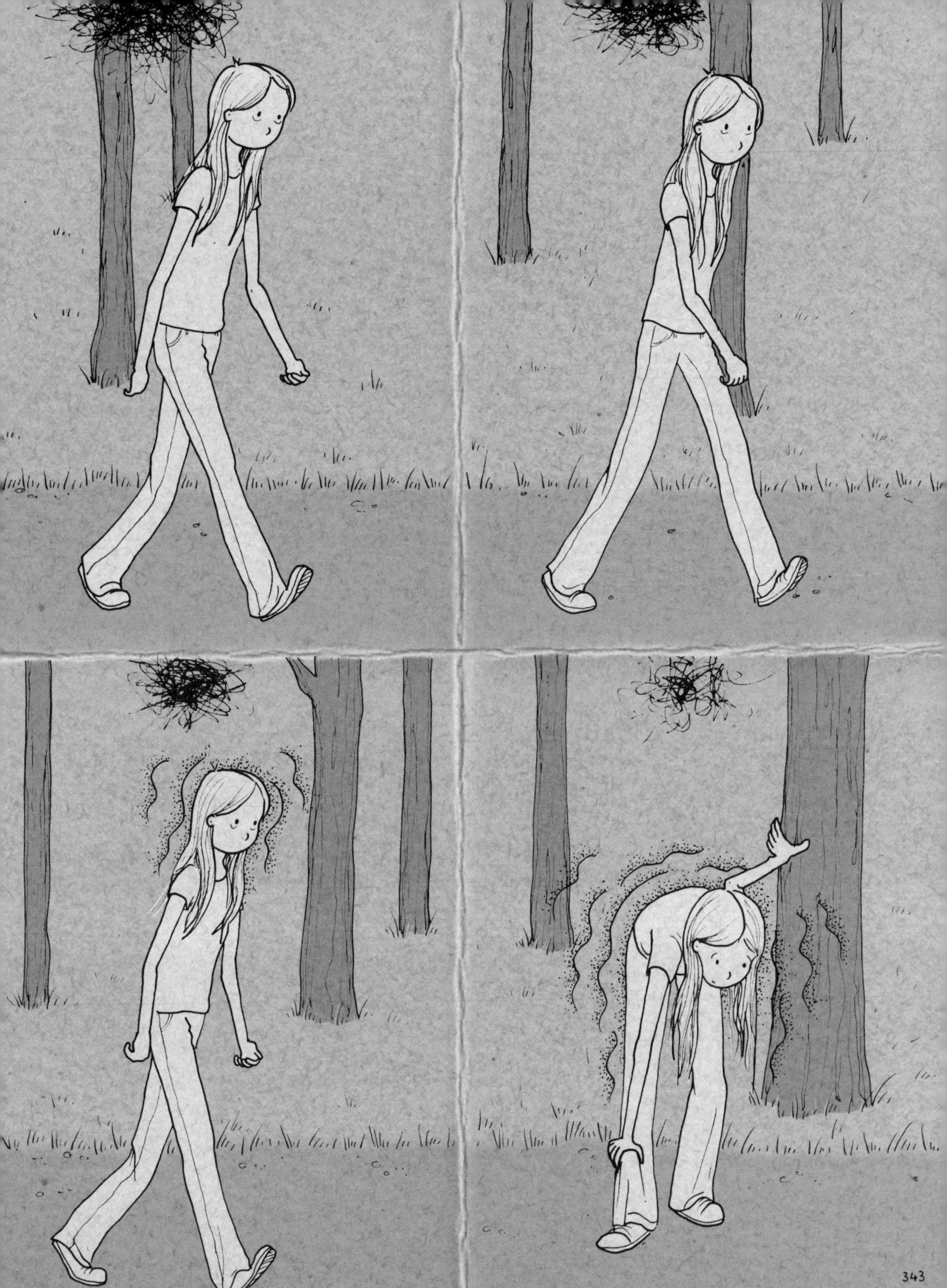

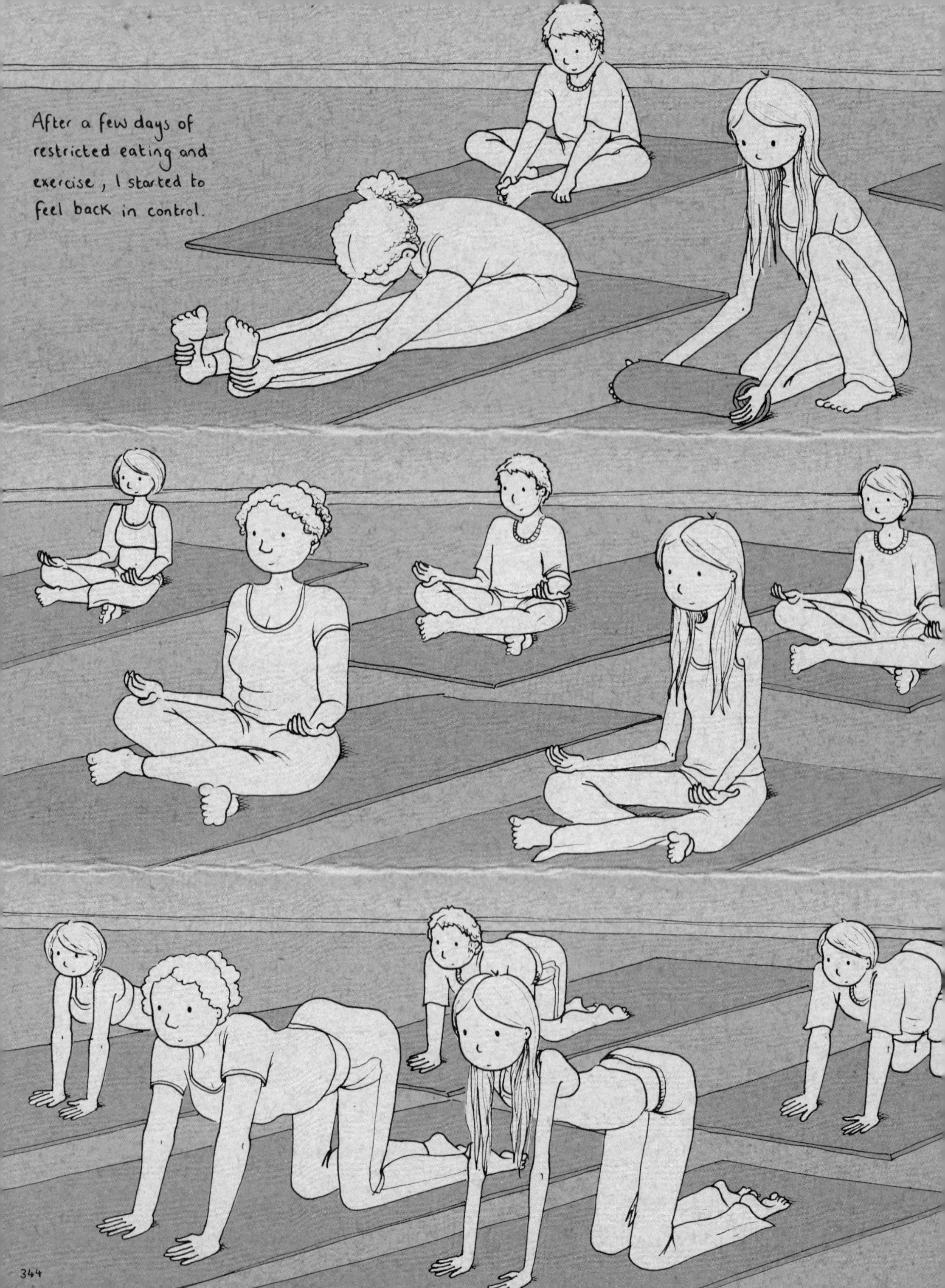
After a few days of restricted eating and exercise, I started to feel back in control.

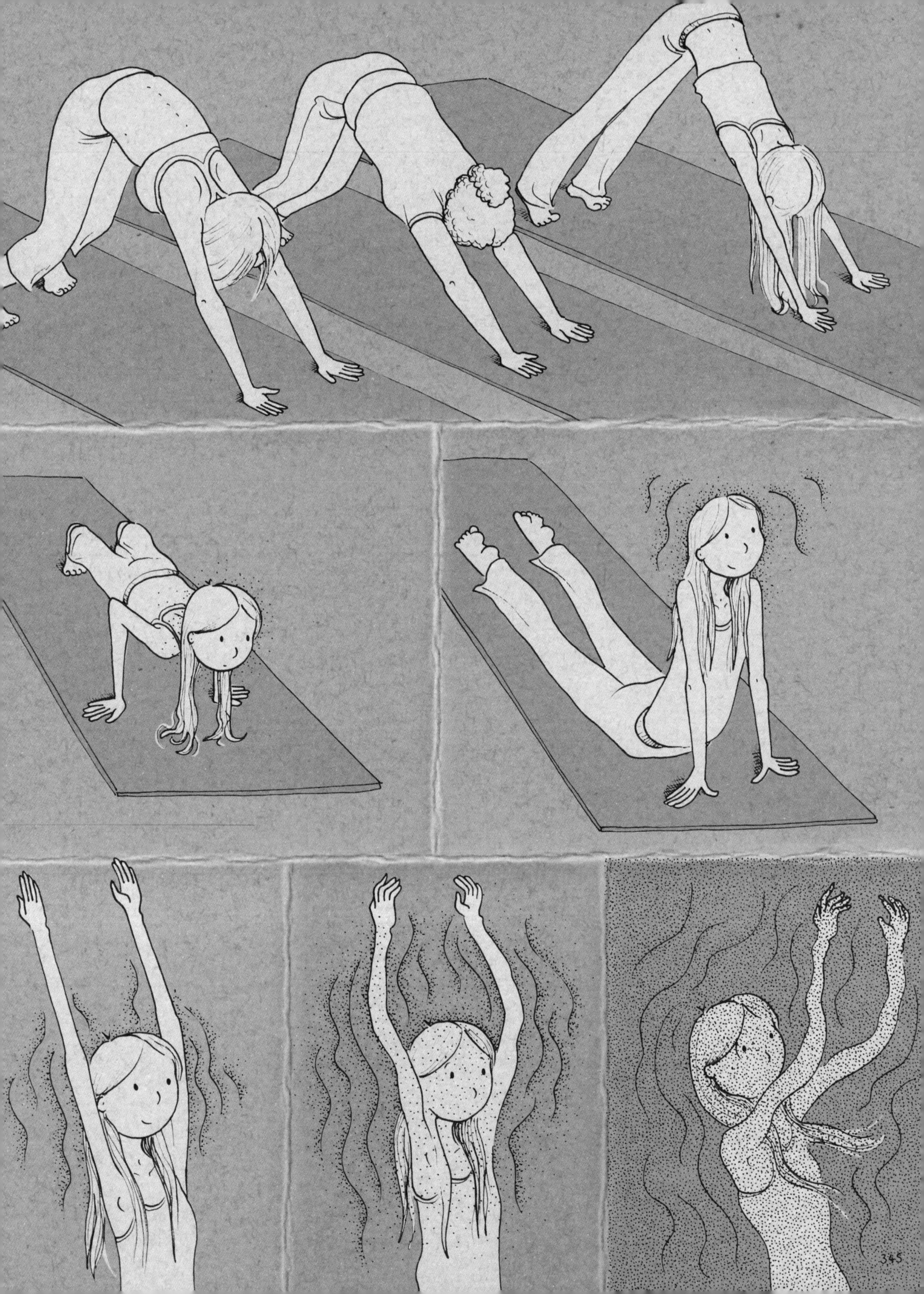

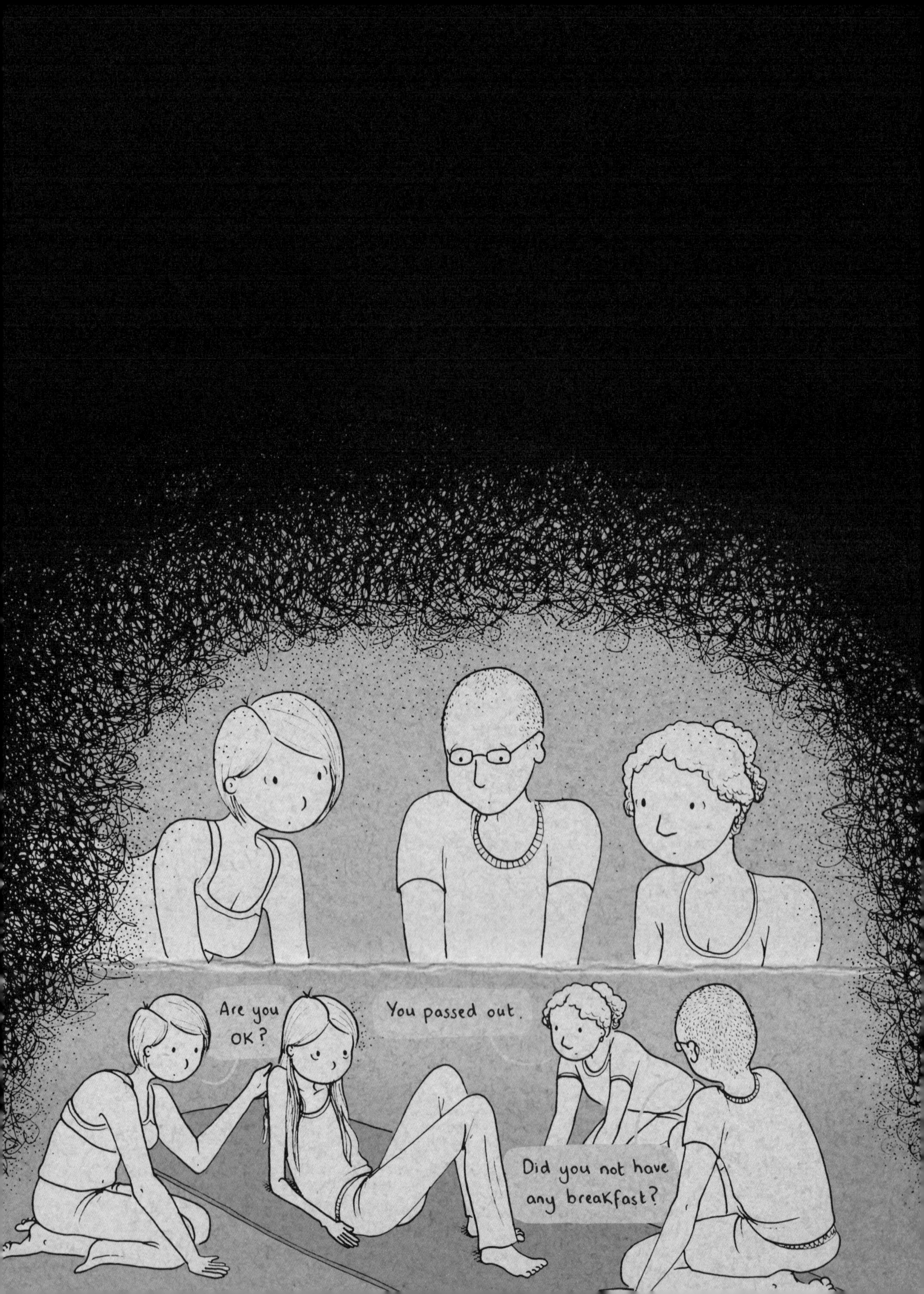
Are you OK?
You passed out.
Did you not have any breakfast?

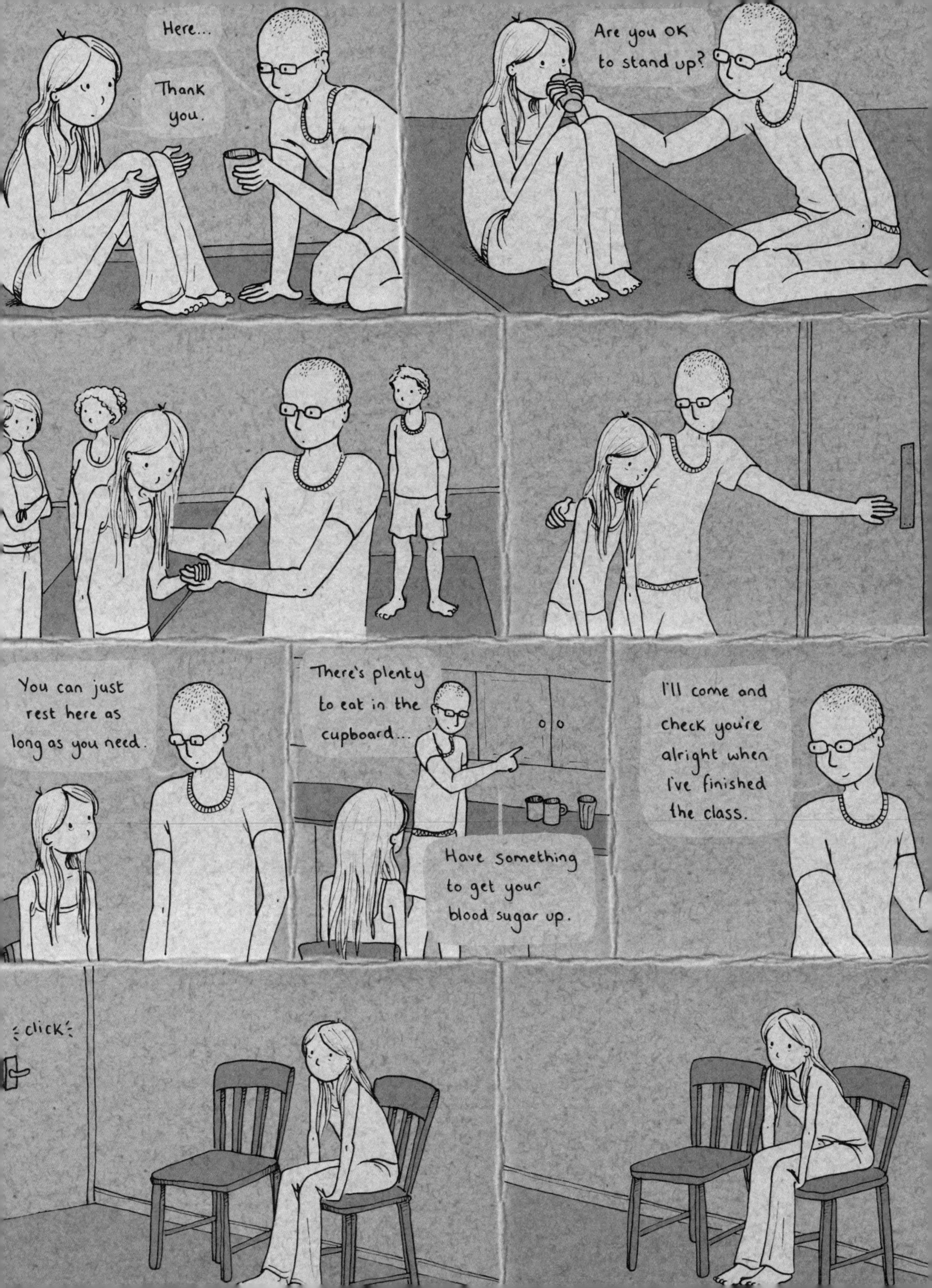
Here...
Thank you.
Are you OK to stand up?
You can just rest here as long as you need.
There's plenty to eat in the cupboard...
Have something to get your blood sugar up.
I'll come and check you're alright when I've finished the class.
click

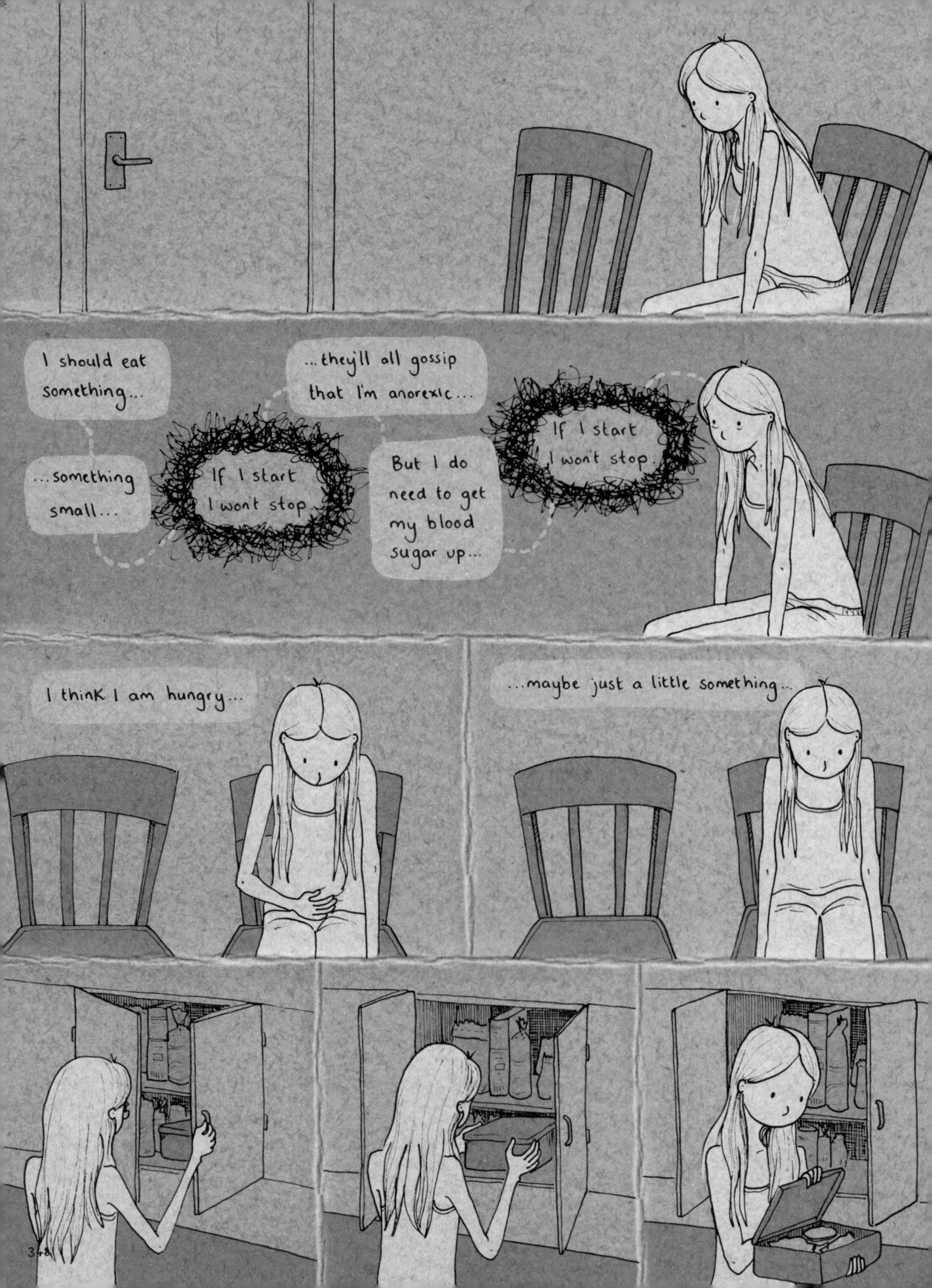
I should eat something...
...something small...
If I start I won't stop.
...they'll all gossip that I'm anorexic...
But I do need to get my blood sugar up...
If I start I won't stop.
I think I am hungry...
...maybe just a little something...

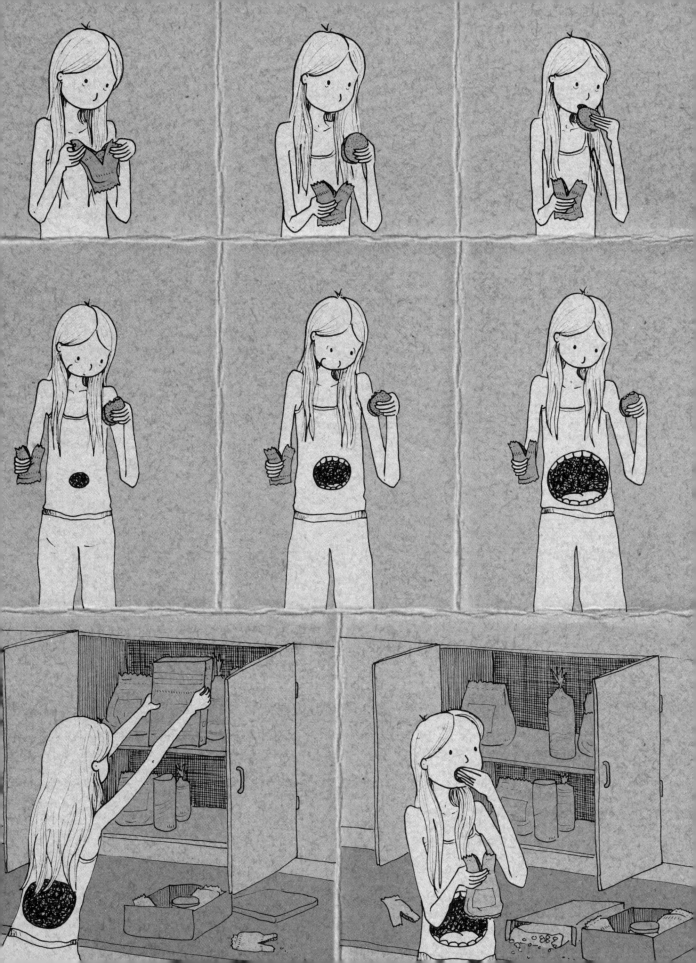

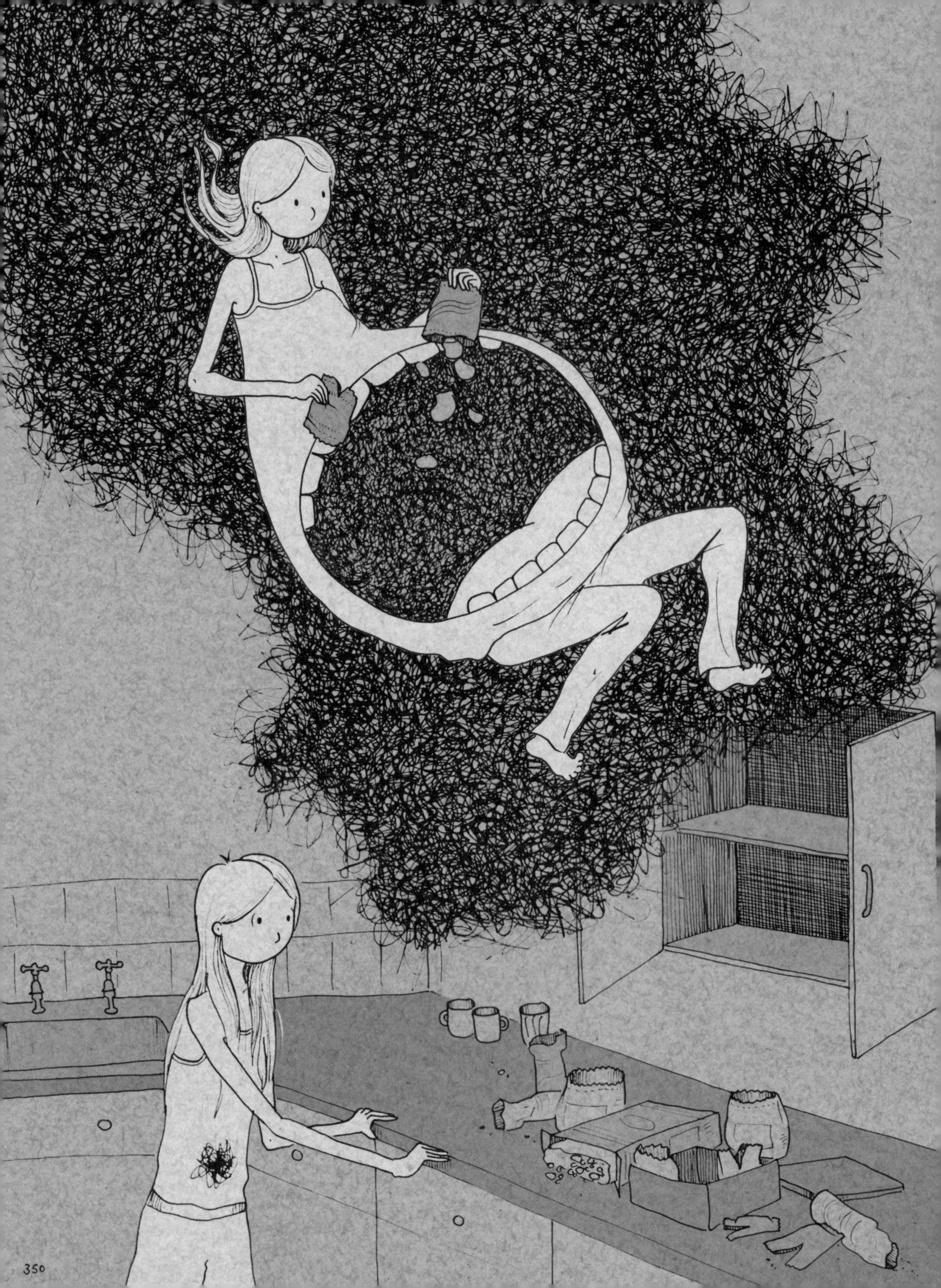

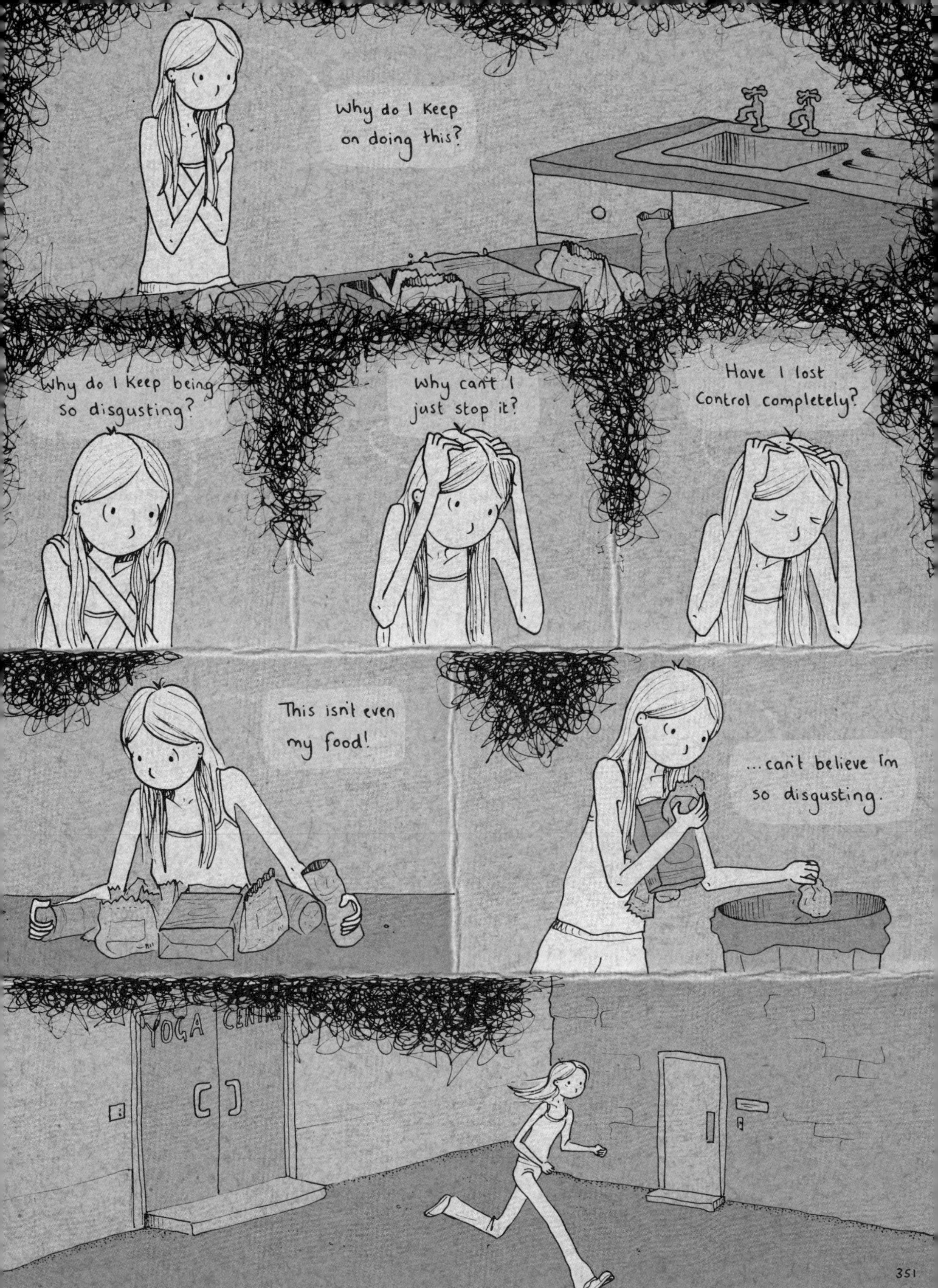
Why do I Keep
on doing this?
Why do I Keep being
so disgusting?
Why can't I
just stop it?
Have I lost
Control completely?
This isn't even
my food!
...can't believe I'm
so disgusting.
YOGA CENTRE

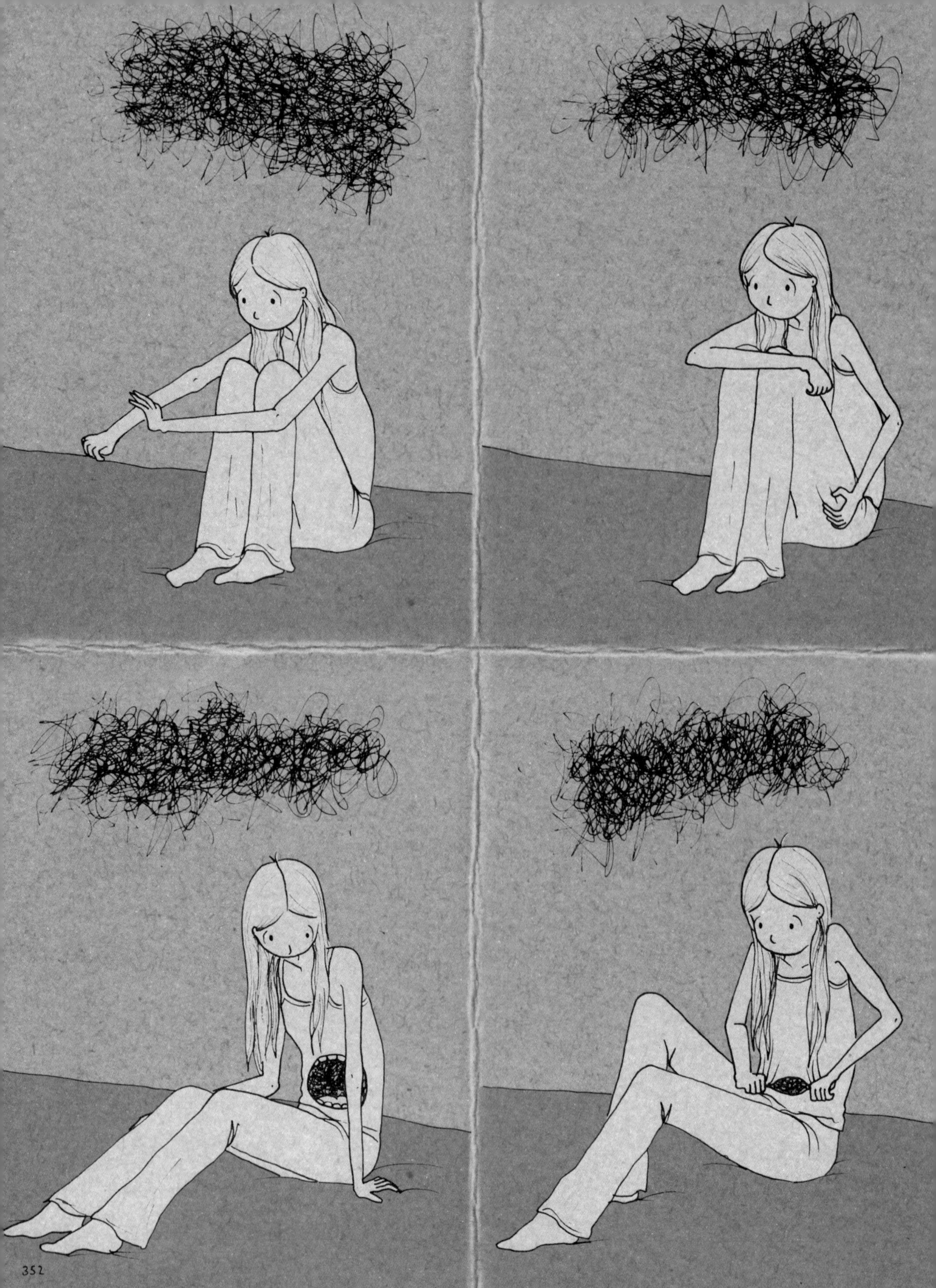

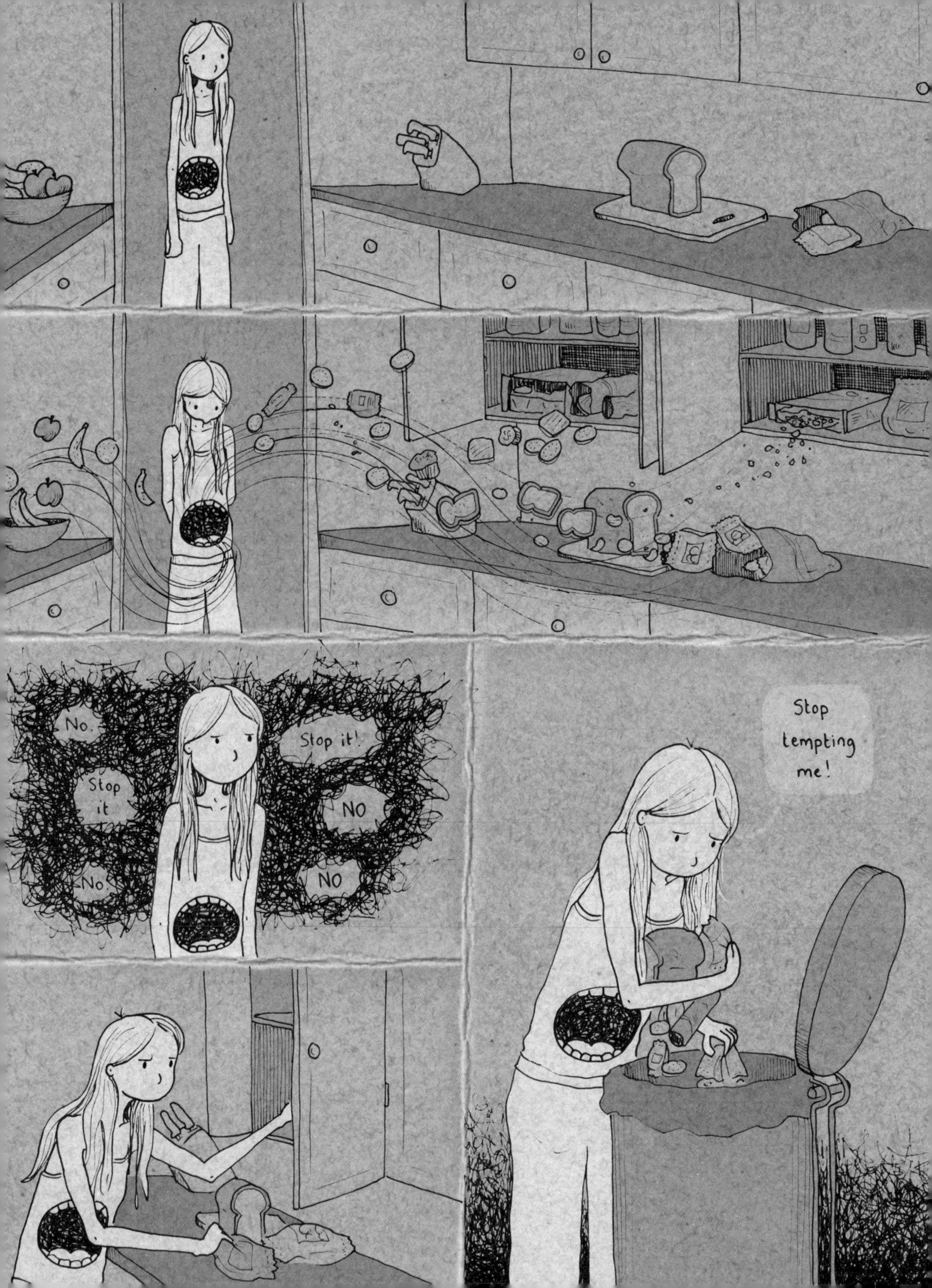
No.
Stop it!
Stop it
NO
No.
NO
Stop tempting me!

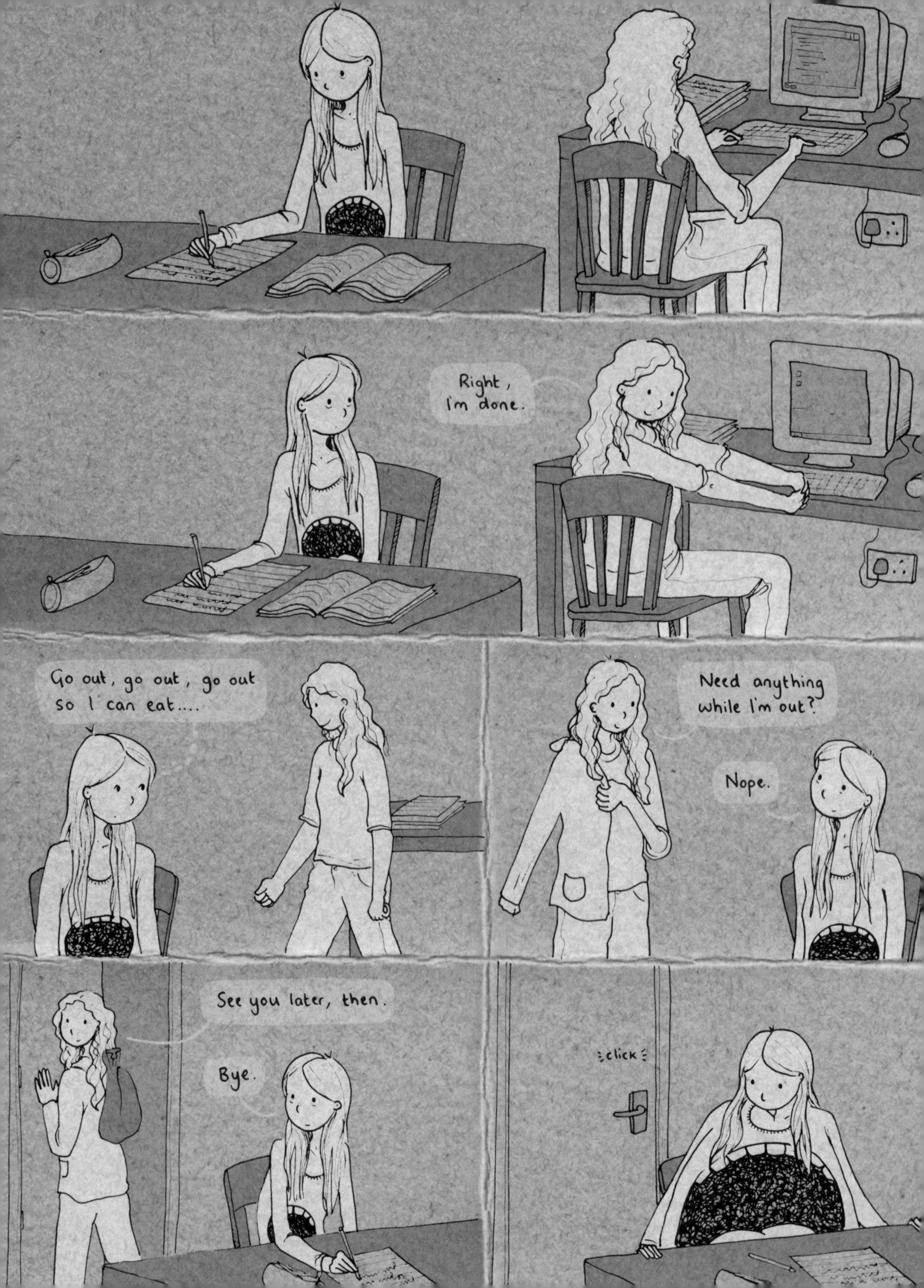
Right, I'm done.
Go out, go out, go out so I can eat....
Need anything while I'm out?
Nope.
See you later, then.
Bye.
click

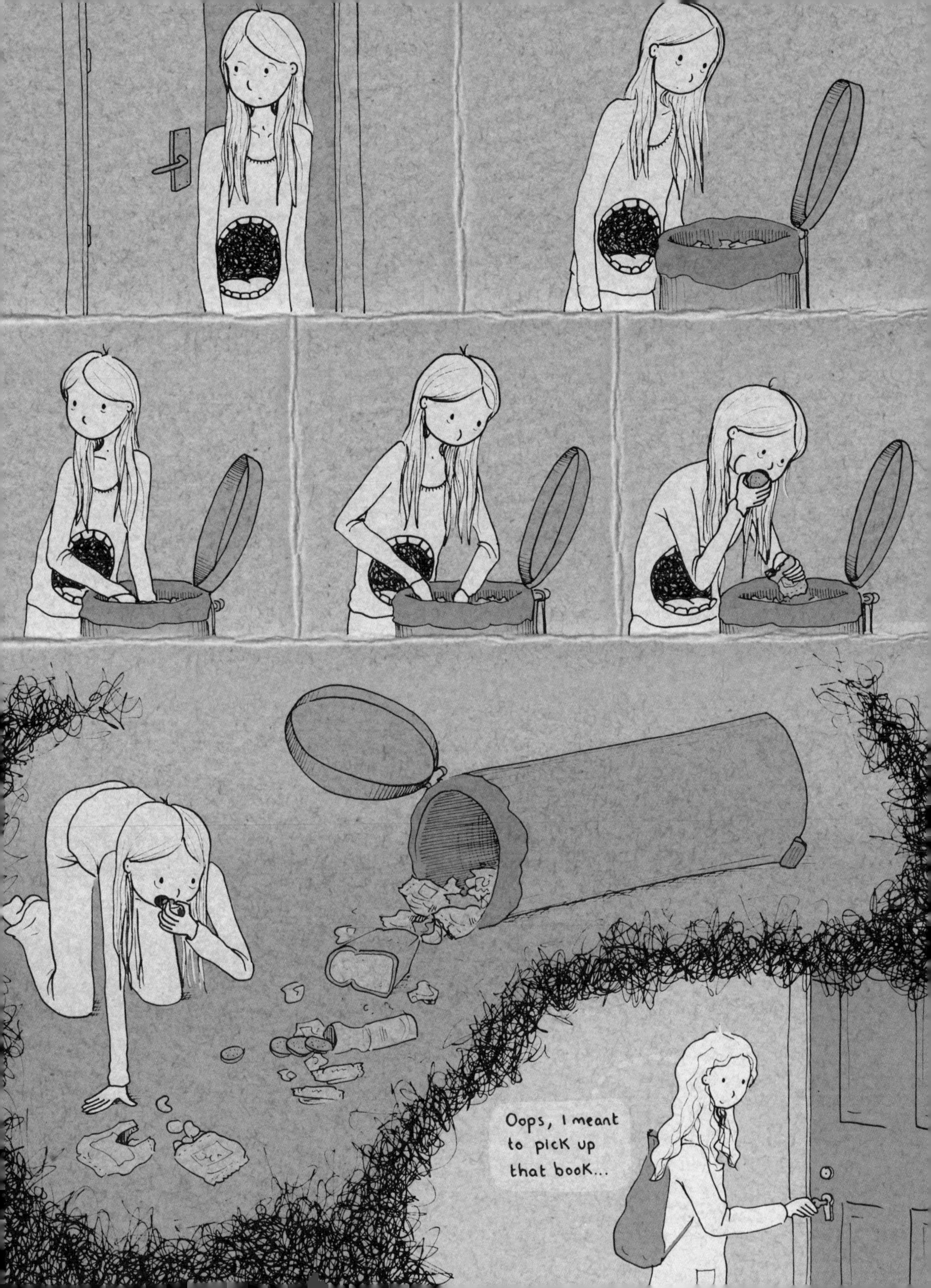
Oops, I meant to pick up that book...

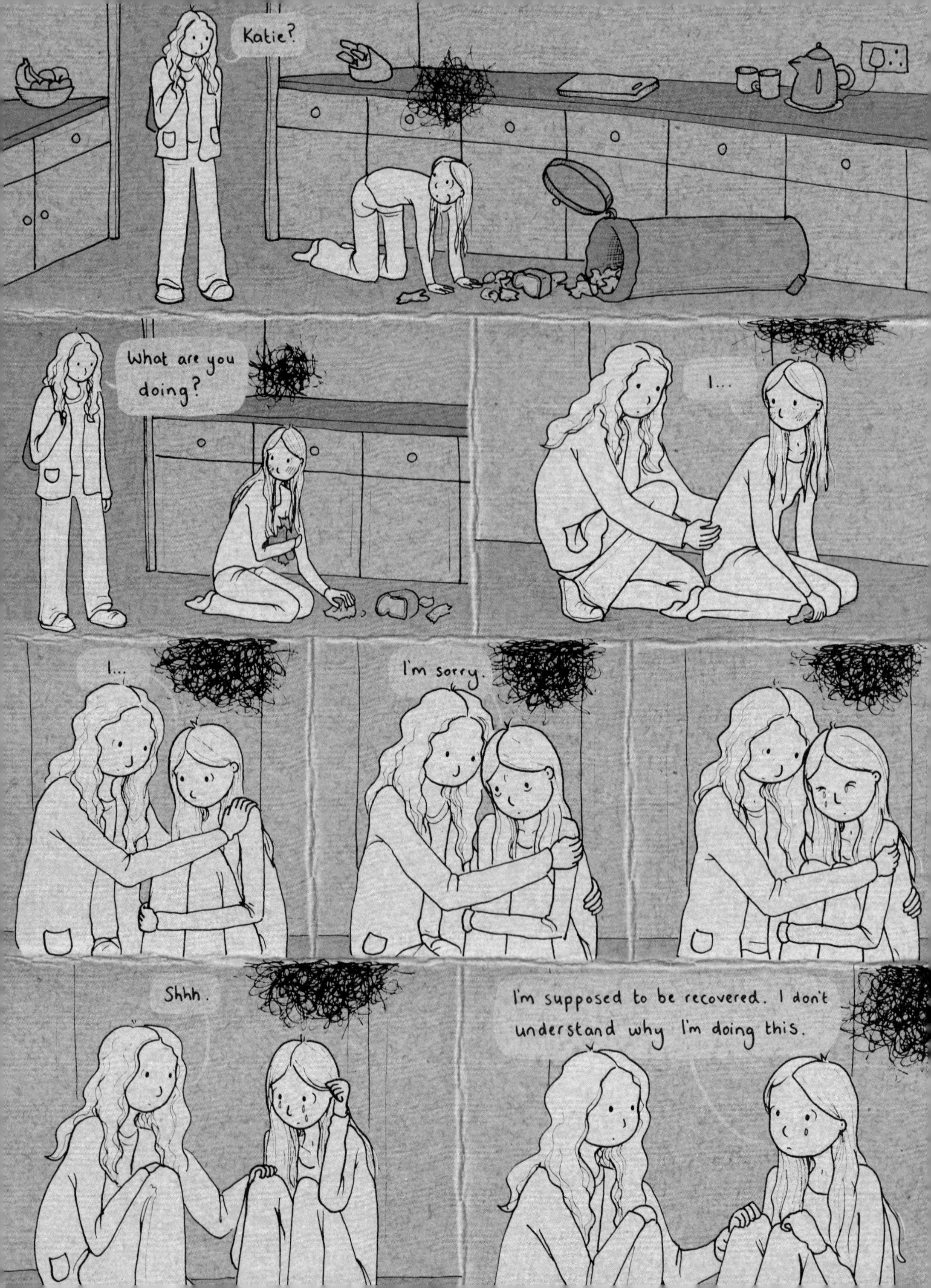
Katie?
What are you doing?
I...
I...
I'm sorry.
Shhh.
I'm supposed to be recovered. I don't understand why I'm doing this.

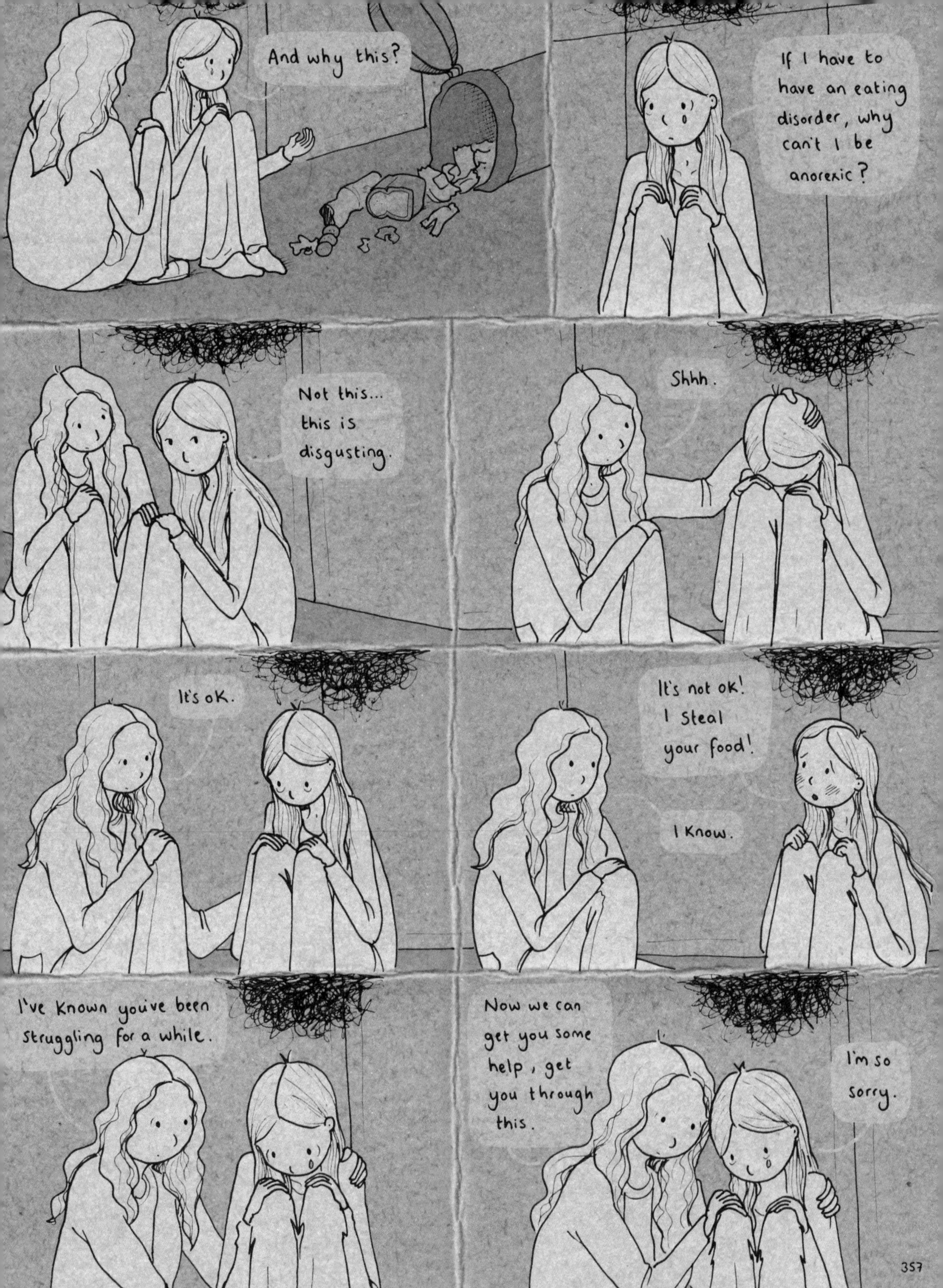
And why this?
If I have to have an eating disorder, why can't I be anorexic?
Not this... this is disgusting.
Shhh.
It's ok.
It's not ok! I steal your food!
I know.
I've known you've been struggling for a while.
Now we can get you some help, get you through this.
I'm so sorry.

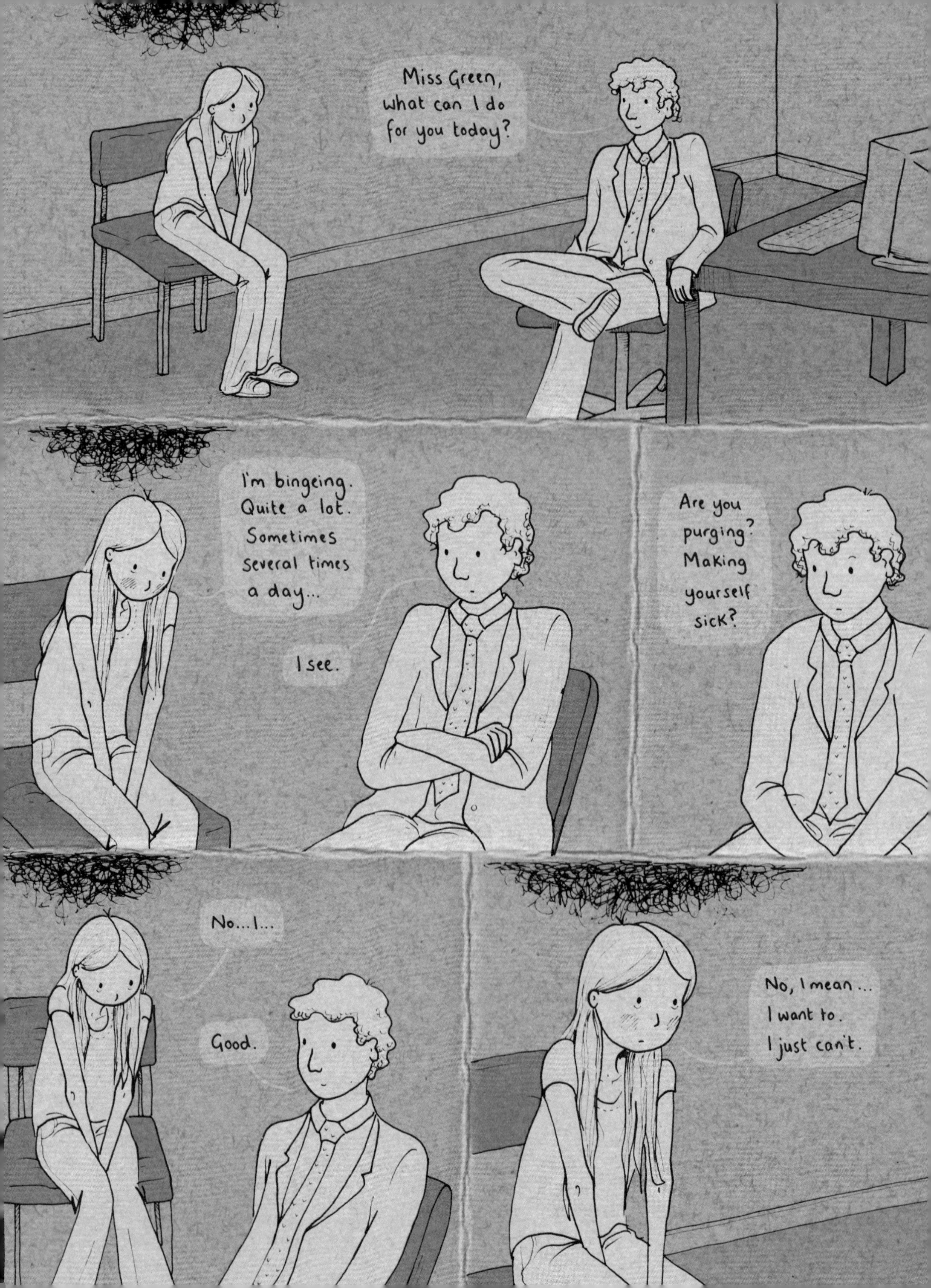
Miss Green,
what can I do
for you today?
I'm bingeing.
Quite a lot.
Sometimes
several times
a day...
I see.
Are you
purging?
Making
yourself
sick?
No... I...
Good.
No, I mean...
I want to.
I just can't.

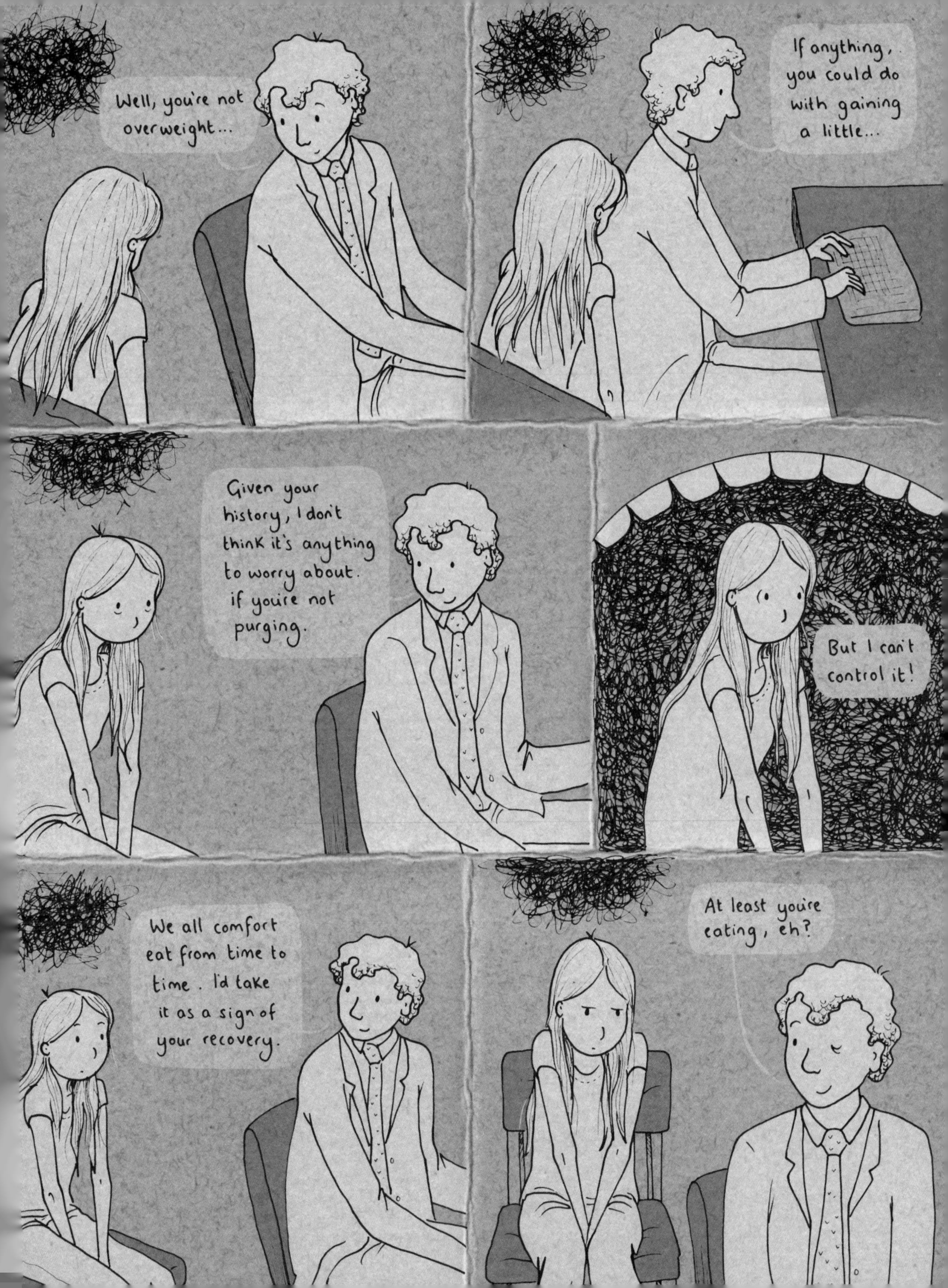
Well, you're not overweight...
If anything, you could do with gaining a little...
Given your history, I don't think it's anything to worry about. if you're not purging.
But I can't control it!
We all comfort eat from time to time. I'd take it as a sign of your recovery.
At least you're eating, eh?

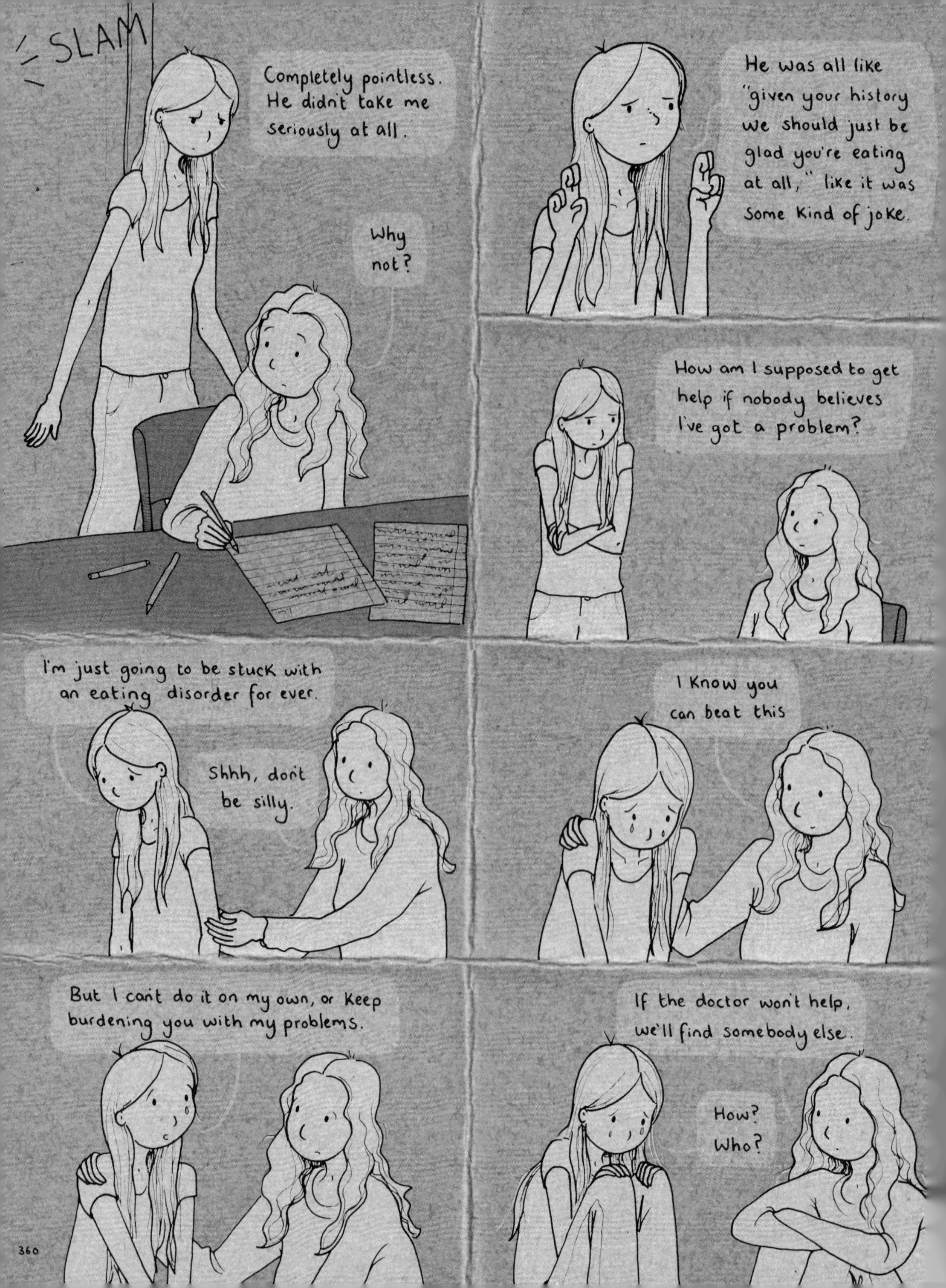
SLAM
Completely pointless. He didn't take me seriously at all.
Why not?
He was all like "given your history we should just be glad you're eating at all," like it was some kind of joke.
How am I supposed to get help if nobody believes I've got a problem?
I'm just going to be stuck with an eating disorder for ever.
Shhh, don't be silly.
I know you can beat this
But I can't do it on my own, or keep burdening you with my problems.
If the doctor won't help, we'll find somebody else.
How? Who?

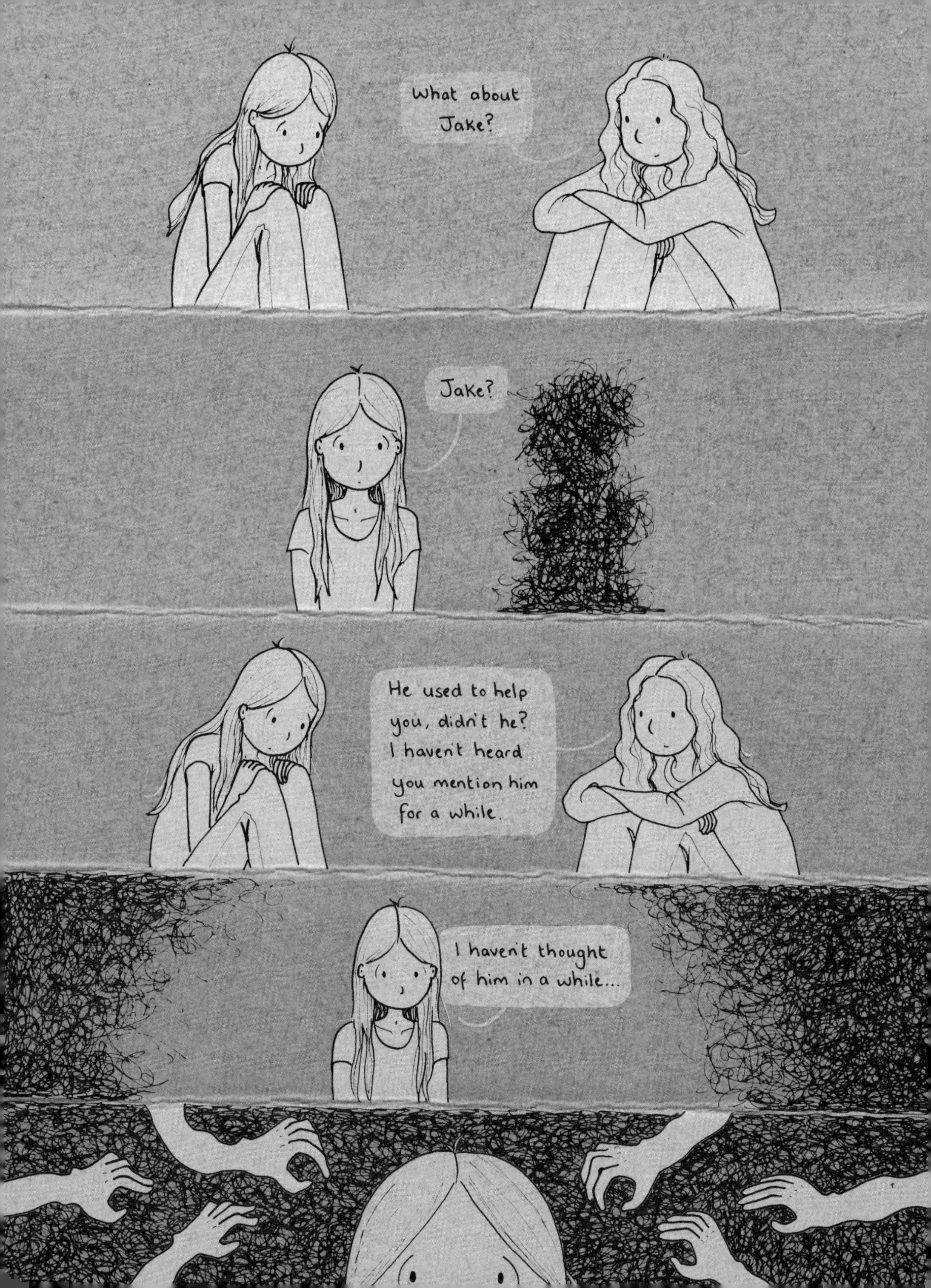
What about Jake?
Jake?
He used to help you, didn't he? I haven't heard you mention him for a while.
I haven't thought of him in a while...

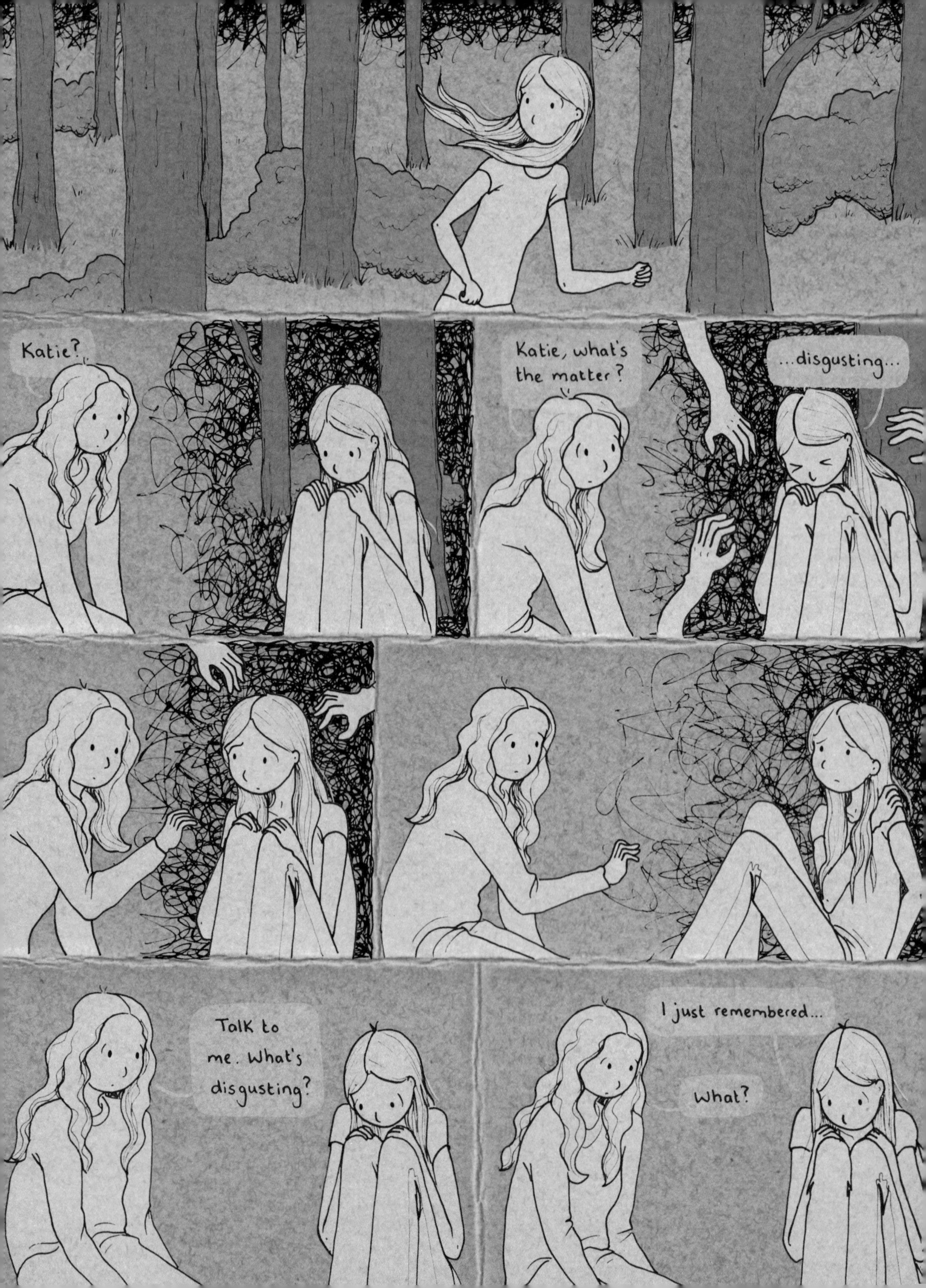
Katie?
Katie, what's the matter?
...disgusting...
Talk to me. What's disgusting?
I just remembered...
What?

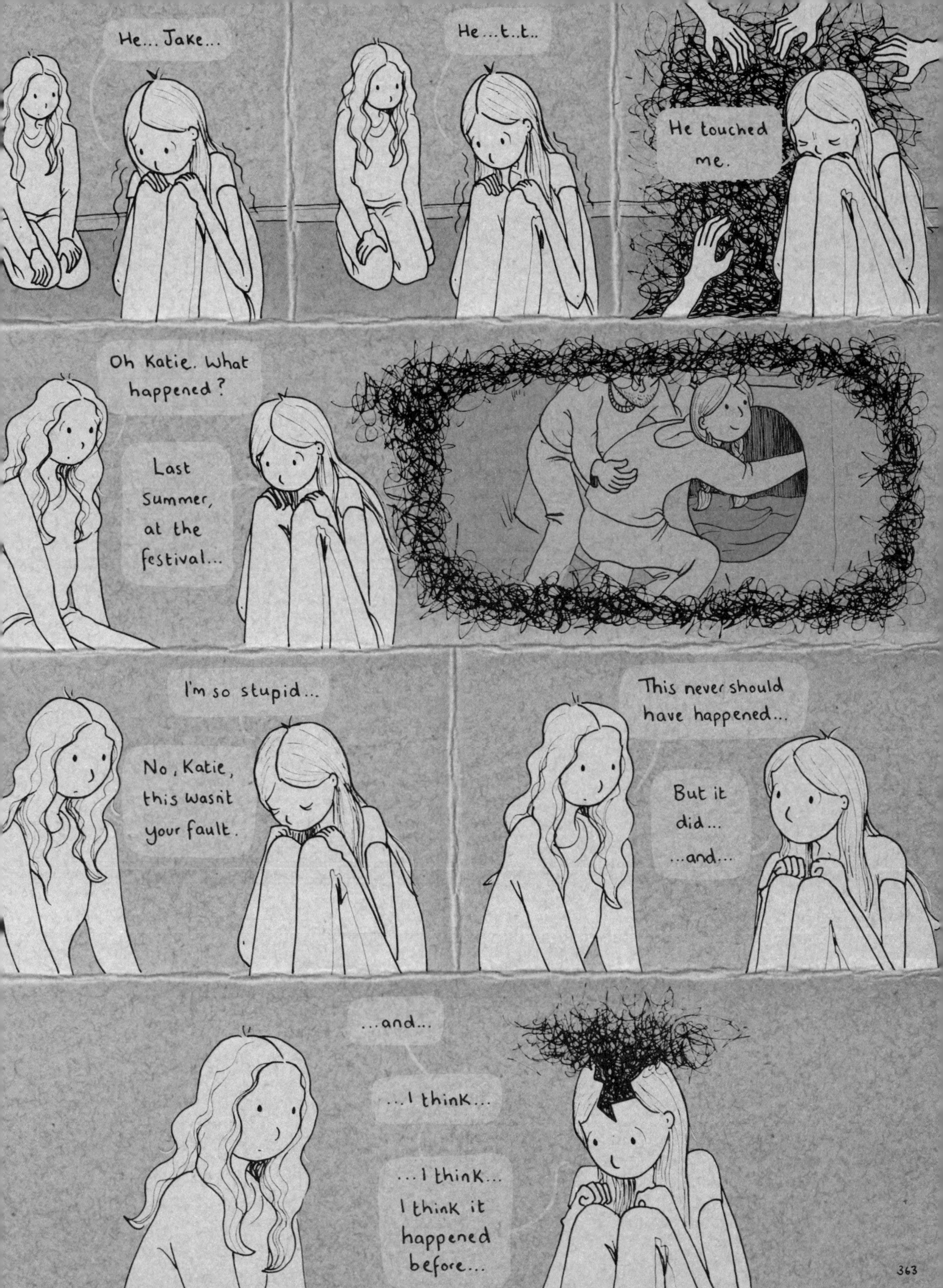
He... Jake...
He...t..t..
He touched me.
Oh Katie. What happened?
Last summer, at the festival...
I'm so stupid...
No, Katie, this wasn't your fault.
This never should have happened...
But it did...
...and...
...and...
...I think...
...I think... I think it happened before...

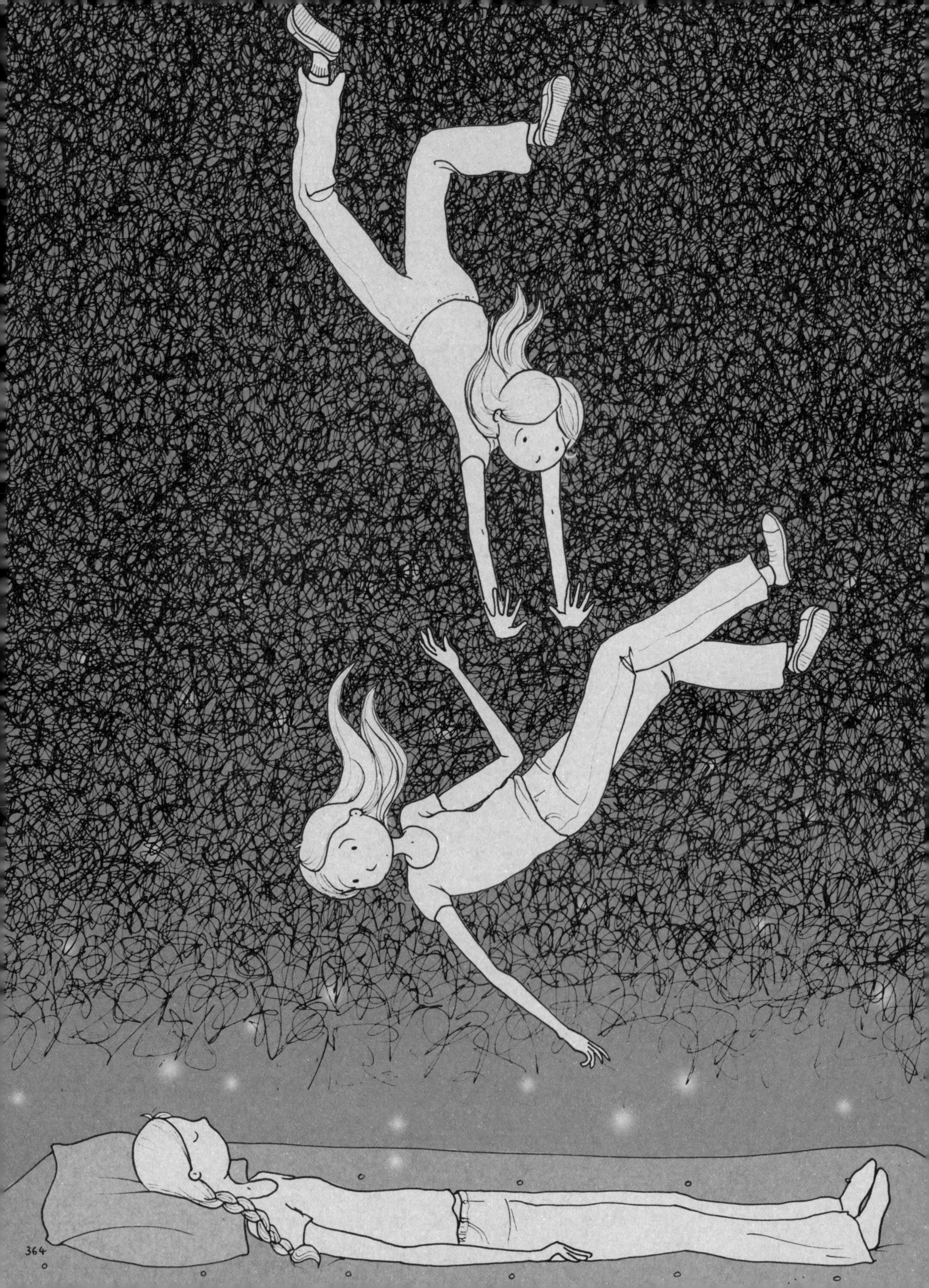

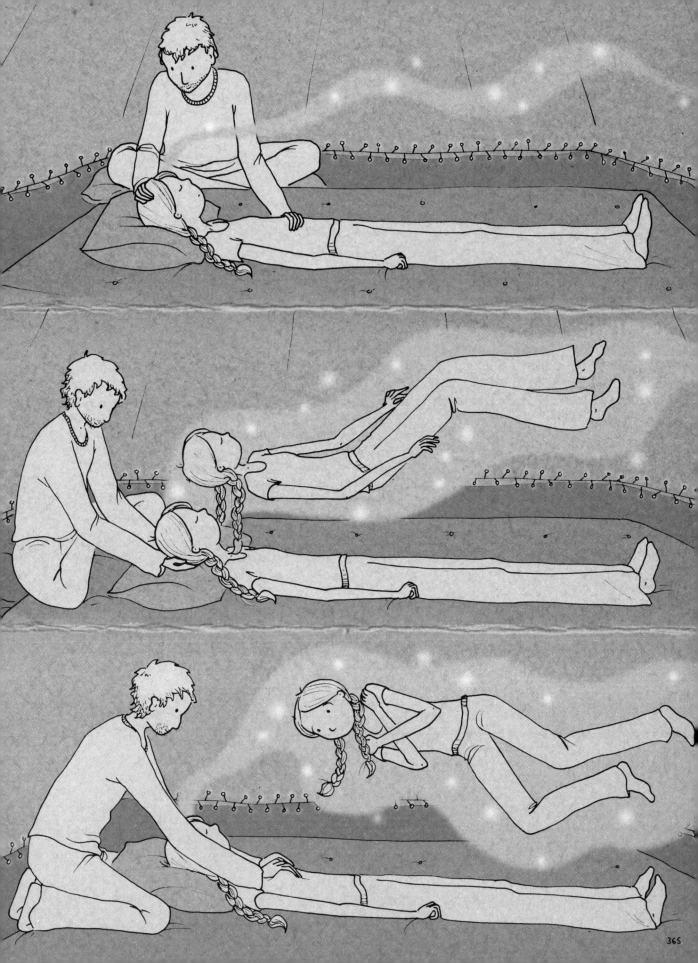

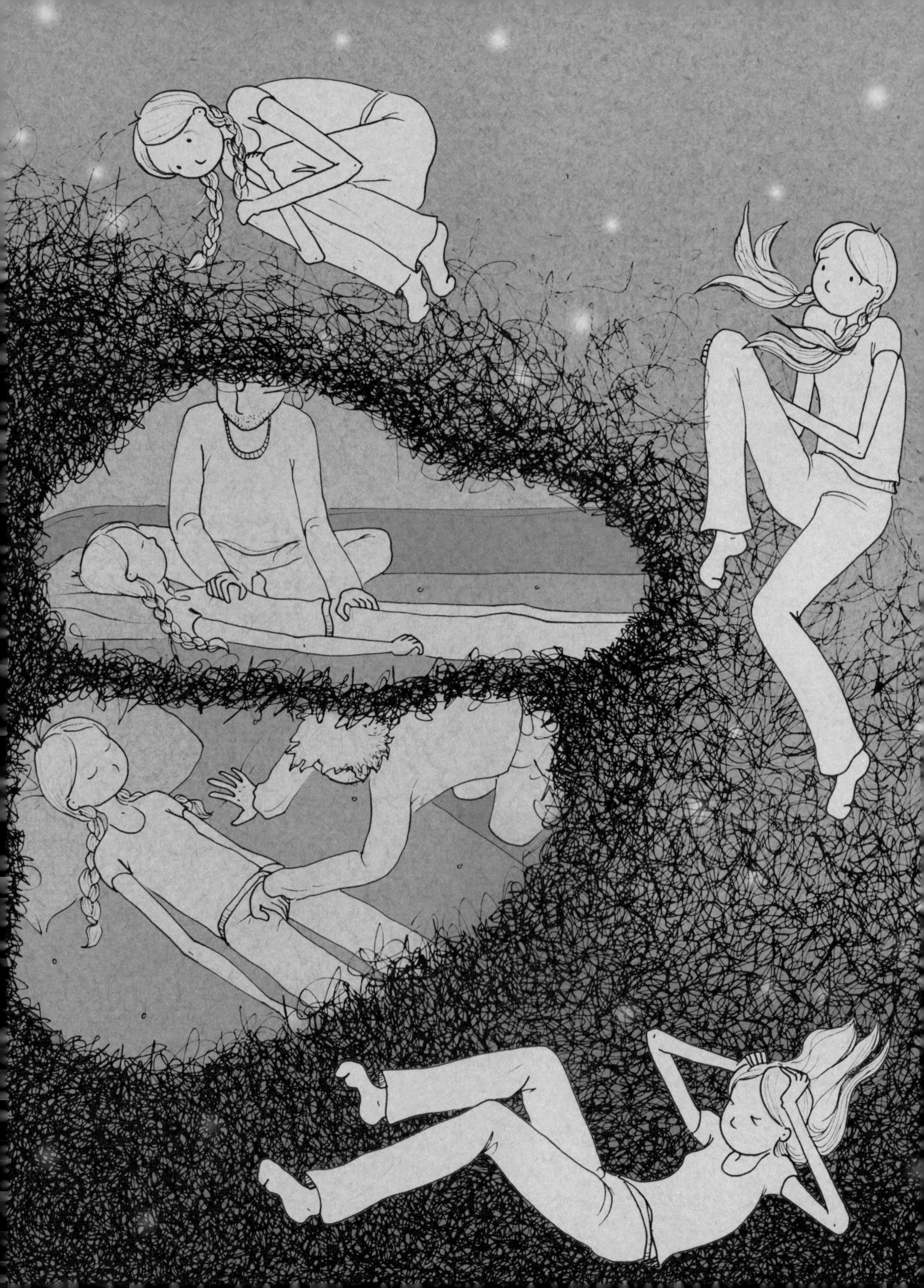

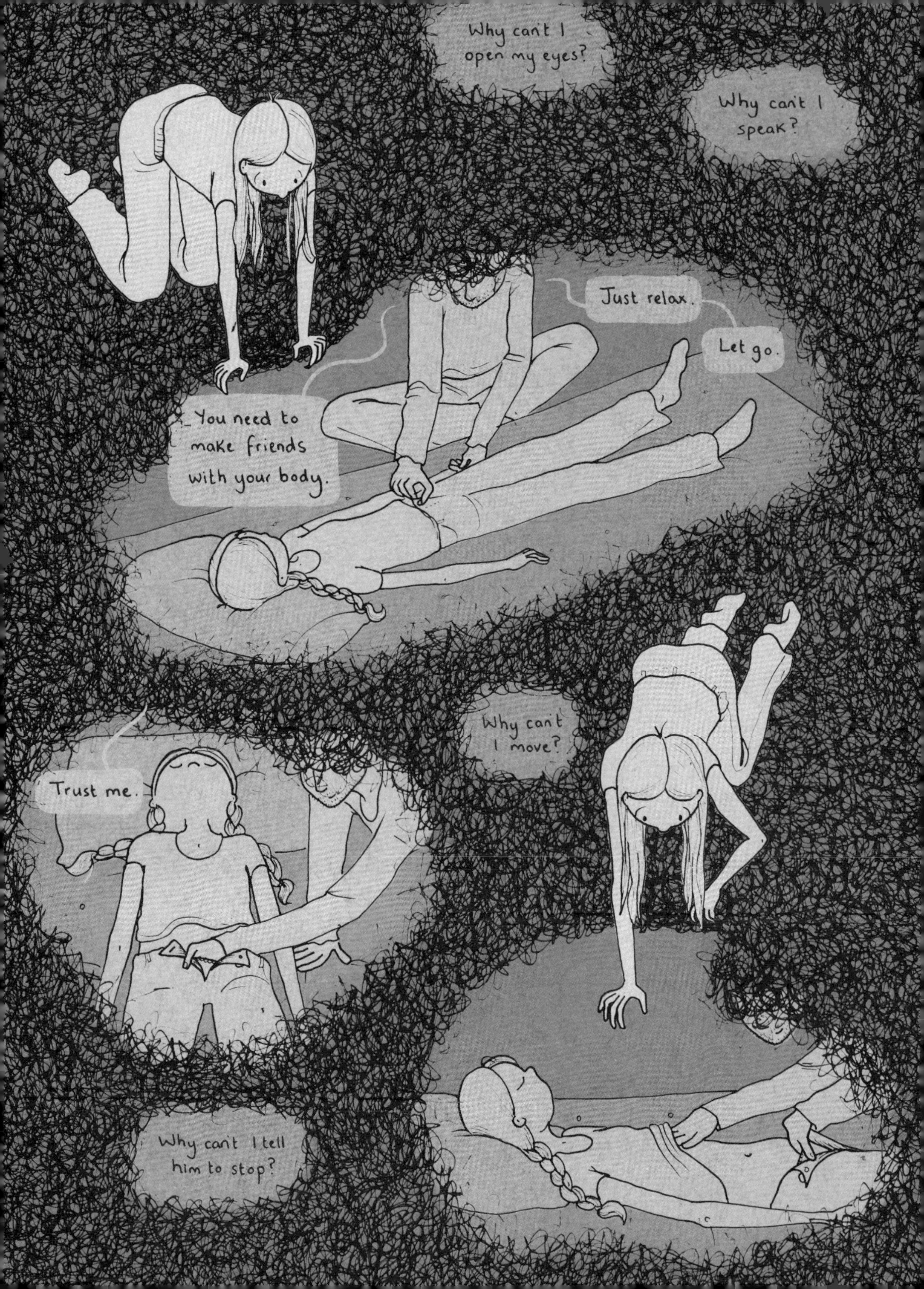
Why can't I open my eyes?
Why can't I speak?
Just relax.
Let go.
You need to make friends with your body.
Why can't I move?
Trust me.
Why can't I tell him to stop?

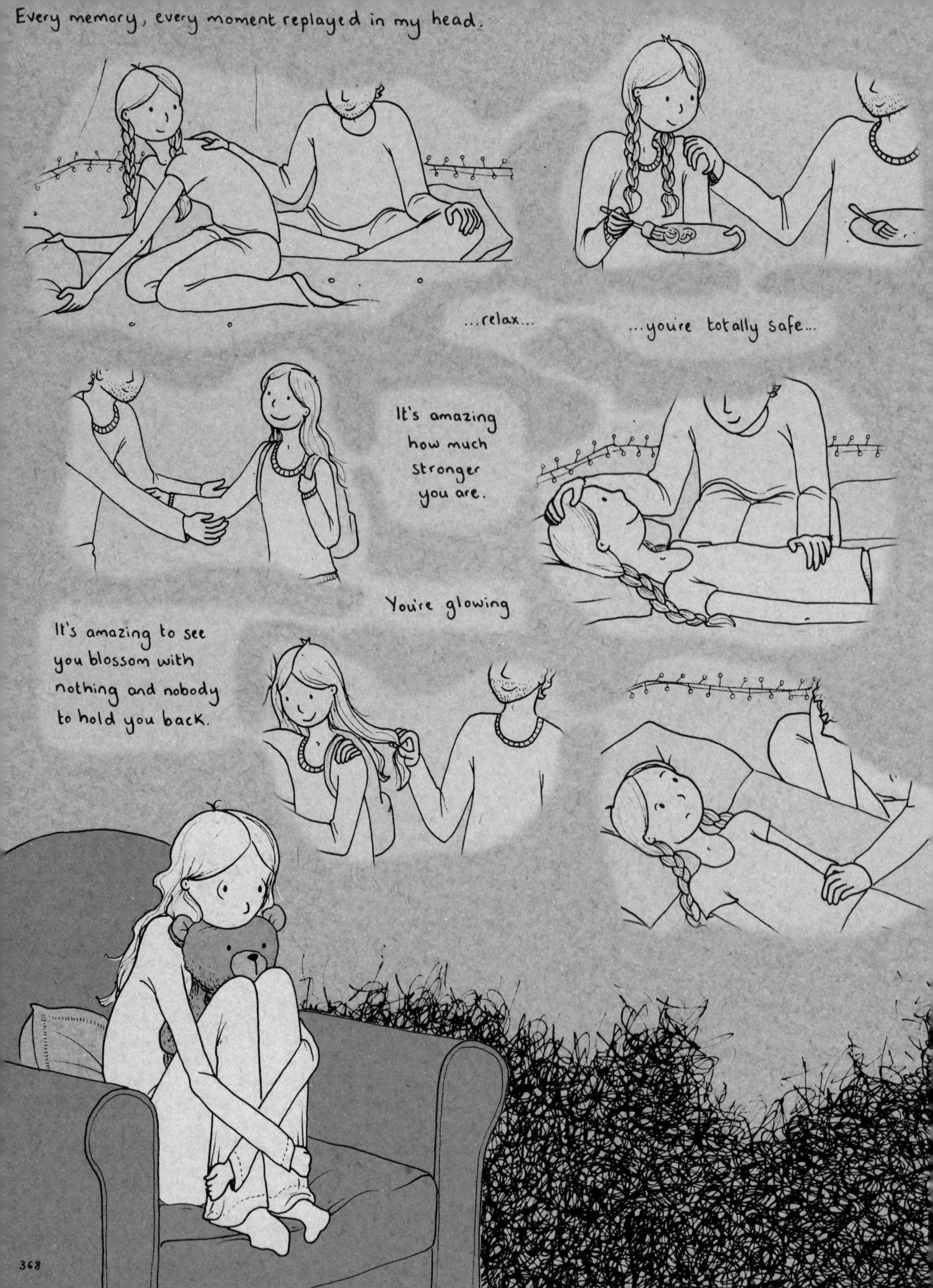
Every memory, every moment replayed in my head.
...relax...
...you're totally safe...
It's amazing how much stronger you are.
You're glowing
It's amazing to see you blossom with nothing and nobody to hold you back.

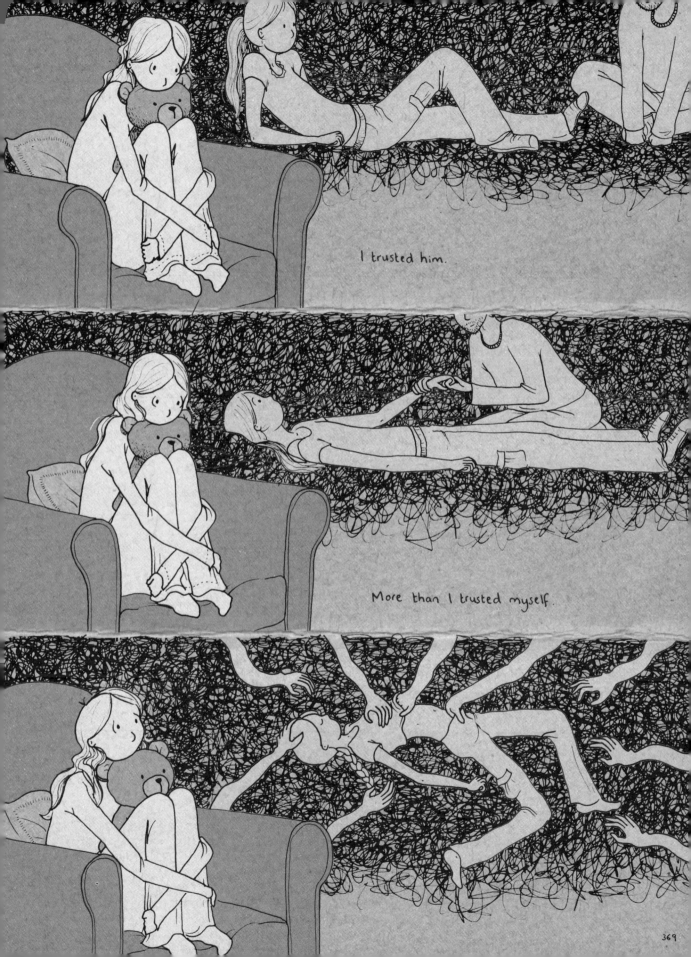

I trusted him.

More than I trusted myself.

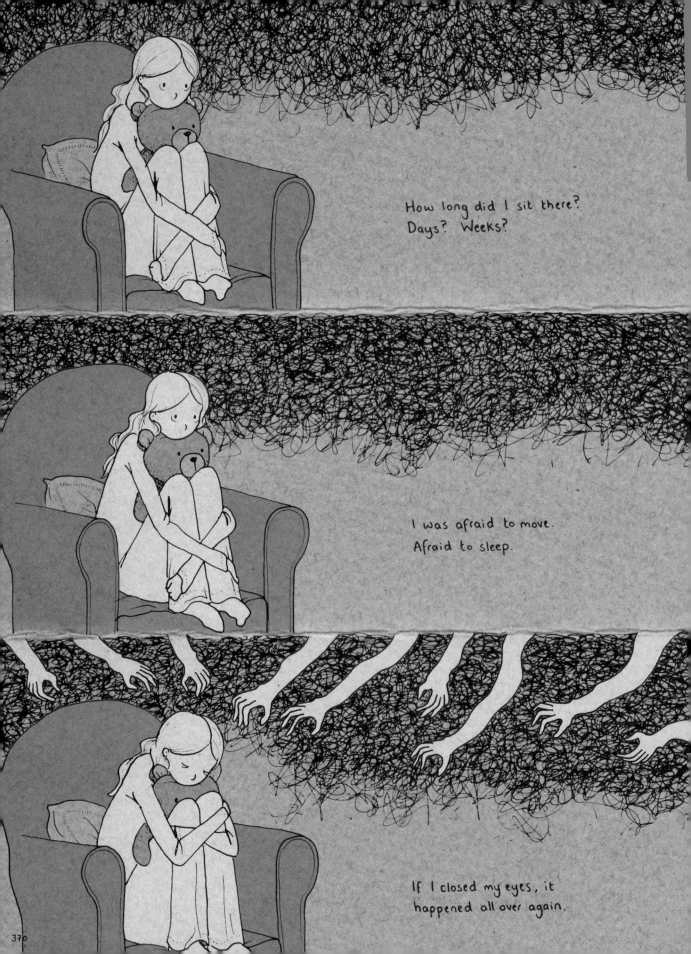

How long did I sit there?
Days? Weeks?

I was afraid to move.
Afraid to sleep.

If I closed my eyes, it
happened all over again.

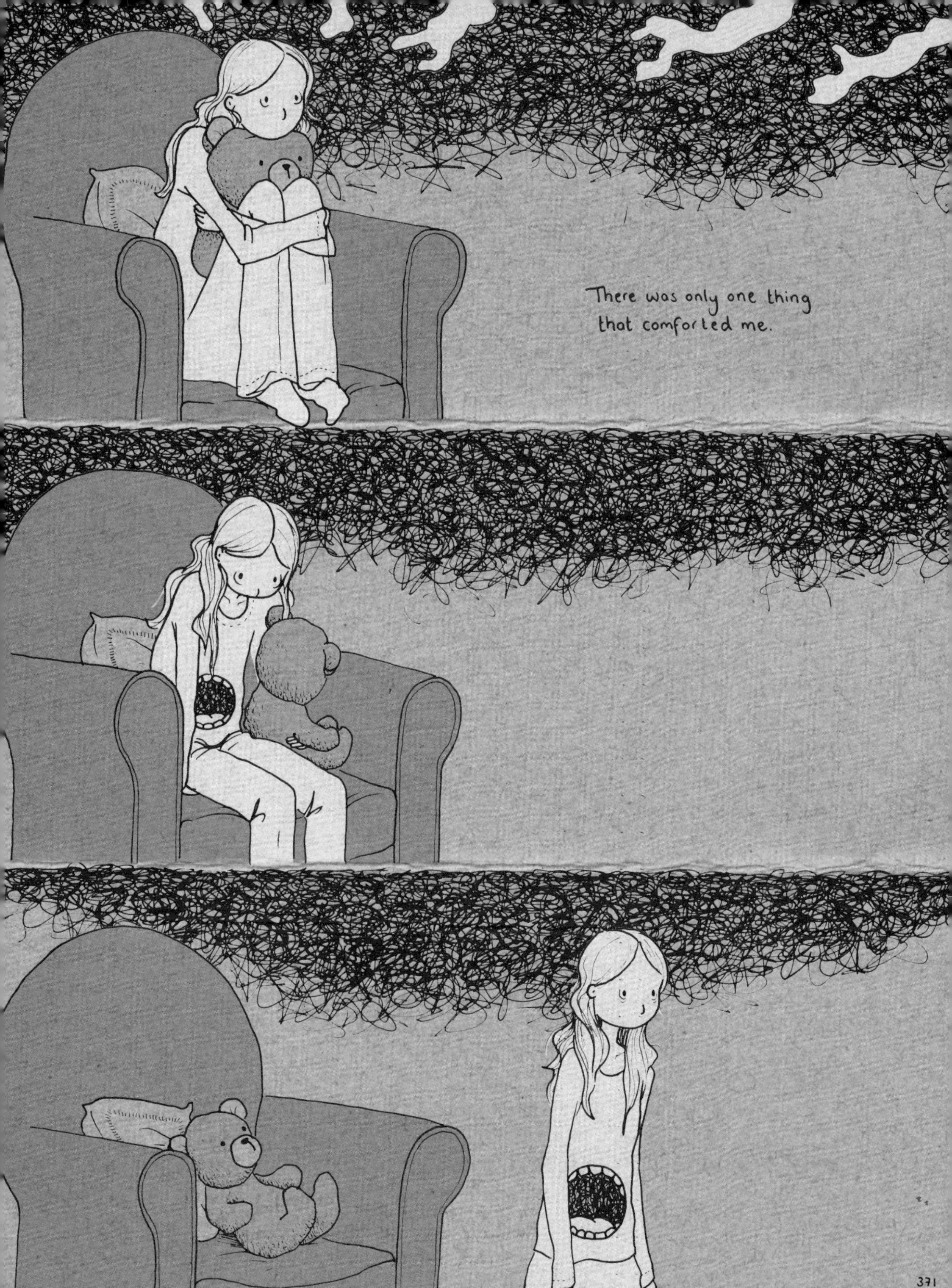
There was only one thing
that comforted me.

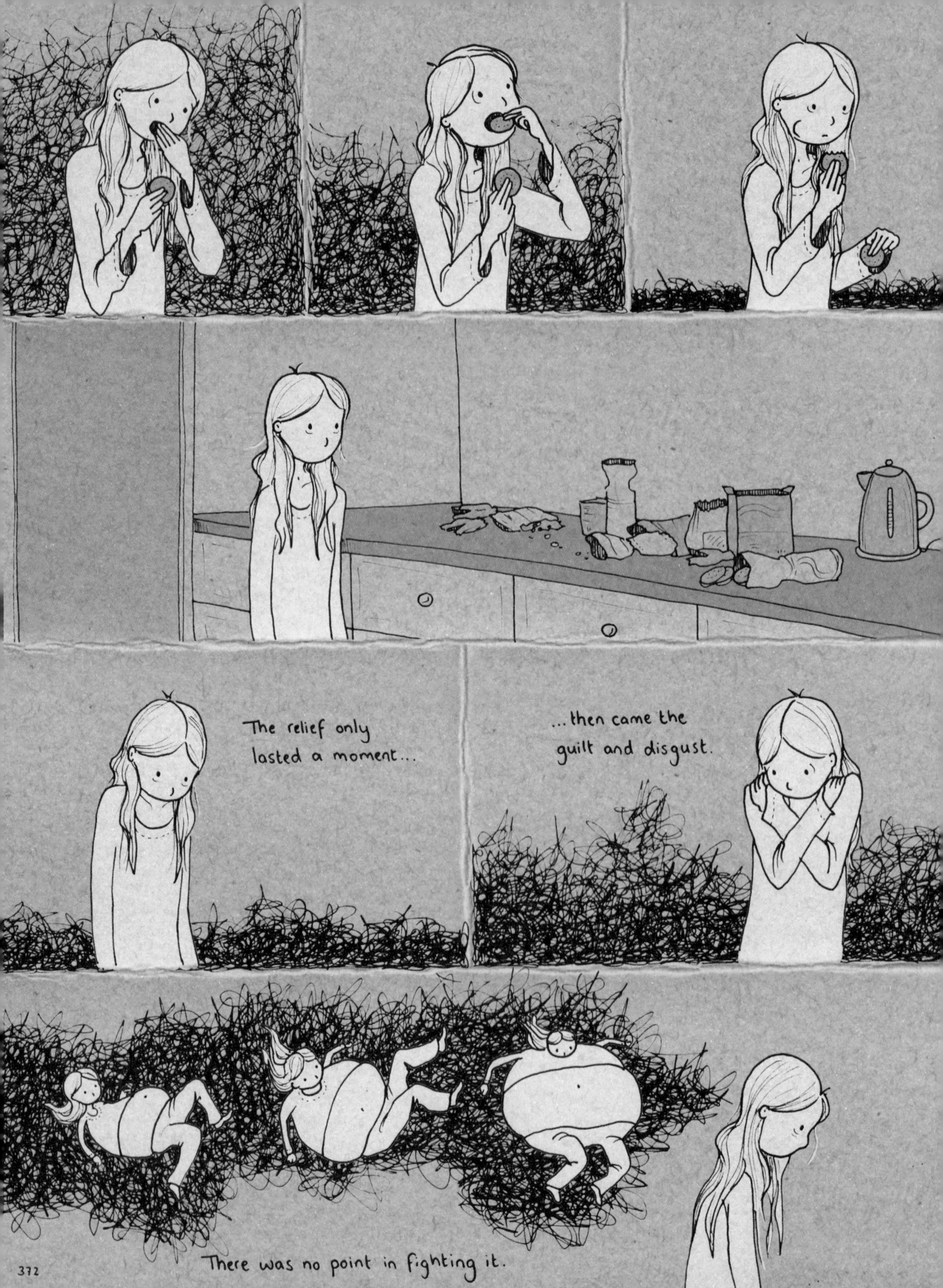
The relief only lasted a moment...
...then came the guilt and disgust.
There was no point in fighting it.

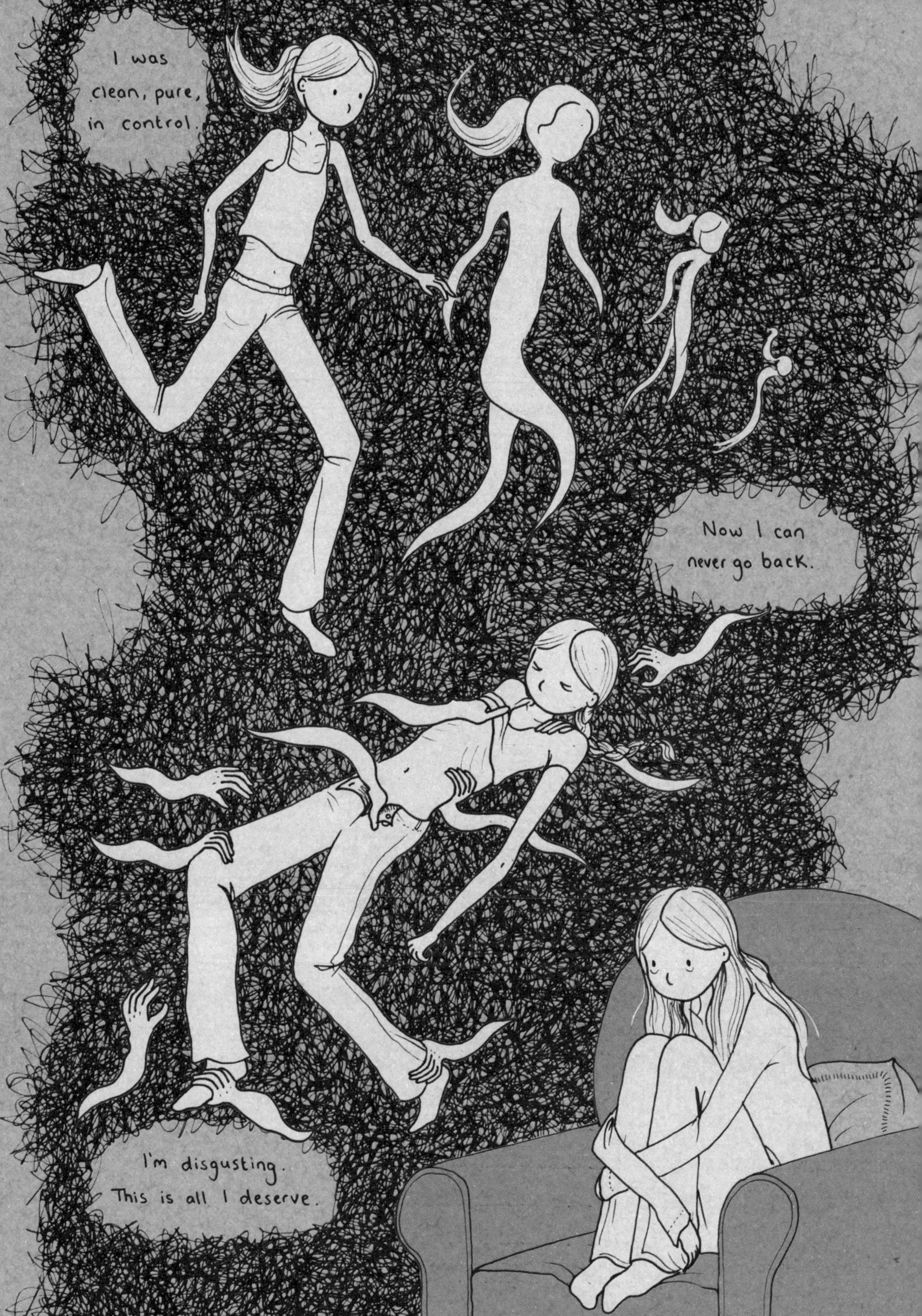
I was clean, pure, in control.
Now I can never go back.
I'm disgusting. This is all I deserve.

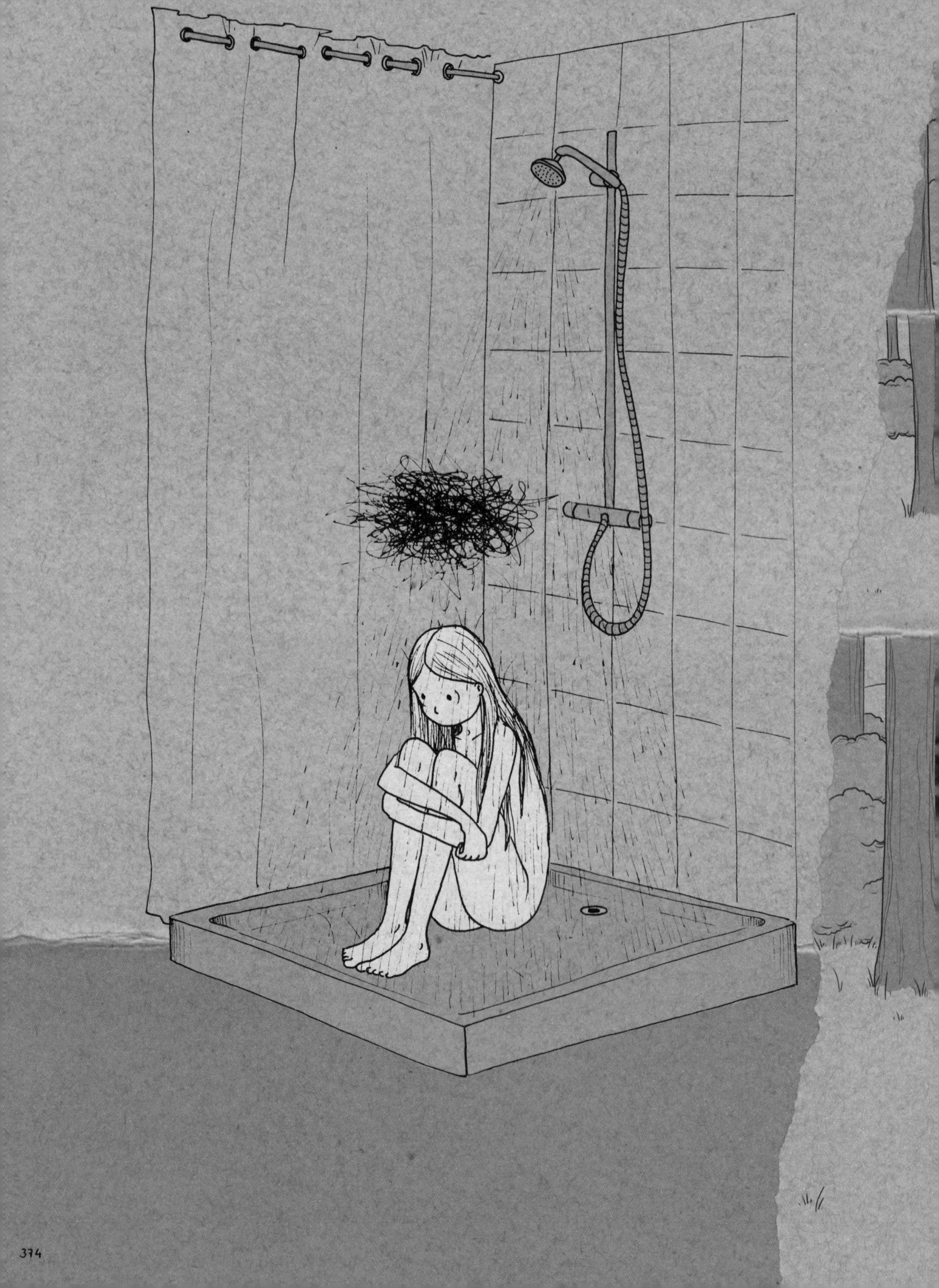

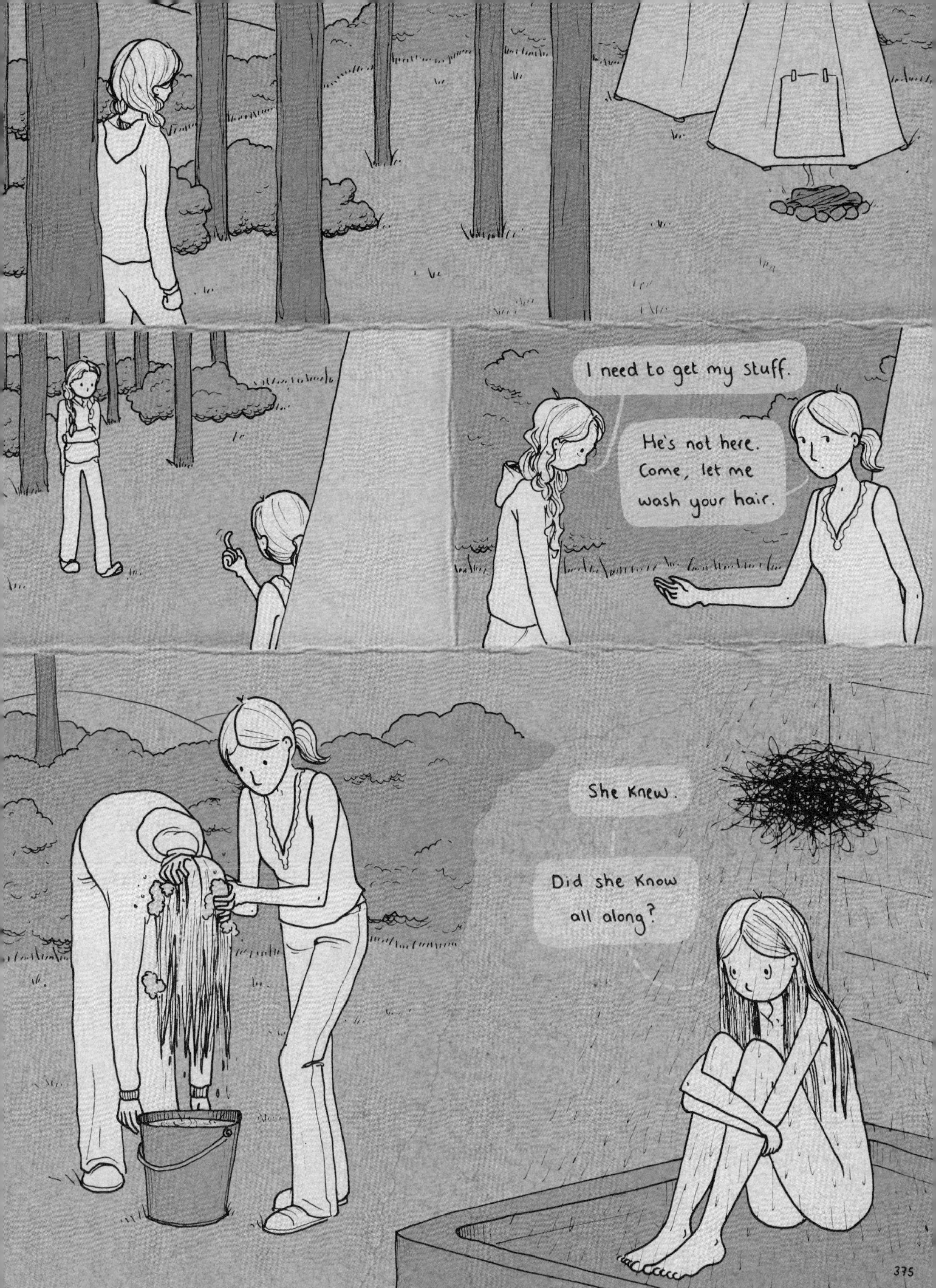
I need to get my stuff.
He's not here. Come, let me wash your hair.
She knew.
Did she know all along?

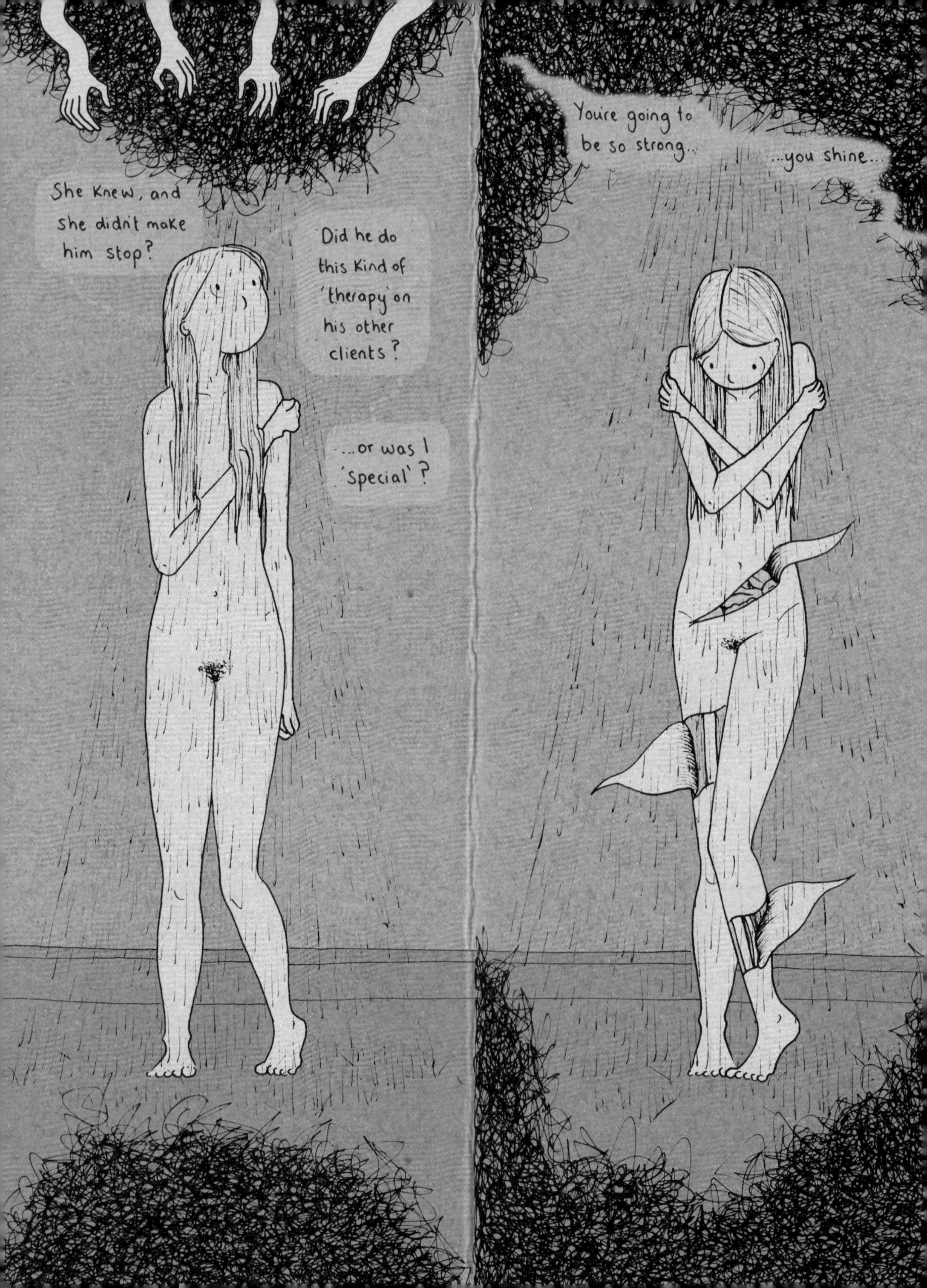
She Knew, and she didn't make him stop?
Did he do this Kind of 'therapy' on his other clients?
...or was I 'special'?
You're going to be so strong...
...you shine...

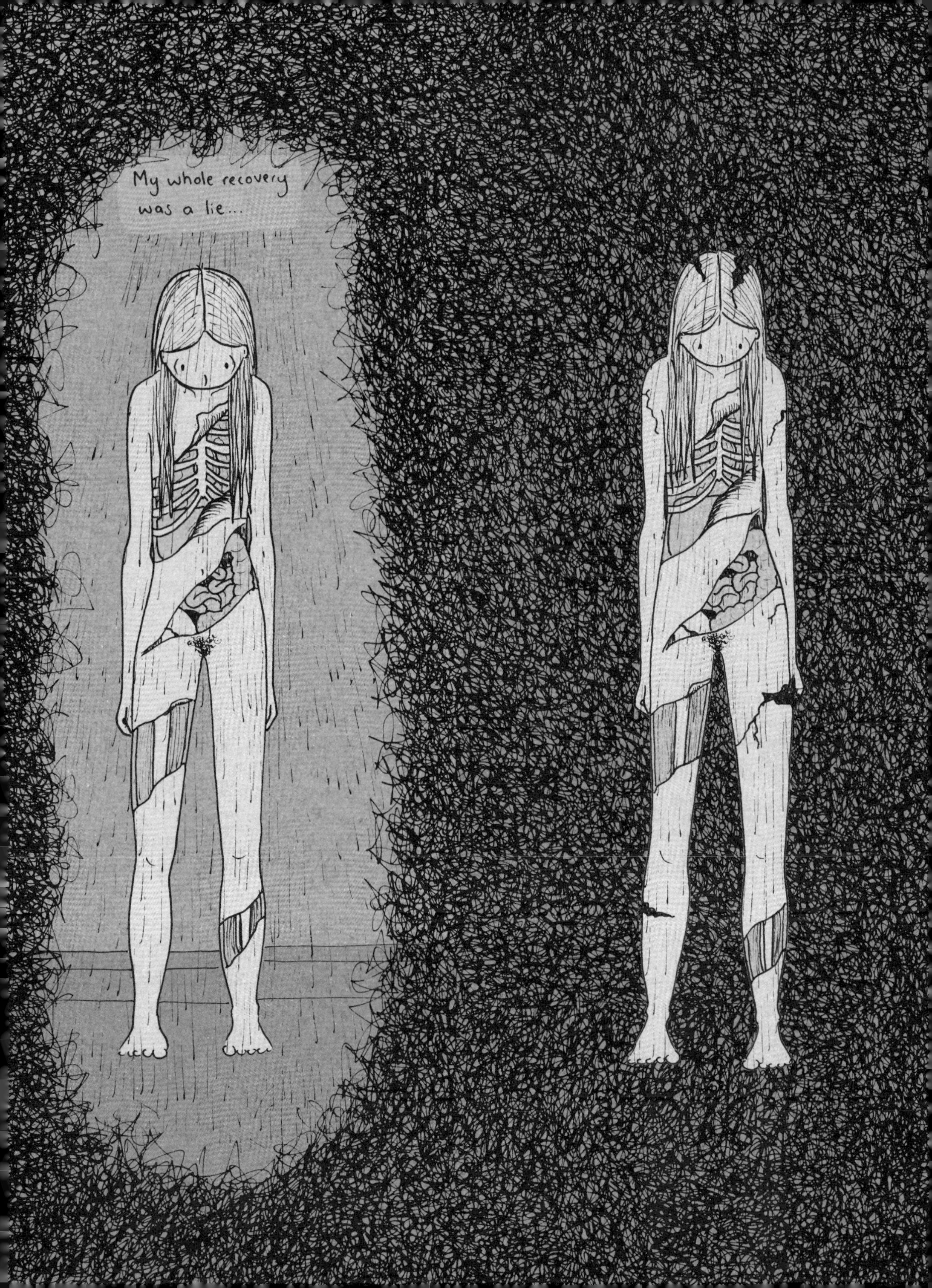
My whole recovery was a lie...

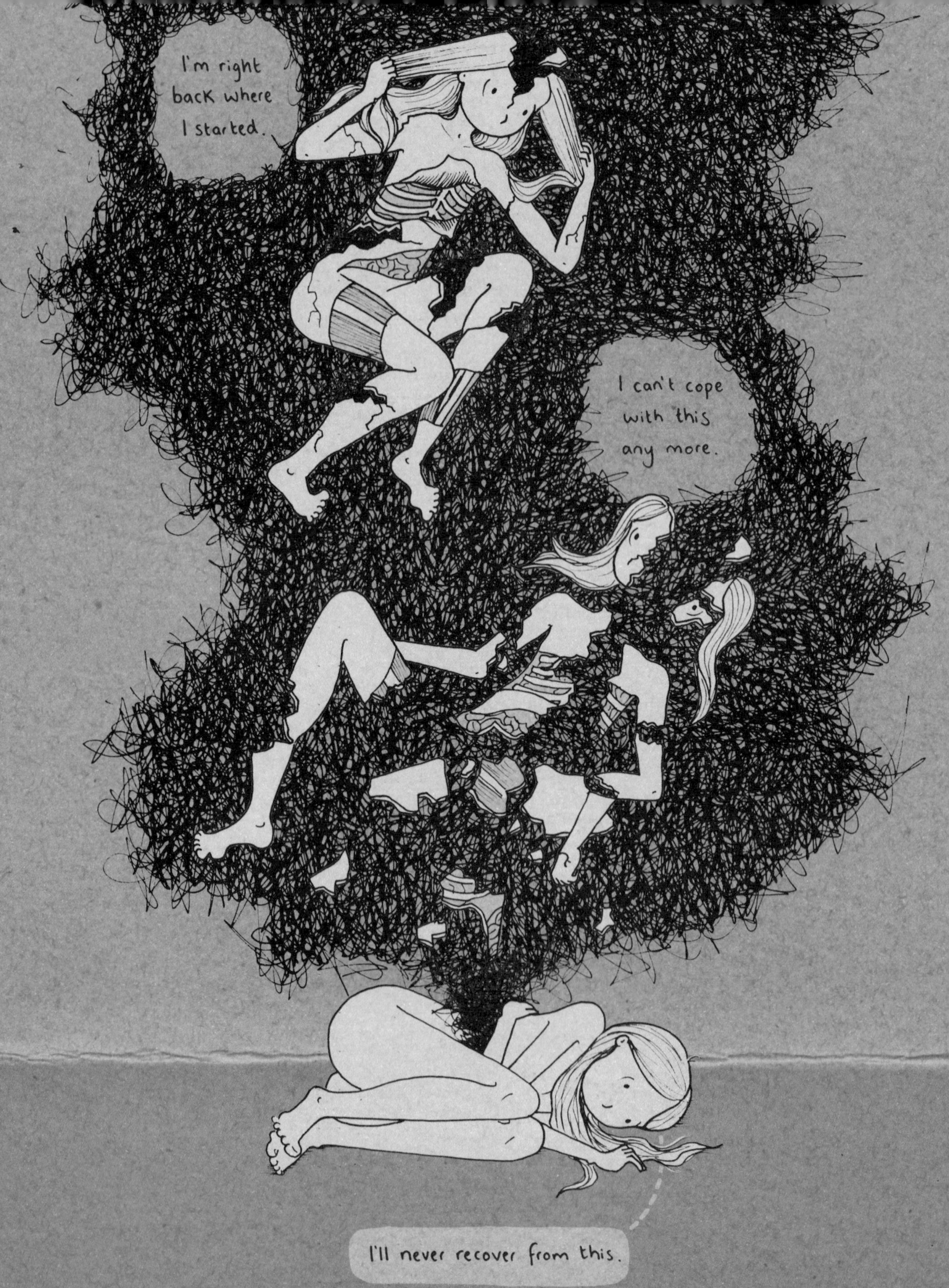
I'm right back where I started.
I can't cope with this any more.
I'll never recover from this.

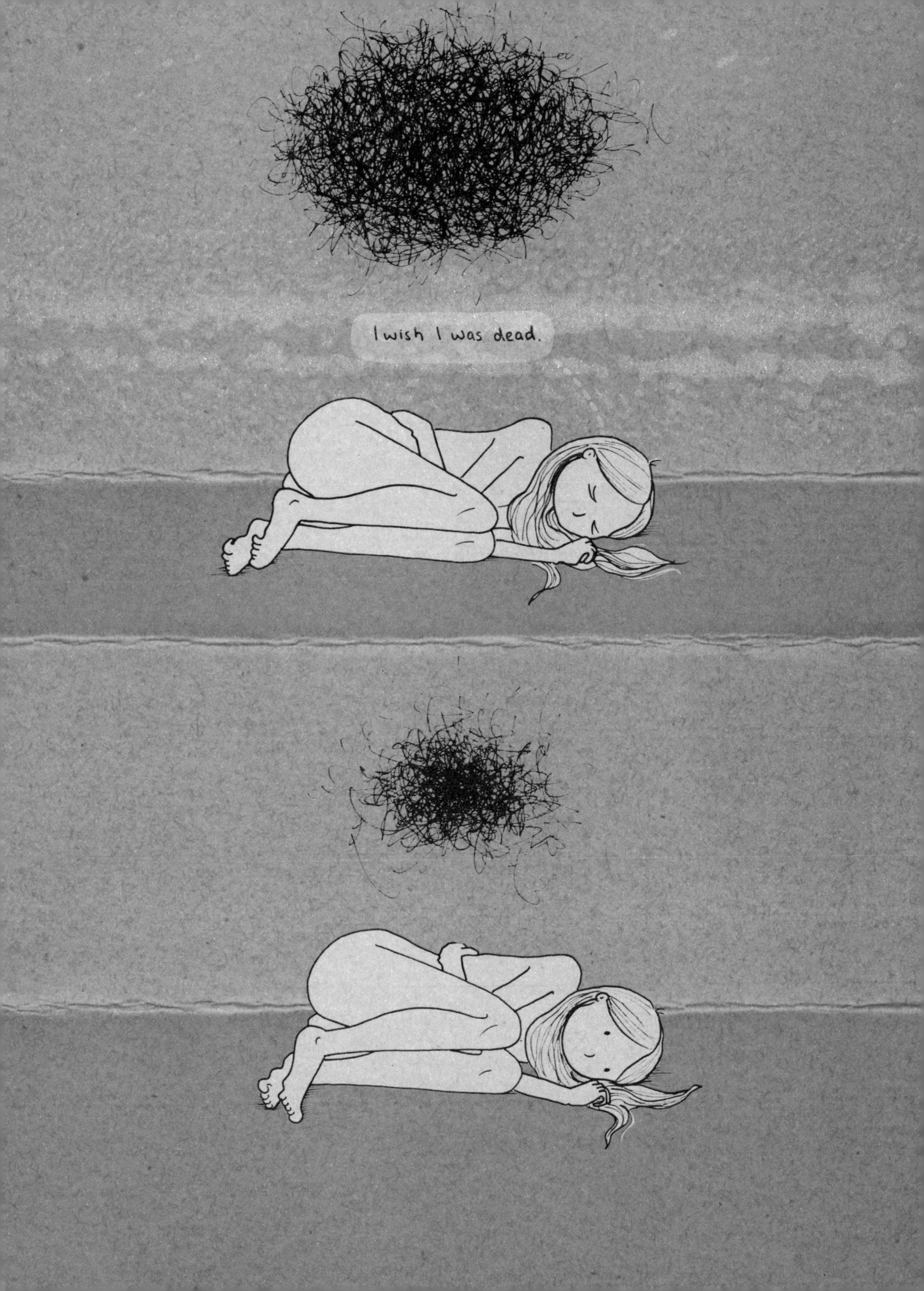
I wish I was dead.

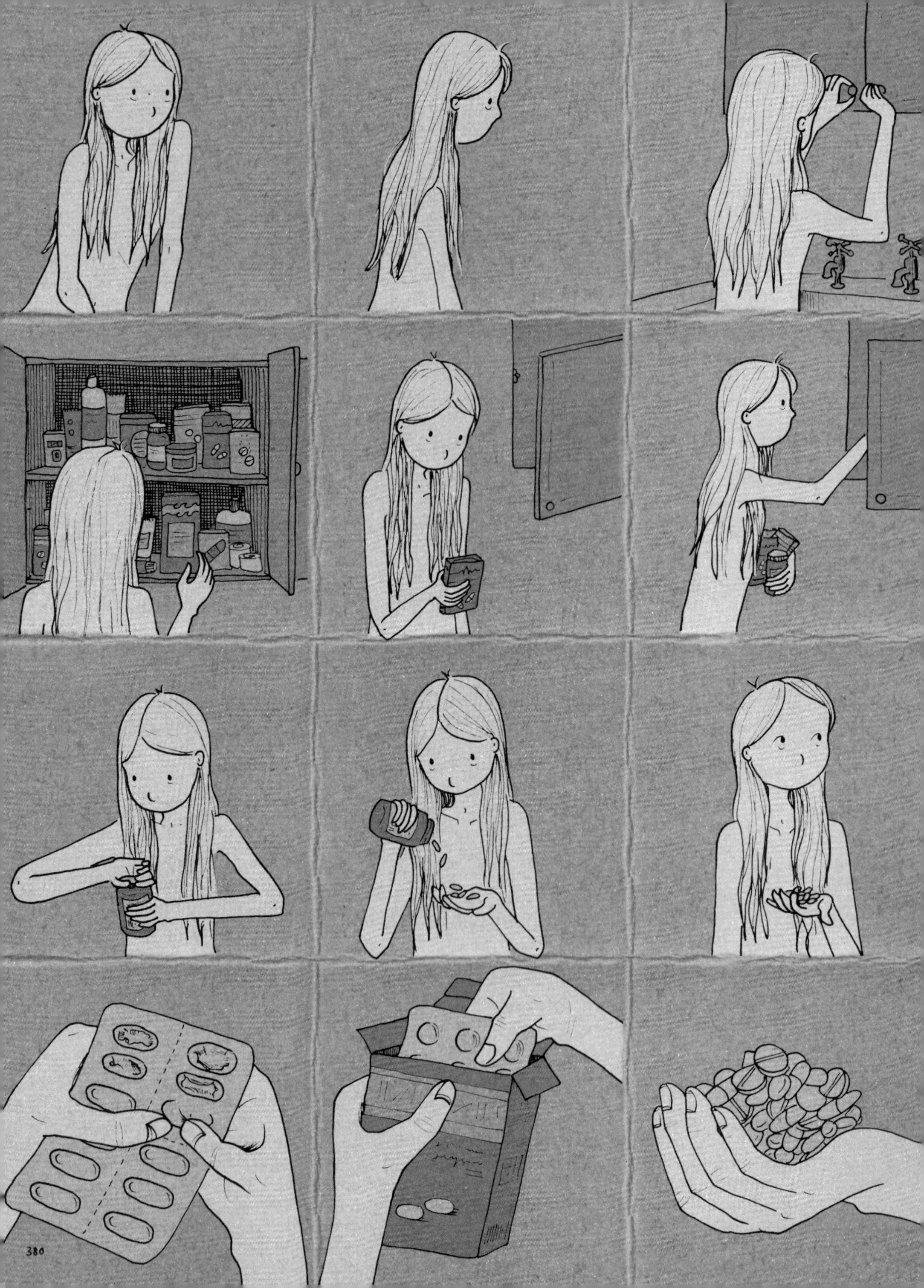

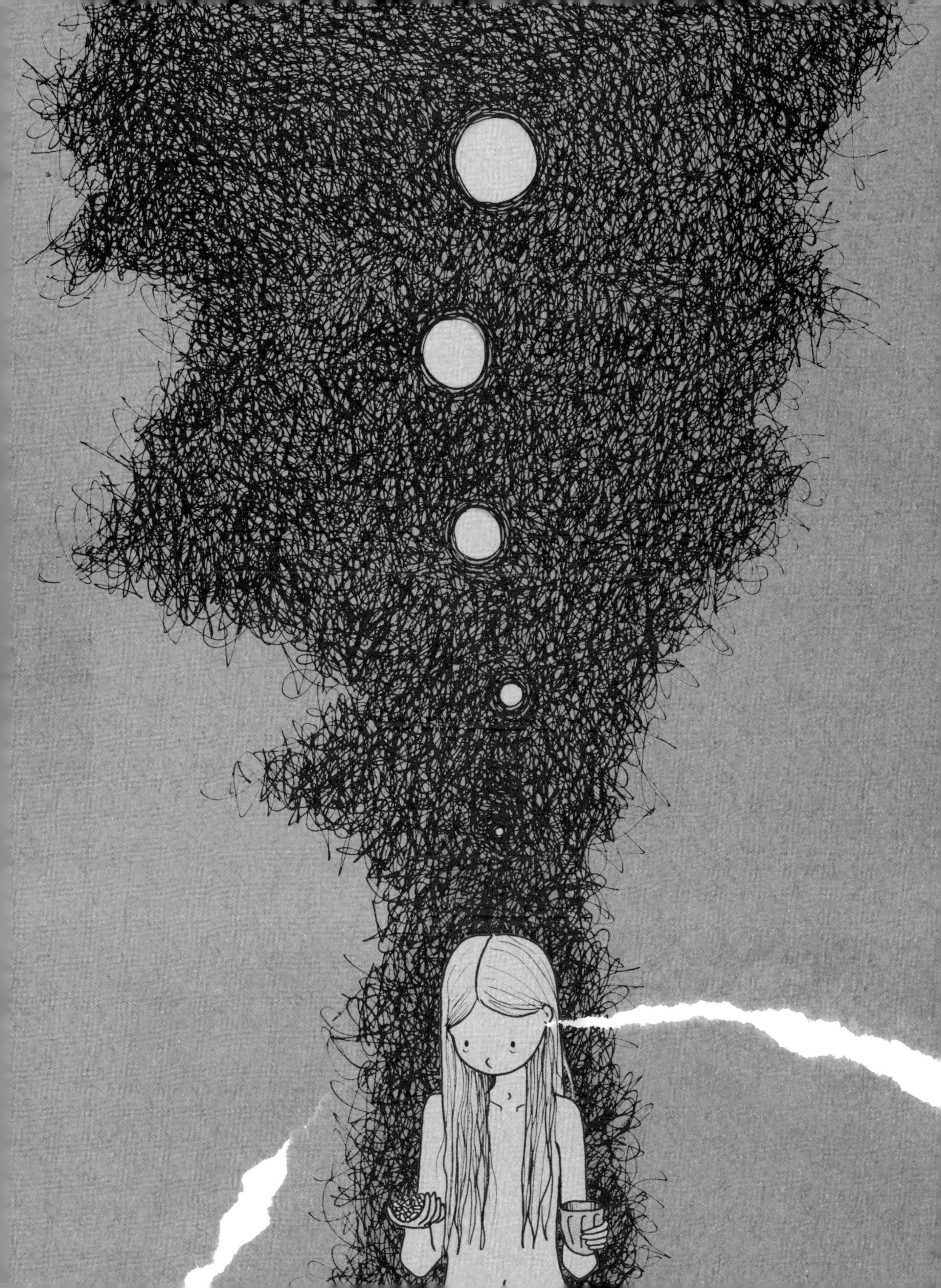

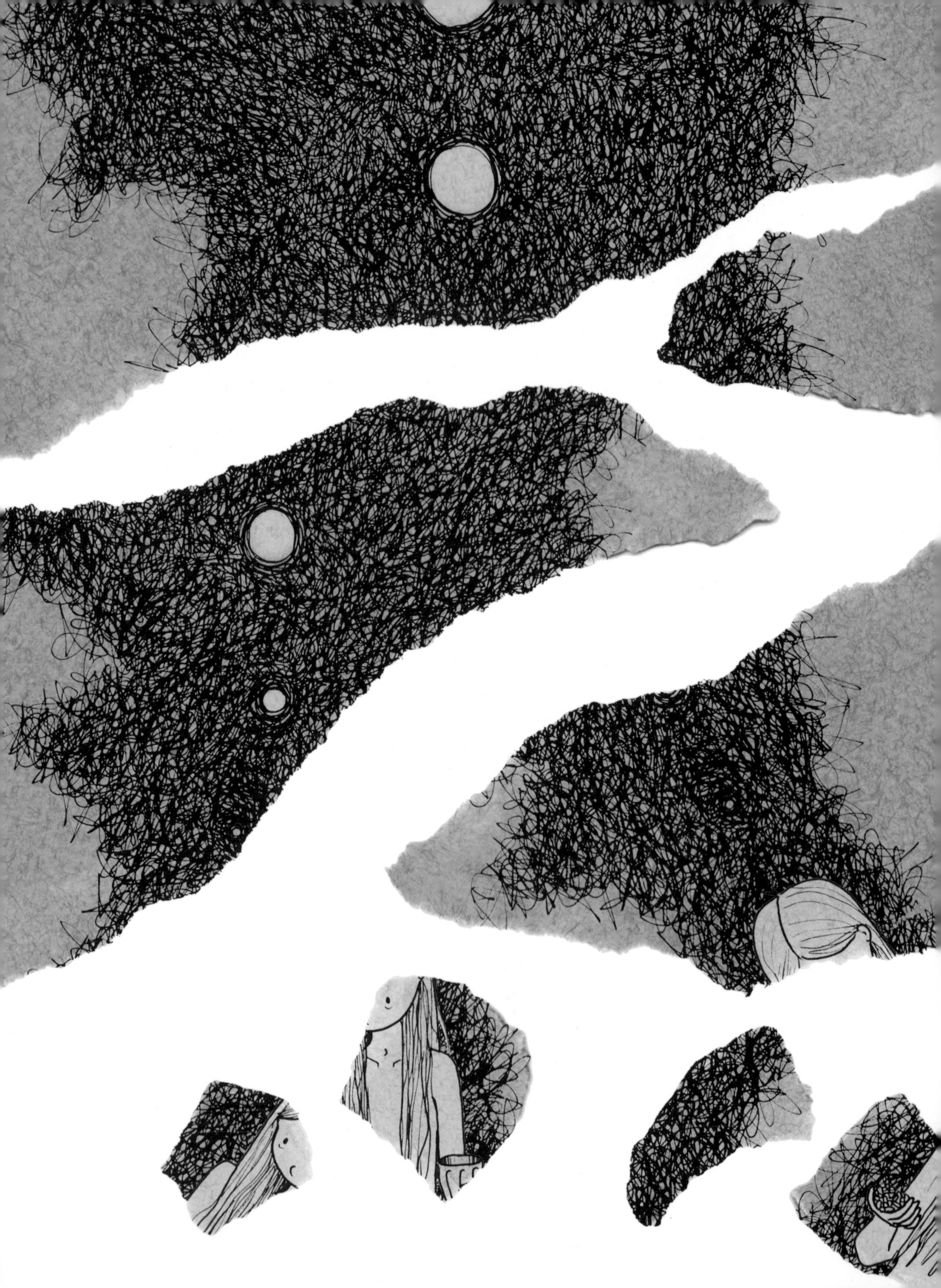

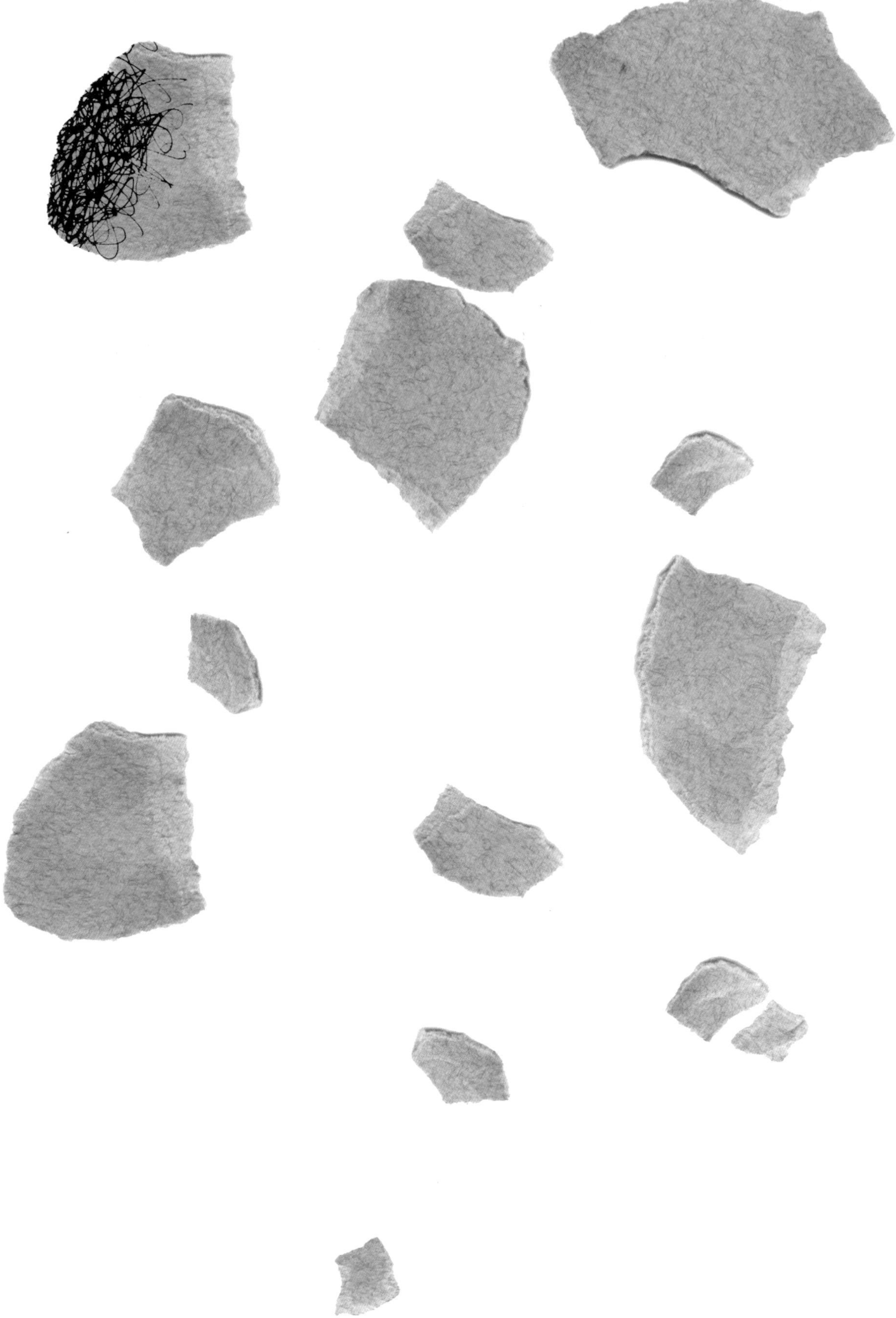

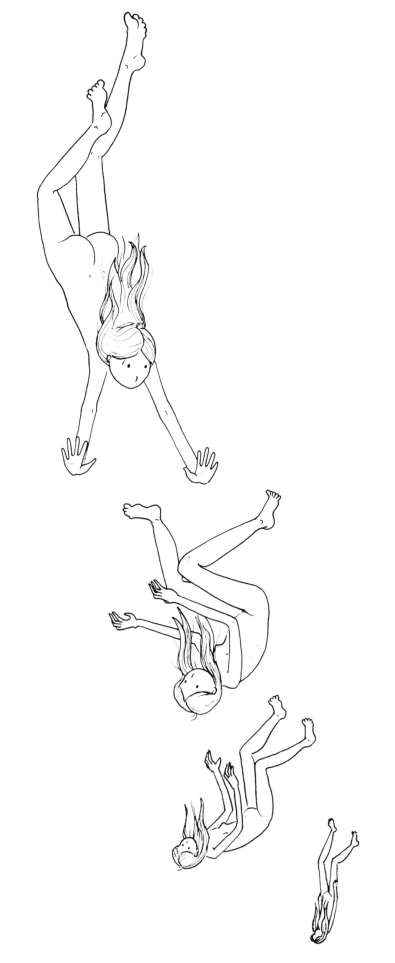

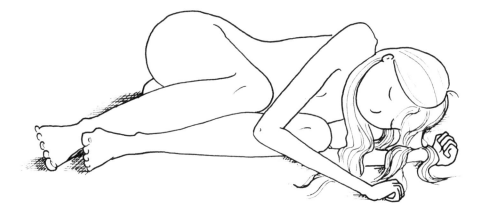

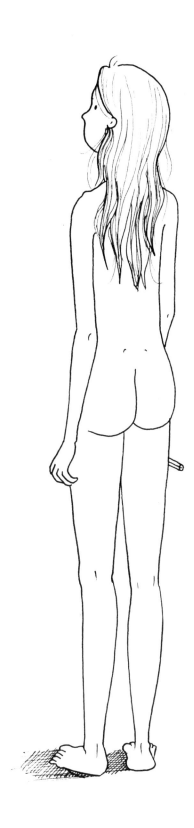

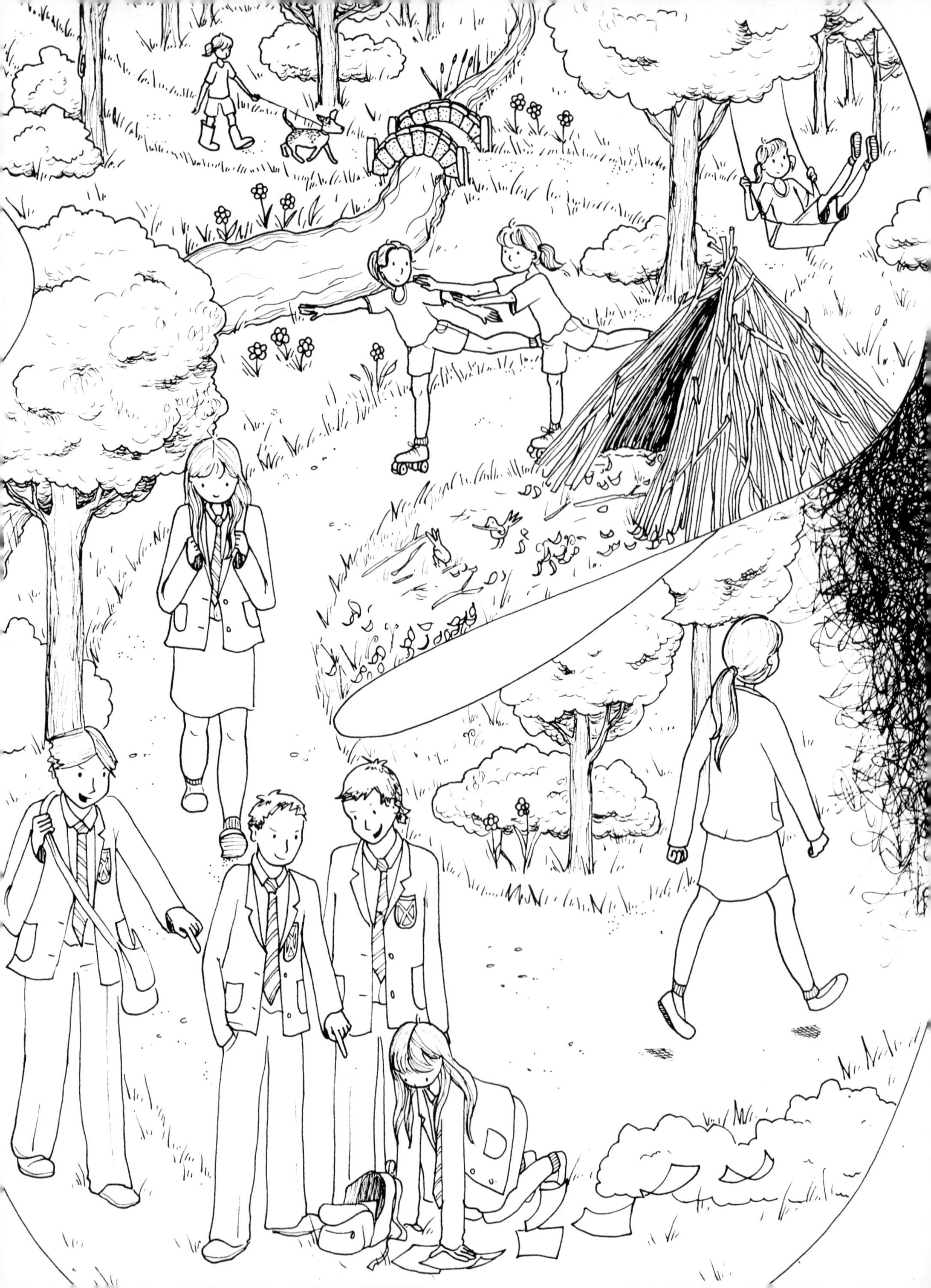

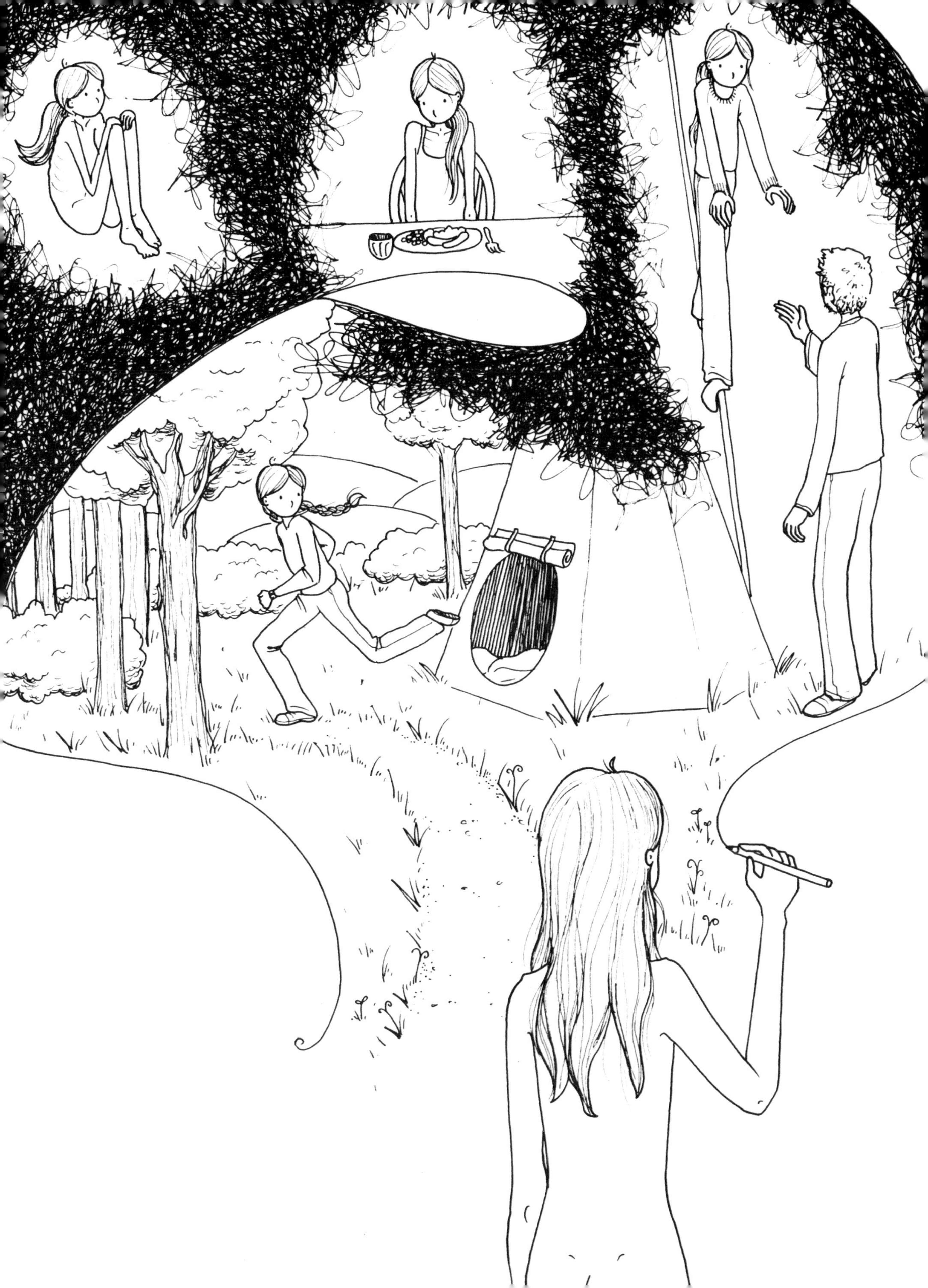

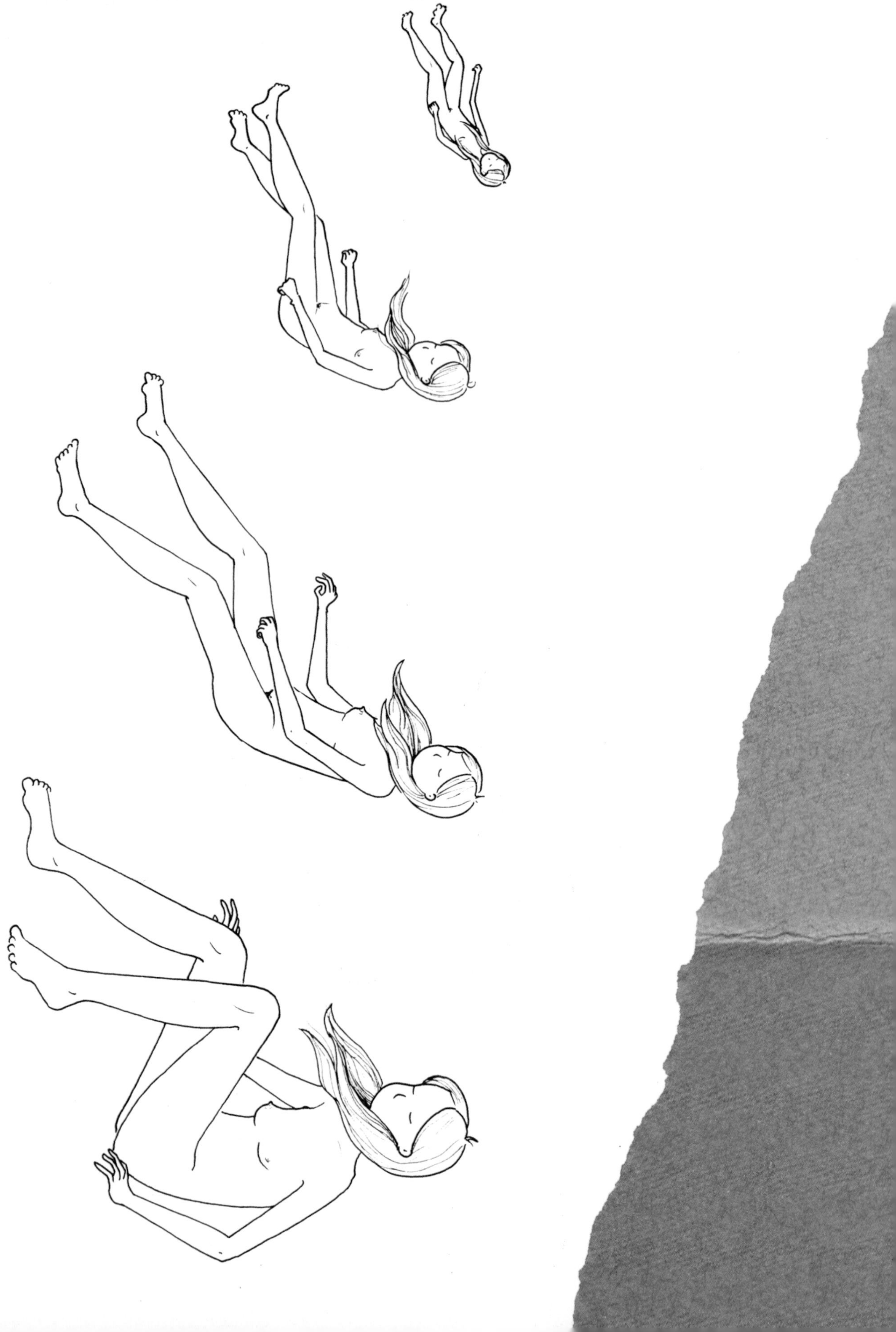

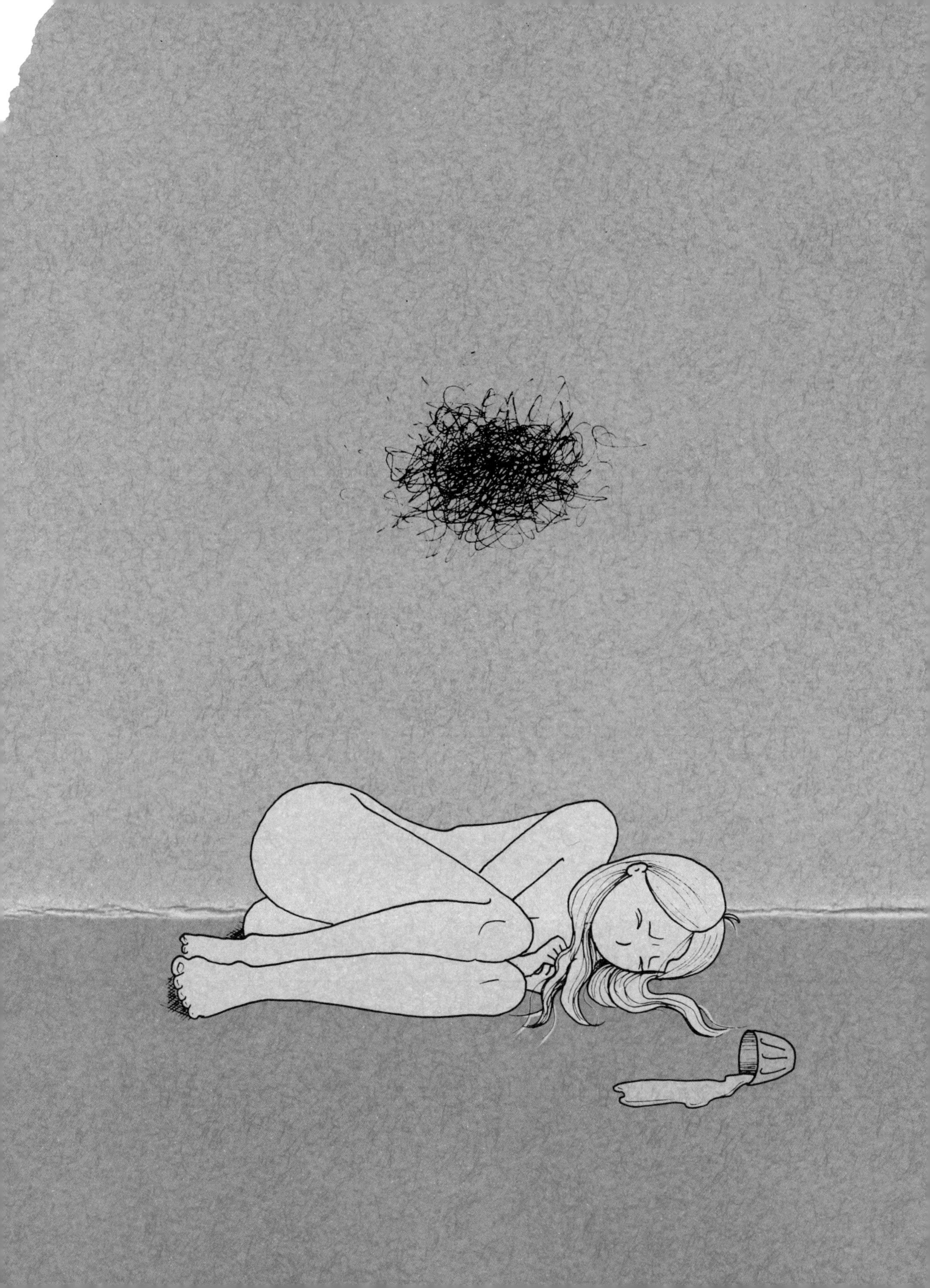

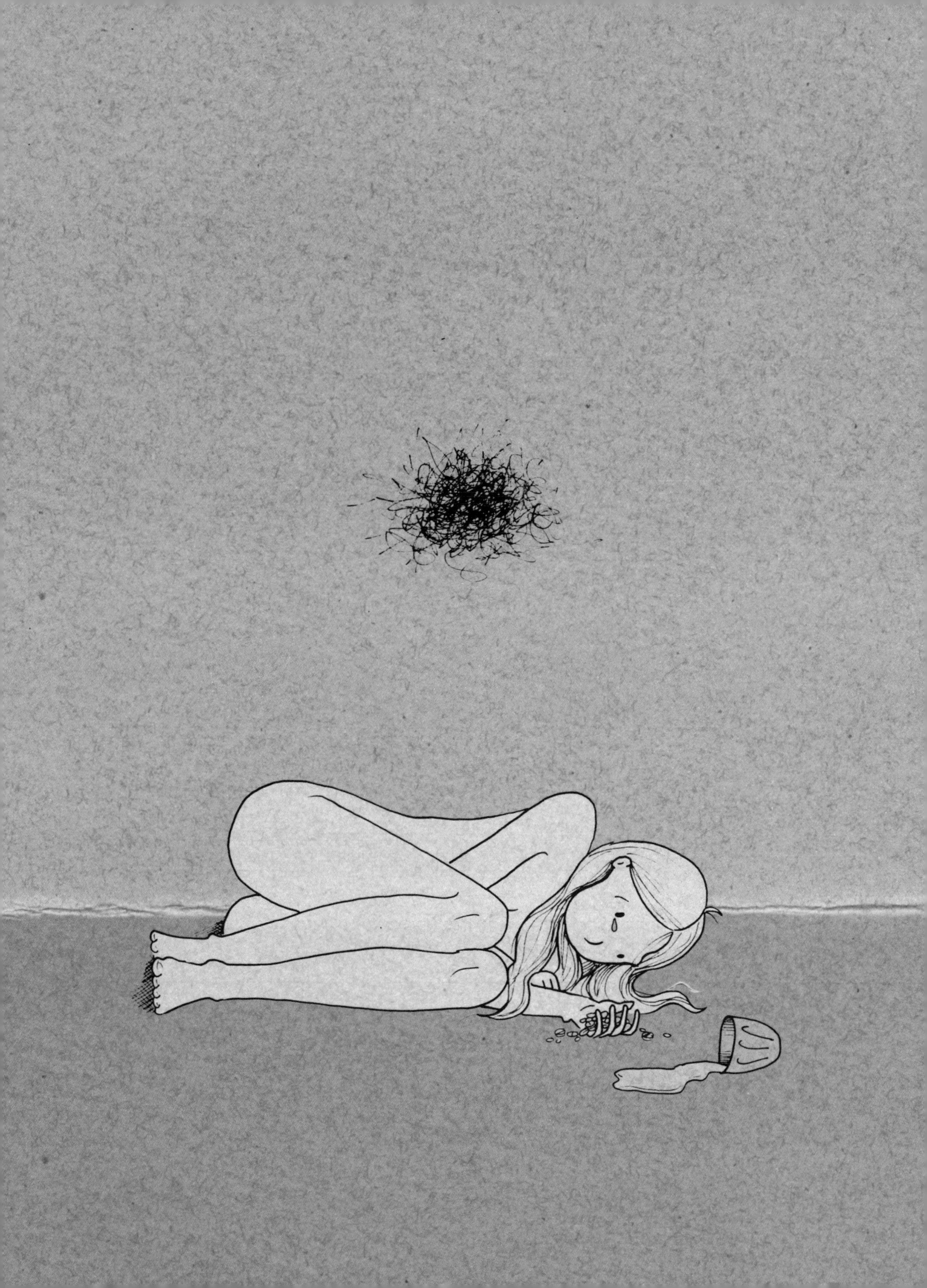

The months around that turning point are a muddle in my memory. Looking back, it's easy to think that things changed in that single moment. Certainly it's more dramatic to tell it that way. Though I don't remember much of when or how, I know I had to make that decision more than once. More than a few times.

In truth it was a process of gently reminding myself, every time I was drawn to the medicine cabinet, to sharp objects or high places: no, this is not what I want.

Sometimes the decision came easily, even with laughter: Oh, here we are again. No, not today thank you. Other times it took every strength I had left. Clutching on, telling myself over and over and over the only things I could hold on to.

I want to live.

I want to draw.

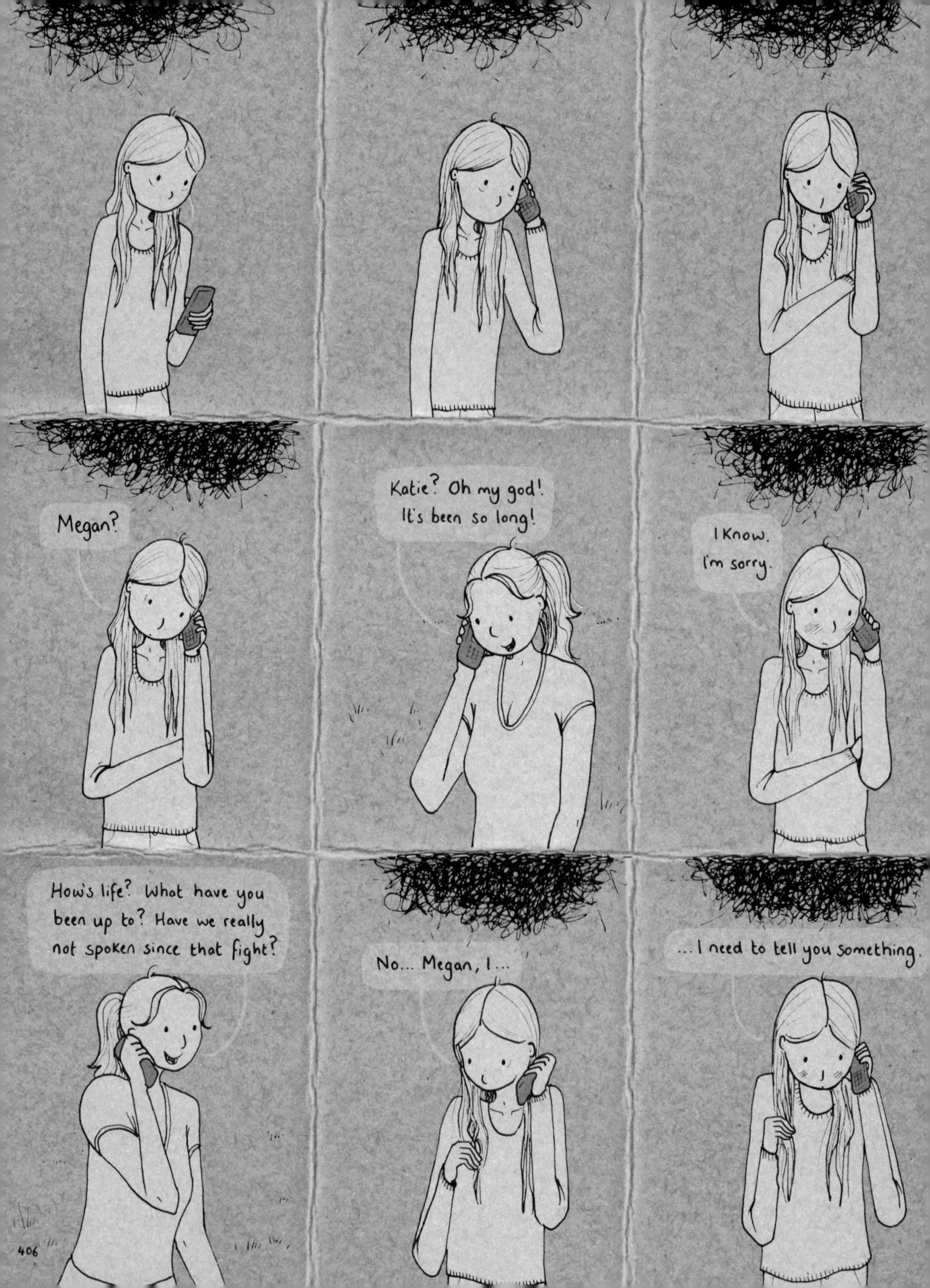
Megan?
Katie? Oh my god! It's been so long!
I Know. I'm sorry.
How's life? What have you been up to? Have we really not spoken since that fight?
No... Megan, I...
...I need to tell you something.

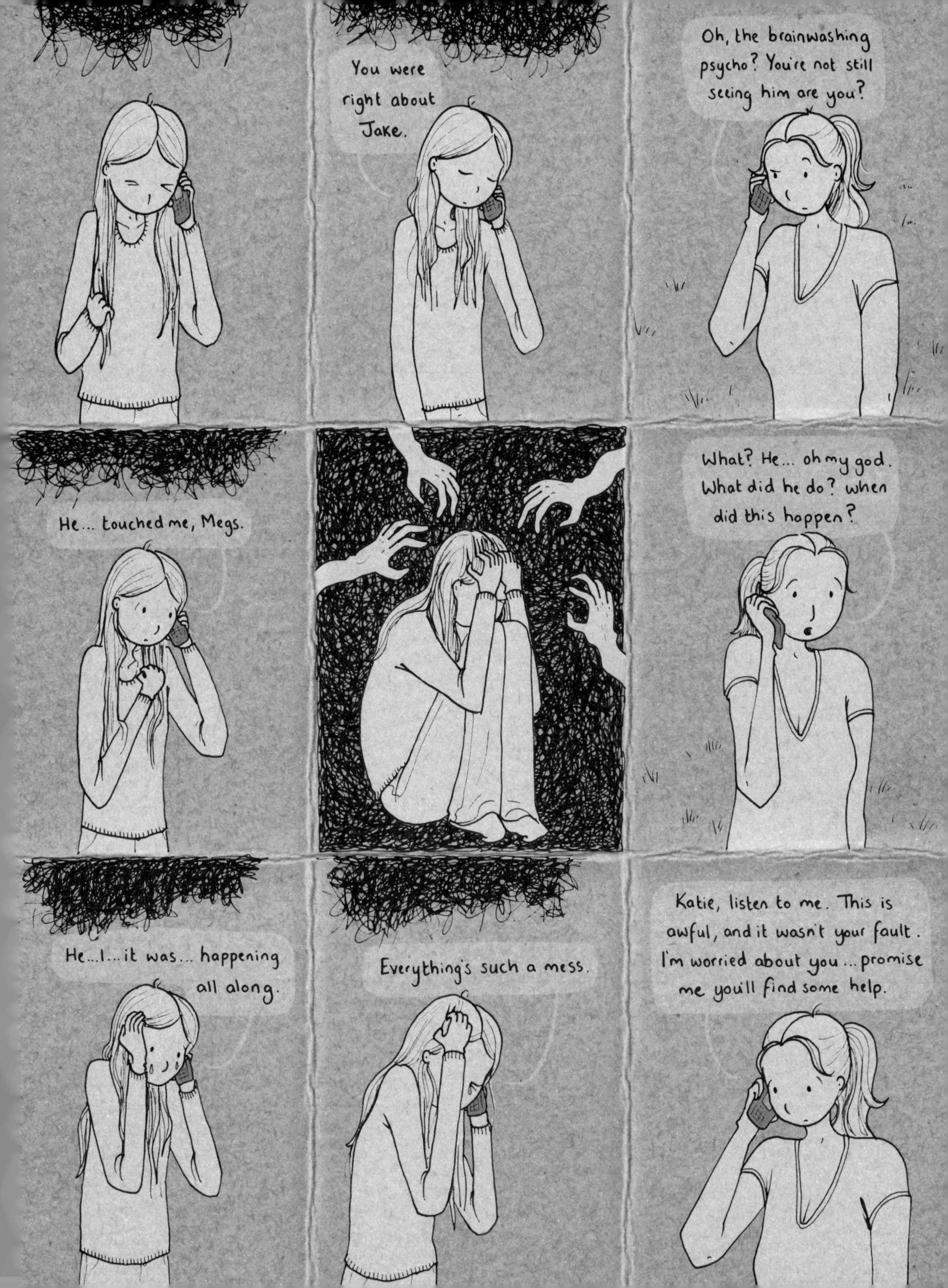
You were right about Jake.
Oh, the brainwashing psycho? You're not still seeing him are you?
He... touched me, Megs.
What? He... oh my god. What did he do? when did this happen?
He...I...it was... happening all along.
Everything's such a mess.
Katie, listen to me. This is awful, and it wasn't your fault. I'm worried about you ... promise me you'll find some help.

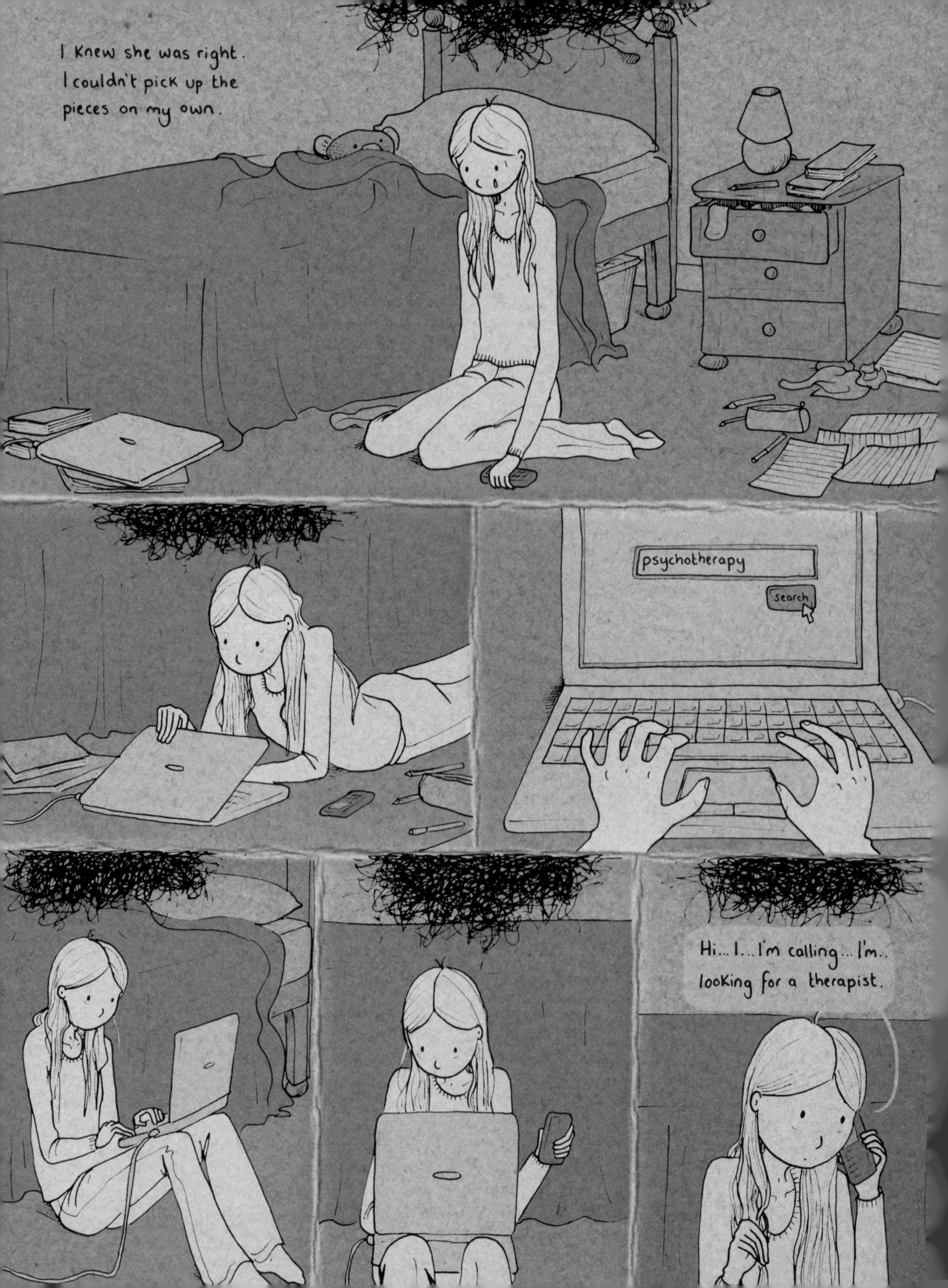
I knew she was right.
I couldn't pick up the pieces on my own.
psychotherapy
search
Hi... I... I'm calling... I'm.. looking for a therapist.

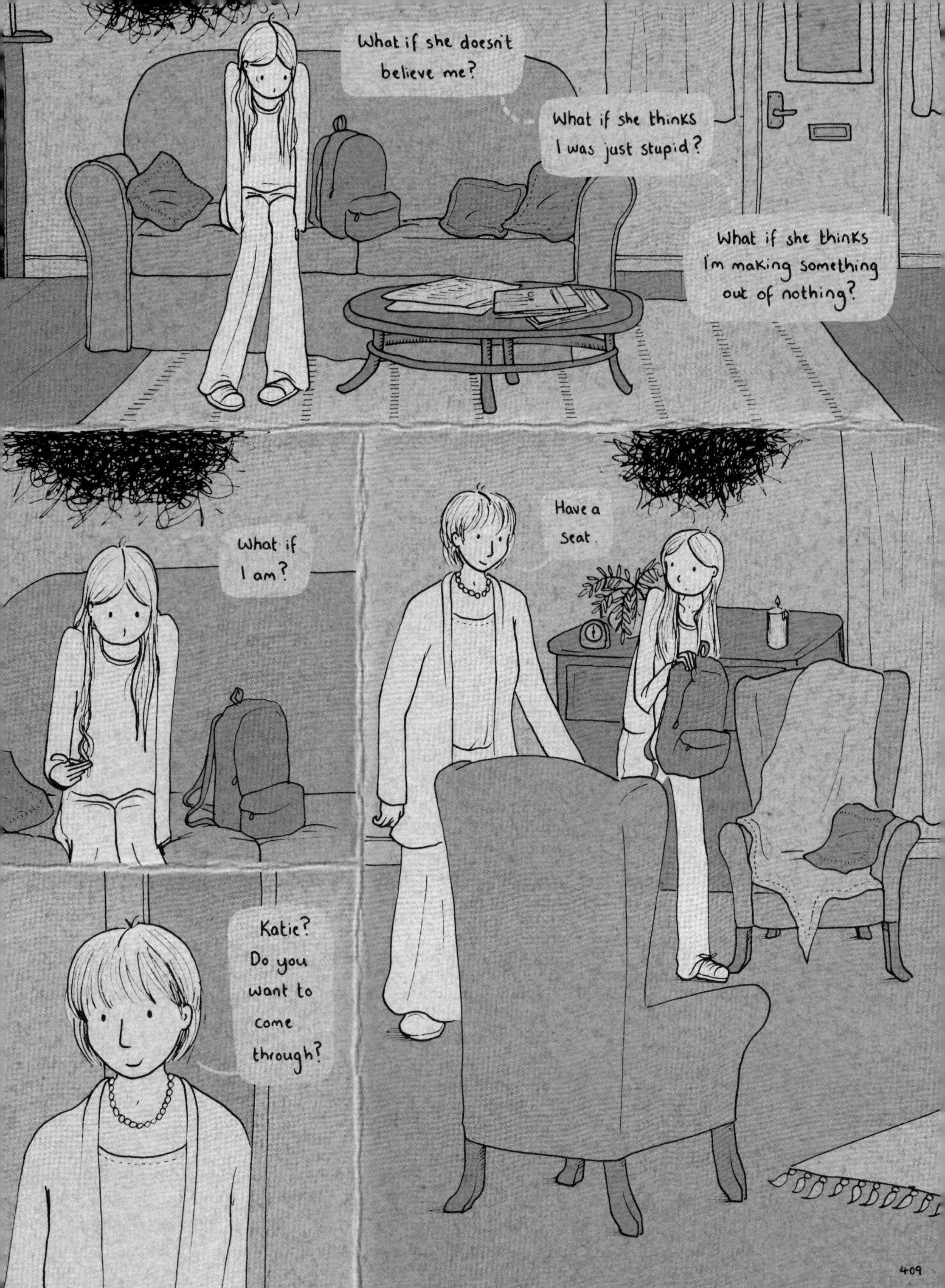
What if she doesn't believe me?
What if she thinks I was just stupid?
What if she thinks I'm making something out of nothing?
What if I am?
Katie? Do you want to come through?
Have a seat.

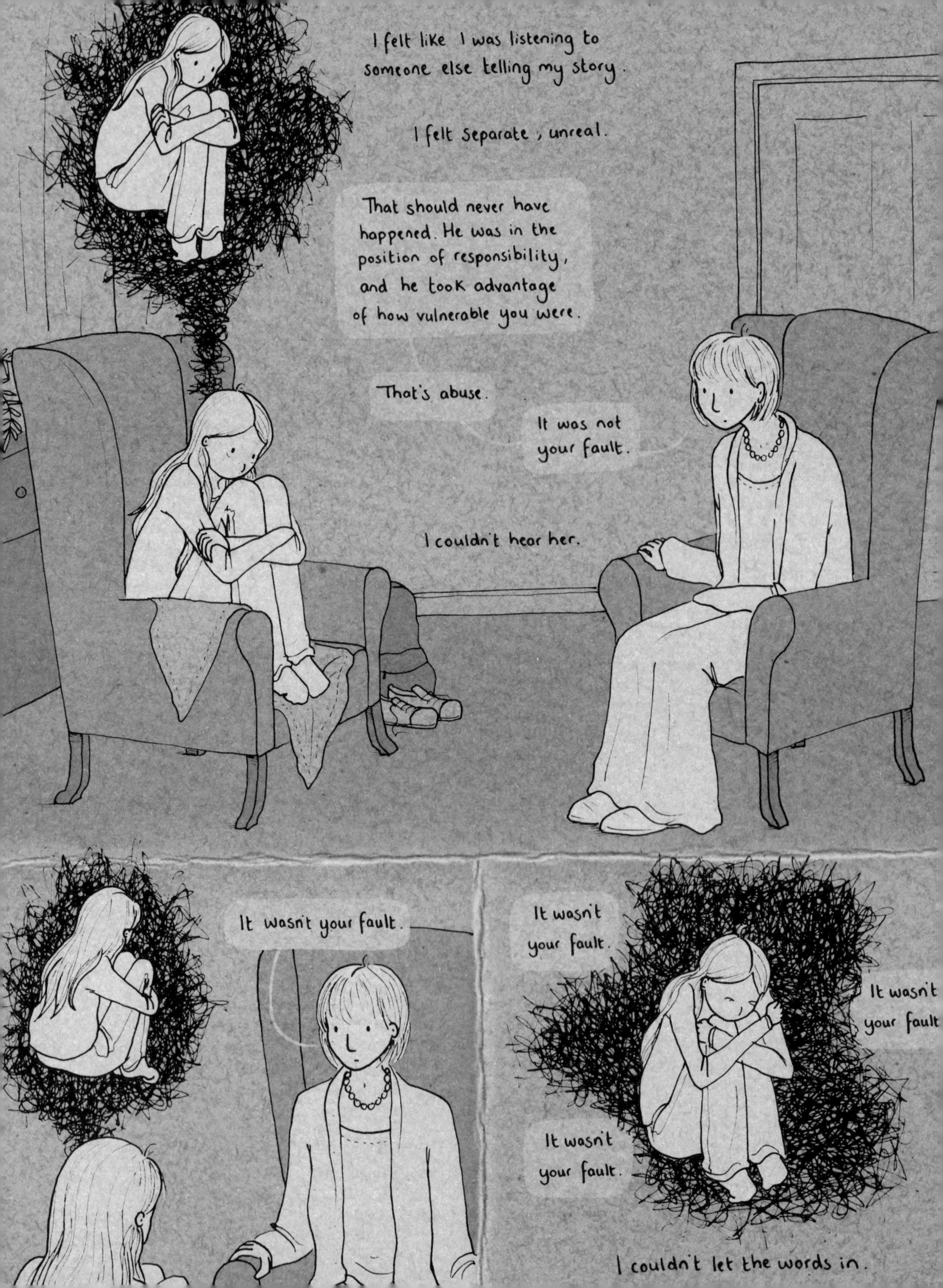
I felt like I was listening to someone else telling my story.
I felt separate, unreal.
That should never have happened. He was in the position of responsibility, and he took advantage of how vulnerable you were.
That's abuse.
It was not your fault.
I couldn't hear her.
It wasn't your fault.
It wasn't your fault.
It wasn't your fault
It wasn't your fault.
I couldn't let the words in.

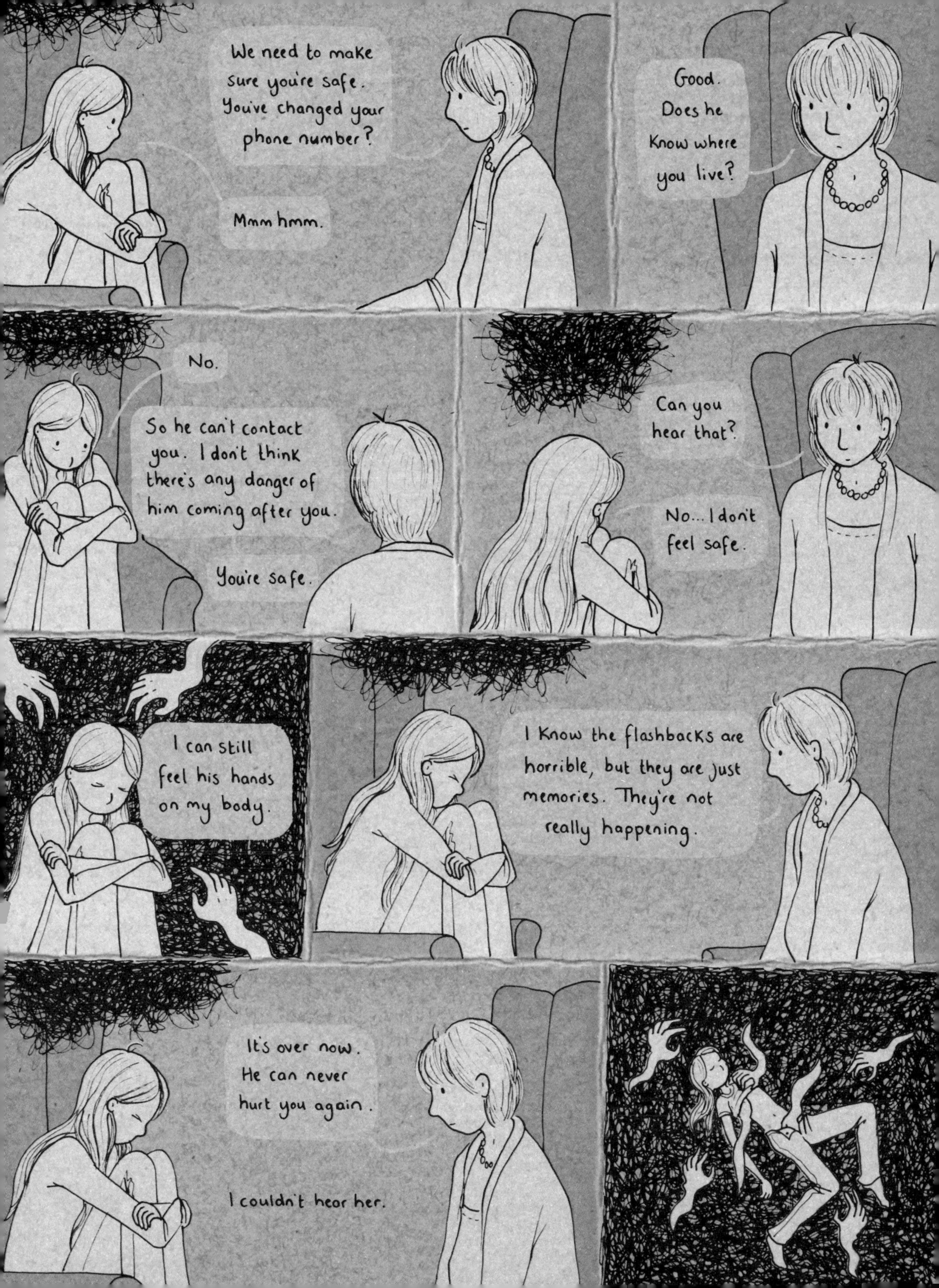
We need to make sure you're safe. You've changed your phone number?
Mmm hmm.
Good. Does he know where you live?
No.
So he can't contact you. I don't think there's any danger of him coming after you.
You're safe.
Can you hear that?
No... I don't feel safe.
I can still feel his hands on my body.
I know the flashbacks are horrible, but they are just memories. They're not really happening.
It's over now. He can never hurt you again.
I couldn't hear her.

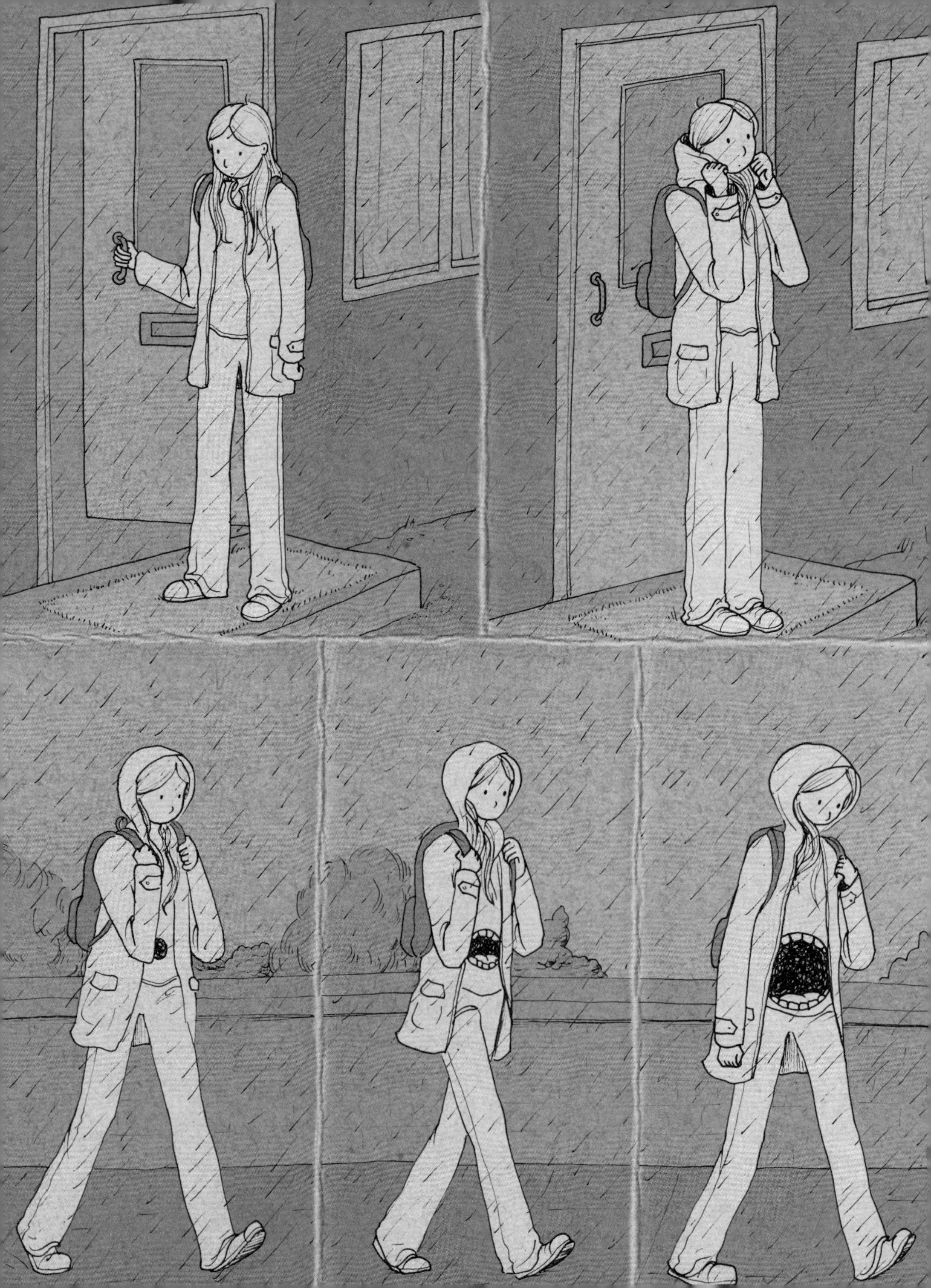

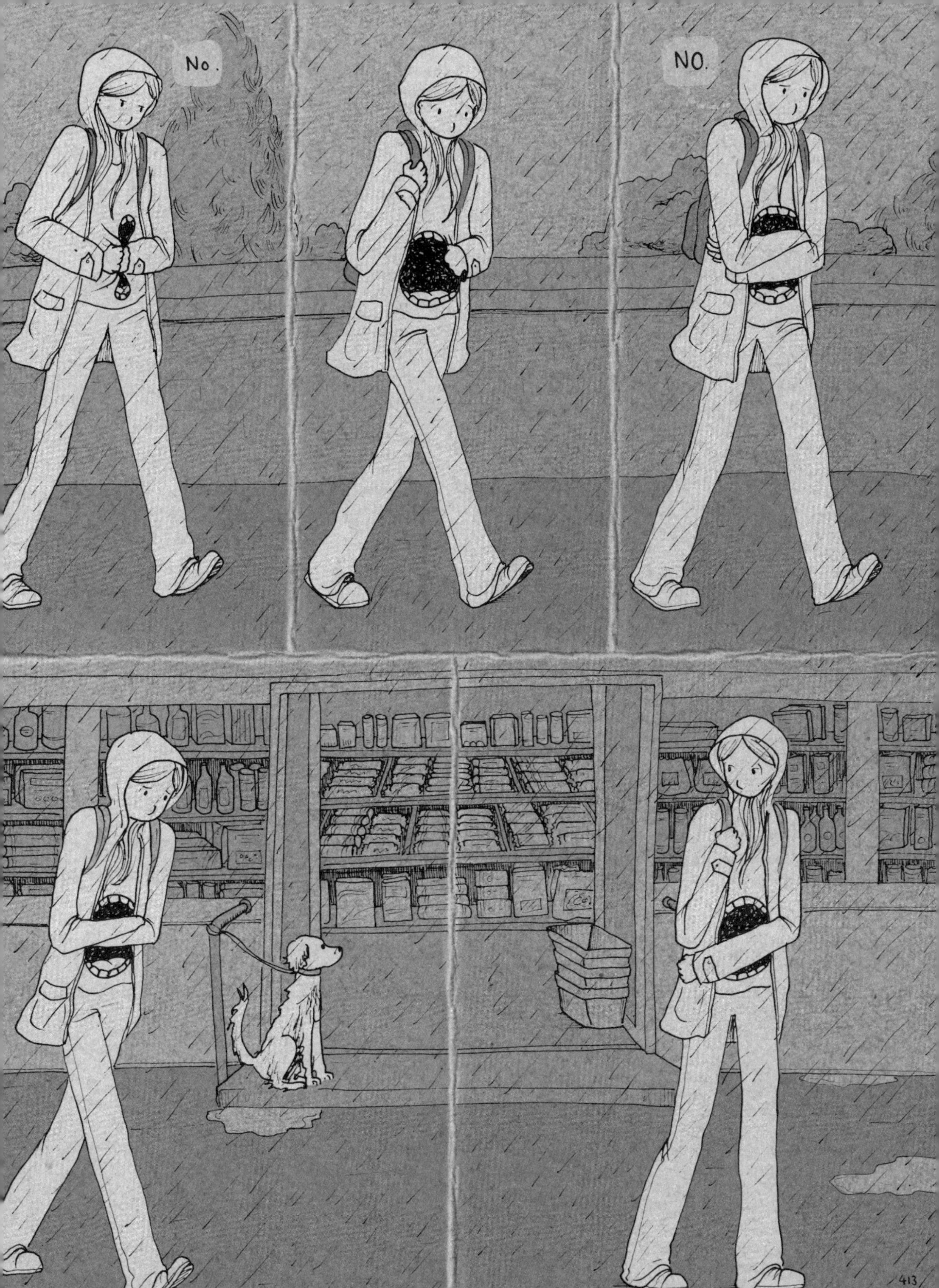
No.
NO.

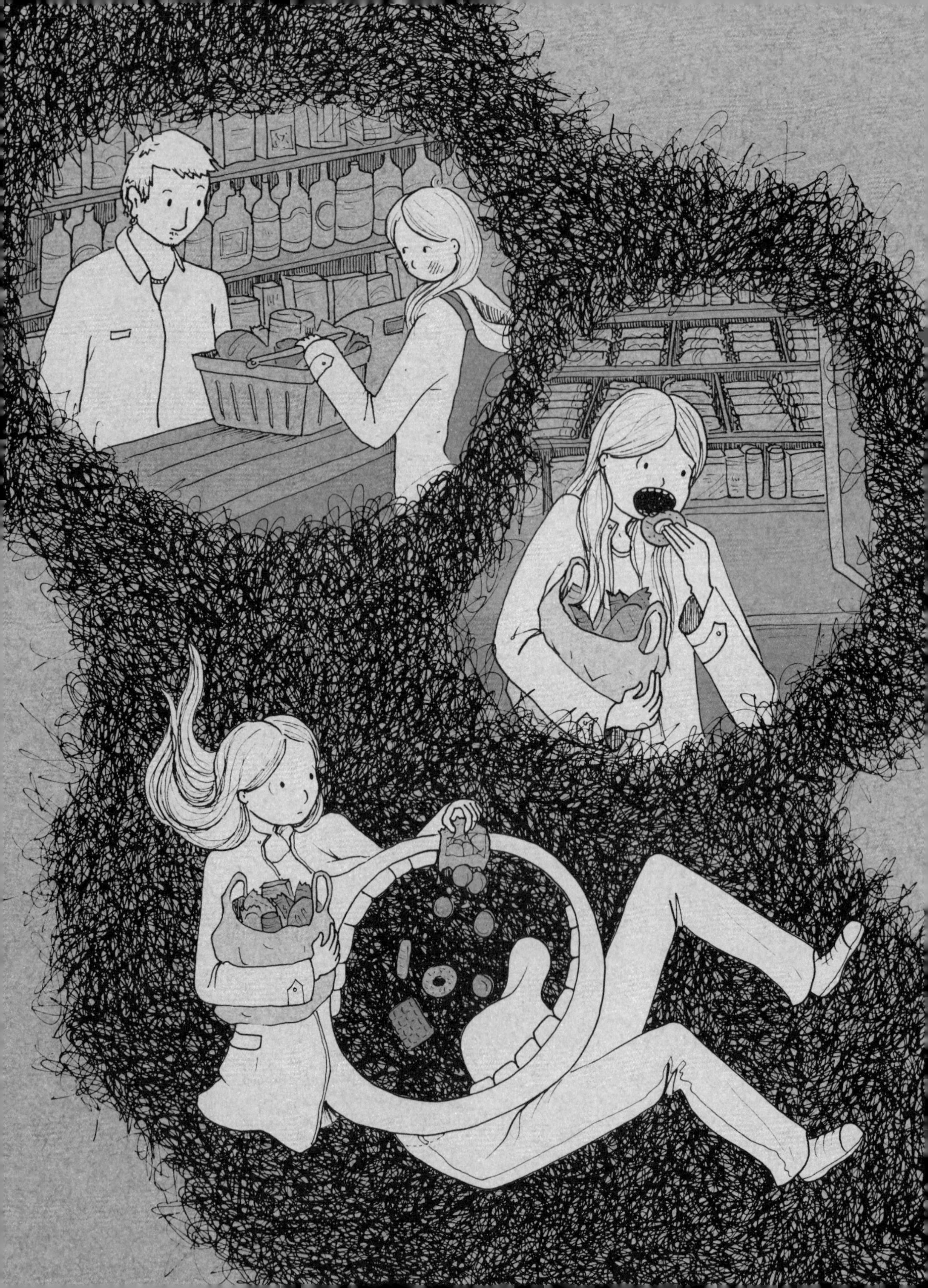

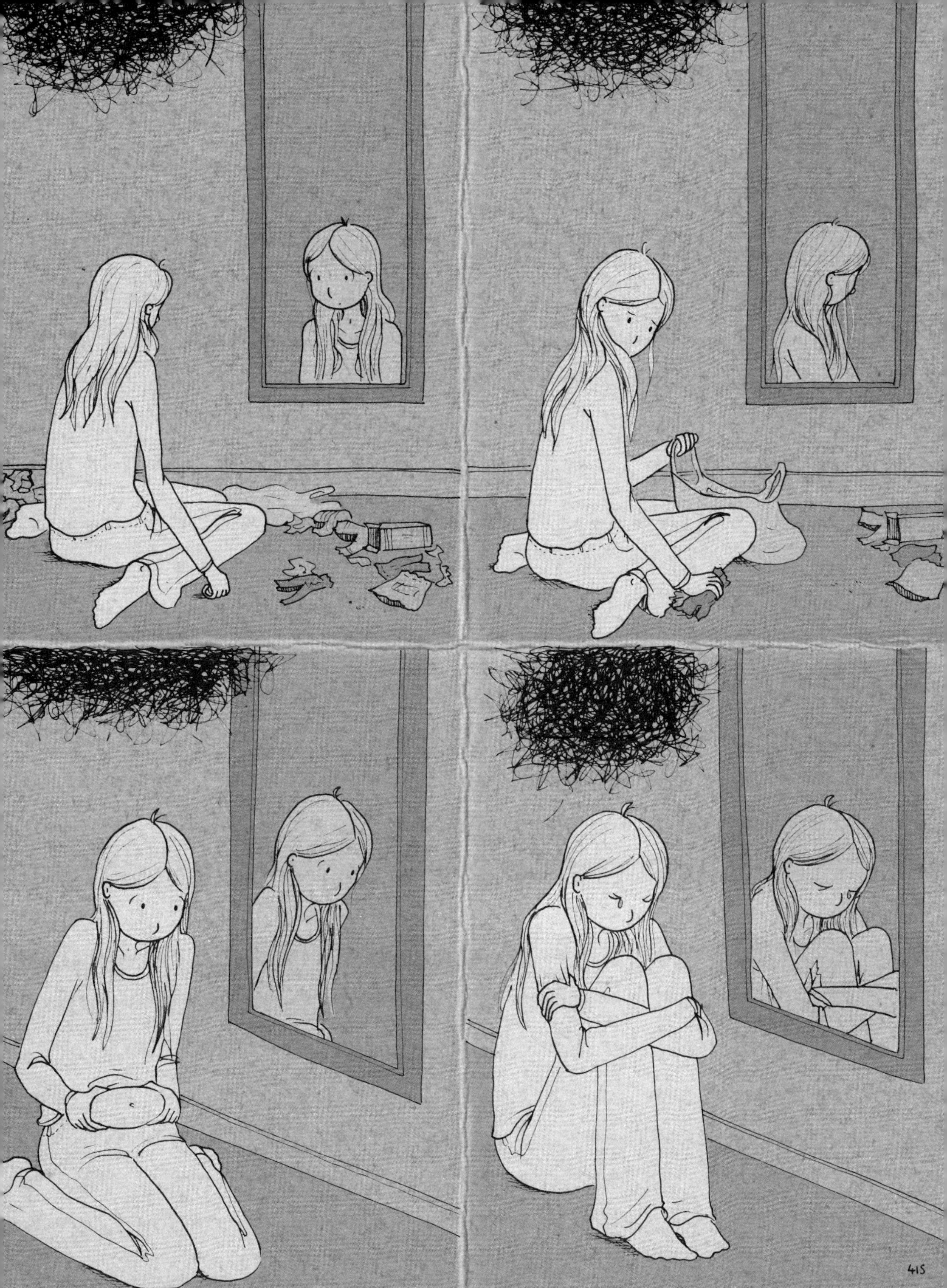

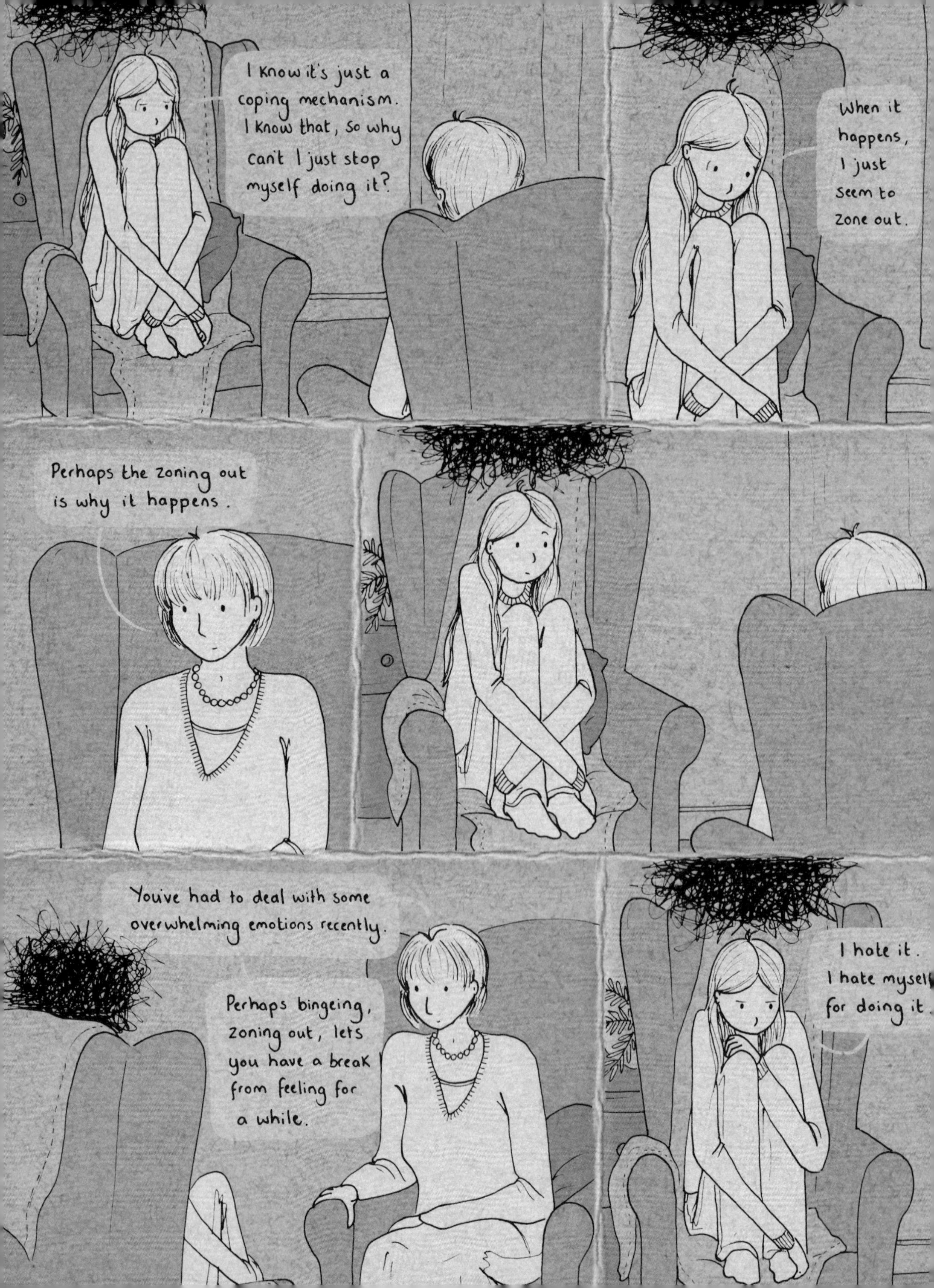
I know it's just a coping mechanism. I know that, so why can't I just stop myself doing it?
When it happens, I just seem to zone out.
Perhaps the zoning out is why it happens.
You've had to deal with some overwhelming emotions recently.
Perhaps bingeing, zoning out, lets you have a break from feeling for a while.
I hate it. I hate myself for doing it.

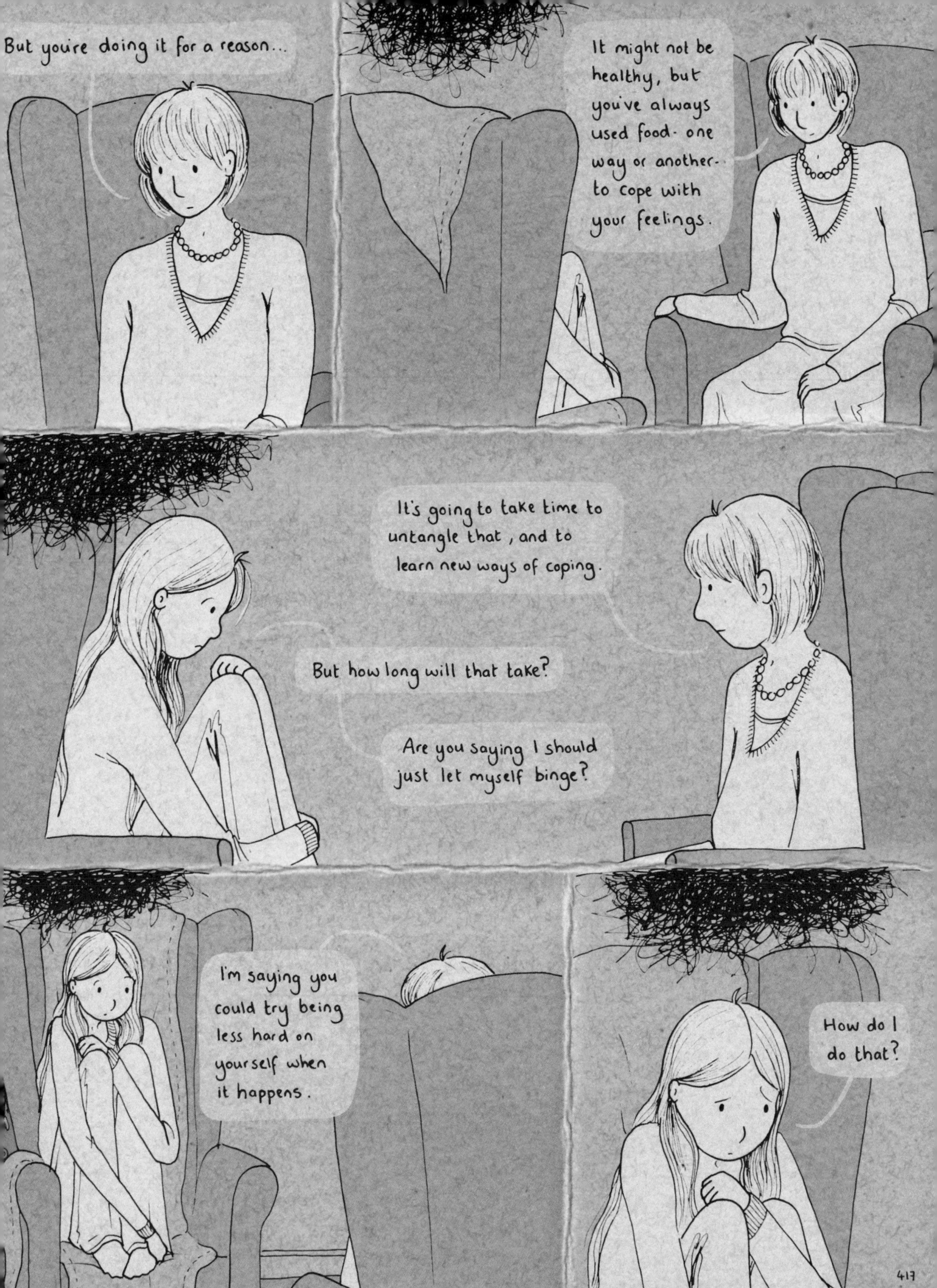
But you're doing it for a reason...
It might not be healthy, but you've always used food- one way or another- to cope with your feelings.
It's going to take time to untangle that, and to learn new ways of coping.
But how long will that take?
Are you saying I should just let myself binge?
I'm saying you could try being less hard on yourself when it happens.
How do I do that?

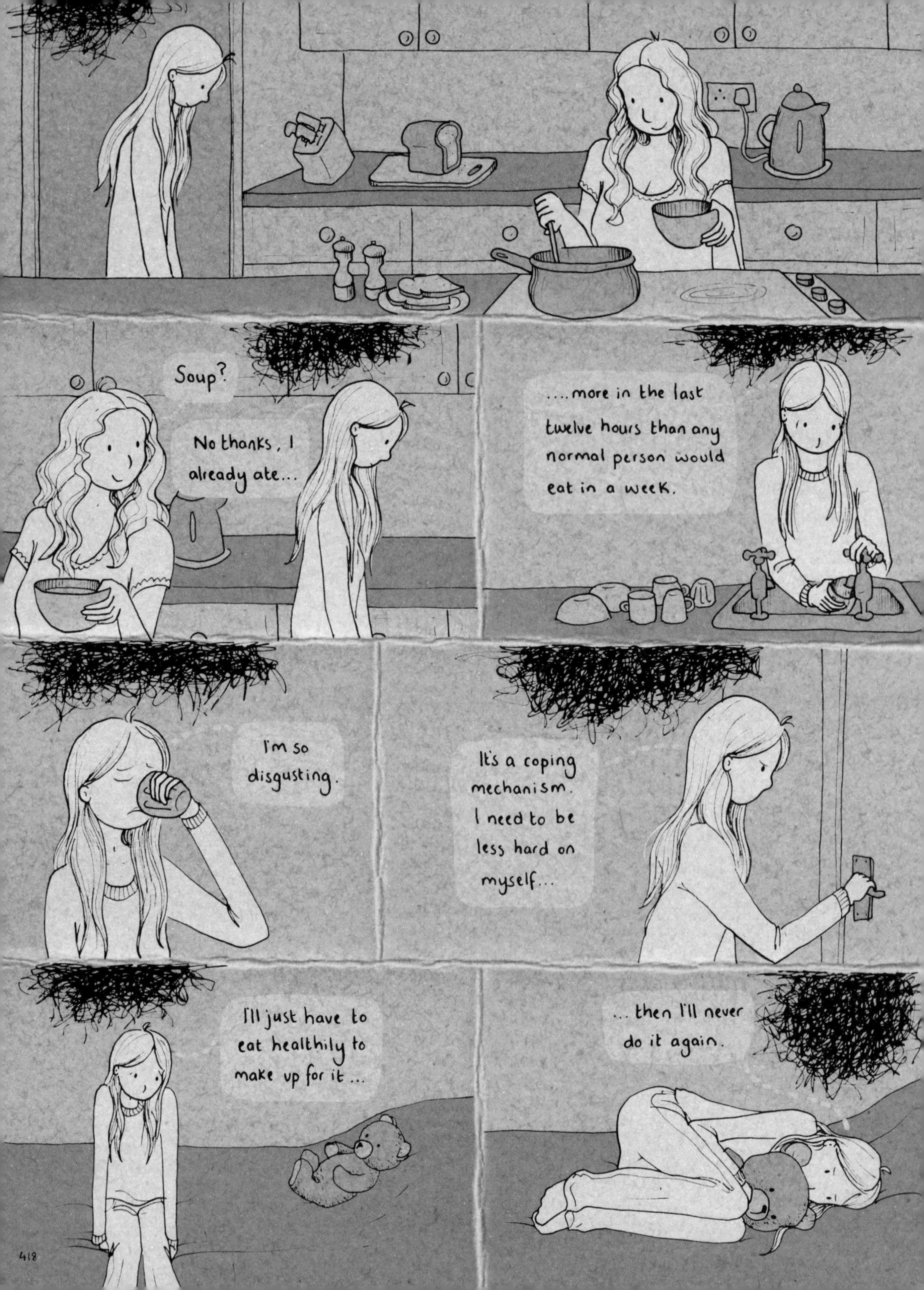
Soup?
No thanks, I already ate...
....more in the last twelve hours than any normal person would eat in a week.
I'm so disgusting.
It's a coping mechanism. I need to be less hard on myself...
I'll just have to eat healthily to make up for it...
... then I'll never do it again.

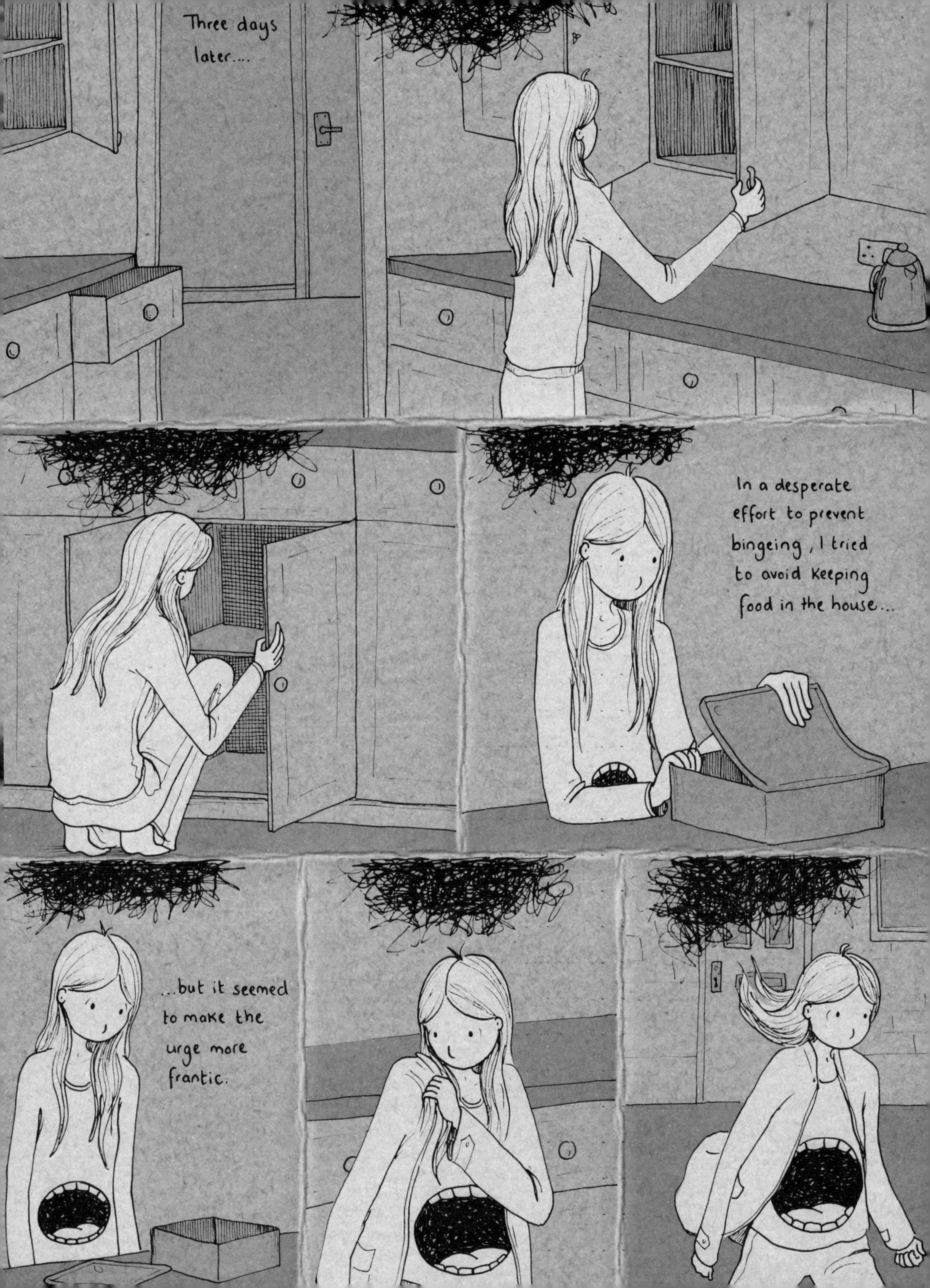
Three days later....
In a desperate effort to prevent bingeing, I tried to avoid keeping food in the house...
...but it seemed to make the urge more frantic.

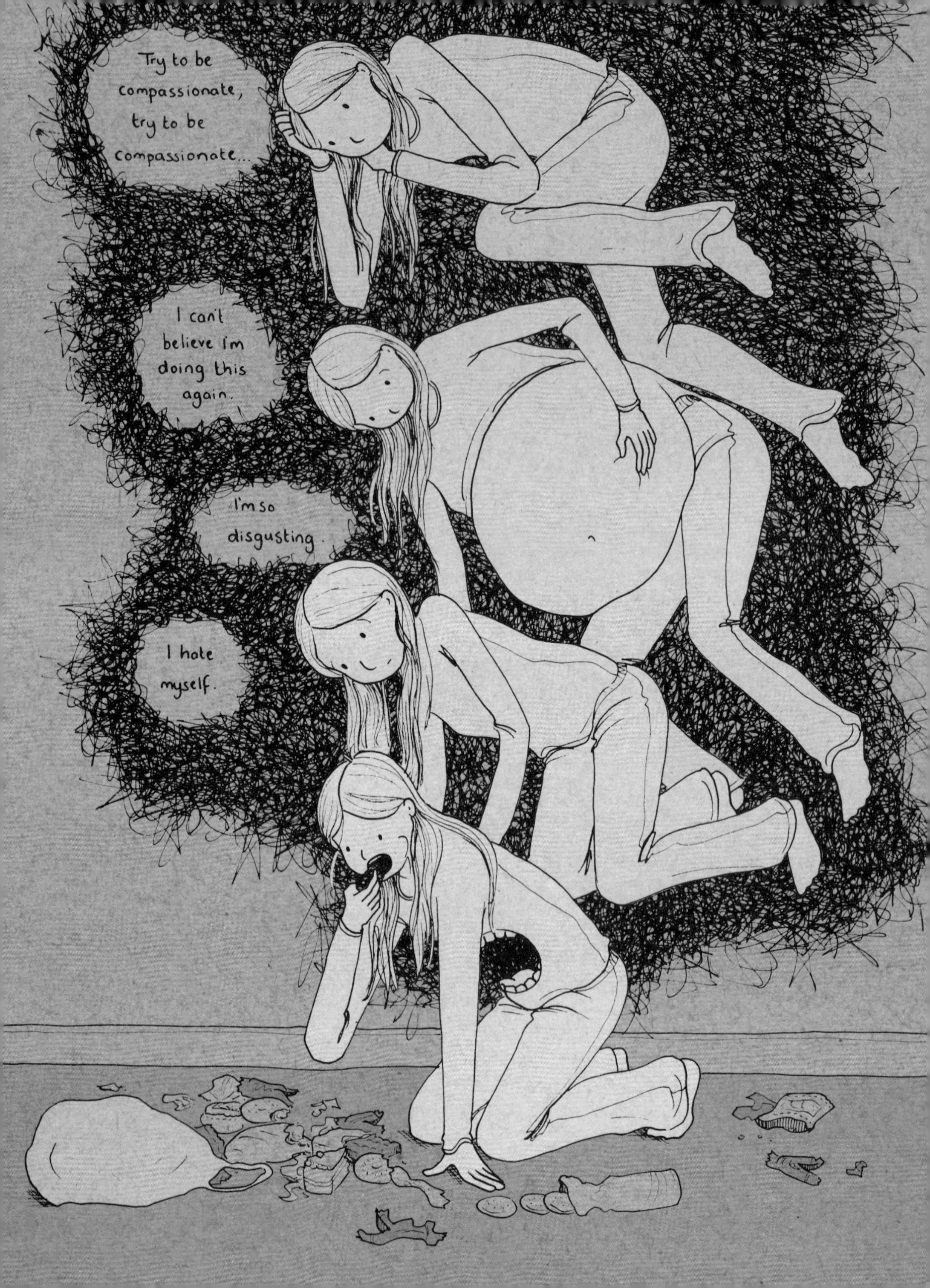
Try to be compassionate, try to be compassionate...
I can't believe I'm doing this again.
I'm so disgusting.
I hate myself.

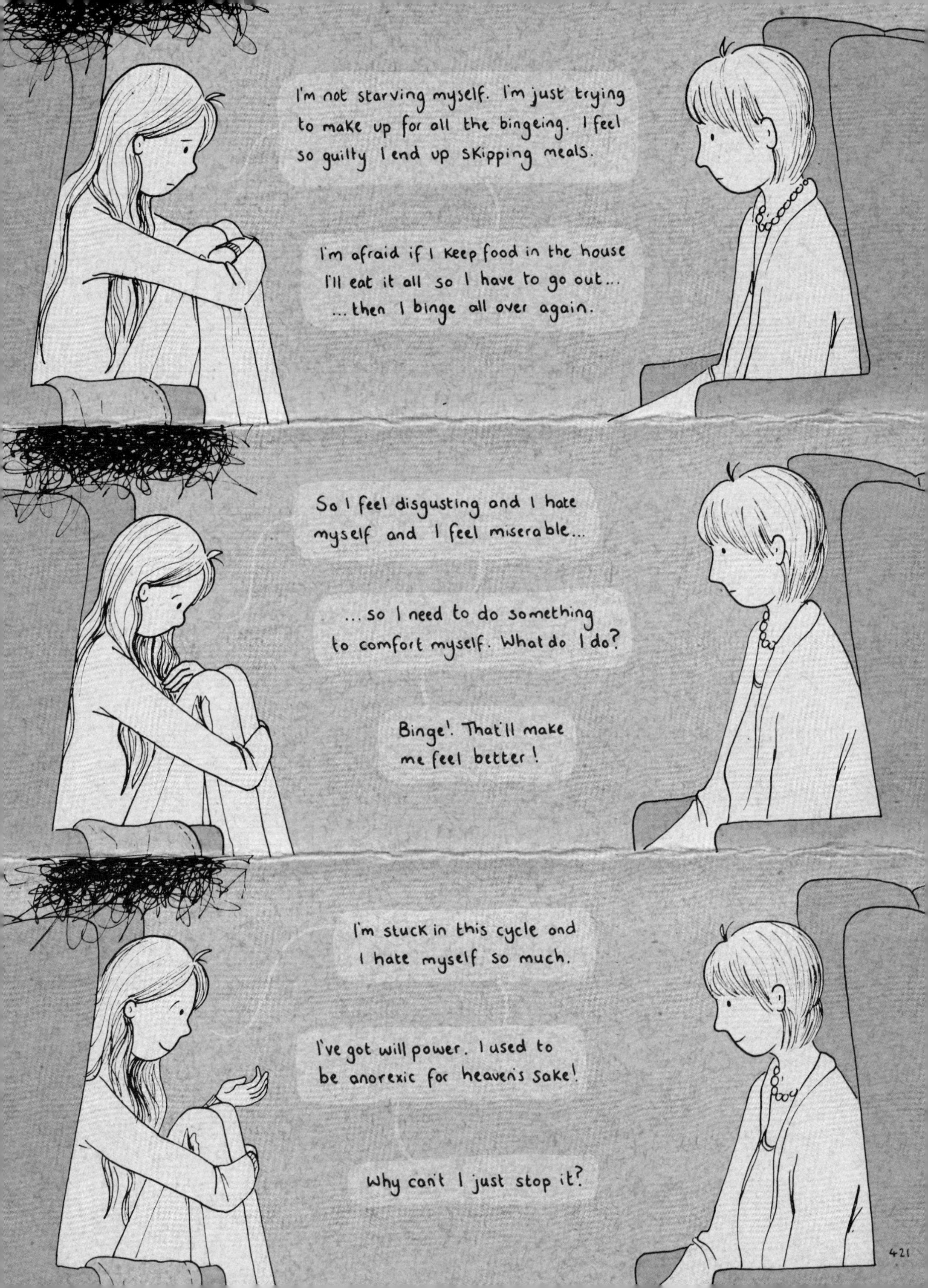
I'm not starving myself. I'm just trying to make up for all the bingeing. I feel so guilty I end up skipping meals.
I'm afraid if I keep food in the house I'll eat it all so I have to go out...
...then I binge all over again.
So I feel disgusting and I hate myself and I feel miserable...
...so I need to do something to comfort myself. What do I do?
Binge! That'll make me feel better!
I'm stuck in this cycle and I hate myself so much.
I've got will power. I used to be anorexic for heaven's sake!
Why can't I just stop it?

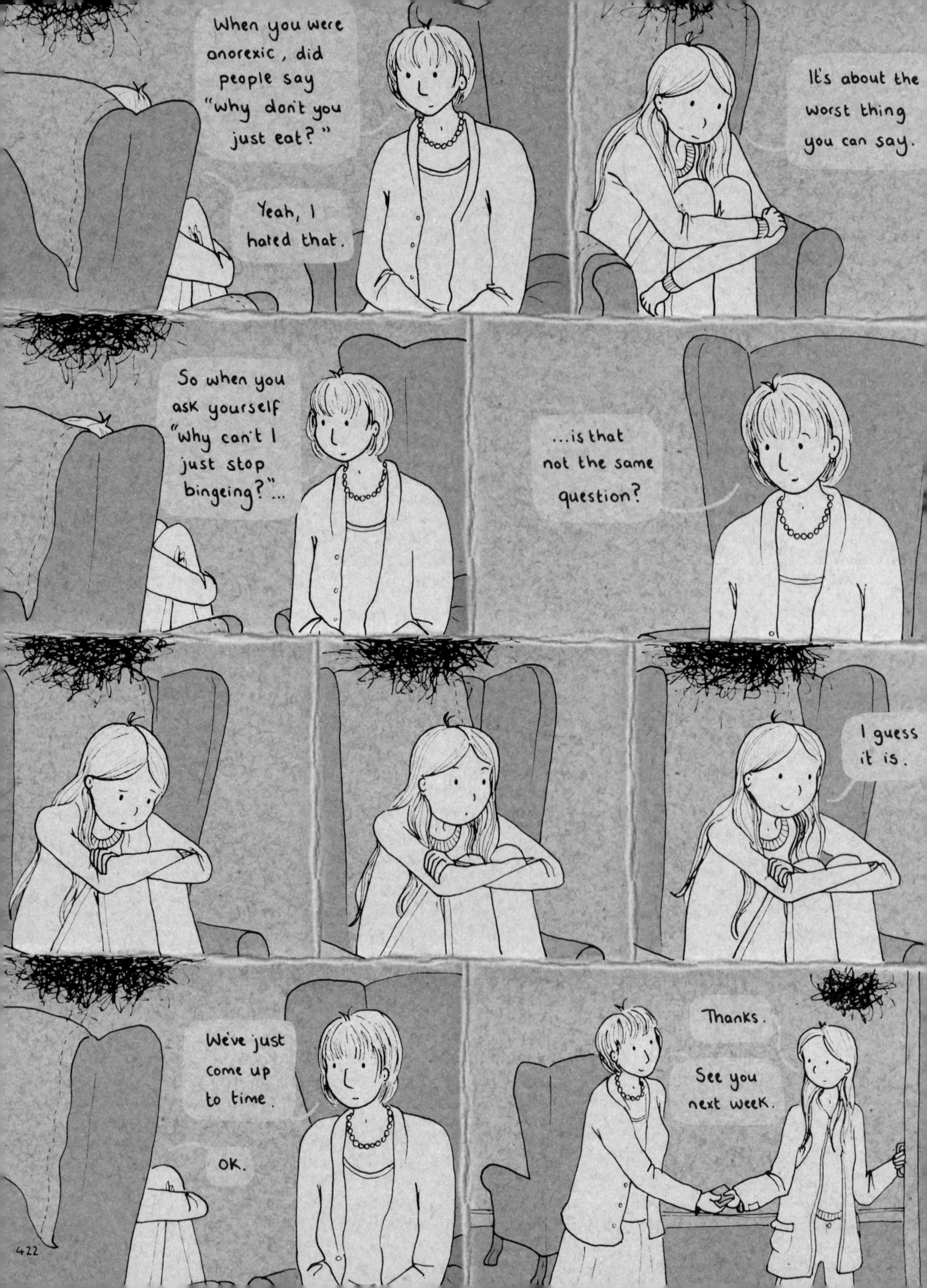
When you were anorexic, did people say "why don't you just eat?"
Yeah, I hated that.
It's about the worst thing you can say.
So when you ask yourself "why can't I just stop bingeing?"...
...is that not the same question?
I guess it is.
We've just come up to time.
OK.
Thanks.
See you next week.

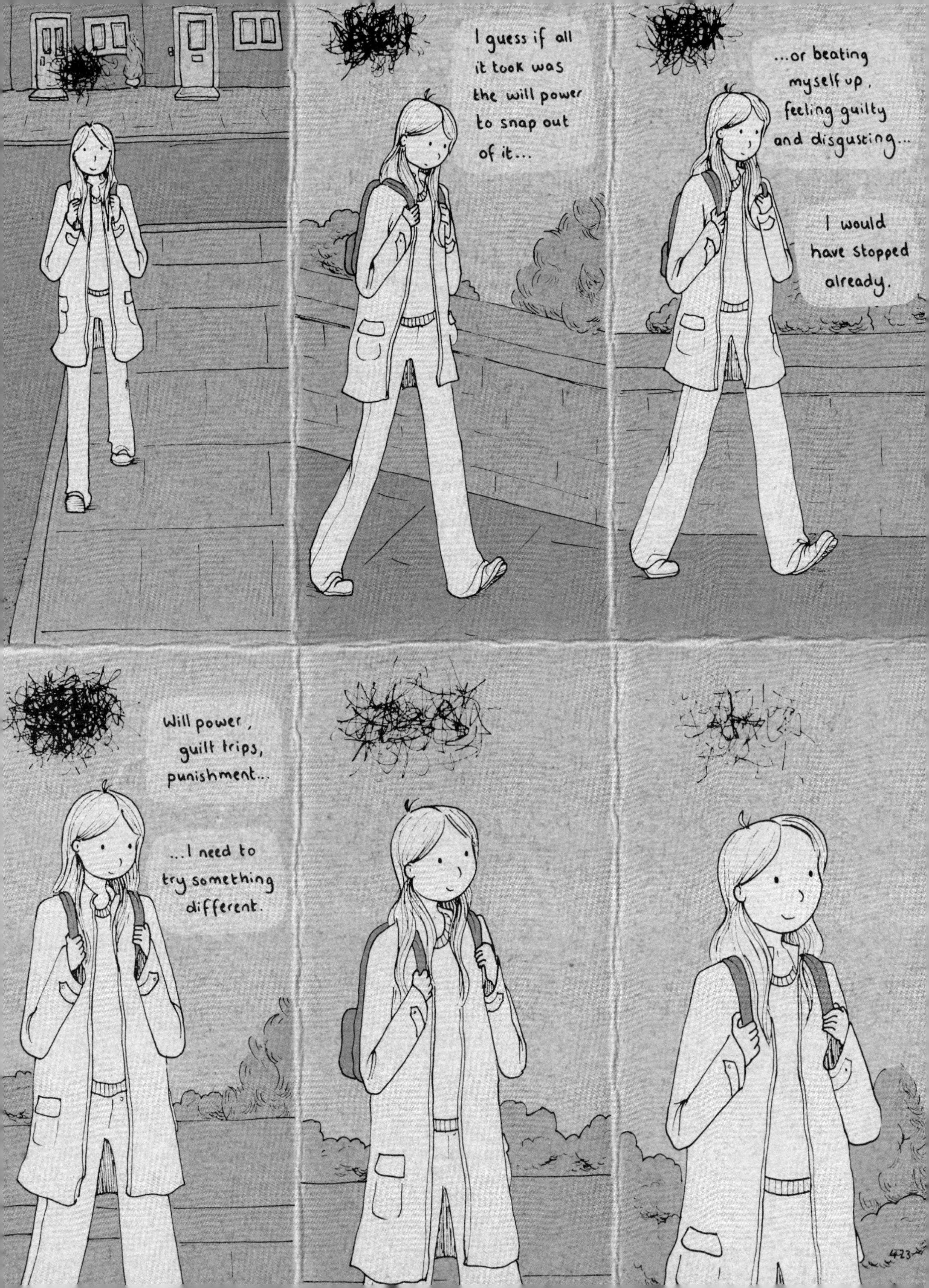

I guess if all it took was the will power to snap out of it...
...or beating myself up, feeling guilty and disgusting...
I would have stopped already.
Will power, guilt trips, punishment...
...I need to try something different.

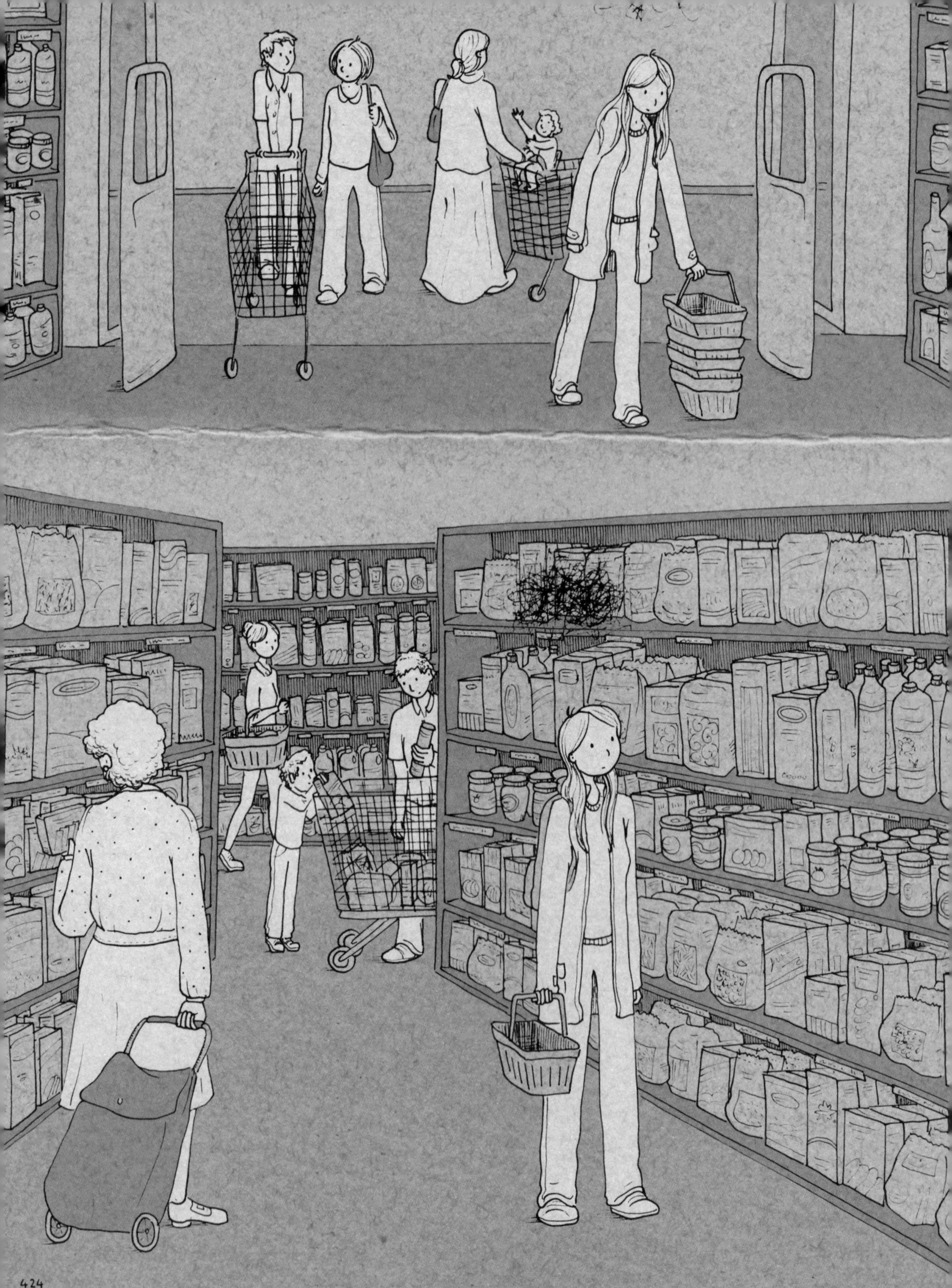

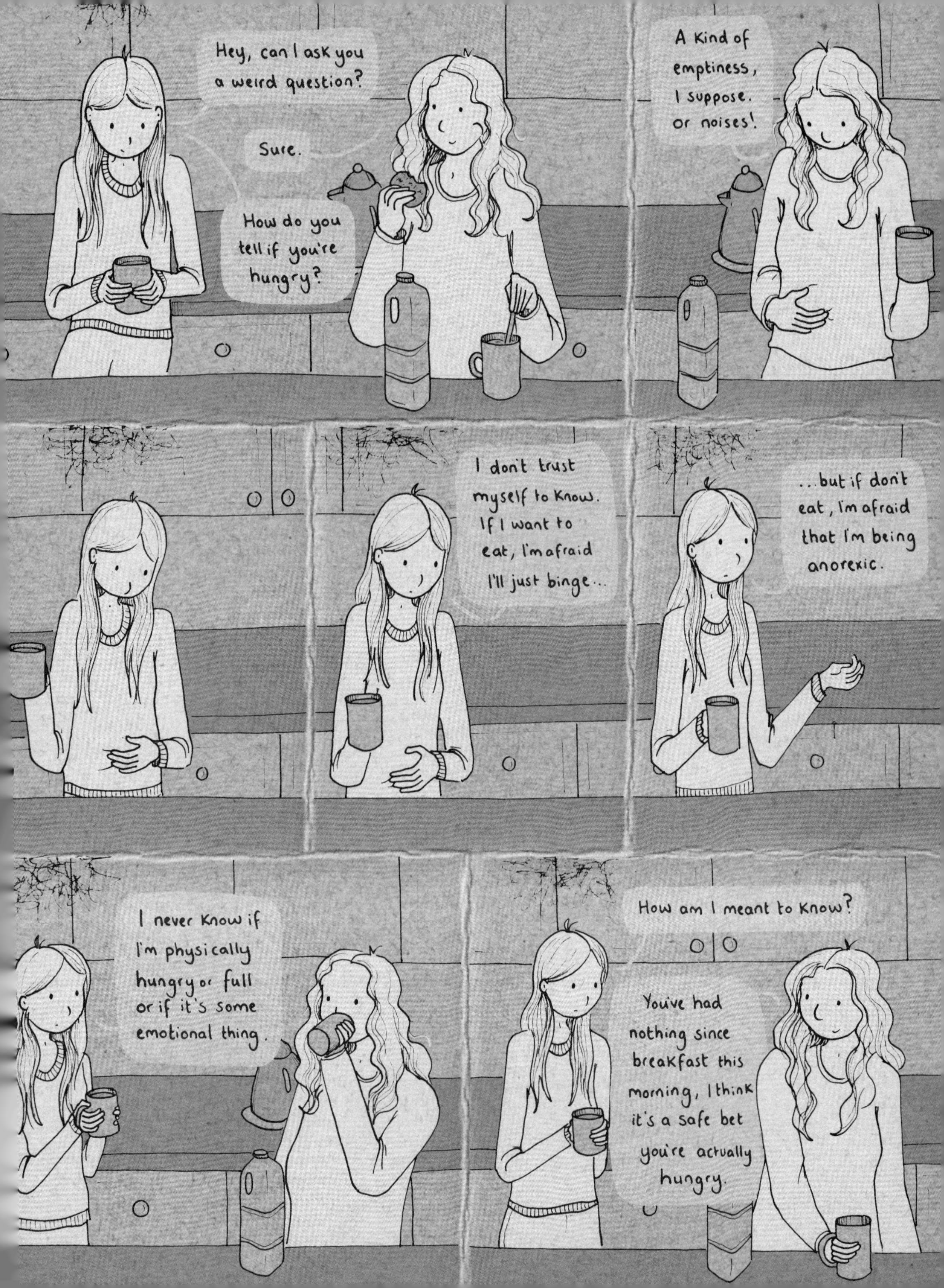
Hey, can I ask you a weird question?
Sure.
How do you tell if you're hungry?
A kind of emptiness, I suppose. or noises!
I don't trust myself to know. If I want to eat, I'm afraid I'll just binge...
...but if don't eat, I'm afraid that I'm being anorexic.
I never know if I'm physically hungry or full or if it's some emotional thing.
How am I meant to know?
You've had nothing since breakfast this morning, I think it's a safe bet you're actually hungry.

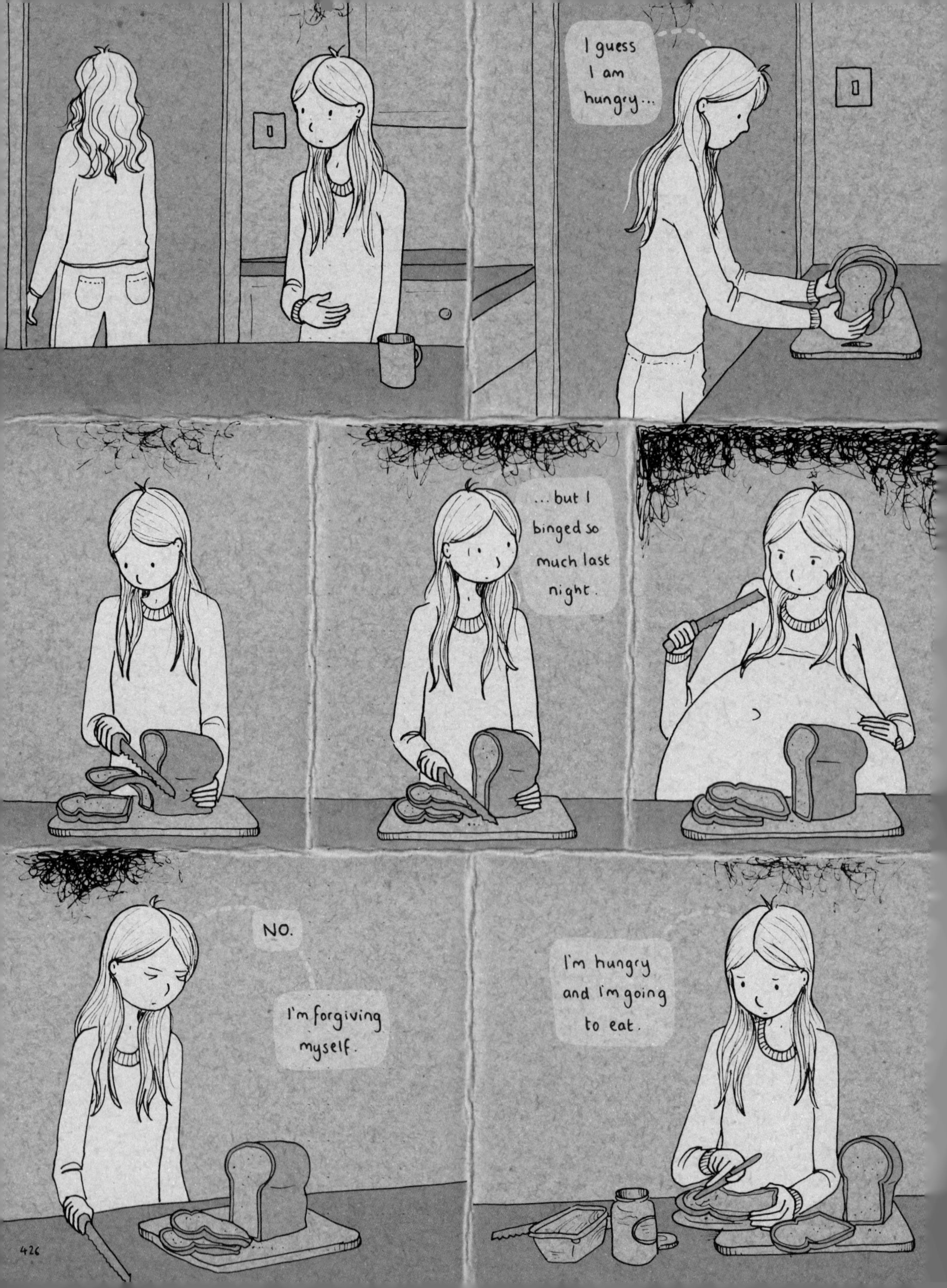
I guess I am hungry...
...but I binged so much last night.
NO.
I'm forgiving myself.
I'm hungry and I'm going to eat.

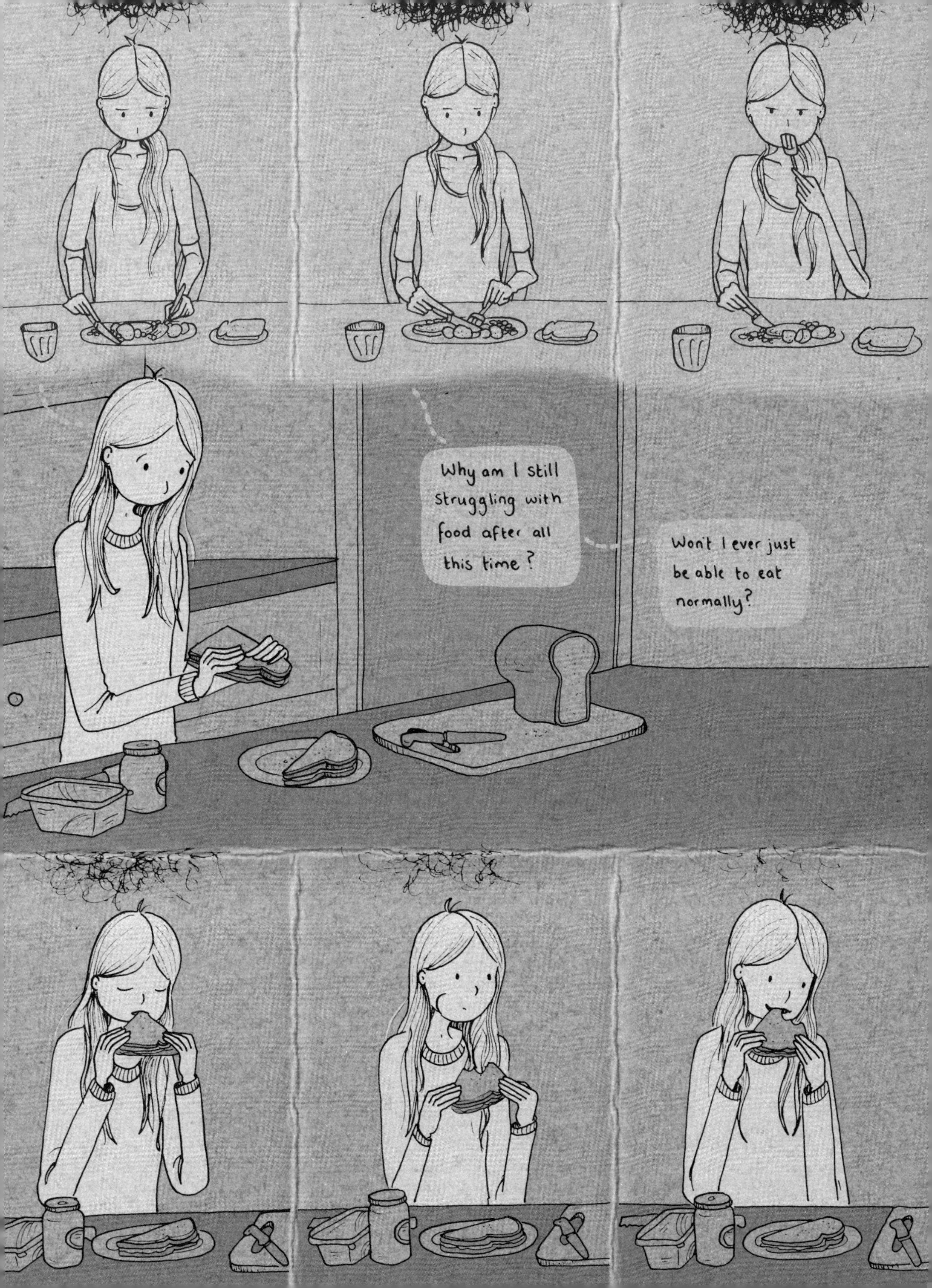
Why am I still struggling with food after all this time?
Won't I ever just be able to eat normally?

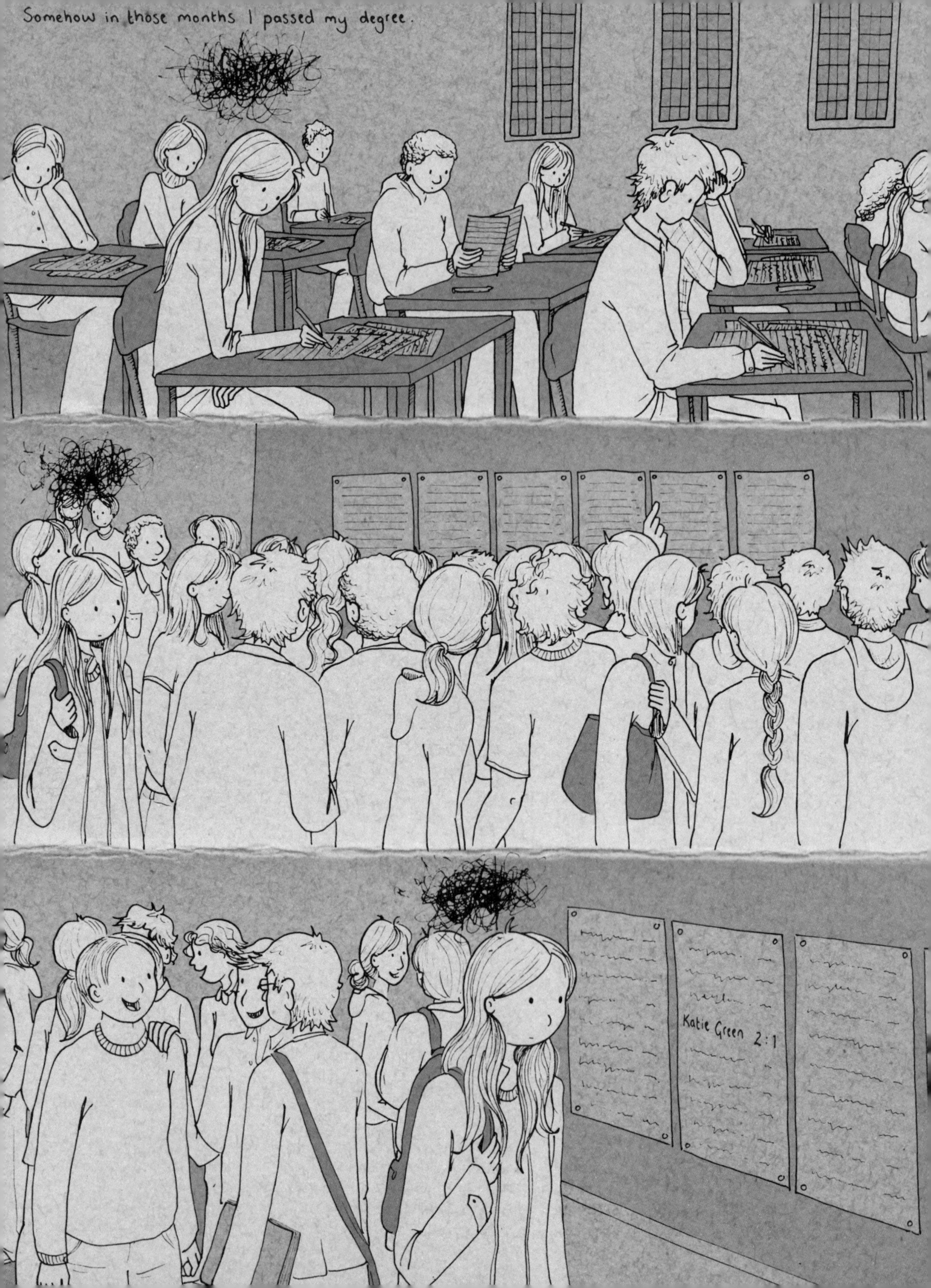
Somehow in those months I passed my degree.
Katie Green 2:1

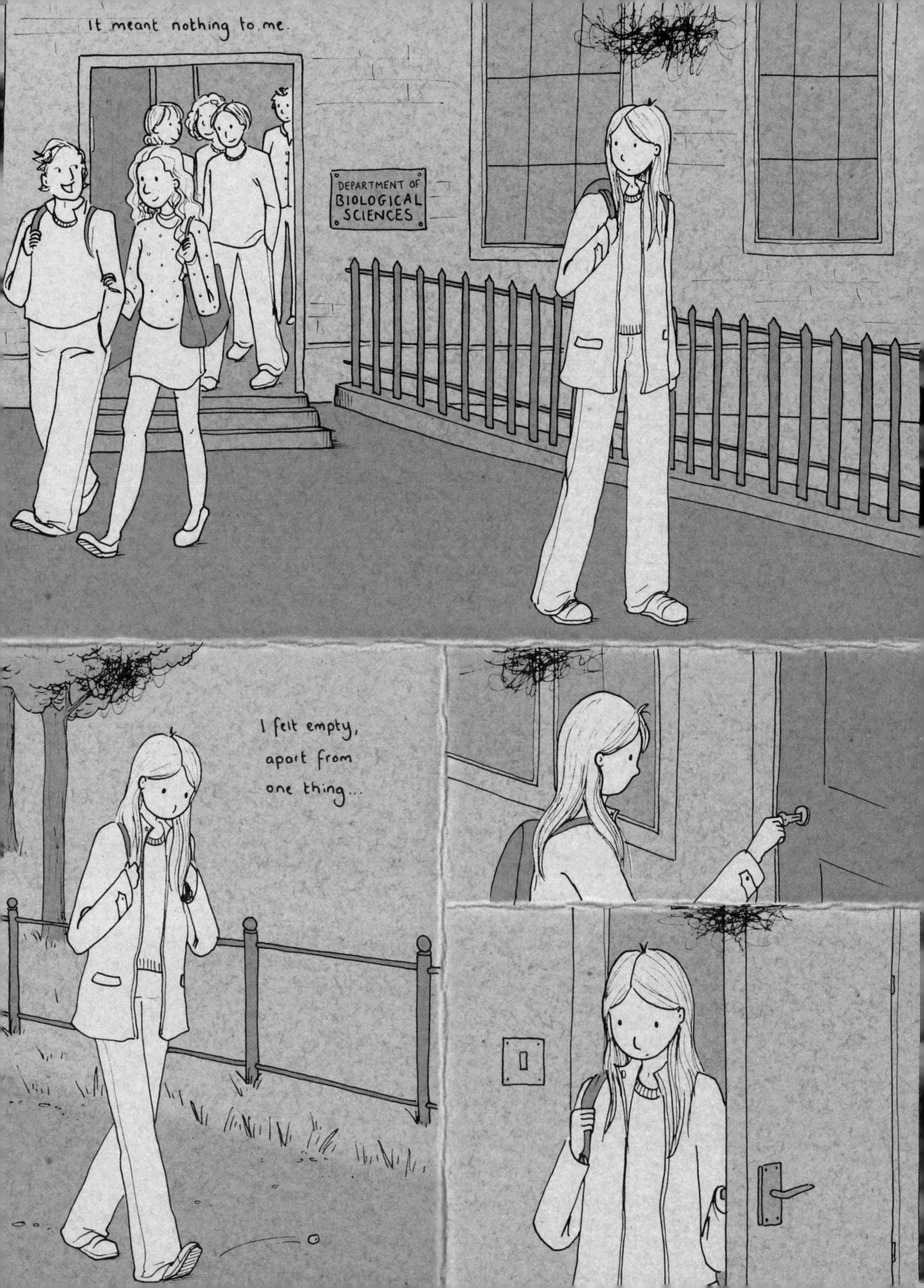
It meant nothing to me.
DEPARTMENT OF BIOLOGICAL SCIENCES
I felt empty, apart from one thing...

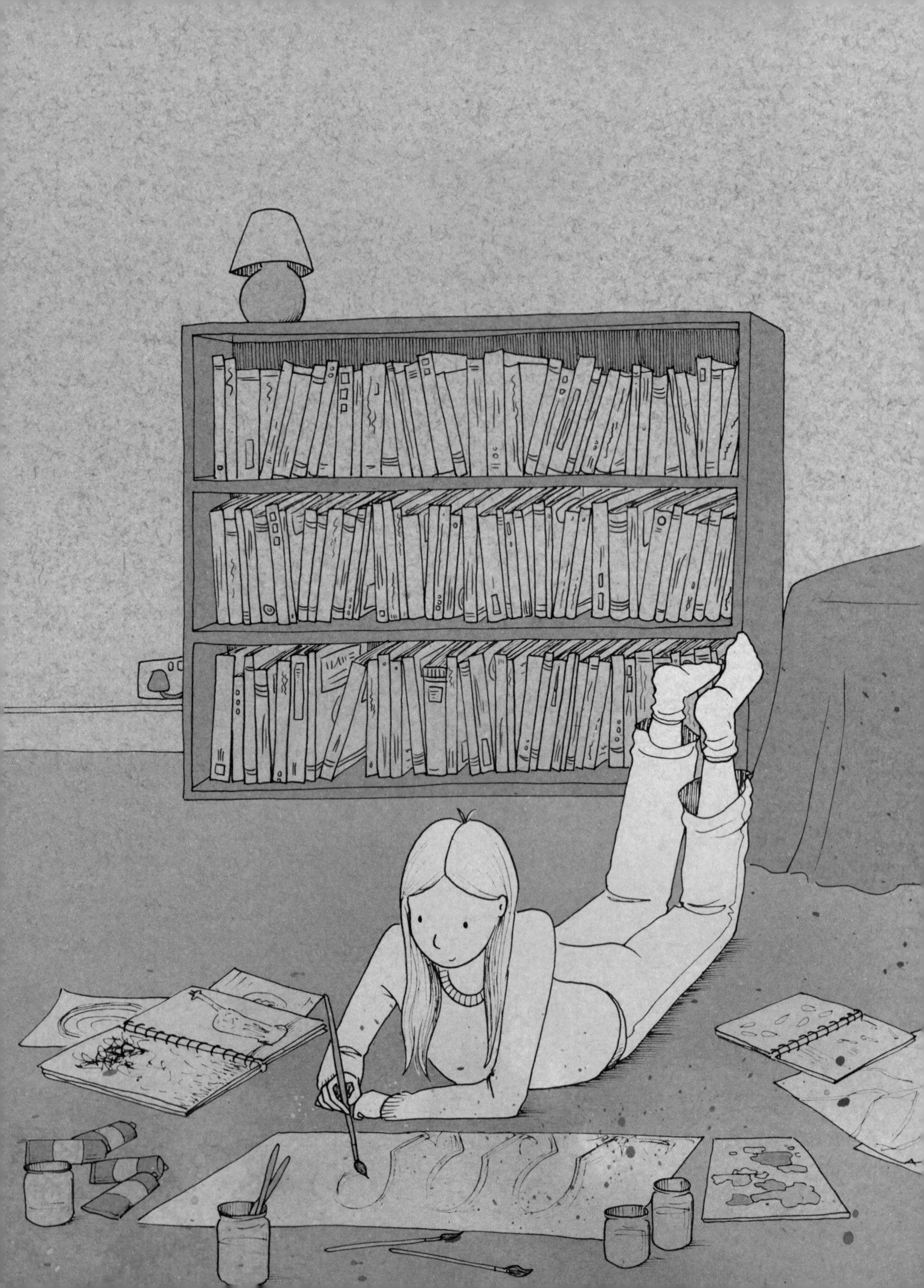

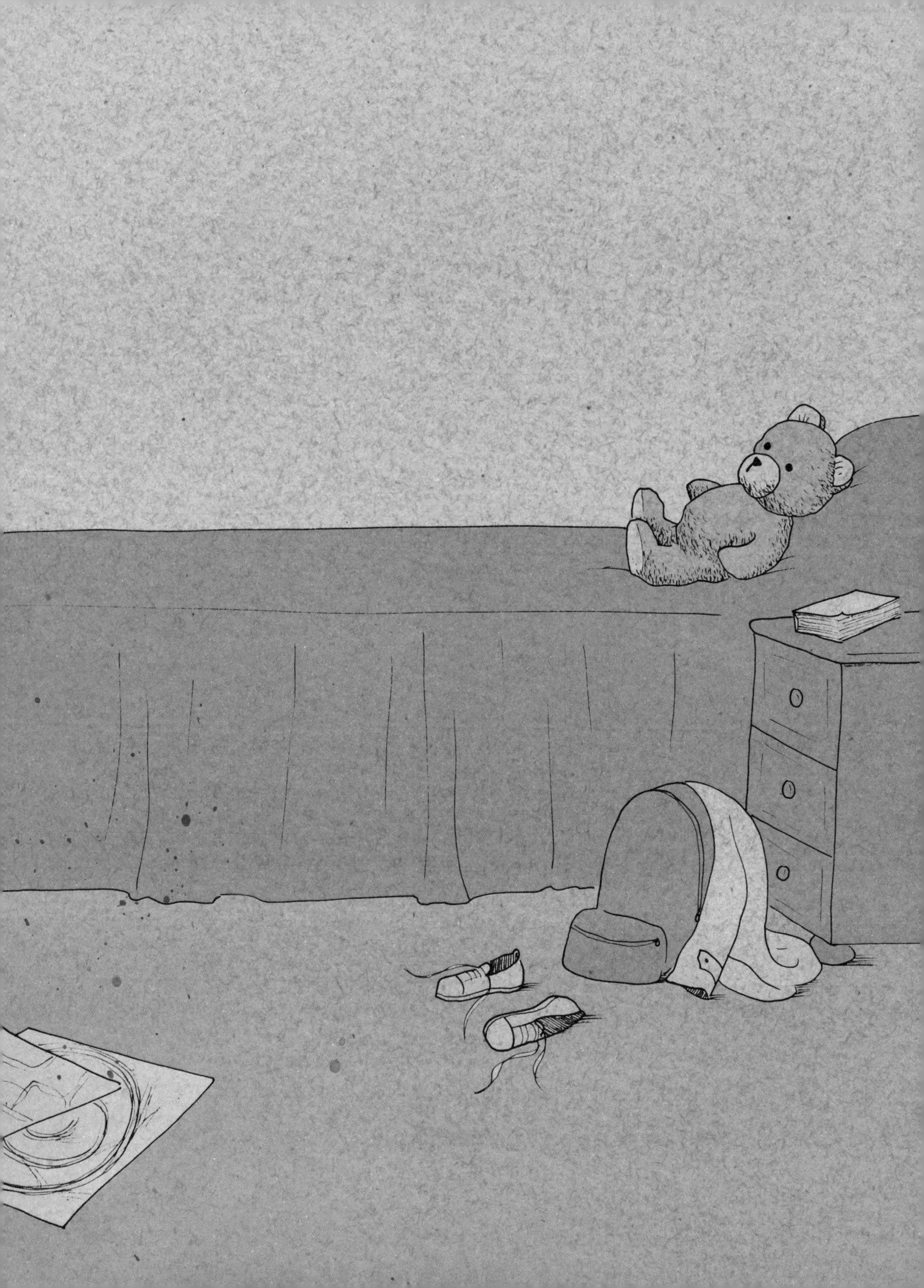

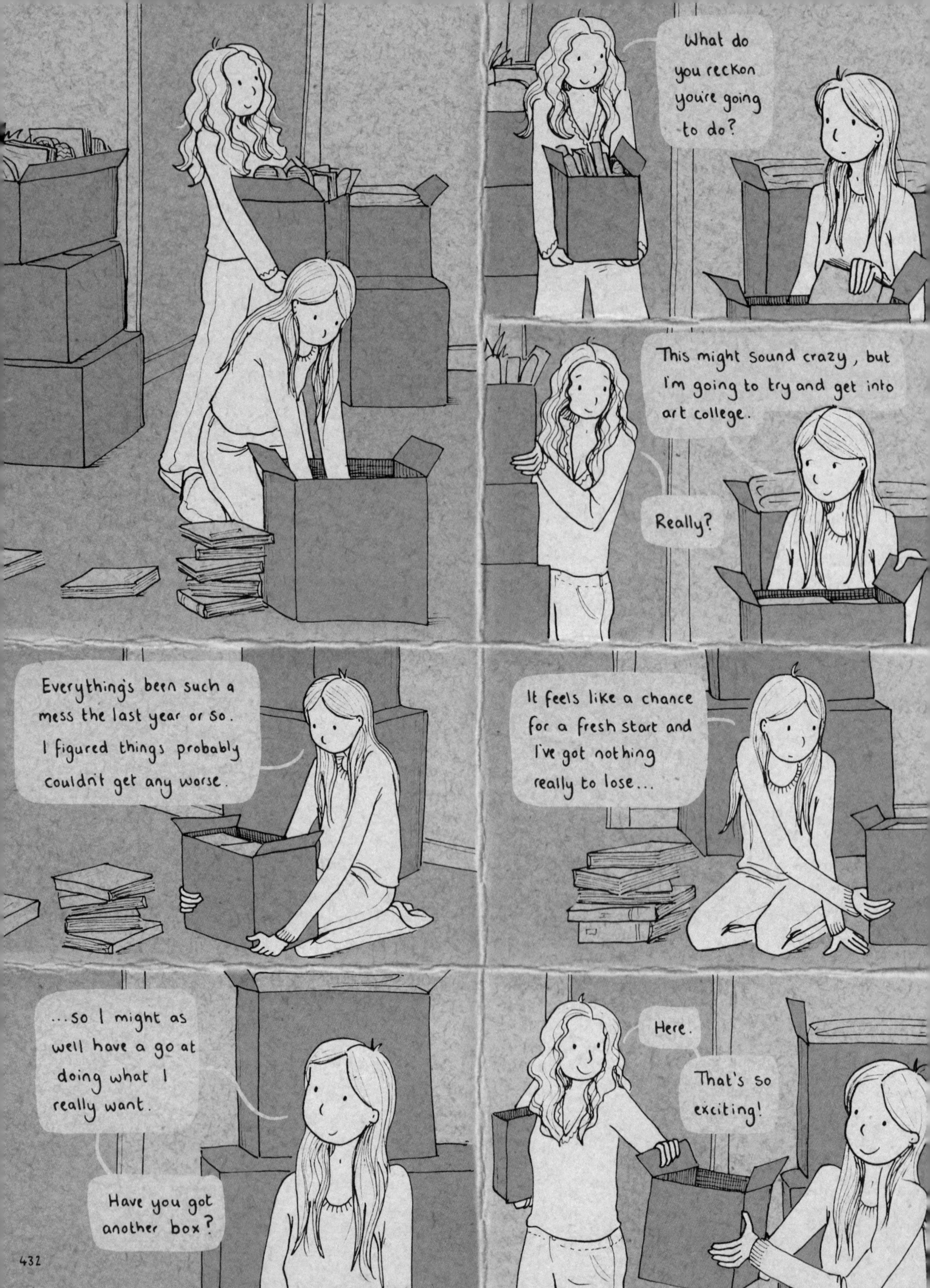
What do you reckon you're going to do?
This might sound crazy, but I'm going to try and get into art college.
Really?
Everything's been such a mess the last year or so. I figured things probably couldn't get any worse.
It feels like a chance for a fresh start and I've got nothing really to lose...
...so I might as well have a go at doing what I really want.
Have you got another box?
Here.
That's so exciting!

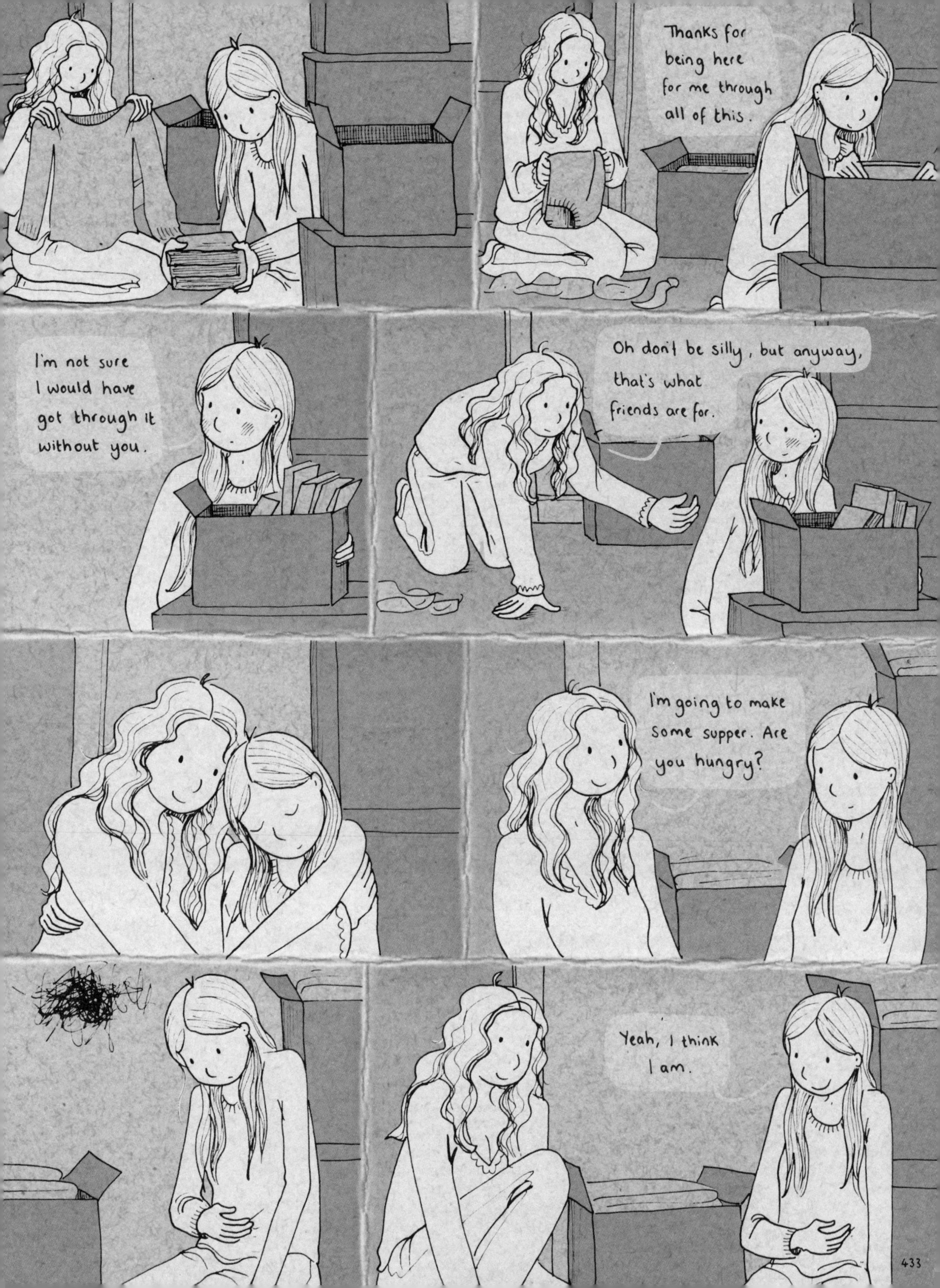
Thanks for being here for me through all of this.
I'm not sure I would have got through it without you.
Oh don't be silly, but anyway, that's what friends are for.
I'm going to make some supper. Are you hungry?
Yeah, I think I am.

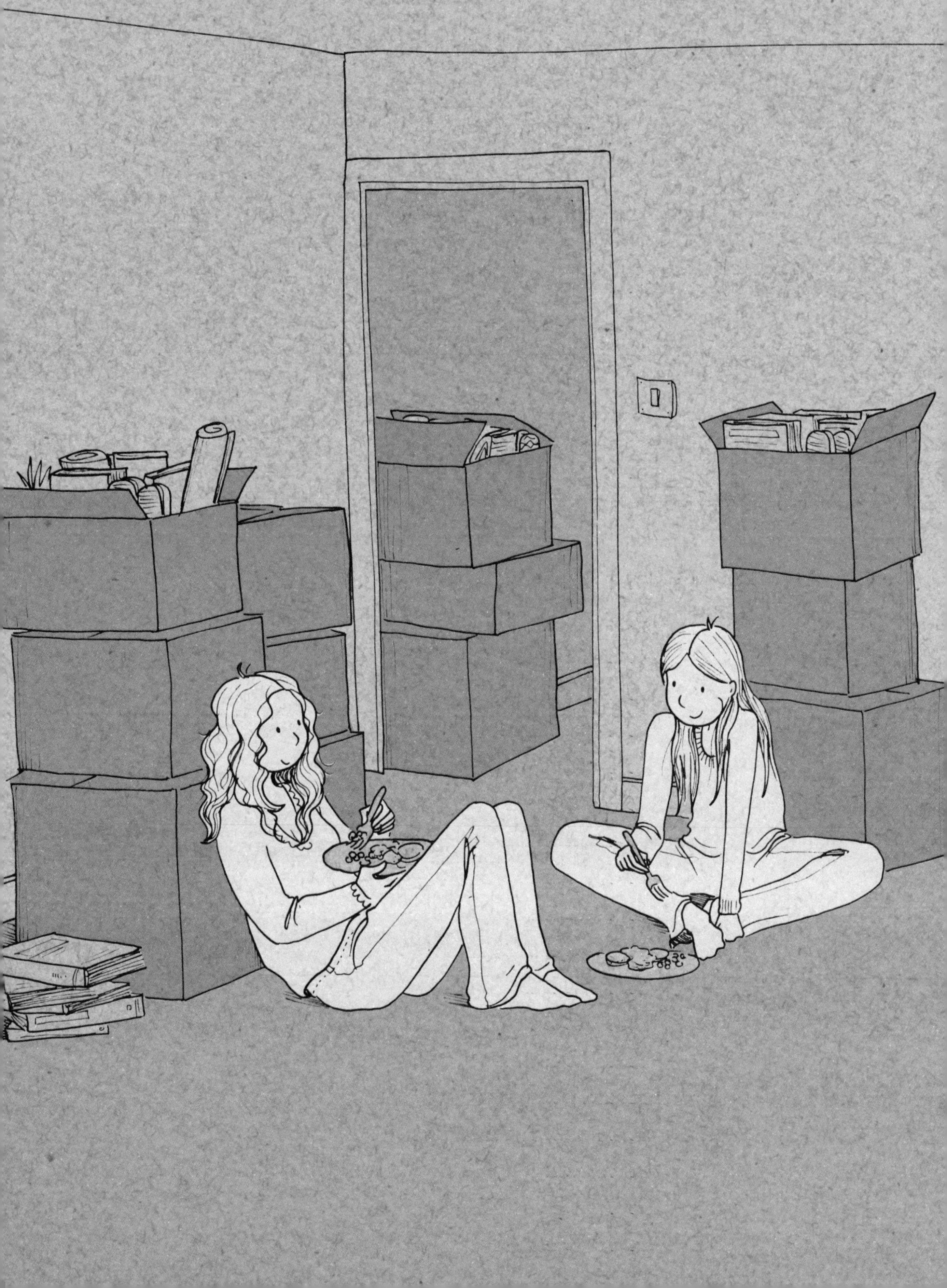

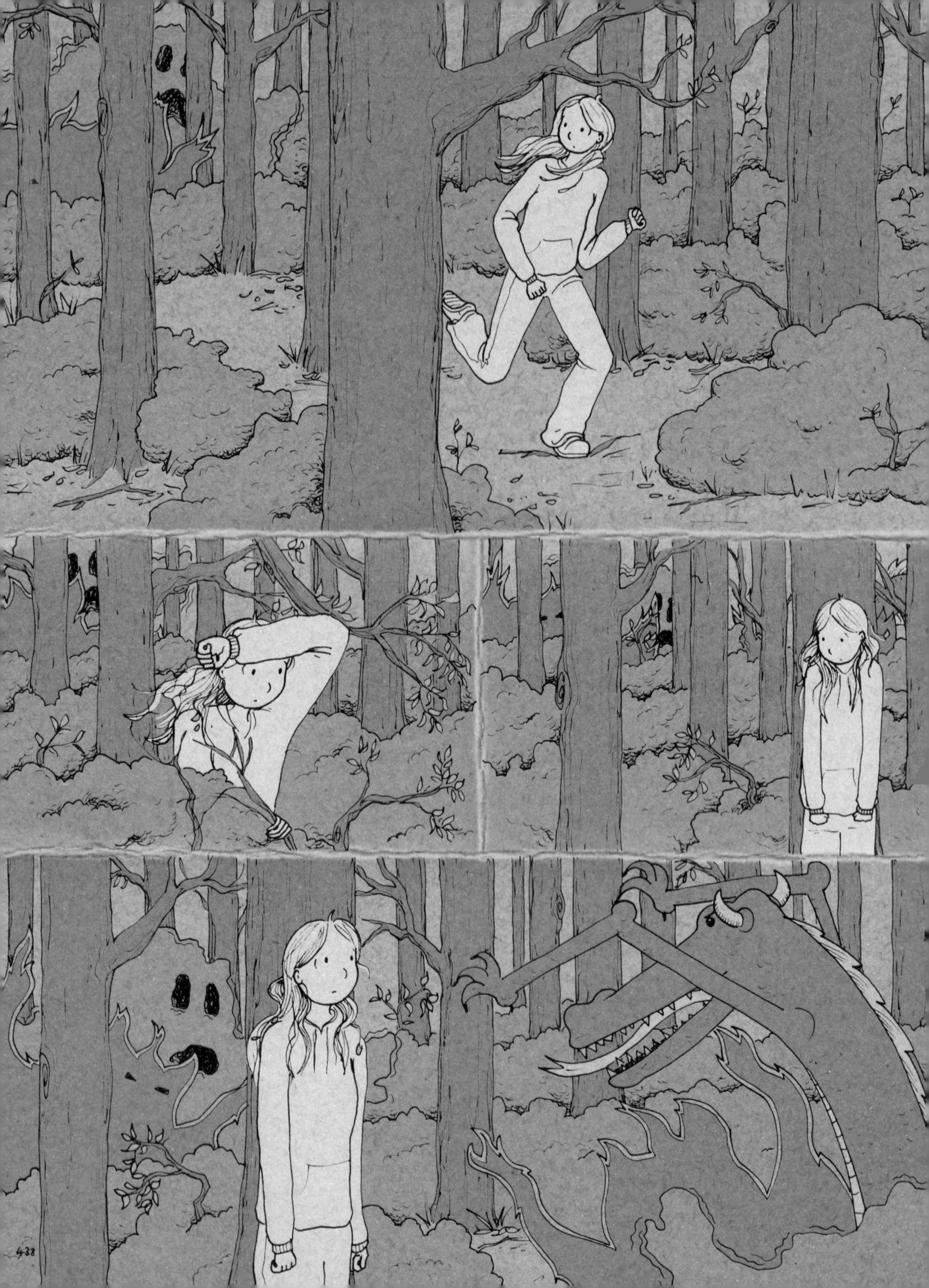

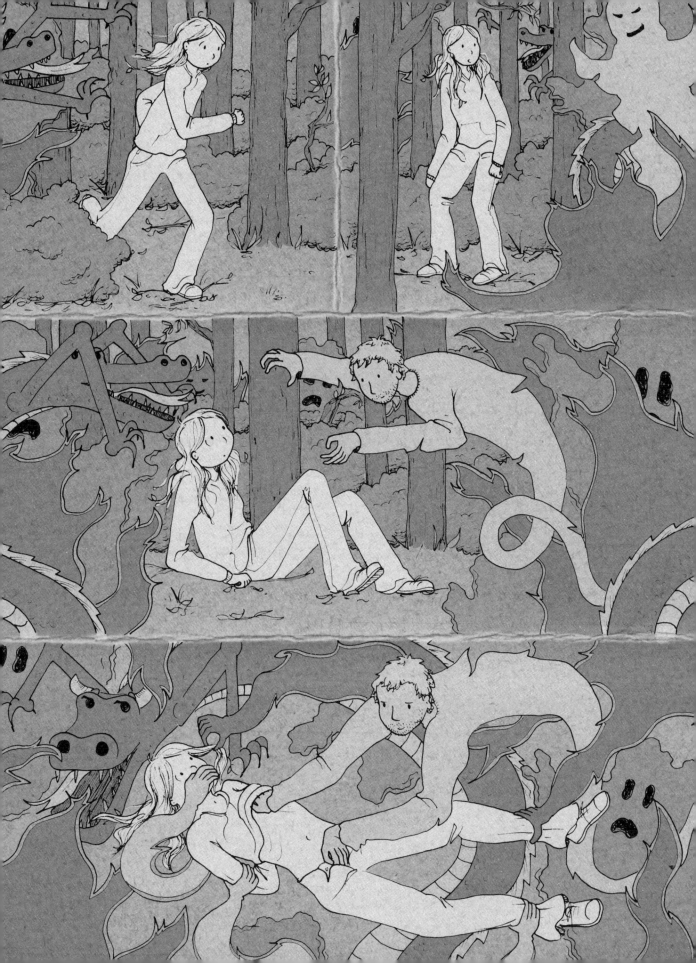

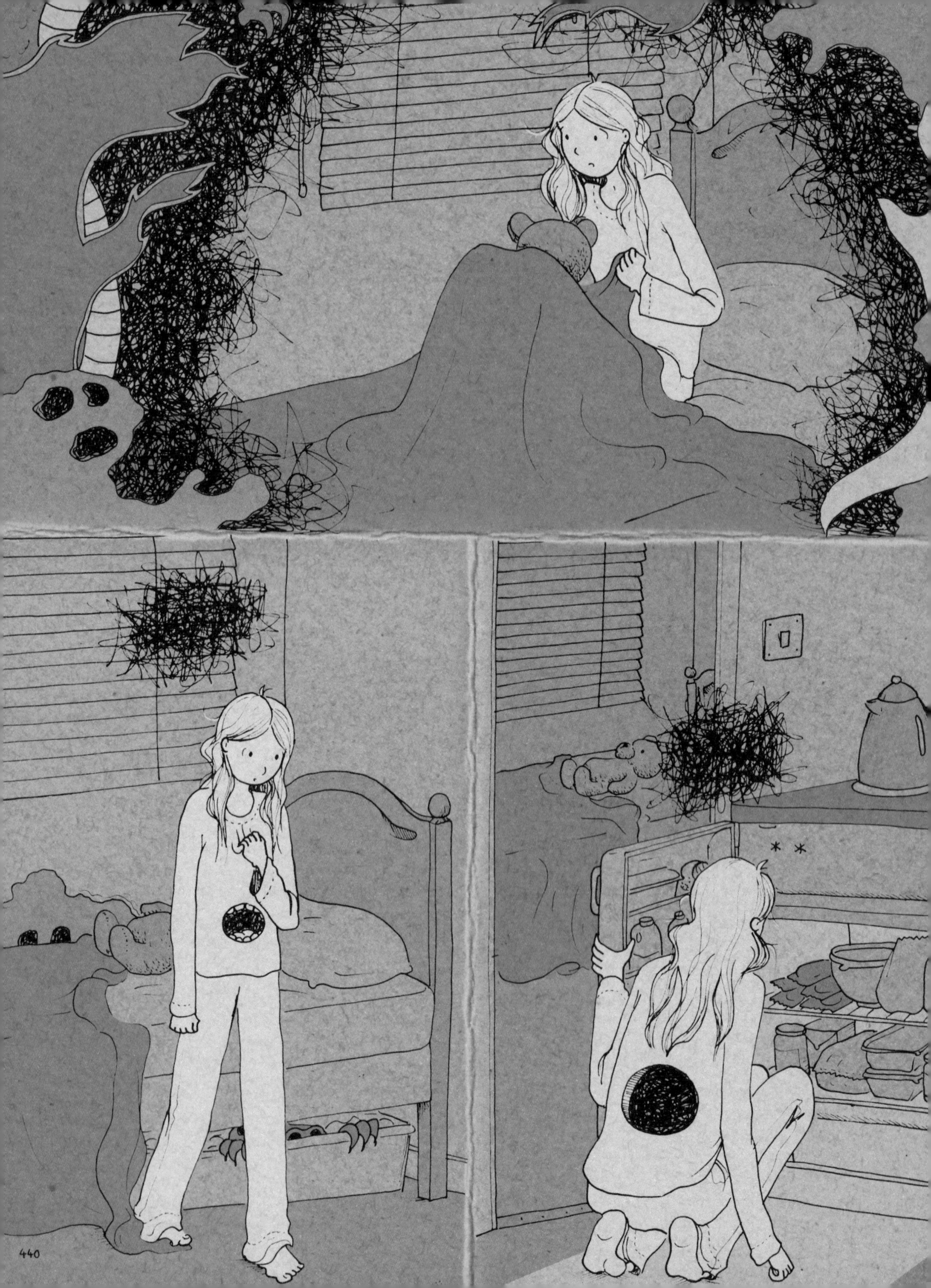

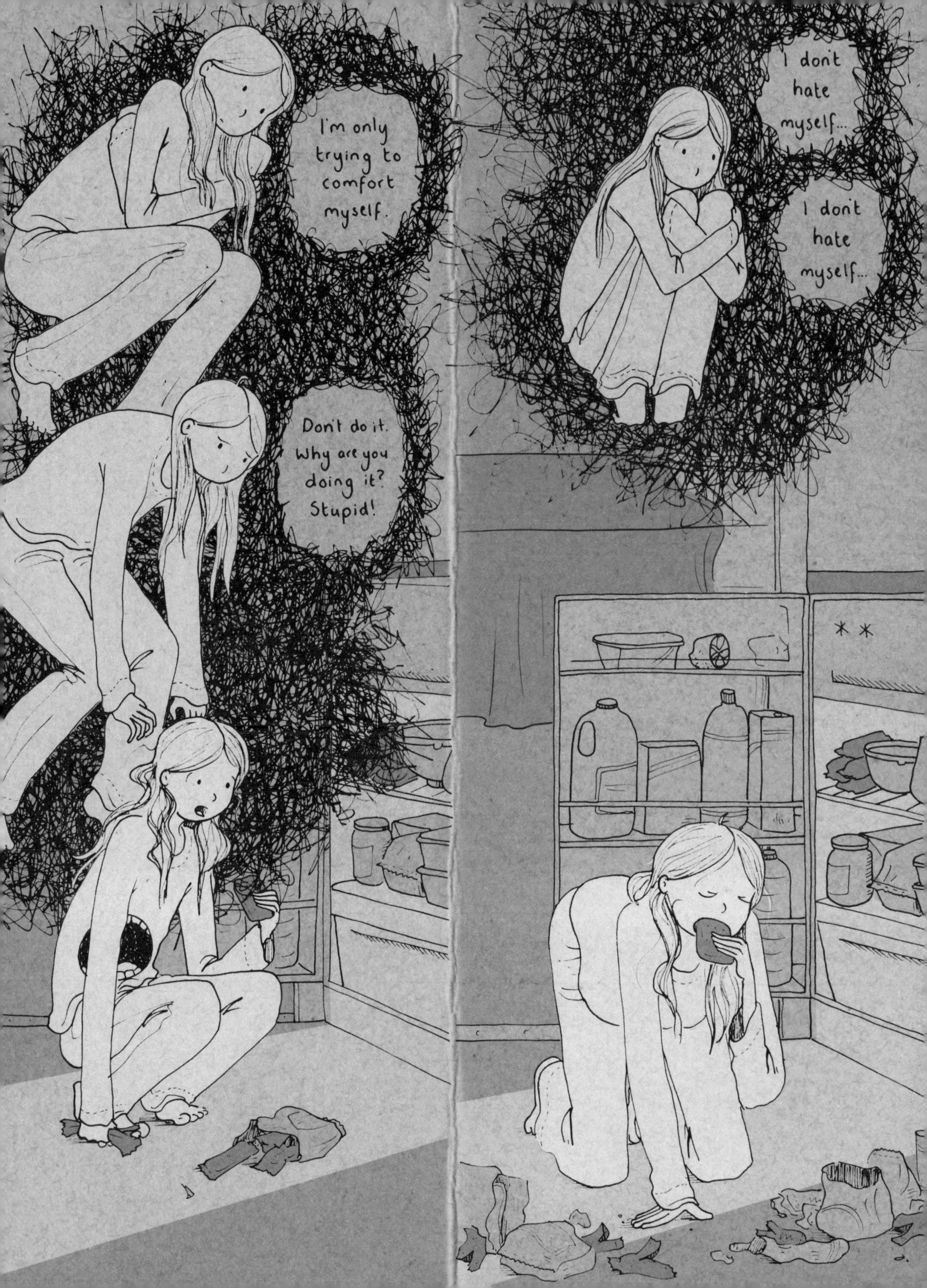
I'm only trying to comfort myself.
Don't do it. Why are you doing it? Stupid!
I don't hate myself...
I don't hate myself...

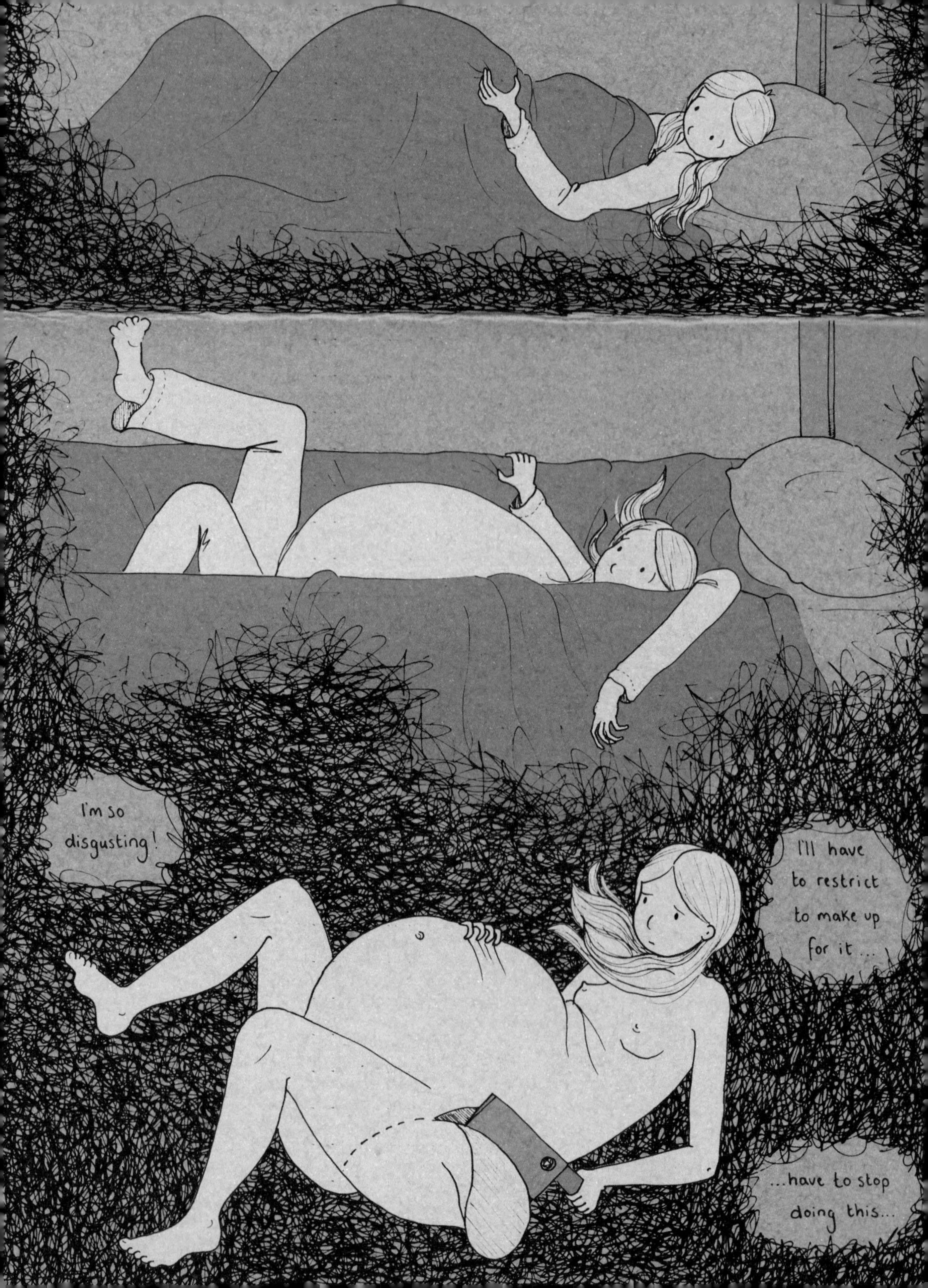
I'm so disgusting!
I'll have to restrict to make up for it...
...have to stop doing this...

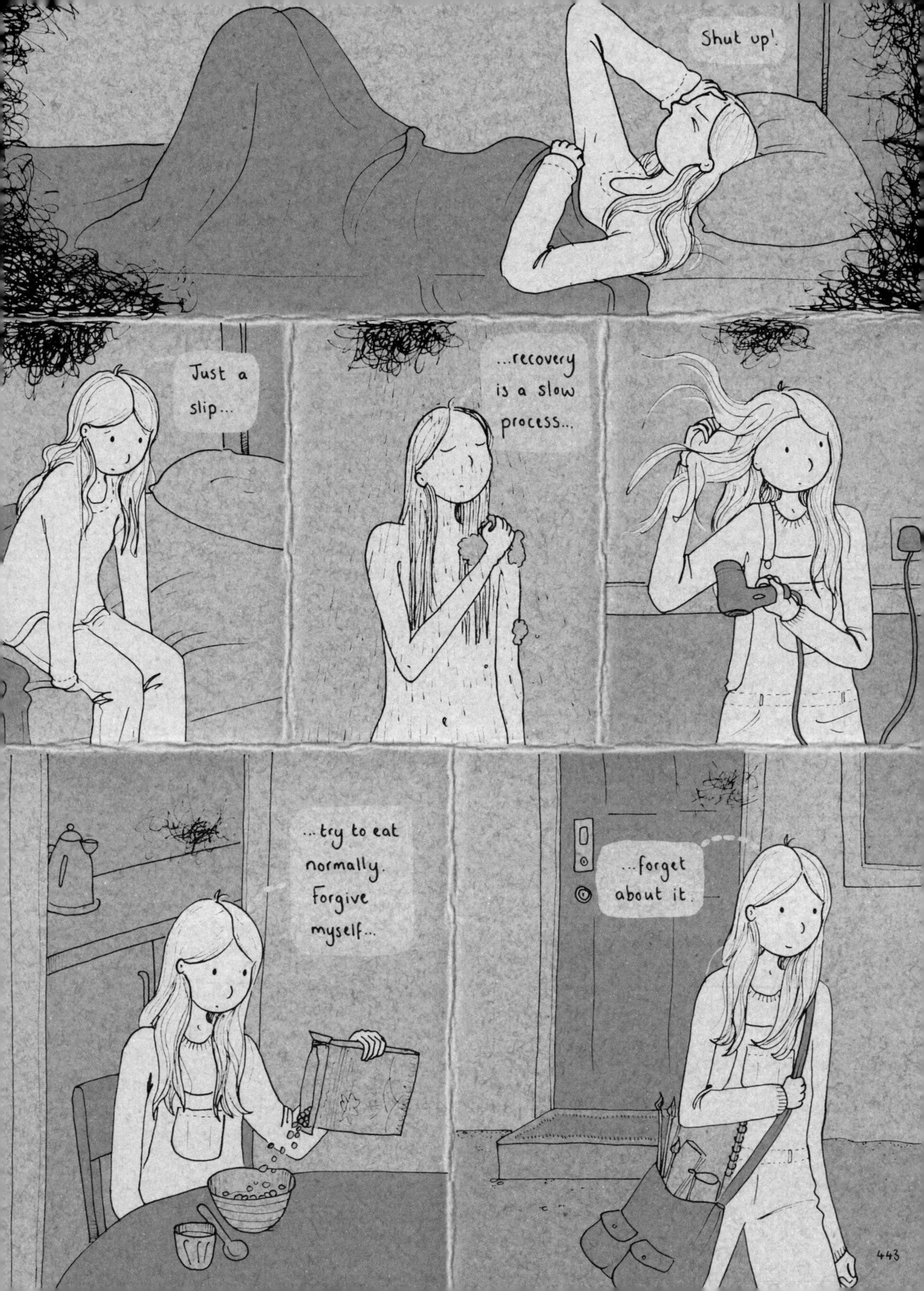
Shut up!
Just a slip...
...recovery is a slow process...
...try to eat normally. Forgive myself...
...forget about it.

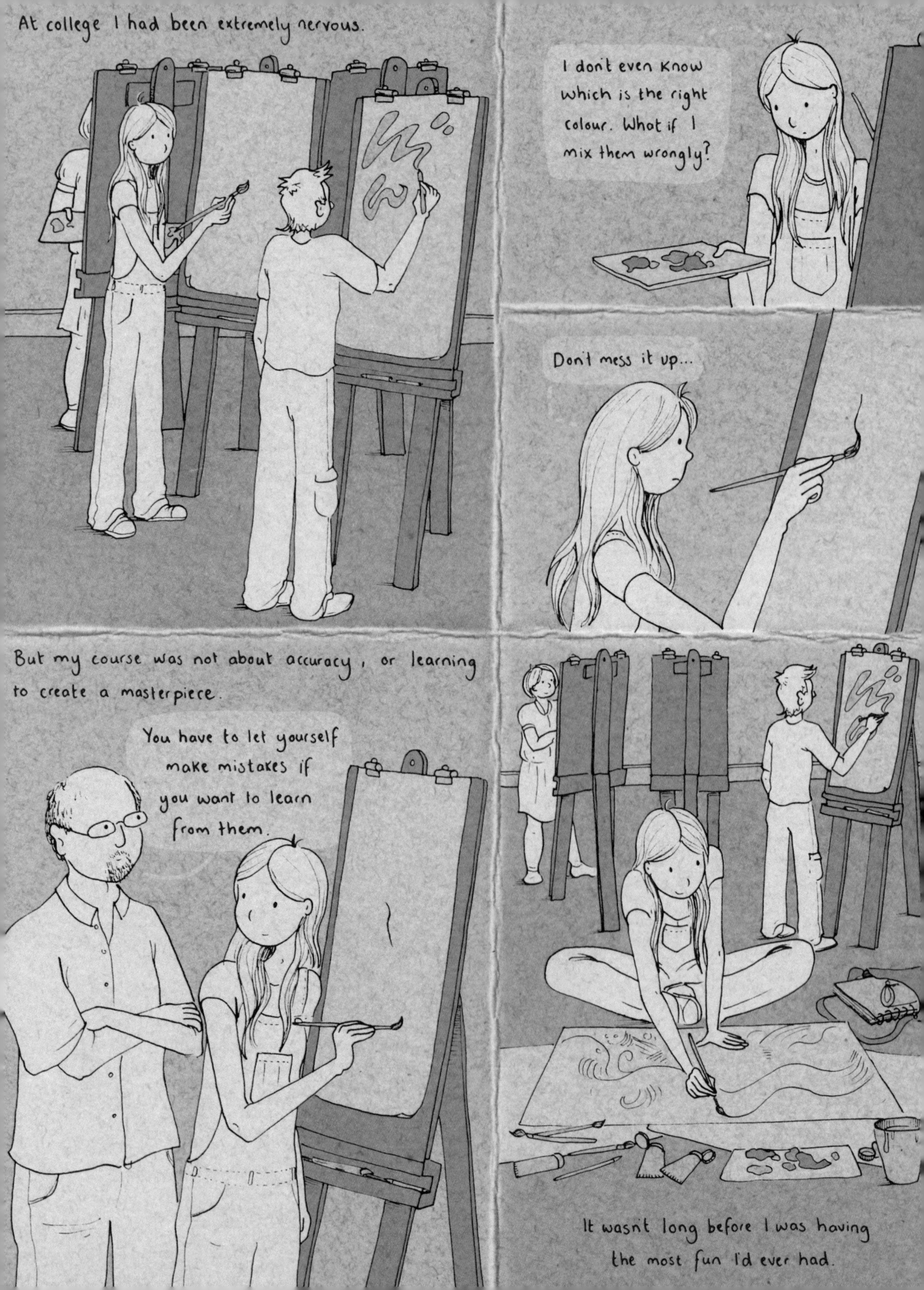
At college I had been extremely nervous.
I don't even know which is the right colour. What if I mix them wrongly?
Don't mess it up...
But my course was not about accuracy, or learning to create a masterpiece.
You have to let yourself make mistakes if you want to learn from them.
It wasn't long before I was having the most fun I'd ever had.

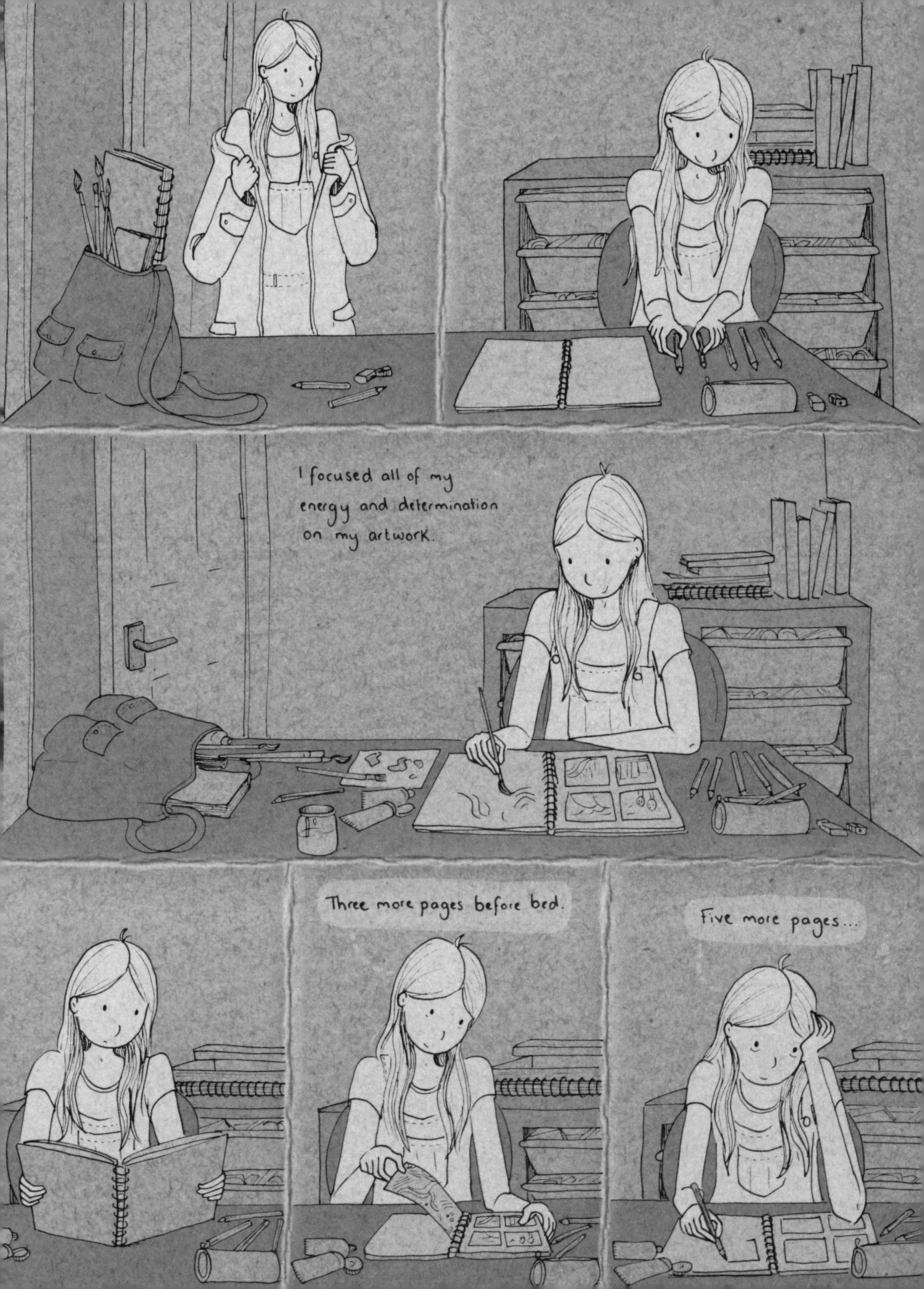
I focused all of my energy and determination on my artwork.
Three more pages before bed.
Five more pages...

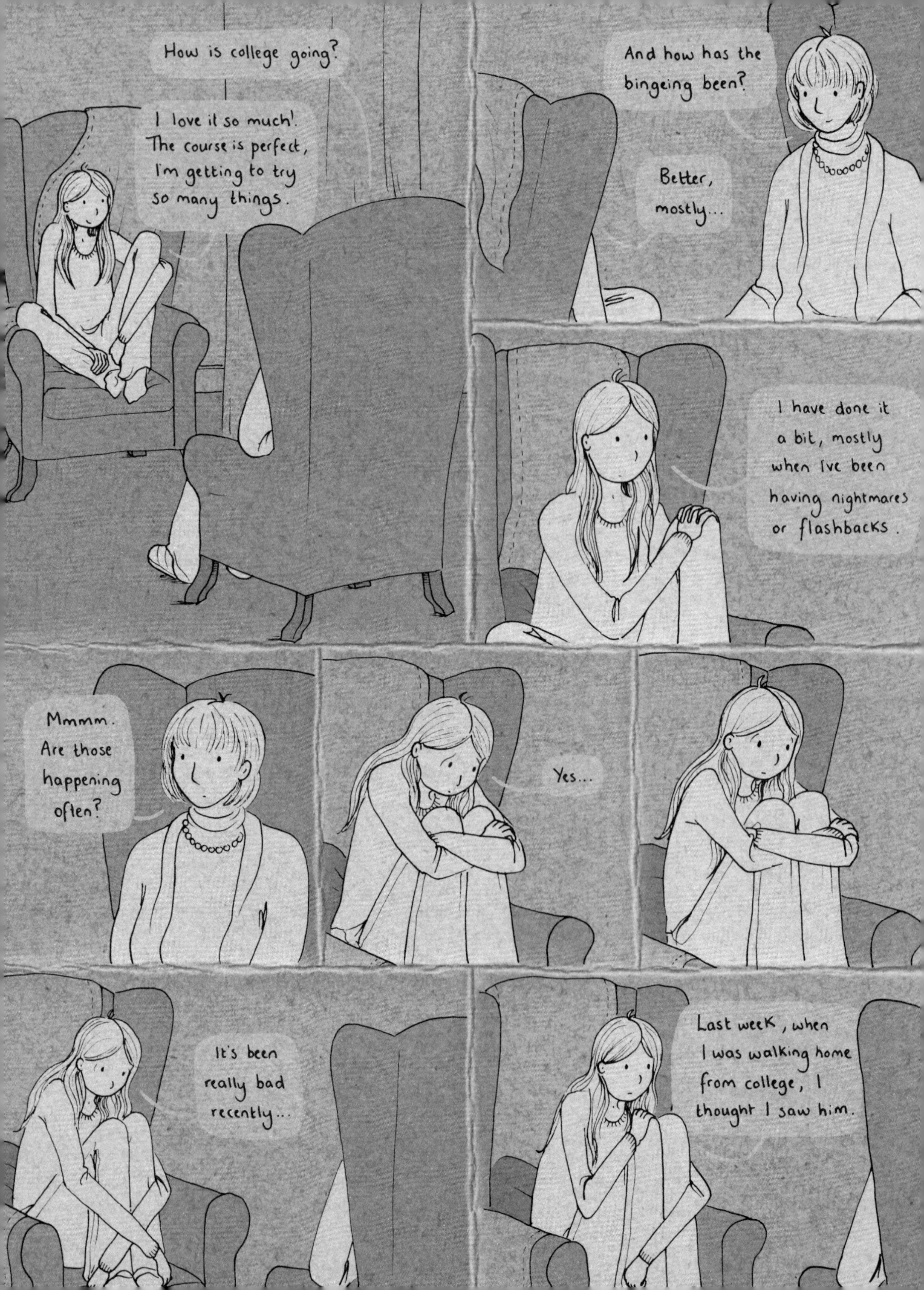
How is college going?
I love it so much! The course is perfect, I'm getting to try so many things.
And how has the bingeing been?
Better, mostly...
I have done it a bit, mostly when I've been having nightmares or flashbacks.
Mmmm. Are those happening often?
Yes...
It's been really bad recently...
Last week, when I was walking home from college, I thought I saw him.

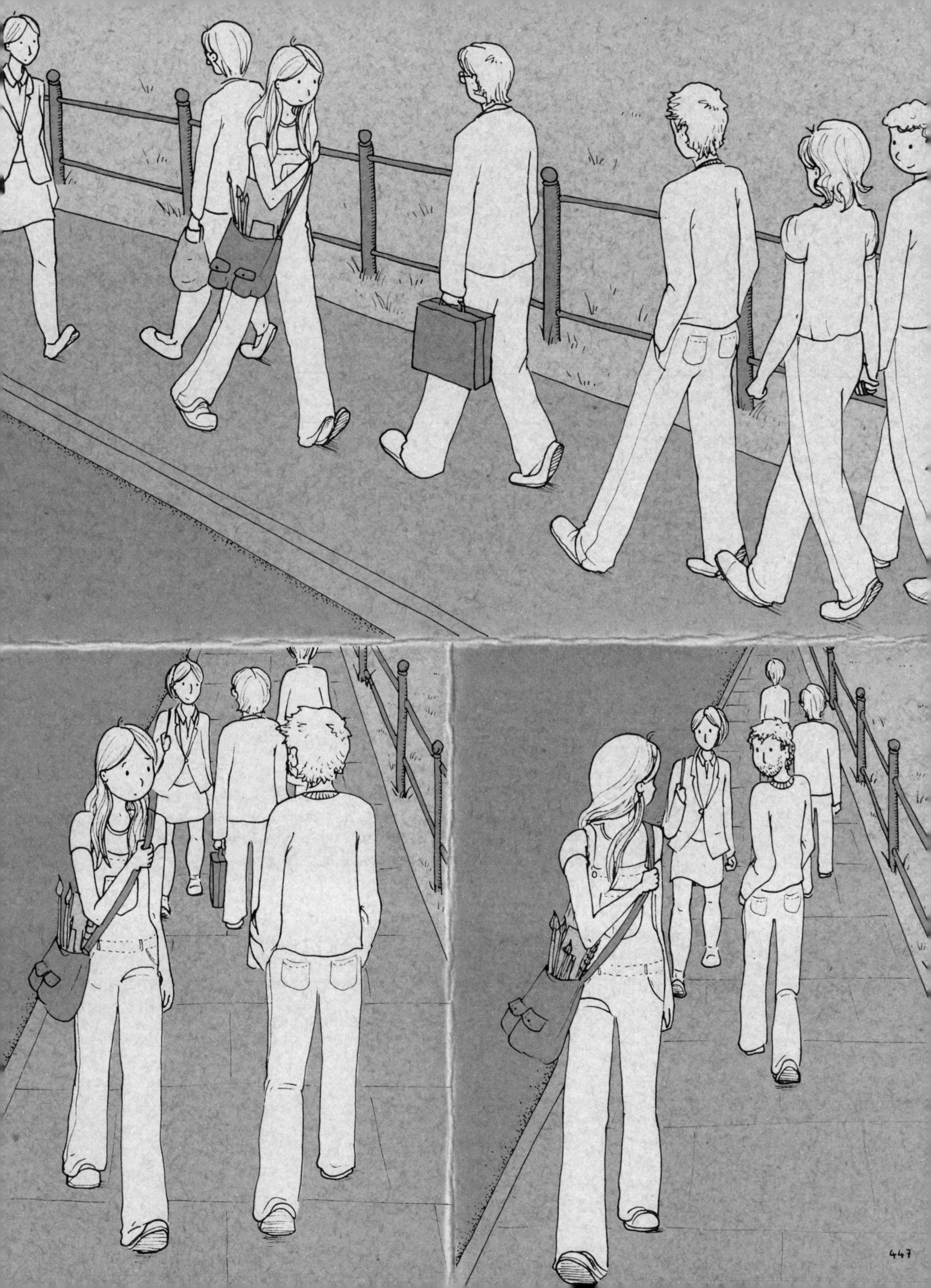

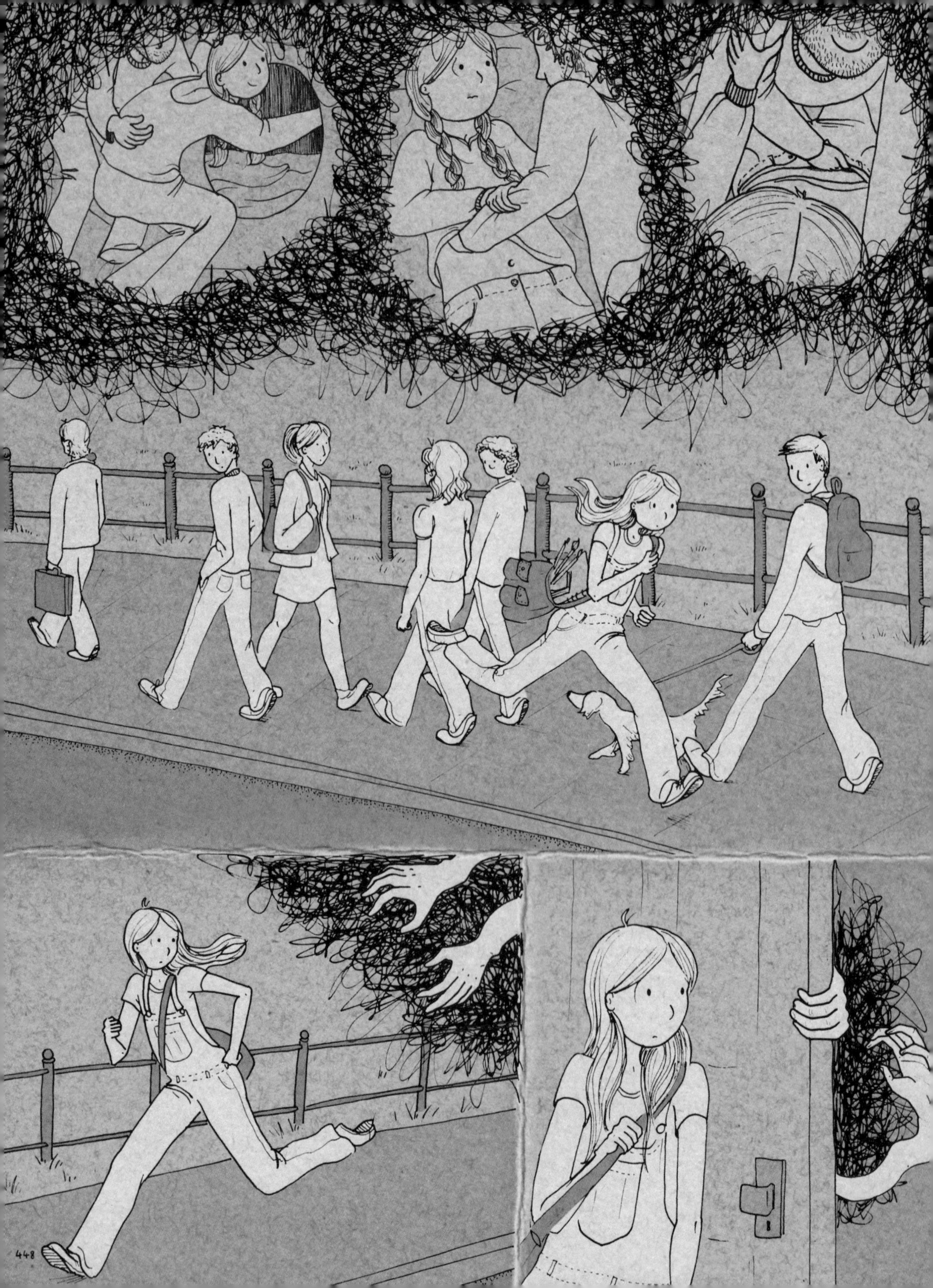

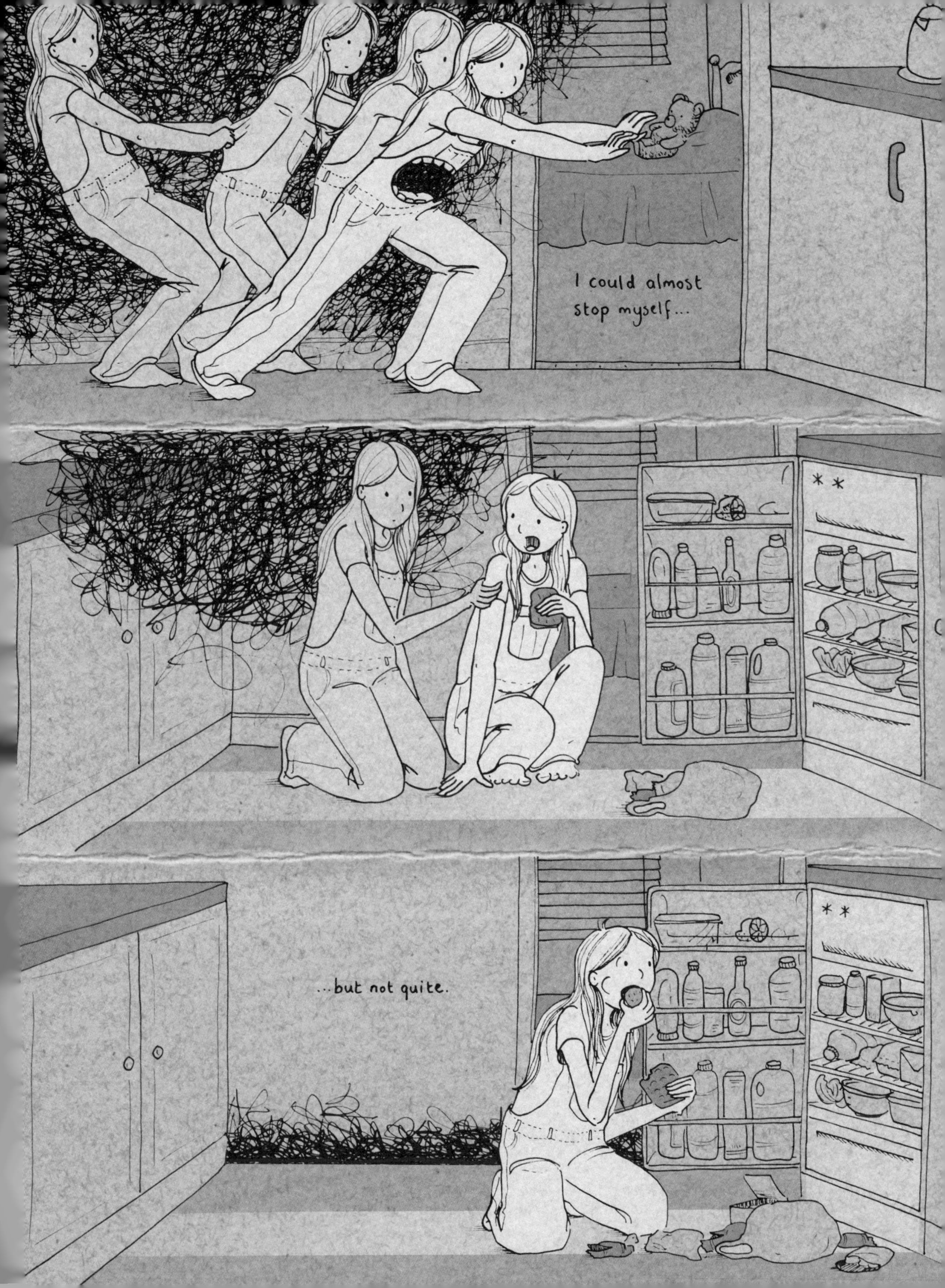
I could almost stop myself...
...but not quite.

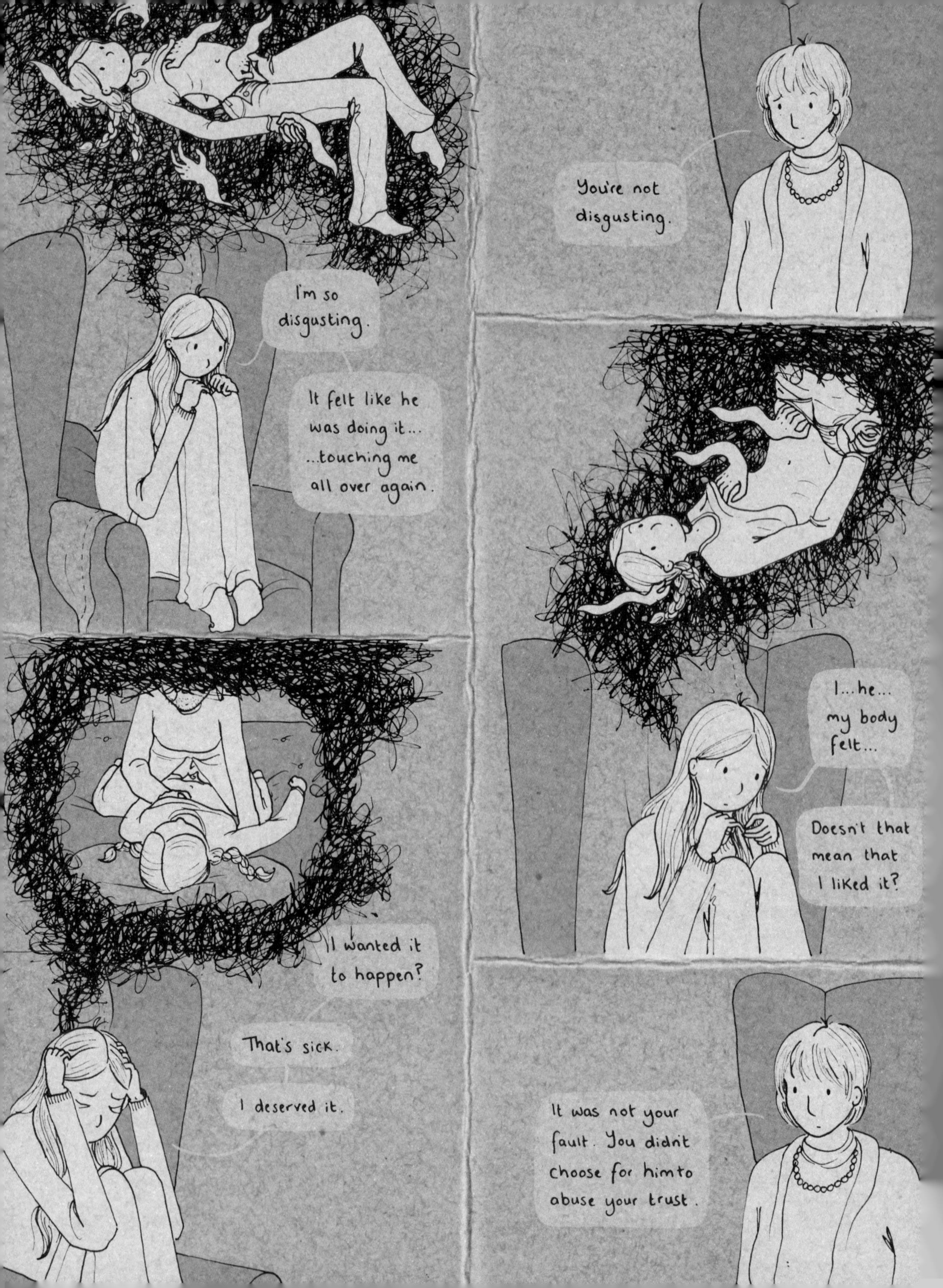

I'm so disgusting.
It felt like he was doing it... ...touching me all over again.
I wanted it to happen?
That's sick.
I deserved it.
You're not disgusting.
I... he... my body felt...
Doesn't that mean that I liked it?
It was not your fault. You didn't choose for him to abuse your trust.

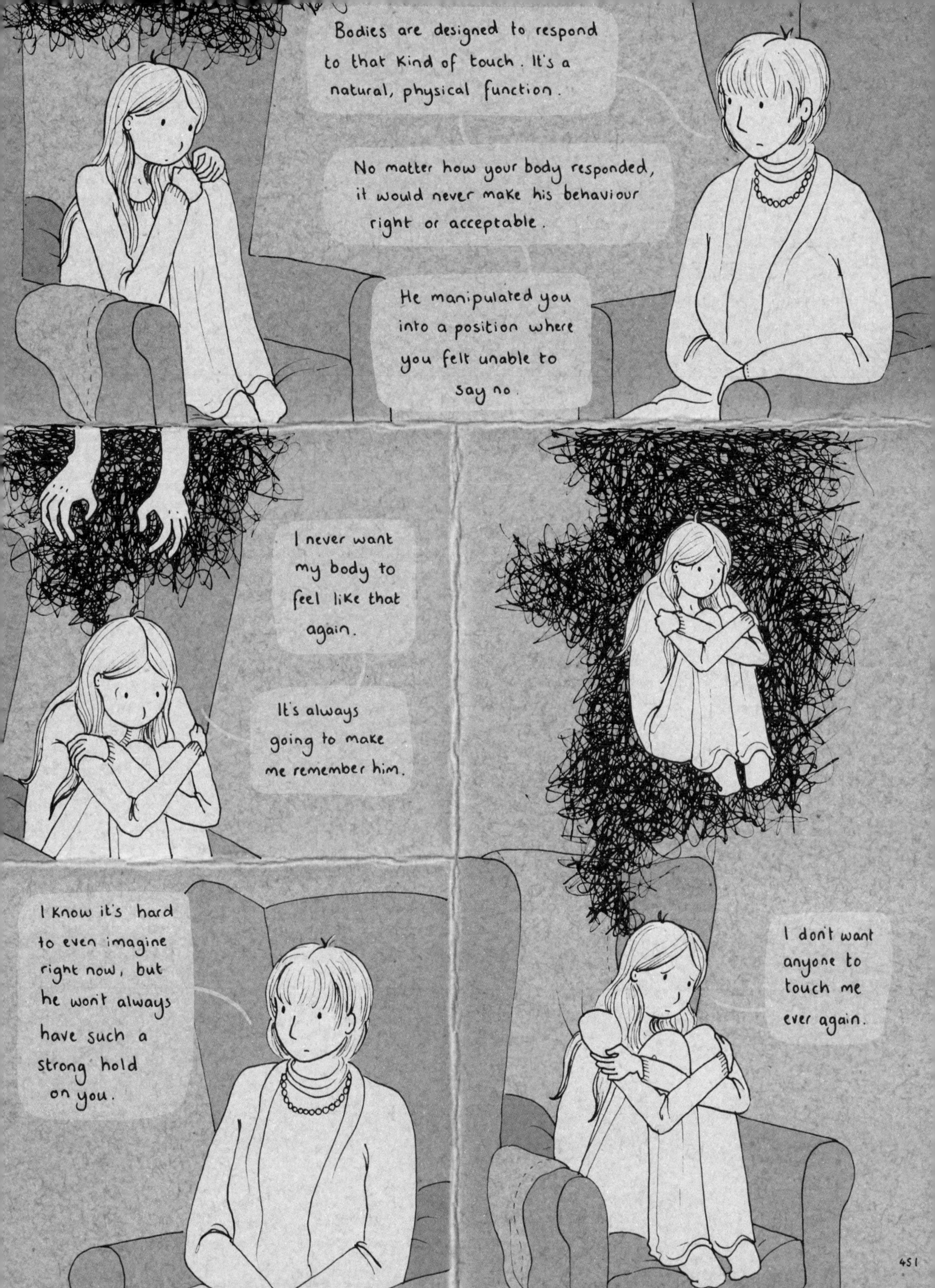
Bodies are designed to respond to that kind of touch. It's a natural, physical function.
No matter how your body responded, it would never make his behaviour right or acceptable.
He manipulated you into a position where you felt unable to say no.
I never want my body to feel like that again.
It's always going to make me remember him.
I know it's hard to even imagine right now, but he won't always have such a strong hold on you.
I don't want anyone to touch me ever again.

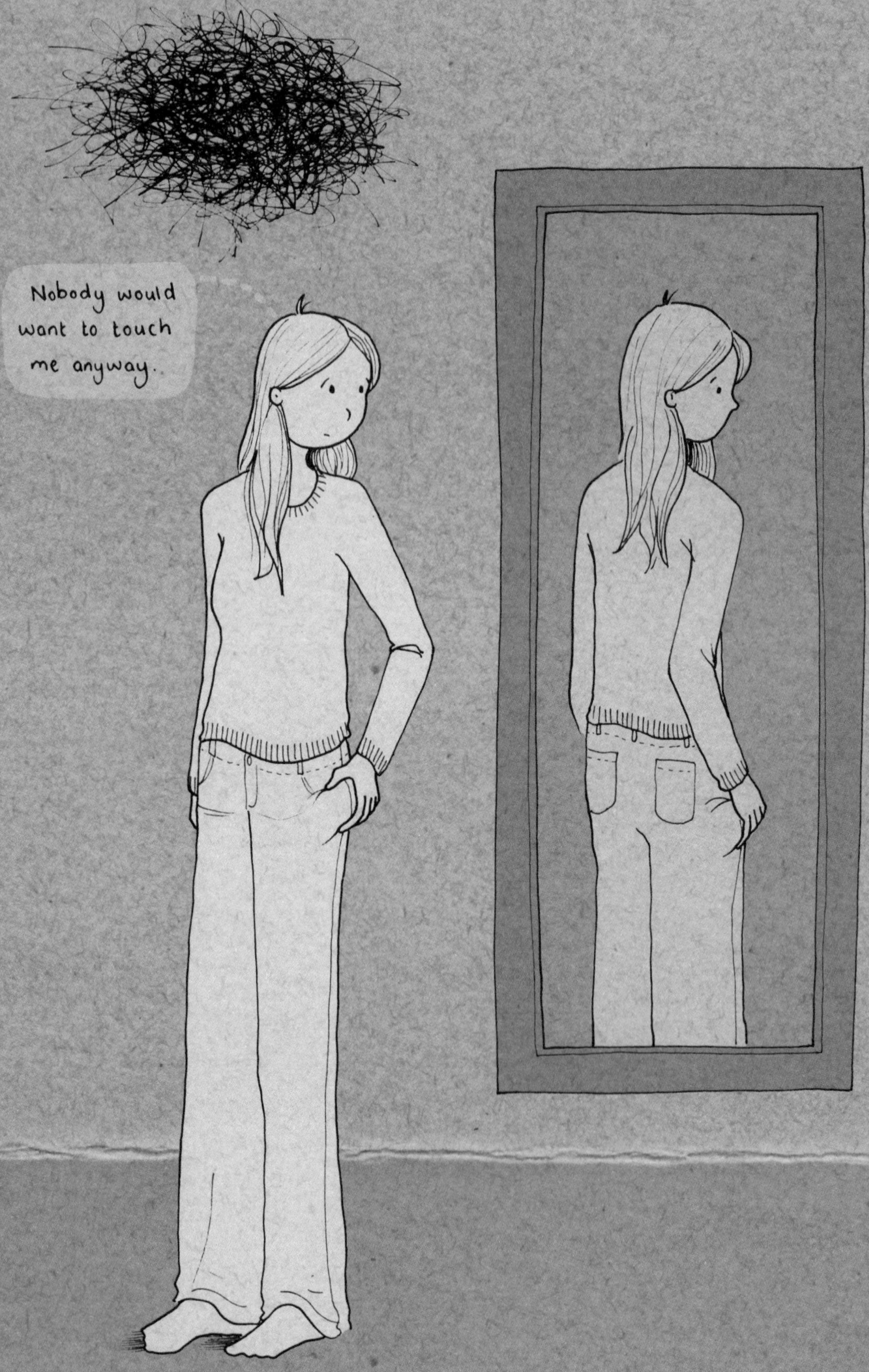
Nobody would want to touch me anyway.

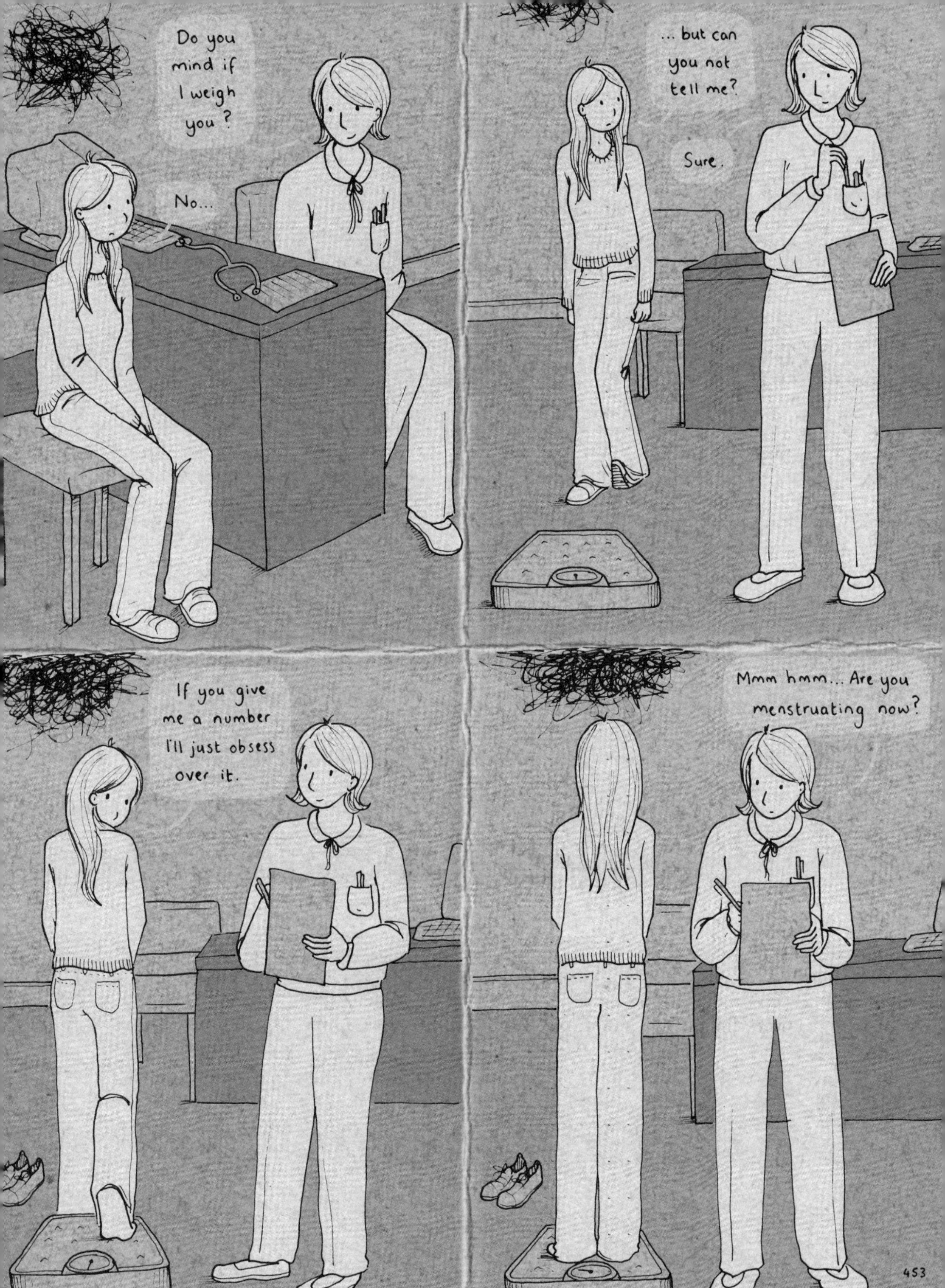
Do you mind if I weigh you ?
No...
... but can you not tell me?
Sure.
If you give me a number I'll just obsess over it.
Mmm hmm... Are you menstruating now?

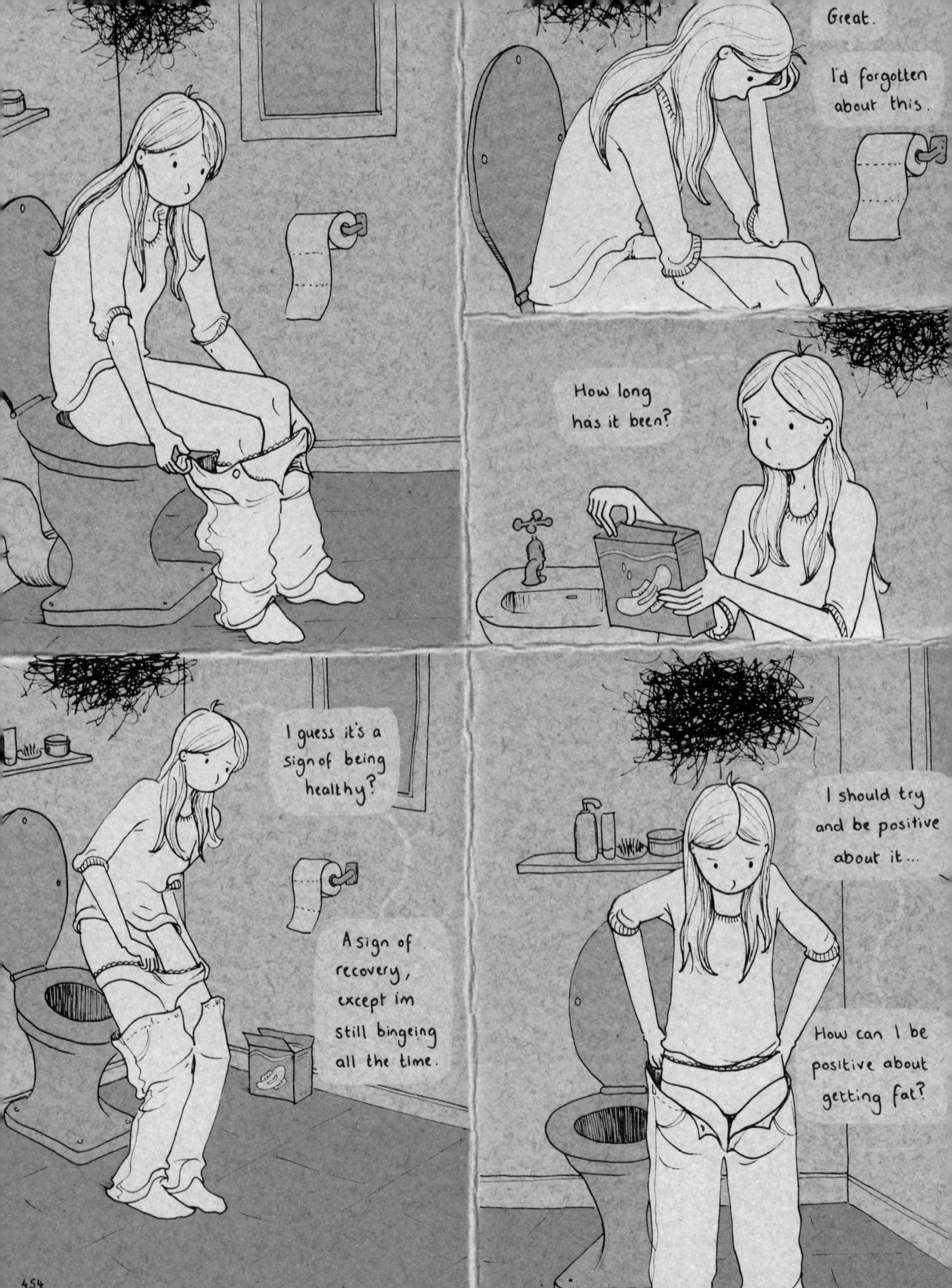

Great.
I'd forgotten about this.
How long has it been?
I guess it's a sign of being healthy?
A sign of recovery, except im still bingeing all the time.
I should try and be positive about it...
How can I be positive about getting fat?

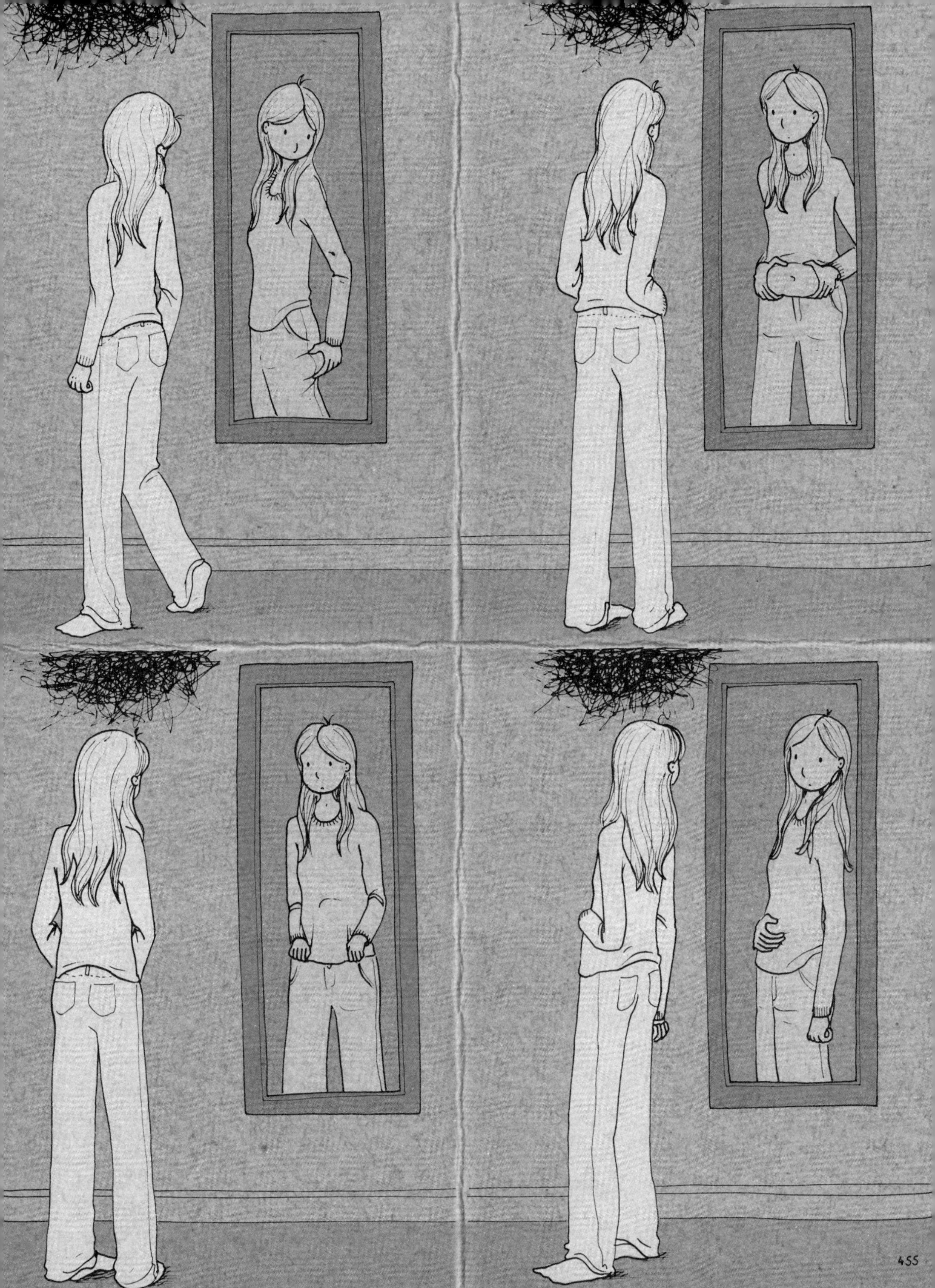

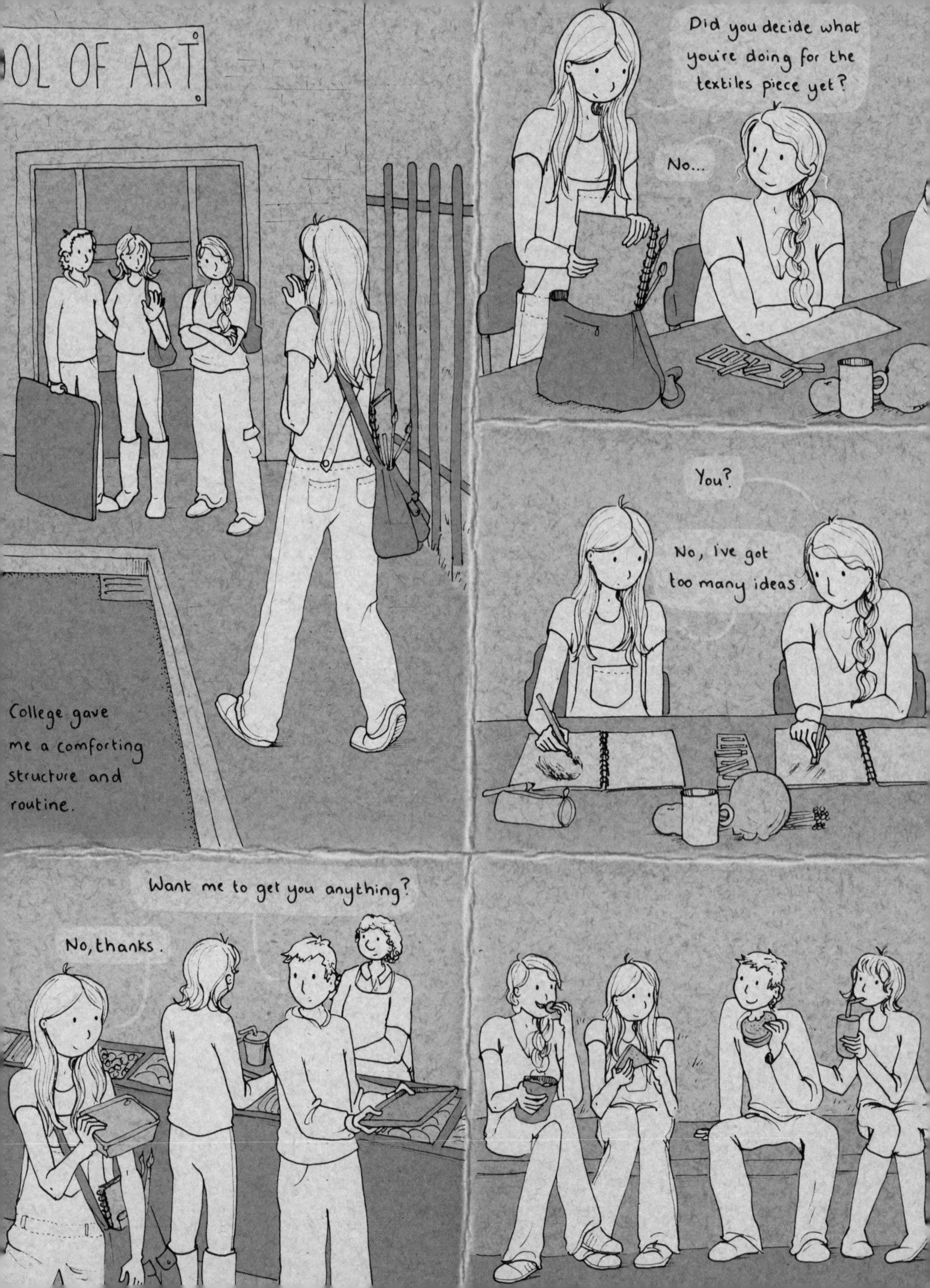
OL OF ART
College gave me a comforting structure and routine.
Did you decide what you're doing for the textiles piece yet?
No...
You?
No, I've got too many ideas.
Want me to get you anything?
No, thanks.

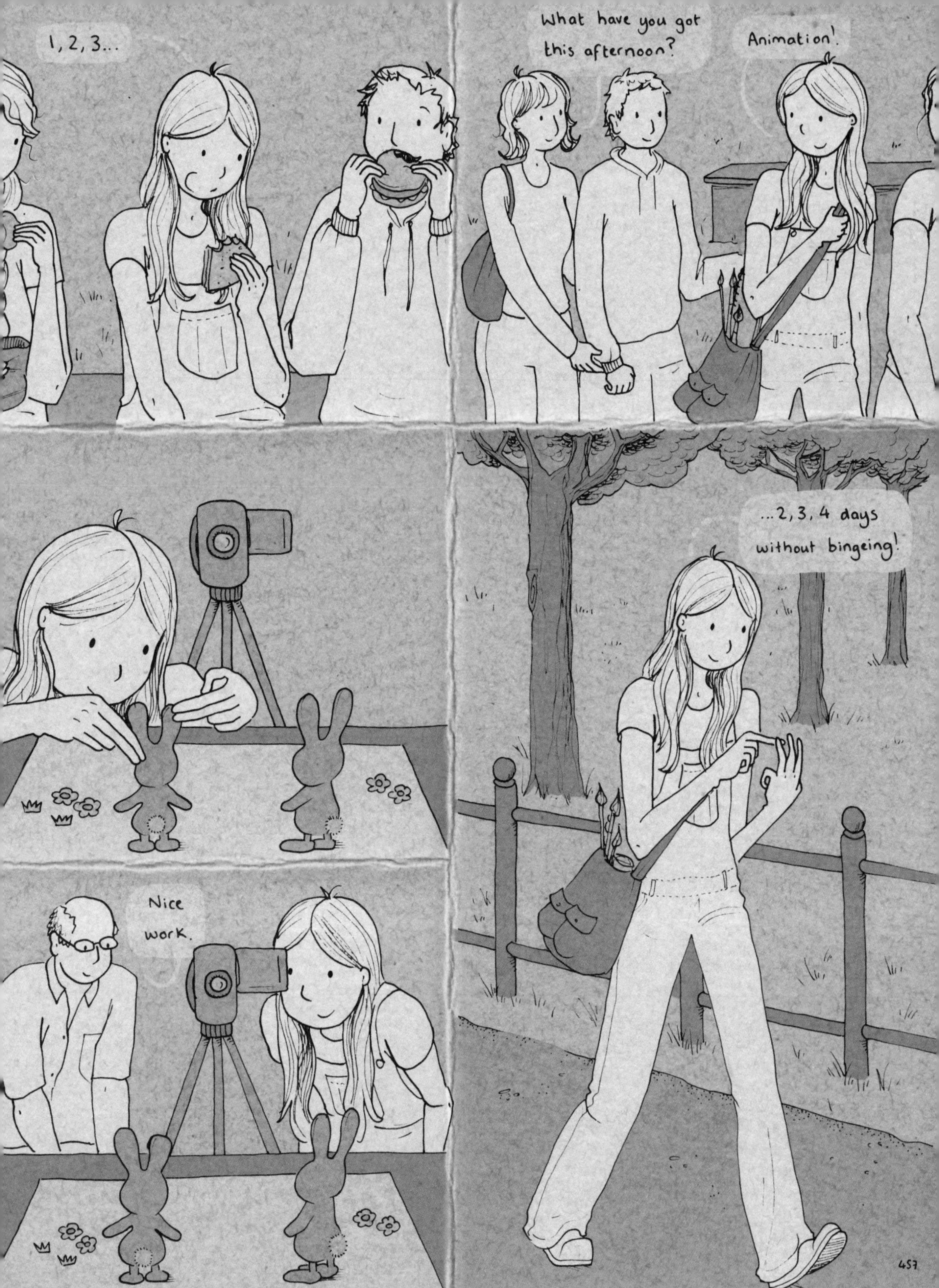
1, 2, 3...
What have you got this afternoon?
Animation!
Nice work.
...2, 3, 4 days without bingeing!

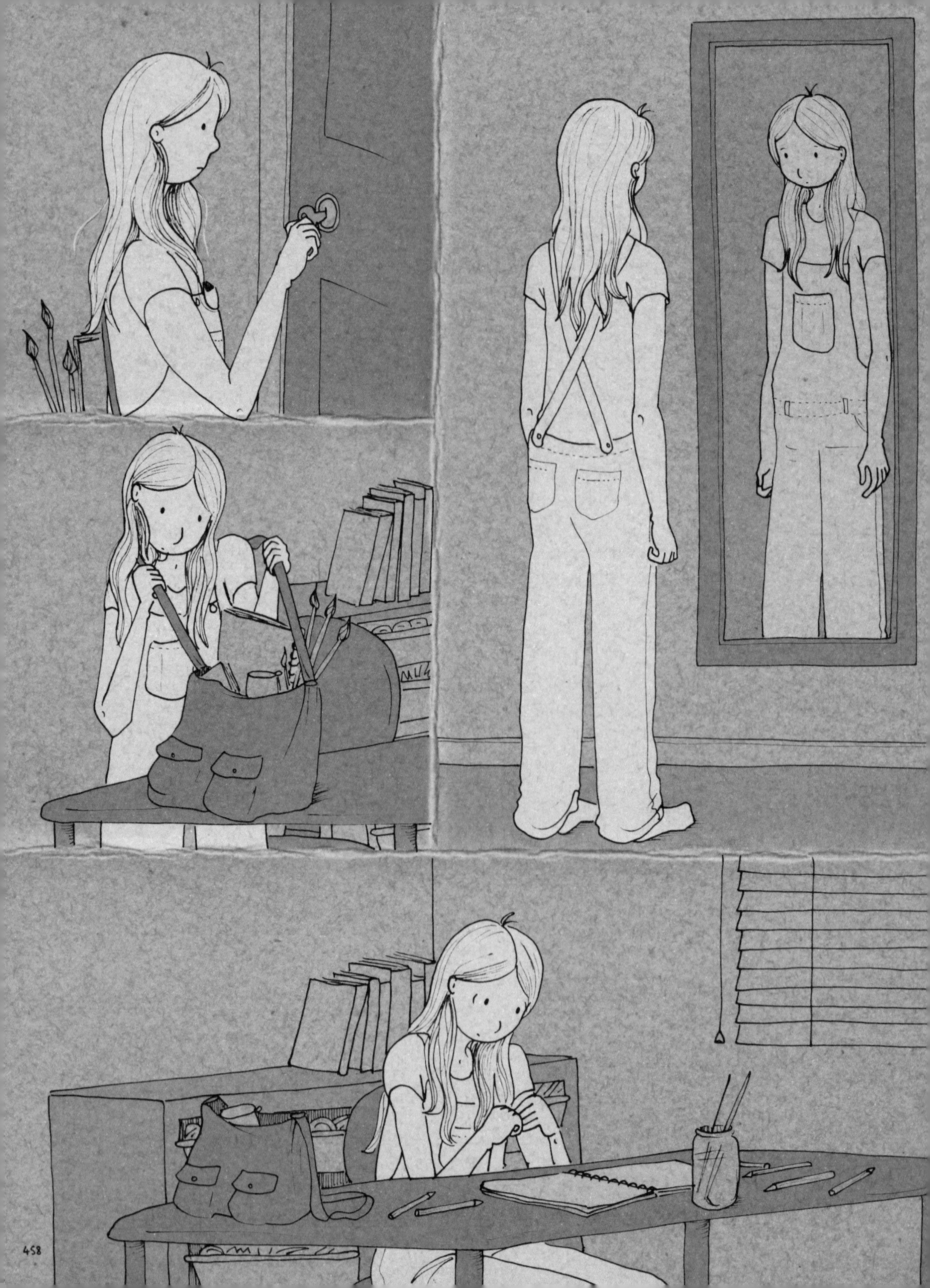

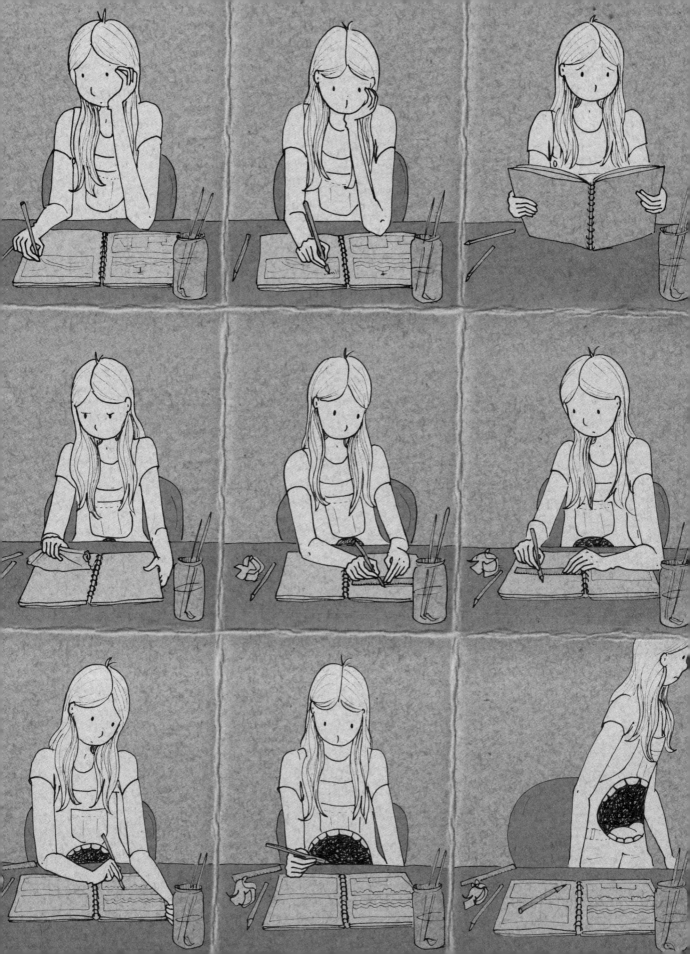

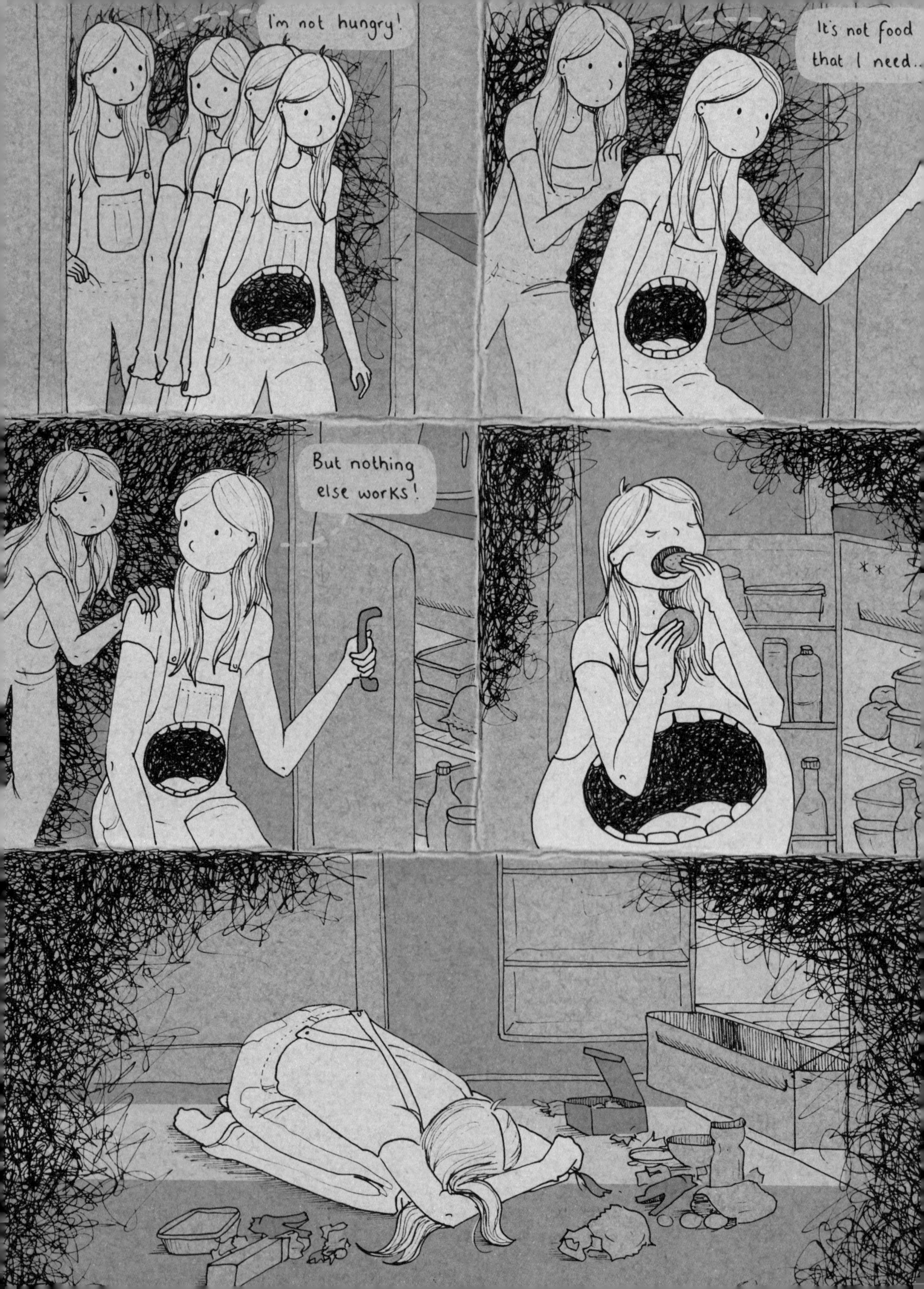
I'm not hungry!
It's not food that I need...
But nothing else works!

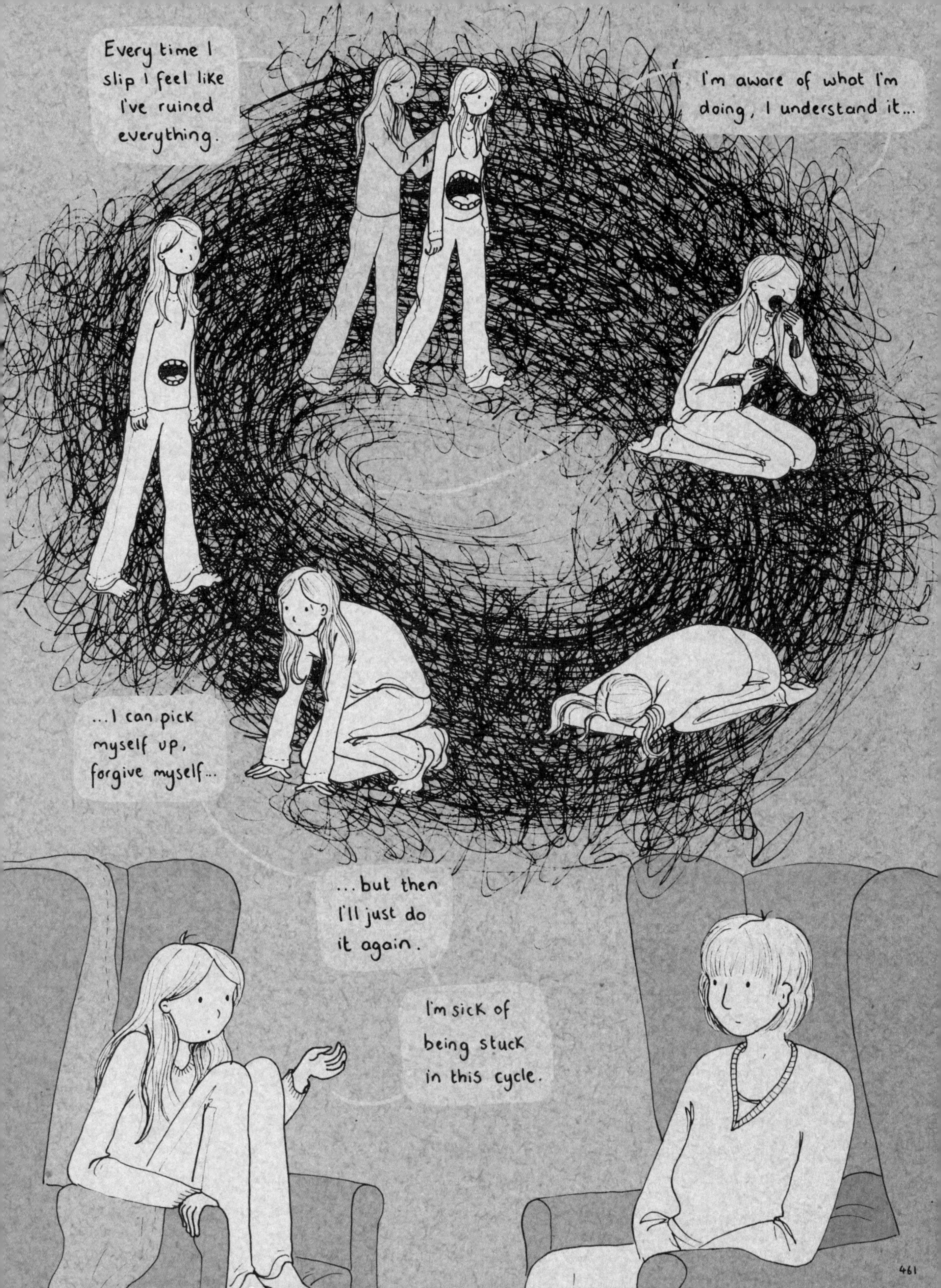
Every time I slip I feel like I've ruined everything.
I'm aware of what I'm doing, I understand it...
...I can pick myself up, forgive myself...
...but then I'll just do it again.
I'm sick of being stuck in this cycle.

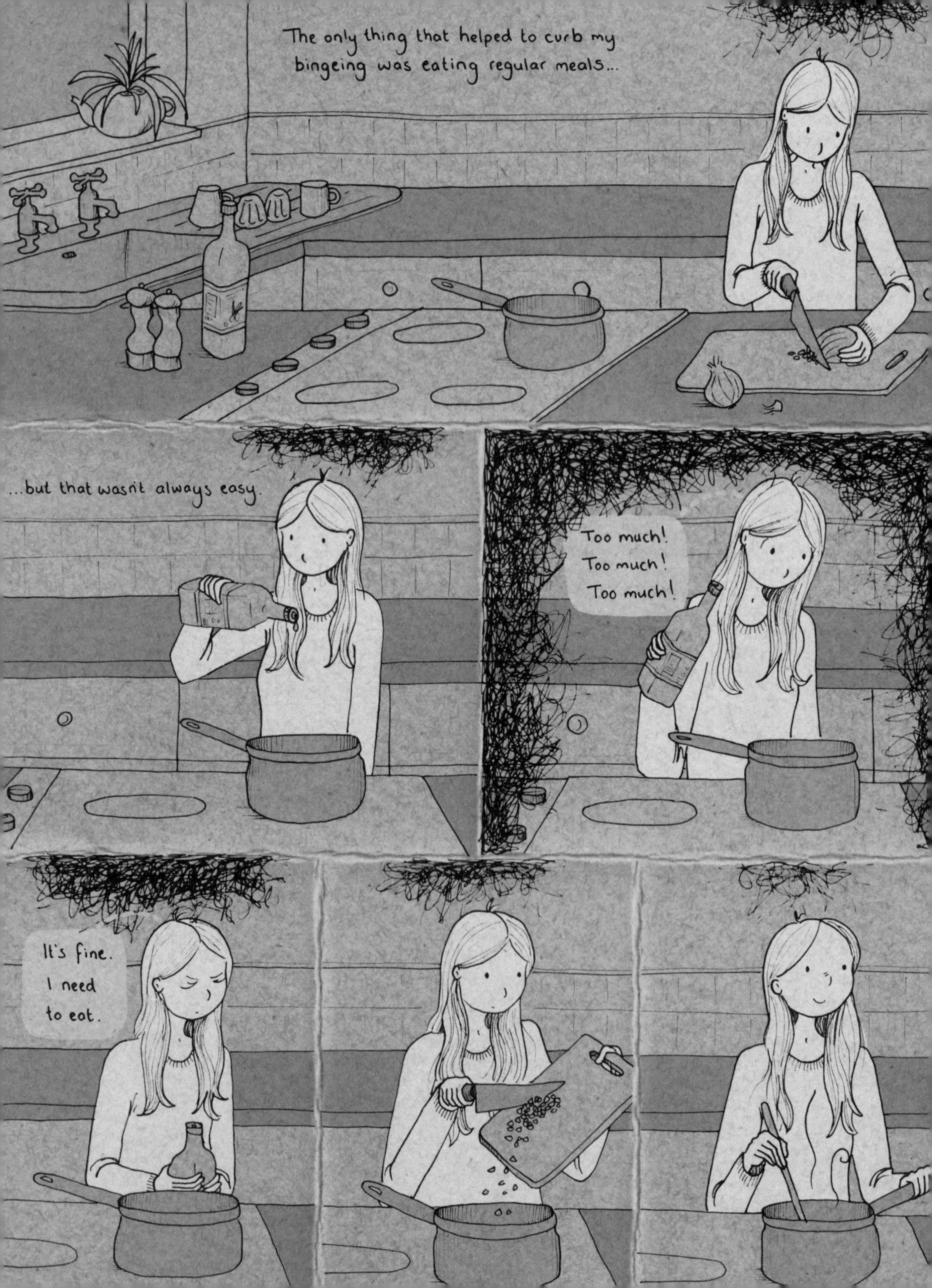
The only thing that helped to curb my bingeing was eating regular meals...
...but that wasn't always easy.
Too much! Too much! Too much!
It's fine. I need to eat.

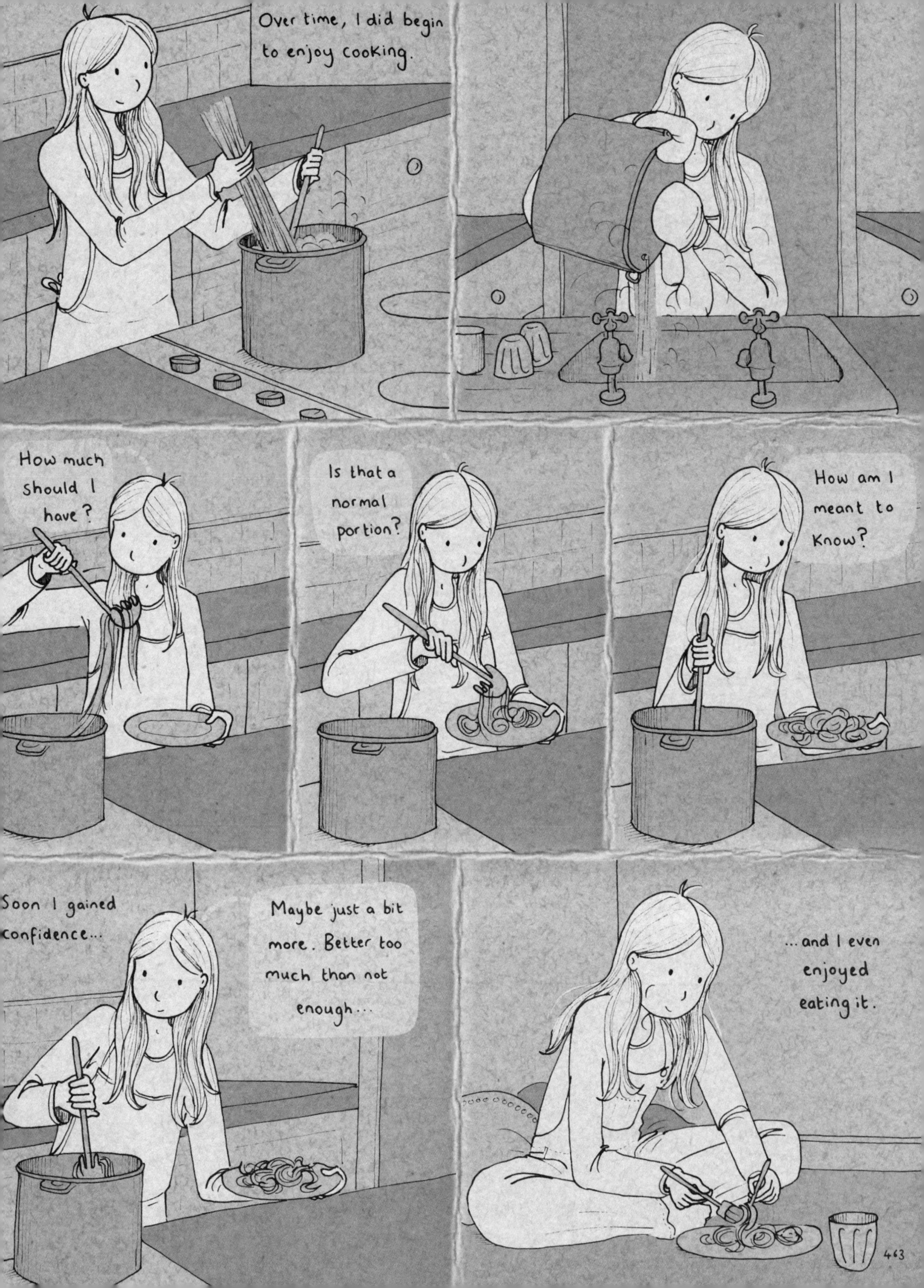
Over time, I did begin to enjoy cooking.
How much should I have?
Is that a normal portion?
How am I meant to know?
Soon I gained confidence...
Maybe just a bit more. Better too much than not enough...
...and I even enjoyed eating it.

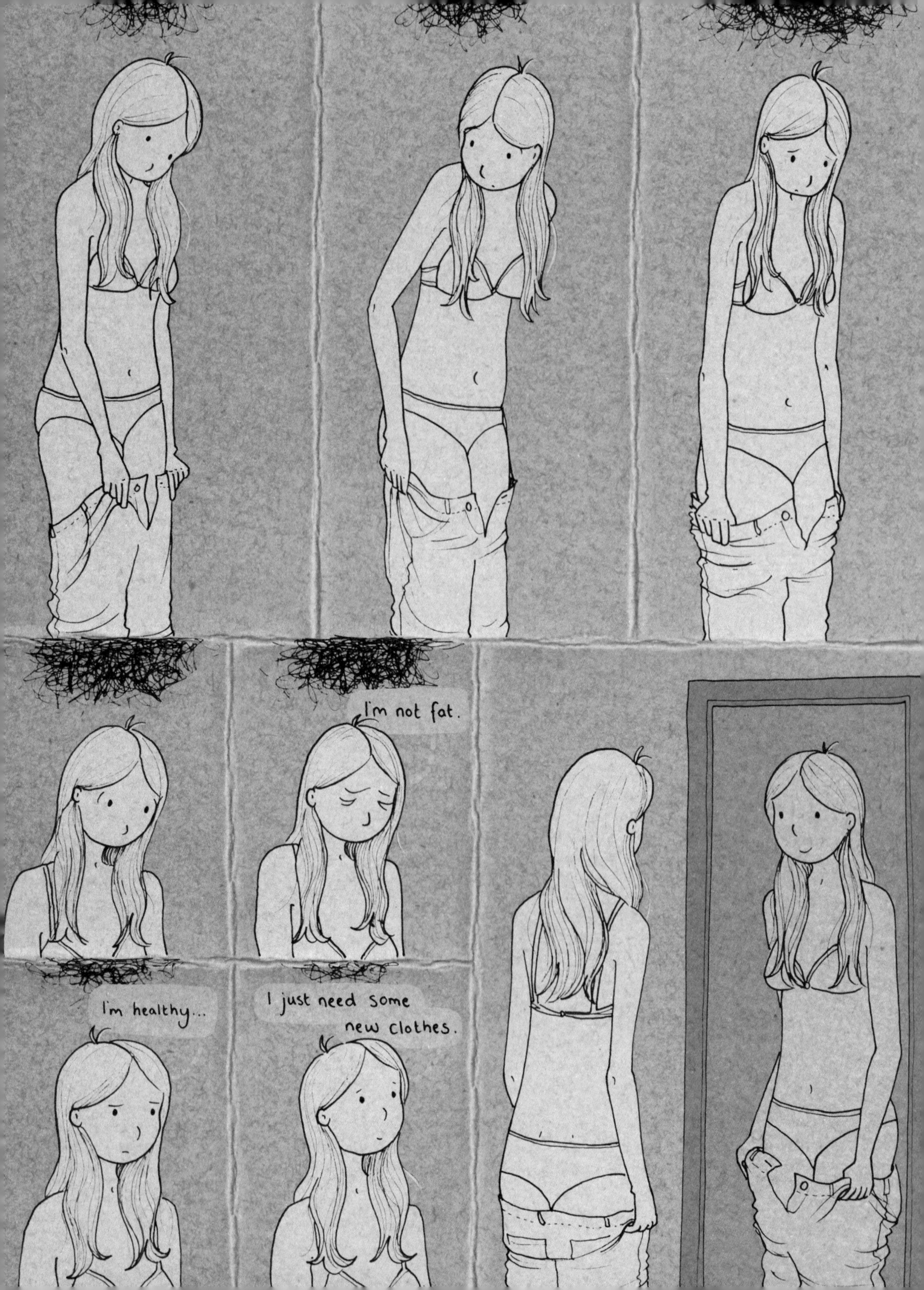

I'm not fat.
I'm healthy...
I just need some new clothes.

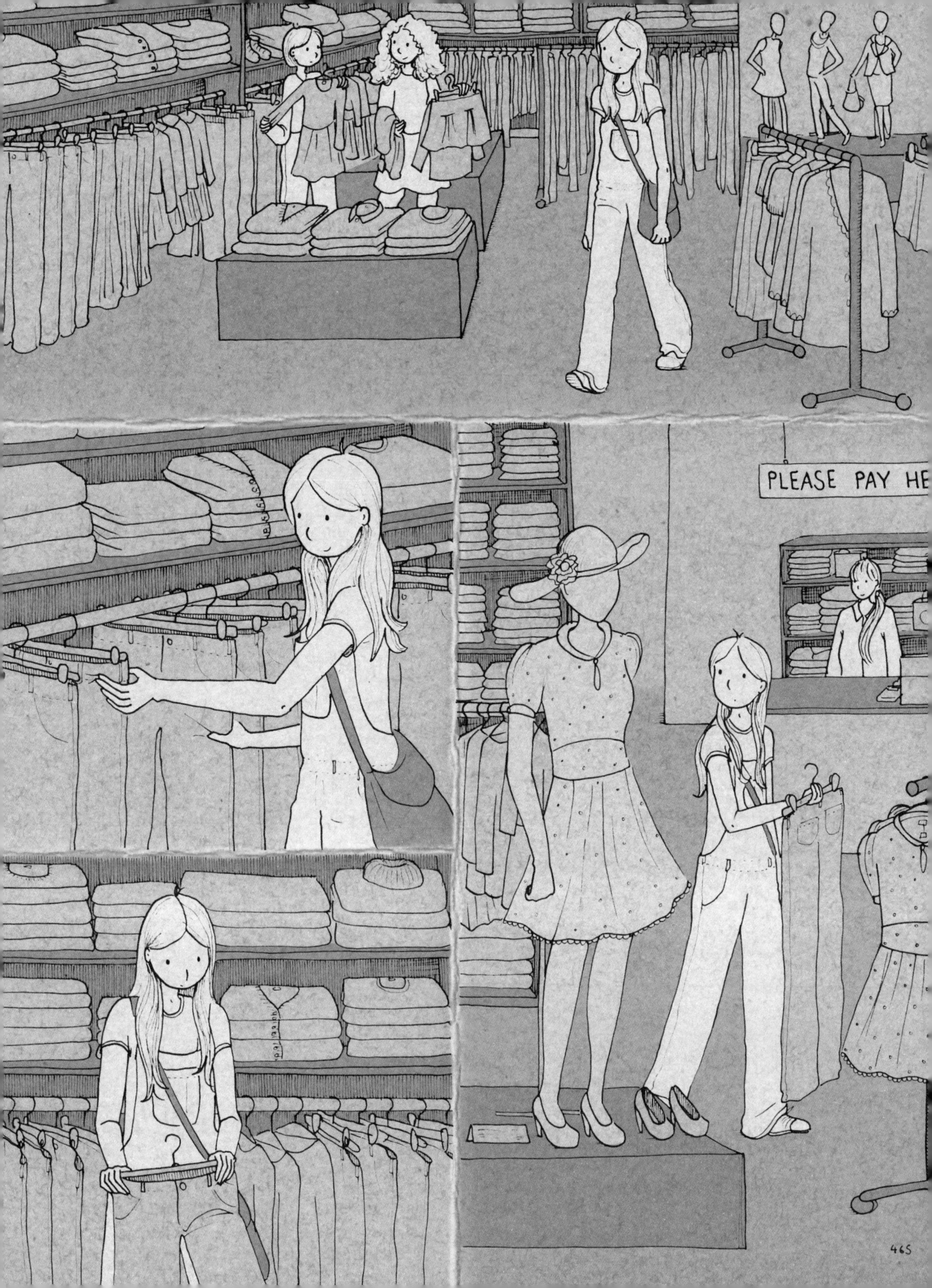
PLEASE PAY HE

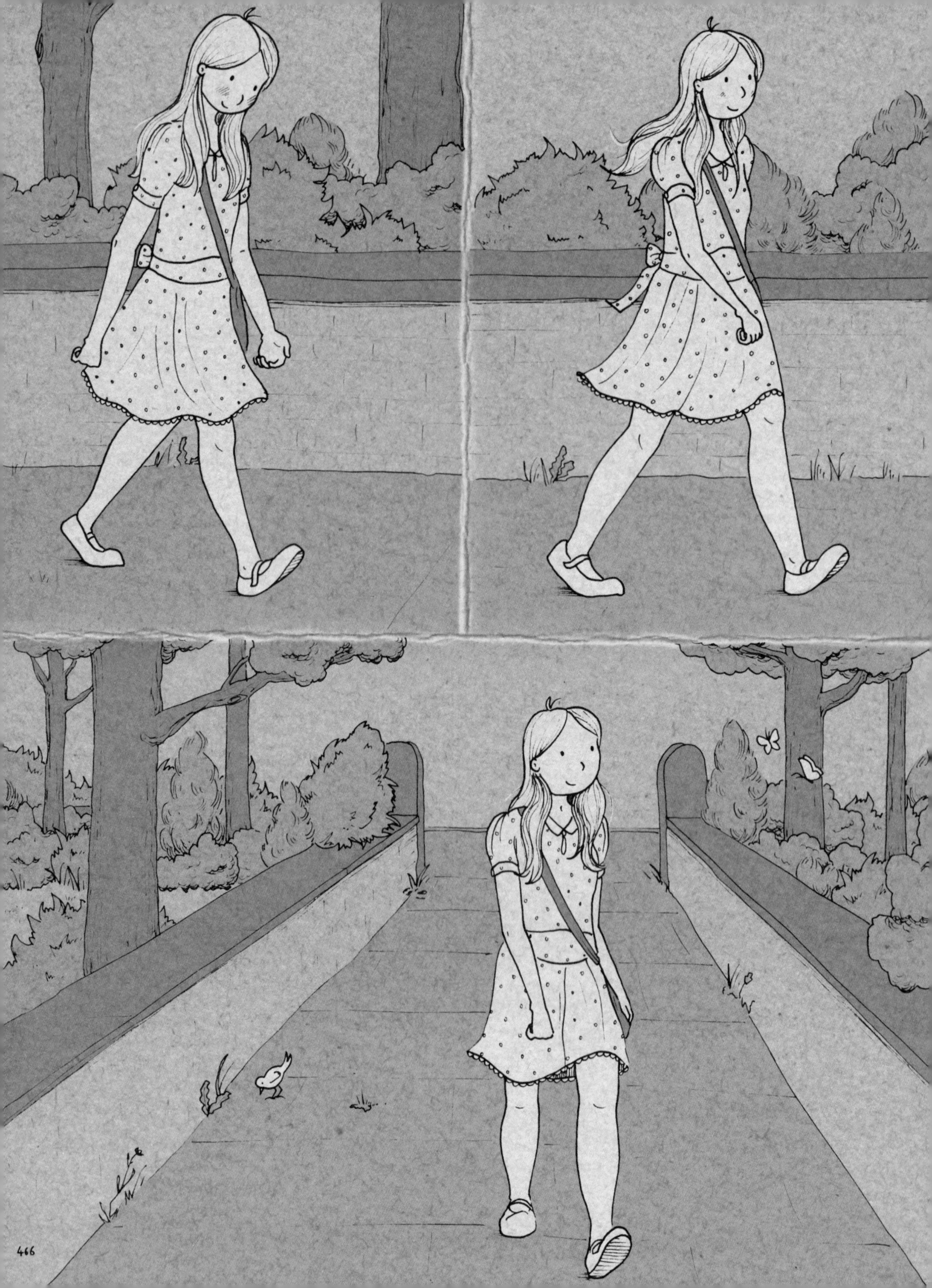

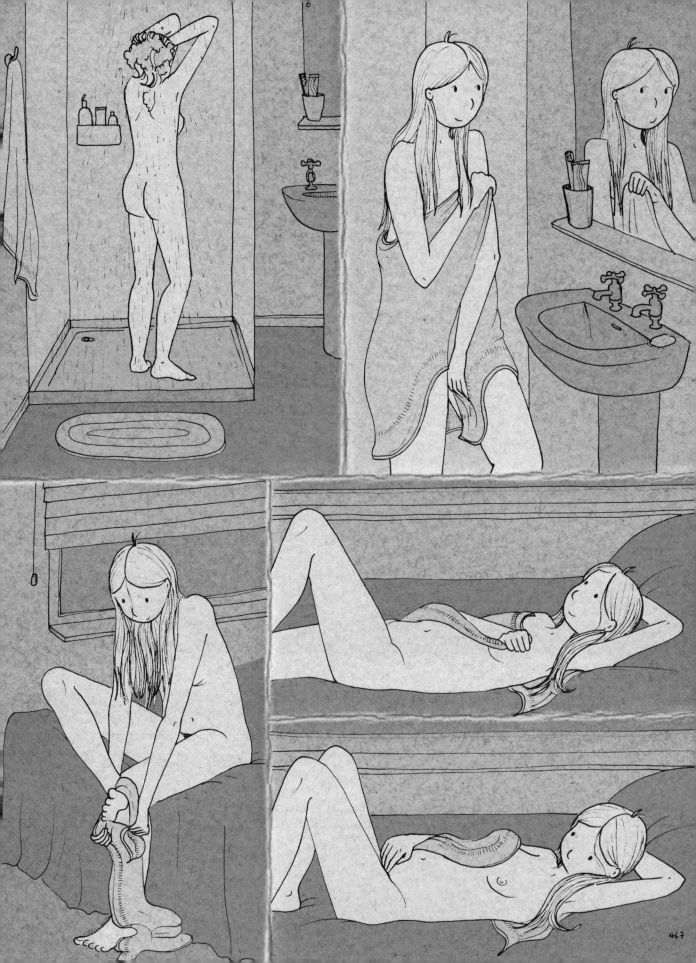

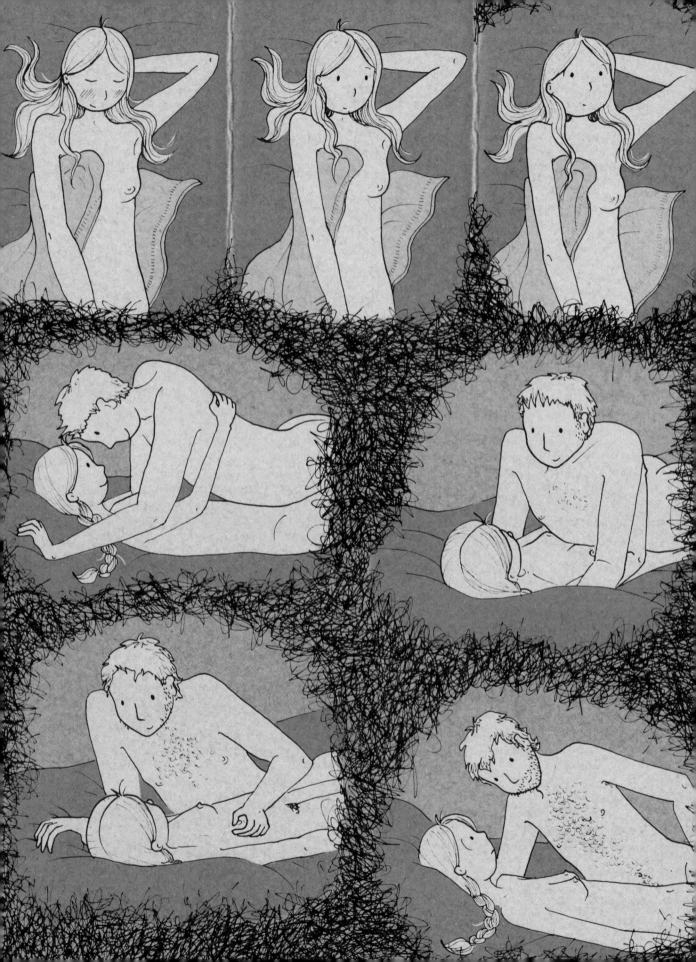

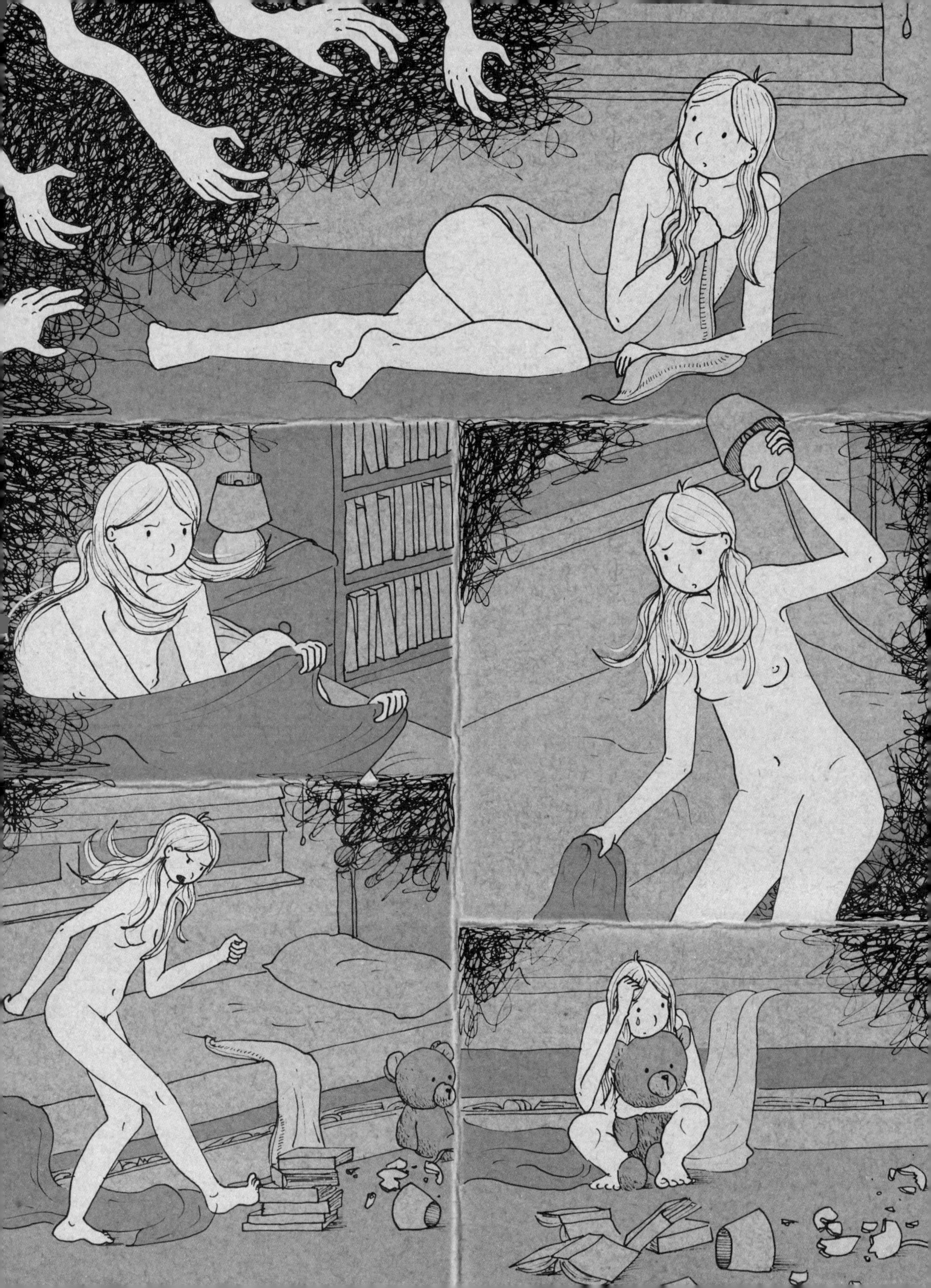

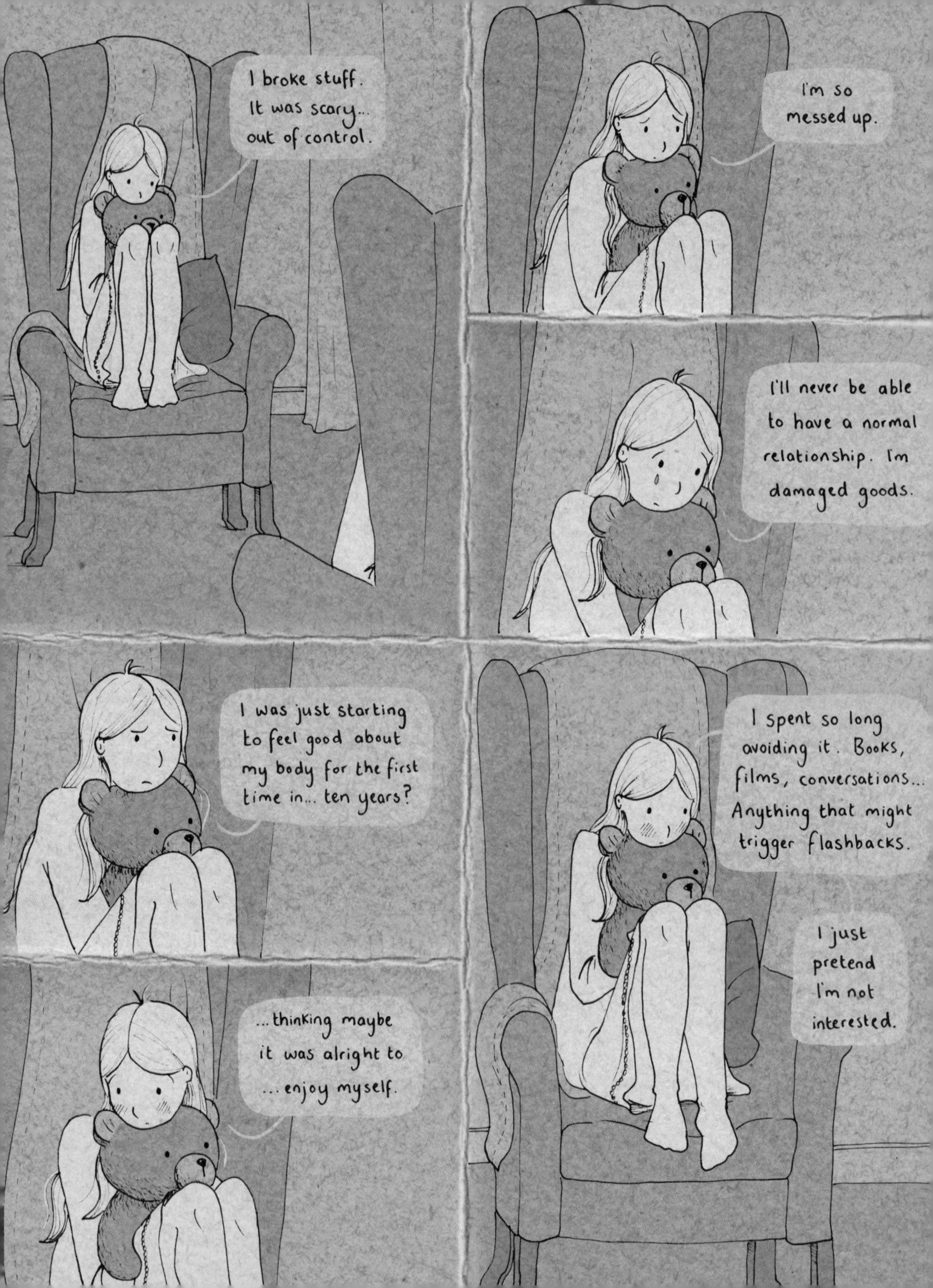
I broke stuff. It was scary... out of control.
I'm so messed up.
I'll never be able to have a normal relationship. I'm damaged goods.
I was just starting to feel good about my body for the first time in... ten years?
...thinking maybe it was alright to ...enjoy myself.
I spent so long avoiding it. Books, films, conversations... Anything that might trigger flashbacks.
I just pretend I'm not interested.

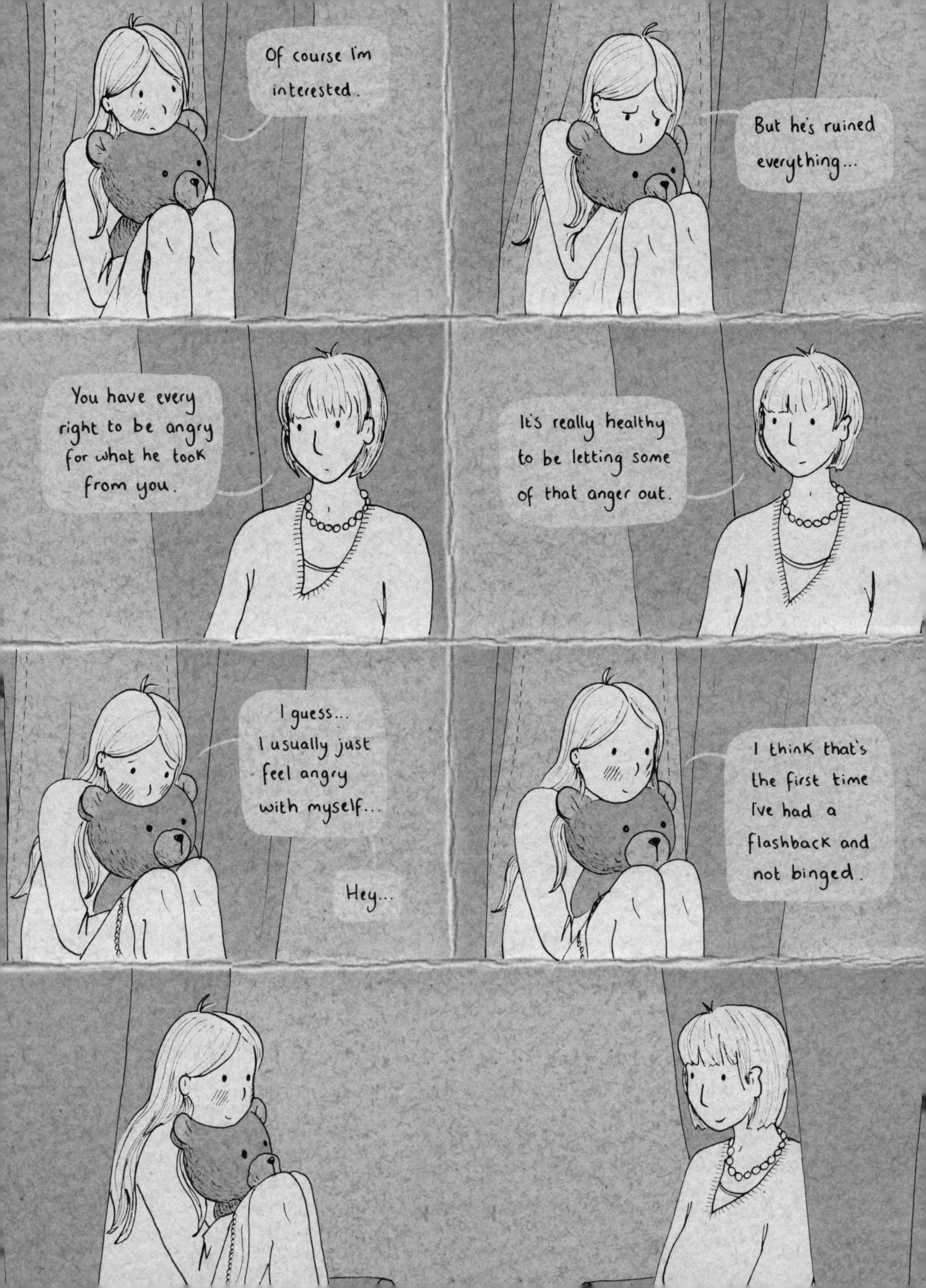
Of course I'm interested.
But he's ruined everything...
You have every right to be angry for what he took from you.
It's really healthy to be letting some of that anger out.
I guess... I usually just feel angry with myself...
Hey...
I think that's the first time I've had a flashback and not binged.

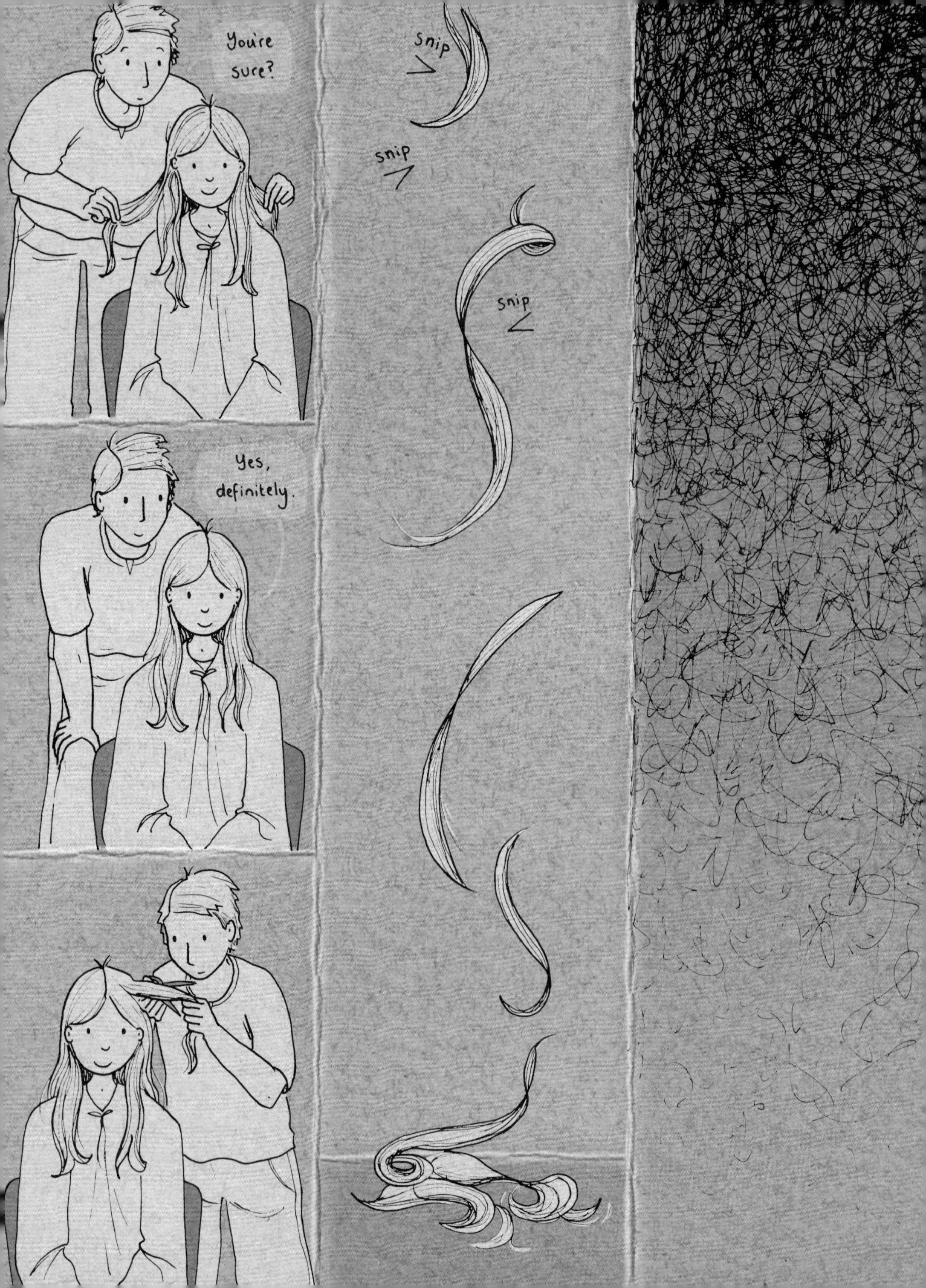
You're sure?
Yes, definitely.
snip
snip
snip

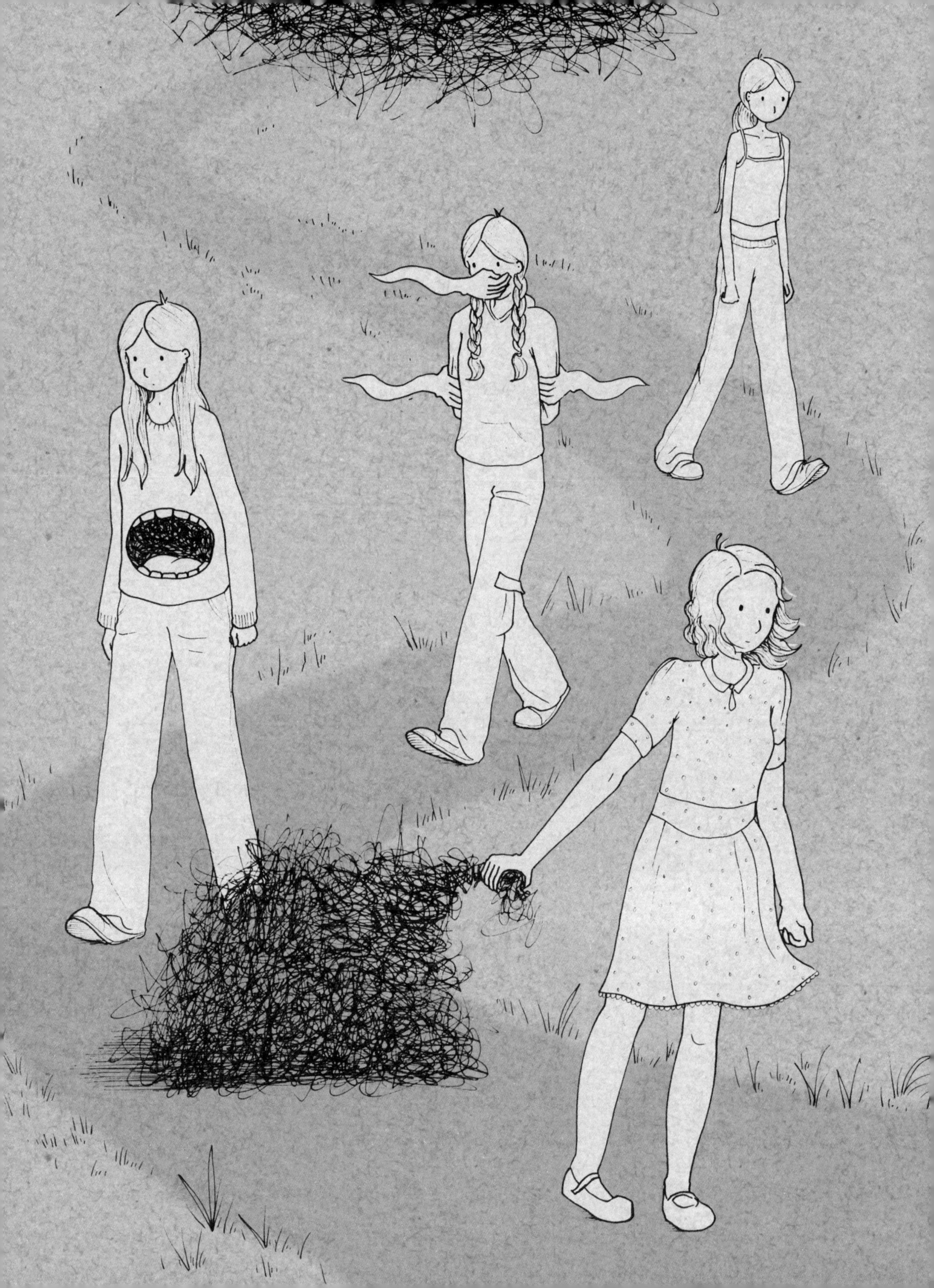

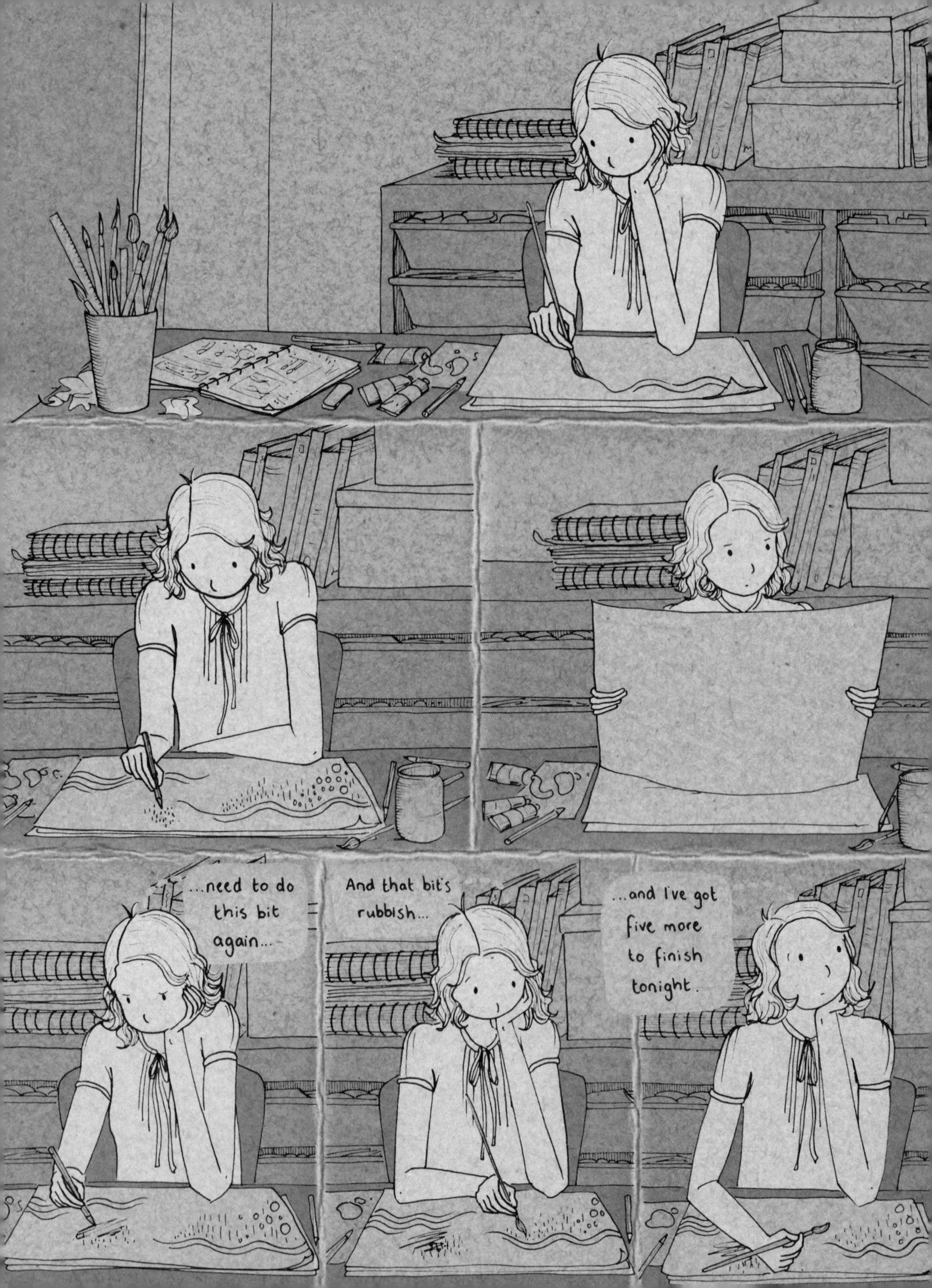
...need to do this bit again...
And that bit's rubbish...
...and I've got five more to finish tonight.

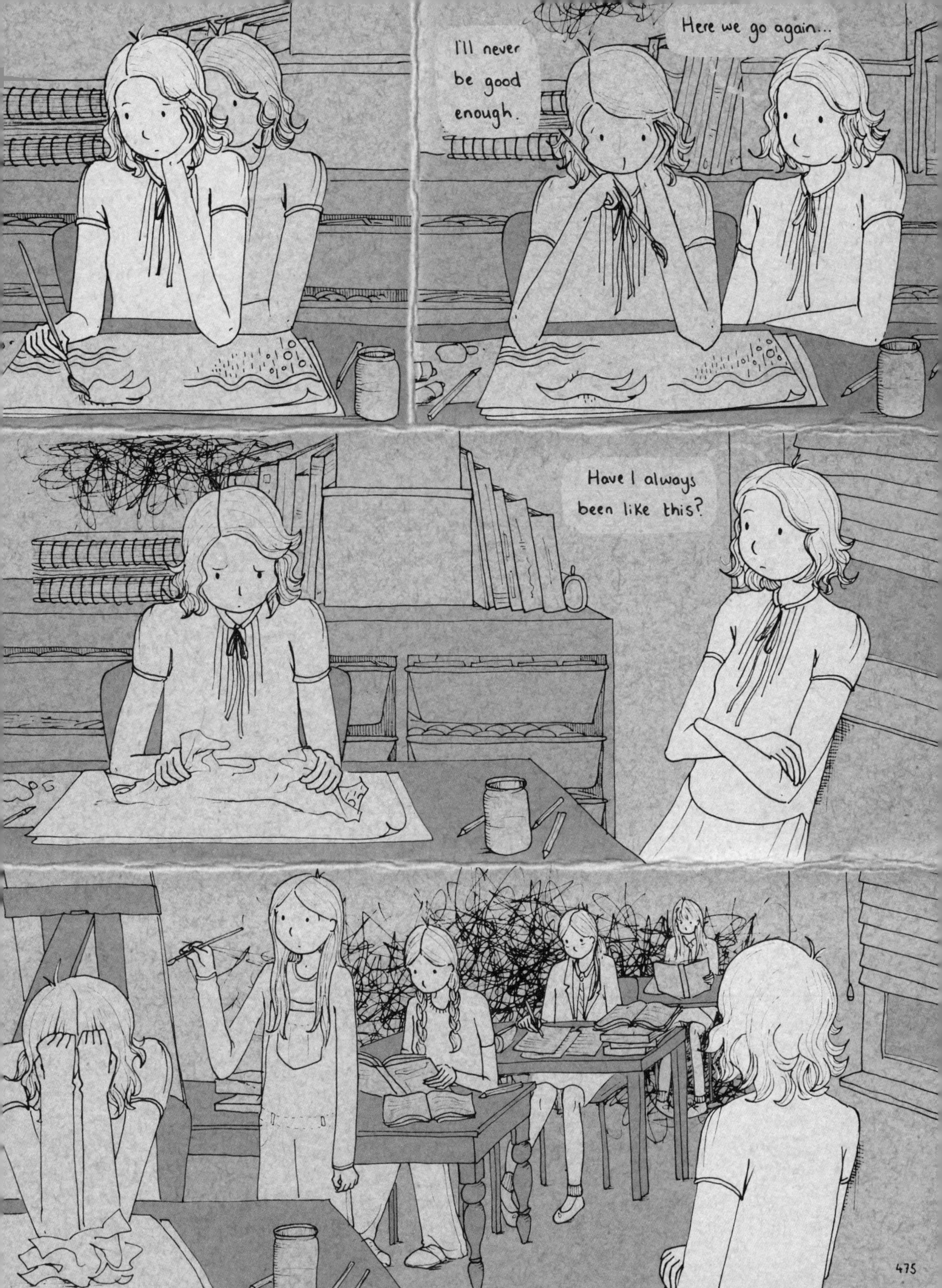
I'll never be good enough.
Here we go again...
Have I always been like this?

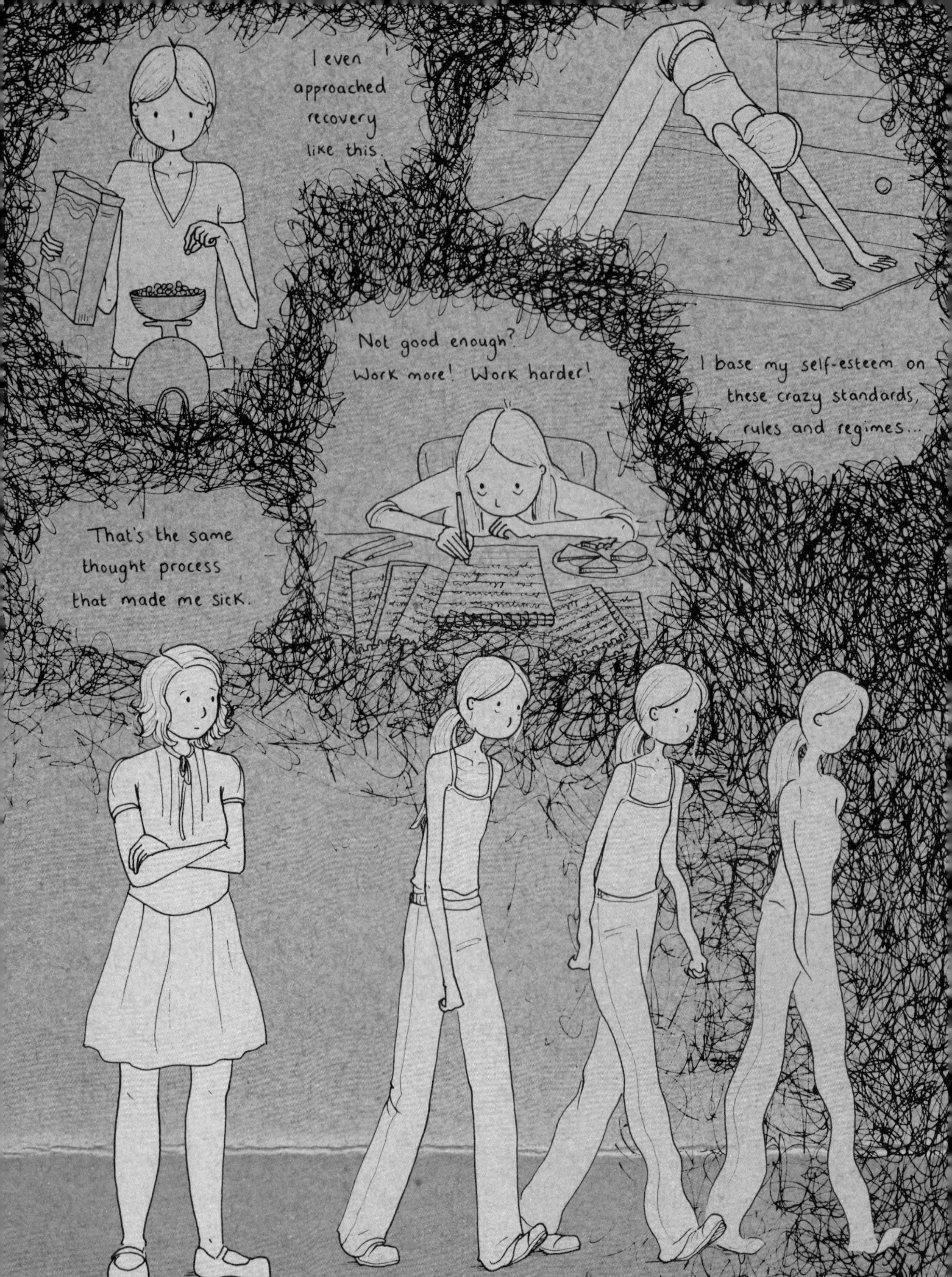
I even approached recovery like this.
Not good enough? Work more! Work harder!
I base my self-esteem on these crazy standards, rules and regimes...
That's the same thought process that made me sick.

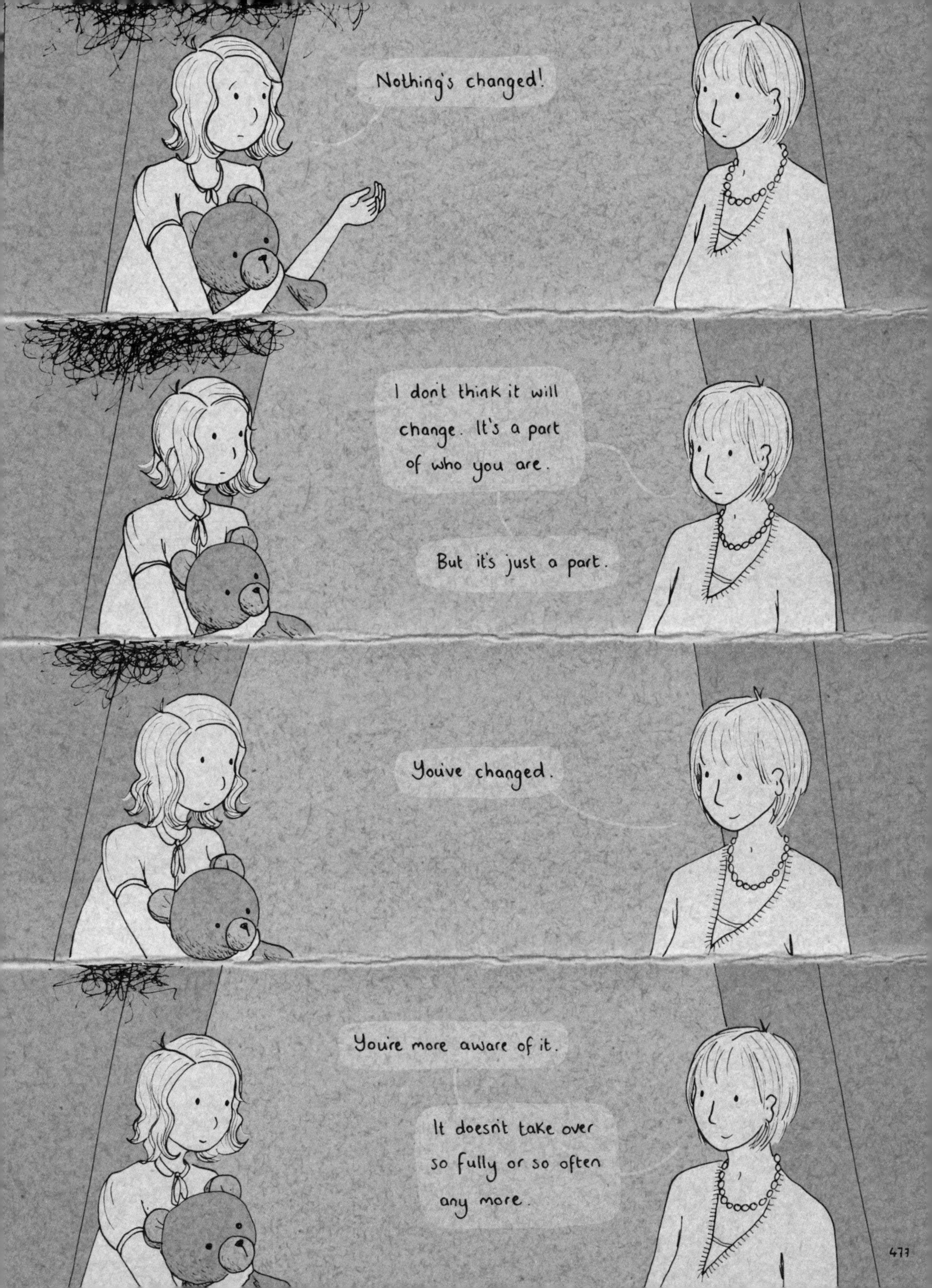

Nothing's changed!
I don't think it will change. It's a part of who you are.
But it's just a part.
You've changed.
You're more aware of it.
It doesn't take over so fully or so often any more.

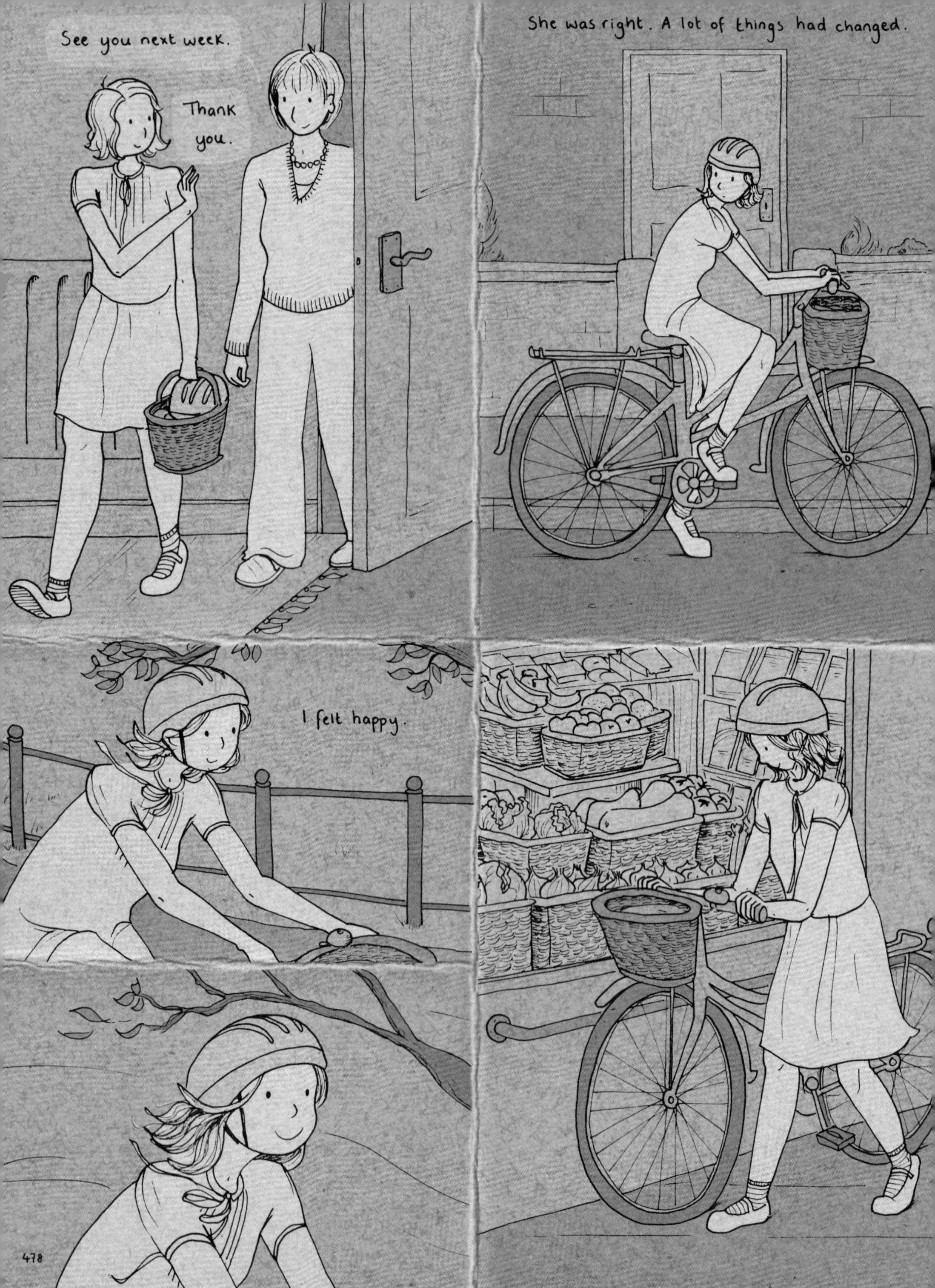
See you next week.
Thank you.
She was right. A lot of things had changed.
I felt happy.

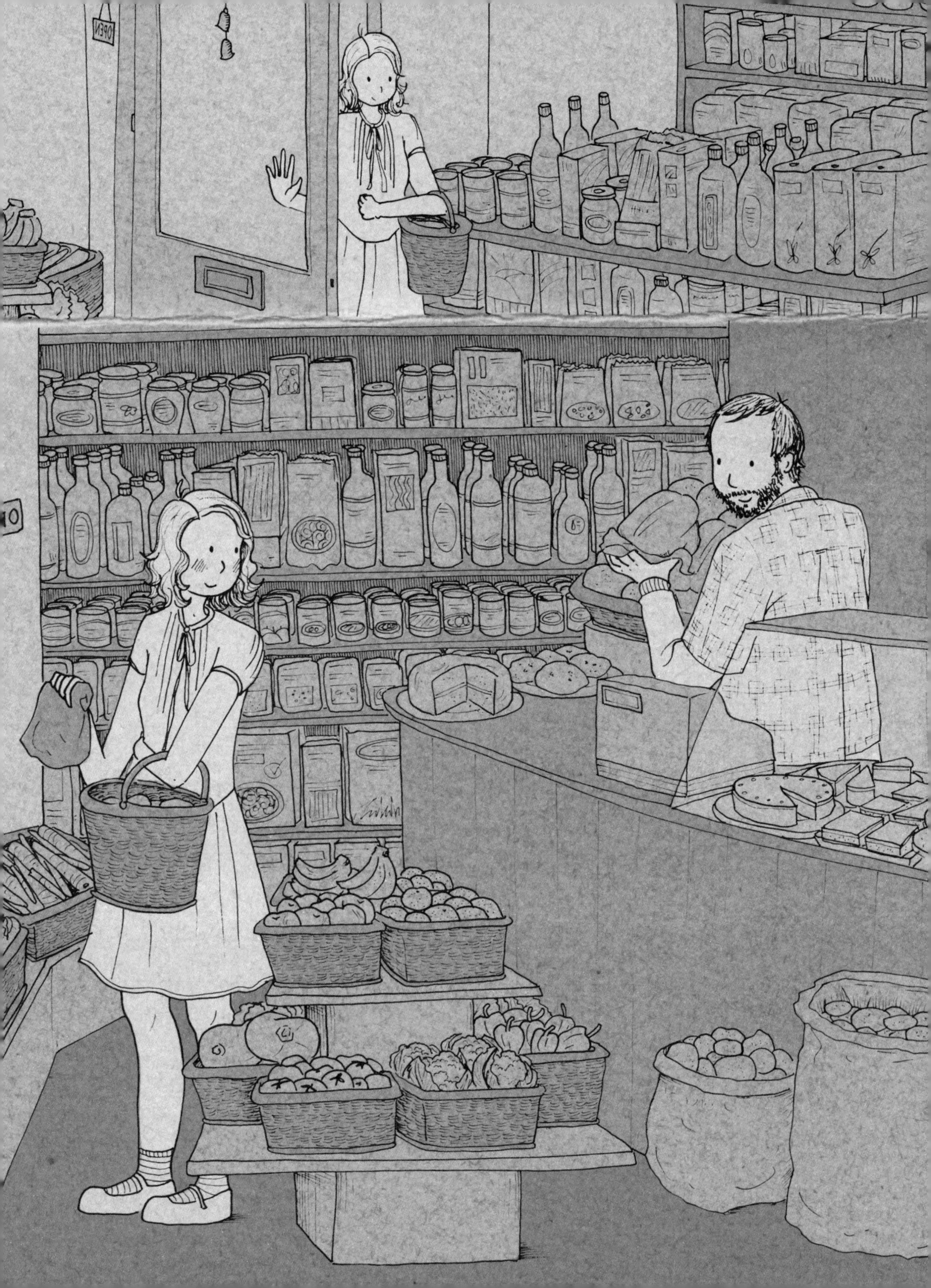
OPEN

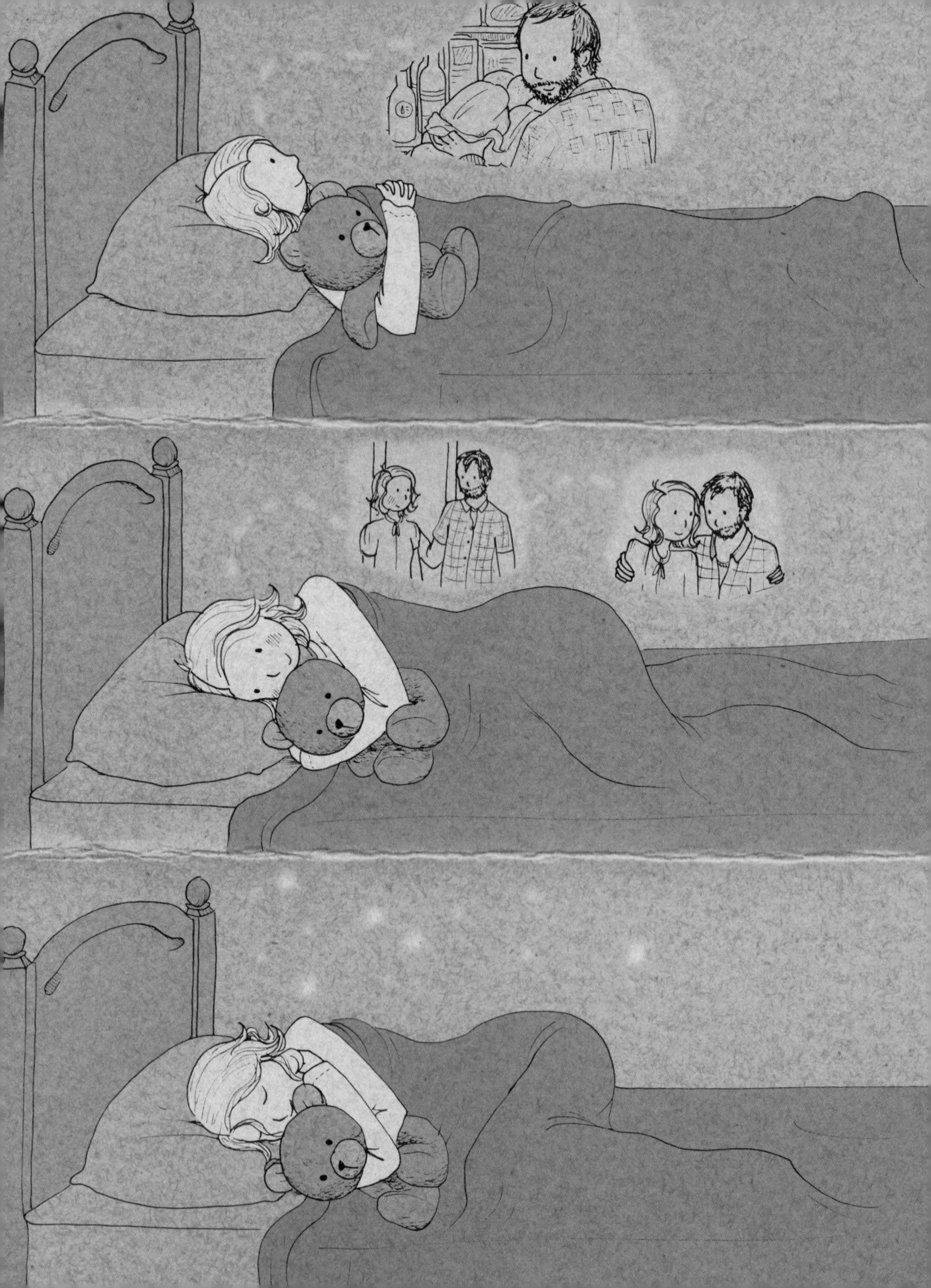

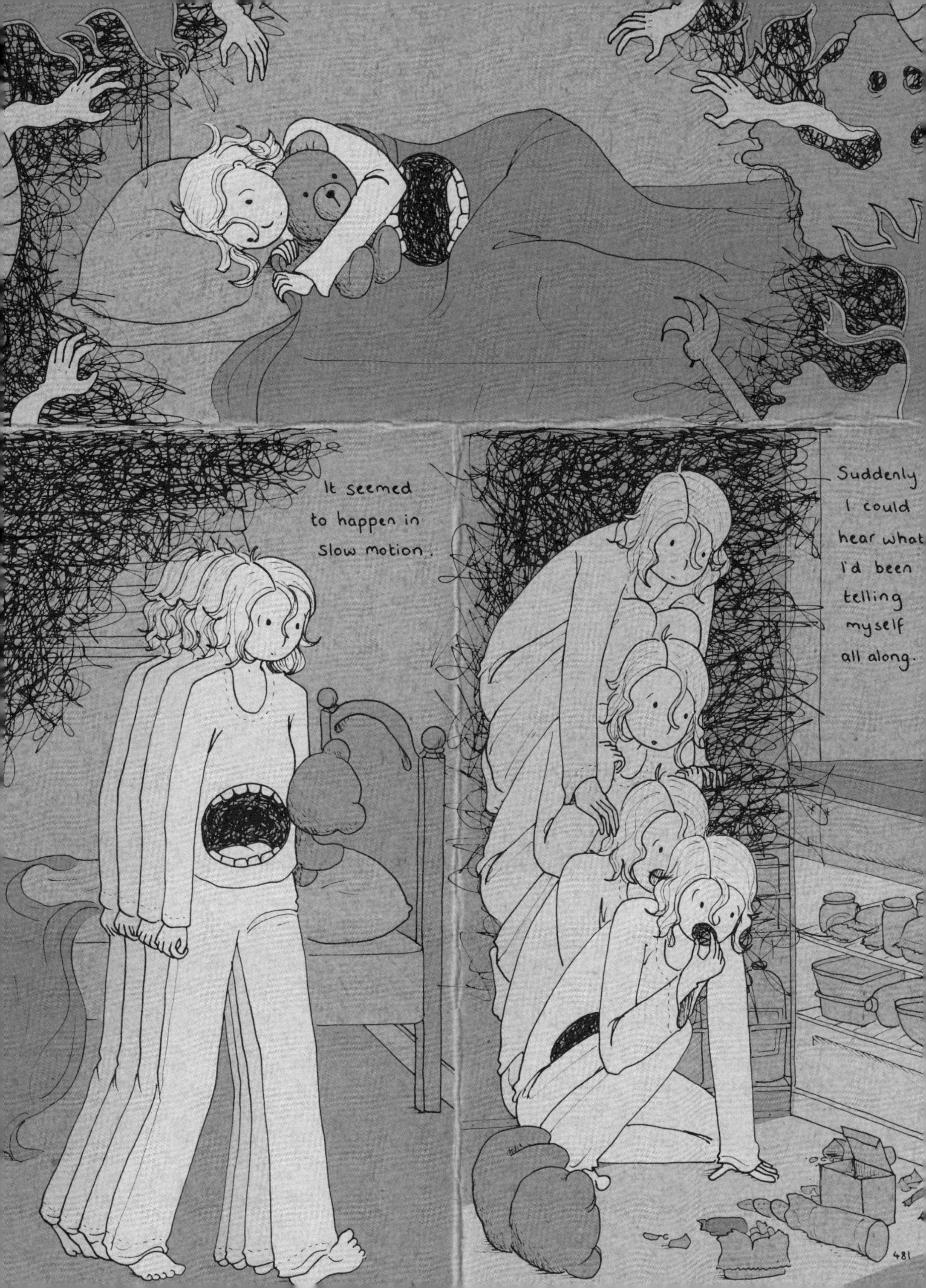
It seemed to happen in slow motion.
Suddenly I could hear what I'd been telling myself all along.

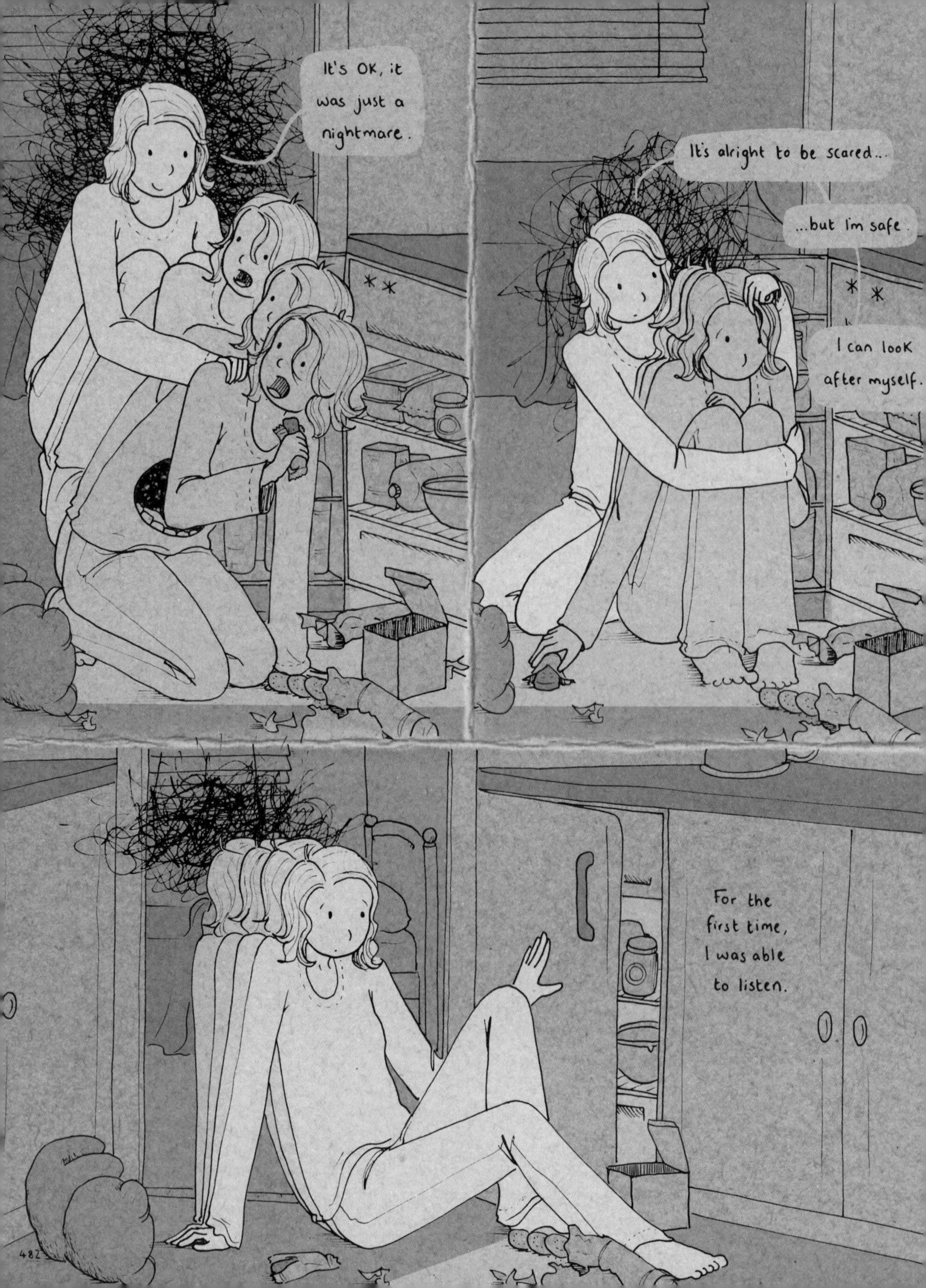
It's OK, it was just a nightmare.
It's alright to be scared...
...but I'm safe.
I can look after myself.
For the first time, I was able to listen.

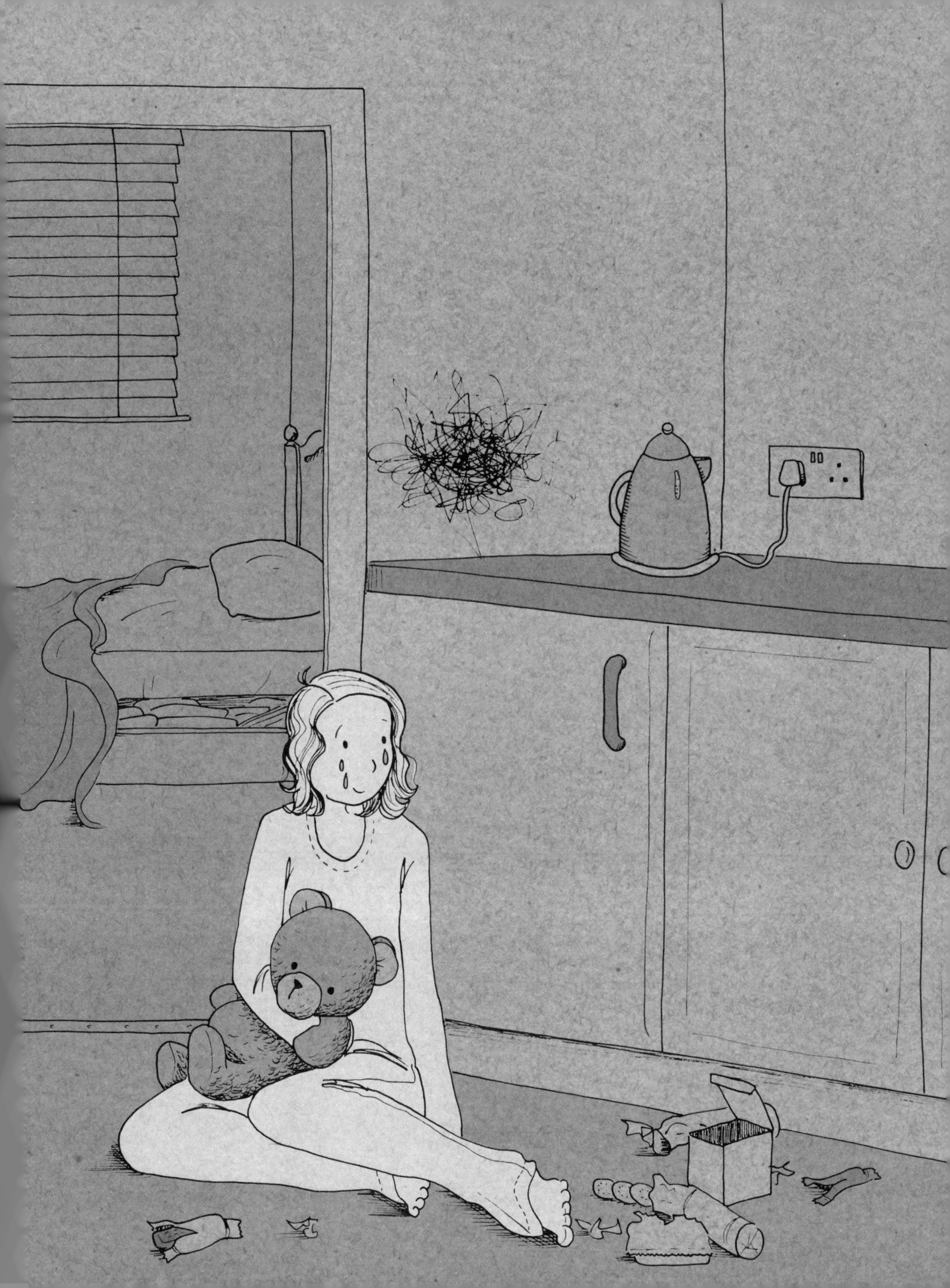

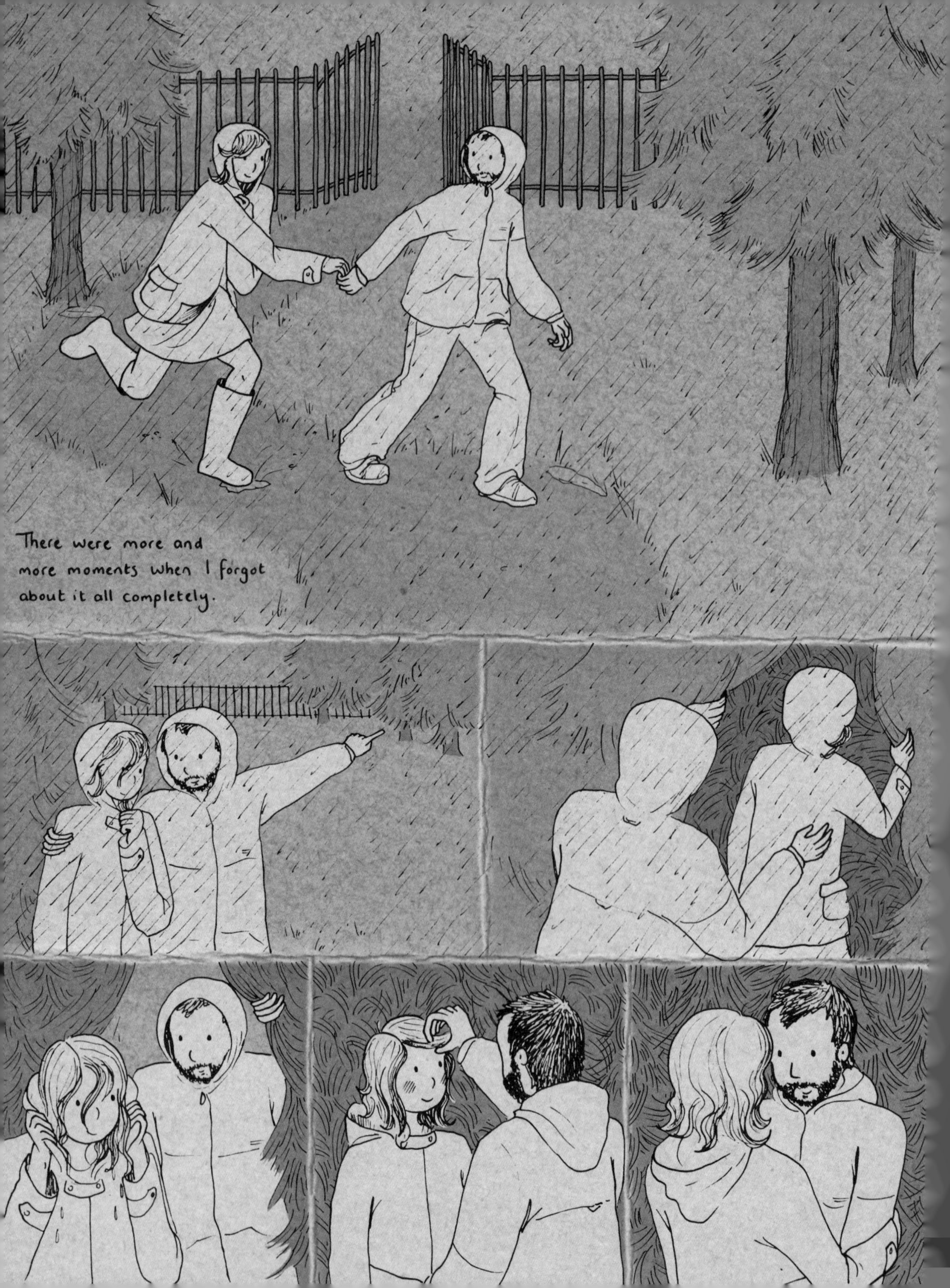
There were more and
more moments when I forgot
about it all completely.

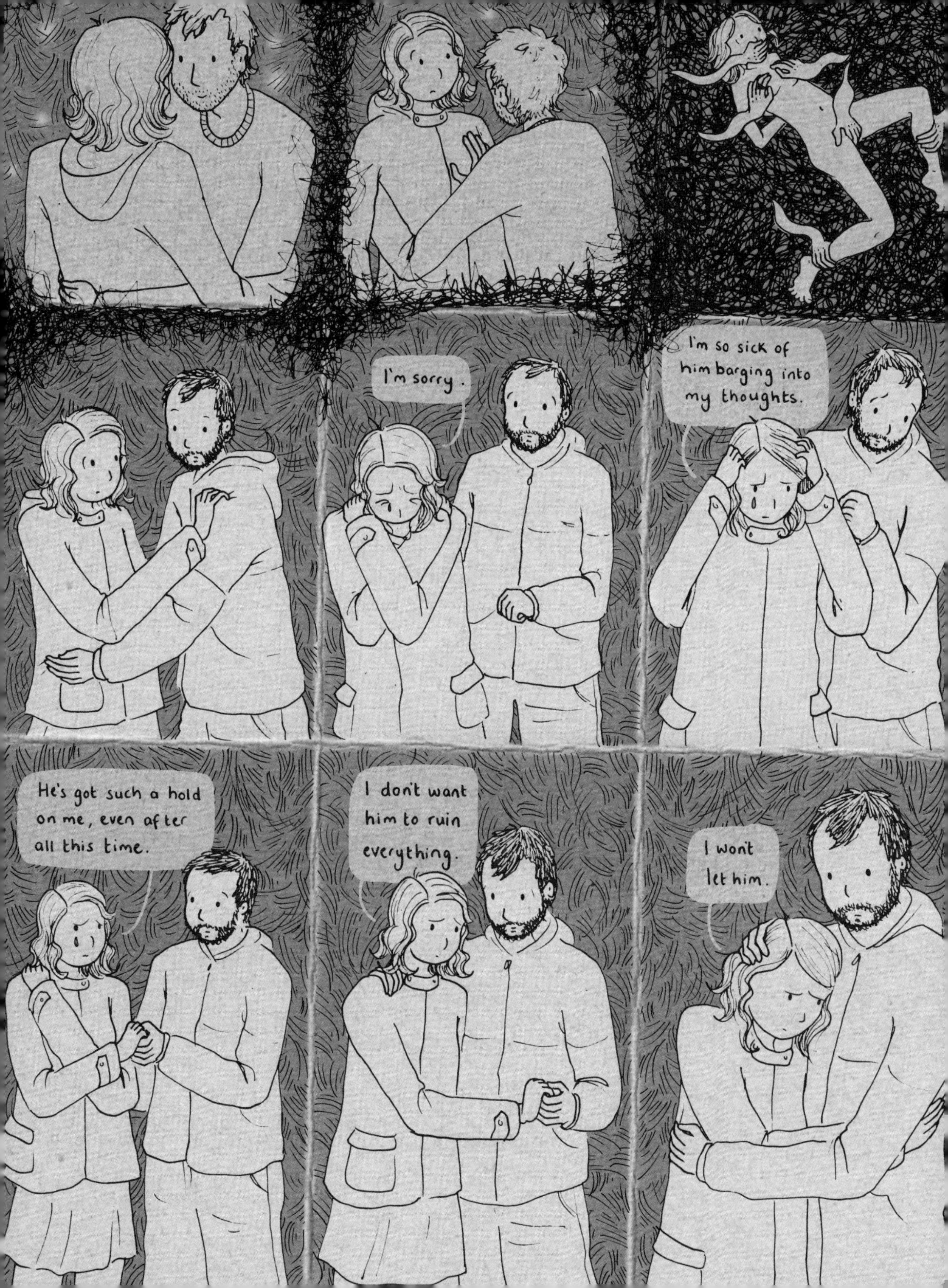
I'm sorry.
I'm so sick of him barging into my thoughts.
He's got such a hold on me, even after all this time.
I don't want him to ruin everything.
I won't let him.

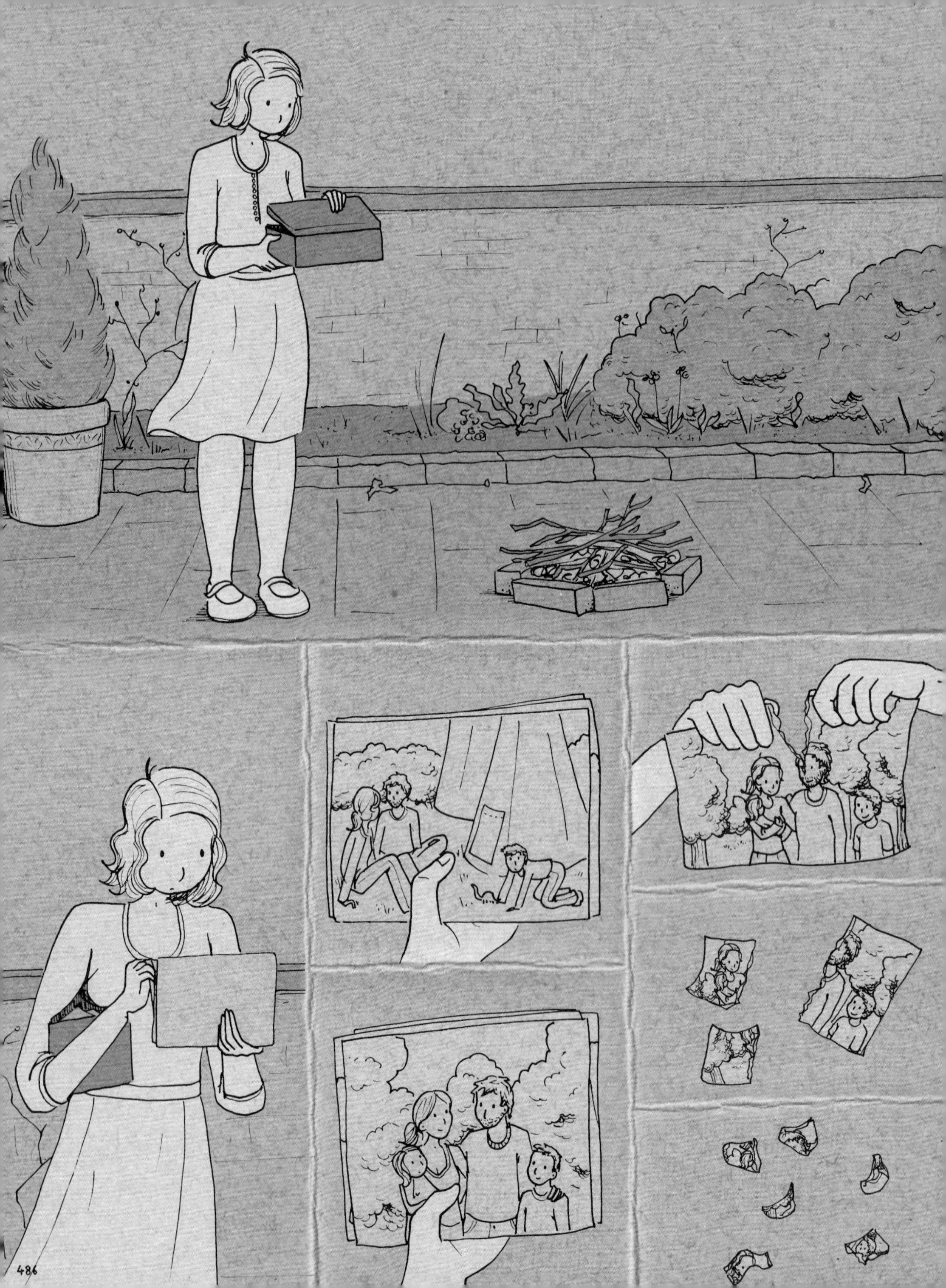

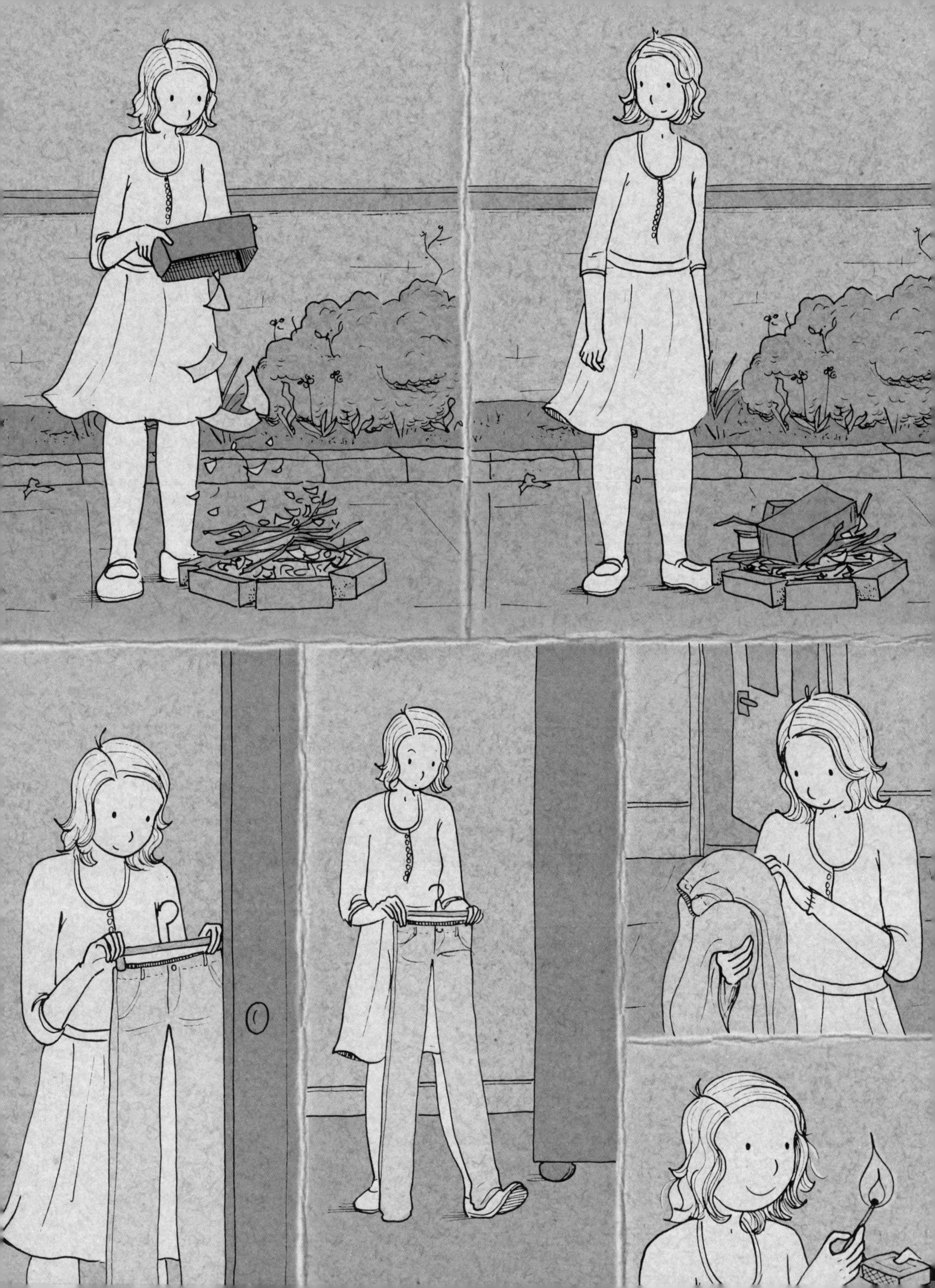

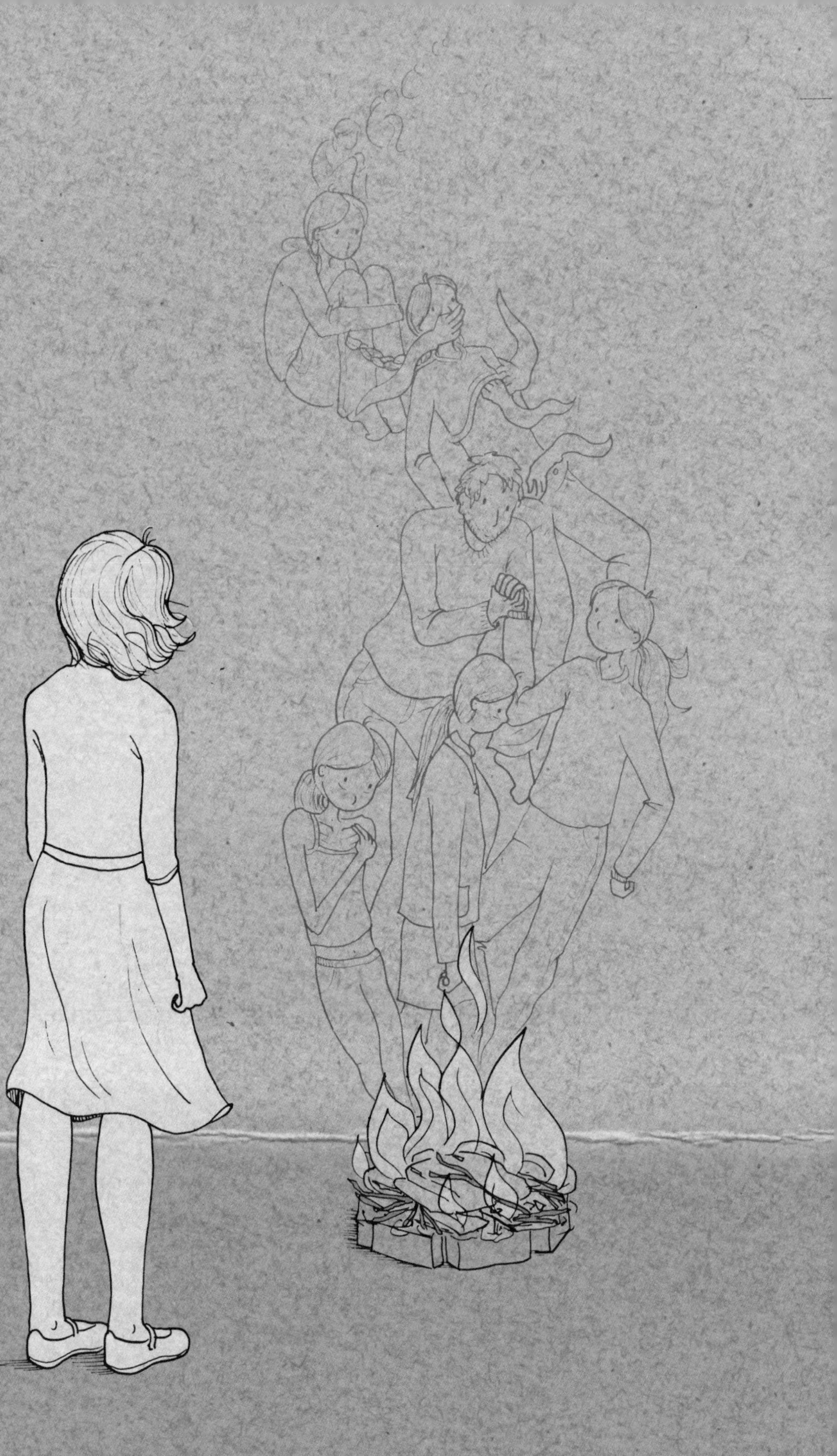

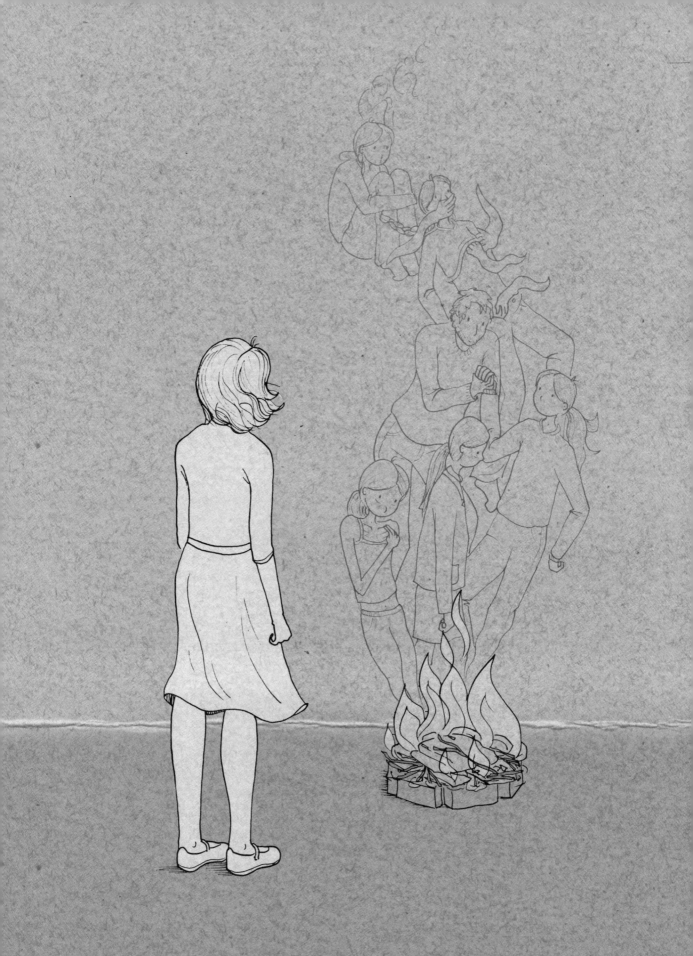

I hoped it would end the day
I burned everything, but I would
need a little more patience.

There were still days I struggled
with what I saw in the mirror,
or with figuring out how to eat.

I held on, waiting to be recovered,
wondering how long it would take.

How would I know when I got there?

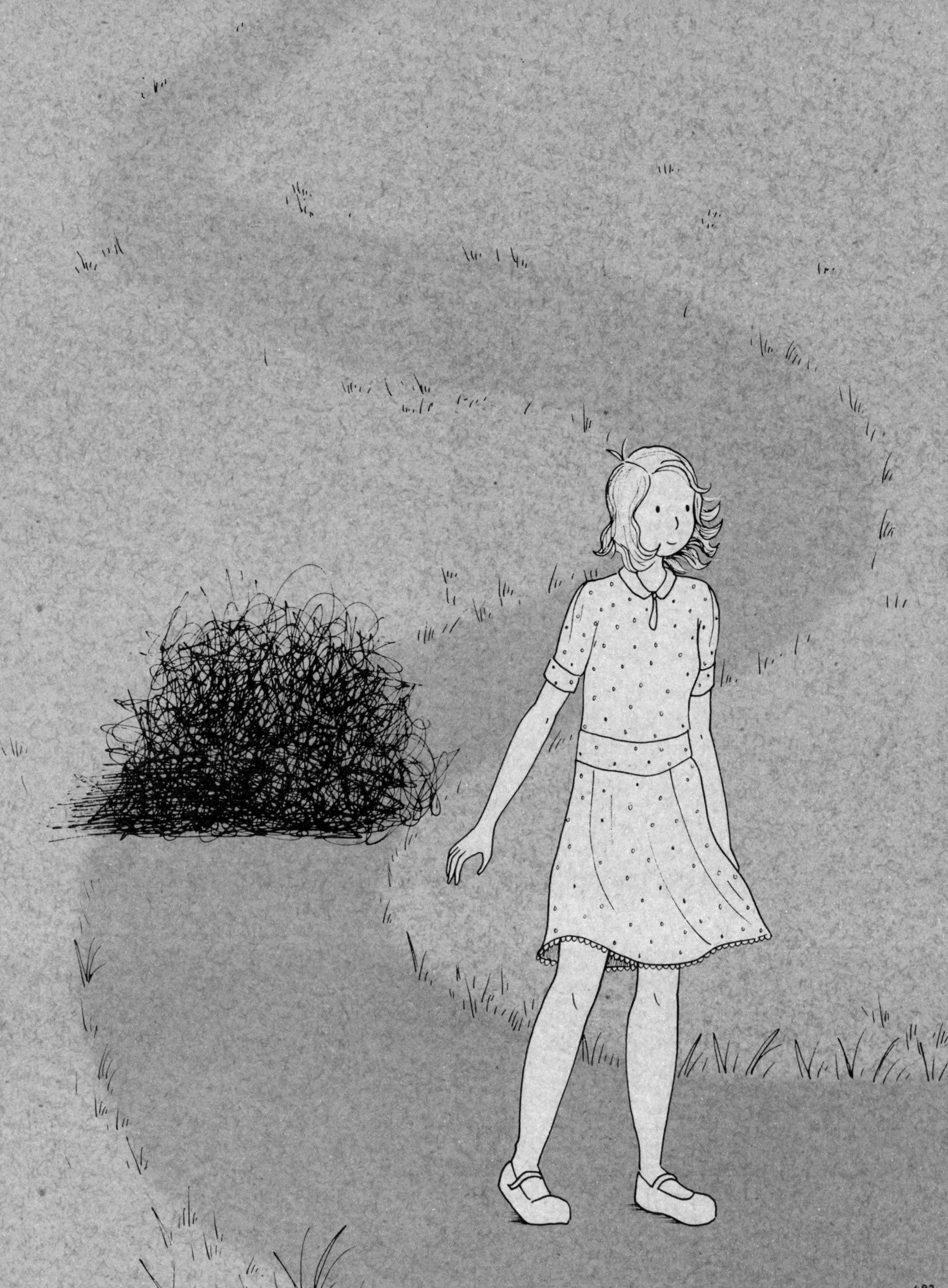

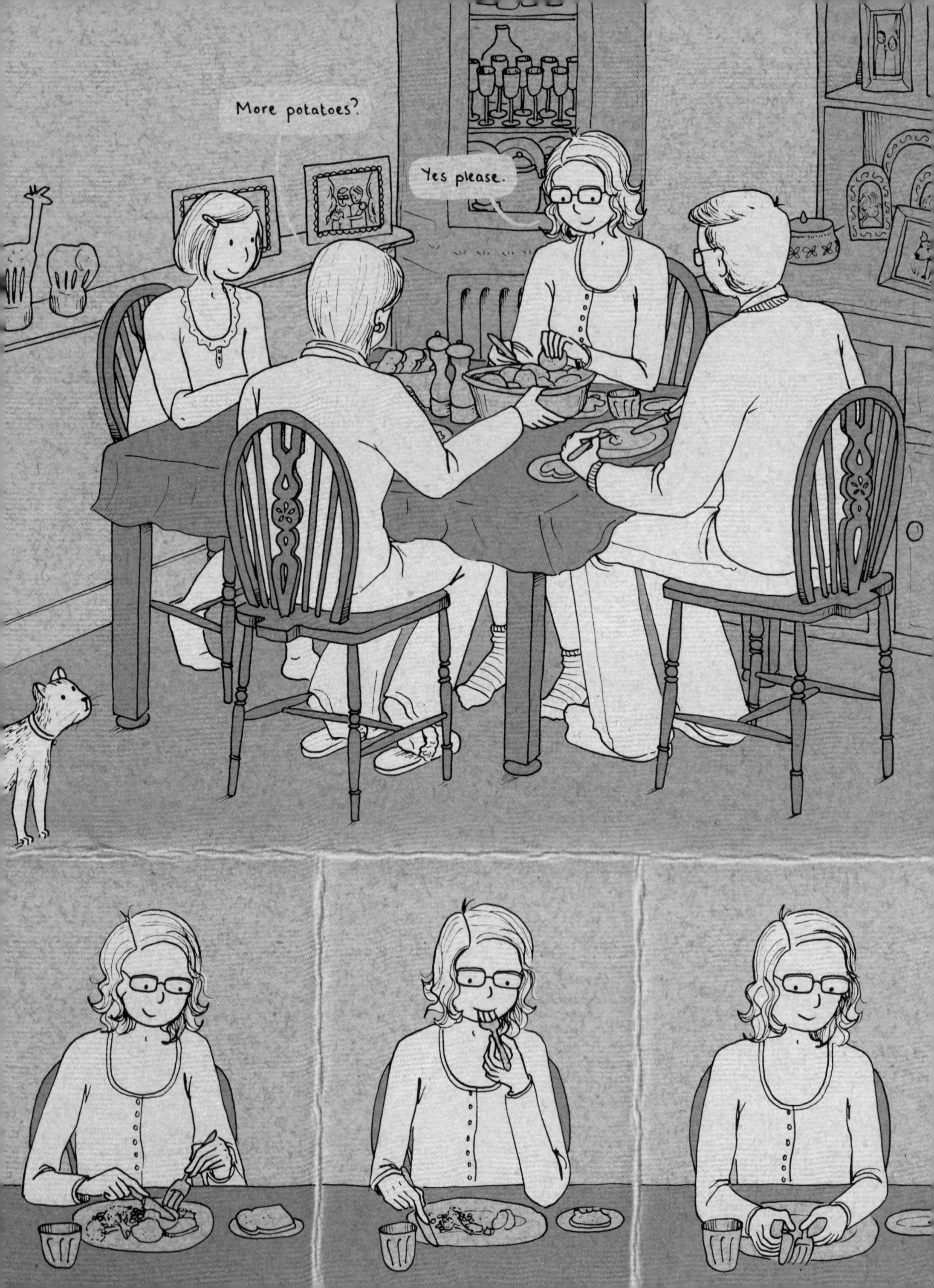
More potatoes?
Yes please.

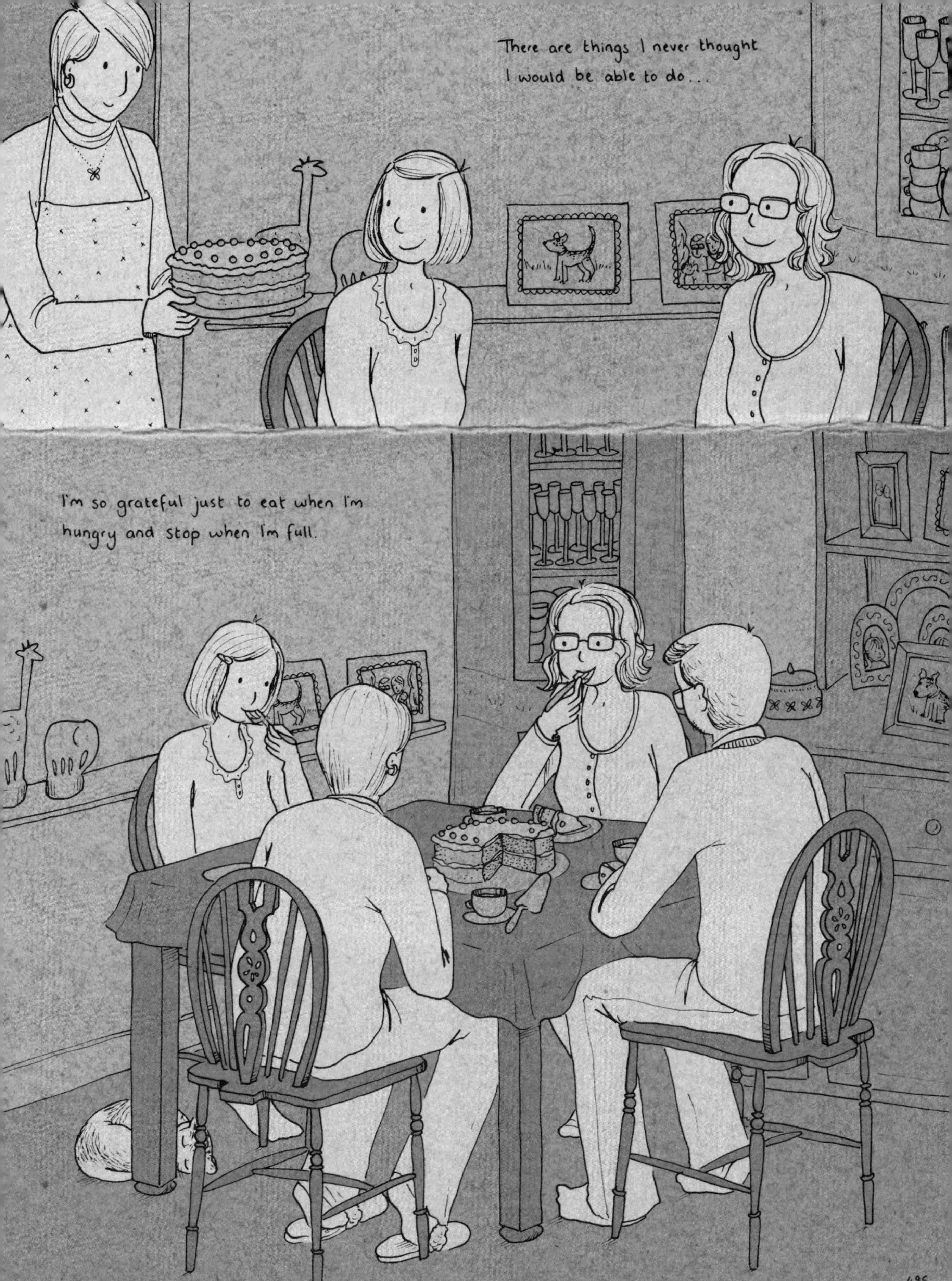
There are things I never thought I would be able to do...
I'm so grateful just to eat when I'm hungry and stop when I'm full.

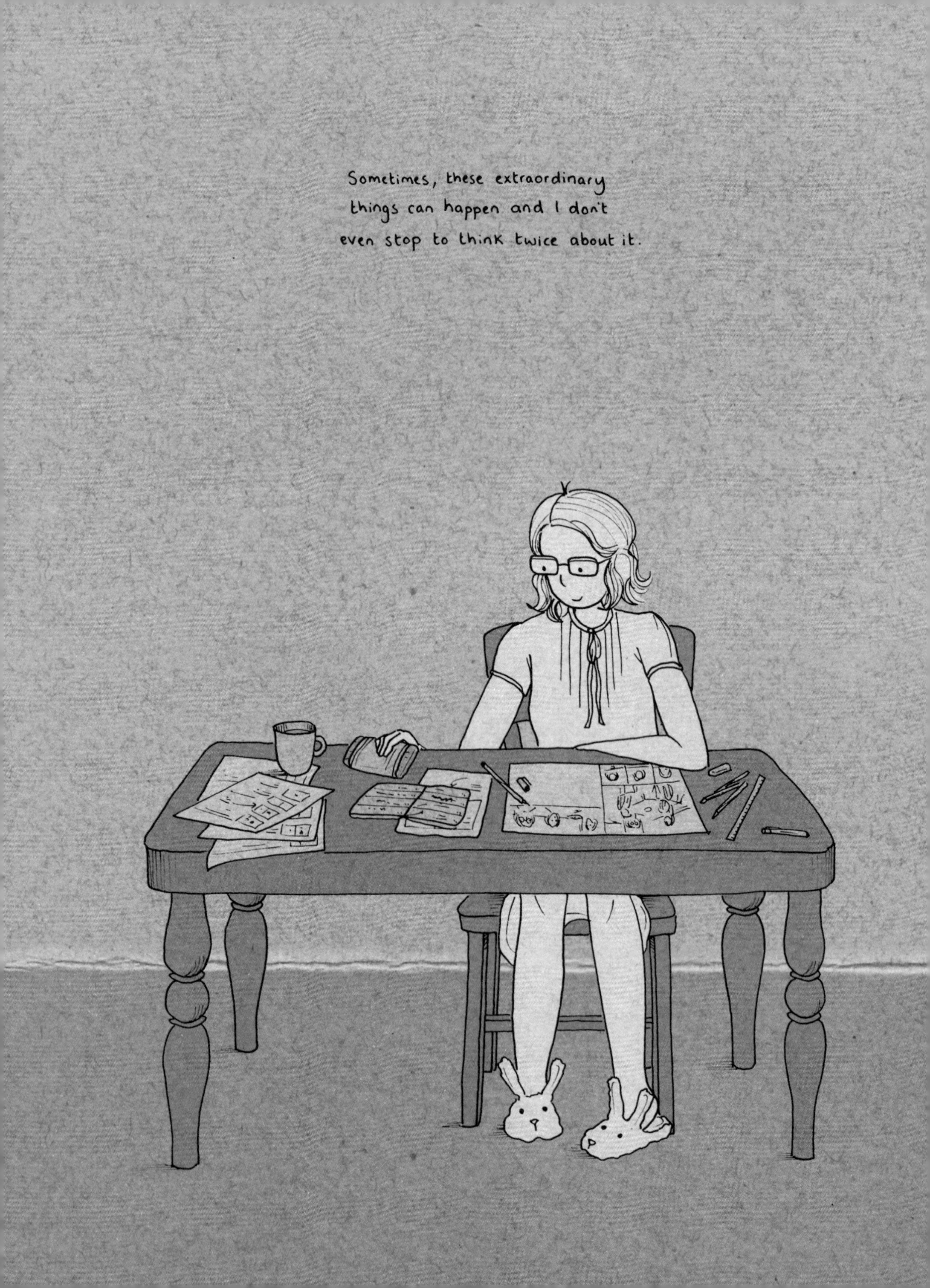
Sometimes, these extraordinary things can happen and I don't even stop to think twice about it.

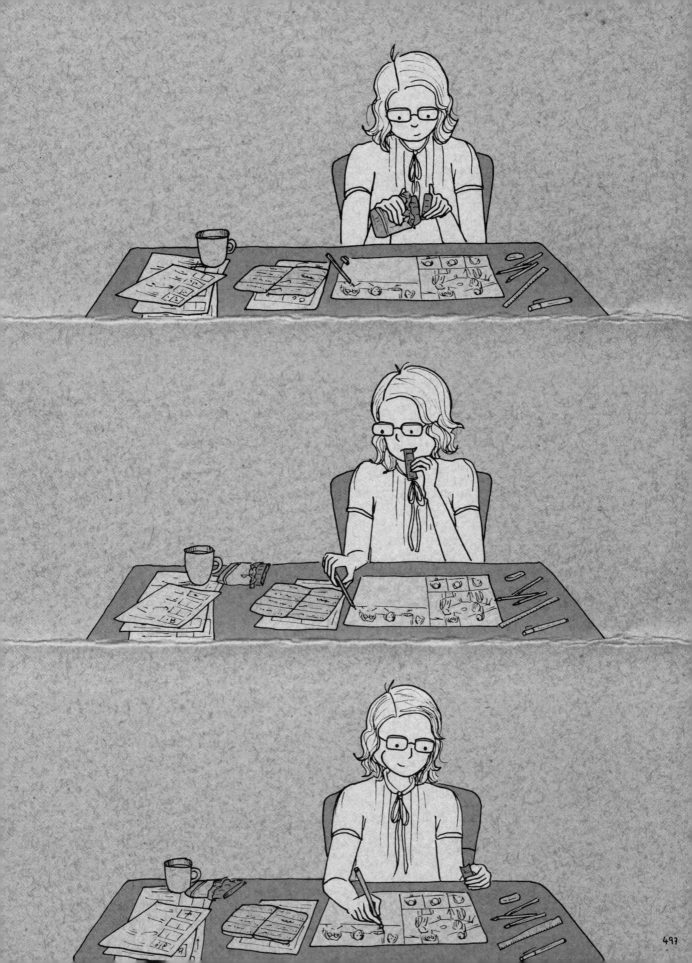

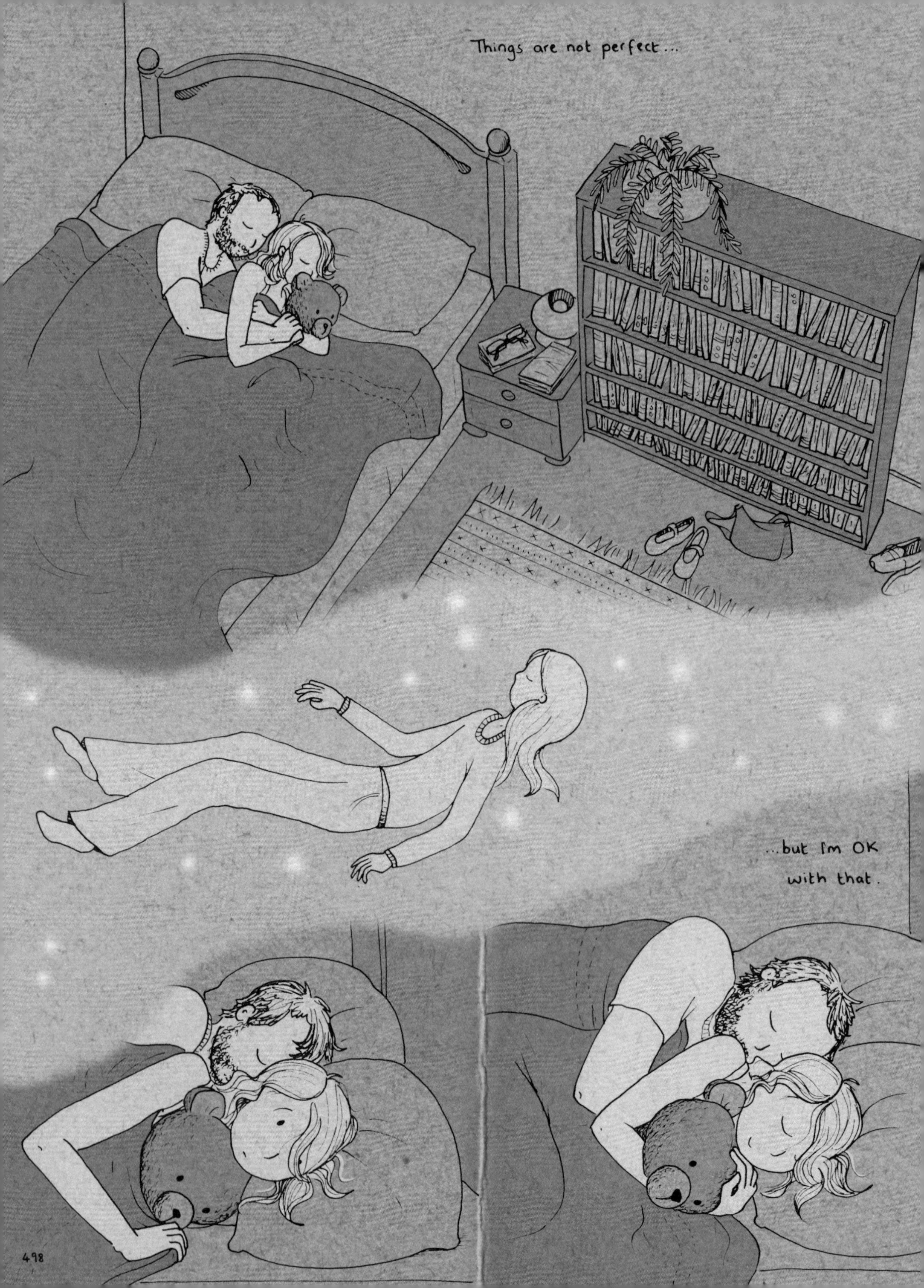
Things are not perfect...
...but I'm OK with that.

Mostly...

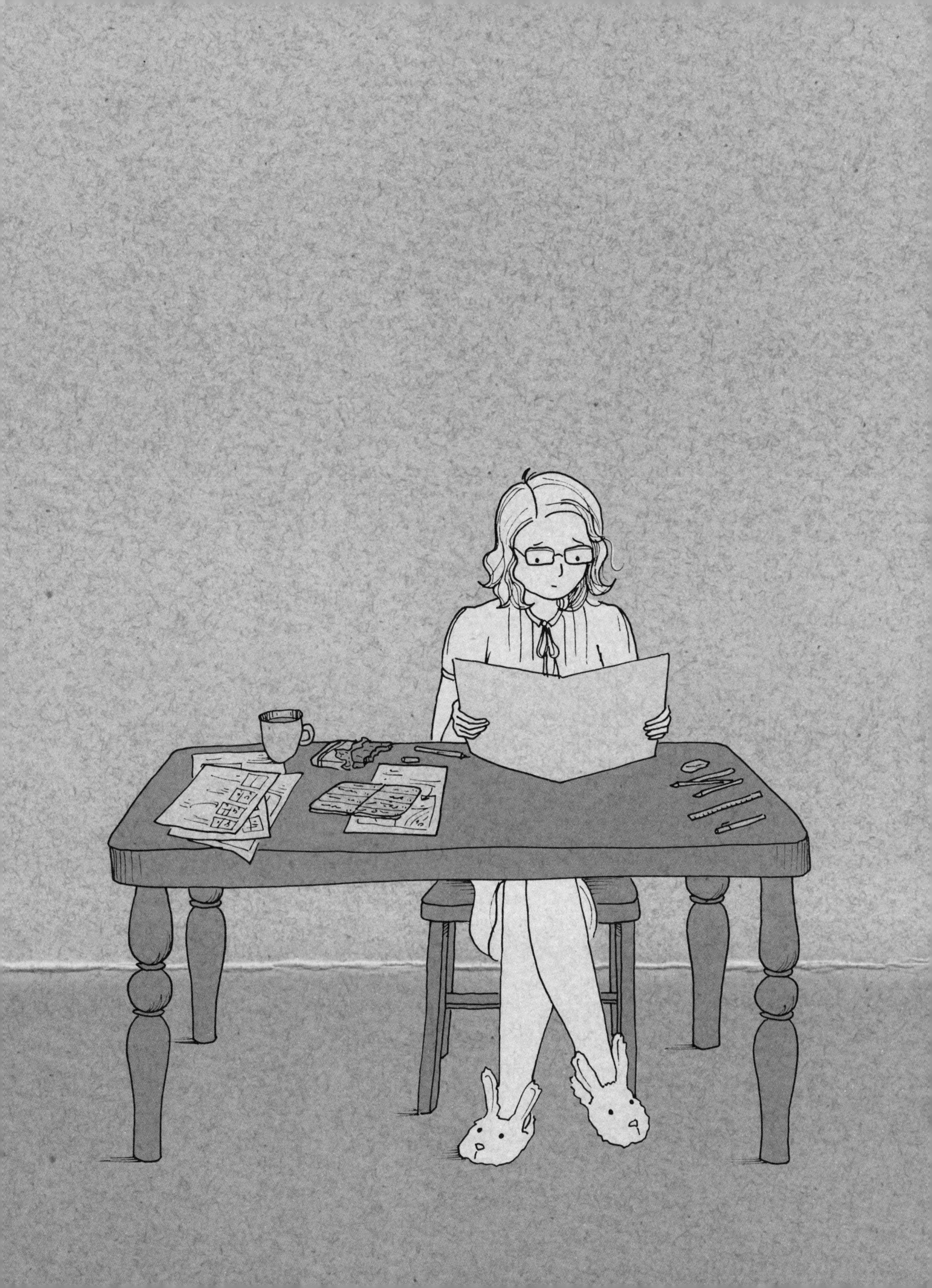

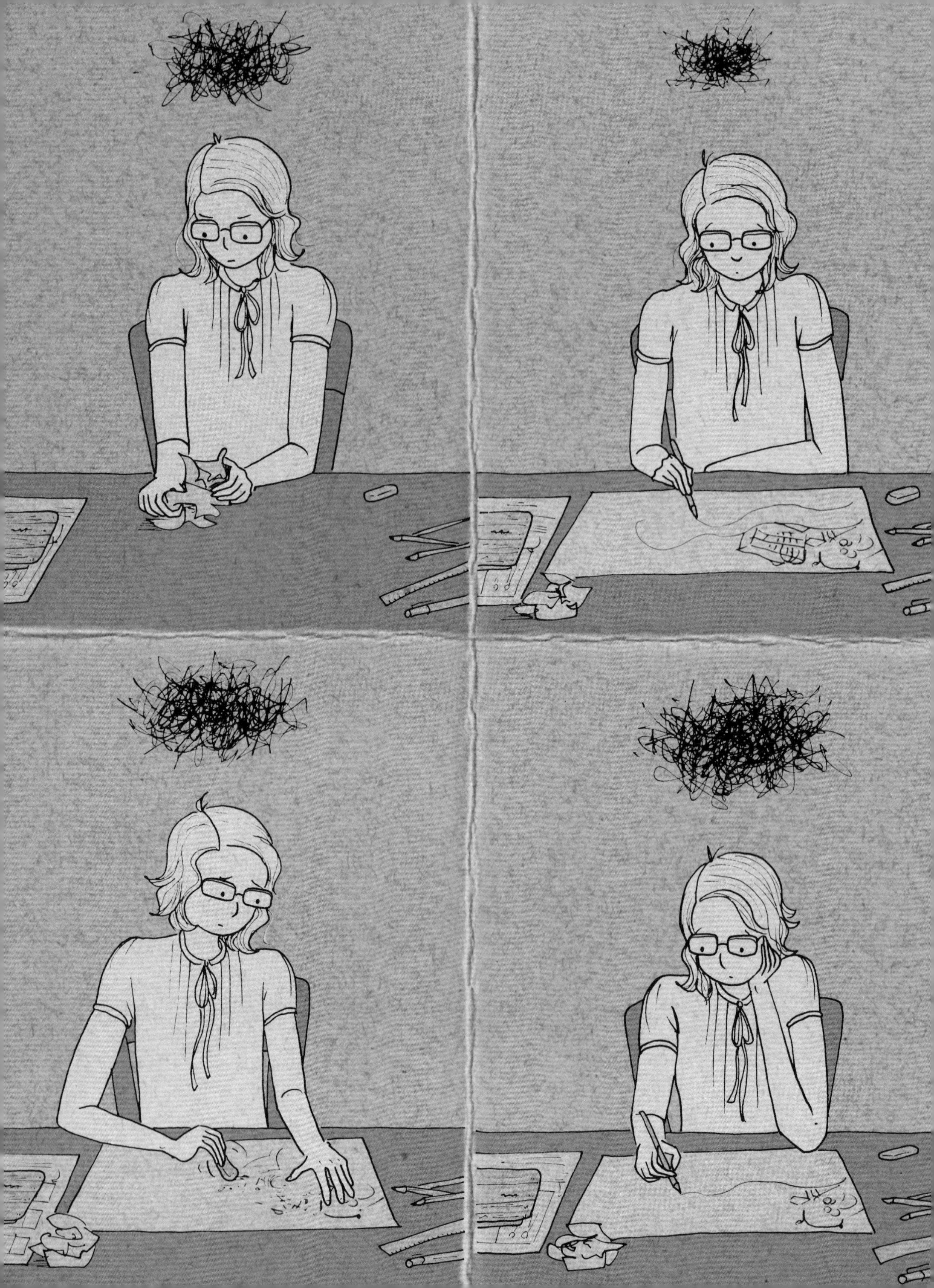

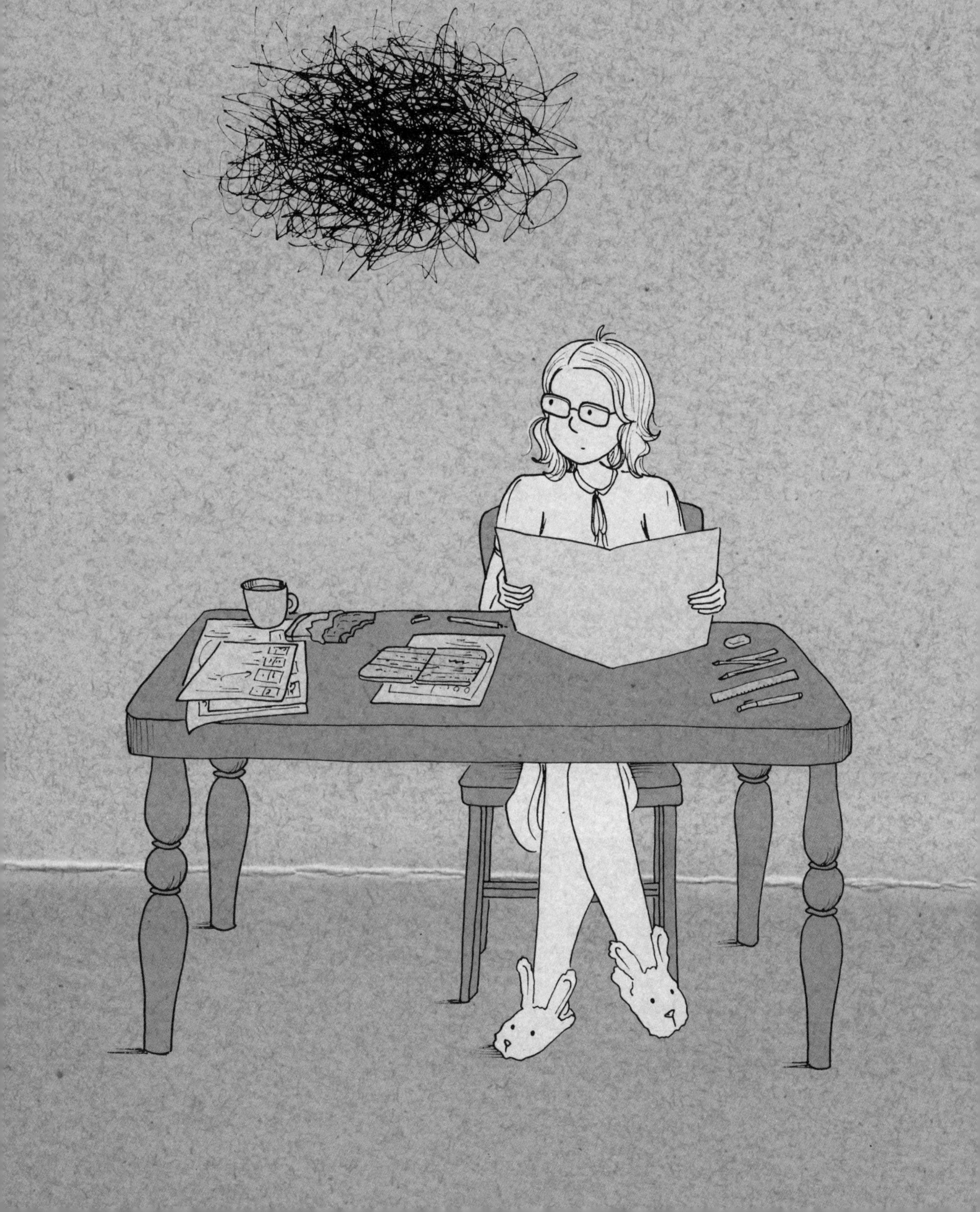

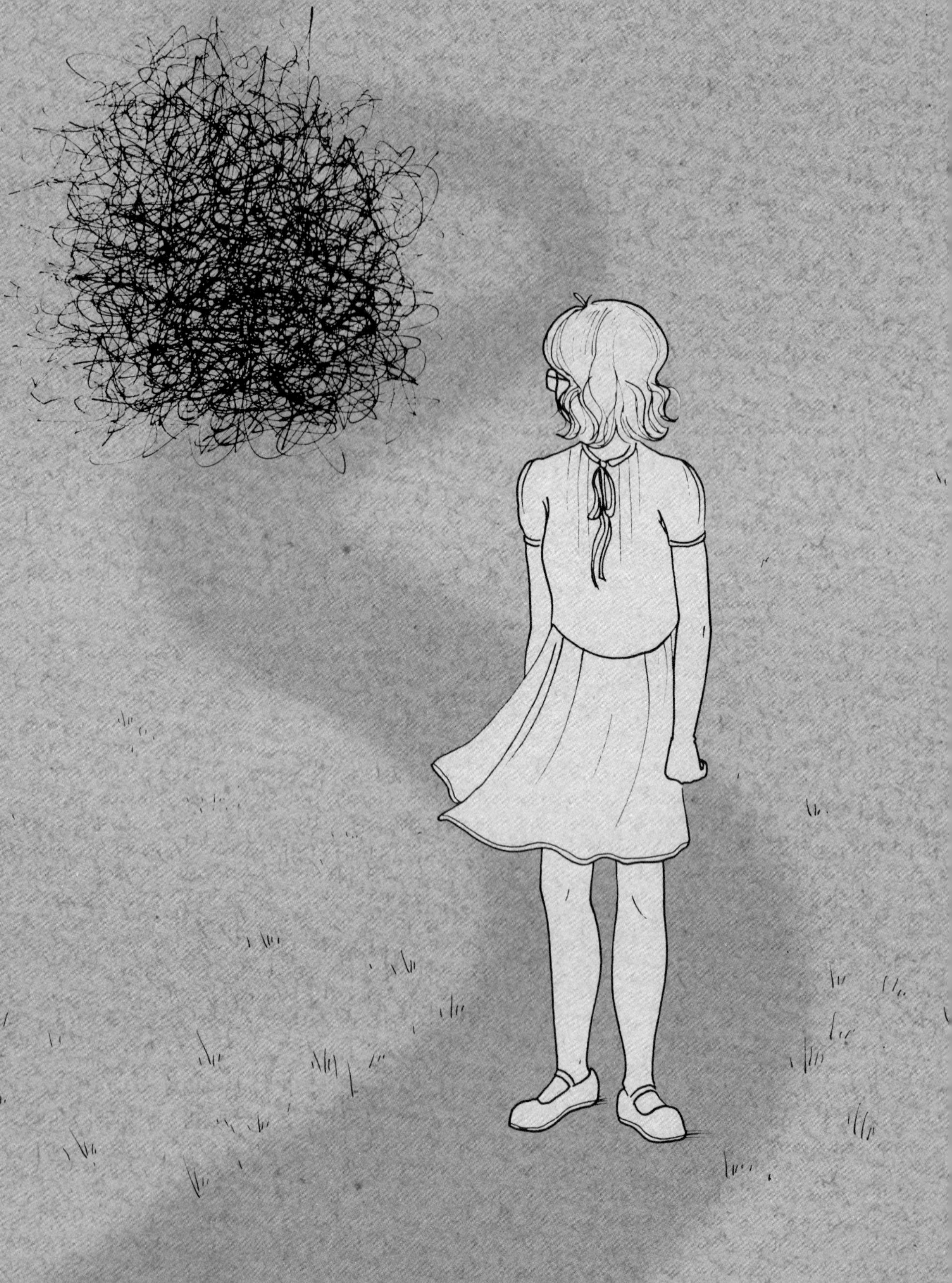

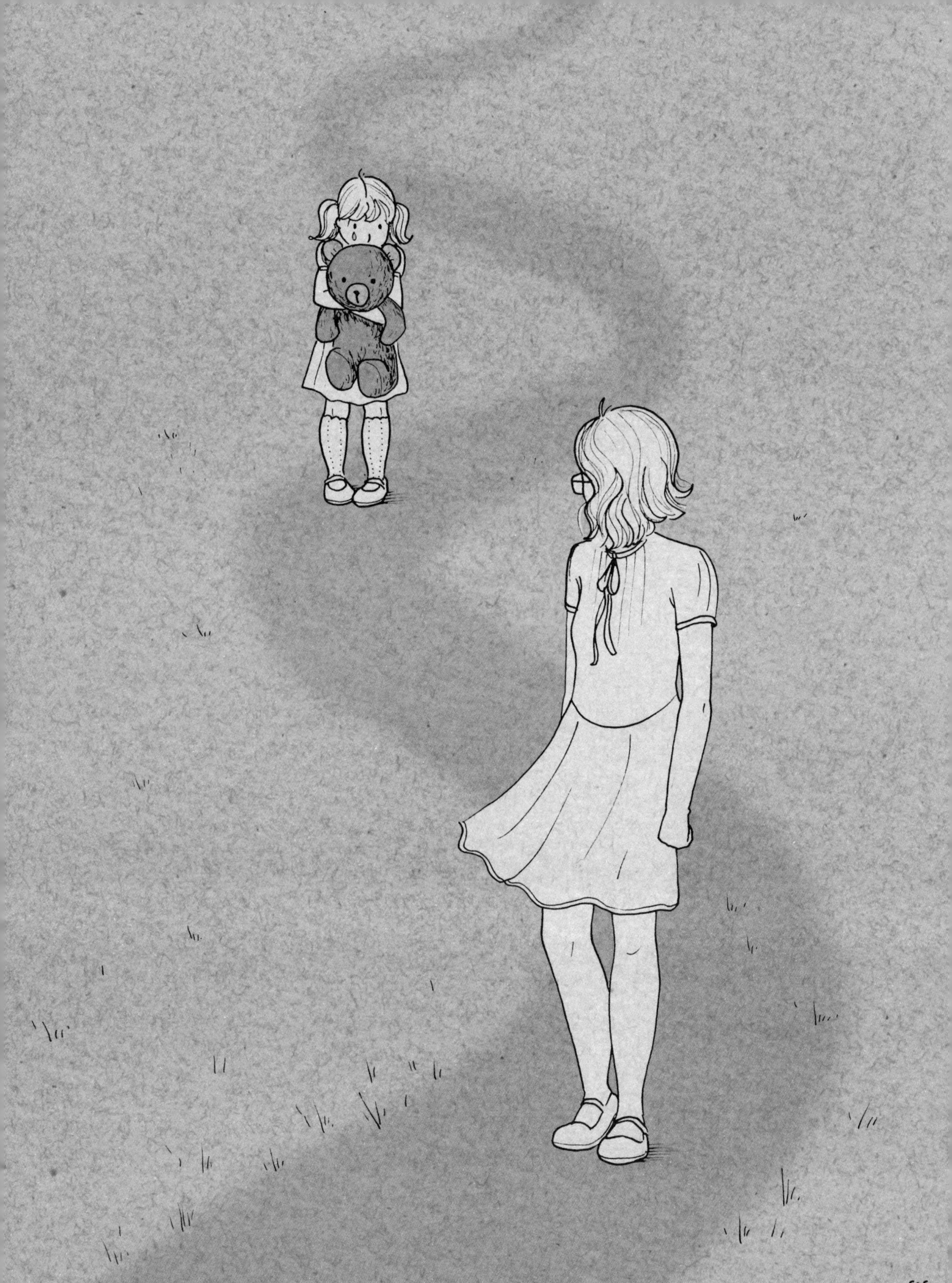

ACKNOWLEDGEMENTS

First and foremost, thank you to my parents for their unconditional love and support, for this project especially.

I can't possibly express enough gratitude to Alex Bowler for saying yes in the first place, for helping me turn it into something book-shaped, and for being unfailingly patient and professional in the face of...
...everything.

I am also deeply thankful to Bryan Talbot for teaching me so much, and for championing the project from the very beginning.

My work on this book was generously supported by funding from the Arts Council England and The Authors' Foundation, for which I'm extremely grateful.

To Shaun Tan, Craig Thompson and Anders Nilsen. None of you have any idea who I am, but if I hadn't found your work I may never have made mine, so thank you.

Heartfelt thanks to Jason Molina, whose music provided a soundtrack to much of my work on this book, and often the courage to keep doing it.

Thank you to Ginny Vollenweider for the perfect title.

To my tutors Louise Brooke, Sarah Blair, Andy Pedlar and Nicky Ackland-Snow, thank you for helping to shape the monster in the very early stages.

Thank you to Paula Knight, Mita Mahato, MK Czerwiec, Joe Decie and Katie Cullinane for helping with some particularly troublesome tangles, and to Simone Lia and Hannah Berry for being lovely.

There are many dear friends who have read bits and given feedback, or who have been tirelessly cheering me on and reminding me why I've been doing this. To attempt to name everyone would only result in accidental omission (and a book twice as long) so please forgive me for not trying. You know who you are and how deeply grateful I am. Thank you all.

There is a further army of family, doctors, nurses, teachers, therapists and friends to whom I am indebted, not for this book so much as my still being here to draw it. To all of you I quite literally owe my life. Thank you for it.

I am very grateful and lucky to have had the generous and steadfast support of Sue Allen, in making this book and so much more.

And to Luke Foster, thank you for everything, and all the wonderful food.

Links, resources and more information can be found at:

www.lighterthanmyshadow.com